REFERENCE

PEOPLES
of the
AMERICAS

PEOPLES
of the
AMERICAS

Volume 1
Anguilla–Belize

MARSHALL CAVENDISH
NEW YORK • LONDON • TORONTO • SYDNEY

Marshall Cavendish Corporation
99 White Plains Road
Tarrytown, New York 10591-9001

Consulting Editor: J. Patrick Gray, Professor of Anthropology, University of Wisconsin

Consultants: Jean-Marc Blais, Senior Interpretive Planner, Canadian Museum of Civilization, Hull, Quebec
        David Frye, Assistant Director, Department of Latin American and Caribbean Studies, University of Michigan

Spanish Consultant: Fran Kaplan

Contributing authors: D. L. Birchfield
                Marion Morrison
                Juliette Radcliffe Rogers
                Philip Steele
                Mary A. Stout

Discovery Books
    Managing Editor: Paul Humphrey
    Project Editor: Helen Dwyer
    Text Editor: Valerie J. Weber
    Design Concept: Ian Winton
    Designers: Barry Dwyer, Ian Winton, and Simon Borrough
    Cartographer: Stefan Chabluk

Marshall Cavendish
    Editorial Director: Paul Bernabeo
    Editor: Marian Armstrong
    Associate Editor: Debra M. Jacobs

The publishers would like to thank the following for their permission to reproduce photographs:
Allsport (David Cannon 25); Andes Press Agency (Stewart Aitchison 43; Hugo Fernandez 15, 21; Veronique Guyomard 4); Anguilla Tourist Office (3 top); James Davis Travel Photography (13, 32, 39); Douglas Donne Bryant Stock Photography (Roberto Bunge cover, 19, 24; Carlos Goldin 18; Suzanne L. Murphy xiii); Greg Evans International (5); Mary Evans Picture Library (29); Eye Ubiquitous (Mike Alkins 35; E. J. B. Hawkins 40; M. W. Smith 8); Hutchison Library (Tony Hardwell 33; J. Henderson 3 bottom); National Library of Wales (23); South American Pictures (20; Hilary Bradt 22; Marion Morrison 9; Tony Morrison 12, 16, 37, 38; Frank Nowikowski 6, 14; Chris Sharp 10, 41); The Stock Market (E. Rekos 11; Zefa-Boutin 27); Tony Stone Images (Doug Armand 34; Cosmo Condina 30; Richard Elliott frontispiece; Alain Le Garsmeur 42; Bob Thomas 31)

(frontispiece) Barbadian girl and boy.

Editor's note: Many systems of dating have been used by different cultures throughout history. *Peoples of the Americas* uses B.C.E. (Before Common Era) and C.E. (Common Era) instead of B.C. (Before Christ) and A.D. (Anno Domini, "In the Year of the Lord") out of respect for the diversity of the world's peoples.

Library of Congress Cataloging-in-Publication Data
Peoples of the Americas.
        p.   cm.
        Includes bibliographical references and index.
        Contents: v. 1. Anguilla–Belize — v. 2. Bermuda–Brazil — v. 3. Canada–Cayman Islands — v. 4. Chile–Costa Rica — v. 5. Cuba–French Guiana — v. 6. Greenland–Jamaica — v. 7. Martinique–Paraguay — v. 8. Peru–Turks and Caicos Islands — v. 9. United States of America — v. 10. United States of America–Virgin Islands

    ISBN 0-7614-7050-6 (set)
    1. Ethnology—America—Juvenile literature. 2. America—History—Juvenile literature. [1. Ethnology—America. 2. America—History.]
E29.A1P46 1999
970'.004—dc21   98-2801
                                                                                                            CIP
                                                                                                            AC

    ISBN 0-7614-7050-6 (set)
    ISBN 0-7614-7051-4 (vol. 1)

Printed and bound in Italy

Contents of the Set

Contents of Volume 1

The Peopling of the Americas

When early European explorers first described the natives of the Americas, they fired the imagination of the public in Europe. Thinkers were fascinated by how the customs of peoples in the "New World" differed from European ways of life and from the lifestyles of other newly contacted peoples in Africa, Asia, and Oceania. People wanted to know how Native Americans were related to the rest of the human species. To answer this question, knowing how they came to the Americas was necessary. This problem has continued to fascinate scientists and the public until the present.

Nobody knows exactly when people first arrived in the Americas or the specific route they took to get there. The first arrival happened so long ago that it is a great challenge to piece together the clues that would solve the puzzle. To understand the peopling of the Americas, scientists must use evidence from many disciplines: archaeology, geology, climatology, linguistics, physical anthropology, biology, and genetics. Sometimes the evidence from one field contradicts that in another field. At other times crucial evidence is missing from one field. In spite of these problems scientists have managed to construct several believable models of how the New World was originally settled. Future research may show that one model fits the facts better than all the others, or it might force us to create new models.

Most American tribes have stories that tell how they were created. Many tribes tell of arriving in what would become their homelands after emerging from beneath the earth. The Yaruro of Venezuela relate how people originally lived under the earth. The snake Kuma threw a thin rope down a hole in the earth, and men and women started to climb out. Unfortunately, only a few people came out before the rope broke under the weight of a pregnant woman. This is the reason there are so few Yaruro people. Other stories tell of North America being created as an island, "Turtle Island," by birds diving in the ocean for mud that they built into land by putting the mud on a turtle's back. Some tribes have migration stories that tell of long journeys that took place in the far distant past. Every tribe has its own stories about how it came to live in its ancestral homelands. The stories are as rich and as varied as the many different kinds of Native peoples in the Americas.

Over the years there have been many wrong guesses about the origins of the Indians. For example, some early Europeans who came to America thought they found the "lost tribes of Israel" that are mentioned in the Bible. Another guess was that the Indians were survivors of the "lost continent of Atlantis," a mythical large island in the Atlantic Ocean supposed to have sunk beneath the waves. These guesses were discarded quickly once scientists started to carefully collect and analyze evidence on the settlement of the Americas.

Scientists have also made wrong guesses. As recently as the 1920s, many prominent scientists held that Indians arrived in North America no more than three thousand or four thousand years ago. However, in the 1930s a series of archaeological finds conclusively showed that people had been living in North America for thousands of years longer than that. Scientists then reexamined the evidence to see how it fit into the new time frame.

Currently, the date the first people entered the New World is a very controversial topic. The best archaeological evidence suggests a date no earlier than twelve thousand years ago. Some archaeologists believe they have identified sites suggesting an even earlier entry, but none have proven to be conclusive. Data from genetics and linguistics also sometimes suggest a date around twelve thousand years ago, but other studies arrive at an earlier date. Usually, scientists do not change a widely accepted model until well-established facts show the model cannot be correct. If the evidence of arrival earlier than twelve thousand years ago proves conclusive, scientists will again adjust their models to make sense of the evidence.

There is widespread agreement that the peopling of the Americas occurred when enough water from the oceans was locked in giant polar ice caps to lower the sea level by as much as 200 or 300 feet (61 to 91 meters). The very shallow Bering Sea, which is 180 feet (55 meters) deep between Alaska (in North America) and Siberia (in Asia), might have been dry land, forming a land bridge between the two continents. Some archaeologists call the connection between Siberia and the New World "Beringia." This land bridge might have been open for long periods, hundreds or even thousands of years, at different times during the last ice age. During the times it was open, animals, and humans who hunted them, would have walked into the New World.

Not everyone believes that the first people to enter the New World came through Beringia. In 1995 a Sioux Indian professor, Vine Deloria Jr., published a book titled *Red Earth, White Lies: Native Americans and the Myth of Scientific Fact*. In this book he calls the Bering Strait theory a scientific myth and says that no scientist had ever published an article in a scientific journal reporting the discovery of any evidence to support the theory. Professor Deloria is correct in that no archaeological site has been found that conclusively shows a migration across the strait. Unfortunately, all the places where archaeologists would look for such sites are currently underwater. However, the evidence from many different fields of research is consistent in support of the Beringia theory, while there is almost no evidence to suggest an alternative entry point. The suggestion that Native Americans originated in the New World would mean that they were not connected to the rest of humanity, an impossibility for scientists who believe that modern humans evolved in Africa and spread to other continents from there.

Some of the strongest evidence for the Bering Strait theory comes from comparing the teeth of prehistoric Asians and prehistoric Native Americans. Physical anthropologists have identified a set of dental features they call Sinodonty (or Chinese-like teeth). Some anthropologists

A current map of the region where Asia and America meet. The superimposed green area represents the probable extent of dry land at times during the last ice age.

argue that Sinodonty originally evolved in southeast Asia and that these people gave rise to the northern Chinese. In turn these northern Chinese gave rise to the Paleo-Indians in the New World. These dental traits are still found in the descendants of these groups but are rare elsewhere in the world. Although the teeth are the most convincing evidence, Native Americans clearly resemble Asian populations in physical features, such as facial structure, more closely than they resemble peoples living elsewhere. The distribution of blood groups also shows that Native Americans resemble northern Asians more closely than other peoples.

While most scientists accept the view that people entered the Americas across the Bering Strait, the questions of when the entry first occurred and how many major migrations took place are still very controversial. Some scattered archaeological sites in Alaska and Canada might date to as early as 15,000 years ago, but the archaeological evidence is not really good until we get to the widespread Clovis cultures that flourished around 11,000 years ago. One theory is that the Clovis people crossed Beringia sometime before 13,000 years ago, rapidly pushed through North America as they followed big game animals (known as megafauna), and reached the northern edge of South America by 10,900 years ago. Some have argued that the Clovis hunters caused the extinction of the megafauna, while others suggest climate changes at the end of the Ice Age caused the extinction. In any event the Clovis culture changed rapidly as people adjusted to obtaining new foods.

Frequently during the past thirty years, people have claimed to have discovered archaeological sites dated far earlier than Clovis sites. Until recently none of these earlier dates has held up to systematic

study. In the past couple of years, however, a growing number of archaeologists have agreed that the Monte Verde site in northern Chile was inhabited around 12,000 years ago and possibly as early as 30,000 years ago.

If the dates for Monte Verde prove to be accurate, the date of entry into the New World will be changed. Linguists analyzing the distribution and spread of Native American languages have suggested that it would take at least 7,000 years for languages to become so different between Alaska and Chile. If Monte Verde was inhabited by 12,500 years ago, that would place entry into Alaska at around 20,000 years ago. However, at that date Alaska was in the middle of a glacial advance that had started about 22,000 years ago. The linguists suggest that entry occurred before the advance, probably before 30,000 years ago. One estimate of how long it would take for all the languages spoken by Native Americans to evolve is at least 40,000 years. This early date is also supported by some genetic studies that estimate it would take at least 30,000 years for the diversity of genes, or inherited characteristics, observed across Native American populations to occur.

One model using the 30,000-year date of entry sees hunters-gatherers rapidly moving to South America to escape the effects of the glacial advance. Archaeological evidence shows that Tierra del Fuego, the southern tip of South America, was reached between 8,000 and 5,000 years ago. When the glaciers retreated, people started to move north again and eventually created the Clovis culture. This original migration produced the vast majority of Native American populations. Around 12,000 years ago another migration from Siberia occurred. These people spoke languages very different from those that were already in the New World. They became the Na-Dene peoples who live mainly in northern North America. Finally, about 5,000 years ago, the speakers of Eskimo-Aleut languages entered the New World, again from Siberia.

Right now, there is no simple answer to the question of when the first peoples entered the New World. If the dates suggested by the linguistic and genetic analyses are correct, we have to ask why there are no well-documented archaeological sites earlier than 12,000 years ago in the New World. If Monte Verde is 30,000 years old, we are left with an 18,000-year gap in the archaeological record. Only more careful archaeological fieldwork can settle this issue.

Archaeologists are on much firmer ground when they discuss what happened in the New World after about 12,000 years ago. The hunting-gathering Clovis culture, widespread in North America, eventually changed into many different regional traditions as groups adapted to their local environments. On the Great Plains of North America, bison hunting on foot was the main economic activity until about 300 C.E., when maize, or corn, which had been domesticated in Mesoamerica before 5000 B.C.E., was introduced. Some groups became farmers, while others continued to hunt bison on foot. When horses were introduced to the Plains after 1640 C.E., some farming groups shifted from agriculture to bison hunting on horseback.

In western North America many groups remained hunter-gatherers until the time of European contact. By around 3500 B.C.E. the rich fishing in a region stretching from Washington State to Alaska had enabled settlement in large permanent villages. The tribes of this northwest coast area were among the most socially complex societies seen among hunter-gatherers. Socially

complex societies based on hunting, gathering, and fishing also developed in southern California.

In modern-day Arizona, New Mexico, Colorado, Utah, and northern Mexico, agriculture led to the rise of the so-called Pueblo traditions starting sometime after 200 B.C.E. The Anasazi constructed complex settlements such as Chaco Canyon and the cliff dwellings of Mesa Verde, while the Hohokam peoples built extensive irrigation canals and ball courts that suggest trading connections to more populated societies in Mexico. Many large communities in this area were abandoned in the late thirteenth and early fourteenth centuries, probably due to climatic changes. Sometime after 1450, the Apache and Navaho (Athabascan speakers whose ancestral homeland was in Canada) reached this area and settled among the Pueblo groups.

Hunter-gatherers in eastern North America were making pottery as early as 2500 B.C.E. Some groups started cultivating plants such as gourds, squashes, and sunflowers as early as 2000 B.C.E., but after 700 C.E. many groups increased their corn crops and became true farmers. Many of these Eastern Woodlands groups also buried their dead under mounds and built large earthworks. These trends culminated in the Mississippian tradition that started around 200 C.E. and reached its height with the building of Cahokia (near Saint Louis), which contained the largest prehistoric earthwork in North America. Although Cahokia was abandoned by 1500, many complex tribes existed in eastern North America when the Europeans entered the area.

People had settled in permanent villages in Central America by 1500 B.C.E. Between 1200 B.C.E. and 500 B.C.E., the Olmec civilization developed, influencing later development to the north in Mexico and in more southern parts of Central America. By 500 B.C.E. the earliest forms of writing had developed. Before 100 B.C.E. the first major city of Monte Albán arose, and central governments formed in the Oaxaca Valley and in the central highlands of Mexico. Around the same time the state system of the Maya developed. Teotihuacán and Monte Albán declined sometime before 750 C.E., and the Toltec Empire dominated a large area of Mexico from its capital city of Tula between 1000 and 1200. After the decline of Tula, the Aztec Empire expanded outward from the capital city of Tenochtitlán (starting about 1400) and was the main power in the area when the Spanish entered the New World.

The Mayan civilizations in southern Mexico, Guatemala, and Honduras rose and fell at different times. The states in the highlands attained peak populations before 250 C.E., while those in the southern lowlands grew until many were abandoned around 1000. Mayan peoples continued to live in the region, but many urban centers were forgotten.

Much more archaeological fieldwork needs to be done before we have a complete picture of the peopling of South America. For many reasons we know more about the Andes than other regions of the continent. First, more archaeology has been conducted in this region than elsewhere. Also, the damp climate in lowland areas like the rain forest is less likely to preserve many cultural objects. Finally, many groups in the lowlands retained hunting-gathering ways of life, sometimes mixing these with slash-and-burn farming, until very recently. These ways of life leave less for archaeologists to find than the groups that build in stone and engage in intensive agriculture.

We do know that by 3000 B.C.E. groups of hunter-gatherers were living in the central Andes. Over the next few centuries peoples of a single valley system united under one government. Sometimes these governments would conquer nearby valleys, and a small empire would rise. Archaeologists can frequently identify cultural traditions that span wide areas. These include Chavín, Tiwanaku, Nazca, Moche, and Sicán. Sometime after 1400 C.E. the Inca Empire started expanding out from the city of Cuzco, rapidly absorbed peoples in much of what became Peru and Ecuador, and was trying to conquer tropical forest peoples of Bolivia when the Spanish arrived.

By 2500 B.C.E. many Caribbean islands had been settled by the Ciboney, but there is still debate over whether these people originally came from Florida or from Venezuela. Between 1000 B.C.E. and 500 B.C.E., Arawak speakers came down the Orinoco River and entered the Caribbean. They displaced the Ciboney everywhere except in a few areas of Haiti and Cuba. In turn Arawak speakers were driven away from many islands by Carib speakers, also originally from northern South America. Wars between Arawak and Carib speakers were ongoing when the Spanish arrived in the area.

The world the Spanish entered was one where population movements were continuing. Unfortunately for the Native peoples, the Europeans were not just a new group of populations entering the mix. Because Native American populations had been isolated from Europeans, they had no immunity to many diseases the colonizers carried. Smallpox, measles, and other infectious diseases often swept through Native populations long before Europeans arrived at particular locations. It is estimated that measles may have caused the death of over one-half of New Spain's Native population by 1531.

This map indicates the most prominent Native American cultures and inhabited sites that developed in the Americas before the arrival of Europeans in the sixteenth century.

World" that forever changed the face of the "New."

People left the Old World to come to the New for many reasons. Many early explorers were looking for new routes for trade between Europe and the markets of India and China. European rulers sent men to the New World to claim land and to search for gold and other wealth. These bands destroyed the Aztec and Inca Empires and, what is more important, spread diseases that killed large numbers of Native Americans. Merchants saw the potential wealth in the New World and sent people to trade with Native American groups. Europeans in the fur trade explored vast areas of North America.

Many European countries established permanent colonies in the New World by giving huge tracts of land to their associates. Sometimes these people migrated to the New World, but often they sent overseers or relatives to farm or mine their lands. In many places these landowners forced Native Americans to work in mines or on plantations. This effort to enforce mass labor usually failed because the Indians died of disease, malnutrition, and mistreatment.

Owners solved this labor shortage by importing slaves, mainly from the west coast of Africa. The slaves who survived the terrible conditions of the voyage from Africa to the New World did much of the work that made European settlement possible in the New World. Their cultural traditions mixed with Native American and European traditions and helped create many new cultures in the New World.

With the loss of so many members, group migrations grew, bringing different Native Americans and Europeans into contact. The weapons of the Native Americans were rarely equal to the guns carried by Europeans, and many groups fell victim to these guns. Other groups escaped by leaving an area as soon as Europeans entered it. They did this to avoid the guns, but also to escape being forced to work in mines or on plantations. The guns carried by the Europeans soon were in Native hands, and frequently warfare between Native groups occurred far ahead of European settlement. The stage was set for the influx of immigrants from the "Old

Although slavery no longer exists in North and South America, the descendants of slaves are frequently at the bottom of the economic ladder and continue to struggle for social justice in many countries of the New World.

For the less wealthy of Europe, the Americas offered a chance to create a new life. Some immigrants were pushed out of Europe, while others were pulled to the New World. Religious persecution pushed members of some religious groups to emigrate. In other cases, members of a religion were pulled to the New World by the desire to follow their religion without interference from the government or from other religious groups. Wars and famine pushed millions of people out of Europe between the sixteenth century and the present. Thousands of people from Southeast Asia immigrated to the United States and other countries in the Americas after the end of the Vietnam War.

The chance for a better economic life has always been a major pull to the New World. Many people in Europe who were forced off the land or lived in crowded cities found stories of vast unsettled lands in the New World irresistible. These immigrants made the middle portion of North America and areas of California some of the most productive agricultural land in the world. When the population of countries in the Old World grew faster than their economies, many people escaped from poverty by coming to the Americas. In recent years, growth in the Pacific Rim economies has also induced wealthy families from Japan, China, and Singapore, to move to the west coast of the New World, not to escape from poverty, but to manage their wealth better.

The story of the peopling of the Americas is not only about groups leaving the Old World and finding a permanent place in the New. People have moved between the countries of the New World to search for wealth, to escape from poverty, to find political freedom, and to build religious communities. Such movement continues to blend cultures that were formerly separate. The many Mexican citizens living or working in the United States, for example, profoundly influence "Anglo" culture. Immigrants from the Caribbean have introduced the music and religions of this region to many cities in the United States, Canada, and South America.

How has this ceaseless movement of peoples affected the already settled inhabitants of the New World? The Europeans who settled in the Americas once thought that the Indians would die out or totally lose their native cultures. Unfortunately, in some places this prediction came true. There are almost no Native American groups found in the Caribbean, for example. In other regions Indian populations declined rapidly, and many people abandoned their traditional way of life.

In the last fifty years, however, some Indian groups have increased in size. Native American groups have become increasingly involved in defending their ways of life. Sometimes this involves winning land claims against the government. In other cases Indian groups are demanding that governments abide by treaties that were frequently ignored. Some groups that had lost much traditional culture are reviving their arts and religions and teaching the next generation about these things in museums and schools operated by members of the tribe. In areas of South America where Native American societies in the denser rain forest areas were contacted by Western culture relatively late, tribal groups have banded together to fight for their land against miners and farmers.

A map of the Americas today. The inset map shows the Caribbean area in more detail.

In this eleven-volume set of books, you will find out about the history and peoples of the Americas. You will learn about how Native American societies were affected by the European settlement of the New World. You will discover how the everyday life of the people in each country was shaped by the cultures of the different peoples who settled it. In the New World the rich cultural traditions of the Americas before the Europeans came and the cultures of Africa, Europe, and Asia have clashed and combined at different times and in different ways. At some times and in some places, the contact of cultures has been tragic, as in the loss of so many Native American lives and cultures and in the institution of slavery. At other times and in other places, the result has been a vibrant mixture that creatively combined elements of different cultures in a unique way and added to the diversity of human life on earth.

J. Patrick Gray
Professor of Anthropology
University of Wisconsin

Reader's Guide

PEOPLES OF THE AMERICAS contains a thorough coverage of the peoples of North and South America, including the indigenous peoples that have inhabited the continents for thousands of years and the more recent immigrants from Europe, Asia, Australasia, and Africa that have made the New World their home.

Volume One contains an introduction by J. Patrick Gray, Professor of Anthropology at the University of Wisconsin and consultant for the whole set. In his introduction, Patrick Gray sets out to map the history of the continents and explain how successive waves of migration, starting at least 13,000 and possibly 30,000 years ago and continuing to the present day, have helped shape their unique character.

The entries are arranged alphabetically by country. Each entry contains a short introduction to the country—its landscape, climate, and a brief general history. It then goes on to look at all the peoples occupying that country today. Larger countries are covered regionally, smaller countries are covered as a whole. We look at how the different groups of people came to be where they are and at their lifestyles in history and today, including the following:

- Religion, myth, and ritual
- Houses and homes
- Clothing and adornments
- Language
- Health and education
- Food and drink
- Family life
- Social life
- Arts and crafts
- Music and dance

For the indigenous peoples, we also examine the challenges to their way of life from outside interests—the oil and mining industries, new settlers, and farmers that threaten the often fragile lands they inhabit. Where groups of indigenous peoples cross national boundaries, they are included under both country entries and cross-referenced.

Most non-English words are followed by a simple pronunciation guide.

At the end of each volume is a **Glossary** with concise definitions of difficult words mentioned in the text, a comprehensive list of **Further Reading**, itemized by country, and an **Index** of about 300 entries.

The Index to the set, found in Volume 11, will help you find references to particular subjects. There is a general index, as well as indexes on the following specific topics:

- Biographical Index
- Geographical Index
- Arts of the Americas
- Festivals of the Americas
- Foods of the Americas
- Peoples and Cultures
- Religions and Religious Ceremonies
- Sports and Games

In addition Volume 11 contains a comprehensive **Pronunciation Guide** with definitions for all non-English words; a complete **Further Reading** list for all volumes, including works of fiction; and a list of **National Days** with explanations.

Each entry opens with a full-color relief map of the country, showing hills and mountains, major rivers, and major regions, towns, and cities mentioned in the text. Another map shows the position of the country within the continent or region as a whole.

The entries are lavishly illustrated with full-color and historical black-and-white photographs, with detailed captions that enhance the text.

Throughout the entries there are color-coded box features with more detailed information on particular topics. Each country has **Facts and Figures** and **Climate** boxes, a **Timeline**, and special boxes on especially fascinating features of life in the country.

The special boxes are just that. They contain those nuggets of information that make each and every country of North and South America special—unique religious practices, interesting food, peculiarites of language, or people and events in history that have shaped that country's destiny.

*The **Facts and Figures** box is a condensed gazetteer of the country, detailing its official name, status, capital and other major cities, its area, population and population density, the makeup of its peoples, its official language or languages, currency, national days, and how it got its name.*

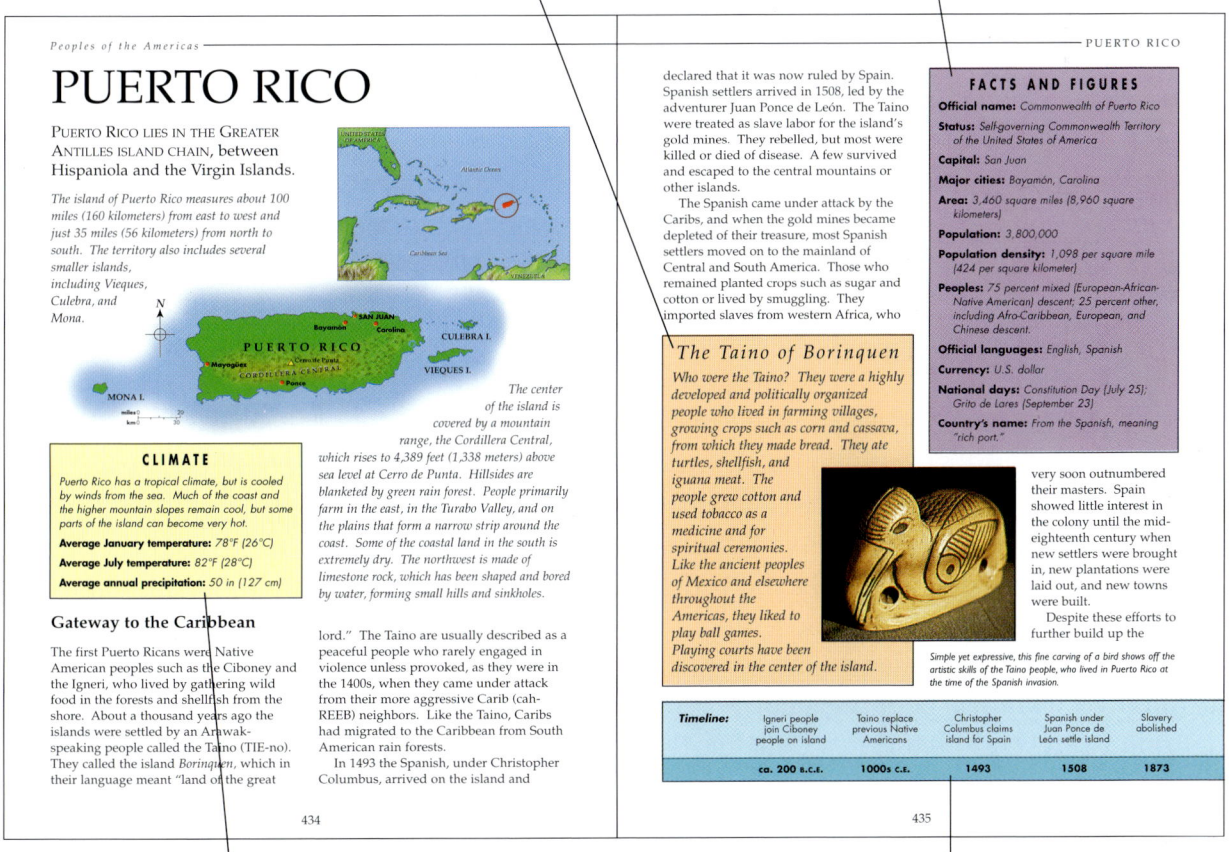

Peoples of the Americas — PUERTO RICO

PUERTO RICO

PUERTO RICO LIES IN THE GREATER ANTILLES ISLAND CHAIN, between Hispaniola and the Virgin Islands.

The island of Puerto Rico measures about 100 miles (160 kilometers) from east to west and just 35 miles (56 kilometers) from north to south. The territory also includes several smaller islands, including Vieques, Culebra, and Mona.

CLIMATE

Puerto Rico has a tropical climate, but is cooled by winds from the sea. Much of the coast and the higher mountain slopes remain cool, but some parts of the island can become very hot.

Average January temperature: 78°F (26°C)

Average July temperature: 82°F (28°C)

Average annual precipitation: 50 in (127 cm)

Gateway to the Caribbean

The first Puerto Ricans were Native American peoples such as the Ciboney and the Igneri, who lived by gathering wild food in the forests and shellfish from the shore. About a thousand years ago the islands were settled by an Arawak-speaking people called the Taino (TIE-no). They called the island *Borinquen*, which in their language meant "land of the great

The center of the island is covered by a mountain range, the Cordillera Central, which rises to 4,389 feet (1,338 meters) above sea level at Cerro de Punta. Hillsides are blanketed by green rain forest. People primarily farm in the east, in the Turabo Valley, and on the plains that form a narrow strip around the coast. Some of the coastal land in the south is extremely dry. The northwest is made of limestone rock, which has been shaped and bored by water, forming small hills and sinkholes.

lord." The Taino are usually described as a peaceful people who rarely engaged in violence unless provoked, as they were in the 1400s, when they came under attack from their more aggressive Carib (cah-REEB) neighbors. Like the Taino, Caribs had migrated to the Caribbean from South American rain forests.

In 1493 the Spanish, under Christopher Columbus, arrived on the island and

434

declared that it was now ruled by Spain. Spanish settlers arrived in 1508, led by the adventurer Juan Ponce de León. The Taino were treated as slave labor for the island's gold mines. They rebelled, but most were killed or died of disease. A few survived and escaped to the central mountains or other islands.

The Spanish came under attack by the Caribs, and when the gold mines became depleted of their treasure, most Spanish settlers moved on to the mainland of Central and South America. Those who remained planted crops such as sugar and cotton or lived by smuggling. They imported slaves from western Africa, who

The Taino of Borinquen

Who were the Taino? They were a highly developed and politically organized people who lived in farming villages, growing crops such as corn and cassava, from which they made bread. They ate turtles, shellfish, and iguana meat. The people grew cotton and used tobacco as a medicine and for spiritual ceremonies. Like the ancient peoples of Mexico and elsewhere throughout the Americas, they liked to play ball games. Playing courts have been discovered in the center of the island.

very soon outnumbered their masters. Spain showed little interest in the colony until the mid-eighteenth century when new settlers were brought in, new plantations were laid out, and new towns were built.

Despite these efforts to further build up the

Simple yet expressive, this fine carving of a bird shows off the artistic skills of the Taino people, who lived in Puerto Rico at the time of the Spanish invasion.

FACTS AND FIGURES

Official name: *Commonwealth of Puerto Rico*

Status: *Self-governing Commonwealth Territory of the United States of America*

Capital: *San Juan*

Major cities: *Bayamón, Carolina*

Area: *3,460 square miles (8,960 square kilometers)*

Population: *3,800,000*

Population density: *1,098 per square mile (424 per square kilometer)*

Peoples: *75 percent mixed (European-African-Native American) descent; 25 percent other, including Afro-Caribbean, European, and Chinese descent.*

Official languages: *English, Spanish*

Currency: *U.S. dollar*

National days: *Constitution Day (July 25); Grito de Lares (September 23)*

Country's name: *From the Spanish, meaning "rich port."*

Timeline:	Igneri people join Ciboney people on island	Taino replace previous Native Americans	Christopher Columbus claims island for Spain	Spanish under Juan Ponce de León settle island	Slavery abolished
	ca. 200 B.C.E.	1000s C.E.	1493	1508	1873

435

*The **Climate** box gives a summary of the general climate of the country and then, depending on the size of the country, gives regional statistical information on seasonal changes in temperature and precipitation.*

*The **Timeline** appears at the bottom of the opening pages of each entry and covers the main political events and movements of peoples that have affected the country from prehistoric times to the present day.*

ANGUILLA

ANGUILLA IS THE MOST NORTHERLY OF THE LEEWARD ISLANDS, a chain of islands lying in the warm waters of the eastern Caribbean Sea.

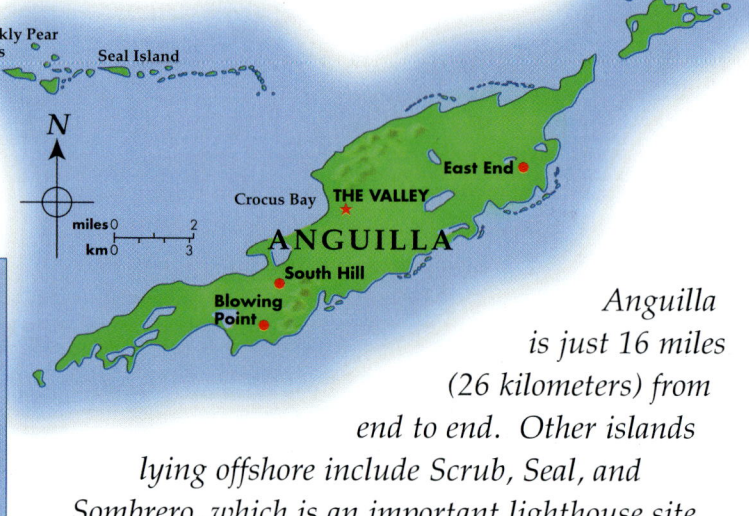

Anguilla is just 16 miles (26 kilometers) from end to end. Other islands lying offshore include Scrub, Seal, and Sombrero, which is an important lighthouse site 30 miles (48 kilometers) north of the main island.

The island is formed of coral and limestone. It is mostly flat, rising to 213 feet (65 meters) above sea level, and dotted with shallow, salty lagoons.

CLIMATE

The island is mostly sunny and dry with cool winds. Rains occur between September and January. Occasional fierce hurricanes sweep in from the Caribbean Sea.

Average year-round temperature: *81°F (27°C)*

Average annual precipitation: *35 in (89 cm)*

Life on a Small Island

Native American peoples are thought to have reached Anguilla (ang-GWIL-uh) in about 1300 B.C.E. Traces of later settlements of people who spoke Arawak have been found at several coastal sites. By the time the first Spanish explorers reached the region in the 1490s, the island was controlled by a Carib-speaking people who had come from South America. During the 1500s, European invaders murdered and enslaved almost all the Arawak-speakers and Carib-speakers. Diseases brought from Europe also killed many Native people. The only reminders of the Arawak-speakers today are their rock carvings in caves at Fountain and Big Spring.

British and Irish settlers arrived in the 1600s. The poor soil and dry climate did little to encourage farming, but these Europeans exported salt and managed to grow some cotton and tobacco. By 1650 the British had claimed Anguilla as a colony and brought in slaves of West African origin to work the land. In 1796 the French invaded the country but were defeated by the British. Slavery was abolished in 1834.

Most islanders today are Afro-Caribbean, descendants of those slaves, and some are of mixed Irish and African descent. In 1967 the islanders rejected a British plan to join together Anguilla with neighboring islands Saint Christopher and Nevis in a single independent nation (see SAINT KITTS-NEVIS).

2

FACTS AND FIGURES

Status: *British dependent territory*

Capital: *The Valley*

Area: *35 square miles (91 square kilometers)*

Population: *10,500*

Population density: *300 per square mile (115 per square kilometer)*

Peoples: *Mainly Afro-Caribbean and Afro-Caribbean-European descent; a few of European descent*

Official language: *English*

Currency: *East Caribbean dollar*

National days: *Anguilla Day (May 30); Constitution Day (August 6); Separation Day (December 19)*

Country's name: *Anguilla is named after its shape—anguilla means "eel" in Spanish.*

Instead, in 1980, Anguilla became a separate British dependency.

Anguillans speak English with a distinctive accent. Many of the islanders are active Christians, and the island has Anglican, Methodist, Baptist, Catholic, and Seventh-Day Adventist churches.

Anguilla is a quiet, peaceful island with a relaxed lifestyle. People mostly wear cool, informal clothes such as T-shirts, jeans, or cotton dresses. The most popular local sport is boat racing. It is a feature of the island's carnival, held each year in August. Carnival also includes fancy dress parades, steel drum bands, and dancing.

The island is not rich. Many Anguillans leave to work overseas, primarily in Great Britain, and send money back to their families at home. Those who stay grow crops such as sweet potatoes, corn, and pigeon peas for local use. Round and red, pigeon peas are a traditional food in the Caribbean. Many families keep chickens and goats. The blue seas of the Caribbean provide a valuable source of seafood, and fine Anguilla lobsters are exported to other Caribbean islands and the United States. In the island's shallow lagoons, the hot sun dries out brackish (salty) water, leaving behind salt that can be collected.

Since the 1980s, more and more people have found work in the growing tourist industry. The island's beautiful beaches and tropical seas have attracted a growing number of tourists.

How do the people keep cool when the temperature rises? An airy veranda welcomes the breeze in The Valley, and the water's edge is always enticing.

Timeline:	People reach and settle Anguilla	English settlers claim Anguilla for Great Britain	French invasion defeated	Slavery abolished	Anguilla rejects independence	Anguilla becomes a separate British dependency
	ca. 1300 B.C.E.	1650 C.E.	1796	1834	1967	1980

ANTIGUA AND BARBUDA

ANTIGUA AND BARBUDA ARE TWO OF THE LEEWARD ISLANDS. Together they make up an independent Caribbean nation.

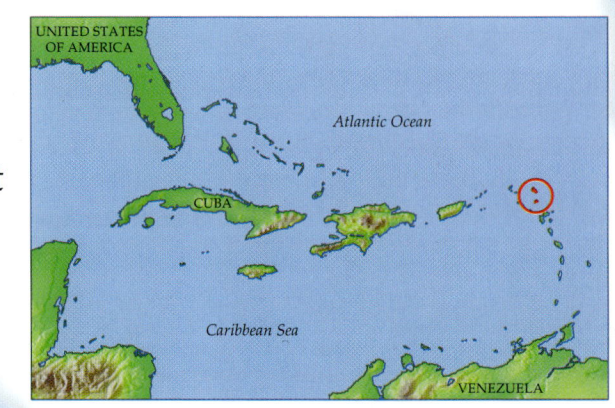

The main island, Antigua, lies 30 miles (48 kilometers) to the south of Barbuda. It is the largest of the Leeward Islands. Offshore lie Green, Guiana, and Long Islands. The territory also includes an uninhabited rocky island called Redonda.

Antigua is a low-lying island formed from coral and limestone. Its coast is fringed with mangroves. Barbuda has highlands in the east and lakes in the north and south. In the west are the calm waters of the Codrington Lagoon.

CLIMATE

The climate is dry for the Caribbean, and droughts are common. Cool winds blow most of the year. The hottest and wettest period is between May and November.

Average January temperature: *81°F (27°C)*

Average July temperature: *86°F (30°C)*

Average annual precipitation: *40 in (102 cm)*

Caribbean Island Life

Antigua (an-TEE-guh) and Barbuda (bahr-BOO-duh) were settled about two thousand years ago by people who spoke Arawak. They made tools of shell, stone, and wood. By the 1200s the region was controlled by the Carib-speaking peoples.

British settlers arrived in 1632. In 1666 the French attacked Antigua during a war with Great Britain. The British won and in 1667 began to rule Antigua. In 1674 they

English Bay, Antigua, was the site of a British naval base from 1743 to 1899. Today many North Americans and Europeans come here for yachting.

FACTS AND FIGURES

Official name: *State of Antigua and Barbuda*

Status: *Independent state*

Capital: *Saint John's*

Area: *170 square miles (441 square kilometers)*

Population: *77,000*

Population density: *453 per square mile (175 per square kilometer)*

Peoples: *90 percent Afro-Caribbean; the remainder are European and Lebanese*

Official language: *English*

Currency: *East Caribbean dollar*

National day: *Independence Day (November 1)*

Country's name: *Christopher Columbus named Antigua after a church in Seville, Spain, called Santa Maria la Antigua. Barbuda means "bearded" in Spanish.*

population of British, Portuguese, and Lebanese. Most islanders are Christians belonging to the Anglican Church.

Almost 76,000 people live on Antigua. It is crowded compared to Barbuda, which has only about 1,100 permanent inhabitants.

Antigua has a good education system and state-run hospitals and clinics. Antiguans enjoy a relaxed, informal lifestyle. The most popular local sport is cricket, and the island's August carnival provides an opportunity for dancing in the street to steel bands and reggae music.

The seas off the islands are famous for their lobsters, and fishing is a way of life for some islanders. Others are farmers; tropical fruits, such as pineapples, grow well here. The chief crop is cotton. Sugarcane was once widely grown, but the sugar industry collapsed in 1972 under competition from rival producers. Factories produce clothing, electric fans, and refrigerators.

imported slaves of African origin to clear the forest and plant sugarcane.

Slavery was abolished in 1834, but the liberated slaves were not given land. Most of them remained poor, while the Europeans controlled the island's economy and land. Great poverty forced many people off farmland and into shantytowns.

Over the next one hundred years, trade developed with the United States. In 1941 the United States began to build military bases on the island, which started a building boom. Independence from Great Britain finally came peacefully in 1981.

Today about nine out of ten Antiguans are Afro-Caribbeans, speaking English with a regional accent. There is also a small

Many visitors come to Antigua to enjoy the beautiful beaches. The growing tourist industry now employs about half the labor force and has made a few islanders wealthy.

Timeline:	Arawak-speakers settle on Antigua and Barbuda	British settle on Antigua	Antigua comes under British rule	Slaves brought to Antigua	Slavery abolished	Full independence from Great Britain
	ca. 1 C.E.	1632	1667	1674	1834	1981

ARGENTINA

ARGENTINA IS THE SECOND LARGEST NATION IN SOUTH AMERICA and the eighth largest in the world.

Argentina stretches from the tropics to the cold seas of the far south. Its western border is formed by the soaring peaks and glaciers of the Andes, while to the east are the stormy waters of the South Atlantic Ocean.

The Andes mountains run the length of the country along the western border with Chile. The Gran Chaco of the north is a wide plain that includes rough scrub, thorny forest, and natural grasslands. Mesopotamia in the northeast contains rain forests, grassy plains, and swamps. The Pampas is an area of natural grassland. Patagonia, the southernmost part of Argentina, is a cold desert of dry, windy plateaus.

Lake Nahuel Huapi is at the center of a large national park near Argentina's border with Chile. This beautiful area attracts huge numbers of visitors each year.

Land of Immigrants

The first people to live in Argentina (ahr-jen-TEE-nuh) were Indians who reached these lands between 12,000 and 14,000 years ago. Over the ages, many different languages and ways of life developed in the region. When Europeans arrived in 1516, it was home to about 300,000 Native

American peoples with at least twenty distinct ethnic groups and cultures.

Soon Spanish settlers were pouring into the region from Bolivia and Peru (see BOLIVIA and PERU). Many of them intermarried with Native Americans, forming the largest part of the colonial population. The land became part of Spain's South American empire and was ruled from Peru until 1776.

The early colonialists brought in large numbers of slaves from western Africa to be servants and to do general labor. Many of the descendents of these slaves joined in the fight for independence from Spain in 1816. Slavery was abolished in 1853. However, Argentina's African population was soon outnumbered by new immigrants and became completely absorbed into the general population. There is no sizeable black community in Argentina today.

The country became independent from Spain in 1816, after a war led by General José de San Martín. The following forty years saw Argentina torn apart by civil wars, in which the cowboys of the Pampas grasslands, the gauchos, played an important part fighting for local warlords. The country was finally united under its current name in 1861.

In the second half of the 1800s, Argentina profited from its growing trade in beef cattle. With the flood of funds, new roads and railways were built.

The promise of land for farming attracted new European settlers fleeing poverty and persecution in their own lands. From the 1850s into the 1900s, large

FACTS AND FIGURES

Official name: *República Argentina*

Status: *Independent state*

Capital: *Buenos Aires*

Major cities: *Córdoba, Rosario, Mendoza, La Plata, San Miguel de Tucumán, Mar del Plata, San Juan*

Area: *1,073,399 square miles (2,780,092 square kilometers)*

Population: *35,600,000*

Population density: *33 per square mile (13 per square kilometer)*

Peoples: *85 percent European descent; 14.7 percent European-Native descent; 0.3 percent Native American*

Official language: *Spanish*

Currency: *Argentine peso*

National days: *May Revolution (May 25); Malvinas Day (June 10); Flag Day (June 20); Independence Day (July 9); San Martín Day (August 17)*

The country's name: *Argentina means "land of silver" in Latin.*

numbers of these new immigrants poured into Argentina. People of Spanish heritage were now outnumbered by immigrants from other European countries. Thousands of Italians moved in and soon became the country's largest ethnic group. There were also British engineers, and farmers from Germany, France, Switzerland, and the Basque homeland along the French-Spanish border. There were Jews and Slavs from the Balkans, eastern Europe, and Russia. Today Argentina has a thriving Jewish

Timeline:	Native peoples reach central South America	Native peoples reach southernmost Patagonia	Spanish discover Rio de la Plata	Spanish found Buenos Aires
	ca. 12,000 B.C.E.	ca. 12,000 B.C.E.	1516 C.E.	1536

La Boca is one of the liveliest districts of Buenos Aires. The neighborhood was originally settled by Basques from France and was later occupied by Italian immigrants.

community of about 400,000. Syrians and Lebanese settled in the north, and Welsh settlers from Great Britain arrived in Patagonia in the south to raise sheep. There were also Dutch, Poles, Hungarians, and Danes. More recently, migrants have arrived from Asia, including Japan and Korea. Many Bolivians and Chileans work on sheep stations or as seasonal laborers (see BOLIVIA and CHILE).

What became of the Native Americans? Some married with the European settlers, became Christians, and took up new ways of life as gauchos and laborers. Many more died of new diseases brought in from Europe. Some fought against the invaders, but in the end, most were murdered, hunted down by the Europeans in a series of brutal raids and wars. Native lands were seized and turned into huge estates owned by a few wealthy landowners. Only about 100,000 Native Americans survive in this large country today.

Modern-day Politicians

Modern Argentina has had a troubled history. Dictators and generals have struggled against democrats for power. One of the most powerful leaders was Juan Perón, who was president from 1946 to

The Spanish separate region from Peru	Independence from Spain	Slavery abolished	European settlement of the Pampas (the plains)	Country united as "Argentina"
1776	1816	1853	1857	1861

CLIMATE

Northern Argentina is a humid area, with hot, wet summers and cold, dry winters. The Pampas have less extreme temperatures, but the eastern part has more rain than the western part. To the south, Patagonia has a mild climate. Tierra del Fuego at the southern tip of the continent has high rainfall all year-round. The Andes mountains are dry in the north, but heavy snows fall in the cold south.

	San Miguel de Tucumán	Buenos Aires	Mendoza	Ushuaia
Average January temperature	79°F (26°C)	74°F (23°C)	75°F (24°C)	50°F (10°C)
Average July temperature	56°F (13°C)	50°F (10°C)	47°F (8°C)	34°F (1°C)
Average annual precipitation	38 in (97 cm)	37 in (94 cm)	8 in (20 cm)	19 in (48 cm)

1955 and again from 1973 to 1974. Perón came up through the ranks of the military to become president of an oppressive political system. He banned free speech, controlled the newspapers and radios, and closed religious schools. At first Perón was popular with the working classes and the poor. But he ran the country into tremendous debt, and prices rose quickly. In 1955, Perón was forced to resign from office and a series of military and civilian governments took over.

In 1976 the armed forces seized power and banned all political parties. They imprisoned or murdered thousands of their opponents. In 1982 the Argentine army invaded the British territory of the Falkland, or Malvinas, Islands, claiming them for Argentina. British troops retook the islands in a brief but bitter war. The following year Argentina returned to democratic rule.

The mothers of those who "disappeared" in the 1970s and 1980s demand information about their children. Many people were tortured and murdered by the military regime.

Since the return of democracy, Argentina has suffered soaring inflation and military unrest. Peronists (members of a political party that supports the ideas of Perón), such as President Carlos Menem, elected in 1989, have moved away from their original policies. The government is now fighting inflation and encouraging free enterprise.

Juan Perón becomes president for the first time	A group of military leaders rules Argentina	War with Great Britain over the Falkland (Malvinas) Islands	Democracy restored	Carlos Menem elected president
1946	**1976**	**1982**	**1983**	**1989**

Dishes from Many Lands

Many different types of cooking are found in Argentina since each group of settlers brought their own favorite dishes with them. Asado con cuero (ah-SAH-doe KONE kwer-oh) is beef barbecued in its hide over an open fire, the traditional food of the gaucho. Italian immigrants brought pasta and potato dumplings, known in Argentina as noquis *(NO-kees). German and central European immigrants brought black puddings, or blood sausages. These became known as* morcillas *(more-SEE-yahs). Locro (LOW-crow) is a dish in the Native Americans' style—a thick soup with meat, beans, potatoes, and peppers.*

Other popular foods are empanadas *(EHM-puh-nah-duhs)—pastries stuffed with meat or seafood—and* pucheros *(poo-CHER-ohs)— stews of chicken or other meats with vegetables.*

The barbecue is one gaucho tradition that is as popular in the suburbs of Buenos Aires as on the Pampas. Asado con cuero—roast beef—tops the menu.

Argentineans Today: The Melting Pot

Of all the countries in South America, Argentina is probably the most like a European country today. Most Argentineans are wholly or partly of European descent. They have all played their part in the creation of modern Argentina, which has acted as a melting pot where languages and cultures of many peoples have mixed together.

The chief language of Argentina is Spanish. This is spoken with a very different accent than the Castilian form of the language spoken in central Spain, and the local accent also differs from other Latin American dialects. For example, the letters *ll* are pronounced *sh* instead of the more common *y*. Spanish is the language of government and is spoken by 97 percent of all Argentineans.

Even so, other languages may still be heard. Native American languages such as Guaraní and Quechua are spoken in the north and west. Many people speak Italian; other communities have also kept alive the languages of the early pioneers, such as English, German, or Welsh.

News is reported in famous papers such as *La Prensa, La Nación*, and *Clarín*. Most publications are in Spanish, and daily newspapers are also published in English, French, and German. There are hundreds of national and regional newspapers. A wide choice of radio and television stations is available, with satellite and cable channels in the more populated regions.

Argentina has a long tradition of learning, with universities dating back to the early days of Spanish settlement. Over the last one hundred years, the education system has raised the percentage of the population who can read and write from 22 percent to over 95 percent today.

Ninety-three percent of people in Argentina are Roman Catholic Christians, but there are also Protestant and Eastern Orthodox Christians, Jews, and people of many other faiths.

As in many largely Catholic countries, the family, which may include grandparents, aunts, uncles, and distant cousins, plays a crucial part in everyday life. Ceremonies such as weddings and funerals are important, and family links extend into the world of business and trade.

Devout Catholics honor saints and shrines with holy days, festivals, and pilgrimages. Over four million pilgrims a year visit the town of Luján, west of Buenos Aires, to pay their respects to the Virgin of Luján, the patron saint of the nation. The northwestern city of Salta celebrates Christmas with festivals of carols.

Some public festivals were brought over to Argentina from Spain, Italy, and Germany. These include carnival, which is a festival held before the Christian time of Lent, as well as local beer and wine festivals. Other festivals mark important moments in Argentine history, often with fireworks and colorful parades.

How do Argentineans make a living? Since 70

Hundreds of thousands of Christians take to the streets of Salta in the northwest. The custom of celebrating Christian festivals with public processions originated in Spain and Italy.

percent of all the country's exports are agricultural products, many work in farming and shipping. Argentine ports ship out wool, vegetable oils, wine, fruit, wheat, and refrigerated beef. In addition, about one in five members of the labor force work in factories, producing textiles, paper, steel, and motor vehicles. Imports include plastics, machinery, and chemicals.

Many families suffered hardships as a result of the country's past political problems, particularly in the period of military government from 1976 to 1983. The Argentine economy has improved in the years since military rule came to an end, but this has not benefited everyone. Buenos Aires is home to some extremely wealthy families, but there are still many poor people in both town and country.

On average, Argentine men can expect to live sixty-eight years and women seventy-five, one of the highest life expectancies in

South America. The country has over three thousand hospitals, and there are more doctors per number of people than in the United States. Health care is paid for by private insurance plans, and there is now also a workers' health plan to help people on low incomes.

Argentina's provinces are linked by air, road, and rail. Many of the roads in country areas are still unpaved. Public transportation is at its best in the capital and major cities. In recent years, the government sold many publicly owned transport systems to private companies in an effort to save tax dollars.

Porteños: People of the Port

The Argentine capital is Buenos Aires, which lies on the southern shores of the Rio de la Plata (River Plate) estuary on the edge of the Pampas, the plains of South America. *Buenos Aires* means "fair winds" in Spanish, and its inhabitants are known as *Porteños,* which means "people of the port."

A fine old steam locomotive stops at Belgrano Station in San Miguel de Tucumán. The country's aging railroad network was built primarily in the nineteenth century.

The Caminito is a popular walk through the southeastern district of La Boca in Buenos Aires. Many of its brightly painted buildings are occupied by artists' studios.

Pedro de Mendoza, a Spanish adventurer, founded the first settlement on this site in 1536. Over the next 350 years, Buenos Aires grew into a major port, its wealth coming from the beef trade. Its merchants were often in political disputes with the big landowners of the countryside. The fact that Buenos Aires remains the center of power today is still criticized by many people from other large cities and from the countryside. They believe that the Porteños look down on them.

Modern Buenos Aires is a sprawling, bustling city built on a grid pattern. Four in every ten Argentineans are Porteños, and it is the big city rather than the wide open spaces of the back country that makes up their world. The streets are busy with taxis and buses, and the capital has its own subway system. The oldest part of town

Big City Slang

Guita (GWEE-tah) means "dough" or "bread" in the sense of money. Pibe (PEE-bay) means "guy." This is Lunfardo (loon-FAR-doh), the street language of Buenos Aires. This dialect of Spanish uses roundabout ways of describing everyday objects. Lunfardo started as a secret language made up by crooks and thieves, but it soon found its way into popular music and poetry. Even so, some of its words should not be used in polite society!

13

The busy traffic of downtown Buenos Aires cuts through the city's main shopping area. The wide avenues 9 de Julio and Corrientes cross at the Obelisco, the tall pillar seen here.

lies around the Plaza de Mayo and the Metropolitan Cathedral, which contains the tomb of José de San Martín, leader of the war for independence from Spain.

Successful businesspeople make their homes in the wealthier suburbs. The richest city-dwellers think nothing of jetting off to their country estates or of owning expensive polo ponies. By contrast, outside the central city, Buenos Aires also has areas of slums and shantytowns—wooden shacks built by poor migrants.

Buenos Aires is a city with a strong European character—hardly surprising since most of its inhabitants are of Italian, Spanish, or other European descent. Cafés are at the center of social life. There, people may linger over a cup of coffee, talk business, play chess, or listen to music. The city stays open late at night, but everything closes down for the weekend, which is a time for the family.

The Nordestinos: People Between Two Rivers

Upstream from Buenos Aires, the Rio de la Plata divides into two great rivers, the Paraná and the Uruguay. The land between the two is known as Mesopotamia. This northeastern part of Argentina includes three provinces—Misiones, Entre Ríos, and Corrientes. Here subtropical rain forests descend to rolling, grassy plains and swamps. Large areas of forest and savannah were cleared for farming in the last one hundred years.

Originally, this region was the territory of a Native American group who spoke Guaraní (gwar-ruh-NEE). Their lands still cross the River Paraná into parts of Paraguay, Uruguay, and southern Brazil (see PARAGUAY, URUGUAY, and BRAZIL). The Guaraní-speakers were once fierce warriors, skilled in the use of bows and arrows. Despite their warlike reputation, some Guaraní-speaking villagers befriended the early Spanish settlers and taught them how to farm local crops such as corn, beans, and a tropical root called manioc (*mandiok* in the Guaraní language). Manioc can be made into tapioca, also a Guaraní word meaning "squeezed out residue."

Jesuit missionaries tried to convert the Guaraní-speakers to the Christian faith, but the mission stations were often raided for slaves. Traditionally, the social groups of Guaraní-speakers were organized into groups through descent from the father; when women married, they went to live in the villages

Who Made the Waterfalls?

The Iguazú Falls are one of the most impressive natural spectacles in South America. Here, on Argentina's border with Brazil, the Iguazú River tumbles over 230 feet (70 meters) through rocks and reefs over a one-and-one-quarter-mile (two-kilometer) wide plateau rim. According to Guaraní mythology, the falls were created when a young warrior called Caroba fell in love with a beautiful young woman called Naipur. Unfortunately, she was already loved by the god of the forest. When Caroba stole away his sweetheart by canoe, the furious god tore the riverbed apart. Raging waters swept the little canoe over the chasm. The warrior was turned into a rock and his lover into a tree.

of their husbands. Villages often contained as many as sixty closely related families.

The largest number of their descendants live across the border in Paraguay (see PARAGUAY), but about fifteen thousand of them still live in the northeastern region of Argentina. Few follow the traditional way of life of their people. But their music survives, as does their language. Some Guaraní words are also used by the

The Guaraní-speaking people live in Brazil, Paraguay, Uruguay, and Argentina. Some follow their ancient traditions, while others have adopted a Western lifestyle.

The scene of gauchos rounding up cattle is traditionally associated with the Pampas, but this is in Entre Ríos province. The Argentine Northeast includes important ranching country.

Spanish-speakers of the region. Most Guaraní-speakers are Roman Catholics whose religious lives center on household rituals and celebrations of saints. They have a rich store of myths and legends, often expressed in song and dance.

Today most Nordestinos, or Northeasterners, are of European or mixed descent. Some are descended from the early Spanish pioneers, others from farmers who arrived more recently. These included Italians, English, Russian Jews, Germans, Poles, and Asians. People of the northeast still mostly live by farming, raising beef cattle or sheep, or by growing grain crops, flax (for making linen), or fruit. Others work in forestry and sawmills. Tourism is important to the region. The beautiful countryside includes several national parks.

At the moment, there are few factories or offices to provide work in the northeastern provinces. A massive dam, built by Argentina and Paraguay, is being completed at Yacyretá, on the River Paraná (see PARAGUAY). Its purpose is to provide hydroelectric power for new industries in the region, but the costs of the plan have proved to be crippling. Many people are forced to move their homes as waters rise in the dammed river valley.

The peoples of the northeast are rural, independent, and proud of their own traditions, particularly their festivals and carnivals. These include *jineteados* (hee-nay-tay-AH-dohs), which means "rodeos," and folk music festivals.

Tamers of the Wilderness: People of the Gran Chaco

A wide plain called the Gran Chaco extends across Argentina's northern borders with Bolivia and Paraguay (see BOLIVIA and PARAGUAY). This region also includes the Argentine provinces of Formosa and Chaco. The landscape varies from rough scrub to thorny forest to natural grassland. Although the Gran Chaco has a cool, dry climate in winter, in summer it is extremely humid and hot. This is the rainy season, when floods cover the plains, creating swamps.

The early European settlers called the furnace of the Gran Chaco a "green hell." The region was very thinly populated, so there were few people to use as a workforce. The few Native Americans who did live on the Chaco fiercely resisted the Spanish arrivals.

Original peoples of the Argentine Chaco included the Chulupí, or Ashluslay; the Mocoví; the Toba; and the Mataco. The Chulupí (CHEW-loop-ee) gathered plants such as wild rice and ate insect larvae and wild honey. Wild cotton and palm fronds provided fiber for their cloth. They fished in the rivers and lived a nomadic life, traveling in bands of about one hundred. Groups were organized through descent in the female line, with membership in kinship groups passed from mothers to their children.

The Mataco (ma-TAH-ko) lived to the south of the Chulupí. They, too, lived by fishing, hunting, and gathering plants. Protestant Christian missionaries converted most Mataco to Christianity.

The Toba (TO-bah) were skilled in textile crafts, weaving beautifully patterned belts of wool on simple looms. They also used cactus fibers to make fabric.

As more and more Europeans settled on the Chaco in the 1800s, the old ways of life began to disappear. Some Native Americans learned to ride horses and found work as ranch hands. Others drifted to the southern cities in search of work. Today some Native Americans on the Gran Chaco are small landholders, growing vegetables and raising their own sheep and goats. However, most are laborers on larger farms or industrial workers, and many are very poor. About 10,000 Mataco and about 15,000 Mocoví and Toba survive on the Gran Chaco today.

The first European settlers to try their luck on the Chaco were Spanish, but in the 1900s, they were followed by new immigrants from central Europe and Italy. These came to grow cotton or to cut down the hardwood tree known as the *quebracho* (kay-BRAH-choh), or "axe breaker." The region is still thinly populated today, and logging remains important for the economy. Sunflower seeds are also a major crop.

Refreshing Maté

Yerba maté is a refreshing hot drink made from the bitter leaves of a shrub called Paraguay holly, which has long been a major crop of northeastern Argentina. The drink takes its name from a Native American word mati *(MAH-tee), which means "gourd." Maté is still drunk from gourd-shaped containers today. It is sipped through a silver straw called a* bombilla *(bohm-BEE-yah), which strains off the leaves. The Native Americans, the first Jesuit missionaries, and then the gaucho cowboys of the Pampas grasslands all drank this precious brew by the gallon.*

Maté is still a very popular drink throughout Argentina, where it is seen as a mark of old-fashioned hospitality. In the northeast, it is sweetened with sugar and flavored with herbs or spices, such as anise seed. On the Pampas and in Patagonia, it is drunk bitter, without sugar. Maté is also drunk in Paraguay and Brazil (see PARAGUAY and BRAZIL).

Córdobans Fill the Heartland

The city of Córdoba lies at the center of the northern half of the country. It dates back to 1573, and over one million people live there today. Since the arrival of the first Spanish settlers, Córdoba has been a center of trade, religion, politics, learning, and culture. The city has many fine old buildings from the colonial period.

The countryside around the city includes fertile farmland and the beautiful Sierras de Córdoba mountain ranges, which are visited by many tourists every year. The name of one range, the Sierra de Comechingones, is a reminder that this was once the territory of the Comechingon peoples. The Comechingones (co-MAY-chee-go-NEEZ) lived in villages, growing corn and herding llamas for their wool and meat. They fought a hard but unequal battle against the Spanish invaders; their warriors were armed only with bows and arrows, and each village fought alone,

A family takes a weekend break by the still waters of a lake set in the beautiful mountains of Córdoba province. The lake was created by the damming of the Rio Ceballos.

rather than uniting with others. Many Comechingones died in battle. In addition, thousands of Comechingones died from diseases brought in by the Spanish.

Very few signs of Native American traditions remain in this region of Argentina. Today's Córdobans are mostly descended from the European immigrants who arrived after railways opened up the region for settlement over one hundred years ago.

Peoples of the Far West

The Andes run down the border between Argentina and Chile. They are a series of massive peaks that soar to 22,834 feet (6,960 meters) above sea level at Aconcagua. The mountain regions are dry in the north, but heavy snows fall in the cold south of Argentina.

Today, the Argentine northwest is a remote region, far from the capital on the coast. However, in the days before the Spanish Conquest, the Andean regions were the most heavily settled, falling under the influence of the great Native American civilizations to the northwest.

The Diaguita (dee-ha-GEE-tah) people of the northwest were farmers who lived in villages and small towns (see CHILE). They irrigated terraced hillsides to grow corn, squash, and beans. On higher mountainsides, they also grew potatoes and quinoa, a grain crop. They made drinks from the pods of the carob tree, hunted the rhea (the South American ostrich), and ate the meat of llamas. Llamas and their relatives, the vicuña and guanaco, also provided wool for the Diaguita, who were skilled weavers of blankets and shirts. They also made beautiful pottery. Their warriors were organized fighters, armed with clubs, bows, and arrows. Their land became an outpost

Las Leñas, in Mendoza province, is an international ski resort set high in the Andes mountains. In the southern part of the world, the winter sports season lasts from June to October.

of the mighty Inca Empire in the 1400s (see Peru), and the Quechua language, dating back to the days of the Incas, is still widely spoken in the region.

The northwestern region was the first to be settled by the Spanish, and old churches and buildings still stand as reminders of its colonial past. Sheep graze on some high pastures, and mines for iron ore and uranium are common. The large plantations at the foot of the mountains produce sugarcane and tobacco; cotton is grown in Santiago del Estero. The northwest has many colorful festivals, many of which are religious, mixing Roman Catholic and Indian traditions.

Life for the poor laborers of the northwest is far from easy. There is little farmwork outside the harvest season. Country roads are often little more than rough tracks, with buses, trucks, or carts lurching from one pothole to another.

To the south, tucked into the foothills of the Andes, are the provinces of Mendoza and San Juan, each named after major cities. This sheltered farming region is known as Cuyo, taking its name from a word of the Huarpe people—*cuyum,* meaning "sandy ground." The Huarpe (oo-AR-pay) were corn farmers who built irrigation channels to their fields in the foothills of the Andes. They passed this valuable knowledge on to the first Spanish settlers. Huarpe skills included basketry and canoe building. Travelers from the east approach Cuyo through the province of San Luis.

Many of the inhabitants of this part of Argentina are of Italian descent, and a larger number of mestizos (people of mixed European and Indian descent) live there than in the eastern part of the country. The region has a dry, sunny climate that is ideal for growing olives, citrus fruits, and grapes. Argentina has been producing good quality wine for hundreds of years, and the grape harvest is celebrated locally with a special festival at which the vines are blessed.

Land of the Gauchos: The Pampas

This sketch, drawn in about 1871, shows indigenous peoples hunting rhea and guanaco with the boleadoras. This whirling weapon was popular with the gauchos of the Pampas.

South of the River Paraná and the mouth of the Río de la Plata lies one of the world's most important areas of natural grassland. The Pampas take up 20 percent of the country's land area. This rolling landscape is moist in the east, which is nearer to the Atlantic Ocean, but drier in the west, which lies in the shadow of the Andes. Parts of the Pampas are marshy, and there are few trees. The climate is mild, and the land is green.

The Pampas were once a sea of grass, the home of scattered bands of Native Americans. These included the Querandí, the Chechehet, and, on the borders of Patagonia, the Puelche, or Guenaken. These Indians hunted the birds and animals of the grasslands, such as the ostrichlike rhea and the wild llama—the guanaco. It was probably the Querandí (kare-rahn-DEE) who invented the *boleadoras* (bowl-lay-uh-DOR-us), a weighted cord used to bring down animals on the run. They also fought with bows and arrows, and spears, aided by spear-throwing sticks.

When the cattle and horses of the Spanish arrivals ran wild and spread across the Pampas, the Querandí learned to ride and hunt the new animals. They formed hunting bands up to a thousand strong. These riding skills served the Querandí well when they became gauchos (cowboys); many of Argentina's gauchos were descended from them.

However, the greatest number of Pampas peoples were slaughtered by the Spanish. Whole tribes were destroyed in a series of wars that took place in the 1800s.

During the last century, the Pampas grasslands became the center of Argentina's international beef trade. Rich landowners with large ranches fenced off the grasslands and hired ranch hands from the new settlers who were pouring in from Europe. Quality beef cattle and sheep were imported from Europe to replace the wild herds.

Today on the Pampas, large areas are devoted to growing crops. The cattle truck, tractor, and four-wheel drive vehicles have taken over many of the cowboy's duties .

Two-thirds of all Argentineans live on the Pampas today. The region includes the big city of Rosario, the major port of Bahía Blanca, and Mar del Plata, a holiday spot on the Atlantic coast that is popular with the Porteños of Buenos Aires.

Gauchos: Cowboys of Argentina

Few groups of people have played such an important part in Argentine tradition as the cowboys of the Pampas—the gauchos. They were famed as some of the world's best horsemen, riding over rough ground at breakneck speed and swimming across rivers with their horses. Many gauchos were mestizos, of mixed European and Native descent.

The first gauchos had long mustaches and often wore their hair long. They wore caps or broad-brimmed hats, neckerchiefs, scarlet red cloaks or ponchos, wide pants called **bombachas** (bohm-BAH-chahs), leather boots with spurs, and belts with heavy silver buckles. Heavily armed with long knives and pistols, they hunted with lassos and the old Querandí weapons of the **bola**, or **boleadoras**, three stones attached to leather thongs that were whirled and thrown, to become entangled in the animal's legs.

The gauchos lived with few comforts, sleeping beneath the stars or in makeshift shelters. They ate little but barbecued beef and used cattle bones as fuel for the campfire. The image of the gauchos is that of tough old rogues, swaggering brigands who loved to drink and gamble and brawl. However, they also became widely admired for their bravery, their courteous manners, their sense of honor, and their hospitality. Stories about them passed into Argentine folklore and song.

The world of the gaucho has virtually disappeared today, but the legend lives on. Many ranch hands still ride with the swagger of the old-timers, and the traditional finery is still worn with pride at cattle fairs and festivals. Even at a city barbecue, people will still roast beef over open fires in the gaucho style.

Riding out in style—a modern gaucho keeps the old tradition alive. The gauchos have become as famous around the world as the cowboys of the North American West.

The Patagonians: People of the South

Patagonia is a huge, sparsely populated region that stretches down to the cold seas and storm-swept rocks at the southern tip of South America. It includes the Argentine provinces of Río Negro, Chubut, Santa Cruz, and Tierra del Fuego.

Patagonia is like a cold desert, made up of dry, windy plateaus with stunted trees and river valleys. However, there is enough pasture here to provide grazing for sheep, and irrigation makes it possible to grow crops.

Patagonia was a harsh home for the indigenous peoples who lived there and also for the European settlers who displaced them in the 1800s.

Most of Patagonia was occupied by the nomadic Tehuelche (tuh-WEL-chee), or Tsoneca, hunters. They wore cloaks made of rawhide and rough, unstitched moccasins. Hide was also used to cover their *toldo* (TOLL-doe), a portable shelter made of long poles. Bodies of the Tehuelche dead were left on hillsides or in caves.

Where Patagonia meets the snowy peaks of the Andes were the lands of the Poya and the Pehuenche Indians (see CHILE). Far to the south, across the Straits of

The port of Ushuaia is the southernmost town in the world. Ushuaia is a naval base; its 40,000 inhabitants make their living from light industry and fishing.

Magellan, were the lands of the natives of Tierra del Fuego, including the Canoe Indians of the coast, whose former territory lies today mostly in Chile (see CHILE). Here, too, were the peoples of the extreme southeast of Argentina, the Ona (OH-nah), or Selknam, and Aush (AUS), or Haush, who were experts at surviving in the bitterly cold climate. Some of the Ona and Aush went naked except for skin cloaks and hoods and a rubbing of grease. They were hunters, armed with longbows and arrows, who lived in small family bands with no chiefs. While the Canoe ate seabirds and shellfish, the Ona and Aush for the most part hunted for guanaco inland. The Fuegian peoples were nearly all killed by the Argentine army in a campaign to exterminate indigenous peoples in the 1880s, or by diseases for which they had no resistance. They had almost completely died out by the early twentieth century.

Native American lands in Patagonia were taken over by settlers—Spanish, Italians, and Welsh. All kinds of people turned up in this wilderness at the end of the world.

A Land of Giants?

The first Europeans to sail these southern coasts reported that the land was occupied by a race of giants. The Portuguese explorer Ferdinand Magellan even called the region Patagonia ("big-foot country"). The legend was widely believed for many years. In reality, the Tehuelche people were only slightly taller than most other Indian populations.

Welsh Valleys in Patagonia

In the nineteenth century, many people emigrated to the Americas from Wales, one of the countries making up Great Britain. In 1865 one small group sailed to the coast of Patagonia in a ship called the Mimosa, *landing at a place they called Porth Madrun (now Puerto Madryn). They settled the valley of the River Chubut.*

The first years were tough and the immigrants barely survived, scraping a living from the harsh landscape. However, the Welsh settlers made friends with the Tehuelche people and learned to hunt. They farmed sheep and became experts at irrigating the dry land. In 1866 they founded another settlement, named Cwm Hyfryd, in the Andes region.

The Welsh-speaking settlements prospered, and the language was used in their newspapers, books, chapels, law courts, government, and on their money. However, during the twentieth century, more and more settlers from Spain and Italy poured into the Chubut Valley. The Patagonian Welsh were outnumbered, and their way of life began to die out. Despite this, cultural links between Wales and Patagonia are still fostered today. The Welsh language is still spoken by several thousand Argentineans, and a bara brith *(BAH-rah breeth), or Welsh fruited loaf, may still be served at a farmhouse tea.*

Today's Patagonians, like their ancestors, mostly live by raising sheep—about thirty million animals total. There are vast sheep stations, or *estancias* (eh-STAHN-syuhs), that produce wool for export. On the South Atlantic coast many people work at the oil production center of Comodoro Rivadavia.

Despite the severe climate, Patagonia has a growing tourist industry, with travelers visiting the southern lake district around San Carlos de Bariloche. The Patagonian Andes include many rivers of ice, such as the spectacular Moreno glacier. Nature lovers also head south to see large colonies of penguins on the rugged coast.

Large areas of Patagonia are lonely places, where sheep farmers must travel long distances to see their neighbors. However, this southern wilderness is beginning to open up to the outside world and is attracting new visitors and settlers.

The high points of the year are often regional festivals. These may celebrate the culture and traditions of the early settlers or horse-riding skills.

In the nineteenth century, many families from Wales settled in Patagonia. They were seeking freedom to worship in the way they wanted and freedom to use the Welsh language.

The Arts of Argentina

Argentina is a land of music and dance, and it takes its inspiration from the peoples who have lived there over the ages. Dances and carnival tunes from the north and west of the country show Native American influences. Spanish song and dance can be heard everywhere, accompanied by the guitar, the most popular instrument in Argentina. Accordion and fiddle music is also popular. Gaucho folk music influenced classical composers such as Alberto Williams and Carlos López Buchardo.

The Porteños are keen operagoers and follow both Argentine and international productions with enthusiasm. Buenos Aires has about seventy theaters of various kinds, the most famous of which is the Teatro Colón, which dates back to 1908. Movies are also very popular in all the big cities, and Argentina has its own film industry, begun in 1897.

The world-famous writer Jorge Luis Borges was born in Buenos Aires. His strange short stories are written in a style sometimes called magical realism, in which

Dance the Tango!

In the 1890s, a new musical rhythm became popular in the slums of Buenos Aires. Soon people were dancing to it, stepping out with all the energy of the Spanish and Gypsy dance tradition. The dance was known as the tango. Men and women danced very closely, clutching each other tightly and bending over low. Polite society found the new dance craze deeply shocking and complained that it was immoral.

At first, the tango was only danced in the seedier bars and cafés of the capital. However, this dance would not go away and was soon being performed in respectable theaters and clubs. Tango tunes and songs written to them became hugely popular. By the 1930s, people were dancing the tango from New York to Paris. It is still popular with ballroom dancers all over the world today—but they say that only in Argentina is it danced with true passion.

A couple demonstrates the true spirit of the tango in a street market in Buenos Aires. This dramatic dance had its origins on the pavements and in the cafés of the capital.

dreams, visions, or myths are woven into tales of everyday people and events. Borges' stories are admired all over the world and have influenced generations of Latin American writers.

Sports Heroes

The most popular sport in Argentina is soccer. The game is said to have been brought to the country by visiting British sailors during the mid- to late nineteenth century. Soccer clubs were founded from 1897 onward, and these included teams that later became famous, such as Rio de la Plata. In 1978 and 1986 Argentina won the international soccer competition called the World Cup.

Argentina defeats Germany in the 1986 soccer World Cup, held in Mexico. It was the second time Argentina had won this competition, and its fourth appearance in the final.

Horses and "Ducks"

In the old days, the gauchos on the Pampas would play a game called pato *(PAH-toe), meaning "duck", in which teams of riders from rival ranches tried to seize a live duck inside a leather basket from a gaucho riding at full gallop. Later, a stuffed hide was used instead. There were few rules, and one player was even allowed to lasso another and pull him down! The game was played over any area, and the aim was to bring "the prize" back to the home ranch. The game was extremely violent and dangerous. It was banned by the government in 1822.*

Even so, it was still being played illegally in the 1900s. In 1937 the game was revived in a safer version, as a kind of basketball played on horseback. Pato is now a national game, and the duck has been replaced by a leather ball with six handles, held out at arm's length.

Argentina also follows another type of football that was first played in Europe—rugby. Its national team is called the Pumas. Other popular sports include cricket, boxing, squash, ice hockey, golf, and tennis.

In the land of the gaucho, it is hardly surprising that horseracing is hugely popular. Argentina is a world leader in the sport of polo and breeds some of the finest ponies. Only the very wealthy can afford to play polo.

Argentina is a great place for all kinds of outdoor pursuits, such as hiking, pony riding, climbing, canoeing, rafting, fishing, sailing, and windsurfing.

ARUBA

ARUBA IS THE WESTERNMOST OF
THE LESSER ANTILLES ISLANDS.

*Aruba lies 18 miles
(29 kilometers) due north of
Venezuela and 50 miles (80 kilometers) to
the west of the island of Curaçao. It lies on the
edge of the shallow waters of South America's
continental shelf. The waters deepen rapidly
north of the island. It is nearly 20 miles
(32 kilometers) long and just 6 miles
(10 kilometers) across at its widest point.*

*The island is rocky, strewn
with large boulders. Sandy
beaches and coral reefs form
the coastline. Inland,
cactus and scrubby bush
cover the poor soil. Aruba is
low-lying, rising to 620 feet
(189 meters) above sea level at its
highest point, Mount Jamanota.*

CLIMATE

*Like the Venezuelan coast to the south, Aruba is
very hot, despite cooling sea breezes, and is
drier than most Caribbean islands.*

Average year-round temperature: *81°F (27°C)*

Average annual precipitation: *23 in (58 cm)*

Staying Dutch

The first people to settle Aruba (a-ROO-
buh) over three thousand years ago were
Native American people, who left behind
pottery and drawings. In 1499 the explorer
Alonzo de Ojeda claimed Aruba for Spain.
However, the Spanish never really settled
the island and left the indigenous people,
an Arawak-speaking tribe called the
Caiquetios, in peace.

In 1636 the Dutch seized the island. It
was granted to the Dutch West India
Company, but little legal trade resulted
because the backwaters of the Caribbean

became a haven for pirates and buccaneers
during the 1660s. In the 1700s horses were
bred here, and the Arawak-speakers and
indigenous laborers from the South
American mainland worked as ranch
hands. Unlike most Caribbean islands,
Aruba never relied on imported slave labor.
Major changes came to the island after
1816, when the Dutch began to settle and
develop the island. The land was never
suitable for food crops, and there was little

FACTS AND FIGURES

Status: *Part of the Kingdom of the Netherlands with independent rule*

Capital: *Oranjestad*

Area: *75 square miles (194 square kilometers)*

Population: *80,000*

Population density: *1,067 per square mile (412 per square kilometer)*

Peoples: *Mainly mixed Native-European or Native-African descent; a few of European or Asian descent*

Official language: *Dutch*

Currency: *Aruban florin*

National days: *Gilberto F. Croes's Birthday (January 25); Aruba Flag Day (March 18)*

Country's name: *Aruba may be a corruption of* Oro hubo, *Spanish for "gold there."*

Arawak-speaking population has largely merged with newcomers, who, over the ages, have included Spanish, Dutch, Afro-Caribbeans, East Indians, Chinese, Southeast Asians, Venezuelans, and refugees from other South American countries. Dutch is still the official language, and English and Spanish are widely understood. As in the Netherlands Antilles, a local dialect called Papiamento has developed. This has been influenced by Spanish and Portuguese as well as Dutch.

The people of Aruba enjoy good health care, and there are excellent schools and colleges. The island's water supply comes from a desalination plant that takes the salt out of seawater.

Like most Caribbean islanders, the people of Aruba stage lavish festivals with music, dancing, and costumes. New Year's Day is a time for celebration, and Carnival is held at its traditional time, before the Christian fast of Lent.

water. In 1828 the island was administered as part of the Dutch West Indies and from 1845 as part of the Netherlands Antilles (see NETHERLANDS ANTILLES). In the 1920s oil refining became a major industry, the island providing oil processing for the Venezuelan oil fields to the south. Oil was the mainstay of the economy until 1985, when the refinery was closed. Tourism then became the chief industry, although the oil industry was revived on a smaller scale in 1990.

In 1954 Aruba was granted self-government, and in 1986 it broke away from the other islands in the Netherlands Antilles, fearing that it would be dominated by neighboring Curaçao.

The population of Aruba today is a melting pot of peoples and cultures. The

Dutch influence is clearly seen in the buildings fronting the square in Oranjestad. The town is named after the Orange family, which has ruled the Netherlands since 1815.

Timeline:	Native Americans settle Aruba	Discovered and claimed by Spain	Taken by the Dutch	Governed as part of the Netherlands Antilles	Aruba separates from the Netherlands Antilles
	ca. 1500 B.C.E.	1499 C.E.	1636	1845	1986

BAHAMAS

THE BAHAMAS ARE A MAZE OF CORAL ISLANDS, reefs, and sandbanks lying off the Straits of Florida.

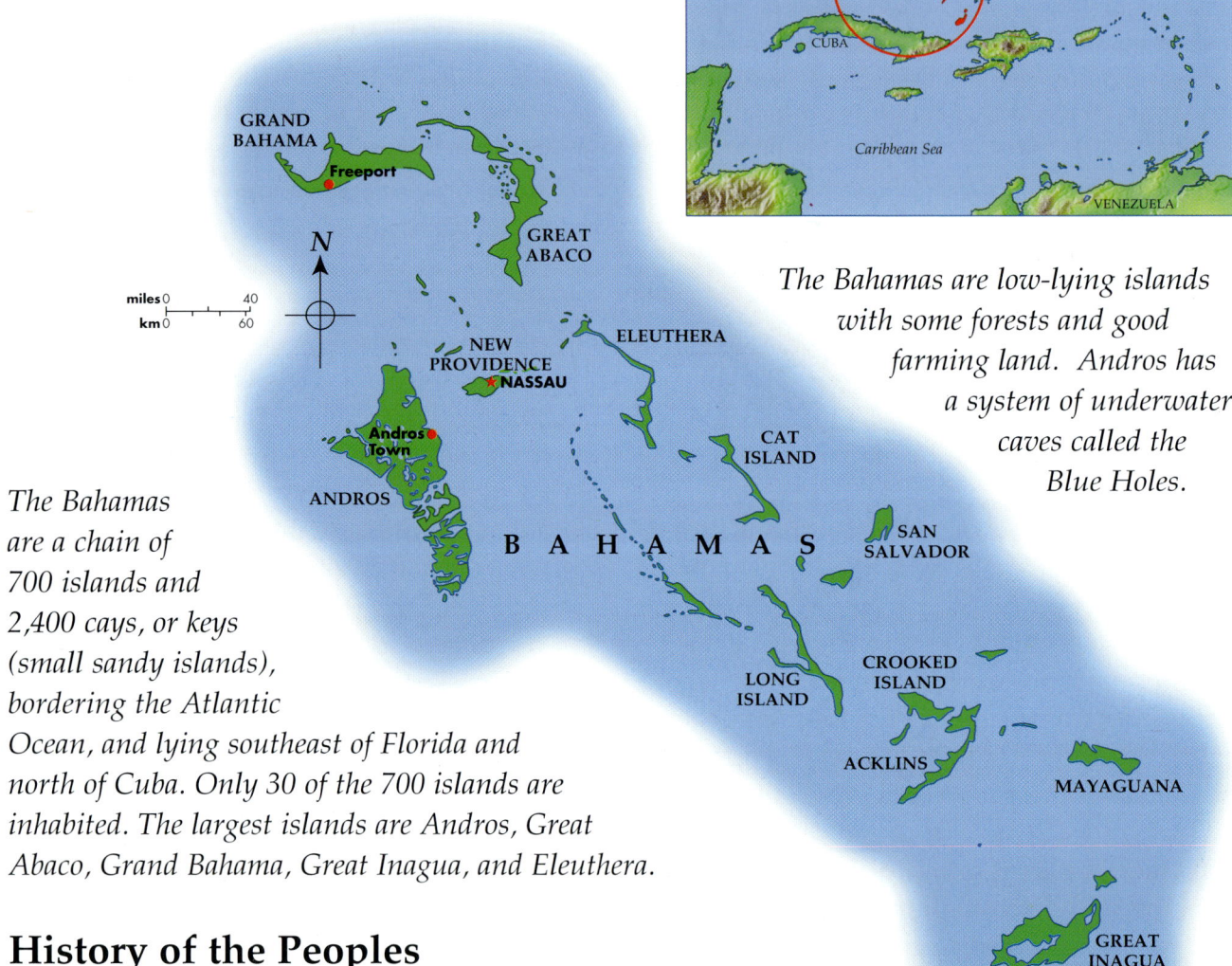

The Bahamas are low-lying islands with some forests and good farming land. Andros has a system of underwater caves called the Blue Holes.

The Bahamas are a chain of 700 islands and 2,400 cays, or keys (small sandy islands), bordering the Atlantic Ocean, and lying southeast of Florida and north of Cuba. Only 30 of the 700 islands are inhabited. The largest islands are Andros, Great Abaco, Grand Bahama, Great Inagua, and Eleuthera.

History of the Peoples

When the explorer Christopher Columbus first landed on San Salvador Island in the Bahamas (buh-HAH-muz) in 1492, he described the Native Americans living there as some of the gentlest and friendliest people in the world. These were the Lucayan (loo-KAY-ehn), an Arawak-speaking people who had been driven north to these islands by their more warlike Carib-speaking neighbors on the South American continent.

CLIMATE

The climate is tropical, with the wettest period being between May and October. Hurricanes often rage across this region between July and December and may wreak havoc along the coasts.

Average January temperature: *71°F (22°C)*

Average July temperature: *81°F (27°C)*

Average annual precipitation: *47 in (119 cm)*

However, the arrival of Europeans in the Caribbean led to tragedy for all the Native peoples. By 1509 the Spanish were sending tens of thousands of Arawak-speakers to work in the mines of Hispaniola, a large Caribbean island nearby (see DOMINICAN REPUBLIC and HAITI). Few survived the ordeal, and today Arawak-speakers have completely disappeared.

The Spanish who raided the Arawak-speaking villages on the Bahamas never colonized the islands themselves. That was left to the British, the next Europeans to arrive, who settled Eleuthera Island in 1646 and New Providence in 1666. Attacks by the Spanish in 1680 and by the French and Spanish in 1703 drove away many British colonialists to the British colonies on the American mainland.

In the 1700s Nassau on New Providence, which was then just a shantytown built from driftwood, became the haunt of

Explorer Christopher Columbus sets foot on San Salvador, or Watlings Island, one of the Bahamas, in 1492. He is met by a band of Lucayans. The Spanish called them "Indians."

FACTS AND FIGURES

Official name: Commonwealth of the Bahamas

Status: Independent state

Capital: Nassau

Area: 5,350 square miles (13,857 square kilometers)

Population: 290,000

Population density: 54 per square mile (21 per square kilometer)

Peoples: 85 percent Afro-Caribbean; 15 percent European

Official language: English

Currency: Bahamian dollar

National day: Independence Day (July 10)

Country's name: Bahamas comes from the Spanish word meaning "shallow sea."

pirates and outlaws from Europe and the North American colonies. In the end the British authorities had to clear New Providence of the pirates and develop the island as a British colony, sending a colonial governor in 1718. The settlers' plantations of pineapples and cotton were worked by slaves from western African until slavery was abolished in 1834.

During the American Civil War (1861–1865), the southern ports on the North American mainland were blockaded by Union forces (the army of the U.S. North). The Bahamas became a trade center that aided the Confederacy (the government of the South), shipping goods into the South.

A similar secret operation was carried out during the 1920s and 1930s, a period

Timeline:	Christopher Columbus reaches San Salvador island in the Bahamas	Spanish take Arawak-speakers to Hispaniola for forced labor	British settle Bahamas	British settle New Providence
	1492 c.e.	1509	1646	1666

when alcoholic drinks were banned in the United States. Illegal liquor was smuggled from the Bahamas across the Straits of Florida to the United States.

After World War II, tourism from the United States grew and grew and became the major source of wealth for the islands. With a successful economy, there were few problems with the Bahamas becoming independent. In 1959 men got the vote, and three years later women were allowed to vote. By 1964 the country had self-government, and in 1973 the islands made up a fully independent nation, known as the Commonwealth of the Bahamas.

Life in the Bahamas

Most Bahamians live on the small island of New Providence, the site of the capital, Nassau. The local population is swollen each year by millions of tourists and other overseas visitors, many of them from the United States.

Today about 85 percent of Bahamians are Afro-Caribbeans or of mixed African-European descent. The Afro-Caribbean population has increased in recent years because of refugees from political unrest in nearby Haiti (see HAITI).

About 15 percent of Bahamians are of European (mostly British) or North American descent. Some of these are descended from the early settlers and outlaws, but most have been attracted here in recent years by tourism or business.

Ninety-four percent of Bahamians are Christian, belonging to Roman Catholic, Anglican, and other Protestant churches.

Cable Beach, Nassau, has everything the tourists want—blue-green seas, white sands, and shady palms. The tourists bring the dollars that are the mainstay of the economy.

English is the language of the Bahamas, sometimes spoken in a local Caribbean dialect. However, the Haitian refugees speak a French Creole.

Various cultural influences meet on these islands. There is the Afro-Caribbean way of life, typical of the other islands lying to the south. This relaxed, informal lifestyle of the Bahamas is typified by the Junkanoo parades, which include dancing and drumming. The parades are part of a winter carnival held between Christmas and New Year. There is the old British colonial influence, seen in the public buildings of Nassau and in the educational system. Great Britain also trains the

Spanish attack Bahamas	French and Spanish attack the islands	British send colonial governor	Slavery abolished	Independence from Britain
1680	1703	1718	1834	1973

Bahamas' defense force and coast guard. There is also the American influence from nearby Florida and the impact of thousands of visiting tourists, yacht owners, and bankers and their tourist dollars. In addition, the United States is the Bahamas' chief source of aid money.

Travel between the scattered islands has to be by boat or aircraft. If you need a hospital, you have to get to Nassau on New Providence or to Freeport on Grand Bahama. Schools are on the main islands, and the College of the Bahamas offers further education through courses held jointly with the University of the West Indies and the University of Miami.

Three newspapers keep the islanders in touch—the *Freeport News*, the *Nassau Guardian*, and the *Tribune*. The islanders have their own radio and television stations and can also receive United States' stations.

There are great contrasts of wealth between the businesspeople of Nassau and the people who live by farming and fishing on some of the outer islands. The Haitian refugees suffer from hunger, unemployment, poor housing, and poverty.

The islands of the Bahamas include some good farm land and produce potatoes, sweet potatoes, pigeon peas, peanuts, sugarcane, and citrus fruit. Crawfish caught off the Bahamas is an important export, as is pulped wood from the island's forests.

Some Bahamians work in light industries, but tourism is the mainstay of the economy. Cruise ships to the Bahamas abound, and tourists flock to the beautiful beaches and coral reefs. Some tourists, especially Americans, come on day trips to gamble at the casinos. The Bahamas are also a base for many foreign banks and insurance companies.

The Junkanoo festival combines elements of ancient European midwinter festivals with the dancing and drumming traditions of western Africa.

BARBADOS

BARBADOS, EASTERNMOST OF THE WINDWARD ISLANDS, is a Caribbean outpost facing the stormy Atlantic Ocean.

Barbados lies to the northeast of Trinidad in the Caribbean Sea. It is 21 miles (34 kilometers) long and 14 miles (23 kilometers) wide.

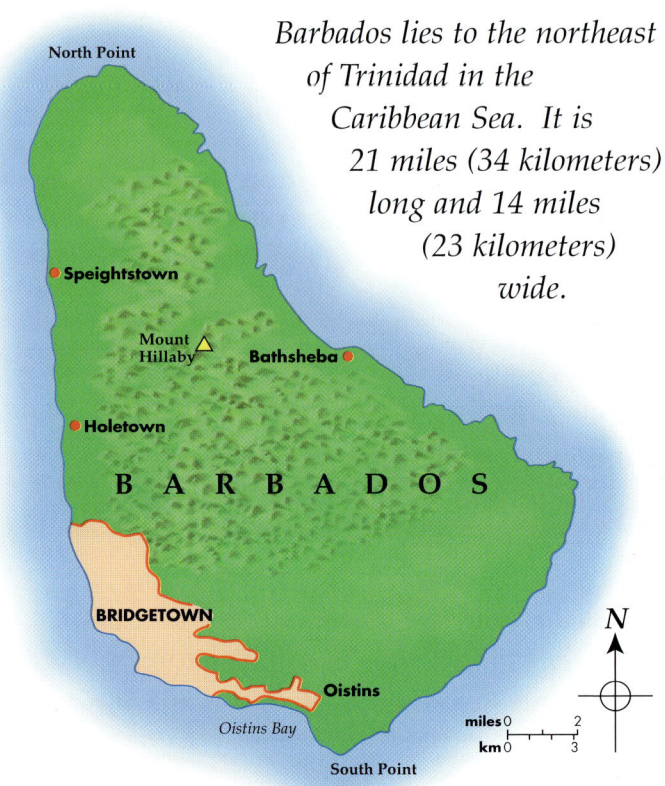

Barbados is an island of coral and limestone, surrounded by reefs. The island is mostly flat, with hills in the northeast rising to 1,113 feet (340 meters) above sea level at Mount Hillaby, the island's highest point.

Women traders selling fruit and provisions outside a drugstore in Speightstown in northwest Barbados. They wear hats to shade themselves from the hot sun.

CLIMATE

The Barbados climate is hot and dry year-round. The rainiest period is in autumn, when fierce hurricanes may build up over the Caribbean.

Average January temperature: 76°F (24°C)

Average July temperature: 80°F (27°C)

Average annual precipitation: 51 in (130 cm)

From Slavery to Independence

The first inhabitants of Barbados (bahr-BAY-dose) were Arawak-speakers, a Native American group. About eight hundred years ago, they came under fierce attack from another Native group, Carib-speakers from the coast of South America. The Carib-speakers themselves may have been driven from Barbados by Spanish slave

FACTS AND FIGURES

Status: *Independent state*

Capital: *Bridgetown*

Area: *166 square miles (430 square kilometers)*

Population: *270,000*

Population density: *1,627 per square mile (628 per square kilometer)*

Peoples: *90 percent Afro-Caribbean; the remainder are European and Asian minorities*

Official language: *English*

Currency: *Barbados dollar*

National days: *Errol Barrow Day (January 21); Kadooment Day (first Monday in August); Independence Day (November 30)*

Country's name: Barbados *means "bearded ones" in Portuguese; the name was given by early European explorers to a species of fig tree that grows on the island.*

Barbadians were in the forefront of Caribbean movements for independence, and democracy was gradually introduced in the 1950s and 1960s, with the right to vote extended to all citizens in 1951. Full independence was achieved at last in 1966.

The Bajans: People with Caribbean Spirit

The capital and chief port, Bridgetown, is in the southwest corner of the island. It is a busy town, the center of the island's business and commerce. The most populated regions are the south and west coasts; 45 percent of the islanders live in towns.

The people of Barbados are known as Bajans (BAY-junz) and speak English. About 90 percent of all Bajans are Afro-Caribbean. About 10 percent of the population is of British or East Asian

raiders in the early 1500s. Both peoples had abandoned the island by 1536, when Portuguese adventurers landed there.

It was the British who first claimed ownership of the island in 1625. The island became a British colony, and people from England and Scotland founded a settlement called Jamestown in 1627 on the west coast. They brought in slaves from western Africa to work the plantations of tobacco, cotton, and sugarcane. Slavery came to an end in 1834, but most of the workers continued to live in hardship and poverty, working on British-owned sugar plantations.

Sugarcane is harvested on Barbados. This has long been one of the most important crops of the Caribbean region. It is turned into molasses (a sweet syrup), refined sugar, and rum.

Timeline:	Carib-speakers raids on Arawak-speakers	Portuguese land on Barbados	Barbados claimed as British territory	African slaves brought to Barbados	Slavery abolished	Full independence from Great Britain
	ca. 1200 C.E.	1536	1625	1627	1834	1966

Cricket Crazy

Barbados, like Jamaica and many other Caribbean islands, is cricket crazy. Wherever there is a patch of clear grass, or even in the street, youths will set up a makeshift pitch. This bat-and-ball game was introduced to the Caribbean from Great Britain in the 1850s. Teams were formed on the islands, while a pan-Caribbean team (the West Indies) fought international matches. As the colonial period came to an end in the 1950s and 60s, West Indian teams became a focus of regional pride, and gained respect internationally by winning matches. This period produced some of cricket's all-time sporting heroes. Perhaps the most famous of all was Barbadian Garfield "Gary" Sobers. Cricket remains very popular throughout the Caribbean, although recently people have also become interested in baseball.

descent. The vast majority are Christians, including Anglicans, Methodists, Pentecostalists, Catholics, and Mormons.

British influence remains very strong today—the island is said to be the most British in the Caribbean, and English is the island's language, spoken with a local accent. Although Barbados is sometimes even called Little England, its way of life is very much that of the Caribbean.

The Bajan lifestyle is easygoing and hospitable, with the year marked by boat racing and street fairs, festivals and carnivals. An annual harvest festival called Crop-Over, held after the sugarcane has been cut, is celebrated with calypso music and street dancing for three weeks.

Many Barbadians today are better off than other Caribbean islanders. However, there is still a large gap between rich and poor, and a lot of the businesses are still run by Europeans. The island is

Bathsheba may be famous for its surfing, but these locals prefer a lively game of cricket. The bowler delivers a rising ball and the batsman responds with a defensive stroke.

Fancy dress is paraded on Kadooment Day, the first Monday in August. This national holiday is the final day of Crop-Over, a festival that marks the end of the sugarcane harvest.

developing as a center for finance companies. Half of the island's income now comes from tourism, but the sugar industry (with its by-products, molasses and rum) is still very important. Barbados has its own oil and natural gas industry, and factories produce textiles, chemicals, cement, and computer parts. One in ten Bajans are farmers, and crops include corn and high-quality cotton. Fishing in local waters yields flying fish, but pollution from shipping has threatened catches.

Barbados has an excellent educational system and a literacy rate among the highest in the world. It is home to one of the island campuses of the University of the West Indies. Health care, too, is well organized, with state-run hospitals as well as private clinics.

Bajan Cooking

The traditional food of Barbados includes fresh and salted fish, hot spicy sauces, plantains (a large type of banana used for cooking), yams and pumpkins, coconuts, and tropical fruits, such as mangoes. Many dishes are similar to western African dishes that slaves brought from their original countries, while the Asian influence shows in Bajan curries and spices. Popular foods include conkies (KOHNG-eez)—sweet potatoes steamed with pumpkin, spices, cornstarch, and coconut—and souse (pickled) belly pork and pig's head mixed with vegetables and spices. Cou-cou (KOO-koo) is a mash of okra and cornstarch. Also popular are flying fish, caught widely in local waters.

BELIZE

BELIZE LIES ON THE YUCATÁN
PENINSULA, bordered to the north
by Mexico and to the west by
Guatemala. To the east is the
Caribbean Sea.

*The low-lying coastline of Belize is shielded
by a long barrier reef of coral (the second
largest in the world) and sandy offshore
islands called cays (KEYS).*

*The north is mostly flat, and includes
logwood swamps, lagoons, savannahs, and
rain forests. The south is a land of tropical
rain forests, mountain slopes and pine
trees, beaches and lagoons.*

CLIMATE

*The country is hot and very humid year-round.
Hurricanes have repeatedly devastated the coast,
killing many people and damaging buildings.*

Average January temperature: *74°F (23°C)*

Average July temperature: *81°F (27°C)*

Average annual precipitation: *76 in (193 cm)*

Land of Ancient Civilization

The early history of Belize (buh-LEEZ) is
that of the Maya (MY-uh), one of the most
remarkable peoples and civilizations in the
world. This Native American people built
great temples and irrigation canals, worked
out a calendar and a system of writing, and
studied astronomy and mathematics. Their
lands stretched right across the Yucatán
peninsula, and their ancient sites are found
in Belize, Mexico, Guatemala, and
Honduras (see MEXICO, GUATEMALA, and
HONDURAS). The ruins surviving in Belize
today are less spectacular than those in
Mexico, but even so the region was very
important to the Maya.

The greatest period of Maya power came
to an end with the rise of the Toltec (TOLL-
tec) people in Mexico in the tenth century.
They broke up the Mayan empire, but

FACTS AND FIGURES

Status: *Independent state*

Capital: *Belmopan*

Other cities: *Corozal, Orange Walk, Belize City, Dangriga, Punta Gorda, San Ignacio*

Area: *8,867 square miles (22,965 square kilometers)*

Population: *200,000*

Population density: *23 per square mile (9 per square kilometer)*

Peoples: *40 percent Creole (Afro-Caribbean); 33 percent mestizo (mixed Native American-European); 10 percent Maya; 8 percent Garifuna (mixed Carib-African); 2 percent Southeast Asian; 7 percent other*

Official language: *English*

Currency: *Belize dollar*

National days: *National Day (September 10); Independence Day (September 21); Garifuna Settlement Day (November 19)*

Country's name: *Belize takes its name from its largest city. The Spanish called the city Belice but the origin of this is unknown.*

Mayan communities in Belize, remote from the old centers of power, survived despite civil wars and conflict. The northern part of Belize was known as Chactemal. The lands to the south were known as Dzuluinicob. The Maya here fiercely resisted the next wave of invaders—the Spanish.

From the 1520s onward, the Spanish made various attempts to bring Belize within their Central American empire. In the 1600s the British built settlements along the coast, which became a center for buccaneers, pirates who preyed on Spanish shipping. In the 1700s the settlers, who came to be called Baymen, began logging hardwood in the forests, using African slave labor imported from Jamaica and Bermuda. Cruelty and injustice resulted in several slave revolts. Slavery was finally abolished in 1833.

In 1798 the Baymen, supported by the British navy, defeated a powerful Spanish fleet off Saint Georges Cay, an island off the northeast coast of Belize. In 1862 Belize became a colony under the name of British Honduras. The Afro-Caribbean (Creole) population was among the first in the Caribbean to demand independence, especially after World War I (1914–1918).

This group of Mayan children lives in the countryside bordering Guatemala. The Mayan people are survivors, having inhabited Belize for thousands of years.

Timeline:	Maya settle in Belize	Toltec invade and destroy the Maya empire	Spanish complete the conquest of the Yucatán peninsula	British buccaneers settle coast, later turn to logging	Slavery abolished
	ca. 2000 B.C.E.	ca. 987 C.E.	1542	1640s	1833

Timber, hammered sheets of metal, and a roof of grooved iron have been assembled to make this cabin in the Belizean countryside.

The Creole people, who had fought for the Allies, were bitterly disappointed with the way in which the British continued to control the colony. The colony also faced economic problems and struggled with Guatemala's claims on the territory and threats of invasion (see GUATEMALA). The British wanted to sign a treaty with Guatemala to ensure a free Belize before granting independence. Finally, in 1981, despite the lack of a treaty, and with British troops present, Belize gained full independence. It was the last country in Central America to become independent.

Peaceful, Green Belize

This is a peaceful country that has largely avoided the political strife common elsewhere in the region. The country is the least crowded in Central America, with over 90 percent of the land being covered in forest. Only in Belize City is there a sense of bustle and urgency.

Almost all Belizeans are Christians, 60 percent of the population being Roman

Guatemala claims the area now called Belize	Belize formally becomes a British colony named British Honduras	British Honduras renamed Belize	Belize becomes fully independent nation	Diplomatic relations between Belize and Guatemala established
1839	**1862**	**1973**	**1981**	**1991**

Belize Food: A Flavorfest

Creole food includes all the Caribbean's favorite ingredients—bananas, coconuts, beans, and rice. Chicken, fish, and beef may be stewed or barbecued. Seafood is outstanding—locally caught lobster, shrimp, red snapper, and shark delight the taste buds. Mayan/Mexican-style food offers tacos, empanadas (pastries), and chili beans. Wild animals, such as armadillos, deer, and boar, are hunted locally. Many restaurants serve Chinese, American, or European food.

Catholic and 35 percent Protestant (mainly Anglican and Methodist).

A mixture of cultures has taken root in Belize over the ages. The official language of English is often spoken in a rich Caribbean dialect, which has borrowed from both Spanish and indigenous languages. Spanish is Belize's second most common language, spoken with a strong Central American accent.

Belize is not a wealthy country, and many of its people live a hard life. The logging industry is no longer as important as it once was, and today more Belizeans work as farmers or as fishermen in the rich coastal shallows. Most of the country's exports are foods such as sugar and molasses (a sweet syrup), honey, cocoa, bananas, rice, citrus fruits, lobsters, and fish products. Textiles are also manufactured for export. Large amounts of food have to be imported, and the United States is Belize's largest trading partner.

Many Belizeans work in the tourism industry. The highest number of overseas visitors come from North America. They come to enjoy the beaches, the coral reefs, the ancient ruins, and the spectacular national parks and wildlife reserves.

A fisherman's T-shirt advertises a fishery cooperative. Conch shells are heaped on the shore behind him. Belize's coasts provide all kinds of seafood as well as tourist souvenirs.

Making Music

Music was very important to the ancient Mayan civilization; religious festivals were marked by flute music, drumming, and dancing. Mayan dance may still be seen at village festivals. Percussion still plays an important role today in Belize. Mestizo (mixed Native American-European) people favor marimba music with bass and drums, and Mexican mariachi music—sentimental folk music played on violin, guitar, and trumpet. A style of music called **brukdown** *(BROOK-down) is a fusion of African rhythms and guitar, banjo, drums, and accordion. Popular among the Creoles over the last one hundred years, brukdown is now played with modern electric instruments.*

Brukdown has been followed by a series of Afro-Caribbean sounds such as calypso, reggae, and **soca** *(SO-kuh). Short for SOul CAlypso, soca is Caribbean dance music that became popular in the 1980s. The most popular music of all is probably Garifuna* **punta** *(POON-tah) rock, which is highly amplified and uses traditional drum rhythms and lyrics in the Garifuna language.*

Outdoor pursuits, too, such as sea fishing, rafting, and exploring caves, are mostly for the tourists. Locals prefer soccer or basketball. There are two television channels, with additional cable channels in some regions, and three radio stations. There are five weekly newspapers.

This is a typical street scene in San Ignacio, at the center of Belize's Cayo district. The town is home to Afro-Caribbeans and Mayans as well as some Asians.

Creoles, Maya, and Mestizos: People of the North and West

The northern frontier of Belize borders Mexico, along the Hondo River. The northern districts of Corozal, Orange Walk, and Belize are mostly flat, including logwood swamps, lagoons, savannahs, and rain forests. Over the years, the land has been cleared in many places by logging companies and farmers.

Belize City, the former capital, lies on the coast opposite Saint Georges Cay. It includes old colonial architecture, such as the courthouse and Saint John's Anglican Cathedral, alongside more modern streets.

The Western Highway leads to Cayo district and the border with Guatemala. The land rises from the coastal swamps to Mountain Pine Ridge, the rain forest of the Vaca Plateau, and the Maya Mountains. The new capital, Belmopan, was founded in 1970 after much of the old part of Belize City was destroyed by a hurricane.

The ancient Mayan ruins of Xunantunich, dating back over one thousand years, lie on the Mopan River, near the Guatemalan border. Mayan people still occupy the region.

Belmopan is a modern center of government, but so far only about six thousand people have chosen to make their homes there.

The largest ethnic group in Belize district is made up of English-speaking Afro-Caribbeans known as Creoles. They make up 40 percent of the total population and play a major role in the economic and cultural life of Belize. Their way of life, food, and music looks to the Caribbean rather than Central America. They speak English, enjoy reggae music, and eat Afro-Caribbean food.

About a third of all Belizeans are mestizos, many of mixed Mayan and European descent. They speak Spanish and/or one of the Indian languages. These mestizos have settled chiefly in the north and west and make their living by farming small plots of land. They tend to eat Central American food and like Latin music or indigenous folk music.

Tens of thousands of immigrants from neighboring countries have also made their homes in Belize in recent years, many of them fleeing civil war or persecution at home. They work as farmers and laborers.

The west of the country is also home to the Maya themselves, the indigenous people of Belize. Remains of their ancient civilization may be seen all over the country at sites such as Altun Ha to the north of Belize City and Xunantunich and Caracol in Cayo district. Today most Maya live by farming, raising chickens and pigs, and growing corn, beans, and rice on land

The Mennonites

The Mennonites are a fundamentalist Protestant group that was founded in Europe in the 1500s. They opposed infant baptism, taking oaths, and fighting, and believed in closed communities and silent prayer. The group was named after their Dutch leader, Menno Simons. The Mennonites set up communities in Switzerland and Germany. Some Mennonites set sail in 1663 for the New World, settling in Canada and later in Mexico. In 1958 some also moved to Belize. They live by farming land in the Orange Walk district, leading extremely simple lives. While some use modern tools and equipment, most reject all modern inventions, such as cars and radios.

cleared from the forest. Many of today's Maya have migrated to Belize during the last 150 years. Many more live across the borders in Mexico, Guatemala, and Honduras (see MEXICO, GUATEMALA, and HONDURAS). The Maya make up about 10 percent of the total population of Belize.

The Garifuna of Central and Southern Belize

In the districts of Stann Creek and Toledo, major roads run through plantations of bananas and other fruits. Much of the south is wild, a land of tropical rain forests, mountain slopes and pine trees, beaches and lagoons. The coastline is shielded from the full force of the ocean by a series of reefs and cays.

A Mennonite farmer drives his traditional horse-drawn cart through the jungle on the road to Upper Barton Creek in the Cayo district of Belize.

The Garifuna (GAR-rif-FOO-nah), or Black Carib people, make up about 8 percent of Belize's population and have their own language and culture. Many live along the southern coasts and in Dangriga, the settlement on the central coast originally known as Carib Town and later as Stann Creek. The Garifuna's original home was on Saint Vincent, one of the Windward Islands in the Caribbean (see SAINT VINCENT AND THE GRENADINES). They are descended from the Carib, or Kalipuna, the Native American peoples after whom the Caribbean is named, and from West African slaves shipwrecked there in 1635.

The Garifuna fought against the British colonial powers in the 1700s and were exiled to the island of Roatán, off the mainland coast. Many came to settle in Belize in the 1800s, especially as political refugees in the year 1832, when they opposed the government of Honduras on Roatán. The Garifuna later settled many other areas of the Central American coast, including Guatemala, Honduras, and Nicaragua (see GUATEMALA, HONDURAS, and NICARAGUA), and today some have found work in the United States.

Over the years, Garifuna have worked as soldiers, sailors, loggers, farmers, and, above all, as fishermen. They are also famous as musicians and dancers. Big celebrations take place in Dangriga on November 19 each year to celebrate the arrival of the Garifuna in Belize.

The majority of the Garifuna are members of the Roman Catholic Church. Both African and Carib religious ideas continue to shape how the Garifuna live. In illness, they often turn to a type of religious specialist called a shaman (SHAH-muhn) for healing. It is believed that the shamans can also magically find lost objects. Shamans are a part of many African and Native American religions.

A drummer beats out Garifuna rhythms at Seine Bight village on Belize's Placencia peninsula. Beaches and coral reefs are attracting tourists to this once-sleepy backwater.

The common African belief in spirit possession, the idea that the spirits of the dead can temporarily take over the body of the living, is also found among the Garifuna. Here ancestors usually possess the living to criticize and threaten people in the village who are misbehaving.

Traveling south toward the small port of Punta Gorda, the climate becomes more humid. The population here is made up of Garifuna, mestizos, Maya, Creoles, and small numbers of Chinese and Lebanese.

Belize is a tiny country, but its independent spirit has helped it to stand up to its larger neighbors and to preserve its rich cultural diversity.

Glossary

Afro-Caribbean: someone born in the Caribbean region of African descent.

Arawak: any of the Native American peoples who spoke one of the Arawak languages. Arawak peoples were indigenous to the Caribbean islands when the Europeans arrived.

Basque: a European people whose homeland lies in southern France and northern Spain. The Basques have their own culture and a language that is related to no other language in Europe.

buccaneer: one of the outlaws, mostly European, who settled on Caribbean islands from the 1630s onward and became pirates.

calypso: a style of Caribbean music and song that first developed in Trinidad in the nineteenth century before becoming popular around the world. Calypso verses, often in dialect, include many references to stories and people in the news. Singers often make up the words as they go along.

Carib: (1) any of the Native American peoples who speak a Carib language. The Caribs are indigenous to Central and South America and to the Caribbean region, which is named after them; (2) Black Carib is another name for Garifuna.

chasm: a great drop, as over the edge of a deep gorge or canyon.

colony: (1) a territory that is governed by another country; (2) an overseas settlement by people of another country.

colonial: relating to a colony.

colonialism: a policy of governing other countries as colonies.

colonist: somebody who lives in a colony.

continental shelf: the land that extends under water from the edge of a continent, forming an area of shallow ocean.

Creole: an English word related to a French, Spanish, or Portuguese term meaning "native to the locality," but it has come to mean very different things at different times and places: (1) most generally, any Caribbean not born in Africa; (2) a Caribbean or Latin American who is descended from the original colonial settlers rather than later arrivals; (3) in the United States, a Louisiana citizen of French descent; (4) various patois, dialects, or accents of French or English as spoken in the Caribbean and the Americas. The Spanish equivalent is *Criollo*.

cricket: a bat and ball game played by two teams of eleven players each. It was first played in England and has spread from there to many parts of the world, including the Caribbean.

dependency: a territory that does not have full independence. It may be ruled by another country as a colony, or it may have limited self-government but not have the right to decide its own foreign policy.

diplomatic relations: the official dealings between the governments of two or more nations or peoples, each represented by their appointed representative (usually an ambassador). When nations quarrel, they may withdraw ambassadors and break off diplomatic relations.

estuary: the place where a river flows into a larger body of water.

free enterprise: an economic system that allows people to trade with as little government interference or control as possible.

fundamentalist: in religion, someone who believes that everything in the holy scriptures is the literal truth.

holy days: days set aside for special religious observance. Christian holy days include Christmas, Easter, and the days honoring saints. The word *holiday* comes from *holy day*.

indigenous: relating to a people who were born within a country or a region as opposed to being immigrants or settlers. Also *aboriginal* or *native*.

lagoon: an area of shallow, calm water surrounded and shielded by reefs and islands.

light industry: the manufacture of electrical goods, toys, or light equipment as opposed to steelmaking, shipbuilding, and manufacture commonly referred to as heavy industry.

mangrove: a tree with tangled roots that form dense vegetation on tropical seashores and salt marshes.

mestizo: a Spanish word for somebody of mixed descent, specifically a person of mixed European and American Indian descent. A *métis* is the French Canadian equivalent.

monarch: a ruler such as a king, queen, or emperor. In modern times, the powers of a monarch are normally limited by laws recorded in a constitution. This is called constitutional monarchy.

peninsula: a piece of land that juts out from the mainland and is surrounded on three sides by water. The word is from the Latin language, meaning "almost an island."

pilgrim: someone who travels to a holy place or a shrine. Muslims go on pilgrimage to Mecca in Saudi Arabia. Christian pilgrims often visit Bethlehem in Israel.

plateau: a high, flat region.

province: a region or division of a country, similar to a state in the United States.

savannah: a grassland dotted with trees.

shaman: a Siberian (Tungusic) word for priest, healer, or holy person. The word now refers to a religious healer or diviner in various cultures.

   shamanism: the beliefs and practices of a shaman and his or her followers, usually associated with communication with spirits of nature and spirits of the dead.

shantytown: an area of makeshift housing, often illegally constructed by poor people on the edge of a town.

subtropical: of, related to, or being the regions bordering the tropics, where the climate is warmer than in temperate regions.

Further Reading

Antigua and Barbuda
Antigua and Barbuda. Broomall, PA: Chelsea House, 1988.
Dyde, Brian. *Antigua and Barbuda.* Edison, NJ: Hunter Publishing, 1990.
Kincaid, Jamaica. *A Small Place.* New York: NAL/Dutton, 1989.

Argentina
Caistor, Nicholas. *Argentina.* Chatham, NJ: Raintree Steck-Vaughn Publications, 1991.
Department of Geography Staff. *Argentina in Pictures.* Minneapolis: Lerner Group, 1988.
Fox, Geoffrey. *The Land and People of Argentina.* New York: Lippincott, 1990.
Gofen, Ethel. *Cultures of the World: Argentina.* Tarrytown, NY: Marshall Cavendish, 1991.
Greenburg, Arnold. *Buenos Aires Alive and the Best of Argentina.* Edison, NJ:
        Hunter Publishing, 1995
Morrison, Marion. *Argentina.* Morristown, NJ: Silver Burdett Press, 1989.
Leibowitz, Sol. *Argentina.* Broomall, PA: Chelsea House, 1990.
Peterson, Marge, and Peterson, Rob. *Argentina: A Wild West Heritage.* Parsippany, NJ:
        Silver Burdett Press, 1990.

Bahamas
Fodor's Travel Staff. *Bahamas 1995: The Complete Guide Including the Turks and Caicos
        Islands.* New York: Fodor's Travel Publications, 1994.
Jeffrey, Nan. *Bahamas Out Island Odyssey.* Birmingham, AL: Menasha Ridge Press, 1995.
McCulla, Patricia E. *Bahamas.* Broomall, PA: Chelsea House, 1988.

Barbados
Broberg, Merle. *Barbados.* Broomall, PA: Chelsea House, 1989.
LaBrucherie, Roger A. *Barbados: A World Apart.* Pine Valley, CA: Imagenes Press, 1993.

Belize
Morrison, Marion. *Belize.* Danbury, CT: Childrens Press, 1996.
Wright, Peggy. *Belize.* Santa Barbara, CA: ABC-CLIO, 1994.

Islands of the Caribbean
Mason, Antony. *The Caribbean.* Parsippany, NJ: Silver Burdett Press, 1988.
Mayer, T. W. *The Caribbean and Its People.* New York: Thomson Learning, 1995.
Springer, Eintou P. *The Caribbean.* Parsippany, NJ: Silver Burdett Press, 1987.
Walker, Cas. *The Caribbean.* North Pomfret, VT: Trafalgar Square Publishing, 1991.

Index

Page numbers in *italic* indicate illustrations.

Page numbers in *italic* indicate illustrations.

PEOPLES
of the
AMERICAS

PEOPLES
of the
AMERICAS

Volume 11
Index

MARSHALL CAVENDISH
NEW YORK • LONDON • TORONTO • SYDNEY

Marshall Cavendish Corporation
99 White Plains Road
Tarrytown, New York 10591-9001

Consulting Editor: J. Patrick Gray, Professor of Anthropology, University of Wisconsin

Consultants: Jean-Marc Blais, Senior Interpretive Planner, Canadian Museum of Civilization, Hull, Quebec
　　　　　　David Frye, Assistant Director, Department of Latin American and Caribbean Studies, University of Michigan

Spanish Consultant: Fran Kaplan

Contributing authors: D. L. Birchfield
　　　　　　　　　　Marion Morrison
　　　　　　　　　　Juliette Radcliffe Rogers
　　　　　　　　　　Philip Steele
　　　　　　　　　　Mary A. Stout

Discovery Books
　　　Managing Editor: Paul Humphrey
　　　Project Editor: Helen Dwyer
　　　Text Editor: Valerie J. Weber
　　　Design Concept: Ian Winton
　　　Designers: Barry Dwyer, Ian Winton, and Simon Borrough
　　　Cartographer: Stefan Chabluk

Marshall Cavendish
　　　Editorial Director: Paul Bernabeo
　　　Editor: Marian Armstrong
　　　Associate Editor: Debra M. Jacobs

The publishers would like to thank the following for their permission to reproduce photographs:
Edward Parker (cover); South American Pictures (Tony Morrison, frontispiece)

(frontispiece) A Mexican artist paints traditional designs on natural bark paper.

Editor's note: Many systems of dating have been used by different cultures throughout history. *Peoples of the Americas* uses B.C.E. (Before Common Era) and C.E. (Common Era) instead of B.C. (Before Christ) and A.D. (Anno Domini, "In the Year of the Lord") out of respect for the diversity of the world's peoples.

Library of Congress Cataloging-in-Publication Data
Peoples of the Americas.
　　　　p.　　cm.
　　　Includes bibliographical references and index.
　　　Contents: v. 1. Anguilla–Belize — v. 2. Bermuda–Brazil — v. 3. Canada–Cayman Islands — v. 4. Chile–Costa Rica — v. 5. Cuba–French Guiana — v. 6. Greenland–Jamaica — v. 7. Martinique–Paraguay — v. 8. Peru–Turks and Caicos Islands — v. 9. United States of America — v. 10. United States of America–Virgin Islands

　　　ISBN 0-7614-7050-6 (set)
　　　1. Ethnology—America—Juvenile literature. 2. America—History—Juvenile literature. [1. Ethnology—America. 2. America—History.]
　　　E29.A1P46 1999
　　　970'.004—dc21
　　　　　　　　　　　　　　　　　　　　　　　　　　　　　　　98-2801
　　　　　　　　　　　　　　　　　　　　　　　　　　　　　　　CIP
　　　　　　　　　　　　　　　　　　　　　　　　　　　　　　　AC

　　　ISBN 0-7614-7050-6 (set)
　　　ISBN 0-7614-7061-1 (vol. 11)

Printed and bound in Italy

Contents

Comprehensive Bibliography

Fiction

Achimoona. Saskatoon, Canada: Fifth House, 1985.
This anthology of short fiction by ten Cree authors reveals a range of topics and writing styles. While some stories feature Native American youngsters facing everyday challenges, other are mystical or surreal. Ages 9 to adult.

Bierhorst, John, ed. *The White Deer and Other Stories Told by the Lenape.* Fairfield, NJ: William Morrow & Co., 1995.
Traditional Lenape (also known as Delaware) Indian tales gathered from ten elders include myths and stories of lost children, tricksters, dogs, and prophecies. Ages 8 to 14.

Bierhorst, John. *The Hungry Woman: Myths and Legends of the Aztecs.* New York: Quill, 1993.
Bierhorst takes sixteenth-century Aztec manuscripts and arranges them in chronological order, beginning with creation myths and ending with several post-Conquest legends. He also includes detailed notes on the stories and their sources and a guide to special terms and Nahuatl pronunciation. Ages 11 and older.

Bruchac, Joseph. *Children of the Longhouse.* New York: Dial Books for Young Readers, 1996.
The story of a fourteenth-century Mohawk village and an adolescent brother and sister who live there. The author also discusses the Mohawk nation and the Iroquois League of Peace. Ages 9 to 12.

Buss, Fran Leeper, and Daisy Cubias. *Journey of the Sparrows.* New York: Bantam Doubleday Dell Publishing Group, 1993.
The poetic yet realistic story of fifteen-year-old Maria who, packed into a crate, makes the dangerous illegal crossing from Mexico to the United States with several other young people. Despite the group's ordeals and their desperate attempts to remain invisible, love blooms amid stories of hope. Ages 10 to 12.

Carlson, Lori M., and Cynthia L. Ventura, eds. *Where Angels Glide at Dawn: New Stories from Latin America.* Madison, WI: Demco Media, 1993.
Ten brief fictional works by writers from nine South and Central American countries use different styles, voices, and adventures to provide lush portrayals of the varieties of Latin American life. Ages 13 to 15.

Castañeda, Omar S. *Among the Volcanoes.* New York: Lodestar, 1991.
A Tzutujil Indian adolescent in Guatemala, Isabel must leave school to take care of her family. Her story takes place against the backdrop of a town undergoing political and social changes. A sequel, *Imagining Isabel*, explores tense political and cultural issues. Ages 13 to 16.

Creech, Sharon. *Walk Two Moons.* New York: Scholastic, 1994.
Thirteen-year-old Sal searches for her mother with her grandparents as they travel from Ohio to Idaho. She tells the story of Phoebe, whose mother has also disappeared. Ages 10 to 13.

Delacre, Lulu, reteller. *Golden Tales: Myths, Legends, and Folktales from Latin America.* New York: Scholastic, 1996.
Twelve classic tales gathered from the lands of the Taino, the Zapotec, and the Muisca. Oil paintings add to the reader's enjoyment of the legends. Ages 8 to 12.

Dorris, Michael. *Morning Girl.* New York: Hyperion Books for Children, 1992.
While twelve-year-old Morning Girl wants to be up to greet the morning, her younger brother, Star Boy, is fascinated by the night. These two perspectives allow the reader to explore Taino life on one of the Bahama Islands in the late fifteenth century and the impact of European exploration. Ages 10 and up.

George, Jean Craighead. *Julie of the Wolves.* New York: HarperCollins Publishers, 1972.
Rebellious Miyax runs away from home, hoping to reach San Francisco. But she finds herself lost in the Alaskan wilderness, without food or compass. Adopted by a pack of wolves, she struggles to survive and, in the process, finds the traditional riches of Inuit life—intelligence, fearlessness, and love. Ages 11 to 15.

Haskins, James. *The Headless Haunt and other African-American Ghost Stories.* New York: Trophy Press, 1995.
The author has collected ghost stories and anecdotes that form part of African American folklore. These tales may chill your blood. Ages 8 to 13.

Hazleton, Hugh, ed. *Jade and Iron: Latin American Tales from Two Cultures.* Toronto, ON: Groundwood Books, 1996. Fourteen illustrated folktales from Latin American and Native American storytellers. Ages 9 to 12.

Jenkins, Lyll Becerra de. *The Honorable Prison.* New York: Viking Press, 1989. Because of the father's journalistic activities in a politically complex South American city, a family, including teenaged narrator Marta, is imprisoned in a rural military outpost. As Marta gradually realizes the seriousness of the family's circumstances, so does the reader, revealed through the crackling narrative and a sense of understated terror. Ages 13 to 15.

McKissack, Patricia C. *The Dark Thirty: Southern Tales of the Supernatural.* Westminster, MD: Alfred A. Knopf/Borzoi Books, 1992. These ten original ghost and horror stories resemble those told in the author's childhood home during the dark thirty, the half hour just before nightfall. These stories from the days of slavery to the civil rights movement incorporate African American history and culture. Ages 8 to 12.

Myers, Walter Dean. *The Glory Field.* New York: Point, 1996. An historical novel tracing the history of an African American family from the arrival of a slave boy in 1753 to the present time. Details the daily life of generations of family members and the social and political climate in which they lived. Ages 12 to 16.

Norman, Howard, ed. *Northern Tales: Traditional Stories of Eskimo and Indian Peoples.* New York: Pantheon Books, 1990. A variety of stories from Native peoples of the far North, including Greenland, Canada, Alaska, and the polar regions. A brief introduction before each type of traditional tale explores the tribal and cultural concerns as well as the diversity of the people who are deeply influenced by and involved in natural occurrences, animals, the supernatural, healers, and religious leaders. Ages 12 and up.

O'Dell, Scott. *Black Star, Bright Dawn.* New York: Hyperion Books for Children, 1990. Bright Dawn, a teenage Inuit, races her father's dogs, including Bright Star, in this tension-filled story of the Iditarod, the dog sled race through the cold wilds of Alaska. A sensitive portrayal of Inuit culture and a vivid adventure. Ages 13 to 15.

O'Dell, Scott. *The Captive* (1979), *The Feathered Serpent* (1981), and *The Amethyst Ring* (1983). Wilmington, MA: Houghton Mifflin. This trilogy follows the life of Julian Escobár, a young Spanish seminarian who is castaway among the Maya and accidentally assumes the guise of a Mayan god in *The Captive. The Feathered Serpent* continues his story with Escobár witnessing the encounter of Montezuma and Hernán Cortés. This fast-paced adventure explores the priest's moral choices. In the final book, *The Amethyst Ring,* Escobár leaves the Maya and joins Francisco Pizarro in the land of the Inca. Ages 12 to 15.

Ross, Gayle, and Joseph Bruchac, retellers. *The Girl Who Married the Moon: Tales from Native North America.* Bergenfield, NJ: Bridgewater, 1994. Folklore celebrating and honoring the varied roles of women in Native American culture. Includes a brief introduction to the Native cultures from which the stories came. Ages 11 to 14.

San Souci, Robert. *Cut from the Same Cloth: American Women of Myth, Legend, and Tall Tale.* New York: Philomel Books, 1993. A collection of fifteen stories about legendary American women from Anglo-American, African American and Native American folklore. The artwork matches the vigorous language of the text. Ages 11 and up.

Taylor, Theodore. *The Cay.* Madison, WI: Demco Media, 1995. A moving adventure story of Phillip, who had always looked down on black-skinned people, whose shipwreck forces him to rely on a wise and loving West Indian on a barren Caribbean island. A forceful portrayal of race relations and personal growth. Ages 8 to 12.

Temple, Frances. *Grab Hands and Run.* Danbury, CT: Orchard Books, 1993. A boy and his sister try to escape from El Salvador with their mother after their father, who has been working against the government, disappears. They flee through Central America and Mexico into the United States, where they remain fugitives. Ages 11 to 14.

Temple, Frances. *Taste of Salt: A Story of Modern Haiti.* New York: Trophy Press, 1994.

A boy injured in political fighting in Haiti tells his story to a friend who has a story of her own. Their loyalty to a country in political turmoil shines through their tale. Ages 12 to 15.

Thomas, Joyce Carol, ed. *A Gathering of Flowers; Stories about Being Young in America.* New York: HarperCollins Juvenile Books, 1992.

This collection of stories by authors of diverse backgrounds covers an immense range of adolescent life in the United States. Writers, including Maxine Hong Kingston, Gary Soto, Gerald Vezenor, Ana Castillo, and Keven Kyung, address what it means to be ethnic and American in diverse racial, regional, and economic situations with a variety of themes, styles, and tones. Ages 14 and up.

Yee, Paul. *Tales from Gold Mountain; Stories of the Chinese in the New World.* Old Tappan, NJ: Simon & Schuster, 1990.

A quirky and imaginative collection of stories using elements of the history and culture of Chinese laborers in Canada and the United States. A full-color drawing illustrates each of the eight original stories. Ages 9 to 12.

Yep, Laurence. *Tongues of Jade.* New York: HarperCollins, 1991.

A retelling of seventeen Chinese American folktales from a variety of Chinese communities in the United States, abounding in witty comments, lush descriptions, and crackling dialogue. Ages 8 to 10.

Nonfiction

General Reference Works
Breaud, Odile. *Cultures of the World.* Mankato, MN: Creative Education, 1998.
Chiarelli, Brunetto, and Anna Lisa Bebi. *The Atlas of World Cultures.* New York: Peter Bedrick Books, 1997.
Gall, Timothy, ed. *Worldmark Encyclopedia of Cultures and Daily Living: Americas.* Detroit, MI: Gale Research, 1998.
Levinson, David, ed. *Encyclopedia of World Cultures.* Old Tappan, NJ: Macmillan Library Reference, 1995.
Peoples of the World: Customs and Cultures. Danbury, CT: Grolier Educational Corp., 1998.

North America
Hirschfelder, Arlene. *Happily May I Walk: American Indians and Alaska Natives Today.* New York: Atheneum, 1986.
Indians of North America (series). Broomall, PA: Chelsea House, 1987-1995.
Katz, Willian Loren. *The Great Migrations, 1880s–1912.* Austin, TX: Raintree Steck-Vaughn, 1993.
Liptak, Karen. *North American Indian Ceremonies.* New York: Franklin Watts, 1992.

South America
Lewington, Anna. *Rain Forest AmerIndians.* Austin, TX: Raintree Steck-Vaughn, 1993.
Newman, Shirlee Petkin. *The Incas.* New York: Franklin Watts, 1992.

Islands of the Caribbean
Bendure, Glenda, and Ned Friary. *Lonely Planet Eastern Caribbean.* Oakland, CA: Lonely Planet, 1994.
Burton, Richard and Fred Reno. *French and West Indian: Martinique, Guadelupe, and French Guiana Today.* Charlottesville, VA: University Press of Virginia, 1995.
Dyde, Brian. *Islands to the Windward: Five Gems of the Caribbean.* Edison, NJ: Hunter Publishing, 1990.
Ferguson, James. *Eastern Caribbean in Focus: A Guide Book to the People, Politics, and Culture.* Northampton, MA: Interlink Publishing Group, 1997.
Mason, Antony. *The Caribbean.* Parsippany, NJ: Silver Burdett Press, 1988.
Mayer, T. W. *The Caribbean and Its People.* Detroit, MI: Thomson Learning, 1995.
Ramdin, Ron. *West Indies.* Chatham, NJ: Raintree Steck-Vaughn, 1991.
Showker, Kay. *Caribbean Ports of Call: Southeastern Regions: From Puerto Rico to the Panama Canal.* Old Saybrook, CT: Globe Pequot Press, 1997.
Springer, Eintou P. *The Caribbean.* Parsippany, NJ: Silver Burdett Press, 1987.
Walker, Cas. *The Caribbean.* North Pomfret, VT: Trafalgar Square Publishing, 1991.

Antigua and Barbuda
Antigua and Barbuda. Broomall, PA: Chelsea House, 1988.

Dyde, Brian. *Antigua and Barbuda*. Edison, NJ: Hunter Publishing, 1990.
Kincaid, Jamaica. *A Small Place*. New York: NAL/Dutton, 1989.

Argentina

Caistor, Nicholas. *Argentina*. Chatham, NJ: Raintree Steck-Vaughn, 1991.
Department of Geography Staff. *Argentina in Pictures*. Minneapolis, MN: Lerner Group, 1988.
Fox, Geoffrey. *The Land and People of Argentina*. New York: Lippincott, 1990.
Gofen, Ethel. *Cultures of the World: Argentina*. Tarrytown, NY: Marshall Cavendish, 1991.
Greenburg, Arnold. *Buenos Aires Alive and the Best of Argentina*. Edison, NJ: Hunter Publishing, 1995.
Morrison, Marion. *Argentina*. Parsippany, NJ: Silver Burdett Press, 1989.
Leibowitz, Sol. *Argentina*. Broomall, PA: Chelsea House, 1990.
Peterson, Marge, and Rob Peterson. *Argentina: A Wild West Heritage*. Parsippany, NJ: Silver Burdett Press, 1990.

Bahamas

Fodor's Travel Staff. *Bahamas 1995: The Complete Guide Including the Turks and Caicos Islands*. New York: Fodor's Travel Publications, 1994.
Jeffrey, Nan. *Bahamas Out Island Odyssey*. Birmingham, AL: Menasha Ridge Press, 1995.
McCulla, Patricia E. *Bahamas*. Broomall, PA: Chelsea House, 1988.

Barbados

Broberg, Merle. *Barbados*. Broomall, PA: Chelsea House, 1989.
LaBrucherie, Roger A. *Barbados: A World Apart*. Pine Valley, CA: Imagenes Press, 1993.

Belize

Morrison, Marion. *Belize*. Danbury, CT: Childrens Press, 1996.
Wright, Peggy. *Belize*. Santa Barbara, CA: ABC-CLIO, 1994.

Bermuda

Raine, David F. *Islands of Bermuda*. Boston: Houghton Mifflin, 1990

Bolivia

Blair, David Nelson. *The Land and People of Bolivia*. New York: Lippincott, 1990.
Department of Geography Staff. *Bolivia in Pictures*. Minneapolis, MN: Lerner Group, 1987.
Ikuhara, Yoshiyuki. *Children of the World: Bolivia*. Milwaukee, WI: Gareth Stevens, 1988.
Morrison, Marion. *Bolivia*. Danbury, CT: Childrens Press, 1988.
Pateman, Robert. *Cultures of the World: Bolivia*. Tarrytown, NY: Marshall Cavendish, 1995.
St. John, Jetty. *A Family in Bolivia*. Minneapolis, MN: Lerner Group, 1986.
Schimmel, Karen. *Bolivia*. Broomall, PA: Chelsea House, 1991.

Brazil

Ashford, Moyra. *Brazil*. Chatham, NJ: Raintree Steck-Vaughn, 1991
Bender, Evelyn. *Brazil*. Broomall, PA: Chelsea House, 1990.
Carpenter, Mark. *Brazil: An Awakening Giant*. Parsippany, NJ: Silver Burdett Press, 1988.
Dawson, Zoe. *Brazil*. Chatham, NJ: Raintree Steck-Vaughn, 1995.
Galvin, Irene. *Brazil: Hard Lives, High Spirits*. Tarrytown, NY: Marshall Cavendish, 1996.
Galvin, Irene. *Brazil: Many Voices, Many Faces*. Tarrytown, NY: Marshall Cavendish, 1996.
Galvin, Irene Flum. *Exploring Cultures of the World: Brazil*. Tarrytown, NY: Marshall Cavendish, 1996.
Haverstock, Nathan. *Brazil in Pictures*. Minneapolis, MN: Lerner Group, 1987.
Lewington, Anna. *Antonio's Rain Forest*. Minneapolis, MN: CarolRhoda Books, 1993.
Marshall, David. *Brazil*. Cary, IL: Rigby Interactive Library, 1996.
Reynolds, Jim. *Amazon Basin: Vanishing Cultures*. San Diego, CA: Harcourt Brace and Company, 1993.
Richard, Christopher. *Cultures of the World: Brazil*. Tarrytown, NY: Marshall Cavendish, 1991.
Schwartz, David M. *Yanomami: People of the Amazon*. New York: Lothrop, Lee and Shepard Books, 1995.
Waterlow, Julia. *The Amazon*. Chatham, NJ: Raintree Steck-Vaughn, 1994.

Canada

Ayer, Elizabeth. *Canada*. Vero Beach, FL: Rourke Publishing Group, 1990.

Bakken, Edna. *Alberta.* Danbury, CT: Childrens Press, 1992.

Barnes, Michael. *Ontario.* Minneapolis, MN: Lerner Group, 1995.

Bender, Lionel. *Canada.* Parsippany, NJ: Silver Burdett Press, 1987.

Campbell, Kumari. *New Brunswick.* Minneapolis, MN: Lerner Group, 1996.

Department of Geography Staff. *Canada in Pictures.* Minneapolis, MN: Lerner Group, 1989.

Emmond, Kenneth. *Manitoba.* Danbury, CT: Childrens Press, 1992.

Gann, Marjorie. *New Brunswick.* Danbury, CT: Childrens Press, 1994.

Hancock, Lyn. *Northwest Territories.* Danbury, CT: Childrens Press, 1993.

Kalman, Bobbie. *Canada Celebrates Multiculturalism.* New York: Crabtree Publishing, 1993.

Kessler, Deirdre. *Prince Edward Island.* Danbury, CT: Childrens Press, 1992.

Law, Kevin. *Canada.* Broomall, PA: Chelsea House, 1991.

Lotz, Jim. *Nova Scotia.* Danbury, CT: Childrens Press, 1992.

MacKay, Kathryn. *Ontario.* Danbury, CT: Childrens Press, 1992.

Malcolm, Andrew H. *The Land and People of Canada.* New York: HarperCollins Children's Books, 1991.

Margoshes, David. *Saskatchewan.* Danbury, CT: Childrens Press, 1992.

Pang, Guek-Cheng. *Cultures of the World: Canada.* Tarrytown, NY: Marshall Cavendish, 1994.

Richardson, Gillian. *Saskatchewan.* Minneapolis, MN: Lerner Group, 1995.

Sateren, Shelley Swanson. *Exploring Cultures of the World: Canada.* Tarrytown, NY: Marshall Cavendish, 1996.

Shepherd, J. *Canada.* Danbury, CT: Childrens Press, 1992.

Sunday, Jane. *Canada.* Chatham, NJ: Raintree Steck-Vaughn, 1992.

Templeman-Kluit, Anne. *Yukon.* Danbury, CT: Childrens Press, 1994.

Thompson, Alex. *Nova Scotia.* Minneapolis, MN: Lerner Group, 1995.

White, Marian. *Newfoundland—Labrador.* Danbury, CT: Childrens Press, 1993.

Cayman Islands

Smith, Hunter. *Cayman Islands—The Beach and Beyond.* Edison, NJ: Hunter Publishing, Inc., 1995.

Chile

Department of Geography Staff. *Chile in Pictures.* Minneapolis, MN: Lerner Group, 1988.

Dwyer, Chris. *Chile.* Broomall, PA: Chelsea House, 1990.

Galvin, Irene. *Chile: Journey to Freedom.* Parsippany, NJ: Silver Burdett Press, 1996.

Galvin, Irene. *Chile: Land of Poets and Patriots.* Parsippany, NJ: Silver Burdett Press, 1990.

Hintz, Martin. *Chile.* Danbury, CT: Childrens Press, 1994.

Pickering, Marianne. *Chile: Where the Land Ends.* Tarrytown, NY: Marshall Cavendish, 1997

Winter, Jane Kohen. *Cultures of the World: Chile.* Tarrytown, NY: Marshall Cavendish, 1991.

Colombia

Department of Geography Staff. *Colombia in Pictures.* Minneapolis, MN: Lerner Group, 1987.

Dubois, Jill. *Cultures of the World: Colombia.* Tarrytown, NY: Marshall Cavendish, 1991.

Morrison, Marion. *Colombia.* Danbury, CT: Childrens Press, 1990.

Pearce, Jenny. *Colombia: The Drug Wars.* New York: Gloucester Press, 1990.

Stewart, Gail. *Colombia.* New York: Crestwood House, 1991.

Costa Rica

Cummins, Ronnie. *Costa Rica.* Milwaukee, WI: Gareth Stevens, 1990.

Department of Geography Staff. *Costa Rica in Pictures.* Minneapolis, MN: Lerner Group, 1987.

Foley, Erin. *Cultures of the World: Costa Rica.* Tarrytown, NY: Marshall Cavendish, 1997.

Forsyth, Adrian. *Journey Through a Tropical Jungle.* Old Tappan, NJ: Simon and Schuster, 1989.

Mallory, Kenneth. *Waterhole: Life in a Rescued Tropical Rain Forest.* New York: Franklin Watts, 1992.

Patent, Dorothy, and William Munoz. *Biodiversity.* Boston, MA: Clarion Books, 1996.

Peduzzi, Kelli. *Oscar Arias: Peacemaker and Leader Among Nations.* Milwaukee, WI: Gareth Stevens, 1991.

Cuba

Crouch, Clifford. *Cuba.* Broomall, PA: Chelsea House, 1991.

Cummins, Ronald. *Cuba.* Milwaukee, WI: Gareth Stevens, 1991.

Haverstock, Nathan. *Cuba in Pictures.* Minneapolis, MN: Lerner Group, 1993.

Morris, Emily. *Cuba.* Chatham, NJ: Raintree Steck-Vaughn, 1991.

Sheehan, Sean. *Cultures of the World: Cuba.* Tarrytown, NY: Marshall Cavendish, 1994.

Staelb, Frank. *Children of Cuba.* Minneapolis, MN: Lerner Group, 1996.
Stewart, Gail. *Cuba.* New York: Crestwood House, 1991.

Dominica
Staib, Frank J. *Children of Dominica.* Secaucus, NJ: Carol Publishing Group, 1998.

Dominican Republic
Foley, Erin. *Dominican Republic.* Tarrytown, NY: Marshall Cavendish, 1995.
Haverstock, Nathan. *Dominican Republic in Pictures.* Minneapolis, MN: Lerner Group, 1988.

Ecuador
Bickman, Connie. *Children of Ecuador.* Minneapolis, MN: Abdo and Daughters, 1996.
Foley, Erin. *Ecuador.* Tarrytown, NY: Marshall Cavendish, 1995.
Lepthien, Emilie U. *Ecuador.* Danbury, CT: Childrens Press, 1993.
Sly, Alexandra. *The Waorani: People of the Ecuadoran Rain Forest.* Parsippany, NJ: Silver Burdett Press, 1993.

El Salvador
Bachelis, Faren M. *El Salvador.* Danbury, CT: Childrens Press, 1990.
Cheney, Glenn Alan. *El Salvador, Country in Crisis.* New York: Franklin Watts, 1990.
Cummins, Ronald. *El Salvador.* Milwaukee, WI: Gareth Stevens, 1990.
Foley, Erin. *El Salvador.* Tarrytown, NY: Marshall Cavendish, 1994.
Stewart, Gaul B. *El Salvador.* New York: Crestwood House, 1991.

Falkland Islands
Strange, Ian J. *The Falklands: South Atlantic Islands.* New York: Putnam Publishing Group Library, 1985.

French Guiana
Morrison, Marion. *French Guiana.* Danbury, CT: Childrens Press, 1995.

Greenland
Alexander, Bryan, and Cherry Alexander. *The Eskimos.* New York: Crescent Books, 1997.
Buell, Janet. *Greenland Mummies.* New York: Twenty First Century Books, 1998.
Lepthien, Emilie U. *Greenland.* Danbury, CT: Childrens Press, 1989.
Levine, Charlotte. *Danish Dependencies.* Broomall, PA: Chelsea House, 1989.

Grenada
Eisenberg, Joyce. *Grenada.* Broomall, PA: Chelsea House, 1988.

Guatemala
Brill, Marlene Targ, and Harry R. Targ. *Guatemala.* Danbury, CT: Childrens Press, 1993.
Cummins, Ronnie, and Rose Welch. *Guatemala.* Milwaukee, WI: Gareth Stevens, 1990.
Hadden, Gerry, ed. *Teenage Refugees from Guatemala Speak Out.* New York: Rosen Publishing Group, 1997.
Nach, James. *Guatemala in Pictures.* Minneapolis, MN: Lerner Group, 1987.

Guyana
Brill, Marlene Targ. *Guyana.* Danbury, CT: Childrens Press, 1994.
Department of Geography Staff. *Guyana in Pictures.* Minneapolis, MN: Lerner Group, 1988.

Haiti
Anthony, Suzanne. *Haiti.* Broomall, PA: Chelsea House, 1989.
Goldish, Meish. *Crisis in Haiti.* Brookfield, CT: Millbrook Press, 1995.
Myers, Walter Dean. *Toussaint L'Ouverture: The Fight for Haiti's Freedom.* Old Tappan, NJ: Simon and Schuster, 1996.
Ngcheong-Lum, Roseline. *Cultures of the World: Haiti.* Tarrytown, NY: Marshall Cavendish, 1994.

Honduras
Norsworthy, Kent, and Tom Berry. *Inside Honduras.* Albuquerque, NM: Interhemispheric, 1994.
Targ, Harry R., and Marlene Targ Brill. *Honduras.* Danbury, CT: Childrens Press, 1995.
Weddle, Ken. *Honduras in Pictures.* Minneapolis, MN: Lerner Group, 1987.

Jamaica

Barraclough, John. *Jamaica.* Crystal Lake, IL: Rigby Interactive Library, 1996.
Capek, Michael. *Jamaica.* Minneapolis, MN: Carolrhoda Books, 1998.
Sheehan, Sean. *Cultures of the World: Jamaica.* Tarrytown, NY: Marshall Cavendish, 1996.

Mexico

Alcraft, Rob, and Sean Sprague. *Mexico.* Crystal Lake, IL: Rigby Interactive Library, 1996.
Arnold, Helen. *Mexico.* Chatham, NJ: Raintree Steck-Vaughn, 1995.
Dahl, Michael, S. *Mexico.* Mankato, MN: Bridgestone Books, 1997.
DuBois, Jill. *Women in Society: Mexico.* Tarrytown, NY: Marshall Cavendish, 1993.
Dubois, Jill, and Eric Siow. *Cultures of the World: Mexico.* Tarrytown, NY: Marshall Cavendish, 1993.
Hopkinson, Amanda. *Mexico.* Chatham, NJ: Raintree Steck-Vaughn, 1992.
Howard, John. *Mexico.* Parsippany, NJ: Silver Burdett Press, 1992.
Irizarry, Carmen. *Passport to Mexico.* New York: Franklin Watts, 1994.
Kalman, Bobby. *Mexico—the People.* New York: Crabtree Publishing, 1993.
Parker, Edward A. *Mexico.* Chatham, NJ: Raintree Steck-Vaughn, 1998.
Rummel, Jack. *Mexico.* Broomall, PA: Chelsea House, 1990.
Shepherd, Donna Watts. *The Aztecs.* New York: Franklin Watts, 1992.
Staub, Frank. *Children of the Sierra Madre.* Minneapolis, MN: Lerner Group, 1996.
Stein, R. Conrad. *Mexico—a Golden Past, A Hopeful Future.* Minneapolis, MN: Dillon Press, 1996.

Montserrat

Dyde, Brian. *Islands to the Windward: Five Gems of the Caribbean.* Edison, NJ: Hunter Publishing, 1990.

Nicaragua

Haverstock, Nathan A. *Nicaragua in Pictures.* Minneapolis, MN: Lerner Group, 1993.
Kott, Jennifer. *Cultures of the World: Nicaragua.* Tarrytown, NY: Marshall Cavendish, 1994.
Malone, Michael. *A Nicaraguan Family.* Minneapolis, MN: Lerner Group, 1998.

Panama

Hassig, Susan M. *Cultures of the World: Panama.* Tarrytown, NY: Marshall Cavendish, 1996.
Presilla, Maricel E. *Mola: Cuna Life, Stories, and Art.* New York: Henry Holt and Co., 1996.
Stewart, Gail B. *Panama.* New York: Crestwood House, 1990.
Vasquez, Ana M. *Panama.* Danbury, CT: Childrens Press, 1991.

Paraguay

Haverstock, Nathan A. *Paraguay in Pictures.* Minneapolis, MN: Lerner Group, 1987.
Morrison, Marion. *Paraguay.* Danbury, CT: Childrens Press, 1993.

Peru

Bickman, Connie. *Children of Peru.* Minneapolis, MN: Abdo & Daughters, 1994.
Deltenre, Chantal, and Martine Noblet. *Peru and the Andean Countries.* Hauppauge, NY: Barron, 1995.
Department of Geography Staff. *Peru in Pictures.* Minneapolis, MN: Lerner Group, 1992.
Falconer, Kieran. *Cultures of the World: Peru.* Tarrytown, NY: Marshall Cavendish, 1996.
Kalman, Bobbie, and Tammy Everts. *Land, People, and Cultures: Peru.* New York: Crabtree Publishing Company, 1994.
Lepthien, Emilie U. *Peru.* Danbury, CT: Childrens Press, 1992.

Puerto Rico

Abodaher, David J. *Puerto Rico: America's 51st State.* New York: Franklin Watts, Incorporated, 1993.
Aliotta, Jerome J. *Puerto Ricans.* Broomall, PA: Chelsea House, 1995.
Aliotta, Jerome J. *The Puerto Ricans.* New York: Franklin Watts, 1993.
Fradin, Judith, and Dennis Fradin. *From Sea to Shining Sea: Puerto Rico.* Chicago: Childrens Press, 1995.
Hauptly, Denis. *Puerto Rico: An Unfinished Story.* New York: Simon and Schuster, 1991.
Johnston, Joyce. *Puerto Rico.* Minneapolis, MN: Lerner Group, 1994.
Johnston, Joyce. *Puerto Rico in Pictures.* Minneapolis, MN: Lerner Group, 1995.
Levy, Patricia. *Cultures of the World: Puerto Rico.* Tarrytown, NY: Marshall Cavendish, 1994.
Press, Petra. *Cultures of America: Puerto Ricans.* Tarrytown, NY: Marshall Cavendish/Benchmark Books, 1996.

Saint Vincent and the Grenadines
Philpott, Don. *St. Vincent & Grenadines.* Lincolnwood, IL: Passport Books, 1996.

Suriname
Beatty, Noelle B. *Places and Peoples of the World: Suriname.* Broomall, PA: Chelsea House, 1988.

Trinidad and Tobago
Bailey, Donna, and Ansel Wong. *Where We Live: Trinidad.* Chatham, NJ: Raintree Steck-Vaughn, 1990.
Urosevich, Patricia R. *Trinidad and Tobago.* Broomall, PA: Chelsea House, 1997.

United States of America
Anderson, Marcie. *Exploring the Fifty States.* Saint Petersburg, FL: Willowisp Press, 1994.
Ashabranner, Brent. *Still a Nation of Immigrants.* New York: Dutton Children's Books, 1993.
Baines, John D. *The United States.* Chatham, NJ: Raintree Steck-Vaughn, 1993.
Birchfield, D. L., ed. *The Encyclopedia of North American Indians.* Tarrytown, NY: Marshall Cavendish, 1997.
Bock, Judy, and Rachel Kranz. *Scholastic Encyclopedia of the United States.* New York: Scholastic, Inc., 1997.
Catalano, Julie. *The Mexican Americans.* Broomall, PA: Chelsea House, 1995.
Cox, Vic. *The Challenge of Immigration.* Springfield, NJ: Enslow Publications, 1995.
Department of Geography Staff. *United States in Pictures.* Minneapolis, MN: Lerner Group, 1995.
Ferry, Steven. *Cultures of America: Russian Americans.* Tarrytown, NY: Marshall Cavendish/Benchmark Books, 1996.
Franklin, Paula A. *Melting Pot or Not? Debating Cultural Identity.* Springfield, NJ: Enslow Publications, 1995.
Gabor, Al. *Cultures of America: Polish Americans.* Tarrytown, NY: Marshall Cavendish/Benchmark Books, 1995.
Galván, Raúl. *Cultures of America: Cuban Americans.* Tarrytown, NY: Marshall Cavendish/Benchmark Books, 1995.
Herda, D. J. *Ethnic America: The North Central States.* Brookfield, CT: Millbrook Press, 1991.
Herda, D. J. *Ethnic America: The Northeastern States.* Brookfield, CT: Millbrook Press, 1991.
Herda, D. J. *Ethnic America: The Northwestern States.* Brookfield, CT: Millbrook Press, 1991.
Jones, Jayne C. *In America: Greeks in America.* Minneapolis, MN: Lerner Group, 1990.
Krone, Chester. *United States of America.* Chatham, NJ: Raintree Steck-Vaughn, 1990.
Kuropas, Myron B. *In America: Ukrainians in America.* Minneapolis, MN: Lerner Group, 1995.
Lee, Kathleen. *Illegal Immigration.* San Diego, CA: Lucent Books, 1996.
Lee, Lauren. *Cultures of America: Japanese Americans.* Tarrytown, NY: Marshall Cavendish/Benchmark Books, 1996.
Lee, Lauren. *Cultures of America: Korean Americans.* Tarrytown, NY: Marshall Cavendish/Benchmark Books, 1995.
Leuzzi, Linda. *Urban Life.* Broomall, PA: Chelsea House, 1995.
Levinson, David, ed. *American Immigrant Cultures: Builders of a Nation.* Old Tappan, NJ: Macmillan Library Reference, 1995.
Marquardt, Arthur H. *The New Americans.* Notre Dame, IN: Cross Cultural Publications, 1994.
Meyer, Carolyn. *In a Different Light: Growing Up in a Yup'ik Eskimo Village in Alaska.* Old Tappan, NJ: Simon & Schuster, 1996.
Morrow, Robert. *Immigration: Blessing or Burden?* Minneapolis, MN: Lerner Group, 1997.
Moy, Tin. *Cultures of America: Chinese Americans.* Tarrytown, NY: Marshall Cavendish/Benchmark Books, 1995.
Payton, Shelia. *Cultures of America: African Americans.* Tarrytown, NY: Marshall Cavendish/Benchmark Books, 1995.
Poynter, Margaret. *The Uncertain Journey: Stories of Illegal Aliens in El Norte.* New York: Atheneum, 1992.
Press, David P., and Elizabeth Kaplan. *Cultures of America: Jewish Americans.* Tarrytown, NY: Marshall Cavendish/ Benchmark Books, 1995.
Press, Petra. *Cultures of America: Mexican Americans.* Tarrytown, NY: Marshall Cavendish/Benchmark Books, 1995.
Press, Petra. *Cultures of America: Puerto Ricans.* Tarrytown, NY: Marshall Cavendish/Benchmark Books, 1996.
Reimers, David M. *A Land of Immigrants.* Broomall, PA: Chelsea House, 1995.
Riehecky, Janet. *Cultures of America: Irish Americans.* Tarrytown, NY: Marshall Cavendish/Benchmark Books, 1995.
Shapiro, William E., ed. *The Kingfisher Young People's Encyclopedia of the United States.* London: Kingfisher Books, 1994.
Stein, R. Conrad. *The United States of America.* Danbury, CT: Childrens Press, 1994.
Stone, Amy. *Cultures of America: French Americans.* Tarrytown, NY: Marshall Cavendish/Benchmark Books, 1995.
Strom, Yale. *Quilted Landscapes: Conversations with Young Immigrants.* Old Tappan, NJ: Simon & Schuster, 1996.
Washburne, Carolyn. *Cultures of America: Italian Americans.* Tarrytown, NY: Marshall Cavendish/Benchmark Books, 1995.

Uruguay
Department of Geography Staff. *Uruguay in Pictures.* Minneapolis, MN: Lerner Group, 1994.
Morrison, Marion. *Uruguay.* Danbury, CT: Childrens Press, 1992.

Venezuela

Fox, Geoffrey. *The Land and People of Venezuela.* Scranton, PA: HarperCollins Juvenile Books, 1991.
Heinrichs, Ann. *Venezuela.* Danbury, CT: Childrens Press, 1997.
Morrison, Marion. *Venezuela.* Danbury, CT: Childrens Press, 1989.
Winter, Jane Kohen. *Cultures of the World: Venezuela.* Tarrytown, NY: Marshall Cavendish, 1994.

Virgin Islands (UK)

Luntta, Karl. *Virgin Islands Handbook.* Chico, CA: Moon Publications, 1997.

Virgin Islands (U.S.)

Aylesworth, Thomas G., and Virginia L. Aylesworth. *Territories and Possessions: Puerto Rico, U.S. Virgin Islands, Guam, American Samoa, Wake, Midway and Other Islands, Micronesia.* Broomall, PA: Chelsea House, 1995.

Pronunciation Guide to Countries, Peoples, and Foreign Terms

Anguilla (ang-GWIL-uh)

Antigua (an-TEE-guh) **and Barbuda** (bahr-BOO-dah)

Argentina (ahr-jen-TEE-nuh)
asado con cuero (ah-SAH-doe KONE KWER-oh): beef barbecued in its hide
bara brith (BAH-rah breeth): a Welsh fruit loaf
boleadoras (bowl-lay-uh-DOR-us): a weighted cord used for hunting
bombachas (bohm-BAH-chahs): wide gaucho pants
bombilla (bohm-BEE-yah): a silver straw
Chulupi (CHEW-loop-ee): a Native American people
Comechingones (co-MAY-chee-go-NEEZ): a Native American people
Diaguita (dee-ha-GEE-tah): a Native American people
empanadas (EHM-puh-nah-duhs): meat- or seafood-stuffed pastries
estancias (eh-STAHN-syuhs): sheep ranches
Guaraní (gwar-ruh-NEE): a Native American people
guita (GWEE-tah): "dough" or money in Lunfardo
Haush (AUS): a Native American people
Huarpe (oo-AR-pay): a Native American people
jineteados (hee-nay-tay-AH-dohs): rodeos
locro (LOW-crow): a thick, Native American soup
Lunfardo (loon-FAR-doh): the street language of Buenos Aires
Mataco (ma-TAH-ko): a Native American people
mati (MAH-tee): a gourd
morcillas (more-SEE-yahs): blood sausages
noquis (NO-kees): Italian potato dumplings
Ona (OH-nah): a Native American people
pato (PAH-toe): a gaucho game on horseback
pibe (PEE-bay): a "guy" in Lunfardo
pucheros (poo-CHER-ohs): chicken or other meat stews
quebracho (kay-BRAH-choh): a hardwood tree
Querandí (kare-rahn-DEE): a Native American people
Tehuelche (tuh-WEL-chee): a Native American people
Toba (TO-bah): a Native American people
toldo (TOLL-doe): a portable shelter

Aruba (a-ROO-buh)

Bahamas (buh-HAH-muz)
Lucayan (loo-KAY-ehn): a Native American people

Barbados (bahr-BAY-dose)
Bajans (BAY-junz): people of Barbados
conkies (KOHNG-eez): steamed sweet potatoes
cou-cou (KOO-koo): mashed okra and corn starch

Belize (buh-LEEZ)
brukdown (BROOK-down): popular Creole music
cays (KEYS): small, low islands

Garifuna (gah-ree-FOO-nah): Black Caribs, descendants of Africans and Caribs
Maya (MAH-yuh): a Native American people
punta (POON-tah): Garifuna music
shaman (SHAH-muhn): a religious healer
soca (SO-kuh): Caribbean dance music
Toltec (TOLL-tec): a Native American people

Bermuda (bur-MYOO-duh)

Bolivia (bo-LEEV-eè-ah)
aguayo (ah-GWHY-o): a striped shawl
aji (ah-HEE): strong-tasting peppers
altiplano (ahl-tee-PLAH-no): a high, treeless plain
Aymara (EYE-mah-rah): a Native American people
balsas (BAHL-sahs): boats made of reed
caja (KAH-hah): a drum
cambas (KAHM-bahs): a lowland group of people
caña (KAHN-yah): a bamboo flute with horn
ch'ullu ch'ullu (ch-OOL-yoo ch-OOL-yoo): an instrument made of bones or shells
chapaco (chah-PAH-koe): a violin
chapaqueada (chah-pah-KEH-ah-dah): a dance
charango (chah-RAHN-go): a small guitar
Chipaya (chee-PAH-yah): a Native American people and village
Chiriguano (chee-ree-GWAH-no): a Native American people
cholas (CHO-las): mestizo women
cholos (CHO-los): mestizo men
chullo (CHOOL-yo): a knit hat
chuño (CHOON-yo): small, hard potatoes
collas (KOL-yahs): a highland group of people
cordilleras (kor-deel-YEH-rahs): mountain ranges
cueca (KWE-kah): a popular dance
diablada (dee-ah-BLAH-dah): a dance
erke (AIR-keh): a wind instrument
huayño (WHINE-yoh): a Native American dance
Kallawaya (kahl-yah-WAY-yah): a Native American people
locoto (lo-KO-to): a green, yellow, or red pepper
Macha (MAH-chah): a Native American people
morenada (mo-reh-NAH-dah): a kind of carnival dance
Paceños (pah-SEHN-yos): the people of La Paz
pinkullo (peen-KOOL-yo): a flute
polleras (poy-YEH-rahs): brightly colored skirts
pututo (poo-TOO-too): an instrument made from a bull's horn
qola (KO-la): "medicine" in Aymara
Quechua (KEH-choo-ah): a Native American people
quena (KEH-nah): a flute
Saya (SAH-yah): a kind of music with drumming and chanting
surazos (soo-RAH-sos): cold winds
tarka (TAHR-kah): a flute

tinkus (TEEN-koos): ritual battles

Todos los Santos (TO-dos los SAHN-tos): All Saints' and Souls' Day

totora (toh-TOH-rah): a reed used for roof thatch, mats, baskets, and boats

tunta (TOON-tah): small, hard potatoes

Yuracaré (yoo-rah-kah-REH): a Native American people

zampona (sahm-POHN-ya): a reed panpipe

Brazil (bruh-ZIL)

acarajé (uh-cur-ruh-JAY): a dish made of garlic, shrimp, and dendé oil

atabaques (uh-tah-BAH-kes): tall drums

baianas (buh-ee-YAHN-us): women of Bahia

bandeirantes (buhn-deh-RUHN-tes): explorers looking for gold and diamonds

batucada (buh-too-CAH-duh): percussion groups

beiju (BAY-zhoe): cassava bread

berimbau (beh-ring-BOW): a string instrument with hollow gourd

bombachas (bohm-BAH-shahs): gauchos' baggy pants

brasil (brah-ZEE-il): a hardwood tree used for dye

caboclos (kuh-BOE-kloos): descendants of Native American peoples and foreign settlers

campos cerrado (KUHM-poos say-HAH-doe): dry grasslands

Candomblé (kuh-dome-BLEH): a religion

capoeira (kup-oh-AY-rah): a dance with African origins

Cariocas (kah-ree-OH-kus): people who live in Rio de Janeiro

caruru (kuh-ru-RU): a dish made of shrimp, peanuts, and ginger

dendé (den-DAY): a kind of palm

favelas (fuh-VEL-uhs): slums

garimpeiros (gah-reem-PAY-rose): mestizo gold seekers

gaúchos (gah-OO-shose): cowhands

jangada (juhn-GAH-duh): a sailing raft

jangadeiros (juhn-gah-DAY-rose): fishermen who use a raft

Karaja (kuh-rah-JAH): a Native American people

Kayabi (kie-yah-BEE): a Native American people

Macumba (Muh-COOM-buh): a religion

mate (MAH-tay): an herbal tea

nordeste (nor-DES-tay): the northeastern region of Brazil

novelas (noh-VEL-as): televised soap operas

orixas (oh-ree-SHAS): Yoruba gods

Passarela do Samba (puh-suh-RELL-uh doe SUM-bah): Rio's carnival stadium

paulistas (pow-LIS-tas): people of São Paulo State

planalto (pluhn-OWL-tow): upland or high plain

quilombos (kee-LUM-bose): groups of runaway slaves

sertão (sehr-TAO): the forested interior region of Brazil

Suyá (soo-YAH): a Native American people

vaqueiros (vah-KAY-rose): cowboys

Xavante (shah-VAHN-tay): a Native American people

yano (ee-ON-oh): a large round shelter made of palm thatch

Yanomami (ee-on-oh-MA-mee): a Native American people

Canada

askimek (AHS-kih-mek): the Ojibwe word for Inuit

Assiniboine (uh-SIN-uh-boin): a First Nations/Native American people

Atsina (at-SEE-nuh): a First Nations/Native American people

Attikamek (uh-TIK-uh-mehk): a First Nations/Native American people

Beothuk (BAY-uh-thuck): a First Nations/Native American people

Blackfeet (BLACK-feet): a First Nations/Native American people

Bonhomme (bun-HUM): a snowman, symbol of Quebec's carnival

bonspiel (BAHN-speel): a curling competition

cabane à sucre (kah-BAHN ah SOOK-ruh): a "sugar shack" or place where maple syrup is made

Chipewyan (chip-uh-WHY-un): a First Nations/Native American people

Cree (CREE): a First Nations/Native American people

Déné (deh-NAY): a group of First Nations peoples

Doukhobors (DUKE-uh-boors): "spirit fighters," a Russian immigrant group

eskimantis (esk-i-MAN-tis): Abenaki word for Inuit

Festival du Voyageur (fest-ee-VAHL due voy-ah-JUR): a Winnipeg festival celebrating the voyageurs

Gros Ventre (grow-VAHN-truh): a First Nations/Native American people

habitants (ah-bee-TAHN): tenant farmers

Hutterites (HUT-uh-rites): an immigrant group from Slovakia and Moravia

Innu: (IN-noo): tribal name for Napaskis and Montagnais together, First Nations/Native Americans from Quebec and Labrador

Inuit (IN-yoo-it): a people formerly called Eskimos

Inuvialuit (in-NOO-vee-ah-loo-it): another name for Inuit

kanata (kuh-NAH-duh): Huron or Iroquois word for Canada meaning "village" or "settlement"

Kutchin (kuch-IN): an indigenous peoples of the Yukon

lacrosse (lah-CROSS): a Native American game

liveyers (LIV-yuhrs): Labrador inhabitants

Maliseet (MAL-uh-seet): a First Nations/Native American people

Métis (MAY-tee): descendants of French and First Nations/Native American peoples

Mód (MAWD): a Scottish festival in Cape Breton

Mohawks (MO-hawks): a First Nations/Native American people

Montagnais (mon-tun-YAY): a First Nations/Native American people

Naskapi (NAS-kuh-pee): a First Nations/Native American people

Nunavut (NOON-ah-vuht): the Arctic section of the Northwest Territories owned by the Inuit and/or the Canadian government

Ojibwe (o-jib-WAY): a First Nations/Native American people

600

Peaux-rouges (poe ROUJ): the European name for Native Americans

Piegan (pee-GAN): a First Nations/Native American people

Saulteaux (SOE-toe): a First Nations/Native American people

seigneurs (sayn-YEURS): landowners

Siksika (SITS-ih-kah): a First Nations/Native American people

sirop d'érable (see-ROW dee ay-RAHBLE): maple syrup

tourtière (tour-tee-YAIR): a pork pie

Tuscarora (tusk-uh-ROAR-uh): a First Nations/Native American people

voyageurs (voy-ah-JURZ): French trappers, explorers, and traders

Cayman (KAY-man) Islands

Chile (CHEE-lay)

almud (ahl-MOOD): a Chilote measuring device

arpillera (ahr-pee-YAY-rah): an embroidered picture or pattern

Aymara (eye-mah-RAH): a Native American people

chicha (CHEE-chah): fermented grape juice

Chilotes (chee-LOE-tayss): descendants of Native Americans and Spanish on the Chiloé Islands

cueca (KWAY-kah): the Chilean national dance

Domingo de Cuasimodo (doe-MEAN-goe day kwah-SEE-moe-doe): an Easter festival

empanadas (em-pah-NAH-thus): pastries filled with eggs, olives, cheese, seafood, or chopped meats

huasos (WAH-soess): Chilean cowboys

Huilliche (wee-YEE-chay): a Native American people

ichu (EE-chew): a type of grass

Incas (EEN-kahs): a Native American people

machis (MAH-cheess): Mapuche female shamans

machitunes (mah-chee-TOO-nayss): Mapuche word for collective prayers to the gods

malones (ma-LONE-ayss): a Mapuche word for meetings to listen to dreams and predict the future

Mapuche (ma-POO-chay): a Native American people

moai (MOE-eye): Easter Island statues

Ona (OE-nah): a Native American people

Pascuense (pahss-KWEN-say): the Polynesian language of Easter Island

Pehuenche (pay-WAYN-chay): a Native American people

Picunches (pee-KOON-chase): a Native American people

porotos granados (poe-ROE-toess grah-NAH-thoess): a traditional dish with Native American origins

ruka (ROO-kah): a traditional Mapuche home made of thatch

tsunamis (tsoo-NAH-mees): huge waves caused by earthquakes in the sea

Yaghan (YAH-gahn): a Native American people

Colombia (koe-LOME-bee-uh)

alabaos (ag-lah-BAH-oess): songs of praise

Arhuaco (ahr-WAH-koe): a Native American people

Bogotanos (boe-goe-TAH-noess): the inhabitants of Bogotá

bombo (BOME-boe): a double-headed drum

castas (KAHSS-tahss): Guajiro family groups

corrido (koe-REE-thoe): a dance

cuatro (KWAH-troe): a small guitar

cumbia (KOOM-bee-ah): a dance with African origins

cununo hembra (koo-NOO-noe EM-brah): a drum

cununo macho (koo-NOO-noe MAH-choe): a drum

currulao (koo-roo-LAH-oe): a dance

gaitas (GUY-tahss): flutes made of cactus and beeswax

galerón (gah-lay-ROEN): a dance

Guajiro (gwah-HEE-roe): a Native American people

Guambiano (gwahm-bee-AH-noe): a Native American people

guasá (gwah-SSAH): a rattle with seeds

hai (HI): Noanama spirit figure

haibana (hi-BAH-nah): Noanama shaman

joropa (hoe-ROE-pah): a dance

juego de la rana (WAY-goe day lah RAH-nah): a game

Kogi (KOE-hee): a Native American people

llaneros (yah-NAY-roess): cattlemen

llanos (YAH-noess): grasslands

malocas (mah-LOE-kahss): Tukano communal houses

mamas (MAH-mahss): Kogi priests

mantas (MAHN-tahss): Guajiro cotton robes

mopa mopa (MOE-pah MOE-pah): a plant used for lacquer

Muisca (moo-EESS-kah): a Native American people

mute (MOO-tay): a Paez Indian soup

Noanama (noe-ah-NAH-mah): a Native American people

Páez (PIE-ayss): a Native American people

palenques (pah-LAYN-kayss): former slave enclaves in the rain forest

pasaje (pah-SAH-hay): a dance

Pijao (pee-HOW): a Native American people

raspas (RAHSS-pahss): instruments made from gourds

redoblante (ray-doe-BLAHN-tay): a double-headed drum

Tairona (tie-ROE-nah): a Native American people

tejo (TAY-hoe): bullfighting

tiple (TEE-play): a small guitar

Tukano (too-KAH-noe): a Native American people

tuma (TOO-mah): a Guajiro necklace

vallenato (bye-NAH-toe): a type of music

zambos (SSAHM-boess): descendants of Native Americans and Africans

Costa Rica (KOESS-tah REE-kah)

chicha (CHEE-chah): a corn drink

gallo pinto (GUT-yoe PEEN-toe): the national dish of Costa Rica

hermanticos (air-mahn-TEE-koess): "little brothers," a nickname for Costa Ricans

meseta central (may-SAY-tah sayn-TRAHL): large central valley

pan bon (PAHN BONE): a glazed sweet bread

polacos (poe-LAH-koess): Jews

rundown (RON-don): a meat and vegetable or fish stew

sabaneros (sah-bah-NAY-roess): cowboys

tamelas (tah-MAY-lahss): a corn dish
ticos (TEE-koess): a nickname for Costa Ricans

Cuba (KYOO-buh)

Azucareros (ah-soo-kah-RAY-roess): "the sugar workers" baseball team
babalawos (bah-bah-LAH-woess): Santería priests
balseros (bahl-SAY-roess): "rafters," people fleeing Cuba
batás (bah-TAHSS): drums
bohios (boe-EE-yoess): wooden country houses
boniato (boe-NYAH-toe): a sweet potato
camellos (kah-MAY-yoess): long, public vehicles
campesinos (kahm-pay-SEE-noess): people living in rural areas
guajiros (gwah-HEE-roess): traditional peasant farmers
Industriales (een-dooss-tree-AH-layss): "the factory workers" baseball team
malanga (mah-LAHN-gah): a root vegetable
nueva trova (noo-AY-bah TROE-bah): ballad music
orishas (oe-REE-shahss): Santería gods
Santería (sahn-tay-REE-ah): a African-Cuban religion
son (SOEN): dance music
Tabacaleros (tah-bah-kah-LAY-roess): "the tobacco workers" baseball team
tres (TRAYSS): a three-stringed guitar
trova (TROE-bah): ballad music

Dominica (dohm-uh-NEE-kuh)

Jounen Kweyol (joo-NEE KWAY-yahl): a Creole festival

Dominican Republic (duh-MIHN-ih-kuhn rih-PUB-lick)

bohíos (boe-HEE-oess): wooden cabins
locrio (LOE-kree-oe): a rice dish
mondongo (moen-DOEN-goe): a stew made of a cow's stomach
sancocho (sahn-KOE-choe): a meat and vegetable stew
tamboras (tahm-BOE-rahss): a double-headed drum

Ecuador (EHK-wuh-door)

aji (AH-hee): chile peppers
alpargatas (ahl-pahr-GAH-tahss): sandals
Aucas (OW-kahss): Quichua word for "savages"
ayahuasca (i-yah-WAHSS-kah): a hallucinogen
blanco (BLAHN-koe): white
bocina (boe-SEE-nah): an instrument made of cow horns
bomba negra (BOME-bah NAY-grah): a mix of Native highland music and African rhythms
bombos (BOME-boess): small drums
Cañaris (kahn-YAH-reess): a Native American people
Cayapas (ki-YAH-pahss): a Native American people
charango (chah-RAHN-goe): a tiny guitar
chupe (CHOO-pay): a thick cream soup
Colorados (koe-low-RAH-thoess): a Native American group, also known as Tsichila
coroneta (koe-roe-NAY-tah): an instrument made of cow horns

Costeños (koess-TAYN-yoess): people of the coastal lowlands
cushmas (KOOSH-mahss): knee-length cotton tunics
cuy (KWEE): guinea pig
el loco (el LOW-coe): "the madman," a nickname for President Abdala Bucaram
Esmeraldeños (ayss-may-rahl-DAYN-yoess): people of the coastal region
fanesca (fah-NAYSS-kah): a soup eaten at Easter
ikat (EE-kaht): a tie-dyeing process
indígena (een-DEE-hay-nah): Native American
locro (LOW-croe): a thick cream soup
montuvios (moan-TOO-bee-oess): people with white, Native American, and black parentage
páramo (PAH-rah-moe): a mountain region
pasacalle (pah-sah-CAH-yay) a dance
Pase del Niño (PAH-say dell NEEN-yoe): a festival celebrating the birth of Christ
pasillo (pah-SEE-yoe): a dance in waltz time
pasodoble (pah-sah-THOE-blay): a Spanish dance
pingullu (peen-GOO-yoo): a kind of flute
quena (KAY-nah): a kind of flute
Quichua (KEE-chew-ah): a Native American group
rondador (roen-thah-DOER): an Ecuadorian panpipe
Salasacas (sah-lah-SAH-kahss): a Native American people
sanjuanito (sahn-wahn-EE-toe): a dance
Saragureños (sah-rah-hoo-RAIN-yoess): a Native American people
Serranos (say-RAH-noess): people of the Andean highlands
sierra (see-EHR-uh): mountains
superfino (soo-pair-FEE-noe): a good Panama hat
tapices (tah-PEE-sayss): wall hangings
toquilla (toe-KEE-yah): a fine straw
Tsichila (ZEE-chee-lah): a Native American group, also known as the Colorados
tupus (TOO-pooss): ornate silver pins
Waorani (wah-oe-RAH-nee): a Native American group
zampoña (sahm-PONE-yah): a kind of panpipe

El Salvador (el SAHL-bah-door)

brujería (broo-hay-REE-ah): witchcraft
chozas (CHOE-sass): thatched cabins
curanderos (koo-rahn-DAY-roess): herbal doctors
pupusa (poo-POO-sah): a kind of pancake
tierra caliente (tee-AY-rah kah-lee-AYN-tay): "hot land," the coastal area

French Guiana: (gee-AH-nah)

fromager (froe-mah-JAY): a kind of tree
gendarmes (ZHAN-dahrm): police officers
les métros (lay may-TROE): metropolitan French people
maluana (mah-loo-AH-nah): a circular piece of wood
marake (mah-RAH-kay): "ant test," a Wayana initiation ceremony
Marrons (mah-RONS): "wild slaves"
tukusipan (too-koo-SEE-pahn): a Wayana hut
Wayana (why-YAH-nah): a Native American group

Greenland
illu (IG-loo): Inuit house
illuigaq (ig-LOO-yee-gahk): an Inuit temporary hunting lodge
Kalaallit (kah-LAH-licht): an Inuit group
Landsting (LAHND-sting): parliament

Grenada (grihn-AY-dah)
parang (pah-RAHNG): a pre-Christmas festival

Guadeloupe (GWAHD-l-oop)
l'hivernage (lee-vair-NAHJ): the rainy season
gwo ka (gwoe kah): country folk music
zouk (ZOOK): a kind of techno music

Guatemala (gwah-tuh-MAH-luh)
criollos (kree-OY-ohs): descendants of Spanish immigrants
Garifuna (gah-ree-FOO-nah): Black Caribs, descendants of Africans and Caribs
huipil (hwee-PEEL): a woman's sleeveless shirt
Itzá (eat-SAH): a Native American people
ladinos (lah-DEE-nose): people of Spanish and Mayan ancestry
Maya (MAH-yuh): a Native American people
metate (may-TAH-tay): a grinding stone
na (NAH): a Mayan thatched house
Popol Vuh (POH-puhl VOO): a book on Mayan myths

Guyana (GUY-ah-nah)
balata (bah-LAH-tah): sap from the bulletwood tree
Lokono (loe-KOE-noe): a Native American people
Macushi (mah-KOOSH-ee): a Native American people
Wai Wai (WHY-why): a Native American people
Wapishana (wah-PEESH-ee-ah-nah): a Native American people

Haiti (HAY-tee)
affranchis (ah-FRAH-shee): freemen
bamboches (BAHM-boesh): dance and drumming sessions
cadance (KAH-dahns): a dance
compas (KOME-pah): a dance
gourde (GOORD): "gourd," the name for Haitian currency
Kreyol (KRAY-awl): Creole, a French dialect
loas (LWAH): Voodoo spirits
ounphor (OEN-fore): a religious building for the practice of Voodoo
rara (RAH-rah): costumed dancers in bands
Taino (TIE-no): a Native American people
taptaps (tap-TAPS): minibuses
tontons macoute (TOEN-toen mah-KOOT): Haitian secret police
Vodun (VOO-doo): a religion with African and Roman Catholic elements
zouk (ZOOK): pop music of the French Caribbean

Honduras (hahn-DUHR-us)
Chorti (CHORE-tee): a Native American people

Garifuna (gah-ree-FOO-nah): Black Caribs, descendants of Africans and Caribs
ladinos (lah-DEE-nose): people of mixed Spanish and Native ancestry
Lenca (LAIN-kah): a Native American people
Miskito (meess-KEE-toe): a Native American people
Sumo (SOO-moe): a Native American people

Jamaica (juh-MAY-kuh)
cimmarón (SIHM-mahr-rahn): "wild," or free Africans
ganja (gahn-JAH): marijuana
kumina (koo-mih-NAH): rituals similar to those of Voodoo
mento (men-TOE): a dance

Martinique (mahr-tih-NEEK)
chouval bwa (choo-VAHL bwah): a kind of music
mornes (MAWRN): low hills
Toussaint (TOO-seh): All Souls religious festival

Mexico (MEK-sih-koe or MAY-hee-koe)
Aztecs (AZ-teks): a Native American people
caribales (kar-REE-bah-layss): small Lacandones communities
charros (CHAH-roess): horsemen
chilaquiles (CHEE-lah-kee-layss): pieces of dry tortilla
chinampas (chee-NAHM-pahs): floating gardens
chirimía (chee-ree-MEE-ah): a wooden drum
hancab (hahn-KAHB): Yucatec "work of the groom," part of the marriage ritual
hetzmek (HETZ-mek): Yucatec baptism
Huastecs (WAH-steks): a Native American people
huehuetl (way-WAY-tull): conch shell instrument
Huichols (wee-CHOLES): a Native American people
huipiles (wee-PEE-layss): tunics
jaripeos (hah-ree-PAY-ohs): competitions with roping and taming horses
Lacandones (lah-kahn-DOE-ness): a Native American people
Maya (MY-uh): a Native American people
Mixtecs (mees-teks): a Native American people
mole poblano (MOE-lay poe-BLAH-no): a chocolate and meat dish
muhul (moo-HOOL): part of the Yucatec marriage ritual
Nahuas (nah-WAHS): a Native American people
Olmecs (AWL-mekss): a Native American people
Otomis (oh-TOE-meess): a Native American people
posadas (poe-SAH-das): a candle-lit procession
rancherias (ran-chair-EE-ahs): groups of several houses
rarpipama (rrahr-PEE-pah-mah): a Tarahumara ball race
rebozos (ray-BOE-soess): shawls
Seris (SEH-rrees): a Native American people
Tarahumara (tahr-uh-hoo-MAHR-uh): a Native American people
Tarascan (tah-rah-SKAHN): "Dance of the Old Men"
Tarascan (tuh-RASS-kuhn): a Native American people
teponaztle (tay-poe-NOTS-lay): a kind of drum
Toltecs (TOEL-tekss): a Native American people

torote (toe-ROE-tay): a fiber used for making baskets
Totonacs (toe-TOE-nahks): a Native American people
Tzeltals (sel-TAHLSS): a Native American people
Tzotzils (SOWT-tseelss): a Native American people
Voladores (boe-lah-DOOR-ayss): Totonac "Flying Pole
  Dance"
Yaquis (YAH-kees): a Native American people
Yucatecs (YOO-kuh-teks): a Native American people
Zapotecs (zah-puh-TEKS): a Native American people

Montserrat (mahn-sur-RAT)
jumbie (JUM-bee): dances to heal the sick

Nicaragua (nih-kuh-RAH-gwah)
bajo (BAH-hoe): a meat and vegetable stew
gallo pinto (GOY-o PEEN-toe): a dish made of white rice,
  red beans, onions, and garlic
Garifuna (gah-ree-FOO-nah): Black Caribs, descendants of
  Africans and Caribs
Miskito (miss-KEE-toe): a Native American people
Nicarao (neek-ar-oe): a Native American people
Purísma (poor-EEZ-mah): a festival
refrescos (ray-frayss-KOESS): fruit drinks
vigorón (bee-go-RON): pork cracklings and cabbage

Panama (PAN-uh-mah)
Buglere (boog-LARE-ee): a Native American people
Chocó (choe-KOE): the name of a forested region in
  Panama and Colombia and the name of the Native
  American inhabitants
corvina (kore-BEE-nah): sea bass
cumbia (KOOM-bee-ah): a dance
Embera (em-BARE-ah): a Native American people
Guaymí (GWHY-mee): a Native American people
Kuna (koo-NAH): a Native American people
molas (moe-LAHSS): Kuna blouses
sancocho (sahn-KOE-choe): a soup with chicken, spices,
  and vegetables
tamborito (tam-bore-EET-oh): the national dance of Panama
Teribe (tare-EE-bay): a Native American people
wini (WEE-nee): bands of colored beads worn by Kuna
  women
Wounaan (woe-NAIN): a Native American people

Paraguay (PAR-uh-gwhy)
Aché (AH-chay): a Native American people
aho-poi (ao-poi): hand-embroidered cotton
Ayoreo (ah-joe-RAY-oe): a Native American people
bombilla (bome-BEE-yah): a metal straw
chipas (CHEE-pahs): a cornmeal bread
Chulupí (choo-loo-PEE): the Nivaclé, a Native American
  people
Guaraní: (gwhar-uh-NEE): a Native American people
Maca (mah-KAH): a Native American people
ñandutí (nyah-doo-tee): handmade lace
sopa Paraguaya (SOE-pah pahr-ah-GWHY-uh): a
  dumpling made of corn and cheese
terere (tare-air-AY): cold Paraguayan tea

Peru (pay-ROO)
achiote (ah-chee-OH-tay): a seed used for paint
antaras (ahn-TAH-rahss): a type of flute
ayllus (EYE-youss): Incan communities
balsas (BAHL-sahss): rafts made of reed
cañawa (cahn-YAH-wah): a cereal
charango (chah-RAHN-go): a small guitar
Chavín (CHAH-VEEN): a Native American people
chicha (CHEE-chah): corn beer
chicha morado (CHEE-chah moe-RAH-tho): a sweet,
  nonalcoholic drink
chifa (CEHH-fah): a Chinese restaurant
Chimú (chee-MOO): a Native American civilization
chullo (CHOO-yo): a knitted hat
costeños (coe-STAIN-yoess): people of the coast
cushmas (COOSH-mahss): long ponchos
El Niño Jesus (el NEEN-yo hay-SOOSS): literally "the
  baby Jesus," the name for a warm current along the
  Ecuadoran and Peruvian coasts
escabeche (ayss-cah-BAY-chay): a fish dish
huaynos (WHY-noess): country music
Limeños (lee-MAYN-yoess): inhabitants of Lima
Moche (MOE-chay): a Native American people
montaña (mone-TAHN-yah): the eastern slopes of the
  Andes Mountains
Nazca (NAHSS-kah): a Native American civilization
padrinos (pah-DREE-noess): godfathers
papas a la huancaina (PAH-pass ah lah wonk-ah-EE-nah):
  potatoes in a spicy sauce
Paracas (pah-RAH-kahss): a Native American civilization
Peninsulares (pay-neen-soo-LAH-rayss): Spaniards born
  in Spain
pueblos jovenes (PWAY-bloess HOE-vane-ayss):
  shantytowns
punas (POO-nahs): grasslands
Quechua (KAY-choo-ah): a Native American language
quipu (KEE-poo): a knotted string used for
  recordkeeping
Sechín (say-CHEEN): a Native American people
selva (SELL-bah): a dense tropical rain forest
Wari-Tiwanaku (WAH-ree tee-wah-NAH-koo): a Native
  American civilization
zampoñas (sahm-PONE-yahss): a kind of flute

Puerto Rico (poo-AIR-toe REE-koe)
alcapurrias (ahl-kah-POO-ree-ahss): crab fritter
arroz con pollo (ah-ROESS cone POY-yo): chicken and rice
asopao (ah-soe-PAH-oe): a meat stew
bacalao (bah-kah-LAH-oe): a codfish fritter
bomba (BOME-ba): a dance style
Carib (cah-REEB): a Native American people
fondas (FONE-thahss): street stalls
frijoles (free-HOE-layss): beans
guneo (gee-NAY-oh): an African word for banana
léchon asado (lay-CHONE ah-SAH-thoe): roasted suckling
  pig
mofongo (moe-FONE-go): plantains fried in batter
pavas (PAH-bahss): straw hats

sofrito (soe-FREE-toe): a spicy sauce
son (SONE): a dance music
surrilitos (soo-ree-LEE-toess): cornmeal cheese fritters
Taíno (TIE-no): a Native American people

Saint Kitts-Nevis (NEE-vihs)

rotis (ROE-teess): pancakes with potato and chicken
     filling

Saint Lucia (SAINT LOO-shee-ah)

cadance (cuh-DASS): a kind of French-Caribbean music
Jounen Kweyol (joo-NEE KWAY-yahl): a festival held in
     October
pouile dudon (PWAY dee-DOH): chicken stew
soupe germou (soop jer-MOO): pumpkin soup
zouk (ZOOK): a kind of techno-funk music

Saint Pierre (SAINT PEER) and Miquelon
(MIK-uh-lohn)

tiaude (tee-ODE): cod chowder

Saint Vincent and the Grenadines
(gren-uh-DEENZ)

Suriname (sue-ree-NAH-muh)

bami (BAH-mee): Javanese fried noodles
cuatro (KWAH-troe): a four-stringed guitar
gamelan (gah-meh-LAHN): a type of Javanese music
kaseko (kah-SICK-oh): a kind of band
kawina (KAH-wee-nah): a kind of music with singing and
     drums
phulawri (pul-LAW-ree): fried chickpea balls
pinda soep (PIHN-dah soup): peanut soup
roti (RROW-tee): a thin bread wrapped around potatoes,
     vegetables, and chicken
samosas (sah-MOE-sahss): pastries filled with meat and
     vegetables
Sranan (srrah-NAHN): a Creole English dialect

Trinidad (TRIHN-ih-dad) and Tobago
(tuh-BAY-goe)

aripa (ah-RAY-pah): a cornmeal pie stuffed with meat
channa (CHAH-nah): split peas fried in batter
chutney (CHUT-nee): a kind of Asian music
cuatro (KWAH-troe): a four-stringed guitar
dhall (DOLL): lentils
Divali (dee-WAH-lee): a Hindu festival
Eid ul Fitr (eed ul FEE-tar): a Muslim feast
Hosay (hoe-ZAY): the Islamic New Year festival
mas (MAHS): costume competitions
parang (pah-RAHNG): Spanish Christmas carols
Phagwa (PAH-gwah): a spring festival
phulori (puh-LAOW-ree): split peas fried in batter
picong (pee-KONG): an insult
pow (PAO): Chinese doughnuts
rapso (RAP-soe): calypso rap
rotis (ROE-tee): a bread filled with curry or lentils
soca (SOE-kah): soul calypso, a kind of dance music

Turks and Caicos (KAY-kuhs) Islands

United States of America

Adena (ah-DEE-nah): a Native American people
Aleuts (a-LOOTS): a Native American people
Anasazi (ah-nuh-SAH-zee): a Native American people
Apache (up-PATCH-ee): a Native American people
Athabascan (ath-uh-BASS-kun): a Native American
     language
Caddoan (KAHD-o-uhn): a Native American people
Catawba (kuh-TAW-buh): a Native American people
Cherokee (CHAIR-uh-kee): a Native American people
Chickasaw (CHIK-uh-saw): a Native American people
Chippewa (CHIP-uh-wah): a Native American people
Choctaw (CHOK-taw): a Native American people
Comanche (cuh-MAN-chee): a Native American people
Creek (creek): a Native American people
Deutsch (DOYCH): German people, mistakenly called the
     Pennsylvania Dutch
encomienda (en-kome-EE-en-dah): a forced labor system
Hmong (hmawng): a Laotian people
Hohokam (huh-HOE-kuhm): a Native American people
Huguenots (HYOO-guh-nots): French Protestant settlers
Inuit (IN-yoo-it): a Native American people
Iroquois (IR-uh-kwoy): a Native American people
Jicarilla (hee-kuh-REE-yuh): a Native American people
Kiowa (KI-uh-wuh): a Native American people
kivas (KEE-vuhs): ceremonial chambers
Kwanzaa (KWAHN-zuh): an African American holiday
Mardi Gras (MAHR-dee grah): "Fat Tuesday," the French
     celebration before Lent
mariachi (mah-ree-AH-chee): a type of Mexican folk music
Marielitos (mar-ee-el-EE-toss): a group of Cuban
     immigrants
Mescalero (mess-kuh-LEHR-oe): a Native American
     Apache people
Mimbres (MIHM-bris): a style of Native American pottery
Mogollon (moe-guh-YONE): a Native American people
Muskogean (muss-KOE-gee-un): a Native American
     language group
Natchez (NATCH-is): a Native American people
Navajo (NAH-vuh-hoe): a Native American people
Ojibwe (o-jib-WAY): a Native American people
Osage (O-saje): a Native American people
Pueblo (PWEB-loe): a Native American people
Shawnee (shaw-NEE): a Native American people
Sioux (SUE): a Native American people
vaqueros (vah-KARE-oes): cowboys
Yakima (YAK-uh-muh): a Native American people

Uruguay (oo-roo-GWHY)

bombachas (boem-BAH-chahss): baggy trousers worn by
     gauchos
Charrúa (chah-ROO-ah): a Native American people
estancias (ace-TAHN-see-ahss): large farms
facón (fah-CONE): a kind of knife
parrilladas (pah-ree-YAH-thahss): large barbecues
yerba maté (YAIR-bah mah-TAY): a tea drink

Venezuela (ven-uh-ZWAY-luh)

arepas (ah-RAY-pahss): corn pancakes

areperas (ah-ray-PAY-rahss): restaurants that specialize in arepas

Caraqueños (kah-rah-CANE-yoess): people of Caracas

charrascas (chah-RAHS-kahss): an instrument with a metal scraper

cuatros (KWAH-troess): four-stringed guitars

furrucos (forr-ROO-koess): a kind of drum

gaitas (GUY-tahss): rhymed verses

Guajiros (gwah-HEE-roess): a Native American people

huallacas (why-YAH-kahss): corn pancakes filled with meat, vegetables, and spices

joropo (hoe-ROE-poe): the national dance

liqui-liqui (LEE-key LEE-key): a traditional outfit for men

llaneros (yah-NAY-roess): cowboys

llanos (YAH-noess): a grassland plain

majobo (mah-HOE-boe): a drink made from palm sap

mamones (mah-MOE-nayss): small, green fruits

mantas (MAHN-tahss): Guajiro dresses

Maracuchos (mah-rah-KOO-choess): residents of Maracaibo

moriche (moe-REE-chay): a kind of palm

pabellon criollo (pahy-bay-YONE cree-OY-yoe): shredded meat with vegetables, beans, rice, and fried plantains

palafitos (pah-lah-FEE-toess): single-room houses

páramo (PAH-rah-moe): a mountain region

Paraujanos (pah-rao-HAH-noess): people who live in the Sinamaica lagoon north of Maracaibo City

ranchos (RAHN-choess): shanty houses

ruanas (roo-AH-nahss): woolen ponchos

tepuís (tay-oee-EESS): "mountains" in the Pemon language

Warao (wah-RAH-roe): a Native American people

National Days by Country

Anguilla

Anguilla Day (May 30):
celebrates the island's historical and cultural identity.

Constitution Day (August 6):
honors the island's legal constitution.

Separation Day (December 19):
marks the Anguilla Act of 1980, which made the island a separate British dependency and severed its ties with Saint Kitts-Nevis.

Antigua and Barbuda

Independence Day (November 1):
commemorates the gaining of full independence as a nation in 1981.

Argentina

May Revolution (May 25):
celebrates the May Revolution of 1810.

Malvinas Day (June 10):
celebrates the establishment of the Political & Military Command of the Malvinas (Falkland Islands) in 1829, when the United Provinces of the River Plate reasserted claim to the Falklands and occupied them. The holiday reinforces the Argentine claim each year.

Flag Day (June 20):
honors the flag.

San Martín Day (August 17):
honors the death of José de San Martín, the general who led Argentina to independence in 1816.

Aruba

Gilberto F. Croes' Birthday (January 25):
commemorates the Aruban politician who founded the Separacion movement in the 1940s. This culminated in autonomy being granted in 1986.

Aruba Flag Day (March 18):
celebrates Aruban historical and cultural identity.

Bahamas

Independence Day (July 10):
commemorates full independence being achieved in 1973.

Barbados

Errol Barrow Day (January 21):
commemorates the first prime minister of an independent Barbados.

Kadooment Day (First Monday in August):
a carnival with fancy dress and calypso, the last day of the three-week Crop-Over (harvest) Festival.

Independence Day (November 30):
commemorates full independence being achieved in 1966.

Belize

National Day (September 10):
commemorates the Battle of Saint Georges Cay in 1798.

Independence Day (September 21):
commemorates the achievement of full independence in 1981.

Garifuna Settlement Day (November 19):
commemorates the arrival of the Garifuna people in Belize in 1823.

Bermuda

Bermuda Day (May 24):
formerly known as Empire Day throughout the British colonies, this is the anniversary of the birthday of Queen Victoria of Great Britain.

Cup Match Day (July 31):
a holiday devoted to a cricket match between teams representing Saint George's and Somerset.

Somers Day (August 1):
is named after Admiral Somers, who was shipwrecked on the island in 1609.

Labor Day (September 1):
honors working people.

Bolivia

Labor Day (May 1):
the traditional day for honoring work and workers.

La Paz Municipal Holiday (July 16):
commemorates July 16, 1809. July 16 is the traditional festival of the Virgin of Carmen, the patron saint of La Paz. In 1809 conspirators, led by Pedro Domingo Murillo, decided to use this date for an uprising against Spanish rule, followed by a proclamation of independence.

Independence Day (August 6):
commemorates the signing of the Act of Independence of the Provinces of Upper Peru on August 6, 1825.

Columbus Day (October 12):
commemorates the day on which Christopher Columbus first set foot in the Caribbean, in 1492.

Brazil

Tiradentes Day (April 12):
commemorates the day of execution in April 1792 of Tiradentes (the Toothpuller), who was the leader of the Inconfidencia, the first anti-Portuguese revolution in colonial Brazil.

Labor Day (May 1):
the traditional day for honoring work and workers.

Independence Day (September 7):
anniversary of September 7, 1822, the day on which Dom Pedro I declared Brazil's independence.

Our Lady of Aparecida (October 12):
Our Lady of Aparecida is the shortened form of Our Lady of the Aparecida of the Waters, Brazil's patron saint. Every year on October 12 the town of Aparecida is the center of pilgrimage for hundreds of thousands of Brazilians.

Proclamation of the Republic (November 15):
anniversary of the proclamation of the Republic on November 15, 1889, after the fall of the monarchy.

Canada

Victoria Day (Monday before May 25):
> *celebrates the birthday of Queen Victoria of Great Britain, born on May 24, 1819.*

Canada Day (July 1):
> *This national day is held on the anniversary of the proclamation of the British North America Act of 1867, which united the country and laid down its constitution.*

Labor Day (First Monday in September):
> *honors working people.*

Thanksgiving Day (Second Monday in October):
> *a day of thanks, celebrated by early Puritans with prayers and feasting, continues as a major harvest feast day.*

Remembrance Day (November 11):
> *commemorates those who gave their lives for their country in two world wars and in other conflicts.*

Cayman Islands

Discovery Day (mid-May):
> *commemorates the discovery of the islands by Christopher Columbus in 1503.*

Constitution Day (July 6):
> *honors the island's constitutional status.*

Chile

Labor Day (May 1):
> *the traditional day for honoring work and workers.*

Navy Day (May 21):
> *commemorates the Naval battle of Iquique in 1881, the important battle that led to the defeat of the Peruvians in the War of the Desert.*

Independence Day (September 18):
> *anniversary of the Battle of Maipú in 1818 and the final defeat of the Spanish.*

Armed Forces Day (September 19):
> *the armed forces hold a large parade attended by the president and other officials.*

Columbus Day (October 12):
> *commemorates the day on which Christopher Columbus first set foot in the Caribbean, in 1492.*

Colombia

Labor Day (May 1):
> *the traditional day for honoring work and workers.*

Independence Day (July 20):
> *commemorates the overthrow of Spanish authority and establishment of a new government in Santa Fé de Bogotá.*

Battle of Boyacá (August 7):
> *anniversary of the decisive battle in 1819 in which Simón Bolívar and his men defeated the Spanish.*

Columbus Day (October 12):
> *commemorates the day on which Christopher Columbus first set foot in the Caribbean, in 1492.*

Independence of Cartagena (November 11):
> *anniversary of the day Cartagena declared its absolute independence from Spain in 1811.*

Costa Rica

Juan Santamaria's Day (April 11):
> *honors the young drummer boy soldier Juan Santamaria shot dead after he set fire to an enemy stronghold at the Battle of Rivas in 1856.*

Labor Day (May 1):
> *the traditional day for honoring work and workers.*

Independence of Guanacaste Day (July 25):
> *marks the annexation of Guanacaste from Nicaragua in 1824.*

Virgin of the Angels (August 2):
> *celebration of the patron saint of Costa Rica.*

Mother's Day and Assumption Day (August 15):
> *honors mothers on the same day as the festival of the Virgin Mary.*

Independence Day (September 15):
> *anniversary of the day Costa Rica became independent in 1823.*

Columbus Day (October 12):
> *commemorates the day on which Christopher Columbus first set foot in the Caribbean, in 1492.*

Cuba

Day of the Triumph of the Revolution (January 1):
> *celebrates the victory of the revolutionaries in 1959.*

Day of the Workers/International Labor Day (May 1):
> *the traditional day for honoring work and workers.*

Day of the Insurrection (July 26):
> *commemorates the attack by the revolutionaries on the Moncada barracks in 1953.*

Anniversary of the War of Independence in 1868 (October 10):
> *commemorates the beginning of the unsuccessful 1868–1878 war of independence.*

Dominica

Independence Day (November 3):
> *commemorates the achievement of full independence in 1978.*

Dominican Republic

Independence Day (February 27):
> *commemorates the end of Haitian rule and the declaration of independence in 1844.*

Restoration Day (August 16):
> *commemorates the end of Spanish annexation (1861–1865).*

Ecuador

Patriotism and National Unity Day (February 27):
> *remembers the battle of Tarqui in 1829 in which the Republic of Colombia defeated Peru.*

Labor Day (May 1):
> *the traditional day for honoring work and workers.*

Battle of Pinchincha Day (May 24):
> *remembers the battle of Pinchincha in 1822 which ensured independence from Spain*

Bolívar's Day (July 24):
> *celebrates the birthday of the man who led the battle for independence in Venezuela, Colombia, Ecuador, and Peru.*

Columbus Day (October 12):
  commemorates the day on which Christopher Columbus first set foot in the Caribbean, in 1492.

El Salvador

Independence Day (September 15):
  commemorates the end of Spanish rule in 1821.

Falkland Islands

Falklands Day (August 14):
  commemorates the first British landing in 1690.

French Guiana

Labor Day (May 1):
  the traditional day for honoring work and workers.
National Day (July 14):
  commemorates the storming of the Bastille in 1789, which marked the beginning of the French Revolution.
Armistice Day (November 11):
  marks the end of World War I.

Greenland

National Day (June 21):
  honors Greenland's historical and cultural identity.

Grenada

Independence Day (February 7):
  celebrates the island's break with British rule in 1974.

Guadeloupe

Bastille Day (July 14):
  commemorates the storming of the Bastille in 1789, which marked the beginning of the French Revolution.

Guatemala

Anniversary of the Victory of the 1871 Revolution (June 30):
  celebrates the revolution which led to Justo Rufino Barrios' accession to power two years later.
Independence Day (September 15):
  commemorates the break away from Spanish rule.

Guyana

Republic Day and Mashramani Festival (February 23):
  is the anniversary of the day in 1970 when Guyana became a cooperative republic within the British Commonwealth
Labor Day (May 1):
  the traditional day for honoring work and workers.
Independence Day (May 26):
  celebrates the day in 1966 when Guyana ceased to be a British colony and became independent.
Caricom Day (First Monday in July):
  celebrates the Caribbean Community formed in 1973.
Freedom Day (First Monday in August):
  celebrates the abolition of slavery in 1834.
United Nations Day (October 24):
  celebrates the day in 1945 that the UN charter came into effect.

Haiti

Independence Day (January 1):
  commemorates the declaration of an independent Afro-Caribbean republic in 1804.
Heroes of Independence Day (January 2):
  commemorates those who took part in the struggle for independence.
Americas' Day (April 14):
  commemorates the First International Congress of American States, held in 1890.
Labor Day (May 1):
  the traditional day for honoring work and workers.
Flag Day (May 18):
  honors the Haitian flag.
National Sovereignty Day (May 22):
  honors the self-determination of the Haitian people.
Dessalines Day (October 17):
  commemorates Jean-Jacques Dessalines, who declared Haiti independent in 1804.
Toussaint-Louverture Day (November 1):
  commemorates Toussaint-Louverture, hero of the Haitian struggle for independence.
Discovery Day (December 5):
  commemorates the day Christopher Columbus sighted Hispaniola in 1492.

Honduras

Day of the Americas (April 14):
  commemorates the First International Congress of American States, held in 1890.
Labor Day (May 1):
  the traditional day for honoring work and workers.
Independence Day (September 15):
  commemorates the break away from Spanish colonial rule in 1821.
Columbus Day (October 12):
  commemorates the day on which Christopher Columbus first set foot in the Caribbean, in 1492.
Army Day (October 21):
  honors the armed forces.

Jamaica

Independence Day (August 1):
  commemorates the granting of independence to Jamaica in 1962.

Martinique

Bastille Day (July 14):
  commemorates the storming of the Bastille in 1789, which marked the beginning of the French Revolution.
Schoelcher Day (July 21):
  commemorates Victor Schoelcher, the French statesman who campaigned for the abolition of slavery.

Mexico

Constitution Day (February 5):
  celebrates the constitution drawn up in 1917 after the Mexican Revolution.

Birthday of Benito Juárez (March 21):
> *anniversary of the birth of Juárez, the Zapotec Indian who was twice president of Mexico between 1857 and 1872.*

Labor Day (May 1):
> *the traditional day for honoring work and workers.*

Anniversary of the Battle of Puebla (May 5):
> *commemorates the battle in 1862 when the Mexican Army made a stand against the French.*

Independence Day (September 16):
> *anniversary of the day in 1810 that Father Miguel Hidalgo y Costilla called for rebellion against Spain.*

Columbus Day (October 12):
> *commemorates the day on which Christopher Columbus first set foot in the Caribbean, in 1492.*

Anniversary of the Revolution (November 20):
> *the official anniversary of the beginning of the Mexican Revolution in 1910.*

Montserrat

St. Patrick's Day (March 17):
> *commemorates Irish heritage and also the slave uprising of 1768.*

Festival Day (December 31):
> *the climax of carnival.*

Netherlands Antilles

Queen's Day (April 30):
> *honors the head of state, Queen Beatrix of the Netherlands, and commemorates the birthday in 1909 of the Queen Mother, Juliana.*

Nicaragua

Independence Day (September 15):
> *celebrates Nicaragua's break with Spanish colonial rule in 1821.*

Panama

Labor Day (May 1):
> *the traditional day for honoring work and workers.*

Discovery of America Day (October 12):
> *commemorates the day on which Christopher Columbus first set foot in the Caribbean, in 1492.*

Independence from Colombia Day (November 3):
> *anniversary of the day Panama declared its independence from Colombia in 1903.*

Flag Day (November 4):
> *honors the riots that took place in November 1959 which led to the flying of the Panamanian flag in the Canal Zone.*

First Call of Independence Day (November 10):
> *anniversary of Panama's first call for independence in 1821.*

Independence from Spain (November 28):
> *anniversary of the day Panama gained independence from Spain in 1821 and became part of Colombia.*

Paraguay

San Blás Day (February 3):
> *the festival day of the country's patron saint.*

Heroes Day (March 1):
> *marks the end of the War of the Triple Alliance in 1870, the bloodiest battle in Latin-American history.*

Labor Day (May 1):
> *the traditional day for honoring work and workers.*

National Day (May 14–15):
> *celebrates the night of May 14–15, 1811 when Paraguayans deposed the Spanish governor.*

Peace of Chaco Day (June 12):
> *celebrates the day fighting ended in the Chaco War in 1935.*

Constitution Day (August 25):
> *anniversary of the promulgation of Paraguay's 1967 constitution.*

Columbus Day (October 12):
> *commemorates the day on which Christopher Columbus first set foot in the Caribbean, in 1492.*

Peru

Labor Day (May 1):
> *the traditional day for honoring work and workers.*

Independence Day (July 28–29):
> *commemorates July 28, 1821 when General San Martín entered Lima and proclaimed independence for Peru.*

Santa Rosa de Lima (August 30):
> *honors Santa Rosa, the patron saint of Lima and one of Peru's most revered saints.*

Battle of Angamos (October 7):
> *commemorates the naval battle off Angamos in 1879 during the War of the Pacific, in which the Chileans defeated the Peruvians and the Peruvian hero Admiral Miguel Grau was killed.*

Puerto Rico

Constitution Day (July 25):
> *marks Puerto Rico being declared a Commonwealth in 1952.*

Grito de Lares (September 23):
> *commemorates a bid for independence in 1857.*

Saint Kitts-Nevis

Independence Day (September 19):
> *commemorates the achievement of independence in 1983.*

Saint Lucia

Independence Day (February 22):
> *commemorates the achievement of independence in 1979.*

St. Lucy's Day (December 13):
> *the festival day of the island's patron saint.*

Saint-Pierre and Miquelon

Bastille Day (July 14):
> *commemorates the storming of the Bastille in 1789, which marked the beginning of the French Revolution.*

Saint Vincent and the Grenadines

Saint Vincent & Grenadines' Day (January 22):
> *commemorates the discovery of Saint Vincent by Christopher Columbus in 1498.*

Independence Day (October 27):
commemorates the achievement of independence in 1969.

Suriname
Labor Day (May 1):
the traditional day for honoring work and workers.
National Unity or Emancipation Day (July 1):
commemorates the abolition of slavery on July 1 1863.
Independence Day (November 25):
anniversary of the date independence was gained in 1975.

Trinidad and Tobago
Independence Day (August 31):
commemorates the achievement of independence in 1962.
Republic Day (September 24):
honors the republican constitution adopted in 1976.

Turks and Caicos Islands
Emancipation Day (August 1):
celebrates the abolition of slavery in 1834.

United States of America
Birthday of Martin Luther King Jr. (Third Monday in January):
honors Martin Luther King Jr., the slain African American civil rights leader.
President's Day (Third Monday in February):
honors the birthdays of Abraham Lincoln and George Washington, two of the early American presidents.
Memorial or Decoration Day (Last Monday in May):
honors those who have died in service to the United States.
Independence Day (July 4):
commemorates the signing of the Declaration of Independence and the resulting birth of a new nation.
Labor Day (First Monday in September):
honors working people.
Columbus Day (Second Monday in October):
commemorates the day on which Christopher Columbus first set foot in the Caribbean, in 1492.
Veterans or Armistice Day (November 11):
created to honor the peace agreement signed by all the countries involved in World War I, it is now a holiday in which all veterans who served the United States in wars are honored.
Thanksgiving Day (Fourth Thursday in November):
a day of thanks, celebrated by early Puritans with prayers and feasting, continues as a major harvest feast day.

Uruguay
Landing of the Thirty-three Patriots (April 19):
remembers the exiles and patriots, who, led by Juan Antonio Lavalleja, crossed the Uruguay river from Argentina in 1825 and fought to free Uruguay of the Portuguese.
Labor Day (May 1):
the traditional day for honoring work and workers.
Battle of Las Piedras (May 18):
commemorates the battle in 1811, the first victory of the rebels against the Spaniards in the fight for independence.
Birth of General Artigas (June 19):
commemorates the birth date in 1764 of José Gervasio Artigas, hero of Uruguay's struggle for independence.
Constitution Day (July 18):
anniversary of the constitution approved for the new Republic of Uruguay on July 18, 1830.
National Independence (August 25):
aniversary of the date independence was achieved in 1828.
Columbus Day (October 12):
commemorates the day on which Christopher Columbus first set foot in the Caribbean, in 1492.

Venezuela
Labor Day (May 1):
the traditional day for honoring work and workers.
Anniversary of the Battle of Carabobo (June 24):
anniversary of the decisive battle in 1821 in which Simón Bolívar defeated the Spanish.
Independence Day (July 5):
commemorates the signing of the Act of Independence in 1811.
Simón Bolívar's Birthday (July 24):
celebrates the birthday of the man who led the battle for independence in Venezuela, Colombia, Ecuador, and Peru.
Columbus Day (October 12):
commemorates the day on which Christopher Columbus first set foot in the Caribbean, in 1492.

Virgin Islands (UK)
BVI Territory Day (July 1):
celebrates the islands' status under the constitution of 1967.

Virgin Islands (U.S.)
Emancipation Day (July 3):
marks the end of Danish rule.
U.S. Independence Day (July 4):
commemorates the U.S. Declaration of Independence in 1776.

National Days by Date

Use the following list to find a national day celebrated on a particular day of the year. See under each country's name in the list, National Days by Country, beginning on page 607, for a description of the events commemorated on that day.

January

Third Monday in January:
United States of America
- 1 Cuba, Haiti
- 2 Haiti
- 21 Barbados
- 22 Saint Vincent and the Grenadines
- 25 Aruba

February

Third Monday in February:
United States of America
- 3 Paraguay
- 5 Mexico
- 7 Grenada
- 22 Saint Lucia
- 23 Guyana
- 27 Ecuador, Dominican Republic

March

- 1 Paraguay
- 17 Montserrat
- 18 Aruba
- 21 Mexico

April

- 11 Costa Rica
- 12 Brazil
- 14 Haiti, Honduras
- 19 Uruguay
- 30 Netherlands Antilles

May

Mid-May:
Cayman Islands
Monday before May 25:
Canada
Last Monday in May:
United States of America
- 1 Bolivia, Brazil, Chile, Colombia, Costa Rica, Cuba, Ecuador, French Guiana, Guyana, Haiti, Honduras, Mexico, Panama, Paraguay, Peru, Suriname, Uruguay, Venezuela
- 5 Mexico
- 14–15 Paraguay
- 18 Haiti, Uruguay
- 21 Chile
- 22 Haiti
- 24 Bermuda, Ecuador
- 25 Argentina
- 26 Guyana
- 30 Anguilla

June

- 10 Argentina
- 12 Paraguay
- 19 Uruguay
- 20 Argentina
- 21 Greenland
- 24 Venezuela
- 30 Guatemala

July

First Monday in July:
Guyana
- 1 Canada, Suriname, Virgin Islands (UK)
- 3 Virgin Islands (U.S.)
- 4 United States of America, Virgin Islands (U.S.)
- 5 Venezuela
- 6 Cayman Islands
- 10 Bahamas
- 14 French Guiana, Guadeloupe, Martinique, Saint-Pierre and Miquelon
- 16 Bolivia
- 18 Uruguay
- 20 Colombia
- 21 Martinique
- 24 Ecuador, Venezuela
- 25 Costa Rica, Puerto Rico
- 26 Cuba
- 28–29 Peru
- 31 Bermuda

August

First Monday in August:
Barbados, Guyana
- 1 Bermuda, Jamaica, Turks and Caicos Islands
- 2 Costa Rica
- 6 Anguilla, Bolivia
- 7 Colombia
- 10 Ecuador
- 14 Falkland Islands
- 15 Costa Rica
- 16 Dominican Republic
- 17 Argentina
- 25 Paraguay, Uruguay
- 30 Peru
- 31 Trinidad and Tobago

September

First Monday in September:

Canada, United States of America

1	Bermuda
7	Brazil
10	Belize
15	Costa Rica, El Salvador, Guatemala, Honduras, Nicaragua
16	Mexico
18	Chile
19	Chile, Saint Kitts-Nevis
21	Belize
23	Puerto Rico
24	Trinidad and Tobago

October

Second Monday in October:

Canada, United States of America

7	Peru
10	Cuba
12	Bolivia, Brazil, Chile, Colombia, Costa Rica, Ecuador, Honduras, Mexico, Panama, Paraguay, Uruguay, Venezuela
17	Haiti
21	Honduras
24	Guyana
27	Saint Vincent and the Grenadines

November

Fourth Thursday in November:

United States of America

1	Antigua and Barbuda, Haiti
3	Dominica, Panama
4	Panama
10	Panama
11	Canada, Colombia, French Guiana, United States of America
15	Brazil
19	Belize
20	Mexico
25	Suriname
28	Panama
30	Barbados

December

5	Haiti
13	Saint Lucia
19	Anguilla
31	Montserrat

Biographical Index

Numbers in **bold** indicate volumes; page numbers in *italic* indicate illustrations.

Numbers in **bold** indicate volumes; page numbers in *italic* indicate illustrations.

Geographical Index

Numbers in **bold** indicate volumes; page numbers in *italic* indicate illustrations; page numbers in **bold** refer to full articles.

Numbers in **bold** indicate volumes; page numbers in *italic* indicate illustrations; page numbers in **bold** refer to full articles.

Numbers in **bold** indicate volumes; page numbers in *italic* indicate illustrations; page numbers in **bold** refer to full articles.

Numbers in **bold** indicate volumes; page numbers in *italic* indicate illustrations; page numbers in **bold** refer to full articles.

Arts of the Americas

Numbers in **bold** indicate volumes; page numbers in *italic* indicate illustrations.

Numbers in **bold** indicate volumes; page numbers in *italic* indicate illustrations.

Festivals of the Americas

Numbers in **bold** indicate volumes; page numbers in *italic* indicate illustrations.

Foods of the Americas

Numbers in **bold** indicate volumes; page numbers in *italic* indicate illustrations.

Peoples and Cultures

Numbers in **bold** indicate volumes; page numbers in *italic* indicate illustrations.

Numbers in **bold** indicate volumes; page numbers in *italic* indicate illustrations.

Numbers in **bold** indicate volumes; page numbers in *italic* indicate illustrations.

Macushi, **6:**320

Makuna, **4:**211

Malaysians in Saint Lucia, **8:**442

Maliseet, **3:**139–40

Mam, **6:**306–7

Manta people, **5:**250–51

Mapuche, **4:**172, 173, 175–76, *176*, 181–82

Maquiritare, **10:**564, 576–77

Maracuchos, **10:**571

Marielitos, **9:**515

Maroons (Marrons): in Dominica, **5:**242; in French Guiana, **5:**277, 279, 282–83, *282*; in Jamaica, **6:**337, 338, 342

Martinique, people in, **7:**350–51

Mataco, **1:**17

Matsés, **8:**431–32

Matuarièrs, **8:**451–52

Maya: in Belize, **1:**36–37, *37*, 40, 41–42, 43; in El Salvador, **5:**268; in Guatemala, **6:**301–4, 306–7, 308, 309, 310–13, *312*; in Honduras, **6:**331–32, 334; in Mexico, **7:**355–56, 374, *374*

Mayoruna, **8:**430

Mbya Guaraní, **7:**402

Mescalero Apache, **9:**521

Mestizos: in Belize, **1:**41, 43; in Bolivia, **2:**58, *58*, 71; in Brazil, **2:**81, 85, 97, 98; in Chile, **4:**172, 176; in Colombia, **4:**192–93, 197, 201, *201*, 211; in Costa Rica, **4:**216; in Ecuador, **5:**253–54, 261; in El Salvador, **5:**271; in Mexico, **7:**359, 361, 363, 365; in Nicaragua, **7:**385; in Panama, **7:**391, 392; in Paraguay, **7:**399; in Peru, **8:**417, *418*, 419, *420*, 425, *433*; in Uruguay, **10:**554, 556; in Venezuela, **10:**562, 564, 565

Métis, **3:**116, 120–21, 145, 153

Métros, les, **5:**283

Mexicans, **7:**352–77; in the U.S.A., **7:**362, **9:**513–14, *513*, 515, **10:**540

Micmac people, **3:**113, 133, 138, 139–40

Middle Eastern people: in Chile, **4:**174; in Colombia, **4:**204. *See also* Lebanese people, Syrians, Turks

Minuané, **10:**553

Miskito, **6:**334, **7:**385

Mississippian culture, **9:**485–86

Mixtecs, **7:**353–54, 368

Moche, **8:**412–13

Mocoví, **1:**17

Mogollon, **9:**482, 485, *485*

Mohawk, **3:**114, 127–128, 133

Montagnais, **3:**113, 132–33, 138

Montserratians, **7:**378–79

Montuvios, **5:**254, 263

Motilones. *See* Barí

Moxos, **2:**69–70

Muisca (Chibcha), **4:**189–90, 195, 198–99, 213

Mulattos: in Brazil, **2:**81–82; in Colombia, **4:***192*, 193, 201, *201*; in Cuba, **5:**234; in Ecuador, **5:**263; in Haiti, **6:**324–25; in Peru, **8:**423; in Uruguay, **10:**556; in

Venezuela, **10:**564, 565

Muskogean-speakers, **9:**487

Nahua (Mexican), **7:**366, *367*

Nahua (Peruvian), **8:**431–32, *432*

Nahuizalco, **5:**270–71

Naskapi, **3:**113, 132, 138–39

Natchez, **9:**486, 496

Native Americans in the U.S.A.: before European contact, **9:**479–87; during colonization, **9:**473–74, 487–88, *488*, 489, *489*, 495–98, *496*, *497*, *498*, 503–4, *504*, 505; in the twentieth century, **9:**519–23, *519*, *520*, *521*, *522*, *523*

Navajo people, **9:**487, 520, *520*, **10:**539

Nawa, **8:**431

Nazca people, **8:**411–12

Netherlands Antilles, people in the, **7:**380–81

Neutrals, **3:**114

Nevisians, **8:**440–41

New Zealanders in Chile, **4:**184–85

Nicaraguans, **7:**382–87; in the U.S.A., **9:**516

Nicarao, **7:**382, 385

Nipissing, **3:**127

Nishga, **3:**148

Nivaclé. *See* Chulupí

Noanama, **4:**203–4, *204*, **7:**392, 394–95

Nootka, **3:**114, 148

Nordestinos, **1:**14–16

Norsemen. *See* Vikings

North Americans: in Bermuda, **2:**52; in Chile, **4:**173; in Costa Rica, **4:**218, 221; in Panama, **7:**391; in Paraguay, **7:**401; in Puerto Rico, **8:**436

Northern Ojibwe, **3:**142

Norwegians in Ecuador, **5:**263

Ojibwe, **3:**113, 126, 127, *127*, 142, 145, **9:**522, **10:**536, *536*

Okanangan, **3:**147–48

Olmecs, **5:**268, **7:**353

Ona, **1:**22, **4:**172, 183, 184–85, *184*

Oneida, **3:**114

Onondaga, **3:**114

Osage, **9:**498

Otavaleños, **5:***257*, *258*, 258–59, *259*

Otomis, **7:**367, *367*

Ottawas, **3:**127

Oxil, **6:**307

Oyampi, **5:**278

Paceños, **2:**64

Páez, **4:**189, 191, 197–98, *197*

Pai Tavytera, **7:**402

Pakistanis in the U.S.A., **9:**515

Palikur, **5:**278

Panamanians, **7:**388–95

Panare, **10:**576–77

Panche, **4:**189

Panchimalco, **5:**270–71

Pankararu, **2:**85

Papago, **9:**482, **10:**539

Paracas, **8:**411–12

Paraguayans, **7:**396–403

Paramaccaners, **8:**451–52

Paraujanos, **10:***560*, 571–72, 579

Pasto people, **4:**199

Patamona, **6:**321

Paulistas, **2:**91

Pehuenche, **1:**22, **4:**172, 181, *181*

Pemon (Pemong), **6:**321, **10:**576–77

Peninsulares, **8:**417

Pennsylvania Dutch, **9:**501, *501*

Peruvians, **8:**410–33

Petun, **3:**127

Piarora, **10:**564, 576–77

Picunches, **4:**172

Piegan, **3:**143–45, 146

Pijao, **4:**189, 191

Pikomchi, **6:**307

Pima, **9:**482, **10:**539

Pipil, **5:**268–69, 270–71, **6:**334

Piro, **8:**430

Plains Apache, **9:**498, 522

Plains Cree, **3:**113, 143–45, 146

Pokoman, **5:**268

Polacos, **4:**219

Poles: in Argentina, **1:**8, 16; in Canada, **3:**117–18, 120, 146; in the U.S.A., **9:**507, 510–11, *511*, **10:**536; in Uruguay, **10:**555

Polynesians, **4:**176, 185–86, *185*

Popayanense, **4:**189

Porteños, **1:**12–14

Portuguese people: in Antigua and Barbuda, **1:**5; in Bermuda, **2:**52; in Brazil, **2:**77–78, 92; in Canada, **3:**120; in Guyana, **6:**315, 318, 319; in Saint Vincent and the Grenadines, **8:**447; in Suriname, **8:**450; in Uruguay, **10:**553–54; in Venezuela, **10:**564

Poya, **1:**22

Pueblo people, **9:**482, 521–22, *522*, **10:**539

Puelche, **1:**20

Puerto Ricans, **8:**434–439; in the U.S.A., **9:**514, *514*; in the U.S. Virgin Islands, **10:**583

Purépechas. *See* Tarascans

Puruhás, **5:**251

Q'eqchi, **6:**307

Q'uanjob'al, **6:**307

Quaquas, **8:**457

Quebec Inuit, **3:**131–32

Québécois, **3:**122, 133–36

Quechua: in Bolivia, **2:**58, *58*, 59, 60, 68, *68*; in Ecuador, **5:**251; in Peru, **8:***410*, *418*, 419, 425–27, *426*, *427*, 432

Querandí, **1:**20

Quiché, **6:**306–7, *312*

Quichua, **5:**264, 265–66

Quijos, **5:**264

Quillacinga, **4:**189

Quimbaya, **4:**189, 190

Numbers in **bold** indicate volumes; page numbers in *italic* indicate illustrations.

Numbers in **bold** indicate volumes; page numbers in *italic* indicate illustrations.

Religions and Religious Ceremonies

Numbers in **bold** indicate volumes; page numbers in *italic* indicate illustrations.

Sports and Games

Numbers in **bold** indicate volumes; page numbers in *italic* indicate illustrations.

Comprehensive Index

Numbers in **bold** indicate volumes; page numbers in *italic* indicate illustrations; page numbers in **bold** refer to full articles.

Numbers in **bold** indicate volumes; page numbers in *italic* indicate illustrations; page numbers in **bold** refer to full articles.

Numbers in **bold** indicate volumes; page numbers in *italic* indicate illustrations; page numbers in **bold** refer to full articles.

Numbers in **bold** indicate volumes; page numbers in *italic* indicate illustrations; page numbers in **bold** refer to full articles.

Numbers in **bold** indicate volumes; page numbers in *italic* indicate illustrations; page numbers in **bold** refer to full articles.

Numbers in **bold** indicate volumes; page numbers in *italic* indicate illustrations; page numbers in **bold** refer to full articles.

Numbers in **bold** indicate volumes; page numbers in *italic* indicate illustrations; page numbers in **bold** refer to full articles.

Numbers in **bold** indicate volumes; page numbers in *italic* indicate illustrations; page numbers in **bold** refer to full articles.

Numbers in **bold** indicate volumes; page numbers in *italic* indicate illustrations; page numbers in **bold** refer to full articles.

Numbers in **bold** indicate volumes; page numbers in *italic* indicate illustrations; page numbers in **bold** refer to full articles.

3:137, 141, *141*, 157; in Chile, **4:**175; in Colombia, **4:**200, 202, 204, 210; in Costa Rica, **4:**222, 223; in Cuba, **5:**240, *240*; in the Dominican Republic, **5:**248; in Ecuador, **5:**258, 263–64, 266; in Grenada, **6:**297; in Guadeloupe, **6:**299; in Guatemala, **6:**308; in Haiti, **6:***328*, 329, *329*; in Honduras, **6:**334, 335; in Jamaica, **6:**339, 343, *343*; in Martinique, **7:**351; in Mexico, **7:**369, 374–75, *375*; in Montserrat, **7:**379; in the Netherlands Antilles, **7:**381; in Nicaragua, **7:**387; in Panama, **7:**395; in Peru, **8:**432–33, *433*; in Puerto Rico, **8:**437; in Saint Lucia, **8:**443; in Saint Vincent and the Grenadines, **8:**447; in Suriname, **8:**455, *455*; in Trinidad and Tobago, **8:**460, 461; in the U.S.A., **9:**495, *495*, **10:**539, *539*, 546–47, *546*; in Venezuela, **10:**574, 578–79, *578*

Música sertaneja, **2:**101

Muskogean-speakers, **9:**487

Muslims: in Canada, **3:**122; in Chile, **4:**176; in Guyana, **6:**318, 321; in Jamaica, **6:**343; in Panama, **7:**392; in Suriname, **8:**454–55; in Trinidad and Tobago, **8:**461, *461*; in Venezuela, **10:**565

Mute, **4:**198

Na, **6:**310

Na-Déné languages, **3:**112

Nahua (Mexican), **7:**366, *367*

Nahua (Peruvian), **8:**431–32, *432*

Nahuatl language, **5:**271; **7:**357, 366, 382

Nahuel Huapi Lake, Argentina, **1:***6*

Nahuizalco, **5:**270–71

Naismith, James, **10:**548

Ñandutí lace, **7:**403

Napoleon III, Emperor, **5:**277

Nascimento, Edson Arantes do "Pelé," **2:**103

Nascimento, Milton, **2:**101

Naskapi, **3:**113, 132, 138–39

Nassau, Bahamas, **1:**29, *30*

Natchez, **9:**486, 496

Native Americans in the U.S.A.: before European contact, **9:**479–87; during colonization, **9:**473–74, 487–88, *488*, 489, *489*, 495–98, *496*, *497*, *498*, 503–4, *504*, 505; in the twentieth century, **9:**519–23, *519*, *520*, *521*, *522*, *523*

Navajo language, **9:**520

Navajo people, **9:**487, 520, *520*, **10:**539

Nawa, **8:**431

Nazca Lines, Peru, **8:**412, *412*

Nazca people, **8:**411–12

Nebraska, U.S.A., **9:**511

Neruda, Pablo, **4:**186–87

Netherlands Antilles, **7:380–81**

Neuland, Paraguay, **7:**401

Neutrals, **3:**114

Nevada, U.S.A., **10:**537–38

Nevisians, **8:**440–41

New Amsterdam, Guyana, **6:**317

New Amsterdam, U.S.A., **9:**472

New Brunswick, Canada, **3:**139, 140

New Brunswick, New Jersey, U.S.A., **9:**511

Newfoundland, Canada, **3:**115, 136–138, *136*, *137*

New Glasgow, Canada, **3:***141*

New Granada, **4:**192

New Hampshire, U.S.A., **10:**530–31

New Jersey, U.S.A., **9:**500, 507, 510, 511, 515, **10:**532

New Mexico, U.S.A., **9:**479, 485, 487, 497, 498, 503, 513, 520–21, **10:**537–38, 539

New Netherlands, U.S.A., **9:**492

New Orleans, Louisiana, U.S.A., **9:**491, 495, 496, **10:**534, *534*

New Paltz, New York, U.S.A., **9:***491*

New Spain, **7:**358–59

Newspaper Rock State Park, Utah, U.S.A., **9:***484*

New York City, New York, U.S.A., **9:***472*, *509*, 510, *517*, **10:**545; African Americans in, **9:**477, 494, **10:**531–32; Europeans in, **9:**500, *500*, *507*, 508–9, 510, 511, **10:**531–32; Latin Americans in, **9:**514, *514*, 516

New York State, U.S.A., **9:**493, 495, 500, 506, 507, 510, 515, 517, 523

New Zealanders in Chile, **4:**184–85

Nicaragua, **7:382–87**

Nicaraguans, **7:**382–87; in the U.S.A., **9:**516

Nicarao, **7:**382, 385

Niemeyer, Oscar, **2:**94, 102

Nieuw Amsterdam, Suriname, **8:**451

Nieuw Nickerie, Suriname, **8:**453

Niño, El, **8:**424

Nipissing, **3:**127

Nishga, **3:**148

Nitassinan, Canada, **3:**132, 133

Nivaclé. *See* Chulupí

Noanama, **4:**203–4, *204*, **7:**392, 394–95

Nootka, **3:**114, 148

Noquis, **1:**10

Nordeste, Brazil, **2:**84–85

Nordestinos, **1:**14–16

Noriega Moreno, Manuel, **7:**391

Norsemen. *See* Vikings

North Americans: in Bermuda, **2:**52; in Chile, **4:**173; in Costa Rica, **4:**218, 221; in Panama, **7:**391; in Paraguay, **7:**401; in Puerto Rico, **8:**436

North Carolina, U.S.A., **10:**533

North Dakota, U.S.A., **10:**536, 538

Northern Ojibwe, **3:**142

Northwest Mounted Police, **3:**118

Northwest Passage, **3:**152

Northwest Territories, Canada, **3:**152–56

Norwegians in Ecuador, **5:**263

Nova Scotia, Canada, **3:**139, 140

Nueva trova, **5:**240

Nunavut, Canada, **3:**120, 152, 153–56

Obregón, Alejandro, **4:**212

Odawa Powwow, **3:**131

O'Gorman, Juan, **7:**377

Ohio, U.S.A., **9:**500, 511

Ojeda, Alonzo de, **1:**26

Ojibwe, **3:**113, 126, 127, *127*, 142, 145, **9:**522, **10:**536, *536*

Oka, Quebec, Canada, **3:**133

Okanangan, **3:**147–48

Oklahoma, U.S.A., **9:**482, 503, 511, 519, 520–21, 523, **10:**534

Olmecs, **5:**268, **7:**353

Ona, **1:**22, **4:**172, 183, 184–85, *184*

One Hundred Years of Solitude, **4:**212

Oneida, **3:**114

Onondaga, **3:**114

Ontario, Canada, **3:**126–31

Orange Walk District, Belize, **1:**40

Oranjestad, Aruba, **1:***27*

Ordóñez, José Batlle y, **10:**555

Oregon, U.S.A., **9:**512, 517, **10:**537–38, 540–41

Oriente, Bolivia, **2:**69–72

Orishas, **5:**236

Orozco, José Clemente, **7:**377

Ortiz, Simon J., **9:**522

Oruro, Bolivia, **2:**73

Osage, **9:**498

Otavaleños, **5:***257*, *258*, 258–59, *259*

Otero, Alejandro, **10:**579

Otomis, **7:**367, *367*

Ottawa, Ontario, Canada, **3:***118*, 130–31, *130*

Ottawas, **3:**127

Ouro Prêto, Brazil, **2:**90

Oxcarts, in Costa Rica, **4:**216, *216*

Oxil, **6:**307

Oyampi, **5:**278

Pabellón criollo, **10:**570

Paceños, **2:**64

Pachacuti, Emperor, **8:**414

Páez, **4:**189, 191, 197–98, *197*

Páez Vilaró, Carlos, **10:**559

Pai Tavytera, **7:**402

Pakistanis in the U.S.A., **9:**515

Palafitos, **10:**571

Palenque, Mexico, **7:***355*

Palikur, **5:**278

Pampas, Argentina, **1:**20–21

Panama, **7:388–95**

Panama Canal, Panama, **7:**390, *390*

Panama City, Panama, **7:**389, 392, *392*

Panama hats, **5:**267, *267*

Panare, **10:**576–77

Pan bon, **4:**222

Panche, **4:**189

Numbers in **bold** indicate volumes; page numbers in *italic* indicate illustrations; page numbers in **bold** refer to full articles.

Numbers in **bold** indicate volumes; page numbers in *italic* indicate illustrations; page numbers in **bold** refer to full articles.

Numbers in **bold** indicate volumes; page numbers in *italic* indicate illustrations; page numbers in **bold** refer to full articles.

Numbers in **bold** indicate volumes; page numbers in *italic* indicate illustrations; page numbers in **bold** refer to full articles.

Numbers in **bold** indicate volumes; page numbers in *italic* indicate illustrations; page numbers in **bold** refer to full articles.

Numbers in **bold** indicate volumes; page numbers in *italic* indicate illustrations; page numbers in **bold** refer to full articles.

REFERENCE

PEOPLES
of the
AMERICAS

PEOPLES
of the
AMERICAS

Volume 10
United States of America–
Virgin Islands (U.S.)

MARSHALL CAVENDISH
NEW YORK • LONDON • TORONTO • SYDNEY

Marshall Cavendish Corporation
99 White Plains Road
Tarrytown, New York 10591-9001

Consulting Editor: J. Patrick Gray, Professor of Anthropology, University of Wisconsin

Consultants: Jean-Marc Blais, Senior Interpretive Planner, Canadian Museum of Civilization, Hull, Quebec
David Frye, Assistant Director, Department of Latin American and Caribbean Studies, University of Michigan

Spanish Consultant: Fran Kaplan

Contributing authors: D. L. Birchfield
Marion Morrison
Juliette Radcliffe Rogers
Philip Steele
Mary A. Stout

Discovery Books
Managing Editor: Paul Humphrey
Project Editor: Helen Dwyer
Text Editor: Valerie J. Weber
Design Concept: Ian Winton
Designers: Barry Dwyer, Ian Winton, and Simon Borrough
Cartographer: Stefan Chabluk

Marshall Cavendish
Editorial Director: Paul Bernabeo
Editor: Marian Armstrong
Associate Editor: Debra M. Jacobs

The publishers would like to thank the following for their permission to reproduce photographs:
Bruce Coleman Collection (Hans Reinhard 538); Corbis (Ed Eckstein 544; Kevin Fleming 530, frontispiece; Natalie Fobes 541; Lynn Goldsmith 549; Philip Gould 534; Judy Griesedieck 531; Reuters/Corbis-Bettmann 547; Phil Schermeister 536; Ted Spiegel 532); James Davis Travel Photography (543); Eye Ubiquitous (Michael George 548; G. Wheatley 545); Getty Images (550; Nicholas DeVore 537; Rich Frishman 542; Jacques Jangoux 578; Alan Levenson 540; Keith Wood 533); Robert Harding Picture Library (K. Gillham 581, 583; Jeff Greenberg 546); Image Bank (Alvin Upitis 535); Panos Pictures (Alfredo Cedeño 564, 565, 569 top); South American Pictures (Charlotte Lipson 539, 551; Kimball Morrison 554; Tony Morrison cover, 552, 555, 556, 557, 558, 559, 560, 562, 563, 566, 567, 568, 569 bottom, 570, 571, 572, 573, 575, 576, 577, 579)

(frontispiece) A boy at a Fourth of July celebration in Wisconsin.

Editor's note: Many systems of dating have been used by different cultures throughout history. *Peoples of the Americas* uses B.C.E. (Before Common Era) and C.E. (Common Era) instead of B.C. (Before Christ) and A.D. (Anno Domini, "In the Year of the Lord") out of respect for the diversity of the world's peoples.

Library of Congress Cataloging-in-Publication Data
Peoples of the Americas.
    p.   cm.
        Includes bibliographical references and index.
        Contents: v. 1. Anguilla–Belize — v. 2. Bermuda–Brazil — v. 3. Canada–Cayman Islands — v. 4. Chile–Costa Rica — v. 5. Cuba–French Guiana — v. 6. Greenland–Jamaica — v. 7. Martinique–Paraguay — v. 8. Peru–Turks and Caicos Islands — v. 9. United States of America — v. 10. United States of America–Virgin Islands

    ISBN 0-7614-7050-6 (set)
    1. Ethnology—America—Juvenile literature. 2. America—History—Juvenile literature. [1. Ethnology—America. 2. America—History.]
E29.A1P46 1999
970'.004—dc21   98-2801
                                                                                                                          CIP
                                                                                                                          AC

    ISBN 0-7614-7050-6 (set)
    ISBN 0-7614-7060-3 (vol. 10)

Printed and bound in Italy

Contents

The United States Today

Today the United States is the most powerful nation on earth, with a rich diversity of cultures. But it also has great regional diversity, brought about by the varying climate, landscape, and patterns of settlement that have shaped the nation over the years.

New England: Land of Rocky Beauty

In the northeastern corner of the United States, the states of Connecticut, Maine, Massachusetts, New Hampshire, Rhode Island, and Vermont form what is known as New England, a region of hilly, rocky terrain with small mountain ranges. The climate within this small area varies widely. The more eastern states experience fierce winters and cool summers, making them attractive tourist destinations; they draw winter skiers and summer refugees from hot, humid areas to the south. New England is home to some of the most beautiful scenery in the United States: the Adirondack Mountains; the annual fall spectacular of colorful forest leaves; and picturesque towns, farms, and covered bridges reminiscent of life a century ago.

The land and its cultures still reveal the stamp of its early settlers, primarily Anglo-Americans (immigrants from Great Britain). The early settlers battled determinedly with the Native Americans already living in the area. Several northeastern tribes were almost completely wiped out, but the Iroquois and several other smaller tribes still maintain a small but strong presence in New England. The European settlers cleared the heavily forested land for farms and used most of the lumber for building materials. They also quarried slate and granite from Vermont.

In the snow-covered mountains of Saint Albans, Vermont, a farmer uses horses and a sled to harvest maple sap. The sap is used to make maple syrup.

Today the area remains heavily populated by Anglo-Americans, and one national holiday, Thanksgiving, honors the English Pilgrims' first harvest in 1621, wrung from the rocky New England soil. All over the United States, people of many ethnic groups take a day off to cook turkey and squash and eat pumpkin pie—whether or not those foods are even native to their area.

Although its soil was not very rich and the growing season is short, the New England area became a rural area filled with family farms. By 1880, over 50 percent of the land in New England was farmland. Since then agriculture has been declining, although eastern New England still maintains its character as a rural economy. Currently dairy farming and poultry production represent the primary agricultural pursuits.

Fishing has always been a key industry in New England, with some of the richest fishing grounds in the world yielding lobster, cod, and many other catches. With the growth of the shipbuilding and the textile mill industries in the nineteenth and early twentieth centuries, New England became the United States' first industrial center. As these industries have declined, New England has attempted to replace them with electronics and other types of manufacturing industries. However, so many other areas and countries are competing in this field that New England has not been very successful.

A Maine restaurant worker helps a family choose lobsters for the pot. The New England coast is renowned for its seafood, and fishing is a small but stable industry.

The modern economy of the New England area is not particularly strong. Modern business is concentrated southwest of the New England area in New York City, although many people who work in New York now purchase second homes in the New England area or vacation there.

Middle Atlantic Region: An Urban Economy

The New York metropolitan area, though geographically small, contains over seventeen million people and is a major business center of the United States. Located in the Middle Atlantic region, it has probably the most culturally mixed ethnic population in the country. For

531

Construction work takes place in Philadelphia, Pennsylvania. The cities of the Middle Atlantic region are growing business centers, replacing what was once farmland.

exception of the rich Pennsylvania and New Jersey farmlands, the soils of the Middle Atlantic region were usually poor. Most of the seaboard area was a swampy lowland, rising to the Appalachian Piedmont and Allegheny Mountains to the west. Prior to the Civil War, the nation's iron industry was centered in Pennsylvania, and coal was mined in the western part of the state. Currently businesses in this region manufacture chemicals and pharmaceuticals as a primary industry.

This region is dominated by spreading cities—New York, Philadelphia, Wilmington, Baltimore, and Washington, D.C. Surrounding farmlands have surrendered inevitably to city landscapes, and the need for more urban real estate has generated skylines of tall buildings.

decades new immigrants have settled in large numbers in New York and the surrounding areas. Irish, Italians, East Europeans, Jews, and African Americans arrived in waves to join the original Dutch, German, and Anglo-American inhabitants.

In addition to being the major port for shipping traffic from Europe, New York also became an important destination for goods coming to the coast from the interior of the United States after the Erie Canal opened in 1830. New York is also a manufacturing center, especially for the garment industry, and functions as an international business center, with more corporate headquarters than any other city. The entire coastal area from Boston to Washington, D.C., is a highly urbanized complex of cities often called the Megalopolis Region.

The eastern seaboard began with an agricultural and rural economy. With the

The South: From Plantations to Manufacturing Plants

Between the Potomac River and the Gulf Coast of Texas lies a large geographic region in the southeastern portion of the United States known as the South. There is some question as to whether Texas is a part of the South or the Southwest, but otherwise, it is a fairly distinctive region. The area consists of a broad coastal plain and the southern portions of two mountain ranges: the Appalachians and the Ozark-Ouachita, drained by the mighty Mississippi River. Many people in the South, whether white or black, were born there, and some can trace their ancestry in the country back before 1850. While the South overall has seen little immigration, people have moved to the edges of the South, to Maryland, Texas, and Florida. In contrast, Atlanta and the Research Triangle area of North Carolina have seen major immigration in the last decade.

Originally populated by many different Native American tribes, most of the Native inhabitants were either forcibly relocated west of the Mississippi, primarily in Oklahoma, or killed. The original Anglo-American settlers in the area began farming cotton and tobacco for export and created the plantation system, which required such large amounts of field labor that they brought in African slaves.

The South was defined by its plantation economy prior to the Civil War (1861–1865). Its agriculture was based mainly on cotton, corn, and tobacco, in an area with a long growing season, ample rainfall, and rich soils. The early plantation economy produced a unique southern colonial architecture, a gracious way of life among the wealthy, and a distinctive variation of American English that is widely shared by Southerners. The Civil War devastated the South: its lands were occupied, much of the South was destroyed, and its plantation economy was dismantled.

Even after the war, the population of the southern United States was the most poorly educated, the most rural, and often displayed a bitter prejudice between whites and blacks. As a result of the overt prejudice and poor rural economy, many southern African Americans moved to urban areas, particularly in the northern states, to find work. The South became a focus of the national civil rights movement in the 1960s. Many people from other states came to the South to join protest marches and rallies to establish and enforce equal rights for African Americans.

Today a more diverse agricultural system has replaced plantation agriculture and crops. Cotton and tobacco, though still

An oil tanker moors in the loading bay of an oil refinery in Houston, Texas, on the Gulf of Mexico. Texas has long been the home of the American oil industry.

important, are grown on a more limited basis, while rice and peanuts are also major crops. More livestock is raised; dairy and beef cattle, hogs, and poultry are large industries. Many of the southern states contain commercial forestland, and the South produces nearly 60 percent of the country's pulpwood. Other significant natural resources include the vast reserves of oil and gas in Texas and Oklahoma. The economy is changing from a rural one to an urban one, and southern cities are booming, as the number of jobs in professional, technical, and governmental fields increase. Industrial growth in the southeastern states is much higher than in any other area of the country. Many companies are moving manufacturing plants to the South because of the lower cost of living, lower taxes, and available labor force.

Viewers pack the streets and decorated balconies of homes in the French district of New Orleans for the annual Mardi Gras festival, the city's most popular annual event for 150 years.

Mardi Gras

Mardi Gras (MAHR-dee GRAH), or Fat Tuesday, is a French celebration that flourishes in New Orleans. Originally a religious event, Fat Tuesday marks the last day of the Carnival period before Ash Wednesday, which begins the fasting days of Lent for some Christians. Carnivals probably had their origins in pagan spring fertility rites, but now combine parades, pageantry, folk drama, and feasting.

New Orleans's Mardi Gras began with private masked balls and parties held by the French in the 1700s. After enduring a ban under the Spanish, the parties commenced again when New Orleans became a part of the United States. Secret societies, such as the Mystick Krewe of Comus, were formed to organize and manage the celebrations. The Mardi Gras Krewes developed from private social clubs, which funded the lavish parades and street fairs, often competing with each other for acclaim. Mardi Gras remains a festive street party, in which costumes, parades, music, hilarity, mockery, and feasting abound.

Florida is a unique part of the South. Its mild subtropical climate and miles of coastal beaches has made it a major tourist destination and a popular retirement area, as well as a primary producer of the nation's citrus crop. Florida has also received many recent immigrants, primarily Cubans and Haitians fleeing economic and political hardships in their home countries.

The Midwest: The Heartland

Located around the Great Lakes, the Midwest is a region of gently rolling hills and flat plains dotted with smaller lakes, streams, and rivers. It is the central lowland of the country, with severe winters and mild summer conditions good for crops. At one time a natural forest and grassland, most of the forestlands have been cleared for agriculture. With miles of

A field of green snap beans is harvested in Wisconsin. The fertile soil of the Midwest was a gift to immigrant farmers, and agriculture is still very important in the area today.

flat land and no mountain ranges, rich soil has made this area a natural agricultural heartland. When the early settlers began moving west of the Appalachians in search of fertile farmlands, the first place they settled was the Ohio Valley. Most farms began as large plots of land cultivated by

The Erie Canal

The Erie Canal is a historic, artificial waterway connecting the Hudson River with the eastern end of Lake Erie near Buffalo, New York. The canal's goal was opening transportation via waterway from New York City to the Great Lakes area. The completion of the seven million dollar, 363-mile- (584-kilometer-) long canal in 1825 effectively opened the entire Midwest region for settlement. The resulting growth in the Midwest was phenomenal, as Midwesterners shipped farm produce and, later, iron ore to the East, while the necessary supplies and manufactured goods came West.

families, and that trend has persisted, despite the fact that it is difficult for a family farm to compete with large agribusinesses in the modern world.

Many different tribes of Native Americans, primarily Algonquian-speaking peoples, originally lived here. The first European settlers in the area were French; they established settlements in order to ply the fur trade in North America. Great Britain gained title to the area after defeating the French in the French and Indian War (1763) and, after the American Revolution (1775–1783), the Native Americans continued to successfully resist the European settlers through a series of battles with the American army. During the War of 1812, Tecumseh, a Shawnee chief, encouraged many of the tribes to ally with Britain against the United States. Native Americans helped the British take Detroit. But the British were eventually defeated, and the Native Americans were deported to the West. At this point settlers began to pour into the region, which had been only sparsely settled by hardy frontiersmen.

The lumber in the northern Midwest brought French Canadians and Scandinavians. The rich farmlands brought Germans. And rich lead and iron ore resources attracted miners, primarily Welsh, Irish, and Slavs. The lakes and rivers made transporting goods easy, which helped in the explosive growth of the Midwestern cities. Detroit, Cleveland, Chicago, Minneapolis-Saint Paul, and Milwaukee became highly industrialized and attracted even more immigrants. Poles and other eastern Europeans came to the cities to work in the mines of Duluth, in the iron and steel industries of Cleveland, and in the meatpacking plants of Chicago. Later, European immigrants and African

Ojibwe Indians gather the wild rice harvest on the Bowstring River. This is part of the Leech Lake Indian Reservation in Minnesota.

Americans from the South came to the Midwestern cities to work in Milwaukee's breweries, Detroit's automobile assembly plants, and for other manufacturers.

Native Americans, particularly the Ojibwe (also known as the Anishinabe and Chippewa), remain a part of the Midwest culture. They cluster in the northern woodlands, while the Sioux retain lands in the Dakotas. In addition, a significant Native American population resides in the cities, particularly Chicago and Minneapolis.

Agriculture has been the first and most enduring business of the Midwest, although it has been overshadowed by its rapidly growing industrial urban areas. Often called the Corn Belt, this area grows a lot of corn—for humans, for cattle feed, and, increasingly, for export to other countries like Japan and Russia. In addition to corn, soybeans now provide another cash crop. The area also produces crops for livestock feed, such as hay and oats. The northern states, especially Wisconsin, have specialized in dairy farming. In addition, in parts of Iowa and Illinois, beef and hog production add to the economy. Some wheat is grown in the Midwest, but it is not a primary crop.

In many ways the Midwest has come to symbolize the United States, the cultural, if not geographic, center of the country. When non-Americans think of rich farmlands combined with industrial cities in the United States, where people are well educated and work hard, what they imagine is the Midwest.

Unfortunately, it is also a place in decline. The population is moving away to the West and the South. The heavy industries are old and fading. The Midwest is struggling to bring some of the new electronic technology-based industries to the region.

The Mountain West

This area of the United States is defined by the massive bulk of the Rocky Mountains, which run roughly from north to south. The Mountain West region includes portions of Montana, Utah, Wyoming, Colorado, New Mexico, Arizona, Nevada, California, Oregon, Idaho, and Washington. Much of this arid land is near or in the mountains.

Creating an enormous geographic barrier, the Rocky Mountains discouraged early immigrants from settling since they were able to find richer, more attractive land elsewhere. Therefore, most of the region was sparsely settled until recently. This area, known for its wide-open spaces, consists of the vast plains and prairies on the east side of the Rockies as well as the rough beauty of the mountains themselves.

The treeless, arid plains are at a higher altitude than the Midwest, and they are battered by temperature extremes and strong winds. Once the settlers reached the plains, they didn't stop but crossed to the Pacific coast. European settlers were looking primarily for farmlands, and the plains would not do. Also the vast prairies were a stronghold of many Native American peoples referred to collectively as the "Plains Indians."

Eventually the plains were settled by miners, ranchers who used the grasslands for livestock grazing, and grain farmers. Beef cattle represented most of the livestock raised in this area, and the occupations of ranching and riding herd were concentrated in the plains and mountains of the Mountain West region. In the late

Much of Wyoming and Montana east of the Rockies is given over to cattle ranching. They are among the largest but most sparsely populated states in the country.

Cowboys

The first cowboys were probably vaqueros (vah-KARE-oes) from Latin America who worked on ranches in Texas around 1820. Skilled horsemen, they handled the herds of cattle on the ranches. In the autumn, cowboys rounded up all the free-ranging cattle and branded them; in the winter they watched over the herd; and in the spring they drove selected cows to the nearest railroad town to be shipped to market. In between they did odd jobs, such as mending fences, repairing equipment, and, if they were the only ones around, doctoring sick animals. The tools of their trade were their lariat (rope), saddle, spurs, branding iron, and, of course, their all-important horse.

Cowboys can still be found working on cattle ranches in the Mountain West area today. Although their occupation has been greatly romanticized, it actually involves a lot of hard, physical labor and a lot of camping out.

nineteenth century, advances in farming techniques and equipment made it possible to farm on the arid, windy plains.

But the farmers and ranchers each had different needs that led to range wars between them. Eventually, both occupations diminished the prairie grasslands, and strong winds began to badly erode soils. This cycle culminated in the dust bowl of the 1930s, when the soil became worn out; wheat farms were abandoned as farmers migrated to the cities for work.

The plains areas have recovered well from this economic depression and are flourishing again. Wheat remains a key crop in the area. Today, however, crops are more diversified, and sugar beets, flaxseed, grain sorghum, barley, and rye have joined wheat as important crops grown in the plains.

Mining is still important to the Rocky Mountain region. Copper in Montana and Nevada, silver in Colorado and Nevada, oil and gas in Wyoming and Colorado, and coal in Montana, Wyoming, and the Dakotas have all contributed to the economy. The Mountain West also relies on its spectacular beauty to lure tourists. Yellowstone and Glacier National Parks draw crowds during the summer, and Colorado offers first-class skiing during the winter.

The Mountain West states have remained fairly homogeneous. Primarily a rural, ranching, and mining economy with far-flung small communities, the Mountain West boasts only one large city—Denver, Colorado. Because of people migrating to urban areas, this region is dotted with "ghost towns," towns that have died or shrunk drastically when a particular business or occupation ceased in that area.

Although many immigrants have passed through these areas or occupied them during mining booms, the population remains predominantly Anglo-American, with a strong Native American presence. Many tribes occupy lands in the Mountain West, including the Flatheads and Crow in Montana and various bands of Sioux in the Dakotas. The Mormons, a religious group, settled in the area of Salt Lake City, Utah, early on and have had a strong role in developing the region. In addition, Hispanics from the Southwest have recently arrived.

In recent years the mountain states of Colorado and Wyoming have seen enormous growth in the number of skiers visiting their snowy winter slopes.

The Southwest

The southwestern United States is a culturally distinct area since it was originally a part of Mexico and settled late by Anglo-Americans. Due to its rural character and lack of people, many different cultures flourish side by side with relatively little mixing compared with the rest of the country.

The continuous history of the Native American peoples of the area is most significant. This arid, hostile land, broken by high plateaus and mountainous bioregions, presents a harsh environment that was unattractive to agriculturally minded settlers. Perhaps that is one reason why Native American cultures have endured, particularly the various Pueblo, Navajo, Apache, and Tohono O'odham (Pima-Papago) tribes. The state of Arizona has a greater percentage of land owned and controlled by Native Americans than any other state in the country.

Miners were the first settlers to move to the Southwest. New Mexico possesses a variety of minerals as well as oil and natural gas. Arizona was heavily mined for its copper. Later, Anglo-American ranchers moved into the Southwest, and livestock ranching became a mainstay. With the start of large-scale irrigation, Arizona became a major cotton-farming state.

Tourism has always been important to the area. The Southwest contains the Grand Canyon and many other beautiful scenic areas, and its warm winters make it a winter tourist destination. Recently, the Southwest has boomed, with many businesses relocating to the area, especially to Phoenix, Arizona, due to its good weather, attractive tax situation, and ready pool of workers.

One issue that continues to plague the area is the water supply for millions of people, animals, and crops. Cities, farms, and Indian reservations must divide up a limited water supply among themselves.

Mariachi music is as popular north as it is south of the Mexican border. This mariachi band is performing for a New Mexico audience.

Mariachi Music

Mariachi (mah-ree-AH-chee) music is a type of Mexican folk music that is commonly heard in the southwestern United States. Composed of violins, guitars, and brass wind instruments, the size of the orchestra varies from three to twelve musicians, and the instruments used may change from song to song. Found at restaurants, weddings, street fairs, and festivals, mariachi groups may play both traditional folk and contemporary music. An international mariachi conference held in Arizona since 1982 draws over thirty thousand participants and sellout crowds to watch the top mariachi groups, with their stylish costumes and upbeat brassy tunes, showcase and share their techniques.

The Pacific Coast

Portions of Washington, Oregon, and California form the Pacific Coast. Climates vary in this area, from cold and rainy in the north to warm and sunny in the south. In general the coastal areas are more moist and humid up to the mountains, and the eastern sides of the mountain ranges tend to be more arid. The coastal area has dry sunny beaches in the south, forests of magnificent redwood trees in northern California, and lush green forests meeting the wild Pacific Ocean in the foggy north.

Various Native American tribes peopled the Pacific Coast before the arrival of Europeans. The Spanish were the first Europeans to settle in California. The Californian gold rush in 1848 lured enormous numbers of settlers into central California, and the Pacific Coast region grew at a fast pace. All types of people from all different states came to California, pushing the Native populations off their land and into the growing towns.

Despite the gold rush, California is fairly poor in mineral resources. It became a major agricultural producer in the United States and a home to agribusinesses. Starting small with ranches, citrus and date groves, and wheat fields, Californian agriculture has exploded; with the help of irrigation, the state has become the number one producer of farm products in all of the United States. Today the leading crops are fruits, nuts, grapes, and cotton, with cattle, vegetables, and dairy farming rounding out the mix. Many of these crops are labor-intensive, and the need for farmworkers has lured immigrants from Pacific Rim countries and Mexico.

Today California is second only to New York as a center of international trade and business. After World War II ended in 1945, food preparation and aircraft

As well as being the most populous, California is also a booming industrial state, boasting electronic and computer industries as well as aircraft manufacture.

industries throve in California. The state also dominates the electronics and computer industries. California has become highly urbanized, as people from everywhere migrate to it. Known as the second Ellis Island, it is the primary destination for immigrants from Asia and Latin America.

The rest of the nation watches California since many consider it to be the trendsetting state for the whole country. Some Californian trends, like nonsmoking areas, health foods, and health clubs, have swept the rest of the country. California's primary issue is how to handle its constantly increasing population and still retain its natural beauty and quality of life.

The Pacific Northwest is blessed with three natural resources: forests, fish, and waterpower. After the fur trappers and the gold miners came the farmers, who settled Oregon's fertile Willamette Valley. Nut and fruit farming, including berries, pears, and apples, combine with wheat farming, dairy farming, and ranching to form the agricultural backbone of the Northwest, while lumbering and fishing add to its economy. Recently the large urban areas have also attracted computer software businesses. Known for social innovation and leadership in government, the Northwest is tackling the problems arising from an economy that lacks diversity.

A Yakima Indian fishing by the Dalles Dam. This dam and others have destroyed many Native American fishing grounds along the Columbia River.

Alaska and Hawaii

Alaska contains the highest mountain in the nation, covers an area twice the size of Texas, and has a coastline longer than those of the mainland states all combined. Though it has poor soil, the area is heavily forested; it becomes swampy in the

Salmon Fishing

Pacific salmon fishing ranks second only to shrimping in terms of commercial value to the United States fishing industry as a whole. It is particularly important to the economy of the Pacific Northwest and Alaska.

Salmon are hatched in freshwater, then they swim to the ocean to complete their adult life. After one to five years, they return to the freshwater where they were born in order to spawn. After the female lays the eggs in the streambed and they are fertilized by the male, the adults die. By the 1930s, dams on Washington's Columbia River prevented salmon from reaching their spawning beds, decreasing salmon production to only one-sixth of the catch harvested by Native Americans a century earlier. In addition, overfishing by Canadian and American commercial fishers in the Pacific Ocean have also diminished the salmon supply.

Another controversy surrounds the fishing rights of the Native Americans in the Northwest, for whom the salmon is not only an important food but a center for their entire culture. With treaties between Canada and the United States in place, and with limits placed on commercial fishing and dam building, the salmon have made a modest comeback. The annual First Salmon Ceremony, held by most of the Northwestern tribes, honors the place of the salmon in their lives.

summer and frozen in the winter. Alaska has a very strong Native American presence, with Inuit (IN-yoo-it), sometimes called Eskimos, Aleuts (a-LOOTS), and Northwest Coast Native Americans.

In the 1890s a gold rush in the Yukon brought abrupt population growth, but today Alaska is sparsely settled and has the flavor of a frontier state, although the people cluster in towns and settlements. The fishing industry and the petroleum industry dominate the Alaskan economy. These are supplemented by the tourist industry, as Alaska is a startlingly beautiful, undeveloped land. In the far west of Alaska, near the Bering Sea, there is virtually no development, and the Aleuts live relatively undisturbed.

Hawaii consists of a chain of volcanic islands in the Pacific Ocean with a tropical climate. Native Hawaiians occupied the islands. They had a culture similar to that found in other parts of Polynesia. When Americans and Europeans came to Hawaii, the Native population declined. This was due to the diseases the incomers brought and to competition for resources with the new settlers, who became plantation owners.

Bananas, pineapples, and sugarcane were grown and harvested for export. The Hawaiian Natives had an established lifestyle of living off the land and were not interested in working as laborers on the plantations. So white plantation owners hired laborers from Japan, China, and the Philippines to pick the crops. Today Hawaii thrives as a premier tourist destination. Large hotels entice tourists to take advantage of Hawaii's balmy climate, sparkling oceans, and beautiful beaches.

Two Inuit greet a gray whale in Barrow, Alaska. With a population of around 550,000 people, Alaska is the least densely populated state in the United States.

Hula

The hula is a native Hawaiian dance, which is now commonly performed throughout Hawaii as a folk dance for entertainment. Originally, trained dancers performed the hula to a chanting accompaniment to honor the gods or praise the chiefs. Whalebone anklets and bracelets and flower necklaces, or leis, were worn by the dancers, along with short skirts for the women and loincloths for the men. The ukulele was borrowed from Portuguese sailors and added as accompaniment.

Today the hula will tell a story or describe a place through gestures and movement. Costumes now include raffia skirts, and percussion and guitar may now join the ukulele. The beauty of this folk dance has made it well known throughout the United States.

At the Kodak Hula show in Waikiki, Honolulu, a Hawaiian woman performs the traditional hula dance to a chanting musical accompaniment.

Living in the U.S.A.

Diverse though it is, modern America is also one nation, with a federal government, a common system for educating its children, and many similarities in lifestyle. Most of its people live in a home that has water, electricity, sewerage, telephone, radio, and television. Almost 85 percent of Americans possess automobiles, and they use them heavily. A very mobile society, Americans move around the country quite a bit; few stay in the same area where they were born.

Americans have income to spend on recreation, and most of them spend it on television, video and computer equipment, sports and sports equipment, magazines, newspapers and books, and spectator amusements. Often there are two wage earners per household, making child care a major issue and expense for working parents. Working people often patronize the fast-food restaurants, which have multiplied rapidly in the United States since the 1950s. As most people reside in nuclear family units, a gathering place for the community is found either in churches or in large indoor malls containing numerous retail stores, restaurants, movie theaters, and other services under a single roof. Most Americans spend several hours per day watching television, which has become a major cultural force in the country.

A high proportion of Americans attend college. These students are attending their graduation at Villanova University in Pennsylvania.

Education in the United States consists of primary and secondary schools and is considered mandatory through twelfth grade. The literacy rate for the country is about 96 percent. Beyond twelfth grade, an elective higher education system is available for those who can pay tuition or qualify for scholarships. About 21 percent of the American population has earned an undergraduate college degree, which is commonly considered to be the amount of education required in order to work in a professional occupation.

A new trend in the United States is reversing the traditional tendency of moving from the farms to the cities. Currently, there is greater migration of people out of the city and back to rural areas that are now somewhat suburban. Another trend is a population shift from the Midwest and Northeast to the South and Southwest (known as the Sun Belt). The warmer weather of the southern and southwestern states has also drawn an aging population.

American Art

The United States has made major contributions to world art, literature, and culture, especially within the last fifty years. Early American architecture was heavily influenced by British styles. After the Revolutionary War, Thomas Jefferson made a concentrated effort to break away from British styles of architecture when he designed buildings. He based his design for the Virginia state capitol on that of a Roman temple and started the neoclassic style of architecture, which modifies an ancient style to suit modern needs. The Capitol building of the United States in Washington, D.C., is built in the neoclassic style.

While different styles proved to be popular over the years, perhaps the most original American contribution to architectural style was the skyscraper. Tall commercial buildings located in urban areas began to be built in earnest after the great fire of Chicago burned down most of that city in 1871. As they rebuilt Chicago, it became the center for the new high-rise architecture, although New York later surpassed Chicago as the home of the skyscrapers.

Frank Lloyd Wright has made the most significant contributions of any single American architect to modern architecture in the United States. His designs of houses reflected the spirit of the Midwest and West, including his famous "prairie house" designs, which were flat and open, often incorporating the outside landscape into the design of the building.

Beginning with portrait painting, then realistic American landscapes and impressionism, artists in the United States followed the dominant European schools of art. But after World War II, the center for experimental art shifted to New York City, and the group of artists whose works became known as abstract expressionism flourished, among them Jackson Pollock and Willem de Kooning. Later, Andy Warhol began the pop art movement, where realistic images of mass culture dominated, such as pictures of Campbell's soup cans and faces of celebrities. In the 1980s and 1990s a diverse mixture of styles, materials, and subjects has emerged.

American Writers

American literature began with diaries, letters, journals, sermons, and true accounts of life in the colonies. After the Revolution, there was an attempt to develop a uniquely American literature. One example was author James Fenimore Cooper, a writer of a series of novels, known as the Leatherstocking Tales, set in the United States containing a hero, Natty Bumppo, who represents the pioneering, independent spirit of the citizens.

From the 1830s to the 1850s, the romantic period of writing saw Henry David Thoreau and Walt Whitman celebrating communion with nature. Mark Twain heralded a new realism in American literature and wrote dialog with uniquely American regional dialects.

Regionalism, or writing about one area of the United States and its culture, began to flourish around the turn of the twentieth century and has continued as an important part of American literature. Here, the minority writers often found their voice:

Frank Lloyd Wright was America's most influential architect. One of his most famous buildings is Falling Water *in Pennsylvania.*

Willa Cather wrote about the West, and Paul Lawrence Dunbar wrote about the South. Social protest novels became popular with Upton Sinclair's *The Jungle*; this novel and others revealed the sordid aspects of American society. After World War I, Sherwood Anderson and Upton Sinclair exposed what they saw as the shallowness of small-town America, while Ernest Hemingway and William Faulkner documented the war and its attendant losses.

During the Great Depression, literature became very political and more aware of social conditions. John Steinbeck's *The Grapes of Wrath*, the story of a farming family fleeing the dust bowl, is an example of this era. The popularity of the short story as a form of literature began and would continue, while Raymond Chandler and Dashiell Hammett perfected the detective story. World War II saw the rise of the American drama, with playwrights Tennessee Williams, Arthur Miller, and Edward Albee.

The social movements of the 1960s and 1970s affected writing in the United States. They gave rise to many feminist and ethnic writers such as James Baldwin, Joan Didion, Betty Friedan, Scott Momaday, Toni Morrison, Leslie Marmon Silko, and Alice Walker.

Novels of many different types are popular currently. While the enormous diversity of popular literature today does not suggest any particular trend, most of the important authors think of themselves as critics of American society in one form or another.

American Music

Religious music dominated the colonial period in the United States, and the British influence was significant. Although there was some interest in classical music, the early Americans preferred popular music

Country music is a uniquely American sound. Here a country band performs at the Red Barn Community Festival in Aldie, Virginia.

and military bands. In the nineteenth century, unique American music consisted primarily of unsophisticated folk tunes. All other musical styles were borrowed from Europeans. All musical training was done in Europe, and particularly Germany. After World War I, dependence upon the German musical culture lessened. Music conservatories sprung up in the United States, along with orchestras and choral groups.

Near the turn of the century, jazz was born, along with ragtime and the blues. Given birth by African American folk music, jazz in its many forms continues as a strong expression of American culture. Musical theater is also popular in the United States, but it is primarily rock and roll that has become a major American industry and influenced music around the world. Another musical form arising out of American folk music is country and

western music, also popular in the United States and another worldwide export. The various forms of popular music are very much a part of life and widely listened to in the United States.

Sports and Leisure

As both spectators and participants, Americans are very interested in sports. Attending a sports event, playing a sport, and exercising are three of the top leisure activities for people living in the United States. The American interest in competition and individual and team achievement has led to increased professional player salaries, which number among the highest salaries in the nation, second only to those paid to top stars in the

Cal Ripken Jr. of the Baltimore Orioles signs autographs for his fans. Because players are so popular, they can make money from advertising as well as from sports.

Basketball was invented by American James Naismith in 1891. The first national league was launched in 1925, and it is now one of the country's fastest-growing sports.

movie industry. Also, sports players are named frequently by American children when asked to identify heroes or role models. Sports stars are now as popular as movie stars in the advertising industry, which creates television commercials of sporting heroes selling shoes, cars, and deodorants.

Baseball has long been considered America's favorite pastime. With its origins in the British game of rounders, baseball is played by participants of all ages throughout the country. In professional baseball, thirty teams, divided into two leagues, each play 162 games from March through October. The winning teams from the National League (founded in 1876) and the American League (founded in 1900) meet in the World Series every October to decide the national championship.

United States-style football is another significant American sport. It is a contact

sport of two eleven-man teams playing on a rectangular-shaped field. Football began as a college sport in the last decade of the nineteenth century and is now played in most U.S. secondary schools, colleges, and at the professional level. Football is played in the fall, and the Super Bowl, the most important game of the season, is played the last Sunday in January. Super Bowl Sunday is regarded as an important holiday by many sports fans, as they gather to feast and watch this battle for the National Football League championship on television.

The other chief sport in the United States is basketball. It is played on both indoor and outdoor courts with two five-player teams attempting to lob a ball through a hoop 10 feet (3 meters) high in their opponents' territory. Basketball can be played by participants of all ages, male and female. It is particularly popular at the college and professional levels because of marketing and television exposure. The college basketball season begins in November, ending in March with a 64-team national tournament that culminates in the Final Four to decide the national championship. The National Basketball Association (NBA), which is the U.S. professional basketball organization, has helped promote basketball as a world sport.

Sports have traditionally provided an arena where members of minority groups who have been excluded from the mainstream business culture can excel in the United States. In the early 1900s, Irish and Italian boxers won the hearts of Americans as they became champions. Jim Thorpe, a Native American, represented the United States in the Olympics as a top runner. Today many American sports, such

as football, basketball, and boxing, are dominated by outstanding African American athletes.

Participation by children in sports leagues, such as Little League, has always been popular. This activity brings together people of all ethnic groups and walks of life to participate in a common activity. Next to sharing education in the public schools, children's sports activities serve to create a common culture. American youngsters participate in baseball, soccer, and basketball teams.

Exercising, another top American leisure activity, is quite popular with most Americans. Great value is placed on good health in the United States, and people are encouraged to exercise as a means of staying healthy. For those who also enjoy being outdoors, jogging, walking, rollerblading, skateboarding, and cycling wherever there is available space are the things to do. Another group of Americans are joining health clubs in record numbers, where they can swim, participate in aerobic exercise classes, use stationary bicycles, lift weights, and run on a treadmill.

Celebrations

The national holidays honor American heroes, the American armed forces personnel, United States independence, and the American worker. In addition, the landing of the original colonists in the United States is celebrated on Thanksgiving Day, a day not celebrated by most Native Americans. And

Christmas in New York City is celebrated with dazzling displays of lights and, here at Saint Patrick's Cathedral, with the lighting of candles.

Martin Luther King Jr.

Martin Luther King Jr. is best known for his leadership of the American civil rights movement. Born on January 15, 1929, in Atlanta, Georgia, King attended Crozer Theological Seminary and Boston University. He went on to become an eloquent Baptist minister in Montgomery, Alabama, where he led a group of civil rights activists. In 1959 he visited India and discussed with Indian leader Mahatma Gandhi's followers the principles of nonviolent resistance, which he was convinced would be the most effective strategy for the civil rights movement. He went on to lead countless sit-ins and protest marches. Arrested in Birmingham, Alabama, after a demonstration to desegregate lunch counters, King wrote a famous letter to

Martin Luther King Jr. addressing the 200,000-strong crowd at the Lincoln Memorial in Washington, D.C., at the end of the 1963 March on Washington.

supporters that spelled out his philosophy of nonviolent action.

King focused the attention of the entire country on the problems produced by segregating races and the unequal treatment received by African Americans. He rallied the African American population and led it in nonviolent protests, such as the 1963 March on Washington, which drew 200,000 protesters, black and white, to the Capitol.

The actions King led had national impact. The Civil Rights Act of 1964 authorized the federal government to enforce desegregation. His demonstrations in Selma, Alabama, resulted in the passage of the Voting Rights Act of 1965. King was killed by a sniper in 1969. He received the Nobel Peace Prize in 1964, and in 1986, the U.S. Congress voted to observe a national holiday in his honor.

Christmas remains as a Christian holiday, celebrated in the United States by a cultural mix of traditions. New Year's Day, January 1, is the day of the Rose Bowl Parade in Pasadena, California, watched by many people on television. Later, the Rose Bowl football game occurs, a game which matches two top college football teams against each other.

The newest holiday is Martin Luther King's birthday. Martin Luther King Jr. led the civil rights movement of the 1960s and devoted his life to improving the status of African Americans in the United States.

The country also celebrates unofficial holidays together. These holidays may be imported from other countries or be 100 percent American: Chinese New Year (honors the home and begins the new year), Kwanzaa (based on African harvest festivals), Saint Patrick's Day (celebrates Irish heritage), Halloween, and various religious holidays.

Kwanzaa

Kwanzaa (KWAHN-zuh) is an African American holiday celebrated each year from December 26 through January 1. Patterned after African harvest festivals, it was created in 1966 by Maulana Karenga, a university professor, as a nonreligious celebration of family and social values.

Over five million people celebrate the seven principles of unity, self-determination, collective responsibility, cooperative economics, purpose, creativity, and faith. A community celebration occurs on December 31, involving feasting and gift exchange.

Halloween is celebrated by children and adults alike across the United States. In New Mexico it is combined with the traditional Mexican Day of the Dead festival.

URUGUAY

URUGUAY IS A SMALL COUNTRY on the east coast of South America.

Uruguay is bounded by the Atlantic Ocean on the east, Brazil on the north, and by the Río de la Plata (River Plate) in the south. To the west the Uruguay River separates it from Argentina.

Uruguay is a land of gently rolling grasslands with two ranges of hills that cover much of the north and east of the country. The highest point is only 1,644 feet (501 meters) above sea level. Within the hills are some low plateaus and broad valleys. Few trees grow here, except along the banks of the rivers and streams. Along the coast lies a narrow plain with tidal lakes, sand dunes, and swamps. Most of the population live in Montevideo, along the coast, and in towns along the Uruguay River.

A rancher with his cattle crosses the grassy slopes of the Cuchilla Grande in eastern Uruguay. Many of the roads in the interior are unsurfaced.

CLIMATE

Uruguay has a temperate climate with occasional cool nights. It seldom freezes and rarely snows. The interior of the country is a few degrees warmer than the coast, which benefits from offshore winds. Tropical winds from Brazil and cold dry winds from Argentina also affect the climate, and violent storms occur if the two meet. April and May are the wettest months.

Average January temperature: 72°F (22°C)
Average July temperature: 50°F (10°C)
Average annual precipitation: 38 in (97 cm)

552

FACTS AND FIGURES

Official name: *República Oriental del Uruguay*

Status: *Independent state*

Capital: *Montevideo*

Major cities: *Salto, Rivera, Las Piedras*

Area: *68,037 square miles (176,216 square kilometers)*

Population: *3,200,000*

Population density: *47 per square mile (18 per square kilometer)*

Peoples: *More than 90 percent of European descent; less than 10 percent mestizos (mixed European-Native descent) and mulattos (mixed European-African descent)*

Official language: *Spanish*

Currency: *Uruguayan peso*

National days: *Landing of the Thirty-Three Patriots (April 19); Labor Day (May 1); Battle of Las Piedras (May 18); Birth of General Artigas (June 19); Constitution Day (July 18); National Independence (August 25); Columbus Day (October 12)*

Country's name: *Uruguay is believed to derive from the language of the original Native peoples; one possible meaning is "the river of shellfish."*

Land of the Charrúa

Charrúa (chah-ROO-ah) Indians once occupied most of today's Uruguay (oo-roo-GWHY). Earlier groups included the Yaró, Bohané, and Minuané or Güenoa, who were either related to the Charrúa or conquered by them. The Charrúa lived by hunting, fishing, and gathering wild fruits and roots.

Many animals throve in the grasslands, including the ostrichlike rhea. The Charrúa hunted these animals with bows, arrows, slings, spears, or a weighted cord called a bolas. They fished from canoes that could hold forty standing men who rowed with long paddles decorated with feathers.

The Charrúa lived in houses built of four poles covered with straw mats. They painted their bodies and wore shells, bones, and feathers as necklaces and in their ears. Furs and skins served as wrap-around clothing in the cold weather; otherwise people went naked. The Charrúa did not have permanent leaders, uniting only in times of war under the bravest or most powerful men. Shamans, or priests, called on spirits for help and guidance in times of illness or war.

Juan Díaz de Solís was the first European to sail up the River Plate. In 1516 he landed on a site near present-day Montevideo but was killed by the Charrúa.

The Spaniards knew Uruguay as the *Banda Oriental*, or "east bank," because it was on the east side of the Uruguay River. Argentina, on the western side of the river, was the "west bank." Explorers who followed Solís showed little interest in the Banda Oriental because the land contained no gold or silver and the Charrúa fiercely resisted any invaders. The Spaniards did not establish a settlement until 1624. In 1680 the Portuguese residing in Brazil founded Colonia on the southern coast of Uruguay. The Spaniards countered by founding Montevideo in 1726.

Rivalry over the Banda Oriental continued between the two colonial powers

Timeline:	Nomadic hunters and gatherers enter northern Uruguay	Charrúa Indians established	Spaniard Juan Díaz de Solís lands in Uruguay	Missionaries found first settlement in Soriano
	ca. 8000 B.C.E.	ca. 2000 B.C.E.	1516 C.E.	1624

until 1776 when it became part of the Spanish Viceroyalty of the United Provinces of the River Plate. In 1807 the British, hoping to weaken Spain's power in its colonies, took Montevideo and occupied the coastal region for several months. From this contact the colonists learned of revolutionary movements in France and North America; the experience gave them a taste for independence and free trade.

The colonial economy was based on cattle, which prospered on the rich pasture. However, the Charrúa learned to ride horses and took to hunting and killing the cattle. In response settlers established *estancias* (ace-TAHN-see-ahss), or large farms, which they fenced off to protect the animals. No longer having the grasslands to themselves, the Charrúa declined rapidly.

A painting of the port of Montevideo in the 1850s by the artist Augusto Borget. Sailors traded goods from Europe and the United States for Uruguayan hides and meat.

Some were forced into labor on the farms, others were killed in conflicts with the Spaniards, but most died from European illnesses to which they had no immunity. A few received help from Jesuit missionaries, who gave them shelter and taught them to grow crops, to read and write, and to carve and weave. When the Jesuits were expelled from South America in 1767, these Native Americans were left to fend for themselves. Today the Charrúa have totally mixed into the mestizo (mixed European and Native American descent) population.

A Land of Immigrants

The Banda Oriental gained its independence and became the República Oriental del Uruguay in 1828. At that time the population numbered only seventy thousand, including the Natives, Spaniards, and Portuguese. Immigrants began

Portuguese found Colonia	Spanish found Montevideo	Jesuit missionaries expelled	Banda Oriental (Uruguay) becomes part of Viceroyalty of United Provinces of the River Plate
1680	1726	1767	1776

arriving, a slow trickle at first, mainly Spaniards and Italians. During the second half of the century, the trickle became a flood and included people from Mediterranean Europe, the Middle East, and Great Britain. By the end of the nineteenth century, Uruguay had more than a million people. Thousands more arrived in the first years of the twentieth century, many escaping problems in their homelands. They included Poles, Romanians, Russians, Turks, Lebanese, Jewish refugees from Germany, and members of the Mennonite religion.

Nineteenth-century immigrants brought new ideas from Europe that helped to expand the economy. Some settled in Montevideo, where they were involved in shipping and in trading goods such as textiles and leather. Others began commercial farming in the coastal zone, growing vegetables and fruits. Swiss farmers produced butter and cheese, while British farmers introduced pedigree sheep and cattle. British engineers also helped develop railroads and gasworks, and in time there was a British school, hospital, and cricket club in Montevideo.

José Batlle y Ordóñez, who was president from 1903 to 1907 and from 1911 to 1915, introduced social reforms giving government help to the sick and unemployed. Thus, Uruguay became the only country in South America to consider the government at least partly responsible

This woman and her grandchild belong to a Russian community that has lived in a small village near the Uruguay River since early in the twentieth century.

for the well-being of its citizens, thus becoming a "welfare state."

Uruguay enjoyed an economic boom during World War II, but afterward, exports of meat and wool dropped and funding the welfare state became a problem. During the 1950s and 1960s the economy declined further, and riots, demonstrations, and general discontent arose, which led to a terrorist campaign by the Tupamaro urban guerrillas. The military took over in 1973 and remained in power until 1985. Since then normal democratic elections have been held, but strikes and protests have continued against the government's failure

Uruguay becomes independent	Tupamaro urban guerrillas emerge	Military government rules country	Julio Maria Sanguinetti becomes president for the second time
1828	**late 1960s**	**1973–1985**	**1994**

Stalls are piled high with flowers at this Sunday market in Montevideo. In this area opposite the university, however, many people prefer to browse among the newsstands.

to revive the economy. In 1989 the conservative Blanco party candidate, Luis Alberto Lacalle, won the elections. In 1994, by a slender majority, Julio Maria Sanguinetti of the Colorado Party became president for the second time. He formed a coalition with the Blancos to try and resolve the country's economic problems.

Uruguay: A Shared Culture

Most Uruguayans are descended from immigrants who began to arrive soon after the country became independent. The rest are *mestizos,* of mixed Spanish and Native American parentage, and *mulattos* of mixed European and African descent, who live near the border with Brazil. Today the mixture of immigrant peoples is obvious

from the variety of peoples' surnames. But in every other sense, it is a Uruguayan society, with people sharing the same language, culture, and problems. Spanish is the official language, although some immigrant families still use their own languages when speaking among themselves.

Education is free and required for children between the ages of six and fourteen, and the literacy rate, at 97 percent, is one of the highest in South America. The welfare state provides help for the unemployed, the sick, and the poor; for people injured at work; family allowances; and some retirement benefits for the elderly.

Most Uruguayans belong to the Catholic Church, but others are Protestants, Baptists, Methodists, or followers of other evangelical groups. Religion is not taught in schools, and divorce has been permitted since the end of the last century.

Parilladas and Maté

Uruguay has plenty of good locally produced food, particularly meat, dairy products, fish, and fruit. Market stalls are stacked with many varieties of cheese, salamis, sausages, and hams similar to those of Spain, Italy, and Germany.

Lunch for working people in Montevideo often means a visit to the converted old Customs House near the port, which is filled with **parrilladas** *(pah-ree-YAH-thahss), which are like very large barbecues. Metal grills, each the size of a door, are propped at an angle over charcoal fires and covered in huge cuts of beef, pork, mutton, veal, and great spirals of spicy sausages. Elsewhere in the city, many restaurants and snack bars sell a wide variety of pizzas and pastas.*

Drinking yerba maté tea (YAIR-bah mah-TAY) is a custom Uruguayans share with Argentineans and Paraguayans. Cold or hot water is poured onto yerba maté leaves, crushed in the bottom of a gourd. The drink is sipped through a metal straw. Uruguayans carry their gourds wherever they go, at work or at home, along with a vacuum flask filled with water to add to the tea whenever necessary.

Uruguayans are becoming more urban; 87 percent of Uruguayans now live in towns. People arrive daily from rural areas looking for work and better educational and medical facilities. Most go to Montevideo, but others have settled in Salto and Paysandú on the Uruguay River and Rivera on the border with Brazil. Often, newcomers can't find work, and they earn what they can from odd jobs or selling trinkets on the streets. Lack of housing is a problem, and in most towns, beyond the wealthier homes and middle-class apartment blocks, stand poor shanty areas, with houses made of wood or flattened oilcans, where supplies of water and electricity are very limited.

This woman is drinking traditional yerba maté tea from a gourd while relaxing on the waterfront in the southern town of Colonia.

Rural Lives

In rural areas people still farm their own small plots and keep animals. There is little money for mechanical equipment, and people use horses or ox-drawn plows.

557

Gauchos find shelter from the midday sun in the shade of a tree. Though many young cowboys prefer jeans and a checked shirt, older gauchos keep the traditional style of dress.

They grow vegetables and many different kinds of fruit, including grapes; wine production is a growing business. Rural homes are built of brick or concrete, usually with one story, and sometimes with a verandah for hanging hammocks.

Gauchos, or cowboys, mostly work on large estancias in the interior. Many generations ago their ancestors were Spaniards who rejected colonial life on the coast for a lonely life in the grasslands herding cattle. They often married Charrúa women. Superb horsemen, they were independent and totally self-sufficient. There was always a good supply of meat— every meal was beef—and ample leather for their clothing and equipment. They worked long days, sleeping in the open and traveling long distances to keep the animals on the move.

Traditional gaucho dress is a broad-brimmed black hat, long-sleeved cotton shirt, baggy pants called *bombachas* (boem-BAH-chahss), and black leather boots. But many younger gauchos prefer jeans and checked shirts. Gauchos carry a lasso and a special knife called a *facón* (fah-CONE) tucked into a leather belt. They use sheepskins over their saddles for extra comfort. Aspects of their work have changed since the old days. Now they seldom sleep in the open, except on long cattle drives. They have dormitory quarters on the estancias and cattle are kept within range.

Today few young men are prepared to commit themselves to this way of life. Like so many others in the countryside, many have left to make a new start in the towns.

Reminders of some of the original immigrant groups still exist. Near Colonia are communities descended from Italian and Swiss settlers, who still celebrate the Swiss national day and sell Swiss cheeses and music boxes to tourists. Near Paysandú is a farming community of Russian descent where eastern European-style horse-drawn carts are still used.

Arts and Leisure

Two well-known works by the Uruguayan sculptor José Belloni are in parks in Montevideo. One is a life-size bronze of a yoke of oxen, and the other a full-size stagecoach and horses. An eye-catching gaucho on horseback, the work of José Luis Zorilla de San Martín, also stands in downtown Montevideo.

Two artists born in the nineteenth century, Pedro Figari and Joaquín Torres García, became world famous. Figari, a child of Italian immigrants, also became the country's vice president in 1904. He devoted the last years of his life to painting landscapes and scenes of everyday life. García was interested in constructivism, an abstract art that used materials such as glass and metal.

Carlos Páez Vilaró is probably the best-known contemporary artist. His mural, "The Roots of Peace," was painted on the walls of the Pan American Union tunnel in Washington, D.C., in 1960.

Uruguay won the soccer World Cup in 1930 and again in 1950, and enthusiasm for the sport has never waned. Any youngster, given the chance, spends hours kicking a ball around.

There are facilities for most organized sports, but many people cannot afford them. Instead they take time off on the beaches, windsurfing or perhaps boating, and spend many hours fishing by the rivers.

A typical family weekend in southern Uruguay is spent on the beaches or near the rivers or lakes. On the Laguna del Diario people enjoy all kinds of water sports.

VENEZUELA

VENEZUELA IS ON THE NORTH COAST OF SOUTH AMERICA,
facing the Caribbean Sea and Atlantic Ocean.

*Venezuela shares borders with Guyana on the east,
Brazil on the south, and Colombia on the west.
It has seventy-two offshore islands; the
largest is Margarita.*

*Venezuela has four very
different regions. The
Venezuela highlands run
along the coast and
southwest to the border
with Colombia, while the
Maracaibo lowlands
surround Lake Maracaibo
near the coast in the northwest.
The vast central grassland plain,
or llanos (YAH-noess), lies
between the Venezuelan highlands and
the Orinoco River, and south of the Orinoco
is the almost uninhabited Guiana, a region of
forest and savannas that covers over half the
country. Over two-thirds of the population and most
of the major cities are in the coastal highland region.*

*In the Sinamaica Lagoon north of
Maracaibo in northwest
Venezuela, houses of the
Paraujanos people are built on
stilts and made of thatch, reeds,
and matting.*

560

Arawaks, Caribs, and the Spanish

The earliest inhabitants of Venezuela (ven-uh-ZWAY-luh) were seminomadic food-gathering and hunting tribes. By about 1000 B.C.E. some of their descendants had settled into communities. Peaceful Arawaks farmed in the Venezuelan highlands using irrigated terraces to grow corn and potatoes. The more aggressive Caribs had a reputation for cannibalism. Some Native Americans lived along the coast, using dugout canoes to fish. In the forests seminomadic tribes hunted and cleared patches of ground to grow cassava, fruit, and cotton.

Christopher Columbus first sighted Venezuela in 1498 on his third voyage to the Americas. His encounter with Native peoples covered in pearls led him to believe the land had great wealth. The first Spanish settlement was at Cumaná on the coast in 1523. The Native tribes resisted the invaders for a time, but by the end of the sixteenth century, twenty towns had been established, including Caracas, which was founded in 1567. The land did not hold great mineral wealth so the settlers turned to farming.

Colonial Venezuela was an agricultural society. Farmers raised cattle and grew corn, beans, and other crops to feed the people. The colony's principal crop for three centuries was cacao, which was exported to the United States and Europe. It was used to make chocolate, which was fashionable and popular. Spanish officials ran the colony, but wealthy Creoles (people born in the colony of Spanish parentage) controlled the commerce. Native Americans were forced to work as slaves on the land. Thousands of them died from European diseases to which they had no immunity. The population grew as marriage between Spaniards and Native

FACTS AND FIGURES

Official name: *República de Venezuela*

Status: *Independent state*

Capital: *Caracas*

Major cities: *Maracaibo, Valencia, Barquisimeto*

Area: *352,145 square miles (912,055 square kilometers)*

Population: *22,600,000*

Population density: *61 per square mile (24 per square kilometer)*

Peoples: *65 percent mestizos (mixed European-Native descent); 20 percent European descent; 8 percent blacks and mulattos (mixed African-European descent); 7 percent Native American*

Official language: *Spanish*

Currency: *Bolívar*

National days: *Labor Day (May 1); Anniversary of the Battle of Carabobo (June 24); Independence Day (July 5); Simón Bolívar's birthday (July 24); Columbus Day (October 12)*

Country's name: *It was called "Little Venice" because the villages of Native American houses built on stilts on Lake Maracaibo reminded the Spanish explorers of Venice, Italy.*

Timeline:	Arawak tribes cultivating corn and other crops	Christopher Columbus sights coast of Venezuela	First Spanish settlement at Cumaná	Caracas founded
	ca. 1,000 B.C.E.	1498 C.E.	1523	1567

CLIMATE

Venezuela has a tropical climate; the main factor affecting temperatures is altitude. Lowland areas are hot and humid, while at the other extreme, snow permanently covers a few high peaks. Between the two the climate is generally warm and sunny during the day but cold at night. The dry season extends from December to April, and the rainy season from May to November. Average rainfall in parts of the Orinoco delta is four times as heavy as that on the coast.

	Caracas	Maracaibo	Ciudad Bolívar
Average January temperature	65°F (18°C)	81°F (27°C)	79°F (26°C)
Average July temperature	69°F (21°C)	85°F (29°C)	81°F (27°C)
Average annual precipitation	32 in (81 cm)	23 in (58 cm)	41 in (104 cm)

Americans produced mixed-race mestizos. Black slaves were imported in the seventeenth century to work on coastal cacao and sugar plantations.

By the end of the eighteenth century, Creoles, frustrated by trading restrictions imposed by the Spaniards, spurred the

A scene from a painting by Martín Tovar y Tovar in the Capitol building in Caracas depicts Simón Bolívar's defeat of the Spaniards at the Battle of Carabobo in 1821.

movement toward independence. In 1810 they deposed the king's representative in Venezuela, replacing him with a council to run the colony's affairs. The Spaniards fought back, and it was not until the Battle of Carabobo in June 1821 that the Creoles, brilliantly led by Simón Bolívar, achieved full independence. Bolívar also led Ecuador and Colombia to independence and, as he desired, the three regions, together with Panama, formed the new Republic of Gran Colombia. In 1829 Venezuela withdrew from Gran Colombia and became an independent republic the following year.

Rivalry between Conservatives and Liberals dominated most of the nineteenth century in Venezuela. Conservatives stood for the old order, with power in the hands of wealthy landowners, while the Liberals wanted change and social reform.

Black slaves imported	Creoles in Caracas depose Spanish king's representative and set up a council to run colony	Creoles defeat Spanish at Battle of Carabobo. Formation of Gran Colombia	Venezuela withdraws from Gran Colombia
1600s	**1810**	**1821**	**1829**

Simón Bolívar

Simón Bolívar helped five South American countries gain independence. Born into a wealthy Creole family in Caracas on July 24, 1783, he was an orphan before he was six years old. He was brought up by an uncle and tutors, one of whom, Simón Rodriquez, influenced the young man with his liberal ideas. Bolívar completed his education in Europe and married in 1801. Tragically, his wife died less than a year later, an event that made him turn to politics as a young man. Greatly affected by European revolutionary ideas, he resolved to fight for independence for Latin America. "I will not rest," he said, "not in body or soul, until I have broken the chains of Spain."

He was a good speaker and soldier who commanded great loyalty from his army. It was a long and bloody campaign to which he devoted his life. He died in 1830, only forty-seven years old.

Simón Bolívar, painted by an unknown artist, probably in 1825 when he was about forty-two years old.

Oil Booms and Busts

In 1920 oil was discovered, and foreign companies invested in the industry. By 1928 Venezuela was the world's leading exporter of oil. Revenue from the oil paid for improving roads, railways, and many public buildings. A few people became very wealthy, while the majority of Venezuelans continued to live in abject poverty. In the late 1950s Rómulo Betancourt was the first president to use oil profits to help the ordinary people.

The 1970s were boom years in Venezuela, when the world oil price was at its peak, and Carlos Andrés Perez (president from 1974 to 1978) nationalized the oil and iron industries. By the 1980s things were very different. Venezuela's economy was badly affected by a world glut of oil and a drop in its world price. Soaring inflation and price rises led to three days of riots in most cities. The military were brought in to restore order, and many people were killed.

The 1990s, too, were difficult years for Venezuela. The economy did not improve, poverty increased, and there were protests and strikes. In 1992 two attempted military coups failed, and in 1993 President Perez was suspended from office on corruption charges. In 1994 Rafael Caldera, who had been president from 1969 to 1974, was re-elected at the age of seventy-eight. So far he has been unable to resolve his country's economic problems.

Oil discovered near Lake Maracaibo	Social reform program introduced	Carlos Andrés Perez president	Recession in oil industry	Rafael Caldera elected president for second time
1920	**1958**	**1974–1978**	**1980s**	**1994**

Living in Venezuela

About 65 percent of Venezuelans are mestizos, mixed-race descendants of Spanish settlers and Native Americans. One-fifth of Venezuelans are of European descent. Approximately 8 percent are blacks descended from African slaves and mulattos of mixed African and Spanish

A child of the Piarora tribe, who live in the upper Orinoco region. Many Native Americans still make necklaces and other decorations from seeds found in the forest.

parentage. Small scattered groups of Native Americans make up about 7 percent of the population. They include the Yanomami, Guahibo, and Maquiritare in the south; the Barí (Motilones) in the Andes near the border with Colombia; the Guajiro on the coast north of Maracaibo; and the Warao in the Orinoco delta.

Few immigrants arrived in Venezuela until just before World War II, when thousands of intellectuals, politicians, and scholars fled from Europe. A second wave followed in the 1950s, when the prospect of work and good salaries in the oil industry attracted nearly a half million people from Spain, Italy, Portugal, and eastern Europe. An unknown number of recent immigrants, many of them illegal, have also arrived from other South American countries and Caribbean islands, looking for work.

The distribution of the population in Venezuela is very uneven. About 85 percent of the people live in cities, most of which are in the Venezuelan highlands and the Maracaibo basin. Only a tiny percentage of people live in the llanos and the Guiana highlands, which together take up over two-thirds of the country.

At the beginning of the century, Venezuela was a backward, agricultural nation. The amazing turnaround from agricultural to urban nation in just a few decades is entirely due to the discovery of oil and the revenue the industry has generated.

The boom years of the oil industry have also been accompanied by an increase in the birth rate. Today Venezuela is a young nation, with two-thirds of the population under thirty years old, and almost 40 percent less than fourteen years old.

Almost everyone in Venezuela speaks Spanish, though immigrant languages such as Italian and German are also used. Many Native American groups have their own languages, which are mostly of the Carib, Arawak, and Chibcha linguistic families.

Education is free and compulsory for all children aged seven to fifteen, and about three-quarters of pupils go to state-run schools. Since the 1950s many new schools have been built in towns and rural areas, though those in remote regions are often no more than a one-room wooden hut.

The Venezuelan Constitution allows for freedom of religion. Venezuela is officially a Roman Catholic country, with 80 percent of the people baptized in that faith, but in practice, only about a quarter of the people attend church regularly. There are small numbers of Protestants, Jews, Muslims, and followers of African religions.

Mestizos live in all parts of Venezuela. In the Venezuelan highlands most live in urban areas or work on large commercial farms producing sugarcane, bananas, cacao, cotton, and other crops. Whites tend to stick to the big cities, where many have executive jobs and an affluent lifestyle. Most blacks and mulattos have stayed on the coast, working in the ports, in small fishing villages, or in mountain villages where they have small farms and cultivate cacao.

Venezuela has a rigid class system, which has its roots in the colonial agricultural economy. It is difficult for people to move socially upward into a higher class. A

People celebrate a special Easter mass in a Caracas church. Although people are free to practice any religion they choose, most Venezuelans are Roman Catholic.

The Cult of Maria Lionza

According to legend, a beautiful Indian girl disappeared into the forest, never to be seen again. She returned as a spirit, living in a golden palace with her servants and riding a tapir, a large, gentle, forest mammal sacred to the Native Americans. She is called Maria Lionza, and her many followers associate her with their own Native American, African, and Catholic beliefs. She is perceived as the goddess of the natural world, its animals, and its mineral wealth. Venezuelans of all classes, but especially the poor from the cities, worship her. In special ceremonies, priests invoking her name use mediums to contact spirits to cure illness and cast off evil spirits. The religion extends to many parts of Venezuela, and in 1968 a society called the Aboriginal Cult of Maria Lionza was formed to bring the different groups of worshipers together.

middle class developed with the end of Venezuela's agricultural economy and the migration to towns. Now Venezuela has a large middle class working either in the professions and commerce or at a lower level in construction and manual jobs.

These children attend a dancing school in Puerto Cabello, Venezuela's second busiest port. The town still has cobbled streets and small colonial-style houses.

Caraqueños: People of Caracas

Caraqueños (kah-rah-CANE-yoess) are the people of Caracas. While all cities and towns were affected by the sudden influx of oil wealth, nowhere was the effect so dramatic as in Caracas. Gone is virtually every trace of the old city, except for a small colonial area with the Congress building and the Cathedral. Situated in a valley, Caracas is now a "vertical" city, as the only place to build is upward. Everywhere are glitzy, glassy, steel and concrete skyscrapers. Modern highways and overpasses, cutting through the apartment and office tower blocks, can barely cope

---

Miss Venezuela

The first week of September each year, Caracas comes to a halt as everyone forgets work, problems, and other pleasures to follow the Miss Venezuela contest on television. Though the issue of judging women primarily on how they look is often a feminist issue in other countries, Venezuelans have no such argument. Beauty in Caracas is big business, and Venezuelans are among the world's highest spenders on personal care products. It is a world center for cosmetics and renowned for its plastic surgeons.

Venezuela has many "Misses" competitions; among others there is a Miss Army, Air Force, Navy, Tourism, Granny, and Feet. The Miss Venezuela pageant has been running for forty years, and in that time Venezuela has produced four Miss Worlds, three Miss Universes, and lots of Miss Internationals. The winners are assured of a good future, a move into high society, and wealth. Some are aspiring actresses and pop singers. Most famous is Irene Saez, a former Miss Universe, twice-elected, highly successful mayor of the richest district of Caracas and picked by many as a future president of Venezuela.

---

with the influx of traffic. About a million vehicles daily belch out black smoke and clog the streets. The city has a serious pollution problem.

The population of Caracas today is about four million, four times greater than that of 1955. Every day, more people come into the city, many of them poor Latin

A subway entrance on Plaza Venezuela in the heart of Caracas. The subway is the best way of getting around the city. It is clean, fast, and efficient, though sometimes crowded.

Americans, who are content to take on jobs Venezuelans prefer not do. They work as taxi drivers, domestic servants, and in the construction industry. Venezuelans arriving from rural areas are generally unskilled but may get jobs in the many factories in Caracas that produce processed foods, leather and hides, glass, chemicals, and pharmaceuticals. Otherwise they try to make a living as street traders.

Land in Caracas is very expensive, and only the very wealthy live in the heart of the city. Rich people live in affluent residential suburbs and, further out, the middle class dwell in housing estates. The poor and the new arrivals live in crowded *ranchos* (RAHN-choess), or shanty houses, that cover the sides of the valley. They are solid, if simple, dwellings made of cement or brick, and many have water, electricity, and sewerage systems.

Culturally Caracas could be North America, with its fast-food chains, latest popular music and films, designer clothes, and huge stores and shopping centers. Baseball, not soccer as in most of South America, is the number one sport.

Andean Peoples

The Andean ranges close to the Colombian border are the coldest and highest mountains in Venezuela. The largest city, Mérida, has a backdrop of several magnificent peaks. The city is connected to one of the peaks by the world's highest cable car. Mérida is an old colonial city, with a tranquil atmosphere. It is also a university city, and more than a quarter of

German Pioneers

The mountain village of Colonia Tovar is only 18 miles (29 kilometers) west of Caracas, but for over one hundred years German settlers lived there in almost total isolation. They arrived in 1843, a group of over 350 from Germany's Black Forest, at a time when Venezuela needed immigrants. Thousands of people had died in the Wars of Independence, which, together with the abolition of slavery, left the colony underpopulated and short of workers. The Germans were carefully selected to include farmers and artisans. They were to settle on land donated by the wealthy Creole Tovar family in a beautiful part of the Venezuelan highlands.

The pioneers got off to a bad start when forty died at sea from smallpox. The news preceded them, and they received a cold welcome in Venezuela. They made the journey into the highlands on foot, carrying their farming tools, animal fodder, and barley seeds that would make beer. They expected more Germans to join them, but no one came. The Venezuelans forbade them to marry outside their community, and each time they wanted to leave it, they had to get signed permission.

Their response was to isolate themselves from the outside world. The community included a priest, tailor, teacher, carpenter, printer, blacksmith, and farmers, and it could be totally self-sufficient. The Germans created a village like those they had left in Europe, married among themselves, and spoke their own German dialect. In time the Venezuelans forgot about them.

And so they would have stayed, perhaps, if an enterprising German family, recognizing the tourist potential, had not built a hotel in the 1930s. By the 1960s the village was very popular with tourists from Caracas. Today thousands of tourists descend on Colonia Tovar every weekend. The village has kept its rustic appearance, with red-tiled houses whitewashed and crisscrossed by black wooden beams. There are many craft shops and stalls selling cuckoo clocks, German sausages, rye bread, strawberries, and locally made beer, and restaurants where blonde, blue-eyed waitresses serve typical German meals.

Inevitably, the village is changing. Spanish is replacing German as the first language; old traditions such as the German carnival have given way to salsa and pop; crime, once unheard of in the community, is on the increase, and people are marrying outsiders. Perhaps most seriously, many of the younger generation are choosing to move away to start new lives in Caracas.

In the Venezuelan highlands people live by growing crops and keeping animals. At higher altitudes life is difficult because the soil is poor and there is little pasture for cattle.

of fruit including oranges and mangoes. But now farmers also grow mustard and flowers such as orchids, dahlias, and carnations, which they sell throughout the country.

Old villages and houses in the mountains are built of adobe (sun-dried mud) bricks with red tile roofs. Many have verandahs covered in brightly colored flowers. Newer houses are usually one story tall, in brick and cement with corrugated iron roofs. These rural homes are simple, but most have electricity and a water supply.

One of the Andean ranges, the Sierra de Perijá, which straddles the border of Venezuela and Colombia, is the home of the Barí, or Motilones, Indians. The tribe

the population, some thirty thousand students, attend the University of the Andes (*Universidad de los Andes*) which is the largest and oldest in Venezuela.

The highest inhabitable level in the mountains is the *páramo* (PAH-rah-moe), a cold, wet, and windy region where life is hard. Not much grows on the páramo. To keep warm, people wrap themselves in woolen *ruanas* (roo-AH-nahss), or ponchos.

Lower down the mountains, between about 2,600 and 4,300 feet (800 and 1300 meters), people farm in the valleys and on the slopes. Most of the farms are small and worked by family members, including the children. The land is very stony, and the people fence off their plots with walls made of stones collected from the fields. On the sloping hillsides they use ox-drawn plows and do much of the planting and harvesting by hand. Traditional crops are potatoes, wheat, onions, carrots, garlic, and a variety

Children play in an Andean mountain village. They are with their grandfathers, who, like many older people, wear the traditional ponchos and hats of the region.

569

Venezuelan Food

The most widely eaten dish in Venezuela is pabellón criollo *(pah-bay-YONE cree-OY-yoe), made of shredded meat with onions and green pepper, beans, rice, and fried plantains.*

Arepas (ah-RAY-pahss), small flat pancakes of fried or baked corn or corn-flour dough, are a staple in the Venezuelan diet. They can be filled with a variety of ingredients, including shredded beef, cheese, avocados, tuna, and beans. Poor people eat several each day. There are also areperas *(ah-ray-PAY-rahss), restaurants that specialize in arepas.*

Huallacas (why-YAH-kahss) are corn pancakes filled with chicken, beef, pork, onion, garlic, olives, raisins, tomatoes, green pepper, capers, and sugar and spiced with cumin, parsley, and black peppers. They are wrapped in plantain leaves, which are not to be eaten, and boiled. Huallacas are made entirely of local ingredients but take a long time to prepare; they are mostly eaten at Christmas.

Venezuela has plenty of fish, fruit, and beef. Sea fish include red snapper and shellfish. Rivers in the Andes teem with trout. A huge variety of fruit ranges from the better-known papaya and mango to the less well known mamones *(mah-MOE-nayss), small, round, green fruits that produce a delicate juice. Beef comes mainly from the llanos grasslands.*

belongs to the Chibcha-speaking language group and once was widespread in both countries (see COLOMBIA). Now just a few hundred are left.

Maracuchos: People of the Maracaibo Lowlands

The Maracaibo lowlands are in the northwest corner of Venezuela. This is where Venezuelan oil was first discovered, and Lake Maracaibo, the largest lake in South America, is now covered with a forest of oil rigs. The city of Maracaibo, the oil capital, stands at the opening to the

Often children have to work to help provide money for the family. This young boy from Coro on the hot Caribbean coast is selling iced drinks.

sea. Where once small colonial settlements stood on the shores, there are now large, industrial oil towns like Ciudad Ojeda.

Before oil was discovered, Maracaibo was an important trading center for coffee from the lowlands and in the 1800s did much business with Dutch islands in the Caribbean. A few houses in Maracaibo still reflect Dutch influence, with tall windows and doors painted in contrasting bright colors with decorated facades. Most have given way to hotels and tall office blocks occupied by oil company executives.

Despite its modernization, Maracaibo still feels like a Wild West town, and *Maracuchos* (mah-rah-KOO-choess), as local residents are called, are a tough breed. They need to be. Many men are oil workers or cowboys on large cattle ranches in the lowlands. Women in the countryside raise animals and crops, while urban women sell from market stalls or work in offices or as domestic servants. It is an excessively hot part of the country, where temperatures seldom drop below 85°F (29°C), with very high humidity and virtually no wind. City workers take the heat seriously by starting the day early and taking a long siesta in the afternoon.

It was on the edge of Lake Maracaibo that early explorers saw the houses built on stilts by the Native Americans that led them to name the land "Little Venice." The same style of houses are still used by the Paraujanos (pah-rao-HAH-noess) people

Many poorer Venezuelans have to make a living as best they can. These two men work as shoemakers on the back patio of their home in Maracaibo.

who live in the Sinamaica Lagoon north of the city of Maracaibo. Known as *palafitos* (pah-lah-FEE-toess), the single-room houses today are built on concrete piles and made of reed mats lashed together. They have thatched roofs, and the Paraujanos (meaning "water" or "boat people") move from one house to another by boat. The Paraujanos are an Arawak

571

people, who now speak Spanish. They live primarily by fishing but also blend in with the mestizo way of life and can often be seen in the city markets.

North of Maracaibo: The Guajiros

Guajiros (gwah-HEE-roess) live on the hot, dry, scrubby Guajira Peninsula north of Maracaibo. They are part of a large Native American group of maybe fifty thousand people that extends across the border into Colombia (see COLOMBIA). Seminomadic and fiercely independent, they refuse to be either Colombian or Venezuelan. They still speak their own language and teach their children the Spanish language as a foreign one. For them, the frontier created by the Colombian and Venezuelan authorities is nonexistent, and they wander across it at

Guajiro Indians at the market in Los Filudos, north of Maracaibo. Here, they trade clothing, pots, and pans, as well as livestock, hides, and meat.

will with their sheep and goats, despite the attempts of the local police to stop them.

On the peninsula they build temporary houses, though sometimes they settle if they find a good supply of water. Women do most of the work, tending the animals, spinning, and weaving. To protect themselves against the harsh sun, they paint their faces with a mixture of fat and charcoal and wear colorful, tent-shaped, ankle-length dresses called *mantas* (MAHN-tahss) and slippers with large pompoms.

Near Maracaibo is a weekly Guajiro market where they buy and sell household goods, food, cattle, hides, medicinal herbs, and hand-rolled cigars. Other goods include ceramics, bags, shawls, and hammocks, which they weave in bright colors. The men make belts and saddlebags.

Some Guajiros have moved into Maracaibo, married mestizos, and gotten work in the city or in the oil industry. Although they adopt a mestizo way of life,

they still think of themselves as Guajiros. Some even choose to return to their traditional way of life.

Llaneros: Cowboys of the Grasslands

The vast grasslands, or llanos, of central Venezuela cover about a third of the country and are crisscrossed by dozens of tributaries of the Orinoco River. Very few people live there, but the plains are home to some five million head of cattle. There are two seasons in the llanos. Either the land is like a desert, with only tiny water holes for the abundant wildlife, or it is flooded and impossible to cross.

Most of Venezuela's millions of cattle are herded on the llanos, the vast grasslands that extend across the center of the country.

The original inhabitants were Native Americans, whose first contact with Europeans was with Spanish missionaries. Settlers followed and introduced cattle onto the plains. The cattle were herded by cowboys known as *llaneros* (yah-NAY-roess), who, during the eighteenth and nineteenth centuries, became romantic figures, admired both for their lonely, arduous lifestyle and for their tough, fighting spirit. Descendants of mixed marriages between Spaniards, escaped black slaves, and Native Americans, they formed the bulk of Simón Bolívar's victorious army.

Small numbers of true llaneros work on large ranches in the llanos today. Their classic dress is a straw hat, wooden stirrups, and ponchos. When the grasslands are under water, the llaneros drive the cattle into mountain foothills or through floods to mesas, small plateaus. In the dry season, when the savannah grass is impossible for the cattle to eat, they herd the animals toward wetter regions near the rivers and into grassy valleys of the Venezuela highlands to fatten them.

The Warao of the Orinoco Delta

The Orinoco River divides the llanos from the Guiana highlands. The Warao (wah-RAOW), or Guaraunos, live in the Orinoco delta, one of the largest in the world. The delta is a region of forests and mangrove swamps formed into islands. Orinoco in the Warao language means "father of our land." About fifteen thousand Warao live in the lower delta, an area that is often flooded. They are dependent on their canoes to move around the delta canals where they fish. They also clear patches of forest on the islands and cultivate a few crops. Children learn to swim and use canoes at an early age. The children's dugouts are about six and one-half feet (two meters) long, but adults use much larger craft carved from tree trunks that can carry forty to fifty people. They use forest woods to make handicrafts, including intricately carved models of birds, fish, and other animals that they sell to tourists

People of Guiana

The Guiana region takes in all of Venezuela south of the Orinoco, including the Federal Territory of Amazonas, and covers over half the country. In recent years an industrial complex known as Santo Tomé de (or Ciudad) Guiana has been developed upstream from the Orinoco delta, which has attracted workers from other parts of the country. But even today only 5 percent of the total population lives in this vast region. Most are Native Americans. The most prominent groups are the Yanomami, or Waika, who live on the border with Brazil

---

Gaitas

Gaitas (GUY-tahss) are improvised, rhymed verses that are now associated with Christmas throughout the country. They were heard first in a suburb of Maracaibo and used to begin on December 13, the Saint's Day of Santa Lucia, patron saint of stone pavers. Now gaitas begin much earlier, on October 15, the day of "getting down the furrucos." Maracuchos use furrucos (foo-ROO-koess) and charrascas (chah-RAHS-kahss) with cuatros (KWAH-troess) and maracas to accompany gaitas. Furrucos are drums with poles attached that, when strummed, make a deep noise; charrascas are metal scrapers played with a rod, and cuatros are small, four-stringed guitars. The season of gaitas finishes in early February when the furrucos are put away.

The origin of the gaita is uncertain. It may have arrived with Spanish priests or come from local folklore. Nor is anyone sure whether the first gaitas were religious, political, or used for propaganda. Early gaitas were certainly political, but today, as gaitas are heard most around Christmastime, themes are often religious, with frequent references to popular saints.

The Moriche Palm

The moriche (moe-REE-chay) palm, which grows on some of the islands in the Orinoco delta, is an indispensable part of Warao life. They use the trunks as pillars on which to build their homes. Other palms are used for the flooring and to provide thatch for the roof, which reaches almost to the ground. The moriche provides the Warao with a flour for making bread, grubs which they eat, and seeds which they prepare with sweet honey as a special dish. They also make a form of wine from the palm, and they turn its sap into a drink called majobo (mah-HOE-boe).

The Warao also make attractive, decorated baskets from the moriche, dyeing the fibers with extracts of nuts and seeds and the bark of various trees.

Some Warao Indians have moved into towns and wear Western-style clothing. In Tucupita in the Orinoco delta, this Warao woman is making baskets of moriche palm.

Children from Santo Tomé de Guiana, the industrial complex around the Orinoco River. Many people have moved from other parts of Venezuela to live and work there.

(see BRAZIL); the Guahibo in the Amazon territory and the upper tributaries of the Orinoco (see COLOMBIA); the Maquiritare, or Yecuana; the Piarora in the Amazon territory; the Panare; and the Pemon.

Basic to the Native American way of life are the forest and the rivers. In the forests they clear small patches of land where they grow cassava, plantains, and bananas. There, they hunt for game with bows and arrows and gather nuts, seeds, and plants with medicinal properties. From the forest they also get wood and palm thatch to make their houses and wood for their canoes. The Piarora people are well known for their thirty-foot (nine-meter) high, conical, palm-thatched houses, and the

Makiritare for their canoes, which can be fifty feet (fifteen meters) long and made from a single hollowed-out tree trunk. They use special hardwoods to make bows, cane and reed for baskets, feathers for arrows, and feathers, seeds, and beads to make necklaces, amulets, and other ornaments.

All the tribes fish in the rivers using bows and arrows, nets, lines and traps, or a poison to stun the fish. Most tribes have a shaman who, with the use of hallucinatory drugs from the forest, makes contact with gods and spirits and relieves sickness. Native Americans have their own languages and rituals that include initiation ceremonies for young boys and girls when they are ready for adulthood.

Most Native Americans have had some contact with Europeans and wear some form of western garment, usually T-shirts or shorts. They often continue to wear strings of beads and still paint their bodies. Only a few, like the Yanomami in the remotest areas, still live a truly traditional life, naked except for feathers and bone decorations.

For many years missionaries have been living among the tribes, learning their languages. Some people believe they are destroying Native culture in the process, and certainly one of the first things they do is to persuade the Native peoples to wear clothes.

The Lost World

The Gran Sabana is part of the Guiana highlands. It is a land of waterfalls and flat-topped rocky outcrops called tepuís *(tay-poo-EESS), which means "mountains" in the Pemon language. Among the tepuís is Mount Roraima, a mysterious mountain often covered in mist, which many believe is the land of ancient dinosaurs described by Sir Arthur Conan Doyle in his famous novel,* The Lost World.

Many men have been lured to the Gran Sabana in the search for gold, but few were as persistent as the North American bush pilot Jimmy Angel. On his fifth journey in 1937, he was forced to land his single-engine plane on the rocky top of Auyán Tepuí. Beneath him, cascading down the perpendicular rock for hundreds of feet, was a massive waterfall. Fortunately, Angel and his party found another way down Tepuí. Now known as the Angel Falls, it is the world's longest waterfall, with a drop of 2,648 feet (807 meters).

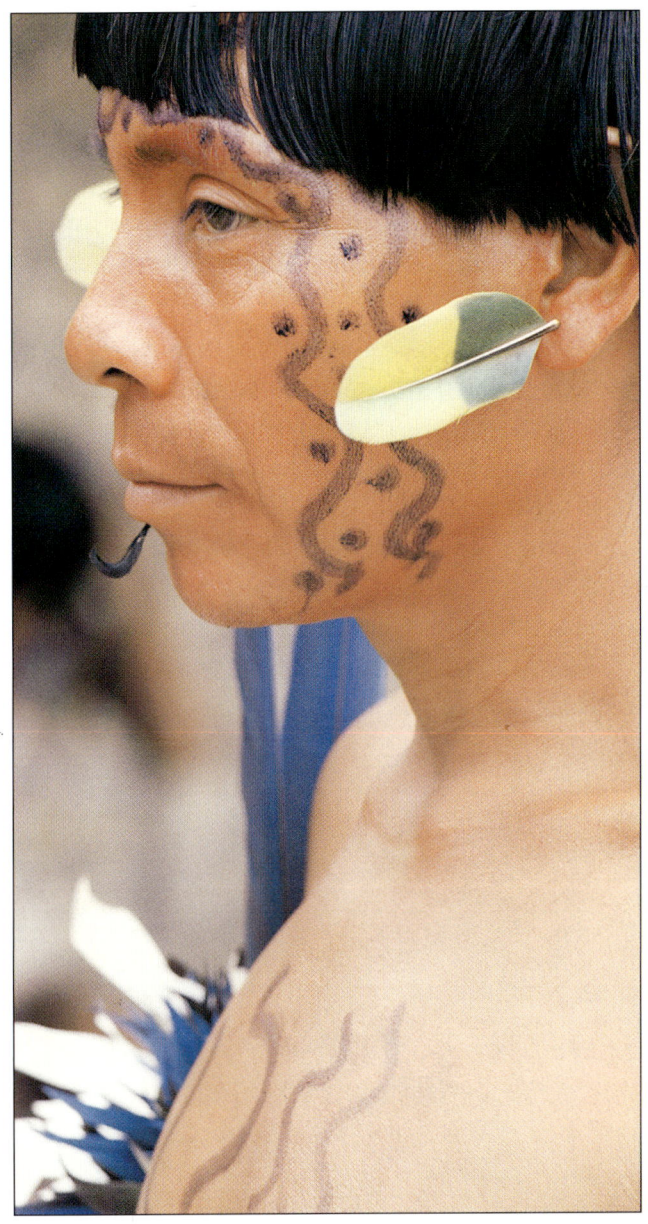

A Yanomami Indian, whose home is on the border with Brazil. His face is painted with the blue-black dye of the genipa plant; the feathers are from a macaw.

On the whole the Venezuelan tribes have been more fortunate than many in South America because governments there have not carried out large-scale development or massive clearance of the forest. However, settlers and speculators, who want land for farming and trees for the timber industry, still invade the territory, and along the southern border, the Yanomami and Guahibo are threatened by gold miners from Colombia and Brazil.

Fiestas and Music

Venezuela's traditional music and dance survive in fiestas held throughout the country. The wide range of instruments reflects the country's mixed heritage and includes Spanish guitars, the four-stringed cuatro, harps, African drums, and Native American flutes. The *joropo* (hoe-ROE-poe), a dance for couples, is the national dance but with variations from region to region. For fiestas, men often don the traditional *liqui-liqui* (LEE-key LEE-key), an outfit consisting of a white cotton shirt, trousers, and boots; women wear colorful skirts with off-the-shoulder embroidered blouses.

Many festivals in Venezuela are religious, celebrating Christmas, Easter, or the patron saint of a village or town. One of the most colorful is on Corpus Christi Day in June in the village of San Francisco de Yare, near Caracas. Dancers representing the devil dress in bright red costumes from head to toe, topped with horned masks. The serious part of the celebrations is the mass held in the local church, but afterward, everyone dances, eats, drinks, and has a good time.

Carnival is Caracas's largest fiesta, held in February or March at the beginning of Lent. The central feature is a large parade with spectacular floats and costumes, bands, and dancers.

One of the most important religious festivals in Venezuela is Corpus Christi. In the village of Chuao in the state of Aragua, revelers dance to the music of drums and maracas.

People of African descent carry a Christian altar through the streets during a festival in Caracas. Elements of African cultures and Catholic beliefs remain in some festivals.

For the mulattos and blacks, the Festival of Saint John in the third week of June is one of the most important. To the sound of African drums, they "baptize" his statue in the sea or river.

A fiesta that characterizes the ethnic mix of Venezuela is held in the Maracaibo region at the end of December and honors Saint Benedict. The festival is essentially African in origin, but mestizos and the Paraujanos also pay homage to the black saint. The Paraujanos sail through the Sinamaica lagoon with his image on their boats, the mestizos dance in the street carrying the saint, while the families of African origin from along the shore of the lake bring out their traditional drums to support the processions.

Venezuelan Artists

The two best-known Venezuelan painters and sculptors of the twentieth century are Jesús Soto (born 1923) and Alejandro Otero (1921–1996). Both have created kinetic art forms, or moving sculpture.

Soto has his own museum, and examples of Otero's work stand in parks and outdoor places in Venezuela. These include the dramatic Abra Solar in Caracas.

Carlos Raúl Villanueva (1900–1975) was Venezuela's foremost architect, and among his many achievements in Caracas were the El Silencio low-cost housing project completed in 1943 and the University City, built in the 1960s.

VIRGIN ISLANDS (UK)

THIRTY-SIX SMALL ISLANDS MAKE UP THE BRITISH VIRGIN ISLANDS.
They lie alongside the American Virgin Islands in the
Leeward group, part of the Lesser Antilles.

*The British Virgin Island chain
includes volcanic rocks and
coral reefs and fifteen inhabited
islands, set around the Sir
Francis Drake Channel. The
largest islands are Tortola (the
site of the capital, Road Town),
Virgin Gorda, Anegada, and
Jost Van Dyke.*

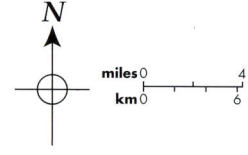

*The islands include long, sandy
beaches with palm trees and
steep climbs inland through
forest and grass. The hills
rise to 1,780 feet (543 meters)
above sea level at the highest
point, Mount Sage, on Tortola.*

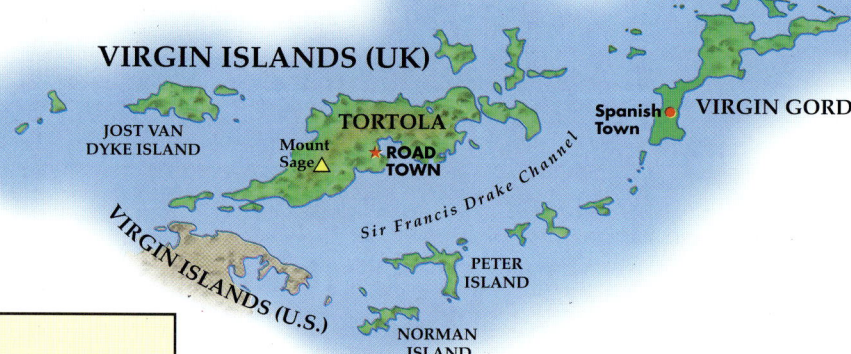

CLIMATE

*The British Virgin Islands have a warm, tropical
climate but are freshened by sea breezes.*

Average January temperature: *76°F (24°C)*

Average July temperature: *83°F (28°C)*

Average annual precipitation: *50 in (127 cm)*

Pirates and Pleasure Boats

The first Virgin Islanders were Arawak-
speakers, Native American hunters and
farmers who entered the Caribbean over
two thousand years ago. They were driven
out by Carib tribes in the 1400s, and the
Caribs were themselves killed by the
Spanish in the mid-sixteenth century.

In the 1600s pirates hid out in these
tropical bays, raiding the fleets of ships
that carried looted treasure from the New
World back to Spain. The first pirates to
settle here were Dutch, but they were
driven out by English pirates and
smugglers in 1672. In the end, Great
Britain brought the Virgin Islands under its
direct rule as a full colony in 1774.

Sugarcane and cotton were planted and
slaves of western African origin brought in
to work the plantations. Slavery was
abolished in 1838. The freed slaves became
small farmers. Most of the European
plantation owners moved elsewhere.

Between 1867 and 1956 the islands were governed as part of the Leeward Islands group, but they then returned to being a separate colony. In the years that followed, rule from Great Britain became largely ceremonial, with the islanders' legislative council making the important decisions. Tourism became the chief source of income and remains so today.

The people of the British Virgin Islands (BVI) are mostly of Afro-Caribbean origin, although the tourist industry has brought in a number of Americans and Europeans. Over half the population lives on Tortola, the busiest of the islands. Their way of life is influenced greatly by their Caribbean neighbors to the east and by their links with Great Britain. They play cricket and celebrate carnival in summer with parades and dancing. However, the currency is the U.S. dollar, and American influence from the neighboring U.S. Virgin Islands is growing fast.

FACTS AND FIGURES

Official name: British Virgin Islands

Status: British dependent territory

Capital: Road Town

Area: 59 square miles (153 square kilometers)

Population: 18,000

Population density: 305 per square mile (118 per square kilometer)

Peoples: 75 percent Afro-Caribbean or mixed Afro-Caribbean-European descent; 25 percent European descent

Official language: English

Currency: U.S. dollar

National day: BVI Territory Day (July 1)

Country's name: From the Spanish Las Virgines, meaning "the Virgins," named by Columbus in honor of Saint Ursula and her eleven hundred companions. Saint Ursula's Day is celebrated on October 21.

A clothing store displays items outside to attract tourists in Road Town on Tortola. Tourism is the mainstay of the islands' economy.

Many islanders are employed in the tourist industry, working in hotels, restaurants, boatyards, and yachting marinas. Other islanders still work as small farmers, raising cattle, sheep, poultry, and goats or supplying the local markets with fruits and vegetables. Some work as fishermen. Traditional cooking includes local prawns and conch, spinach soup, coconut flavoring, and pork, chicken and goat meat.

The islanders are mostly Christian, with Methodist, Church of God, Anglican, Seventh-Day Adventist, Baptist, and Roman Catholic represented among the island's churches.

Timeline:	Islands settled by Arawaks	Arawaks driven out by Caribs	Caribs wiped out by Spanish	Islands become an official British colony	Slavery abolished	Islands given increased independence
	ca. 1 B.C.E.	1400s C.E.	1555	1774	1838	1977

VIRGIN ISLANDS (U.S.)

THE AMERICAN VIRGIN ISLANDS LIE ON THE NORTHEAST EDGE OF THE CARIBBEAN SEA, about forty miles (sixty-four kilometers) east of Puerto Rico.

The islands are rocky or sandy, with green hills. The coasts have fine sandy beaches, fringed by groves of coconut and tangled mangrove swamps. Offshore coral reefs teem with marine life.

There are three main islands. The largest is Saint Croix, with an area of 84 square miles (218 square kilometers). It lies in the south of the island group. The capital, Charlotte Amalie, is on the northern island of Saint Thomas, with the island of Saint John to the east, across Pillsbury Sound. Most of the fifty other small islands are too small to support settlements.

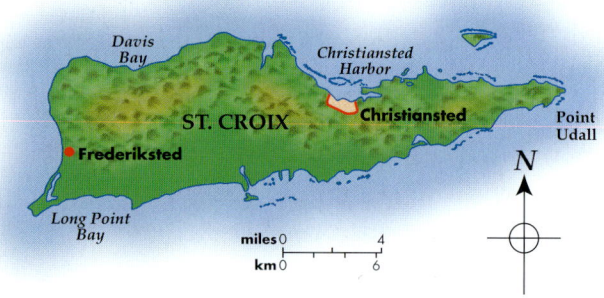

CLIMATE

The U.S. Virgin Islands have a warm climate with a low humidity. Most rain falls during tropical storms in late summer.

Average January temperature: *82°F (28°C)*

Average July temperature: *88°F (31°C)*

Average annual precipitation: *45 in (114 cm)*

An American Paradise

Like other islands in this part of the Caribbean, the American Virgin Islands were first occupied by Arawak-speakers. These came under attack from another Native American people, the Caribs, about six hundred years ago.

Spanish ships under Christopher Columbus reached the islands in 1494.

There was soon a running war between the Spanish, who had settled Puerto Rico to the west, and the Caribs. Most of the Caribs were killed during the 1500s.

The first European settlers included Dutch and English pirates and smugglers. The French settled and claimed Saint Croix, but from the 1660s onward, it was the

FACTS AND FIGURES

Official name: *Virgin Islands of the United States*

Status: *United States dependency*

Capital: *Charlotte Amalie*

Area: *133 square miles (344 square kilometers)*

Population: *107,000*

Population density: *805 per square mile (310 per square kilometer)*

Peoples: *40 percent Afro-Caribbean originally from other islands; 25 percent Afro-Caribbean Virgin Islander; 20 percent Puerto Rican; 10 percent people from the mainland United States; 5 percent European descent*

Official language: *English*

Currency: *U.S. dollar*

National days: *Emancipation Day (July 3); U.S. Independence Day (July 4)*

Country's name: *From the Spanish* Las Virgines, *meaning "the Virgins," named by Columbus in honor of Saint Ursula and her eleven hundred companions. Saint Ursula's Day is celebrated on October 21.*

Caribbean through the Anegada Passage, bound for the Panama Canal. The islanders became full citizens of the United States in 1927 and, from 1970 onward, could choose their governor in direct elections.

Only about 25 percent of the population were born on the island, and these are mostly of Afro-Caribbean descent. Another 40 percent are Afro-Caribbeans from other islands, but there are also minorities of European descent (including some Danes), as well as many Americans and, on Saint Croix, Spanish-speaking Puerto Ricans.

The local population is completely outnumbered by the tourists who pour into the islands from the mainland United States each year. The goods on sale in smart shopping malls are paid for in U.S. dollars, and people play pool and eat hamburgers. Some street names, however, are still in Danish, and attractive architecture in stone and clapboard with red roofs dates back to the days of the Danish colony. The Caribbean atmosphere comes from the warm climate, the local rum, and the sounds of reggae or calypso music. Traditional Caribbean food includes snapper, lobster, conch, curried chicken, and goat stew.

Tourist developments and hotels cover the two main islands. Tourism is the biggest industry by far, employing many people.

Danes who chiefly settled the islands, and they ended up ruling them. They planted sugarcane and imported slaves to work on the plantations. The slaves were given their freedom in 1848.

In 1917 the United States bought the islands from Denmark for use as a naval base. The base was in an ideal position to control Atlantic shipping entering the

This U.S. Virgin islander has the dreadlocks first worn by Jamaican Rastafarians and now seen in many parts of the Caribbean.

Timeline:	Islands settled by Caribs	Caribs destroyed by Spanish	Danes settle Saint Thomas	Slavery abolished	Islands purchased by the United States	Hurricane Hugo leaves 22,500 homeless
	1400s C.E.	1555	1665	1848	1917	1989

Glossary

abject: in a bad way or miserable condition; showing utter hopelessness.

abstract expressionism: a style of painting that occurred primarily between World War II and the 1960s in which objects are not painted realistically.

agribusiness: farming organized as a large-scale business operation.

Anglo-American: a person from the United States whose language and ancestry are English.

bioregion: an area that is defined by similar life forms such as plants, animals, and birds.

clapboard: overlapping wood planking nailed on exterior walls of buildings to protect against the weather.

coup: a change of government brought about by force.

cricket: a bat and ball game played by two teams of eleven players each. It was first played in England and has spread to many parts of the world, including the Caribbean.

depose: to remove a person from office.

desegregation: the act of opening schools, businesses, and housing to people from all races and ethnic backgrounds.

elective: involving a choice; optional.

facade: the face or front of a building.

fasting: eating very little or not eating certain foods, especially for religious reasons.

fodder: food for domestic animals.

gasworks: an industrial plant where coal is heated to release gas.

hilarity: great merriment and fun.

homage: the act of paying respect or allegiance, sometimes with money or gifts.

initiation: admitting someone to a society, usually with some sort of ritual ceremony.

labor-intensive: requiring a large amount of physical labor.

mandatory: not optional; required.

nationalization: making an industry the property of a nation or state.

neoclassic: a term used to describe a movement in architecture in which buildings are based upon the styles of the monuments and temples of ancient Greece.

overt: open and observable by everyone; not concealed or secret.

pagan: a word used to describe the belief in or worship of more than one god; sometimes used to describe a person without a religion.

poncho: a garment made from a square or rectangular piece of cloth with a slit for the head.

propaganda: ideas or information deliberately spread to influence the thoughts of others.

pulpwood: soft wood, such as spruce, aspen, or pine, used in making paper.

raffia: the leaf fibers from an African palm tree, used to make mats and other woven products.

Rastafarian: a member of a religious movement called Rastafarianism, which started in Jamaica in the 1930s. Rastafarians believe that Africa is the promised land and that they are one of the biblical lost tribes of Israel.

segregation: the separation of people of different races or ethnic heritages in schools, businesses, and housing.

shaman: a Siberian word for priest, healer, or holy person. The word now refers to a religious healer or diviner in various cultures.

sniper: someone who shoots at other people from a hiding place.

social reform: to change and improve institutions, for example, education and health facilities, for the benefit of the people.

welfare state: a country that provides government help and finance for people who are poor, sick, elderly, retired from work, or unemployed.

Further Reading

United States of America

Anderson, Marcie. *Exploring the Fifty States.* Saint Petersburg, FL: Willowisp Press, 1994.

Baines, John D. *The United States.* Chatham, NJ: Raintree/Steck-Vaughn, 1993.

Bock, Judy, and Rachel Kranz. *Scholastic Encyclopedia of the United States.* New York: Scholastic, Inc., 1997.

Department of Geography Staff. *United States in Pictures.* Minneapolis, MN: Lerner Group, 1995.

Krone, Chester. *United States of America.* Chatham, NJ: Raintree/Steck-Vaughn, 1990.

Leuzzi, Linda. *Urban Life.* Broomall, PA: Chelsea House, 1995.

Marquardt, Arthur H. *The New Americans.* Notre Dame, IN: Cross Cultural Publications, 1994.

Morrow, Robert. *Immigration: Blessing or Burden?* Minneapolis, MN: Lerner Group, 1997.

Shapiro, William E., ed. *The Kingfisher Young People's Encyclopedia of the United States.* London: Kingfisher Books, 1994.

Stein, R. Conrad. *The United States of America.* Danbury, CT: Childrens Press, 1994.

Uruguay

Department of Geography Staff. *Uruguay in Pictures.* Minneapolis, MN: Lerner Group, 1994.

Morrison, Marion. *Uruguay.* Danbury, CT: Childrens Press, 1992.

Venezuela

Fox, Geoffrey. *The Land and People of Venezuela.* Scranton, PA: HarperCollins Juvenile Books, 1991.

Heinrichs, Ann. *Venezuela.* Danbury, CT: Childrens Press, 1997.

Morrison, Marion. *Venezuela.* Danbury, CT: Childrens Press, 1989.

Winter, Jane Kohen. *Cultures of the World: Venezuela.* Tarrytown, NY: Marshall Cavendish, 1994.

Virgin Islands (UK)

Luntta, Karl. *Virgin Islands Handbook.* Chico, CA: Moon Publications, 1997.

Virgin Islands (U.S.)

Aylesworth, Thomas G., and Virginia L. Aylesworth. *Territories and Possessions: Puerto Rico, U.S. Virgin Islands, Guam, American Samoa, Wake, Midway and Other Islands, Micronesia.* Broomall, PA: Chelsea House, 1995.

Islands of the Caribbean

Mason, Antony. *The Caribbean.* Parsippany, NJ: Silver Burdett Press, 1988.

Mayer, T. W. *The Caribbean and Its People.* New York: Thomson Learning, 1995.

Springer, Eintou P. *The Caribbean.* Parsippany, NJ: Silver Burdett Press, 1987.

Walker, Cas. *The Caribbean.* North Pomfret, VT: Trafalgar Square Publishing, 1991.

Index

Page numbers in *italic* indicate illustrations.

Page numbers in *italic* indicate illustrations.

REFERENCE

PEOPLES
of the
AMERICAS

PEOPLES
of the
AMERICAS

Volume 9
United States of America

MARSHALL CAVENDISH
NEW YORK • LONDON • TORONTO • SYDNEY

Marshall Cavendish Corporation
99 White Plains Road
Tarrytown, New York 10591-9001

Consulting Editor: J. Patrick Gray, Professor of Anthropology, University of Wisconsin

Consultants: Jean-Marc Blais, Senior Interpretive Planner, Canadian Museum of Civilization, Hull, Quebec
   David Frye, Assistant Director, Department of Latin American and Caribbean Studies, University of Michigan

Spanish Consultant: Fran Kaplan

Contributing authors: D. L. Birchfield
   Marion Morrison
   Juliette Radcliffe Rogers
   Philip Steele
   Mary A. Stout

Discovery Books
   Managing Editor: Paul Humphrey
   Project Editor: Helen Dwyer
   Text Editor: Valerie J. Weber
   Design Concept: Ian Winton
   Designers: Barry Dwyer, Ian Winton, and Simon Borrough
   Cartographer: Stefan Chabluk

Marshall Cavendish
   Editorial Director: Paul Bernabeo
   Editor: Marian Armstrong
   Associate Editor: Debra M. Jacobs

The publishers would like to thank the following for their permission to reproduce photographs:
Bruce Coleman Collection (John Cancalosi 485, 522; Jules Cowan 483, 484; Jeff Foott 482); Corbis (477; Morton Beebe 471; Richard A. Cooke 481; Kevin Fleming 521, cover; Raymond Gehman 486; Hulton Deutsch 474; Library of Congress 497, 498, 504, 506, 507, 509, 510, 512, 513; Museum of History and Industry 496; The National Archives 499; Richard T. Nowitz 479; Lee Snider 491, 492; UPI/Corbis-Bettmann 515; Patrick Ward 516; Nik Wheeler 508; Michael S. Yamashita 517); Getty Images (519; Mark Harris 523; Andy Sacks 518; Penny Tweedie frontispiece; David Young Wolff 478); Robert Harding (500); Hutchison Library (Melanie Friend 503); Peter Newark (472, 475, 476, 488, 489, 490, 493, 494, 502, 505, 511); David Simson (495, 501, 514); South American Pictures (Charlotte Lipson 520)

(frontispiece) A man sells garlic and pumpkins in a market stall in New Orleans, Louisiana.

Editor's note: Many systems of dating have been used by different cultures throughout history. *Peoples of the Americas* uses B.C.E. (Before Common Era) and C.E. (Common Era) instead of B.C. (Before Christ) and A.D. (Anno Domini, "In the Year of the Lord") out of respect for the diversity of the world's peoples.

Library of Congress Cataloging-in-Publication Data
Peoples of the Americas.
   p.   cm.
   Includes bibliographical references and index.
   Contents: v. 1. Anguilla–Belize — v. 2. Bermuda–Brazil — v. 3. Canada–Cayman Islands — v. 4. Chile–Costa Rica — v. 5. Cuba–French Guiana — v. 6. Greenland–Jamaica — v. 7. Martinique–Paraguay — v. 8. Peru–Turks and Caicos Islands — v. 9. United States of America — v. 10. United States of America–Virgin Islands

   ISBN 0-7614-7050-6 (set)
   1. Ethnology—America—Juvenile literature. 2. America—History—Juvenile literature. [1. Ethnology—America. 2. America—History.]
E29.A1P46 1999
970'.004—dc21

98-2801
CIP
AC

   ISBN 0-7614-7050-6 (set)
   ISBN 0-7614-7059-X (vol. 9)

Printed and bound in Italy

Contents

UNITED STATES OF AMERICA

THE UNITED STATES OF AMERICA IS THE FOURTH LARGEST
COUNTRY IN THE WORLD.

The United States stretches from the cold of the Arctic Circle to the subtropics of the Florida Keys, from temperate rain forests of the Northwest to the deserts of the Southwest. It includes flat prairies and some of the world's highest mountains, 12,383 miles (19,928 kilometers) of coastline, some of the world's largest freshwater lakes, and one of its longest rivers. Among its fifty states are the Hawaiian Islands, in the Pacific Ocean, over 2,000 miles (3,200 kilometers) off the coast of California.

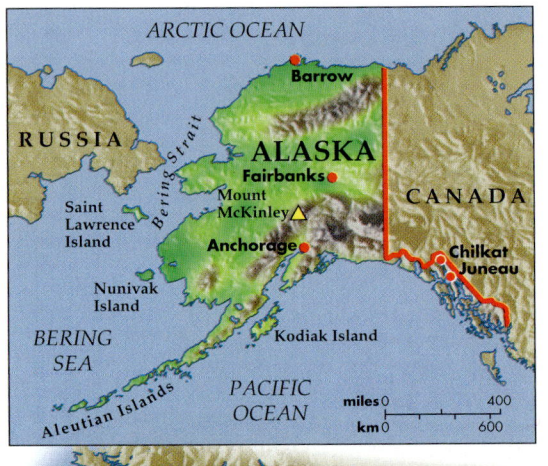

470

Land of Immigrants

The United States is unique in its growth and development. No other country in the world has been populated by so many immigrants from so many different places. United States residents come from almost every country on the globe and represent nearly all ethnic groups. The United States has symbolized hope and a second chance for millions of people from other countries. As a nation, it has achieved a place of importance in the world and is considered a world leader, yet it counts its origins among the poorest, humblest, most despised peoples of the world who made their way to its shores.

New citizens attend a naturalization ceremony in Seattle. The United States is a land of immigrants, and people continue to arrive, seeking a new life in the country.

FACTS AND FIGURES

Status: *Independent state*

Capital: *Washington, D.C.*

Major cities: *New York, Los Angeles, Chicago, San Francisco, Philadelphia, Boston, Detroit, Dallas-Fort Worth, Houston, Miami, Atlanta, Minneapolis-Saint Paul, San Diego, Saint Louis*

Area: *3,787,319 square miles (9,809,156 square kilometers)*

Population: *267,700,000*

Population density: *71 per square mile (27 per square kilometer)*

Peoples: *74 percent European American; 12 percent African American; 10 percent Hispanic; 3 percent Asian, Arab, and Pacific Islander; 1 percent American Indian, Inuit (also known as Eskimo), and Aleut*

Official language: *None, although English is the most common language*

Currency: *U.S. dollar*

National days: *Birthday of Martin Luther King Jr. (third Monday in January); President's Day (third Monday in February); Memorial or Decoration Day (last Monday in May); Independence Day (July 4); Labor Day (first Monday in September); Columbus Day (second Monday in October); Veterans or Armistice Day (November 11); Thanksgiving Day (fourth Thursday in November)*

The country's name: *America is named after Amerigo Vespucci, an Italian navigator and explorer of the South American coast. United States of America came into official use in the Declaration of Independence (1776) and described the union of the thirteen original British colonies into an independent federated republic.*

Timeline:	Clovis culture widespread in North America	Anasazi, Mogollon, and Hohokam cultures of the Southwest collapse	Christopher Columbus reaches the Caribbean Sea	Spanish establish Saint Augustine, Florida
	9000 B.C.E.	**1276–1299 C.E.**	**1492**	**1565**

The First Colonies

The entire North American continent was already occupied by over five hundred different nations of Native peoples for many centuries when the British established their first settlement in 1607. European exploration and "discovery" of North America, however, began almost a century earlier. Ponce de León, a Spanish explorer following in Columbus's footsteps, landed in Florida first in 1513 and later in 1521, when he was driven away by Native Americans. Another Spaniard, Hernando de Soto, entered Florida in 1538, intent on conquest. He spent years crossing the continent in search of gold; his followers finally reached Mexico in 1543. In 1565 the Spanish Jesuits established a small colony in Saint Augustine, Florida, but abandoned it five years later. Sir Walter Raleigh attempted to establish the first British colony on Roanoke Island, North Carolina, which disappeared by 1590. Meanwhile, French fur traders and trappers were gaining a foothold in Canada and the northern United States.

In 1607 John Smith established the first successful British colony at Jamestown, Virginia. Others followed rapidly, and soon individual British colonies dotted the east coast of what is now the United States, joined by a couple of Dutch colonies and a Swedish colony. The colonies, desperate for workers, welcomed people from all nations, although most remained primarily British in origin. When the plantation economy began to take hold in the southern colonies, there were not enough laborers to work on large tobacco and cotton estates. This led the colonists to bring in black slaves from western Africa to work on the plantations.

New York City (then called New Amsterdam) was just a little town on the Hudson River when this picture was painted in the 1650s.

English settle Jamestown, Virginia	First African slaves arrive in Virginia	Pilgrims found Plymouth Colony, Massachusetts	France cedes all territory east of the Mississippi to Great Britain	Start of American Revolution
1607	1619	1620	1763	1775

CLIMATE

The United States has great extremes of climate, depending on the region's latitude, altitude, and distance from the sea.

	New York, New York	Barrow, Alaska	Miami, Florida	Phoenix, Arizona	Honolulu, Hawaii
Average January temperature	32°F (0°C)	–13°F (–25°C)	67°F (19°C)	54°F (12°C)	80°F (27°C)
Average July temperature	77°F (25°C)	39°F (4°C)	83°F (28°C)	94°F (34°C)	88°F (31°C)
Average annual precipitation	43 in (109 cm)	5 in (13 cm)	58 in (147 cm)	7 in (18 cm)	23 in (58 cm)

A Nation Is Born

In 1776 the colonies, each governed separately by a governor sent from Britain, sought to establish themselves as a separate country to avoid the heavy taxes imposed by Britain and to control their own affairs. After joining together to send a Declaration of Independence to Britain's King George, the colonists fought and won the Revolutionary War against the British. They established the new country of the United States of America and created a means of self-government outlined in the Constitution of the United States. But they also inherited the problems that the British had in dealing with their own citizens, who were brutally taking anything that they wanted from the Native population. The Native Americans, pushed ever farther west by the colonists, could do little except retaliate occasionally against the overwhelming number of new people entering the country.

Before 1800 the vast majority of the immigrants were from Great Britain, but they included some Germans, Dutch, and Scandinavians as well. No laws governed immigration to the United States at this time; the country had an open-door policy. And just by being first, the British laid many of the country's foundations; the English language and British law and customs became established as the official "American" way of life.

The Country Grows

Between 1800 and 1881 most people entering the United States came from northwestern European countries. Changing economies, the Napoleonic Wars, soaring birthrates, and famines prompted millions of Irish and Germans to come to the United States. By now the United States had an established economy and still had land available for people, as well as jobs. The Louisiana Purchase of 1803 from France opened up millions of acres for settlement. The United States, which had originally adopted a policy of pushing the Native Americans west of the Alleghenies,

Continental Congress adopts the Declaration of Independence and names the country *United States*	Continental Congress adopts the Articles of Confederation	Britain recognizes the independence of the United States	U.S. Constitution drawn up
1776	**1777**	**1783**	**1787**

reserving the East Coast for themselves, now began to push entire tribes to areas west of the Mississippi River. The settlers rapidly moved into these new lands as well and forced out the resident tribes.

The United States finally stretched to the Pacific Ocean with the annexation of Texas in 1845, the Mexican cession of 1848, the Gadsden Purchase of 1854, and the Alaska Purchase of 1867. The Texans, both Mexican and American, battled General Antonio López de Santa Anna of Mexico in order to establish their own independent state of Texas, later joining the United States. The United States fought Mexico for the southwestern states gained in 1848 and purchased more territory in the Southwest a few years later. Conflict with

Texas's last president, Anson Jones, declares the end of the Republic of Texas. The former Mexican province joined the United States as the twenty-eighth state.

Canada resulted in the 1846 Oregon Compromise, which divided the Northwest territories between the two countries. The 1867 purchase of Alaska from the Russians completed the United States' acquisition of territory on the North American continent.

The discovery of gold in California in 1848 prompted more people to move west. Immigrants now completely overran the territories occupied by Native Americans, so the government set aside little-desired tracts of land—the reservations—and assigned these few pitiful acres to the Native Americans.

First session of the U.S. Congress	United States purchases Louisiana Territory from France	Indian Removal Act forces most eastern Native American tribes west to Oklahoma	Thousands of settlers move west on the Oregon Trail	California gold rush begins
1789	**1803**	**1830**	**1843**	**1848**

Second Thoughts on Immigration

The Civil War (1861–1865) caused a slump in immigration. After the war millions more immigrants came to the United States, but this time they were mostly from southern and eastern Europe. Arriving in huge numbers, these new immigrants were often met with discrimination. They were visibly different from the Anglo-American majority and spoke different languages. And they competed for jobs. The established citizens began, for the first time, to think that immigration into the United States should be limited somehow.

In 1882 the United States passed the first law restricting immigration. No paupers, convicts, and physically or mentally defective persons were allowed to enter the country, and all incoming immigrants were required to pay a tax of fifty cents. This law was followed by others in the late nineteenth century and first quarter of the twentieth century. In 1924 Congress passed the Johnson-Reed Act, which established quotas based upon each country of origin. The number of immigrants to be allowed in from each country was based upon existing ethnic populations in the United States. This highly restrictive system thus favored immigrants from northern Europe over those from southern Europe.

The end of World War I saw the United States move onto the world stage as an important international power. The country flourished and was the center of many new inventions: the airplane, the mass-produced automobile, the mass-produced camera, radio, ready-to-wear clothing, and many other technologies.

The country continued to become more urban. People left the farms that they had spent the nineteenth century carving out of

By 1880, when this cartoon was published, immigration had pushed the United States' population up to fifty million. Two years later the first act restricting immigration was passed.

Civil War begins	Civil War ends; Eighteenth Amendment to the U.S. Constitution abolishes slavery	United States purchases Alaska from Russia	Dawes Allotment Act forces Indian tribes to allot their land in small parcels to tribal members and sell the remainder to American settlers
1861	**1865**	**1867**	**1887**

the wilderness and, in the twentieth century, moved into the cities, where there were more job opportunities.

The Great Depression of the 1930s brought massive unemployment and a momentary halt in the rush of immigration to the United States. Following the Depression, World War II created another boom in the United States' economy. Immigration was now controlled, but the Displaced Persons Acts passed by Congress allowed for the entry of refugees and persons whose lives had been disrupted by the war. In one of the country's most shameful incidents, 110,000 Japanese Americans were confined in internment camps after Japan bombed Pearl Harbor, Hawaii, in 1941.

World War II also accelerated a great migration within the United States that had

Ellis Island: The Immigrant Experience

In 1892 Ellis Island replaced Castle Garden, New York, as the port of entry for all immigrants arriving in the United States. Millions of immigrants shared the experience of being processed through Ellis Island. From 1892 to 1943 it is estimated that seventeen million immigrants landed at Ellis Island. All passed through the great Registry Room, where their names were recorded. On some days over ten thousand people would go through in a single twenty-four-hour period, meeting rushed and impatient immigration officials. About 40 percent of all Americans can trace their ancestry to someone who entered the United States through Ellis Island.

Immigrants from Europe are examined by nurses on Ellis Island before being allowed to enter New York City in this photograph from the early 1900s.

Hawaii is made a U.S. territory	U.S. Supreme Court rules that Congress has full power to do whatever it wants in Native American affairs	United States enters World War I. The Jones Act gives all Puerto Ricans the right to U.S. citizenship
1900	**1905**	**1917**

Migration and Discrimination

A house in an African American ghetto in Chicago, 1941. In the 1940s thousands of African American farmers moved to the big cities, looking for work in factories.

As people immigrated to the United States over the years, great tension always developed between the various ethnic groups. The newest immigrants were often hated; established groups resented them for accepting even less money for some of the lowest-paying jobs, and for their differences in language, dress, and culture. Whatever their social status in their homeland, they tended to be at the bottom of the economic and social ladder when they arrived in the United States. In time an ethnic group would learn the customs of the United States and work hard to move out of their original low status. Often it seemed that the better an ethnic group could "fit into" the Anglo-American culture, the more quickly they would prosper. Also, a new ethnic immigrant group would always come along and move into the position of the lower-class laborers, thus bumping up the previous immigrant group's status. This pattern repeated itself over and over again.

In postwar America, however, clear discrimination still existed against some ethnic groups in terms of hiring, housing, schooling, and social interaction. This type

started some years before. African Americans, lured by jobs in the newly created defense industries, left sharecropping (farming on rented land) in the South in order to move north and work in the factories. They congregated in Chicago, Philadelphia, New York, Detroit, Los Angeles, and many other cities. Like other new immigrants, they clustered in ghettos, partly to live near people they knew in a strange place and partly from economic necessity—they couldn't afford to live anywhere else. In the 1940s about 1.5 million African Americans left the South.

Congress passes Indian Citizenship Act, making all Native Americans citizens	Japan bombs Pearl Harbor, Hawaii; United States enters World War II	The Bracero Program encourages Mexicans to come to the U.S. to work as agricultural laborers	World War II ends
1924	1941	1942–1964	1945

of racism was primarily directed at African Americans and Latinos. Their resentment at this unequal treatment, and the rising awareness of most Americans about the inequalities between people, led to the civil rights movement of the 1960s. Eventually, Congress passed legislation that insured that no one could be treated differently because of their ethnic background. The long process to desegregate all the schools, businesses, and services that had previously been "white only" then began.

The 1970s saw the arrival of legal immigrants from Southeast Asia after the Vietnam War. From the 1980s onward, illegal immigration, especially from Latin America and the Caribbean, has been a great problem for the immigration authorities.

Change is happening in the United States. There is a growing appreciation for cultural diversity. In the early centuries of immigration, immigrants eagerly learned a new language, new dress, and new customs in order to fit in with the majority culture.

A young Chinese American celebrates Chinese New Year in Los Angeles. Like other immigrant groups, Chinese Americans are proud of their heritage.

United States enters the Korean War	Racial segregation prohibited in U.S. public schools	Alaska and Hawaii become the forty-ninth and fiftieth states	United States severs diplomatic relations with Cuba	United States enters the Vietnam War
1950	**1954**	**1959**	**1961**	**1964**

Jewish boys at a morning service in a synagogue. Jews and many other peoples have emigrated to the United States to be free to practice their religion.

Often they were quick to discard their former culture for a new one. Ethnic customs, languages, and background were suppressed.

Now one can sense a new pride in ethnic heritage. People in the United States are eager to find out about their roots and participate in cultural events that celebrate their unique heritage. They are more interested in what makes them different from other Americans, rather than what makes them the same. The whole country is recognizing the enormous cultural diversity that exists within its boundaries and is celebrating its multiethnic roots.

First People in North America

In 1926 American archaeologist Dr. J. D. Figgins found spear points, delicately crafted and made from stone, mixed in with animal bones in northeastern New Mexico. They were buried deep under the ground in a layer of earth about ten thousand years ago. The discovery came to be known as evidence of the Folsom culture. Soon after, similar finds were made at other sites. The truth became clear. People had been living and hunting in North America for at least ten thousand years, more than twice as long as the scientific community had previously thought.

Not long after the discovery of the Folsom culture, an even older human culture, called Clovis, was unearthed in the 1930s. At a place called Blackwater Draw, near Clovis, New Mexico, more stone spear points were found. They were not as finely crafted as the Folsom spear points, but there was enough similarity to see that Folsom points had probably developed from the earlier Clovis points.

Excavations in nearly every state soon uncovered either Clovis or Folsom spear points in layers of earth eight thousand to eleven thousand years old.

Today, scientists are busy looking in even older layers of earth. Nobody knows when a new discovery will be made that might push the clock back even further.

The widespread distribution of Clovis and Folsom points tells us that humans were in contact with one another all across the land. The nearly identical shape of their spear points, finely and delicately crafted with unnecessary artistry, tells us that their culture was fairly similar over great geographical distances. This is in sharp contrast to the great diversity among Native peoples that Europeans would find in North America thousands of years later.

American Indian Movement occupies Wounded Knee, South Dakota; Withdrawal of U.S. troops from Vietnam	New wave of Cuban refugees embarks for United States	NAFTA Treaty, a trade agreement between the United States, Canada, and Mexico, goes into effect
1973	**1980**	**1994**

Staying in One Area: New Cultures Emerge

The end of the last ice age, roughly ten thousand years ago, brought great changes to North America, changes that deeply affected human culture. As glaciers retreated and the climate warmed, plants that had been at a disadvantage during the ice age now found themselves in their element. Trees especially found the new climate ideal for their needs.

Forests began to flourish as a result of the warmer climate, and large species of animals became extinct. Humans had to adapt to hunting other species of game. New hunting methods and weapons had to be invented. Gathering nuts, berries, and other wild crops became more important. The need to store and preserve what had been gathered led to the crafting of basketry and later to the discovery of techniques to make pottery.

The biggest change, however, was that it became easier to survive by remaining in one localized area and learning all of its seasonal resources than by roaming the earth in search of food.

As human populations became more tied to one region, they lost contact with one another. Separated from other people, their languages began a slow process of change that would eventually make them unintelligible to distant people. Separate cultures developed. The end of the ice age produced a continent of rich cultural and linguistic diversity.

The First Mound Builders

By 1000 B.C.E. the Ohio River Valley in the heart of the eastern woodlands had become home to a remarkable culture known as Adena (ah-DEE-nah). The Adena became the first Mound Builders in North America.

The culture flourished for more than one thousand years, until about 200 C.E. During that long period it left many monuments to itself in the form of earthen mounds.

Built one basketful of earth at a time, the Adena mounds give evidence of a highly organized society capable of directing great amounts of labor for a common goal. These accomplishments are all the more remarkable because agriculture, the cultivation of plants to produce crops, had not yet become an important part of life in the eastern woodlands. The Adena might have cultivated a few plants, such as gourds, sunflowers, and pumpkins, but they remained dependent upon hunting wild game and gathering wild plants, nuts, and berries.

Their mounds were of two types—burial mounds and effigy mounds. Burial mounds were often conical or dome-shaped. New burials were placed on top of the older ones and fresh layers of dirt added, the mounds growing ever larger. Effigy mounds were built in the shape of animals and birds. Many of the Adena effigy mounds were destroyed by farming practices and road building when Americans settled the Ohio River Valley.

Hopewell Culture

Also in the Ohio River Valley, another mound-building culture, called Hopewell, began to flourish by about 300 B.C.E. It lasted about one thousand years.

Though the two cultures were very similar, both building large numbers of earthen mounds, there were important differences. While the Adena people were content to stay near their homes in the Ohio River Valley, the Hopewell people spread out across most of the huge Mississippi River Valley. The Hopewell people also established trade routes that left behind objects that had originated from practically every portion of the continent except the far western Pacific coast.

Generally, Hopewell mounds were larger than Adena mounds. Hopewell culture must have also been more highly organized to build such large monuments. The Hopewell culture surpassed the Adena in the variety and complexity of both its

artistic and practical items. The Hopewell people also made much more extensive use of agriculture.

Basket Makers

While mound-building cultures were beginning to flourish in the eastern woodlands, very different cultures were developing in what is now called the American Southwest. This region lacked the abundance of plants and animals to sustain population growth and the development of complex societies. But the region was close enough to the highly advanced civilizations of central Mexico to learn about something very important—the cultivation of corn. Called maize, these early varieties of corn spread to the American Southwest along the trade routes from Mexico.

Great Serpent Mound

The Great Serpent Mound in southern Ohio is one of the most spectacular remaining Adena effigy mounds. A low mound of earth in the form of a snake, it stretches for 1,330 feet (405 meters), is 15 to 20 feet (nearly 5 to 6 meters) wide, and stands about 4 feet (over 1 meter) tall.

Though the mound today is preserved as a historic site, its immediate surroundings along Brushy Creek have been repeatedly threatened by developers who have sought to build lakes and golf courses near the mound. Each time such plans have been proposed, people who want to preserve the mound's surroundings in their natural state have banded together to defeat the projects.

The spectacular Great Serpent Mound of the Adena culture was built more than two thousand years ago. It snakes for over 1,300 feet (over 400 meters) through the Ohio woods.

Known as Basket Makers because of their skill at that craft, these people who adapted agriculture as a way of life were descended from the very small populations who had been able to survive as hunters and gatherers in the area for thousands of years. Agriculture allowed them to settle along the rivers and streams.

They developed a style of house called a pit house, which was sunk into the ground. This eventually evolved into the ceremonial chambers called *kivas* (KEE-vuhs), a characteristic of later cultures in the area.

Archaeologists date the end of the Basket Maker period in this region with the development of pottery. With that change, new cultures would flourish, known as Anasazi, Mogollon, and Hohokam. Eventually, these cultures would develop into the modern-day Pueblo, Pima, and Papago peoples of the region.

A ruined dwelling and underground chamber, or kiva, part of an Anasazi archaeological site at Grand Gulch in Utah. The Anasazi are the ancestors of today's Pueblo people.

Cliff Dwellers

Another part of the Basket Maker story is the beginning of building some villages on the sides of cliffs. People in the region had long made use of caves and overhanging rock ledges for shelter. But the Cliff Dwellers turned this idea into an architectural art form that eventually led to some of the most spectacular constructions on the continent.

The Cliff Dwellers at first merely used stone tools to cut hand and toe holds into rock cliffs to climb to a cave high above or to a high overhanging ledge. Here they found safety from enemies, a safe place to sleep. The cliff dwellings were always within easy walking distance of their cultivated fields of corn along the banks of a nearby stream.

When people of the region developed the craft of stone masonry (building houses with blocks of stone), the Cliff Dwellers began applying the technique to their homes. In time, they refined the practice to an art, building spectacular cliff palaces at numerous locations throughout the Southwest. This art reached its peak during the Anasazi (ah-nuh-SAH-zee) period.

In the Southwest three great cultural traditions reached their peaks and had declined just before Europeans entered the continent. These were the Anasazi, the Mogollon, and the Hohokam.

The magnificant Anasazi cliff dwellings at Mesa Verde in Colorado are over 800 years old. They were built high up the cliff for security.

Mesa Verde

The most spectacular cliff dwellings are located at Mesa Verde (in southwestern Colorado), which is now a national park. There, Cliff Palace, the most spectacular of them all, has more than two hundred rooms and twenty-three kivas. Mesa Verde National Park contains many other cliff dwellings, some of which can be toured under the direction of a park guide. Mesa Verde is an abandoned Anasazi site. Constructed by about 1150, it was abandoned near the end of the fourteenth century. Why the Anasazi abandoned all of their villages within a period of about one hundred years has been one of the great puzzles of American archaeology, but we have a better idea today why this happened.

Anasazi: Ancestors of the Pueblo Peoples

The Anasazi ("Ancient Ones") are a people of great mystery. Developing from earlier Basket Maker peoples, they achieved great feats of social organization, building multistory, stone apartment complexes in the region now known as the Four Corners (where the states of Colorado, Utah, Arizona, and New Mexico meet). The Anasazi (also known as the ancestral Pueblo) also built spectacular cliff dwellings in many of the canyons in the region. Then, over a fairly short period of time, they abandoned all that they had built and moved away. For a long time nobody had any idea why they had left. Scientists now believe they know why the Anasazi left, but other mysteries about them remain.

The development of a technique called dendrochronology (tree-ring dating) has provided much information about the Anasazi. From this technique, scientists now know that the great achievements of Anasazi culture, which reached its height about 1150, occurred during a long period of relatively abundant rainfall in the Southwest. Then came a great drought that lasted from 1276 to 1299. It seems likely

Anasazi wall paintings, or petroglyphs, from Newspaper Rock State Park in Utah. The secrets of the Anasazi remain a mystery to this day.

that the prolonged, intense drought made it impossible for the the Anasazi people to maintain their way of life.

If the Anasazi abandonment of their homeland seems less of a mystery today, hardly any of the other mysteries about them have been solved. One of the most puzzling of those mysteries was not discovered until airplanes were invented. Nobody suspected that the Anasazi built elaborate networks of roads and irrigation channels in the Southwest until airplanes flew over their homeland. The old structures had drifted over with dust so that people on the ground did not notice them. But they were easy to see from an airplane.

The remarkable thing about these roads is that all of them follow precise, straight lines for mile after mile. They do not

detour around any barrier in their path but go straight over it, regardless of whether it might be a steep hillside or a deep canyon. The great network radiates out like spokes on a wheel from the main center of Anasazi life, Chaco Canyon, in northwestern New Mexico. The roads lead to many outlying Anasazi towns. Nobody has ever been able to figure out why the Anasazi built roads in such straight lines. They had no wheeled vehicles.

Perhaps, someday, the discovery of some new scientific technique will help solve some of the puzzles of Anasazi culture, like the development of dendrochronology has helped us to understand why they abandoned their homeland.

Mogollon: Makers of Mimbres

At the same time the Anasazi culture was flourishing, another great cultural group called the Mogollon was at its height. The Mogollon (moe-guh-YONE) people lived in the area that is now southwestern New Mexico and southeastern Arizona. They are considered the finest pottery makers of ancient North America, for a style of pottery called Mimbres (MIHM-bris).

Unlike the Anasazi, the Mogollon lived in mountain valleys, surrounded by well-timbered slopes with sparkling mountain streams. But like the Anasazi, they abandoned their homeland at about the time of the great drought at the end of the thirteenth century.

This beautifully decorated Mimbres bowl from New Mexico shows two intertwining insects. It was made by a member of the Mogollon culture that flourished eight hundred years ago.

Hohokam: Irrigation Engineers

The Hohokam (huh-HOE-kuhm) were true desert dwellers, living in the area where the city of Phoenix, Arizona, now stands. They were among the greatest engineers of antiquity. Their specialty was building elaborate canal irrigation systems, diverting water from rivers to turn the desert into productive cropland.

Many of their old canals were cleaned out and put back into use by the American settlers in the region in the middle of the nineteenth century. Recently, excavations have revealed that the Hohokam were deeply influenced by Mexican culture, especially regarding ball games. Many Mexican-style ball courts have been found throughout their old homeland.

The Hohokam were at the height of their culture at the same time that the Anasazi and the Mogollon cultures reached their peaks. And like the Anasazi and the Mogollon, the Hohokam also abandoned their achievements during the great drought.

Mississippian or Temple Mound Culture

Halfway back across the continent from the desert Southwest, another great mound-building culture was flourishing in the eastern woodlands of the Mississippi River Valley at the same time that the Anasazi, Mogollon, and Hohokam cultures were at their peaks. Called Mississippian, or Temple Mound culture, the people worked hard building earth mounds much larger than the earlier Adena and Hopewell Mound Builders. These mounds had large buildings on the top of them. They are believed to have been used for ceremonial purposes and to have been the homes of priests who ruled the towns.

Agriculture allowed the Mississippian peoples to produce enough food so they could live together in large towns of dense populations. One of those towns, Cahokia, was the home of more than ten thousand people, making it the largest city north of Mexico at that time. Corn was their main crop, but also very important was a recent import—beans from Mexico. Beans provided protein that had previously been supplied by hunting wild game.

Population density caused the Mississippian people to pay a high price in poor health. Recent studies have discovered that many of them died from diseases caused by poor sanitation and other conditions associated with urban crowding.

Many Mississippian centers of population were still flourishing when the first Europeans entered what is now known as the southeastern United States, during the expedition of Hernando de Soto in

The Great Temple Mound at the Etowah Indian Mounds State Historic Site in Georgia. The burial mounds were built between 1000 and 1500 C.E.

1540. By 1700, however, when the French founded New Orleans, only one Mississippian Temple Mound culture still survived, the Natchez on the lower Mississippi River. In 1731, the French destroyed the Natchez (NATCH-is), selling many of them into slavery in the Caribbean islands and chasing away the remnants of the tribe to live with the Chickasaw.

Cahokia

Cahokia, a Mississippian Temple Mound city in present-day southern Illinois, was built near the Mississippi River, across from present-day Saint Louis, Missouri. It was founded about 600 C.E. and reached its peak about 1200. The city contained more than one hundred mounds. Seventeen of the mounds were located within a high palisade wall made of logs.

The largest mound, now known as Monks Mound, is larger than the Great Pyramid of Egypt. Its base covers an area about the size of thirty football fields, and it stands more than 100 feet (30 meters) tall. Archaeologists have discovered that it was built in fourteen different stages over a period of several hundred years.

Nobody knows why Cahokia was abandoned. People did not leave all at once, but beginning about 1200 people left every year until finally, by about 1350, everyone was gone.

Distribution of Tribes on the Eve of European Contact

When Europeans entered the North American continent at the end of the fifteenth century, they found Native peoples settled in every portion of the land. Some had been in their homes for a long time, others were more recent arrivals. Many of the tribes had migrated over long periods of time.

Of the more recent arrivals, the Cherokee (CHAIR-uh-kee) had migrated to the Southeast from the northeastern homeland of their Iroquoian-speaking kindred nations at some time in the past. The Cherokee adopted the culture and lifestyle of the other southeastern tribes.

In the Southwest the Athabascan-speaking Apache (up-PATCH-ee) and Navajo (NAH-vuh-hoe) were recent arrivals. The Athabascan (ath-uh-BASS-kun) language is one of the most widely distributed in North America, reaching into the far north in Canada and to the Pacific coast in California.

Some Siouan-speaking peoples seem to have been in the process of migrating across the Midwest. It is a large language family consisting of many different tribes, and the travels of its speakers are reflected in pockets of Siouan language tribes, such as the Catawba (kuh-TAW-buh), left behind in the Deep South during some earlier period of migration.

The Muskogean (muss-KOE-gee-un)-speaking peoples of the Southeast, especially the largest tribes, the Creek (CREEK), Choctaw (CHOK-taw), and Chickasaw (CHIK-uh-saw), all tell a migration story of a great journey toward the east, always following the rising sun, until they had arrived in their homelands in the Southeast. The Shawnee (shaw-NEE) of the Ohio River Valley are known to have had a special relationship with the Creek in the Southeast, at intervals going to live among the Creek for long periods of time. Kiowa (KI-uh-wuh) oral tradition tells of moving to the southern Great Plains (Oklahoma, Texas, New Mexico) from the area of the Black Hills (South Dakota) and before that from the Rocky Mountains in the Montana region.

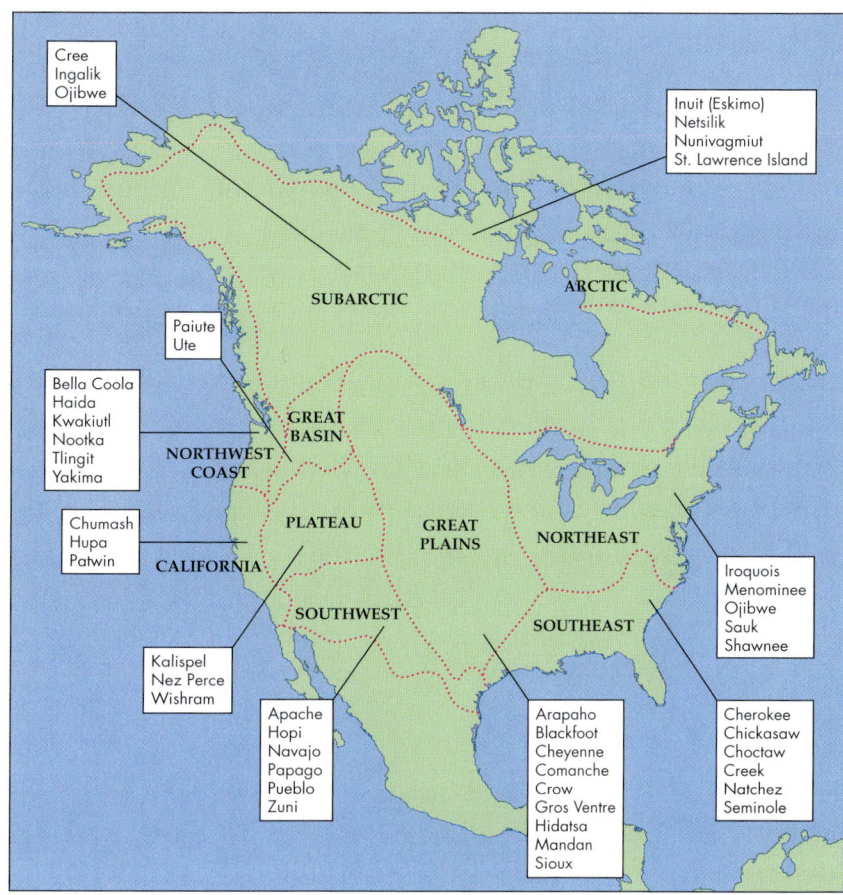

This map shows the main Native American cultures and their major tribes at the end of the fifteenth century, when the first Europeans arrived in the Americas.

Some of the migrations, such as the Kiowa, probably occurred not long after Europeans entered the continent. Some, such as the Apache and Navajo, probably occurred at about the same time that Europeans were first entering the continent. And some, such as the Cherokee, probably occurred in the distant past. Most tribes, however, had been in their historic homeland long enough by the time Europeans arrived to have lost the memory of ever having lived anywhere else.

Colonization and Conquest of North America

In 1492 Christopher Columbus sailed into the Caribbean Sea while attempting to reach China. His voyage was preceded by a long line of sea explorations by Europeans trying to open faster trade routes with the Orient. Henry the Navigator of Portugal had made great strides in this regard by sailing down the coast of Africa to find a faster way to get to India. When Spain financed Columbus's voyage, it was attempting to catch up with its bitter rival—Portugal.

Columbus set an ominous precedent for Native Americans when he returned to Spain with five hundred Indian slaves. Spain quickly conquered the islands of the Caribbean Sea, then the Aztecs in Mexico, and the Incas in Peru. It explored and claimed both the American Southeast and the Southwest.

Native American forced labor, called an *encomienda* (en-kome-EE-en-dah), became

In 1513 Juan Ponce de León claimed Florida for Spain. When he returned in 1521 to establish a colony, he met resistance from Florida's Native Americans, as this engraving shows.

the mainstay of the Spanish Empire in the Americas. Spanish settlement fell into a pattern of picking places with large populations of Natives, who provided labor. Natives died in great numbers.

Colonial Era Immigration Before 1800

After Columbus and the Spanish, it wasn't long before other Europeans came to settle in what is now the United States. When settlers first came to North America, there were no rules or laws about who was allowed to come. It was a "new country," and workers were desperately needed. Anyone who could survive the long ocean voyage was eagerly welcomed.

North America was not a desirable place to live for most Europeans in the early days. The people who came to this harsh

and demanding place were usually poor or desperate to get away from religious persecution, famine, or a prison sentence.

These newcomers thought that the Native Americans were inferior to them because their appearance, their languages, their homes, and their communities didn't look like anything the Europeans had ever seen. The Europeans also feared the Natives and tried different strategies for dealing with them: they traded with them, fought with them, and lived with them under European rules. But their main object was always to gain control of Native land.

Since the land was so vast, there was much work to be done and not enough people to do it. Businesses, called charter companies, owned most of the land and were always seeking new immigrants to work or buy that land, thus making a profit. Back in Europe, the charter companies printed and distributed flyers proclaiming the wonders of North America. They gave no warning of the enormous hardships that would face the new settlers.

When advertising didn't draw enough settlers to North America, the charter companies tried using another strategy—indentured servitude. Europeans who had nothing to lose became indentured servants. Their passage to North America was paid for by the company, and they had to work for free for a certain period of time (such as seven years). At the end of that time, they were released and given a sum of money or a small piece of land. This drew more people to the colonies, but labor was still needed.

William Penn, the Quaker who founded Pennsylvania, signs a peace treaty with Native Americans in 1682. The pacifist Quakers tried to maintain good relations with local peoples.

British Immigrants

The British people (English, Welsh, and Scots) were the first to set up large, permanent colonies of people in what would become the United States. Almost half of the earliest British immigrants were either convicted drunks and debtors avoiding prison, or runaway servants. The first U.S. Census, taken in 1790, recorded that over 75 percent of the total non-Native American population were British immigrants. As the first majority group in the colonies, they established the basis of American society. They decided that the common language used for business would be English, and they established laws

Roanoke Colony

The first English settlement in the United States was established by Sir Walter Raleigh on Roanoke Island, North Carolina, in 1585. The conditions were so harsh at Roanoke that the colonists barely survived, and they convinced Sir Richard Grenville, whose ship arrived the following year, to take them back to England. In 1587 Raleigh sent three ships and 117 more people to Roanoke in a second attempt to settle in North America. During that time the first American, Virginia Dare, was born in August 1587 in Roanoke.

John White, leader of the Roanoke colony, sailed back to England for supplies, but when he returned in 1591 all of the colonists, including little Virginia Dare, had vanished without a trace. What happened to all of the people at Roanoke remains a mystery to this day.

based on English common law and property law.

The people of British descent are often referred to as WASPs (White Anglo-Saxon Protestants). They have always represented the most powerful ethnic group in the country, even when they were no longer a majority.

Located on the east coast of Virginia, Jamestown was the first English settlement that survived in North America. It was started in 1607 to earn money for its charter company, which it never did. The people at Jamestown were too busy trying to exist in a strange, new land to engage in profitable trade or to search for gold and silver. In fact, the only reason the British survived in the American colonies is due to the skills they learned from the Native Americans, such as how to grow tobacco, as well as other food crops. In time, tobacco became a profitable cash crop that was sent back to England.

Another well-known settlement was founded in the northeastern United States, in the New England area at Plymouth, Massachusetts. In 1620 members of a religious group called the Puritans arrived from England to start a new colony where they could worship as they wished. They were sponsored by another charter company. Over half their group perished on the voyage to North America. Sixty years later, in 1681, William Penn founded a new colony in what is now Pennsylvania where another group, the Quakers, could settle and worship freely. The early colonists established a strong sense of religious freedom that is reflected in the U.S. Constitution.

British immigrants eventually settled all over the United States as it grew. British immigration peaked in the decade of 1881

A drawing of the colony of Jamestown as it appeared in 1607. Of the 144 colonists that left England to establish Jamestown, only 105 reached the New World.

to 1890, when 800,000 British entered the country. Since then British immigrants have represented only a modest portion of the entire immigration picture.

Today the United States still reflects its British roots. The chief language spoken in the United States is English. The legal and justice systems in the United States are strongly based on English ideas of property law, common law, and a jury formed of one's peers. Although the American system of government is unique, the U.S. Congress borrows much from the British Parliament.

Since the British came first, other non-British immigrants who followed were often treated as outsiders. They were required to speak English, obey the laws, and participate in a government based on the British tradition to be accepted in their new country.

French Immigrants

Most of the French immigrants to the United States during the early years were fur trappers. Fur was a valuable commodity in Europe, which had exhausted its population of fur-bearing animals. Young men came to the animal-rich North American wilderness to take furs, intending to make their fortune and return to France. Few brought their families to the wilderness, but many ended up marrying Native American women and settling in the United States.

During the French and Indian War, when Britain and France fought over who would control North America (1754–1763), there were just fifty-five thousand French and over one million British settlers. After the British won the war, large numbers of French settled in Canada, Saint Louis, and New Orleans. Some of these became instant U.S. citizens after the Louisiana Purchase in 1803.

A French Huguenot church in New Paltz, New York. Thousands of Huguenots (Protestants) fled France in the 1680s to escape persecution by French Catholics.

About fifteen thousand French settlers were Protestants called Huguenots (HYOO-guh-nots), who came to the United States in the 1680s to escape religious mistreatment at home. They settled everywhere along the East Coast, but a group of them stayed in South Carolina and became businessmen when their plans to farm silkworms, olives, and grapes failed. The Huguenots no longer survive as a religious sect in the United States, but many of their descendants are members of Huguenot societies that celebrate their culture and preserve historical data.

French immigrants have provided a rich cultural heritage for the United States. In New Orleans, for example, the French influence dominates in the architecture, food, and even the street names. Elsewhere, good food has always been associated with French cuisine, and many of the most famous chefs in the United States have a French background. Also, many of the philosophers and politicians that inspired the early settlers with ideas of democracy were French. From 1776 to 1777 the French government secretly supplied the American patriots with guns, ammunition, and clothing. The following year France signed formal treaties of commerce and alliance with the United States and became the first country to acknowledge the new nation. The Statue of Liberty, perhaps one of the most important symbols of the United States, was a gift from the people of France.

Spanish Immigrants

Spain was one of the most powerful countries in the world through the sixteenth to eighteenth centuries and one of the first to explore new continents. Although the Spanish founded a small settlement in Florida in 1565, Saint Augustine, it never grew very large and was traded to Great Britain for the return of Havana, Cuba, in 1763. The greatest Spanish influence in the United States can be found in the Southwest. A Spanish settlement was established at Santa Fe, New Mexico, in 1610, although very few Spaniards actually moved there to live.

The Spanish introduced horses, pigs, and cows to the Americas, and these animals became very important to the Native Americans and the new settlers. Horses provided the main form of personal transportation in the United States before the twentieth century, and the other animals became important food sources for the immigrants. Although few Spanish families

emigrated to North America, the Spanish colonized Central and South America. The Spanish influence in the United States came primarily through the emigrants from Latin America. The Spanish language is spoken by over twelve million people in the United States, particularly in the Southwest and in Florida.

Dutch and Swedish Immigrants

In the 1620s the Dutch began a colony called New Netherlands along the Hudson River in what is now New York. The Dutch West India Company also started a little town called New Amsterdam on Manhattan Island. Both towns were created as business centers from which the trade with their South American and Caribbean colonies could be conducted. The Dutch traders wanted to make their fortune in North America and return home, but many ended up staying.

The Swedish immigrants established an early colony in 1638 on the Delaware River, which they called Fort Christina, now Wilmington. The new Swedish colony, established by a commercial company, never grew very large.

A log cabin built by early Swedish settlers at Fort Christina, Delaware. This style of building was widely copied on the frontiers of the new country.

An overseer with a whip stands watch over slaves cutting sugarcane in the American South of the 1850s. At that time, there were over three million slaves in the United States.

In 1655 the Dutch took over the struggling Swedish colony and in 1664 the British absorbed all of the Dutch colonies in a bloodless takeover. The second wave of Dutch immigration to the United States began in the 1800s as a result of the Napoleonic Wars, religious persecution, and economic problems at home. Many of them settled in Michigan to farm.

Unemployment, low wages, and crop failures in Sweden prompted a second wave of immigration in the 1840s, and the Swedish immigrants found homes in Minnesota, Illinois, New York, and Washington. Swedish lumberjacks and farmers cleared and plowed so much land in their new country that it was said their labors affected more acreage than existed in the entire country of Sweden.

Although the Dutch and Swedish settlers initially maintained their native languages and customs, as early settlers they have become well-integrated into mainstream America. Many place-names in New York have a distinctive Dutch flavor, and modern descendants may don traditional clothing and prepare traditional foods on holidays and special occasions.

Africans: The Forced Immigrants

The majority of Africans who came to the United States were unwilling immigrants. The first Africans brought to the colonies in 1619 were sold into slavery by Dutch traders who were on their way to the West Indies.

Some Africans who arrived were indentured servants, like the poor European immigrants, and got their freedom after completing their term of labor. But most were sold into slavery by other African tribes after they had lost a battle or were kidnapped from their homes by European traders. The people who came to the United States were from many different African tribes, but most came from the western coast of Africa.

Once the large plantation system was established in the southern United States, there was even more need for workers. The institution of slavery grew rapidly, like a bad cancer, to satisfy the need for labor. By 1790 there were over 690,000 black slaves and only 59,000 free blacks according to the U.S. Census.

When the Civil War broke out, there were almost four million slaves in the United

A family of former slaves pose outside their sod house in Nebraska around 1870. Most freed slaves leaving the South headed for the northern industrial cities.

immigrants. Laws legitimized this discrimination with segregated schools, transportation, restaurants, and businesses. In spite of this, some African Americans made great progress just as members of other immigrant groups did. They began their own businesses, became educated and entered the professions, and fought with honor in the American armed services.

Prejudice against this ethnic group eventually led to the rise of the civil rights movement of the 1960s. This resulted in the passage of laws and policies that outlawed discrimination against people

States, practically all of them residing in the southern states and counting for 89 percent of the total African American population. Of the nearly half million free African Americans, 45 percent resided in the northern states. After the Civil War many African Americans, now free but destitute, became sharecroppers in the rural south.

By the end of nineteenth century, the United States was changing from a country that depended mainly on farming to one of businesses and factories. As jobs became available in the northern cities, poor rural African Americans migrated to places like New York, Chicago, Saint Louis, and Baltimore in large numbers. There, they competed with new immigrants for unskilled jobs in the factories and lived side by side with them in crowded city tenements, facing the same problems that poverty dealt to all recent arrivals.

In many ways they encountered the same prejudice that all new immigrants experienced. However, the deep-seated prejudice against African Americans lasted longer than that against more recent

The Middle Passage

Africans were transported to the New World aboard slave ships, crossing the Atlantic Ocean to the Caribbean Islands, then onward to the North American mainland. Africans were packed tightly into ships' holds. Locked in chains, unable to turn or stand up, they survived in foul conditions with no fresh air and a little rotten food. Having no immunity to European diseases, many sickened and died on the trip.

While millions of Africans were transported this way to the New World, it is estimated that at least a million died on the way—victims of disease, starvation, beatings, suicide, uprisings against the ship's crew, and death at sea when whole ships were lost.

based upon their race or ethnicity. During this time schools, transportation, and businesses were desegregated, and everyone was supposed to be treated the same under the law. Unfortunately, laws did not end personal acts of discrimination against individuals.

A jazz band playing in New Orleans, the cradle of American jazz. Jazz has produced such legendary performers as Duke Ellington, Louis Armstrong, Ella Fitzgerald, and Charlie Parker.

Jazz

Jazz is a uniquely American contribution to the world of music. Although many people throughout the world play jazz and have made it their own, this style of music was largely created and nurtured in the African American community. It all began in the late 1800s, when a form of jazz known as Dixieland was being played in New Orleans by African Americans. Other types of jazz soon followed: boogie-woogie, swing, and bop.

So many African American jazz musicians contributed something different to the music, often a showcasing of a new instrument for that form. Jazz, like folk music, also often reflects the lives and times of the performers. For example, Billie Holiday's haunting song "Strange Fruit" is about the lynching of African Americans by whites in the early 1900s.

Because of their history, African Americans were concentrated in the southern states and in large cities in other states, although they live all over the country. African Americans have made many contributions to the United States, and their rich and varied heritage continues. They have introduced fashions, hairstyles, and music based upon their African heritage.

Their distinctive style of food, called "soul food," can be found throughout the United States. African American contributions to music have been huge, as blacks have been instrumental in inventing and promoting blues, jazz, rock and roll, and rap music.

Colonization and the Native Peoples

The influx of so many new settlers into the country had profound, long-lasting, and tragic consequences for the Native peoples that had preceded them.

The Dutch were active in North America only from 1614 to 1664, but their influence spread over much of New York and Pennsylvania during that time. At first, during a brief fur-trade era, the Dutch presence did not cause the local Native Americans much loss of land. But the Dutch soon became land speculators, and

Native Americans in Chilkat, Alaska, around 1895. These dancers are dressed for a potlatch, a ceremonial feast at which a tribal chief gives away gifts to his guests.

war broke out with Native peoples in 1639. Warfare flared off and on until Britain took over the Dutch colony in 1664.

The French established a strong presence in the Saint Lawrence River Valley in Canada (see CANADA) and in the lower Mississippi River Valley. They founded New Orleans in 1700 and also established a post at Mobile Bay. Until Britain expelled them from the North American continent in 1763, they exerted a great influence on the tribes in the lower Mississippi River Valley. The French generally were more interested in conducting trade with the Native Americans than in displacing them from their homes, but some smaller tribes, such as the Natchez, suffered terribly at the hands of the French.

Where Spain wanted Native labor and France wanted Native trade, Britain wanted Native land. With settlements all along the Atlantic coast, plus claiming great stretches of the interior of the continent, the British colonies posed a great threat to Native Americans. The British also had no place for Native Americans within their society. They must adopt British habits and customs or move away or die.

Russia entered North America late, in the 1740s, by way of Siberia, Alaska, and the California Pacific coast, motivated by the fur trade. In 1864 it ended its North American exploits with the sale of Alaska to the United States. In the 120 years that Russians were active in North America, the Native peoples suffered greatly. They were forced into virtual temporary slavery whenever Russian ships visited their shores. From time to time Russians attempted to establish rules of conduct governing their relations with Native peoples in an attempt to correct the worst abuses. But the reforms were rarely put into practice.

Expansion and Trade

Much of the jockeying for empire in North America among European colonial rivals came as a direct result of threats to a country's holdings from another country. Spain was especially jealous of other rivals.

In 1598 Spain authorized a colonizing expedition to New Mexico, 1,500 miles (2,415 kilometers) north of Mexico City, to build an entire colony and guard against other countries' colonizing efforts. Spain was worried that its rich silver mines in Mexico might become a target of conquest by its European rivals. After Russians showed up along the coast of California in the middle of the eighteenth century, Spain finally moved to establish a colony in California, something it had shown little interest in doing until the Russians appeared.

Native Americans became caught in a vicious trade system that demanded they have only one trade partner. France, for example, would not tolerate any English traders in their sphere of influence during the decades the French ruled the lower Mississippi Valley. This put the Indians at a terrible disadvantage —French goods were inferior to and more expensive than English goods, plus they were not always available because the French experienced terrible problems in their

supply system to their colonies in North America. But Native Americans in French areas had no choice. They had to conduct trade exclusively with the French or face military action.

Disease and Displacement Decimate Native Americans

European diseases, against which indigenous peoples had no resistance, killed most of the Native population of North America before Europeans had even entered a particular region. Fatal diseases were spread along the Native trade routes by Native traders long before Europeans could spread diseases by direct contact. The death toll in some areas has been estimated as high as 90 percent.

Pilgrims, for example, found the coast of New England empty when they arrived in the seventeenth century. The entire local Native population had been killed by a smallpox epidemic, spread by ships trading along the coast.

A Creek house from around 1791. By this time disease and displacement had devastated many Indian tribes, while pressure on their lands intensified.

The arrival of Europeans displaced indigenous peoples in many different ways. When the Iroquois obtained guns from the English, they pressured tribes to the west of them to such an extent that the Chippewa (CHIP-uh-wah) were forced westward until they pushed the Sioux (SUE) out of the Minnesota woods and onto the northern Great Plains. Osage (O-saje) obtained guns from the French and drove Caddoan (KAHD-o-uhn) peoples south onto the southern Great Plains.

Comanche (Cuh-MAN-chee) in the Wyoming area obtained Spanish horses and transformed themselves into an entirely different culture. By 1700 they had left Wyoming and migrated south down the front range of the Rocky Mountains onto the southern Great Plains. They completely displaced the Plains Apache from the Great Plains, driving them into the mountains of New Mexico.

Early United States Indian Policy

Most of the Native tribes sided with the British in the American Revolution from 1776 to 1783. By the Royal Proclamation of 1763, the British had established a boundary between their colonies on the Atlantic seaboard and the Native Americans in the Ohio River Valley. Most Native leaders believed they would fare better with the British as neighbors than with independent American colonists, who had no sense of restraint in settling upon Native lands.

The Indian fears proved justified after the Revolution, when increasing numbers of Americans poured over the Appalachian Mountains. With the Louisiana Purchase from France in 1803, the United States doubled the amount of Native land that it claimed as its own.

This portrait of Austenaco, a chief of the Cherokee Nation, was painted in 1792. Soon the Cherokee would be forcibly removed from their lands in the east.

Old Immigration: 1800–1899

The years 1800 to 1899 are known as the period of "old immigration." By this time people were beginning to want to come to the United States. During this century several things changed. Europe experienced a population explosion at the same time that its economies were changing from a rural base to an industrial one. Then there were crop failures as well, such as the great Irish potato famine of 1845. These elements combined to create a situation where there were too many people to feed in Europe. Many looked westward to the new land of hope and opportunity.

The earlier immigrants who sent money back to their native lands helped convince their countrymen that the United States was a place where anyone could get a job and earn good wages. Also, modern steamships had replaced the ships of earlier times, cutting the time of an ocean voyage from Europe to North America in half. All in all, the United States was looking much better as a destination than it had the previous century.

During the nineteenth century the United States added more than fifteen million immigrants and their children to its population and grew from coast to coast in order to make room for all of its new citizens. People continued to come from countries that had settled in the United States during colonial times, but many people from different countries began to migrate to the United States as well, most notably the Irish and the Germans.

Irish Immigrants

In their homeland Irish peasants could barely make a living off the small amount of land that they rented. During the 1840s many were evicted from their homes by English landlords who consolidated their uneconomic patchwork of tenant farms. In addition, the great potato famine of 1845 left thousands starving and launched a mass migration of Irish people to the United States. Between 1820 and 1880, almost 3.5 million Irish came to America.

Boston became home for many poor Irish immigrants escaping the potato famine of 1845. These clam diggers were photographed on a wharf in Boston in 1882.

Although willing to work, these Irish peasant farmers had no money to buy land, so many of them moved to the cities where there were jobs for unskilled laborers. They laid railroad tracks, worked in mines and mills, built homes and streets, hauled freight, and did laundry. They represented up to 30 percent of the populations of New York, Boston, Philadelphia, and Baltimore. Many lived in ghettos in the cities, their hard lives softened by their devotion to family and to the Catholic Church.

Since the majority of the established immigrants were Protestant, Irish Catholics experienced religious discrimination, and many businesses refused to hire Irish workers. Soon the Irish became active in forming labor unions and learned how to use the American political system in order to better their lives. They voted Irish people into government and started newspapers that helped the new immigrants to get along in the United States.

The Irish settled close to where they entered the United States, living mainly in Massachusetts, New York, Pennsylvania, and New Jersey. They brought their style of lace making to the United States, and many communities in the United States celebrate Ireland's patron saint on Saint Patrick's Day, March 17.

German Immigrants

The Germans who migrated to the United States were Catholic, Protestant, and Jewish and represented all walks of life. Germans began to immigrate to the United States during colonial times, when they came to North America via the Netherlands. They settled primarily in the Pennsylvania area to farm. The Germans maintained their own separate communities, and some of these isolated communities still exist as Amish settlements in Ohio and Pennsylvania.

Since 1820 over seven million Germans have moved to the United States, making them the largest immigrant group. They arrived in New Orleans and journeyed up the Mississippi River to settle in the Plains and Great Lakes regions of the Ohio Valley, Iowa, Wisconsin, Missouri, and Illinois. During the 1800s the Germans maintained their separate communities and became known as the best farmers of the time, although many craftsmen and artisans entered the United States as well. They were brewers, lens makers, butchers, carpenters, piano makers, and printers.

Young Irish Americans dressed "in the green" for the traditional Saint Patrick's Day parade in New York City. The March 17 parade provides a popular celebration for Americans.

The Amish continue to live simple lives in modern America. Their plain mode of dress and a lifestyle that avoids the use of modern technologies set them apart from most Americans.

Pennsylvania Dutch

One group of people who settled in the United States beginning in 1683 were called the Pennsylvania Dutch, but they weren't Dutch at all! This name was given to a group of Germans because in their own language they called themselves **Deutsch** *(DOYCH), meaning German, and it was mispronounced by the British settlers.*

The original Pennsylvania Dutch were Mennonites, who came to Pennsylvania seeking religious freedom. Later they were joined by other Germans, including the Lutherans, Amish, Calvinists, and Dunkers (a Baptist group). They settled in southeastern Pennsylvania on the frontier because land was cheap, risking the danger of Indian attack. The "plain Germans" (Mennonites, Amish, and Dunkers) were distinctive for their simple dress and their refusal to adopt modern technologies such as electricity and automobiles, as well as their unique dialect. They can still be seen today, driving along the Pennsylvania roads in their horse-drawn wagons.

When the United States declared war on Germany during World War I, the loyalty of the German Americans was openly questioned. Many of them suffered from the prejudice and suspicion brought about by intense anti-German feelings on the part of their fellow Americans. After World War I many altered their names and became more integrated into American society.

Chinese Immigrants

When gold was discovered in California in 1848, people quickly rushed to the area to search for the precious ore, but no one wanted to do the other jobs involved in the building of cities and towns for the rush of newcomers. Chinese companies arranged to send young men, both willing and unwilling, to California to work. They hoped to participate in the gold rush but were driven from the lawless goldfields by the white Americans who resented the

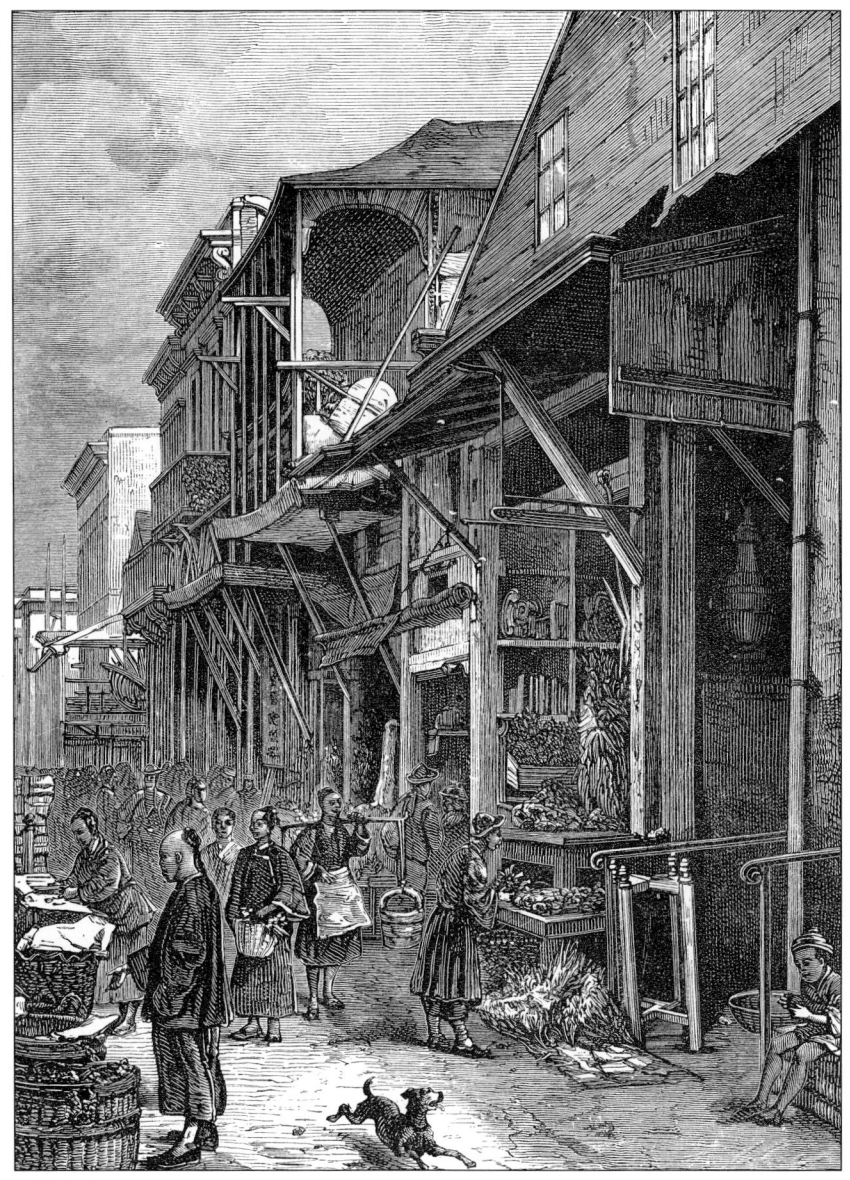

The Chinese quarter of San Francisco in the 1880s. At this time hostility against Chinese immigrants was growing, resulting in the Chinese Exclusion Act of 1882.

nine thousand out of ten thousand railroad workers were Chinese.

Chinese immigrants were welcome so long as their labor was needed. But after 1869, when the railroad work ended, an economic depression caused massive unemployment. The Chinese were seen as competition for all kinds of unskilled work, and people began to resent them and threaten them with violence. Chinese businesses were heavily taxed, and in 1882 the United States passed a law called the Chinese Exclusion Act to prevent further emigration from China.

The act had a devastating effect on the male Chinese immigrants who became stranded in the United States. They were not allowed to bring in wives, children, and families; many were too poor to pay their way back to China. Legally, they were not allowed to marry non-Chinese American women. The violent prejudice and restrictions were such that many of the Chinese lived together in ghettos called Chinatowns in many cities. Most Chinese worked in their own businesses or in the restaurant and food trade in order to succeed. In turn, their children were able to use education and hard work to enter the professional fields.

The old Chinatowns are being refurbished as tourist attractions and as cultural centers where Chinese Americans celebrate their New Year and other aspects of their culture.

competition. So the Chinese immigrants found other jobs, both in California and Hawaii, serving as agricultural laborers until they could start their own businesses.

The Chinese immigrants, almost exclusively male, worked to make money and return to China. Many labored in the gold camps or began their own laundries and restaurants. Others became domestic servants. In the 1850s, when the Union Pacific Railroad was built between California and Utah, it was estimated that

Chinese New Year

The chief holiday for Chinese Americans is New Year's Day, but they don't celebrate it on January 1. Their New Year is based on the Chinese calendar, which was developed sometime around 1300 B.C.E. Their year has twelve months, which are based on the phases of the moon. The Chinese year begins with the second new moon after the winter solstice, sometime between January 21 and February 19. Each year is associated with one of twelve animals: horse, ram, monkey, rooster, dog, boar, rat, ox, tiger, hare, dragon, or serpent.

Traditionally, the New Year is a time for purifying and honoring the home, and many people engage in a thorough housecleaning. New Year's Day is usually a big celebration after all that cleaning and may feature parades, fireworks, food, music, and costumes in a festive street party. The Chinese New Year celebrations can be experienced in many large U.S. cities each year.

This store in San Francisco's Chinatown sells traditional Chinese teas and other necessities. Chinatowns in many U.S. cities are now major tourist attractions.

Native American Policy in the Nineteenth Century

Displacing Native Americans farther and farther west became official government policy in the nineteenth century. In 1830 Congress passed the Indian Removal Act. Under that act President Andrew Jackson forced many of the Native American tribes in the East to move west of the Mississippi River to land now known as Oklahoma.

After the Mexican War (1846–1848), Native Americans in California, Arizona, and New Mexico became subject to U.S. Native American policy. The California Gold Rush of 1849 sent Americans streaming across the lands of the Plains Indians. Wars soon broke out between the settlers and the Native Americans.

With the end of the American Civil War in 1865, the United States was able to turn its military power against the Plains Indians and others, notably the Apache in the Southwest. Before the end of the century, all armed Native resistance had ended.

In 1871 Congress announced that it would no longer enter into treaties with Native tribes. Congress now would simply pass laws to regulate Native life, and the

Female African American and Native American students at an anatomy lecture in the early 1900s. Native Americans were forced to adopt "American" dress and customs.

Native Americans would not be allowed to participate in the decision-making process.

After 1871 Native Americans found themselves powerless, a people ruled by the U.S. Congress. Practicing Native religion was made a crime. Native children were taken from their parents and sent away to boarding schools, where they were forbidden to speak their Native languages. The United States tried to force indigenous peoples to adopt the habits and customs of Americans, a process called assimilation and acculturation. The impact on Native American culture was devastating. Many Native people grew up not knowing their language, and Native religions had to be practiced in secret. Congress did not extend U.S. citizenship to Native Americans until 1924.

New Immigration: 1900–1964

The years from 1900 to 1964 are known as the "new immigration" period. During the first decade of the twentieth century (1900–1910), more people immigrated to the United States than during any other time in history. The country welcomed over 8.5 million new citizens during that decade, and although immigration slowly decreased from then on, many people continued to pour into the land of opportunity.

People immigrated to the United States for many different reasons. But a global change from agricultural to industrial economies resulted in many peasant families being evicted from rented land. With this shift came political changes in Europe as well. Increasing birthrates and decreasing opportunities led to hardship in Europe; many people began to look for a better life.

With the enormous rush of new immigrants into the United States in a short period of time, the westward movement that had populated the country intensified, as did the clashes between immigrant Americans and Native Americans. During this era the United States government began to confine many Native American tribes onto small areas of land called reservations.

During the era of new immigration, people came to the United States from diverse places. Previous immigrants were primarily from northern Europe, but this era saw mass migrations from southern Europe, eastern Europe, and elsewhere. Distinctive in their looks, languages, cultures, and religions, new immigrants were always viewed with suspicion. This led to prejudice against the new arrivals and the establishment of social programs to "Americanize" them, primarily through education and training in the English language. Earlier immigrants feared that the newcomers would take both their jobs and control of the country. As a result of this prejudice and fear, the U.S. government passed a series of laws to control the number of new people entering the country.

In 1917 Congress passed a literacy law, requiring all immigrants over age sixteen to be literate in some language. Congress finally passed a law in 1921 that established quotas of immigrants to be accepted from each European country. These immigration quotas, which were to last for a year, were finally made permanent in the Johnson-Reed Immigration Act of 1924. This ended the open-door policy of immigration that had been a United States tradition.

Immigration restrictions did not allow people to come who had been uprooted in wars or punished by oppressive governments. This became a problem before and during World War II, when thousands of Jewish people persecuted by Adolf Hitler's Nazi government or fleeing Communist governments found themselves unable to immigrate to the United States because of the immigration quotas. As a result, the Displaced Persons Act (1948) and then the Refugee Relief Act (1953) were passed, allowing refugees fleeing oppressive governments to enter the United States. Other laws were passed to allow refugees to enter the United States as special one-time exceptions to the restrictive immigration policy.

Weary immigrants get some air on deck as their ship enters New York Harbor in 1905. A year earlier the cheapest fare from Europe to North America had dropped to ten dollars.

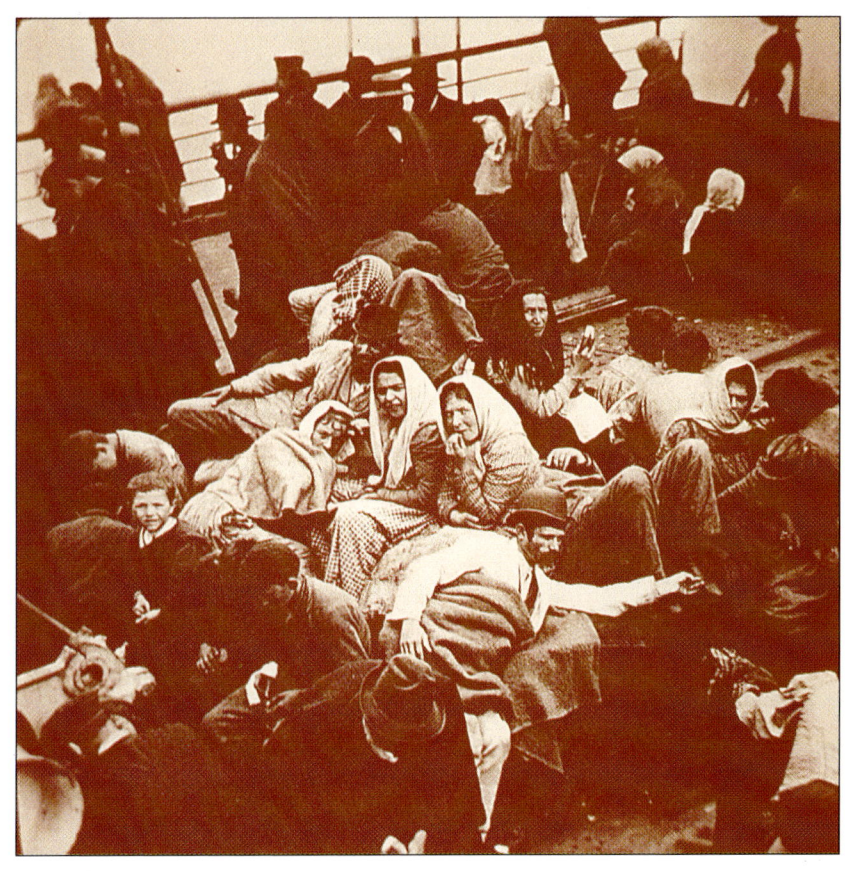

Italian Immigrants

During the era of new immigration, more people came from Italy than from any other country. Between 1901 and 1910 over two million Italians immigrated to America. They were usually peasants from southern Italy who suffered from poor economies, epidemic diseases, and a lack of opportunity for a decent life in their own country. The Italians came to the United States where they heard that jobs were plentiful and wages were high. They settled mainly in New York, Pennsylvania, and the New England area, as they couldn't afford to move further west.

Many Italians worked on the railroads, in construction, and in the mining camps. Often the newcomers were single men who came to labor for a season, returning to Italy with their wages. Known as "birds of passage," they were often controlled by a

Young Italian child workers at a factory in Lawrence, Massachusetts, in 1911. At that time it was not unusual for children as young as six to work in mines and factories.

boss, or padrone, who would arrange for their job and their transportation in return for payment.

Many of the newly arrived Italians lived together in the cities, crowded in tenement housing and often taking in boarders. Like other non-English-speaking immigrants, they found help in a strange new country by banding together with their fellow countrymen and founding mutual-aid societies. Also, the Catholic Church played an important part in helping the new immigrants to adjust to life in the United States.

Though the new immigrants initially thought of themselves as members of a certain Italian province or peninsula, in the United States they were simply Italians. They put aside many differences in order to create Italian newspapers, Italian opera companies, churches, and self-help groups that they could all use and work with. Since many of them intended to eventually return to their own country, the Italians had a lower rate of citizenship and maintained their own language and culture for a longer time than many other groups.

The family unit was of utmost importance to the Italians. Many Italians participated in home sweatshops, where family members worked at home and were paid for piecework.

As generations passed, Italians found positions in politics and government. Italian Americans moved into business in a big way, and Bank of America, the largest bank in the United States, was started by an Italian (A. P. Giannini) in order to finance his countrymen's farming efforts.

East European Jewish Immigrants

Jewish worshipers leave a synagogue on Rivington Street in New York City during Jewish New Year, 1911. New York City was home to an estimated 540,000 Jews during that decade.

During the new immigration era, two million Jews made up the second largest group of immigrants to arrive in the United States. After arrival, over 75 percent of them remained on the eastern seaboard in New York, New Jersey, Pennsylvania, and the New England states. Most of the Jews came from Russia, Poland, and Romania, where they had also lived as a minority group. Since they came from many different national backgrounds, their religion was the feature that united them in their new country. A large number of the Jews stayed in the United States since they were unwelcome in the countries they had left.

At this time a small German Jewish community already existed in the United States. They were a part of mainstream America, and the fact that they had a different religion wasn't considered important since the various immigrants had all brought different religions with them. The established Jewish community was initially bothered by the great influx of East European Jews. There were so many of them, and they spoke their own language, Yiddish.

The Jews had suffered extreme prejudice and deprivation in their home countries, which unfortunately, did not end when the Jews entered the United States. Like the earlier Catholic Irish immigrants, Jews were often excluded from some jobs, colleges, businesses, and organizations

The Garment Industry

The American clothing industry grew through the backbreaking work done by thousands of new immigrants, many of them Jewish Americans. During the nineteenth century much of the ready-to-wear clothing was produced in the tenements of Boston and New York, where bundles of garment pieces were given to families to sew together at home. In the twentieth century, clothing factories were built in the large cities to take advantage of immigrant labor. People worked in crowded, dirty factories, sewing for up to eighteen hours a day to make fourteen dollars a week (worth about 260 dollars today) if they were good. Beginning workers usually made about four dollars a week (about 75 dollars today) at this job.

because of their religion. They countered this by starting their own businesses, banks, and organizations, and eventually the barriers diminished.

Like many other immigrants, the Eastern European Jews settled primarily in cities on the eastern seaboard. With the help of aid societies, relatives, and friends, they worked as peddlers and in the clothing manufacturing business, just as they had in Europe. The women often sewed at home so they could earn money while watching their children.

Jewish people respected education and encouraged their children to stay in school. Many went on to own the businesses for which their fathers had worked, becoming department store owners and successful executives. Today, about 40 percent of the world's Jewish population resides in the United States.

Greek Immigrants

Greeks came to the United States after a war with Turkey and poor farming conditions depressed their chiefly rural economy. The peak decade of Greek immigration to the United States was 1911 to 1920, and many who came were single men intending to work and return to Greece with their wages. They settled in the large cities and took jobs as workers in steel mills and meatpacking plants. New York, Chicago, and Boston boasted the largest Greek populations, where

A 1990 parade in Tarpon Springs, Florida, commemorating Epiphany, which, in the Greek Orthodox Church, is a religious celebration recalling the baptism of Christ.

A vendor sells cool drinks in the Syrian quarter of New York City in 1900. Like the Greeks, many Syrians were Christians who felt threatened by Muslims in their own country.

Greeks also entered service occupations, becoming clerks and restaurant workers.

Like other immigrant groups, Greeks discovered that it was easier to make progress if you were your own boss. So they worked and saved in order to begin their own small businesses, opening diners, pizza parlors, restaurants, and grocery stores.

It was difficult for Greeks to practice the Greek Orthodox religion in the old country, where they were surrounded by Turkish Muslims. Greeks worked hard to establish their religion in the United States. Like other new immigrants, the Greeks were subjected to discrimination.

After immigration quotas by country of origin were lifted in the 1960s, there was a resurgence of Greek immigration to the United States. These immigrants tended to be professionals, such as engineers and doctors.

Syrian and Lebanese Immigrants

The Syrians and Lebanese, from an area in the Middle East once part of the Turkish Ottoman Empire, have a common language, Arabic. They brought a variety of religions to the United States, but the majority of the immigrants from Lebanon and Syria were Christians. In 1919 there were an estimated 400,000 Arab Americans in the United States, many of them in New York.

Primarily peasants in the old country, they became laborers and traders in the United States. They worked in the mills or became peddlers of dry goods and notions. As they amassed some money, they began to open shops and become small business owners. One New York City street, Washington Street in lower Manhattan, became known as "Little Syria." Other small Arab American communities are located in Boston, Philadelphia, Toledo, and Detroit.

Armenian Immigrants

Armenia has been alternately controlled by the Turks and the Russians for most of its existence. In 1915 Turks massacred many of Armenia's native people, sparking massive immigration to several countries, including the United States. There is no accurate record of how many Armenians entered the United States, as they were often listed by immigration officials as Russians or Turks.

Armenians worked in textile mills and shoe factories in the Northeast, as well as in agriculture in the Fresno area of California.

A portrait of an Armenian farming couple in West Andover, Massachusetts, in 1941. Persecution in their homeland led many Armenians to seek a new life in the United States.

One Armenian immigrant introduced the casaba melon, which became a major agricultural crop in California. However, many of the immigrants were already businesspeople with established skills in commerce. Today there are important Armenian communities in New York, New Jersey, Chicago, Massachusetts, and California.

Eastern European Slavic Immigrants

The third largest group to immigrate to the United States during the new immigration era, the Slavs included Poles, Czechs, Russians, Ukrainians, Bulgarians, Serbs, Croatians, and Slovenians. It is possible that over four million Slavs came to the United States, but the exact number is difficult to determine because as many as half of them returned to their native lands.

The Slavs are an extremely varied group of people in terms of language, religion, and lifestyle. They came from different geographical regions in eastern Europe and were often on poor terms with each other. Most lived under the control of Russia, Germany, or Austria. Slavic immigrants were largely peasants who had been displaced after agriculture was modernized and the industrial revolution began. A great number of Slavic immigrants found work in U.S. steel mills, mines, and slaughterhouses. They settled in the industrial heartland of the United States and spread through New York, Pittsburgh, Cleveland, Chicago, Detroit, and Milwaukee.

More is known about the immigrants from Poland and former Czechoslovakia (now the Czech Republic and Slovakia) than the other groups because they remained in the United States in larger numbers. The Poles came to the United

A Polish community in Chicago, 1903. Today, approximately 300,000 Polish Americans still live in Chicago, where they originally settled to work in the meat-packing plants.

The Hungarians, like the Greeks, came to the United States with the intention of earning money and returning home. It is estimated that less than half of them stayed in their new country. They settled in New York City as well as in the mining and steel-furnace areas of Pennsylvania, Ohio, New Jersey, and West Virginia. New Brunswick, New Jersey, once had the distinction of being the "most Hungarian" city in the United States.

States to escape the repressive Russian regime that had stifled their national identity. They tended to settle around New York, Buffalo, and Chicago.

Few Poles came to the United States after the immigration restrictions were put in place, but World War II brought many Poles fleeing the devastation of the Nazi regime.

In 1946, October 11 was declared a day to honor General Casimir Pulaski, a Revolutionary War hero. Since then, an annual parade is held in New York City, becoming a celebration of Polish heritage for many people.

The Czechs, who immigrated with their families, often were skilled workers and artisans as well as farmers. They fled their native Czechoslovakia after a potato famine and political uprisings created bad economic and social conditions. Although many Czechs remained in the major cities to work, large groups of them migrated to Iowa, Wisconsin, Nebraska, Oklahoma, and Texas.

Treats from Other Lands

The following foods were introduced into American cuisine by people from other cultures:

- **Chinese:** *Bing cherries*
- **Dutch:** *cookies, doughnuts, waffles*
- **German:** *beer, frankfurters (hot dogs), hamburgers, sausages*
- **Irish:** *corned beef and cabbage, soda bread*
- **Italian:** *bologna, cantaloupes, pasta, french fries*
- **Mexican:** *Caesar salad, chewing gum, tamales, enchiladas, tortillas*
- **Middle Eastern:** *chickpeas, ice-cream cones, pita bread*
- **Native American:** *potato chips, corn*
- **Swedish:** *meatballs, puffed rice and wheat cereals*

Japanese Immigrants

After the United States halted Chinese immigration, the need for agricultural labor on the West Coast and in Hawaii again became an issue. The Japanese government handpicked some of their best young men to come to the United States to work as agricultural stoop labor. The wages and ideas that were sent home to Japan helped that country modernize and industrialize. However, only about half of the agricultural laborers returned to Japan. The remainder sent for their families and stayed in the United States. Most settled in Hawaii and southern California, but Washington, Oregon, and northern California also had large settlements of Japanese.

Since there were so many single Japanese men in the United States, many of them sent home for brides. Arranged marriages were the norm in their culture. Families would select a bride and send a picture of her to her prospective husband in California or Hawaii. These women came to be called "picture brides." Other people found this practice to be very strange, and it increased their prejudice against the Japanese newcomers.

The difference in their appearance from earlier immigrants made them easy targets for discrimination, and soon a movement grew to keep Japanese out of the country. This became a tricky political issue as Japan was a strong country, and the United States wanted to maintain good relations with it. Thus, the 1907 Gentlemen's Agreement came about. The United States passed no law to restrict Japanese immigration but got the Japanese government to agree to do so itself. In return the United States allowed families of the existing Japanese immigrants to continue to enter the country.

The Japanese were not allowed to own land in the United States, but their children could. Since they were born in the United States, these children were automatically granted citizenship, and they were able to buy land for farming. Japanese Americans produced just about all the strawberries and celery in the United States prior to World War II.

After Japan bombed Pearl Harbor, Hawaii, in 1941, prejudice against Japanese Americans escalated to an all-time high. Deemed a military threat, 110,000 Japanese Americans were interned in camps in the desolate interior portions of the United States, from California to Arkansas.

This Japanese mother and daughter were farm workers in California in 1937. Five years later they were interned when war broke out between the United States and Japan.

They were forced to sell businesses, land, and belongings at enormous losses. In the internment camps the Japanese worked at more diverse jobs than farming and were located in different areas of the United States. Upon their release, they continued to work in a wide variety of occupations and live in more dispersed areas of the country.

Mexican Immigrants

Many Mexicans were living in the Southwest before it became part of the United States. However, the bulk of the five million Mexicans living in the United States today emigrated from Mexico after World War I. Prior to this the Mexican immigrants who came to the United States worked on the railroad or in the mines. After World War I the expansion of irrigated agriculture in Texas, Arizona, and California, combined with the disruptive effects of the Mexican Revolution, resulted in the migration of many Mexicans to the United States seeking agricultural work.

When immigration restrictions slowed Asian immigration to a trickle and a dire need for farmworkers arose, labor contractors, similar to the Italian padrones of an earlier generation, arranged for Mexicans to enter the United States legally or illegally to work. Most Mexicans could earn higher wages in the United States than in Mexico and then return home with their earnings. The closeness of the border made this lifestyle possible for many people, who saw no need to become citizens.

With the Great Depression in the 1930s, many Mexicans were deported so Americans could take their jobs. Later, however, Mexicans were once again encouraged to come to the United States to work when World War II provided employment for so many citizens. In 1942

A Mexican boy bunching carrots in a Texas field in 1939. Throughout the twentieth century millions of poor Mexicans sought farmwork across the border in the United States.

a guest-worker program was begun to fill labor shortages, again primarily in agriculture. But when the labor shortage ended with the return of soldiers from World War II, more than four million Mexicans were deported between 1947 and 1954.

The third wave of Mexican immigration began in the 1970s and continues today. The continuing depressed Mexican economy, changes in immigration laws, the inability to effectively police the United States border with Mexico, and the rise of activist groups created to help Mexican immigrants have all contributed to ongoing migrations. Mexican Americans continue to cluster in the southwestern states of California, Arizona, New Mexico, Texas, and Colorado, although there are many Mexican Americans in other large urban areas such as Chicago.

Hardworking Mexican immigrants contributed greatly to their new homeland, just like the other immigrant groups. What is interesting is that the different waves of migrations have left us with different generations of Mexican Americans living in the United States who have different values. One example of this is the current debate over whether the preferred term is *Mexican American*, *Hispanic*, *Latino*, or *Chicano* to refer to someone whose ancestors immigrated to the United States from Mexico.

Many Mexican Americans have maintained their own cultural groups, speaking their own language, Spanish. They have brought their foods and traditions with them to the United States. Over time they have become more urban and more educated. Working and caring for the family have remained their strongest values. Fewer women than average entered the workforce, perhaps due to a high rate of childbirth, which, because of the cost of child care, makes it less cost-effective to work outside the home.

Puerto Rican Immigrants

In 1917 the people of Puerto Rico became American citizens. As such, their immigration to the mainland was never restricted. They were relatively late immigrants, with their numbers peaking in 1946, when seventy thousand Puerto Ricans arrived on the mainland. Two-thirds of them settled in New York, where they became the most recent ethnic group to move to that city to satisfy the demand for minimum wage labor. Today many Puerto Ricans move from island to mainland and back several times during their lifetime.

All dressed up for the show, young Puerto Ricans take part in a Dia del Niño (Day of the Child) parade in Spanish Harlem, New York City.

Modern Immigration: 1965–Present

In 1963 President John F. Kennedy called for eliminating all immigration quotas based upon national origin. The quotas were discriminatory and especially excluded immigrants from the Asian countries. But it was President Lyndon B. Johnson who signed into law the immigration reforms of 1965, which established numerical quotas for immigration without mention of national origin. Preference was given to relatives of people already in the United States and to professionals, scientists, and artists. Other preferences were given to skilled workers in areas where the United States was weak. Still another segment of the immigration quota was reserved for refugees—those people fleeing political

turmoil in their countries where remaining could endanger their lives. Although the new laws do not discriminate against immigrants by ethnic origin, it is clear that the United States is not interested in accepting all of the world's poor, a change from the original open-door policy.

Another change is that large groups of new immigrants entering the United States are more likely to be dispersed throughout the country these days, rather than gathering at their common port of entry. This strategy was used with the Indo-Chinese refugees entering after the Vietnam War and some of the Cuban and Haitian refugees from the Caribbean. One reason for this policy is to avoid one part of the country having to absorb all of the new people.

In the late twentieth century the ethnic groups with the largest number of recent immigrants to the United States were the Hispanics from the Caribbean, Mexico, and Central and South America, followed by East Asians (Chinese, Koreans, Filipinos) and South Asians (Indians and Pakistanis). Asian immigrants have benefited most from the changes in the 1965 Immigration Act. In 1980, Asian Americans represented 1.5 percent of the total United States population. One prediction is that by the year 2000, Asian Americans will be 4 percent of the population, which would more than double their numbers in less than twenty years.

Immigrants entering the country illegally have become an increasing problem, and in 1978 the government estimated that there were 8.2 million illegal immigrants in the country, 90 percent of them from Mexico. There have been numerous attempts to stem the flow of illegal immigrants from its southern neighbor, although controlling the 2,000-mile (3,220-kilometer) long border is nearly impossible.

Joyful Cuban refugees packed on board the Big Babe cheer as it enters Key West, Florida, on May 20, 1980. In September the Cuban authorities halted the Boat Lift.

Cuban Immigrants

Most Cuban Americans are recent immigrants to the United States. After Fidel Castro came to power in Cuba in 1959 and established a Communist government, thousands of Cubans fled to their northern neighbor. They settled in southern Florida in the Miami area or in New York. Most of the early immigrants were middle-class professional and technical workers.

The second wave of Cuban immigration began in the 1980s and consisted chiefly of unskilled refugees who undertook the trip from Cuba to Florida in small boats. This migration is commonly referred to as the Mariel Boat Lift. The Marielitos (mar-ee-el-EE-toss) represented an influx of 125,000 Cubans into the United States and consisted of people that the Castro regime found undesirable. Today the Cuban Americans live in enclaves in Florida, New York, and New Jersey, where they maintain their culture, language, foods, and music. One section of Miami, referred to as "Little

Havana," features Cuban music, food, and language and thousands of retail businesses owned by Cuban Americans. Cubans have contributed greatly to the revitalization of Miami and to the emergence of the city as an important commercial center specializing in international trade with Latin America.

A young Cuban from Dade County, Florida, at her Quinceañera, or fifteenth birthday celebration. This is considered the birthday when Cuban girls come of age.

Central American Immigrants

The poor countries of Nicaragua, Guatemala, Honduras, and El Salvador have long had unstable authoritarian governments. Poverty, violence, and repression have encouraged an estimated two million people to flee these Central American countries. Many of the refugees have gone to Mexico or to Central American nations, which are poorly equipped to handle a large influx of immigrants. A small number have been granted asylum in the United States but many have not; others enter the United States illegally through Mexico. In some cases they are aided by people in the American Sanctuary Movement, which assists them in entering the country illegally since they believe that these immigrants should be allowed entry as refugees.

Haitian Immigrants

Most of the Haitian immigrants are political or economic refugees from François (father) and Jean-Claude (son) Duvalier's dictatorial government, which flourished from 1957 to 1986. The first wave came early in the regime and consisted of urban, middle-class, professional Haitians. Many of them settled in New York, Philadelphia, and Washington, D.C.

However, the people immigrating in great numbers in the 1970s and 1980s were mostly poor, unskilled workers. Large groups of desperate Haitians descended upon the Florida coast in flotillas of boats and were known as the boat people. This method of illegal immigration became so prevalent in the 1990s that the United States government began intercepting the boat people at sea and detaining them in refugee camps or sending them back to Haiti. This treatment of the Haitian refugees became very controversial in the United States, where some said that harsher immigration standards were applied to Haitians because of their black skin color. Recently, Haitians have settled primarily in Miami, where they struggle to make a living in the poorer sections of the city.

Filipino Immigrants

Filipinos came to the United States in several waves. After the United States annexed the Philippines in 1898, groups of students came to the United States and some remained. In the 1920s and 1930s more Filipinos came to work in the fields of California and Hawaii, like the Chinese and Japanese, where they experienced the same

Filipino women don traditional clothing for the Philippine Day parade in New York City. Many immigrants from the Philippines already speak English as a second language.

anti-Asian discrimination. The largest number of Filipinos immigrated after 1965 and consisted of professionals and small business owners.

While California and Hawaii remained the destination of choice for Filipinos, many more began migrating to Southern states, the Midwest, and the Northeast. Many of the Filipino professionals immigrating are nurses and other medical personnel, who can easily find jobs in American hospitals. A large number of Filipino immigrants already speak English as well as Spanish and their native language. They bring a traditional style of dress, folk songs, dances, and Filipino foods.

Southeast Asian Immigrants

Southeast Asian immigrants, primarily from Vietnam and Laos, have immigrated to the United States as a direct result of U.S. involvement in the Vietnam War, which ended in 1975. Upon the takeover of

Saigon by the Communist North Vietnamese, the southern Vietnamese and the Laotians, primarily from the Hmong (HMAWNG) tribe, who assisted the American efforts in Vietnam were evacuated as refugees and brought to the United States. Many of these refugees were educated business and professional people who were able to adjust fairly rapidly to their new country.

A second wave of immigration occurred in the late 1970s and early 1980s, when Southeast Asians, fleeing the economic hardship and authoritarian government of Vietnam, traveled in homemade wooden boats. Also known as boat people, they were taken to refugee camps throughout Southeast Asia. Eventually they immigrated to a number of different countries, including the United States. The Refugee Dispersion Policy used social agencies to help the refugees settle throughout the United States. Most of the Southeast Asian immigrants went to Washington, Oregon, California, Texas, Minnesota, Illinois, New York, Pennsylvania, Massachusetts, and Virginia.

A group of Hmong farmers display their produce in Fresno, California. Many Hmong assisted the United States in the Vietnam War and feared persecution at war's end.

A large number of Vietnamese fishermen settled on the Gulf Coast in Texas. Others clustered in California, where almost 35 percent of them make their home in Orange County.

Many of these Southeast Asians live below the poverty level, as they struggle to adjust to a strange urban economy for which they are unprepared.

The Southeast Asians have brought with them their rich and ancient culture, including their foods, holiday observances, language, and literature.

Asian Indian Immigrants

Asian Indian immigration has also increased dramatically since the 1965 immigration law reform. Although immigrants from India have come to the United States for many years in small numbers, the greatest number of immigrants arrived after 1965. These recent immigrants are, for the most part, well-educated and trained professionals who may be underemployed in the United

States. For example, many Asian Indians operate motels and newspaper stands, as well as becoming owners of restaurants and import-export businesses. Many others have been able to get work in their professions and have quickly moved into

---

American English: A Rich Mix

American English has been heavily supplemented by words from a variety of native languages of people who originally lived in or immigrated to North America. Various Native American languages have contributed over five hundred words to American English, and Spanish, Dutch, and German are other major contributors. However, American English has gained vocabulary from almost every other language and continues to add new words every day. Here are some examples:

- **Arabic:** *alcohol, algebra*
- **African American:** *banana, jazz, jukebox*
- **Chinese:** *tea, typhoon*
- **Dutch:** *bedspread, business, luck, smoke, wagon*
- **French:** *prairie*
- **German:** *cookbook, dumb*
- **Hebrew:** *cherub*
- **Indian:** *bandanna, loot*
- **Irish:** *boycott, hooligan*
- **Italian:** *bank, concert, laundry, piano*
- **Native American:** *moose, pecan*
- **Polynesian:** *tattoo*
- **Turkish:** *tulip*

the middle class. They bring with them a rich and ancient heritage, including their Hindu and Sikh religions, and unique music, food, and distinctive dress.

Native Americans in the Twentieth Century

Many Native Americans resisted the massive changes of the twentieth century and clung to their cultures. They lived in poverty, while most Americans forgot about them or assumed they had all disappeared at the end of the nineteenth century. In 1928 a government study, known as the Merriam Report, revealed the despair, poverty, and hopelessness of many Native people in the United States. The report sparked a series of reforms in Native education and helped bring about other changes.

In 1934 Congress passed the Indian Reorganization Act, which allowed Native Americans to organize tribal governments with limited powers. During the Great Depression in the 1930s, a U.S. government Indian Commissioner named John Collier, who was sympathetic to the problems of Native Americans, brought about reforms in the Bureau of Indian Affairs.

In the 1950s U.S. Native American policy sought to terminate the United States' treaty obligations to Native tribes, such as providing health care and education. During this period, some tribes were "terminated," which brought their official relationship with the country to an end.

By the early 1970s, with living conditions on Native reservations as bad as ever, a Native activist movement sprang up that brought media attention to the plight of Natives. Native Americans occupied Alcatraz Island in San Francisco Bay in California. They occupied the headquarters of the Bureau of Indian Affairs in Washington, D.C., and they occupied Wounded Knee, South Dakota, which had been the scene of a massacre of Sioux men, women, and children by the U.S. Army in 1890.

These protests brought a change in U.S. policy, and an era of Native self-determination began. Congress enacted laws protecting the civil rights of Native Americans and allowing them to practice some Native religions. Self-determination acts allowed tribes in Oklahoma to form tribal governments again, for the first time since Oklahoma achieved statehood in 1907.

Today, nearly a generation later, the era of Native American self-determination is continuing. Many Native nations are operating large tribal businesses, tribal health care facilities, their own schools and

A group of Native Americans rally for human rights, justice, liberty, and equality outside the White House during the bicentennial celebrations in July 1976.

colleges, and other enterprises. There are still many problems, but increasingly, it is Native people who are trying to find ways to deal with them rather than have others tell them how to live their lives.

Contemporary Native Peoples

There are more than 535 federally recognized Native tribes in the United States. There are many other tribes that are not federally recognized and others that are only recognized by state governments.

There are vast differences among the tribes. Several hundred different Native languages are still spoken in the United States. Some tribes have long traditions as agricultural people; others do not. Some have more than 100,000 members; others consist of only a few small communities. In the space available here, it is only possible to note a few of the individual tribes.

The Navajo Nation, with 24,000 square miles (62,400 square kilometers), is the largest reservation-based Indian nation. Their country is bigger than the combined states of Massachusetts, New Hampshire, and Vermont. More than 200,000 Navajo live on the reservation, in Arizona, New Mexico, and Utah. The Navajo was the first Indian nation to open a tribally owned college, Navajo Community College, in 1969. Today two dozen other Indian nations also operate their own colleges. The Navajo have also been leaders in many other fields of endeavor. They offer a formal, college-level training program for Navajo who want to become medicine men. The Navajo language is spoken by more than 80 percent of the Navajo population.

With more than 300,000 members, the Cherokee Nation of Oklahoma is the largest nonreservation-based Indian nation. In the 1820s a Cherokee named Sequoyah invented a way of writing the Cherokee

language, and the Cherokee have been publishing in their own language ever since. Today in Tahlequah, Oklahoma, the capitol of the nation, some street signs are written in both English and Cherokee. The Cherokee have found many things about American culture worthy of adoption into their culture. Academic education is one of those things. Northeastern State University, in Tahlequah, has the largest enrollment of American Indian students of any university in the United States. Today the Cherokee are among the most skilled professional people in Oklahoma—doctors, lawyers, engineers, and educators. Many other Cherokee remain very traditional.

The Apache live in southwestern Oklahoma and on reservations in Arizona and New Mexico. Oklahoma Apache were taken there as prisoners of war in the late-

A New Mexico Navajo artist decorates a pot with traditional designs. More than 200,000 Navajo live on the reservation that spans three states in the Southwest.

nineteenth century. Jicarilla (hee-kuh-REE-yuh) Apache in New Mexico have won some of the most important Supreme Court decisions for Indians in recent times, decisions regarding their oil and gas reserves. Mescalero (mess-kuh-LEHR-oe) Apache in New Mexico operate a ski resort that is famous for its fine powder snow. The Apache in Arizona and New Mexico have been leaders in participating in the planning of their children's public school education, where Apache children learn pride in their culture.

The Choctaw Nation of Oklahoma and the Mississippi Band of Choctaw Indians are both federally recognized Choctaw tribes. In Mississippi the Choctaw language is still the first language in the homes of more than 80 percent of the people in the tribe. The Choctaw Nation of

Cherokee dancers in Native costume at the annual Chehaw National Indian Festival held at Chehaw Park in Albany, Georgia. Today most Cherokee live in Oklahoma.

Hawaii

Hawaiian Native people spell their land Hawai'i. They are a conquered people who are trying to reclaim at least some portion of their nation from the United States. Their struggle has produced two of the most dynamic Native women leaders in the world: Mililani, who is the elected governor of the Hawai'ian Native people, and her sister, Dr. Haunani Kay Trask, who is director of Hawaiian studies at the University of Hawaii. Dr. Trask, who is also one of Hawaii's most distinguished poets and scholars, is an electrifying public speaker. The two sisters are an inspiration to Native people throughout the world.

Oklahoma has more than 100,000 members and is many times larger than the Mississippi tribe. Both, however, are leaders in tribal economic enterprise. The Mississippi Choctaw operate an assembly plant for automobile parts and a factory that makes greeting cards. In Oklahoma several large truck plazas and a large bingo casino are operated by the tribe. The Mississippi Choctaw host the World Championship Stickball Tournament each year in July.

Pueblo (PWEB-loe) peoples today live in nineteen pueblos in New Mexico. One of them, Acoma Pueblo, might be the longest continuously occupied town in the United States. It was built during the twelfth century and sits atop a mesa that is 350 feet (110 meters) high. Pueblo peoples are among the best farmers of dry land in the world. Each pueblo has a feast day to celebrate the annual harvest, where ancient ceremonies are performed. Pueblos have produced some of the most influential Native American writers in U.S. literature, especially Simon J. Ortiz of Acoma Pueblo and Leslie Marmon Silko of Laguna Pueblo. The nineteen pueblos join together to pursue their common interests in the All-Indian Pueblo Council.

A people of the forest, the Ojibwe (o-jib-WAY), also known as the Chippewa or Anishanabe, are one of the largest tribes in North America. For as long as other peoples have known them, they have lived in the same general area where they are found today, near the Great Lakes. Wild rice has been an important crop for Ojibwe and is still harvested today. In the 1970s

they won an important legal battle, forcing the state of Minnesota to honor their treaty rights to spear fish in waters outside the present boundaries of their land. The Ojibwe's land has shrunk greatly in size. For example, the reservation of the White Earth Band of Chippewa, which is one of the largest of the Chippewa reservations, today consists of only 57,000 acres (23,000 hectares), only about 7 percent of the 837,120 acres (338,765 hectares) when the reservation was formed by a treaty in 1867.

The Sioux are also one of the largest tribes in North America. Their reservations are located mostly in the northern Great Plains region. The Black Hills, known to the Sioux as Paha Sapa, are their sacred ground. Many of the contemporary struggles of the Sioux with the U.S. government are a result of the occupation of the Black Hills by the United States. U.S. courts have ruled that the Black Hills were illegally taken from the Sioux by the United States, but the courts have offered only money in exchange for the loss. The Sioux have refused to take the money. They want the land. Some of the most dramatic events of the period of Native American activism in the 1970s took place on Sioux reservations.

The Comanche were virtually unknown to Europeans until their historic southward migration from the region of present-day Wyoming brought them to the northeastern frontiers of Spanish New Mexico by about 1700. The Spanish tried to stop the Comanche migration by going to the aid of the Plains Apache, who were being pushed off the Great Plains by the Comanche. But nothing could stop the Comanche. They became lords of all the southern Great Plains, until American buffalo hunters exterminated the southern buffalo herd in the 1870s, starving the Comanche into surrender. Today the Comanche are a thriving people with tribal headquarters near Fort Sill in

Native American children from the Taos Peublo in Taos, New Mexico, lovingly display their crop of vegetables. The Pueblo people have mastered the art of dry land farming.

Alaska

Alaska has the highest percentage of Native peoples of any state (15 percent in the 1990 census). Alaskan Native communities are located in every part of the state. There are more than 220 tribal bands, many of them organized into tribal corporations, with members holding shares in the corporation. Major tribal language groups include Athabascan, Tlingit, Aleut, and Inuit (who are also known as Eskimos).

A young Alaskan Inuit. Alaska has the highest percentage of Native peoples of any state. Their lives have been changed by the discovery of oil in the Arctic.

southwestern Oklahoma. They are among the leaders in Native American education, art, and many other fields.

The Sac and Fox were the first Indians in Oklahoma to begin making their own car license plates for tribal members, emphasizing their status as a nation within the United States. Recent court decisions have upheld the power of the tribe to do so.

The Iroquois (IR-uh-kwoy) tribes in the Northeast, largely in New York and across the border in Canada, are among the most influential of all the tribes in North America. Some scholars believe that the Iroquois Confederacy was an important influence on the structure of the government of the United States. They have been leaders in insisting on their rights to operate tribal businesses without interference from the state government. They are also in the forefront in pressing the claims of Native peoples in the United States to the United Nations, attempting to get all the nations of the world to hear their appeals for justice. Like many tribes in North America, the women play powerful roles in the life of their people. Iroquois

clan mothers are leaders, not just within their nations, but for all Indian people.

The Yakima (YAK-uh-muh) in Washington State in the Pacific Northwest are not among the largest tribes, but they are among the most influential. Their traditional form of government was an almost pure form of democracy, a general meeting of the tribe, with each person having both a voice and a vote. Those ideas are still in force today. The annual meeting of the people elects the tribal leaders. The Yakima have been steadfast in insisting that the United States uphold its 1855 treaty with the tribe. Rather than merely complaining about the pollution of the Columbia River and the decline in salmon fishing, the tribe has sought to operate its own fish hatchery.

Glossary

acculturation: the process of adopting customs from another culture.

altitude: height above the ground or above sea level.

armistice: a truce or temporary peace agreement between countries.

assimilation: a process by which one minority group of people becomes mixed within a predominant group of people.

asylum: protection offered by a country to political refugees from another country.

authoritarian: a person or government that favors absolute obedience to an authority. Under an authoritarian government, people lack individual freedoms and control of their government's leaders.

commodity: a product that can be traded or sold for a profit.

common law: a system of laws that began in England that is based on the results of court decisions and on cultural customs instead of on specific written laws.

cost-effective: economical; a good deal in terms of what was received for the amount of money paid.

deport: to forcibly return people to the country from which they came, usually because they have entered the new country illegally.

desegregate: to eliminate segregation in; the practice of opening schools and businesses to people from all races and every ethnic background.

destitute: desperately poor; without money or hope.

diplomatic relations: the formal relationship between two nations, including all communications and agreements between them.

dry goods: textiles, cloth, clothing, and related items.

economic depression: a period of decline in business and trade, marked by debt, bankruptcy, and unemployment.

federal republic: a country with a central government that shares power with individual state governments and where the people rule by electing their political leaders. The United States is an example of a federal republic.

flotilla: a group of boats.

ghetto: a part of a city where members of an ethnic or religious group live because of poverty or discrimination against them. Ghettos are often crowded and dilapidated.

Great Depression: a period of time from 1929 to 1941 in which the worldwide economy was bad, and people lost their homes, farms, and businesses.

intern: to confine people in a small area, especially during wartime.

internment camp: a temporary confined area, surrounded by fences and guards, where people were imprisoned during the war because the government thought they might be enemies.

kindred: people who are related to one another in some manner, such as by blood, marriage, or a common language.

labor union: an organization of workers formed to benefit workers by pursuing higher wages and better working conditions.

latitude: a measurement in degrees of a place in relation to its distance from the equator. Lines of latitude run east and west on a globe.

linguistic: pertaining to language.

mesa: a rock with steep walls and a flat top. Mesas are often found in the southwestern part of the United States.

militia: a group of ordinary citizens organized for military service; they are not a part of the regular army of a country and are used only in emergencies.

Nazi: pertaining to the National Socialist German Worker's Party, which controlled the government of Germany from 1933 to 1945 under Adolf Hitler.

notions: small, lightweight items for household use, such as buttons and sewing needles.

ominous: threatening or frightening.

palisade: logs planted in the ground and close together to form the walls of a fort.

pauper: a person who is extremely poor and qualifies for public charity or welfare; a very poor person.

precedent: an example that is used in dealing with similar situations in the future.

pueblos: Native American villages of the southwestern United States. Their inhabitants, also called Pueblos, are descendants of the Anasazi peoples.

quota: the maximum number, especially of people, that may be allowed to enter a country, a group, or an institution.

repressive: a word used to describe a government that denies individual rights or forcibly rejects the will of the people.

Sanctuary Movement: a movement to help illegal immigrants find safety and refuge in the United States.

sharecropper: a farmer who rents land and gives a share of the crops to the landlord instead of rent.

speculator: a person who takes risks investing in business or finance in hope of gaining.

stickball: a Native American ball game similar to lacrosse, in which a small ball is thrown from a webbed pocket at the end of a stick; also a form of baseball played with a stick and a lightweight ball.

stoop labor: work that involves bending over in agricultural fields, usually in order to tend or pick fruits or vegetables.

tenement: a usually crowded apartment building in poor condition.

Further Reading

United States of America

Ashabranner, Brent. *Still a Nation of Immigrants.* New York: Dutton Children's Books, 1993.

Birchfield, D. L., ed. *The Encyclopedia of North American Indians.* Tarrytown, NY: Marshall Cavendish, 1997.

Catalano, Julie. *The Mexican Americans.* Broomall, PA: Chelsea House, 1995.

Cox, Vic. *The Challenge of Immigration.* Springfield, NJ: Enslow Publications, 1995.

Ferry, Steven. *Cultures of America: Russian Americans.* Tarrytown, NY: Marshall Cavendish/Benchmark Books, 1996.

Franklin, Paula A. *Melting Pot or Not? Debating Cultural Identity.* Springfield, NJ: Enslow Publications, 1995.

Gabor, Al. *Cultures of America: Polish Americans.* Tarrytown, NY: Marshall Cavendish/Benchmark Books, 1995.

Galván, Raúl. *Cultures of America: Cuban Americans.* Tarrytown, NY: Marshall Cavendish/Benchmark Books, 1995.

Herda, D. J. *Ethnic America: The North Central States.* Brookfield, CT: Millbrook Press, 1991.

Herda, D. J. *Ethnic America: The Northeastern States.* Brookfield, CT: Millbrook Press, 1991.

Herda, D. J. *Ethnic America: The Northwestern States.* Brookfield, CT: Millbrook Press, 1991.

Jones, Jayne C. *In America: Greeks in America.* Minneapolis, MN: Lerner Group, 1990.

Kuropas, Myron B. *In America: Ukrainians in America.* Minneapolis, MN: Lerner Group, 1995.

Lee, Kathleen. *Illegal Immigration.* San Diego, CA: Lucent Books, 1996.

Lee, Lauren. *Cultures of America: Japanese Americans.* Tarrytown, NY: Marshall Cavendish/Benchmark Books, 1996.

Lee, Lauren. *Cultures of America: Korean Americans.* Tarrytown, NY: Marshall Cavendish/Benchmark Books, 1995.

Leuzzi, Linda. *Urban Life.* Broomall, PA: Chelsea House, 1995.

Moy, Tin. *Cultures of America: Chinese Americans.* Tarrytown, NY: Marshall Cavendish/Benchmark Books, 1995.

Payton, Shelia. *Cultures of America: African Americans.* Tarrytown, NY: Marshall Cavendish/Benchmark Books, 1995.

Press, David P., and Elizabeth Kaplan. *Cultures of America: Jewish Americans.* Tarrytown, NY: Marshall Cavendish/Benchmark Books, 1995.

Press, Petra. *Cultures of America: Mexican Americans.* Tarrytown, NY: Marshall Cavendish/Benchmark Books, 1995.

Press, Petra. *Cultures of America: Puerto Ricans.* Tarrytown, NY: Marshall Cavendish/Benchmark Books, 1996.

Reimers, David M. *A Land of Immigrants.* Broomall, PA: Chelsea House, 1995.

Riehecky, Janet. *Cultures of America: Irish Americans.* Tarrytown, NY: Marshall Cavendish/Benchmark Books, 1995.

Stone, Amy. *Cultures of America: French Americans.* Tarrytown, NY: Marshall Cavendish/Benchmark Books, 1995.

Washburne, Carolyn. *Cultures of America: Italian Americans.* Tarrytown, NY: Marshall Cavendish/Benchmark Books, 1995.

Index

Page numbers in *italic* indicate illustrations.

Page numbers in *italic* indicate illustrations.

REFERENCE

PEOPLES
of the
AMERICAS

PEOPLES

of the

AMERICAS

Volume 8
Peru–Turks and Caicos Islands

MARSHALL CAVENDISH
NEW YORK • LONDON • TORONTO • SYDNEY

Marshall Cavendish Corporation
99 White Plains Road
Tarrytown, New York 10591-9001

Consulting Editor: J. Patrick Gray, Professor of Anthropology, University of Wisconsin

Consultants: Jean-Marc Blais, Senior Interpretive Planner, Canadian Museum of Civilization, Hull, Quebec
    David Frye, Assistant Director, Department of Latin American and Caribbean Studies, University of Michigan

Spanish Consultant: Fran Kaplan

Contributing authors: D. L. Birchfield
        Marion Morrison
        Juliette Radcliffe Rogers
        Philip Steele
        Mary A. Stout

Discovery Books
    Managing Editor: Paul Humphrey
    Project Editor: Helen Dwyer
    Text Editor: Valerie J. Weber
    Design Concept: Ian Winton
    Designers: Barry Dwyer, Ian Winton, and Simon Borrough
    Cartographer: Stefan Chabluk

Marshall Cavendish
    Editorial Director: Paul Bernabeo
    Editor: Marian Armstrong
    Associate Editor: Debra M. Jacobs

The publishers would like to thank the following for their permission to reproduce photographs:
Barrett and MacKay (445); James Davis Travel Photography (436, 450, 453, 455, 456); Douglas Donne Bryant Stock Photography (Suzanne L. Murphy 435); Eye Ubiquitous (Bruce Adams 439); Robert Harding Picture Library (Ken Gillham 437; Robert Harding 459; Louise Murray 441); Hutchison Library (James Henderson 447); Panos Pictures (Trygve Bølstad 460; Ron Giling 454 top; Eduardo Márguez 418; Max Whitaker 458; Philip Wolmuth 443); Edward Parker (421, 429, 430, 431); David Simson (423, 438, 461); South American Pictures (Claire Leimbach 414, 433; Tony Morrison 410, 412, 413, 415, 416, 419, 420, 422, 424, 425, 426, 427, 428, 432, 448, 451, 452, 454 bottom, cover, frontispiece); Travel Ink (Nigel Bowen-Morris 463 bottom; Abbie Enock 463 top)

(frontispiece) Quechua mayor from Pisac, near Cuzco, Peru.

Editor's note: Many systems of dating have been used by different cultures throughout history. *Peoples of the Americas* uses B.C.E. (Before Common Era) and C.E. (Common Era) instead of B.C. (Before Christ) and A.D. (Anno Domini, "In the Year of the Lord") out of respect for the diversity of the world's peoples.

Library of Congress Cataloging-in-Publication Data
Peoples of the Americas.
        p.   cm.
        Includes bibliographical references and index.
        Contents: v. 1. Anguilla–Belize — v. 2. Bermuda–Brazil -— v. 3. Canada–Cayman Islands — v. 4. Chile–Costa Rica — v. 5. Cuba–French Guiana — v. 6. Greenland–Jamaica — v. 7. Martinique–Paraguay — v. 8. Peru–Turks and Caicos Islands — v. 9. United States of America — v. 10. United States of America–Virgin Islands

    ISBN 0-7614-7050-6 (set)
    1. Ethnology—America—Juvenile literature. 2. America—History—Juvenile literature. [1. Ethnology—America. 2. America—History.]
E29.A1P46 1999
970'.004—dc21   98-2801
                                                                                CIP
                                                                                AC

    ISBN 0-7614-7050-6 (set)
    ISBN 0-7614-7058-1 (vol. 8)

Printed and bound in Italy

Contents

PERU

PERU, THE THIRD LARGEST COUNTRY IN SOUTH AMERICA,
borders the Pacific Ocean in the west.

To the northwest, Peru shares a border with Ecuador, to the northeast with Colombia, to the east with Brazil, to the southeast with Bolivia, and to the south with Chile.

The land of Peru falls into three very distinct zones. In the west, between the Pacific Ocean and the foothills of the Andes Mountains, is a long coastal plain that is 90 miles (145 kilometers) wide at its broadest point. In the central area, which is mountainous, three ranges of the Andes cross the country from north to south with an average altitude of almost 10,000 feet (over 3,000 meters). Here lies Huascarán, which, at 22,205 feet (6,768 meters), is the highest mountain in Peru. This mountainous area is also home to many volcanoes.

To the east of the Andes lie the montaña (mone-TAHN-yah) and selva (SELL-bah). These zones include the forested eastern slopes of the Andes and extensive Amazon rain forests.

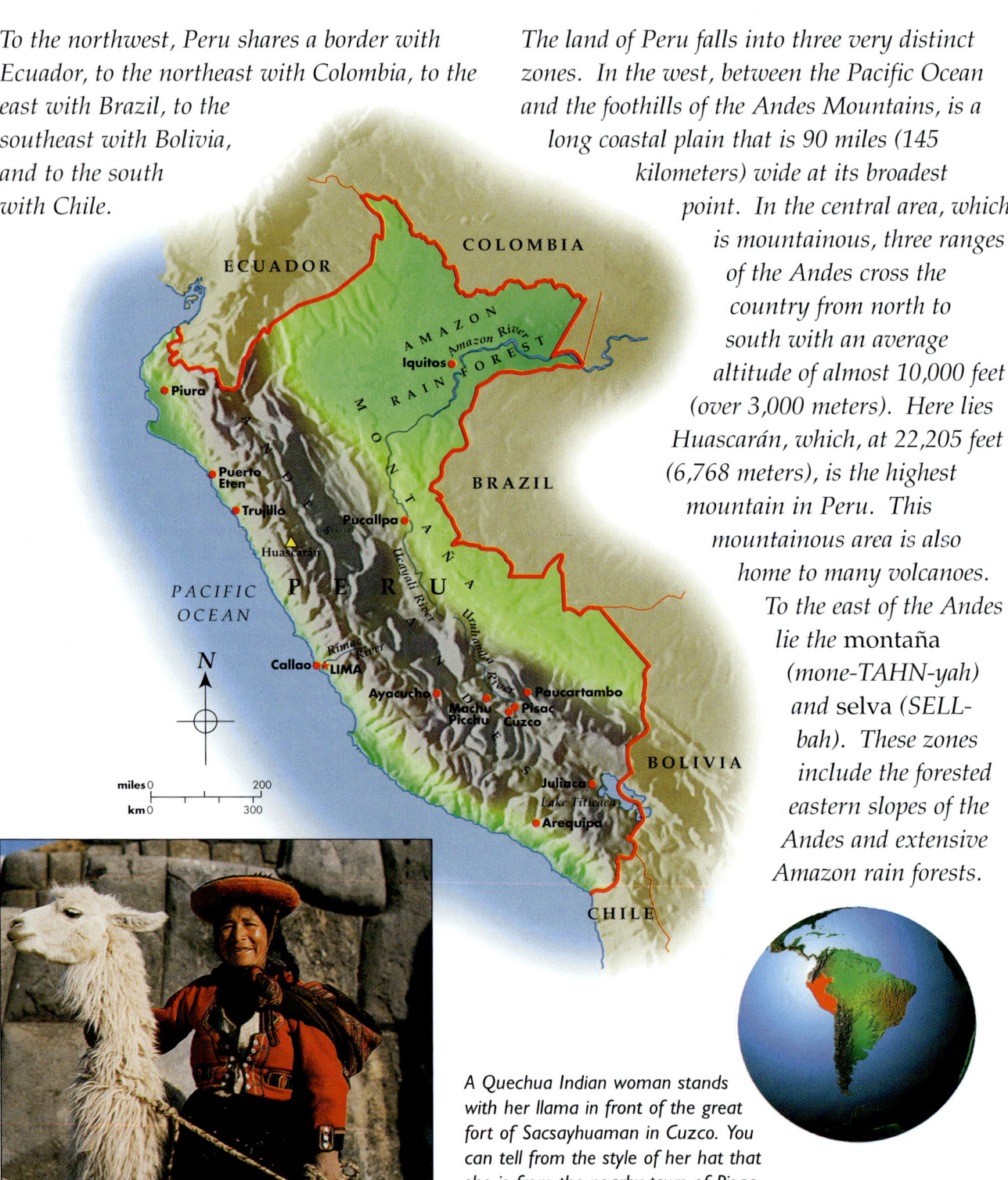

A Quechua Indian woman stands with her llama in front of the great fort of Sacsayhuaman in Cuzco. You can tell from the style of her hat that she is from the nearby town of Pisac.

Early Peoples, Cultures, and Civilizations

The earliest people to inhabit what we now call Peru (pay-ROO) probably arrived in the Andes about 13,000 B.C.E. These people were hunters and gatherers. On the coast they fished and collected shellfish, in the lowland forests they found plenty of game to hunt, and in the mountains they hunted wild vicuña and guanaco (both are mammals similar to the llama and common to South America).

Farming probably began about 2000 B.C.E. In the coastal river valleys and highlands, people cultivated corn, potatoes, beans, squash, and some fruits. They built canals to irrigate land on the desert coast and to bring water to the higher land during the dry season. They also built agricultural terraces on steep mountain slopes. Farmers herded llamas and alpacas to provide wool and meat and to use as pack animals. They also had dogs and kept guinea pigs for food.

These people lived in simple adobe-mud brick or rough stone houses. Pottery making developed as the people needed containers for storing, cooking, and brewing their produce. At the same time, as supplies of cotton and wool increased, people learned the art of weaving.

Separate civilizations developed with their own cultures and languages, particularly in the river valleys. By 1200 B.C.E. the Sechín (say-CHEEN) people had built the largest ceremonial center in the Americas, a huge, stone-faced platform standing 132 feet (40 meters) high. Parts of the walls, carved with macabre heads and torsos, have survived. The Sechín civilization is usually linked with a highland culture, that of the Chavín (chah-VEEN), which is well known for its stone carvings, often of jaguar and other animal themes. Both the Sechín and the Chavín cultures developed farming, domesticating animals, and ceremonial centers around the same time.

The south coast Paracas (pah-RAH-kahss) and Nazca (NAHSS-kah)

FACTS AND FIGURES

Official name: *República del Perú*

Status: *Independent state*

Capital: *Lima*

Major Cities: *Arequipa, Trujillo, Callao, Piura, Cuzco*

Area: *496,225 square miles (1,285,223 square kilometers)*

Population: *24,400,000*

Population density: *49 per square mile (19 per square kilometer)*

Peoples: *45 percent Native American; 37 percent mixed-race mestizo; 15 percent European descent; 3 percent African, Japanese, Chinese, and other descent*

Official languages: *Spanish, Quechua, Aymara*

Currency: *Nuevo Sol*

National days: *Labor Day (May 1); Independence Day (July 28–29); Santa Rosa de Lima (August 30); Battle of Angamos (October 7)*

Country's name: *Derives from a Quechua word meaning "land of plenty."*

Timeline:	Native people settle in and near the Andes	Early tribes begin farming in coastal river valleys and highlands	Sechín civilization completes the largest structure in the Americas at the time
	ca. 13,000 B.C.E.	ca. 2000 B.C.E.	ca. 1200 B.C.E.

The Nazca Lines—Things of Beauty and Mystery

South of Lima the desert coastal land becomes progressively drier. In one isolated region the surface is virtually level, its yellow earth covered with dark brown stones polished smooth by exposure to the wind and sun. Long ago the Nazca people made patterns by clearing the stones. "Lines" cross the desert for mile after mile, as straight as an arrow flies. The Nazca people also constructed immense designs of animals and a variety of other shapes and designs, including rectangular and triangular clearings, spiral designs, and heaps of stones.

The patterns have puzzled archaeologists for many years and have been the object of much speculation, some of it a bit outrageous. In the late 1960s, for example, some people speculated that the patterns could have been landing grounds for early space voyagers. Recent research has come up with more reliable evidence that Nazca people from adjacent valleys used the desert area as a sacred place—a kind of temple where they worshiped their many gods.

The hummingbird figure is one of several animals and birds drawn on the Nazca pampa. Among other designs are spirals, large rectangles, trapezoids, and a human figure.

civilizations emerged around 200 B.C.E. Mummies of the Paracas culture have been found wrapped in some of the finest weavings ever produced by early peoples, while pottery of both cultures was well advanced in style, design, and color. Today people of the Nazca culture are best known for the Nazca Lines—a huge set of extraordinary lines and animal designs—including birds, a whale, a spider, and a monkey—that they drew on the desert. Many experts have puzzled over the significance of these drawings, which are so large they must be seen from the air to be fully appreciated.

Between 100 C.E. and 800 C.E., the Moche (MOE-chay) people created a great empire

Paracas and Nazca civilizations emerge on the south coast	Moche people create an empire on the north coast	Wari-Tiwanaku civilization in central and southern Peru
ca. 200 B.C.E.	100–800 C.E.	600–1000 C.E.

CLIMATE

Peru has a wide range of climates. Although humidity is high in the desert coastal area, that region sees very little change in temperature. Much of the coast is mist-covered from May to November, but because inshore winds pick up little moisture from the cold offshore waters, it seldom rains. In the mountains, temperatures are generally high during the day, but often drop below freezing at night. The highest mountains are covered with permanent ice and snow. The selva, which consists of dense rain forests, has a hot and humid climate, with heavy rainfall year-round.

	Lima	Cuzco
Average January temperature	74°F (23°C)	56°F (13°C)
Average July temperature	62°F (17°C)	50°F (10°C)
Average annual precipitation	2 in (5 cm)	32 in (80 cm)

on the north coast. Many of the Moche were skillful engineers who built roads, irrigation canals, and aqueducts. They constructed two of the world's largest adobe-mud pyramids, the Huaca del Sol and the Huaca de la Luna (Temples of the Sun and Moon). Their craftspeople produced fine ceramic pots and objects in gold, silver, and precious stones.

Other great civilizations included the Wari-Tiwanaku (WAH-ree tee-wah-NAH-koo), which dominated much of central and southern Peru from about 600 to 1000 C.E., and the Chimú (chee-MOO), which extended over most of Peru's north coast. Wari developed around Ayacucho in the Peru highlands, and Tiwanaku developed south of Lake Titicaca (see BOLIVIA).

Despite the distance between the two cultures, they share significant similarities in design, weavings,

Gold objects of the early civilizations have been found in many graves, particularly along the northern Peru coast. This mask is a product of the Moche culture.

Inca emperor Pachacuti reigns	Incas invade Chimú empire on the north coast	Inca emperor Topa Inca Yupanqui reigns
1438–1471	1462–1470	1471–1491

413

ceramics, and architecture. The capital city of Tiwanaku was located near Lake Titicaca in present-day Bolivia. The city was built up out of wetlands through a process called raise-field agriculture. In this process, huge beds of earth are removed from dry areas and placed in swamps and lakes for the purpose of transforming wetlands into land suitable for farming. Some anthropologists have suggested that Tiwanaku's expansion into Wari territory in present-day Peru was motivated by a need for more land for growing crops.

The origins of the Chimú people are steeped in legends about people who came from the sea. The center of their empire was Chan Chan, a sprawling mud-brick city that housed thousands of artisans— women who were weavers of fine cloth and men who crafted metal objects and jewelry. Chimú was a highly developed civilization but was not strong enough to resist an Inca invasion sometime between 1462 and 1470.

The Rise and Fall of the Incas

In the thirteenth century the Incas were one of several small tribes living in the region of the present-day Peruvian city of Cuzco. It was not until the fifteenth century that they began to emerge as one of the most powerful nations in the Americas. Most of their conquests took place under their emperor Pachacuti, who reigned from 1438 to 1471, and then his son Topa Inca Yupanqui, who died in 1491. In a little less than one hundred years, the Incas created an empire that extended from present-day

The pageant of Inti Raymi takes place every year in June in Cuzco. It is a re-enactment of the Inca Festival of the Sun, and hundreds of Peruvians take part.

southern Colombia to central Chile, including Ecuador, Peru, and most of Bolivia.

Pachacuti was a brilliant soldier and administrator. His armies had plenty of food and clothing and fought with slings, bows, spears, and wooden clubs. He built good roads along which the army could transmit messages by a relay of runners or move quickly if it ran into trouble.

Inca empire split by civil war	Arrival of Spaniards	Francisco Pizarro founds Lima
ca. 1525–1532	1532	1535

Alongside the roads, storehouses were kept full of grain to feed the armies or official travelers. The Incas had no wheeled vehicles, but they transported officials or other important travelers in litters, which were carriages on poles carried on the shoulders of strong young men.

All roads converged on Cuzco, the Incas' main city. The main square stood at the center of Cuzco, with the royal palaces nearby. Only royalty, nobles, priests, and other important people were allowed into the heart of the city. Not far from the square was the Incas' most important shrine, the Temple of the Sun. Most buildings were of stone blocks fitted together without mortar, so precisely shaped that even today one cannot pass a knife blade between the stones.

When the Incas conquered a new territory, they took account of the number of people living there, especially young men who might be fit for the Inca army. They also noted whether the land was good for farming or mining. Sometimes whole populations were moved from one part of the empire to another, perhaps because they were troublemakers or perhaps because a workforce was needed. This policy of relocation was also a deliberate attempt to spread the Quechua (KAY-choo-ah) language of the Cuzco region throughout the Inca empire.

Government of the empire was strictly in the hands of the Inca emperor and Inca nobles of royal blood. The rest of the people were commoners who lived in *ayllus* (EYE-youss), or communities, in which everyone knew his or her place and had a specific job. The state dictated when and what workers should do, how they should run their households, and what goods they could own. It even ensured that people married and had children. The state also looked after the sick and elderly. Most people worked on the land or in the mines and had to undergo a period of enforced labor as a form of tax to the state.

In the towns a few people worked as potters, weavers, and jewelers. They fashioned the finest textiles, vicuña skins, and gold and silver objects for the Inca emperor and his nobles. The commoners wore simple clothing of tunics and skirts, with a cloak or mantle over the shoulders. Shoes were made of crude cotton, wool, or leather. The Incas had no form of writing. To keep their records and accounts they used a device of colored, knotted strings called a *quipu* (KEE-poo).

This Inca wooden drinking vessel is known as a k'eru (KAIR-roo). It is about six hundred years old and painted in natural vegetable dyes. Designs featuring feline heads were popular with the Incas.

Spain appoints first viceroy of Peru	African slaves brought in to work on the land and in the mines	Revolt by Native Americans against the Spanish authorities
1544	**mid-1500s**	**1780–1783**

The Lost City of Machu Picchu

Every year over a quarter of a million people visit Machu Picchu, "The Lost City of the Incas," isolated above the Urubamba River in the mountain forests of the Andes. Machu Picchu became known worldwide in 1911 when a young American, Hiram Bingham, was led to the site by local farmers. Bingham was searching for Vilcabamba, the last retreat of the Incas as they withdrew from the Spanish invaders. Bingham became convinced that Machu Picchu was the secret hideout. Recent research has shown that he made a mistake. Later in 1911 he was shown more ruins even deeper in the forest. Modern historians now believe that the second site, though not as impressive as Machu Picchu, is Vilcabamba.

Machu Picchu is a wonderful, nearly intact Inca settlement complete with temples, sacred fountains, and fine masonry. The people cultivated crops on the many stone-built terraces on the hillsides and had contact with neighbors via a series of stone-paved roads. One of these roads leads up high above the Urubamba River. Surrounded by snowcapped peaks, it is a magnificent approach to the realm of the Incas.

The Incas' principal god was the Sun god, from whom they believed the Inca emperor was descended. But they also worshiped other gods who controlled the weather and the land, brought good harvests, or helped them in war. Many of their festivals were related to the agricultural year, in which both the Sun god and Pachamama, or Mother Earth, were supremely important.

Sometime between 1525 and 1527, the Inca Emperor Huayna Capac died. He had not named a successor, and civil war broke out between his surviving sons, Atahualpa, who controlled the northern part of the empire, and Huascar, who had declared himself emperor in Cuzco. In 1532

The extraordinary Inca city of Machu Picchu sits on a hilltop above the valley of the Urubamba River. Surrounding the site is the Cordillera Central range of the Andes.

Peruvians declare independence	Spanish defeated at battles of Junín and Ayacucho	Peru begins exploitation of guano deposits and nitrate beds
1824	**1824**	**1840s**

Atahualpa had just defeated and imprisoned Huascar, when news came that a small group of Spanish adventurers had arrived on the coast of Peru.

The Spaniards in Peru

Francisco Pizarro led a band of only 180 men, but by ambush, deceit, and treachery they captured Atahualpa, acquired a huge gold ransom meant to secure his release, and then killed him. In 1533 the Spaniards occupied Cuzco and two years later founded Lima on the coast. The first years after the conquest were filled with Native rebellions and with bitter conflict among the Spaniards themselves, resulting in Pizarro's death in 1541.

The Spanish crown appointed viceroys to govern the territory. Land was divided among the Spanish conquerors, and Native Americans were forced into slave labor on the land and in the silver and copper mines. They lived a miserable existence, working under appalling conditions underground or toiling for long hours on the farms. They were badly nourished, but worst of all, they were vulnerable to the diseases brought in by the Europeans. Smallpox, influenza, measles, and other illnesses killed tens of thousands of Native people. For extra labor, the Spaniards kidnapped Africans and brought them to South America as slaves.

At the other extreme, wealthy Spanish colonists enjoyed a luxurious lifestyle, especially in Lima, which became the capital city for a territory that included all of South America with the exception of Brazil and Venezuela. In time a division appeared in the colonial society between the *Peninsulares* (pay-neen-soo-LAH-rayss), who were Spaniards born in Spain (which is on the Iberian Peninsula), and the *Creoles*, who were born in the colonies of Spanish parentage. While the Peninsulares usually occupied high positions in administration and government, the Creoles became successful traders.

Into this society another group of people emerged. As few women accompanied the original Spanish conquerors, the Europeans married Native women. They produced the mixed-race *mestizos*, who in colonial times became the equivalent of the middle class and today form a large part of the population.

During the eighteenth century the power and prestige of the viceroyalty of Peru began to decline as the Spanish government—which had previously forbidden colonial trade with any nation other than Spain—now allowed ports on the Atlantic side of the continent to trade with Europe. Output from the silver mines was falling, and in 1780 a Native rebellion caused considerable disruption to the Spanish authorities.

In 1808, events in Europe, including the occupation of Spain by France, led some Spanish colonies to declare independence from Spain. This was not the case in Peru, however, where large numbers of Spaniards remained loyal to the viceroyalty and the Spanish crown. Peru did not become independent until 1824, and only then because General José de San Martín, who had liberated much of the southern

Chinese workers arrive	Slavery abolished	War of the Pacific; Peru loses land to Chile
1849–1880s	1855	1879–1883

South American continent, and Simón Bolívar, who was responsible for freeing much of the north, brought their armies into the struggle.

From 1836 to 1839 Peru and Bolivia became a confederation. The exploitation of coastal guano deposits (dried bird droppings) as fertilizer brought a boost to the economy. Slavery was abolished in 1855, and Chinese laborers were brought in to work on the coastal estates. Another new industry also developed with the exploitation of rich nitrate beds in the Atacama Desert, but this led to the War of the Pacific (1879–1883), in which Peru lost part of its desert territory to Chile.

By the turn of the twentieth century, Peruvian society was still essentially feudal, with large estates owned by wealthy Creoles using Natives and some mestizos as labor. It was not until the 1960s, during the presidency of Fernando Belaunde Terry, that agricultural reform broke up the big estates and redistributed land to the ordinary people. The government also introduced some educational reforms and planned roads to open up the dense rain forest so people from the highlands could settle there.

President Belaunde Terry was forced from office in 1968 by the military, who remained in power until 1980. The military continued many of his social and educational reforms, introduced the use of the Native Quechua and Aymara languages in schools, and built rural schools. But the government incurred large foreign debts. Belaunde Terry returned as elected president in 1980, but he failed to resolve

the country's economic problems. Two guerrilla movements, the *Sendero Luminoso*, or Shining Path, and the *Tupac Amaru*, were also creating trouble. The aim of both the Senderos and the Tupac Amaru was to overthrow the Lima-based government. (Tupac Amaru was named after the last Inca emperor killed by the Spaniards in the

A local union of Quechua and mestizo farmers protests against measures to reduce the cultivation of coca, their livelihood. Their banner reads "Coca or death."

sixteenth century.) Although their methods have often been disruptive and violent, they have gained some support among poverty-stricken residents of many highland and rural communities.

In 1990 and again in 1995, Alberto Fujimori, whose parents were Japanese immigrants, was elected president. His priorities were improving the economy and fighting the guerrillas, whose activities had led to thousands of deaths, bombs, and a

Amazon rubber boom begins	Agricultural reform act under President Belaunde Terry	Military in power	Belaunde Terry re-elected as president
1880s	**1964**	**1968–1980**	**1980**

general disruption of industry and everyday life. The guerrillas were also connected to the illegal drug trade, which has been another major problem for the government.

In his first term as president, Fujimori enjoyed considerable success as the economy improved and the leader of the Senderos was captured. Many felt this would finish the guerrillas, but during Fujimori's second term the Tupac Amaru staged a bold attack on the Japanese Embassy, taking almost five hundred people hostage. After a standoff lasting several weeks, the military killed all the terrorists and freed the hostages. By the mid-1990s the president was no longer as popular as he once was, mainly because he had done little to help the mass of poor people who continue to face rising prices and unemployment.

Life in Peru Today

Almost twenty-five million people live in Peru today. More than one-third of these people are mixed-race mestizos. About three million Native Quechuas and Aymaras live in the highlands, and another 150,000 to 200,000 Native people are estimated to live in the tropical lowlands. It is difficult to be precise about the Native population. In recent years many have migrated from the highland regions to the coast and from rural areas to the cities and towns. In the process, many Native people have taken on characteristics of the mestizo way of life by the way they dress or by speaking Spanish. The rest of the population consists of whites, mainly

Many people in Lima live in the shantytowns on the outskirts of the city. The huts are made of reed and cardboard, and the people are lining up at the only faucet for water.

Sendero Luminoso and Tupac Amaru guerrilla groups carry out terrorist campaigns	Alberto Fujimori elected president	Alberto Fujimori re-elected as president	Attack on Japanese Embassy by Tupac Amaru guerrilla group
1980s	**1990**	**1995**	**1996–1997**

Young mestizo schoolchildren take part in a parade in Cuzco. They are wearing sashes in the colors of Tawantinsuyu, the original name of the Inca empire.

descendants of European immigrants and the original Spanish settlers, and descendants of African, Chinese, Japanese, and other Asian immigrants. The most widely spoken language is Spanish, but about one-fifth of all Peruvians speak Quechua or Aymara as their main language. Other Native people also continue to use their own languages, which are principally of the Arawakan family.

The number of people living in the cities has increased greatly in the last two decades, and today about 70 percent of the people live in urban areas. One-third of all Peruvians now live in Lima, the capital. The densely wooded selva, which covers 60 percent of the country, is home to just 5 percent of the people. Few people have settled there because the forested land is difficult to clear and work, there are few roads, and the main transportation routes are rivers. The central mountain ranges create a formidable barrier to transportation, and thus movement from one part of Peru to another has never been

easy. The development of railroads led to easier access between the coast and the highlands, but it was only the arrival of aircraft that made regular contact with the selva and other remote areas possible.

Free schooling is available to all children from the age of six to fifteen. On the college level, Peru has a number of state-run, private, and Catholic universities. The best-equipped and most heavily attended schools are in the cities and towns. Many children in remote villages can't attend; they are simply too far away to walk to the nearest school, while others are needed to work at home, helping with farming and caring for animals. In the eastern lowlands, missionaries have introduced schooling into some Native villages.

Spanish priests and missionaries brought Catholicism to Peru, but people today are free to practice other religions as well. Although most Native people accepted the

Catholic faith, they combined many of its teachings and beliefs with their own ancient beliefs. According to this practice, known as syncretism, many festivals celebrating Native gods became associated with celebrations on the Christian calendar. For example, in the third week of June, Corpus Christi in Cuzco is observed at much the same time as Inti Raymi, the Inca Festival of the Sun. During this century some evangelical Protestant groups have been hard at work in Peru, including Mormons, Jehovah's Witnesses, and Seventh-Day Adventists.

Food, Served Hot or Not

Most Peruvian dishes are hot and spicy or have a mixture of hot peppers served as a side plate. Papas a la huancaína *(PAH-pahss ah lah wonk-ah-EE-nah), potatoes with a spicy sauce, is a favorite dish. Many traditional dishes on the coast are based on fish, and many dishes in the highlands include potatoes and corn.*

The most popular fish dishes are seviche, raw fish marinated in lemon juice with onions and red peppers, and escabeche *(ayss-cah-BAY-chay), fish with onions, hot green peppers, red peppers, shrimp, eggs, olives, and cumin.*

In the highlands, soups and stews are widely eaten. Cooked for many hours and containing every type of vegetable, often with pieces of pork, chicken, or perhaps beef, they are the warmest and most sustaining food in the cold climate. Tamales, boiled corn dumplings filled with meat and wrapped in a banana leaf, are a traditional food. Something of a delicacy, and reared in Native homes for special occasions, is guinea pig, which is usually roasted.

In the smart suburb of Miraflores in Lima, office workers take their lunch break. This sidewalk snackbar is offering ice cream, coffee, and some alcoholic and fruit beverages.

Costeños: People of the Coast

The mainly mestizo coastal people, or *costeños* (coe-STAIN-yoess), as they are known, have traditionally settled in the irrigated valleys between long stretches of desert. Cities and towns, including the capital Lima, have grown in the larger valleys and offer all the comforts of modern life, such as restaurants, supermarkets, movie theaters, and discos. These provide work for many people. Others are employed in the manufacturing industries that surround most of the larger cities. The

421

The Lord of the Miracles

Every October for over four hundred years, the people of Lima have celebrated the miraculous survival of an image of Christ. The story began on November 13, 1655, when an earthquake struck Lima and caused tremendous damage to the churches and main buildings. Many valuable treasures were lost. Miraculously, one image of Christ survived in a small adobe church in the poor district of Pachacamilla. The image of a black Christ had been painted on a mud-brick wall by an African slave. The piece of wall was taken to another church, where on October 20, 1687, another earthquake struck. Again the image survived.

Every year a replica of this image, known as the Lord of the Miracles, is taken on a tour of the city. October in Lima is known as the "purple month," when members of the "Brotherhood" in charge of the image dress in purple cassocks and parade through the streets. Huge crowds, estimated at two million people, follow the procession, which takes many days to visit different parts of the city. Along the way people light candles, weep, and desperately try to touch the image. In the surrounding streets the spirit is festive. Traditional sweetmeats are sold from stalls, while the crowd celebrates along the processional route deep into the night.

principal positions in government and business tend to remain in the hands of the small but powerful white elite.

In the past twenty-five years Lima has grown dramatically from a city of slightly under two million to about seven million. Much of the growth has come with the general trend of people moving from rural to urban areas, but in the late 1980s this trend was compounded by refugees fleeing terrorist groups in the countryside.

Lima is now a sprawling city straddling the River Rímac. The old city still contains fine colonial buildings, while the modern suburbs are being filled with glass-faced, high-rise offices, hotels, and apartments. Beyond this urban core lie lower-cost suburbs and the countless poor shantytowns, where thousands of families live, often without sanitation or water. Life in these *pueblos jovenes* (PWAY-bloess HOE-vane-ayss) is far removed from the discos and lights of the central city. Most people have no work and live on the very margin of society, selling trinkets in the city streets, doing odd jobs, or even begging.

The growth of Lima has also changed the view of the coastline. For almost 100 miles (160 kilometers) south of the capital, every accessible beach now has vacation chalets and houses where *Limeños* (lee-MAYN-yoess)—the people of Lima—spend long summer weekends swimming and surfing, returning to the city late on Sunday in long lines of traffic.

In parts of Lima it is hard to walk down a street without finding a Chinese restauarant, or *chifa* (CHEE-fah). The section of Lima known as Chinatown has a particularly high concentration of Chinese Peruvian residents and businesses, but Peruvians of Chinese descent also live in other towns, especially Trujillo on the northern coast and Iquitos on the Amazon River. The first Chinese came to Peru as

Two Chinese children in Lima dress like most other poor Peruvians. Only their faces reveal their heritage. These days, few young people speak Chinese; at school they learn Spanish.

contract laborers in the middle of the nineteenth century. Often their living conditions were terrible and they were treated harshly. Nonetheless, most of the Chinese stayed in Peru and married mestizo wives, often from the lower social classes of the time. Now some Chinese occupy senior professional jobs or own restaurants and small shops, and Lima has a Chinese-language newspaper.

Africans came to Peru in small numbers in Spanish colonial times as slaves. At the beginning of the seventeenth century, almost half of the capital's population of twenty-five thousand was black or mulatto (of mixed African and European parentage). By the end of the next century, over 44 percent of all the black slaves in Peru were in Lima Province. In later years, before the abolition of slavery, some blacks gained their freedom by agreeing to fight with the separatist forces against the Spanish crown. Today the few black Peruvians are an accepted part of Peruvian society and tend to live in the coastal valleys, where they work on farms.

El Niño

Along the Peruvian coast the sea is cold because its water originates in the Antarctic and in deep undersea trenches off the coast of Peru. In certain years, however, El Niño, a warm current, sweeps southward, changing the climate. Peruvians know the Niño is on the way when instead of the mist, they see unusually warm and sunny weather long before Christmas. Because the Niño usually arrives close to Christmas, Peruvians call it El Niño, *the shortened form of* El Niño Jésus *(el NEEN-yo hay-SOOSS)—"the baby Jesus."*

Niños have caused immense damage along the Ecuadoran and Peruvian coasts, flooding land and destroying roads and villages. As far as some coastal Peruvians are concerned, El Niño is a mixed blessing. Surfers and sunbathers get to enjoy a long warm summer, but the fishermen see fish shoals disappearing as the surface plankton, on which they feed, dies. As the shoals move away the huge colonies of sea birds that have always been a feature of the coast's wildlife also die of starvation.

Today scientists are concerned that global warming is leading to more frequent Niños and that their effects will be more far-reaching.

There are many fishing villages along Peru's coast. Here at Puerto Eten, wives and children of the fishermen sort the early morning catch. Any surplus is sold in the local market.

Until the 1960s, when agricultural reforms redistributed land to ordinary people, many of the coastal farms were very large. Today farmers work on small plots or on a cooperative basis with other farmers, growing citrus fruits, particularly oranges, and corn, cotton, rice, and vegetables. Although farming the valleys has been the principal work for generations, the sea has become increasingly important as a source of income. One major product of the sea is the anchovy, a small fish that is treated, dried, and ground to form fishmeal, one of Peru's bigger exports.

People of the Highlands: The Quechua

When the Incas began to expand their empire, more than forty separate tribes occupied the highlands of Peru and neighboring Bolivia. With the spread of Inca influence, the Quechua language became almost universal, with as many as thirty separate variations and dialects. The only other Native American language that is still used in the highlands, Aymara, is spoken by the people of the same name, who live mostly around Lake Titicaca.

Today the majority of Native people in the Peruvian highlands are known as Quechua, after the language. Their way of life can vary slightly depending on which region they inhabit. In the *punas* (POO-nahs), or higher places with mountain grasses, the Quechua economy depends on herding llamas, the domesticated Andean relative of the camel. Llama wool is used for weaving fine garments. Quechuas on the fertile mountain slopes usually farm potatoes, while Quechuas living in the warmer, sheltered, or lower valleys depend on their corn harvest. In many parts of the Peruvian highlands, ancient terraces on the steep hillsides are still used for agriculture, and often the original stone-lined irrigation channels carry water from mountain streams.

In the highlands today mestizos far outnumber the Quechua, even though they may speak Quechua as a second language. The most traditional Quechua live in isolated areas, often many days walking from the nearest town. They continue to farm much as they have for centuries. They use simple digging instruments such as a short hoe or stick pressed with the foot.

At fiesta time in Cuzco, a big market usually bustles in the main square. There is always plenty to eat, especially delicacies like cooked guinea pig and spicy sausages.

Often they use large sticks for threshing corn, while the winnowing to separate the chaff is done by hand in the wind. Animals and implements introduced centuries ago by the European colonizers, such as donkeys, bullocks, and wooden plows, are also common.

As the Quechua are primarily farmers, their life follows the seasons of the farming year. Although they followed the moon for their calendar, the Incas also used a simple sun calendar and held festivals when the sun rose or set at special points on the horizon. The Quechua follow the same pattern but with slight variations added by

the Spaniards, so it is now common for the ancient festivals to be linked with a Christian saint's day. In mid-July, for example, the Fiesta del Carmen has replaced the old festival of "cleaning the fields of impurities," and in Paucartambo near Cuzco hundreds of people from local Quechua communities crowd into the town's small square. An image of La Virgen María del Monte Carmeo (Our Lady of Mount Carmel), the patron saint, is paraded around, and the day is filled with dancing, music, and plenty of food.

The modern, often very colorful, Quechua dress is largely based on European designs introduced by the Spaniards. Women wear long skirts that are homespun from sheep's wool or

Young Quechua mothers with their children. The women and girl wear local traditional hats, while the two young boys are wearing chullus *that cover their ears.*

Corn: The Pan-American Plant

Corn (maize) originated as a wild plant in the Americas. Its cultivation probably began in Mexico about eight thousand years ago, and the seeds were gradually introduced to the Andes as people settled there. The planting season in Inca times was August, a month they named Yapakis, *and the harvest was in May, the month of Aymoray, "the great cultivation." Special festivals were held in both months. Animals such as guinea pigs and llamas were sacrificed to placate the gods. Today, the May harvest is marked by the Festival of the Cross, when Quechua women provide large quantities of corn beer, or* chicha *(CHEE-chah), made by boiling corn in water and allowing the liquid to ferment naturally. Chicha was a special drink at most Inca festivals as it was believed to possess sacred properties. Lumps of cornflour paste (lumps of flour mixed with blood and given to the people to eat by the priests) were also used in Inca rituals. In modern Peru a favorite drink is* chicha morado *(CHEE-chah moe-RAH-tho), which is sweet and nonalcoholic. The original recipe used purple corn, resulting in a purple drink, but artificial flavors and colors are often used today.*

cotton. Above this they have a short jacket or bodice. Their hats are especially colorful. Silver jewelry is normally worn by the women, even if it is only a simple spoon-shaped pin to fasten a shawl. Both men and women usually wear sandals made of old automobile tires. Men's dress includes knee-length homespun pants, a short jacket, and a woolen cape, or *poncho*. The patterns used in the weaving of ponchos are highly individual, especially in the central and southern parts of the highlands. It is possible to know which community a man comes from by the designs. They often represent spiritual symbols from ancient times, and some even tell folk stories.

In some ways Quechua family life is changing. At one time all the family, including the children, worked from dawn to dusk. Now, where there are schools, children attend lessons first before working in the fields.

Children always have *padrinos* (pah-DREE-noess), or godfathers, to help or advise them on any number of issues. When a boy or girl reaches five years old, the godfather arranges a hair-cutting ceremony to raise money for the child. The padrino cuts the first lock of hair and gives his godchild a gift such as a sheep or money. Other guests are then invited to cut other locks in return for gifts.

Around their fifth birthday children in some mountain communities have their hair cut. Friends are invited to cut a lock and give a gift, usually of money.

427

This Aymara woman in her traditional derby hat comes from the region of Lake Titicaca. She is selling alpaca wool items and woven ponchos to tourists.

The Aymara of Lake Titicaca

The women of the Aymara today are generally recognized by their derby hats, while the men mostly wear a simple trilby (a soft felt hat) over a knitted hat, or *chullo* (CHOO-yo). Before the derby hat, the Aymara wore a variety of hats dating from Spanish times. A few of these are still worn by elderly women in remote places. The derby has become the preferred headwear for many of the mestizos around Lake Titicaca and in neighboring parts of Bolivia.

The Aymara have traditionally been settled close to Lake Titicaca, and the majority now live south of the lake, in Bolivia (see BOLIVIA). In both Peru and Bolivia the Aymara occupy mainly the land around Lake Titicaca and the flanks of the surrounding mountain ranges. They farm the flatlands around the lake and raise large flocks of sheep. On the mountain slopes they raise alpacas. The alpaca is a relative of the llama that is renowned for its wool.

The many Catholic priests who followed the Spanish soldiers organized the Aymara to build monasteries and large, elaborate churches around Lake Titicaca that have survived to modern times. Aymara festivals combine such Christian symbols as the cross with elements of ancient Aymara spiritual practices, such as pouring liquid offerings to Pachamama, or Mother Earth. Coca, better known today as the leaf from which cocaine is derived, has been used for centuries by both the Quechua and Aymara in their rituals. Participants select coca leaves and use them as offerings to the spirits. Depending on the spirit, coca is used in different ways, sometimes spread on the ground with alcohol, laid in the foundation of a house, or placed on the diseased part of a body. Native people also chew the leaf to help relieve feelings of hunger and cold.

In addition to elements of the Catholic faith, the Spaniards left the Aymara with other remnants of Spanish and European culture. They introduced the Aymara to many domesticated animals, such as sheep, cows, donkeys, and mules. New plants, such as barley, beans, and onions, arrived from Europe, and the Aymara were introduced to the plow, iron tools, glazed pottery, and a new type of loom.

The Aymara also grow domesticated plants native to the Andes, such as potatoes and the cereals quinoa and *cañawa* (cahn-YAH-wah), which are rich in protein. Native plants have been important in Aymara life for centuries, and after the potato perhaps the most important is the totora reed that grows in the shallow water of Lake Titicaca's bays. The delicate white roots and shoots of totora are gathered to feed both people and cattle. The dried reed itself has countless uses, including making reed bundle rafts, known as *balsas* (BAHL-sahss), that are still used by fishermen. At one time houses with totora walls and roofs were common around part of the lake, but now they are used only by a few Aymara who live on large, floating mats of cut reeds.

These lake dwellers used to depend for their livelihood on fishing and totora. The native lake fish were tiny, but the Aymara caught plenty and sold any surplus in mainland markets. The fish supply is now dwindling, but economically times are better as lake dwellers and their unusual islands have become a major tourist attraction in recent years.

Native Americans and Mestizos of the Montaña

To Peruvians the land of ravines, rushing rivers, and cloud-soaked forest on the eastern slopes of the Andes Mountains is known as the montaña. Until the early twentieth century only mule trails led into the wilderness. That isolation has been changed with roads and many small airports.

The modern montaña is dotted with small settlements and a few towns, mostly populated by mestizos. These residents are largely migrants from the highlands who have moved into the territory to farm coffee, cacao, and coca and trade in lumber and forest products. Life in the small settlements is unhurried. Many people do not have telephone connections, and physical contact with the outside world comes mostly from passing traffic.

Aymara Indians living on the Island of Taquile in Lake Titicaca are expert knitters. It is mostly the men that knit, making traditional items of alpaca and sheep wool.

A Shipibo Indian family with crafts they have made. They use a distinctive geometric style in their art that can be seen here on the pots and on the cloth of the women's skirts.

Native people have always lived in these forests, often beside the rivers or in clearer spaces where there is some grassland. They mixed very little with the highland people in the mountains above or with the Amazon people in the tropical forests below so they developed a unique way of life.

The principal groups still living in the montaña are the Ashaninka, or Campa, the Machiguenga, the Piro, the Shipibo-Conibo, the Mayoruna, and the Amahuaca. Many of these peoples lead similar lifestyles. Those in isolated places still wear long, cotton, cloaklike ponchos, or *cushmas* (COOSH-mahss). Often they paint their faces, sometimes with no more than a simple line drawn with a blue-black staining juice, sometimes with much larger patches of red stain from ground achiote (ah-chee-OH-tay), which is a seed. Ornaments include seed necklaces and small bracelets made of hundreds of tiny colored glass beads threaded on cotton to form geometric patterns. The Shipibo-Conibo people are noted for pottery made of fine clay and covered with a white paint. Against this background they draw red or black designs.

The Native Americans of the montaña live in simple houses thatched with palm. The raised floor and sides are generally made from split palm wood. The women keep gardens in patches of cleared forest, where they grow several crops, especially yucca, which has tubers that are used like potatoes. Men make bows and arrows for hunting and fishing, though this is not as common as it once was because many people now own shotguns. Schools and medical clinics have been built, especially in the larger centers. These are run both by the state and by missionary groups.

Much of the montaña is now being exploited by mestizos, and huge areas are in the control of cocaine producers. This has led to the retreat of many of the last traditional Native Americans in the region to the most inaccessible areas of Peru.

Peoples of the Amazon

Huge rivers meander eastward away from the montaña toward Brazil through a vast region entirely covered by rain forest. This is Amazonia. Over the past 150 years mestizo and European pioneers have established many small settlements. Many of the settlements are beside rivers, the natural highways of the area. Today two of these settlements have grown into cities. Pucallpa on a tributary of the Amazon River has 200,000 inhabitants, and Iquitos on the Amazon has almost half a million. Pucallpa is connected by a road to Lima, but Iquitos is totally surrounded by forest and is accessible only by air or by river. All the trappings of modern life exist in these

cities—banks, hotels, restaurants, movies, schools, and hospitals—but their economic life revolves around trading and the drive to open up more of the forest for agriculture. Only occasionally, people from the Native forest tribes visit the cities, but most keep to their distant homes. Few have remained completely untouched by outside influences, however, and the Yaminawa, or Nawa, are perhaps the last with whom contact is rarely made. Many fear, however, that even their private world of total dependence on the forest and rivers for food may soon vanish as oil exploration extends into their territory.

The true forest people, who also include the Nahua, the Matsés, the Yagua, and the Huitoto, maintain close contact with the natural world. Their original spiritual beliefs are based on spirits of the forest and river; they gather or grow their food in gardens; and they make their clothing, which is usually minimal, from forest fibers. Ornaments such as necklaces are made from tiny seeds or the teeth of animals. Facial

The most common transportation on Peru's Amazon is a boat. There are many hazards in the rivers; here a young boy is on the lookout for tree trunks and hidden rocks.

This Nahua man is making a decoration of feathers to wear. His necklace is of forest seeds, and he wears a palm-fiber covering around his waist.

Native Americans in Amazonia, is changing quickly. Missionaries, schools, medical posts, and river traders of all kinds are everywhere, even though the forest wall may seem impenetrable.

Peruvian Music

The ancient music of the central Andes was played on drums and a variety of flutes made from reeds, ceramic, or bone. The haunting sound is still heard occasionally in some Quechua communities, but most of the Quechua music in Peru has been influenced strongly by instruments introduced by the Spaniards. A thirty-six-stringed harp, the violin, accordion, and a small guitar called a *charango* (chah-RAHN-go) are the favored instruments at most fiestas. In recent years there has been a revival of music played on flutes, particularly the *antaras* (ahn-TAH-rahss), or *zampoñas*

decoration comes from natural colors, and medicines are extracted from forest plants. This unique way of life, like that of many

The Rubber Boom

Until the middle of the nineteenth century, Europeans and forest people had little contact with one another. As Europe became more and more industrialized, however, the demand for rubber grew, first for waterproofing clothes and later for making automobile tires. The rubber trees of the Amazon forest yielded a sap that could be hardened by a process known as vulcanization. The best trees were in Peru's Amazonia, and by the end of the nineteenth century, the Peruvian rivers were bustling with activity spawned by the rubber industry. The people running the industry became wealthy—so wealthy that they could even afford to send their dirty clothes to Europe to be laundered—but the rubber industry needed cheap labor to fuel its productivity and huge profits. Although poor Brazilians arrived by the boatload, the main source was the Native people. The methods of rounding up workers were harsh, and Native resistance to "recruiting" incursions was often met with unspeakable brutality. Whole tribes were decimated, and people were subjected to horrendous torture. One U.S. observer reported an incident in which a victim was wrapped in the national flag, doused with gasoline, and burned to death.

Mario Vargas Llosa

Mario Vargas Llosa is one of the most famous Peruvians of recent times. Born in 1936 in the city of Arequipa, he studied at San Marcos University in Lima and eventually turned to a career as a novelist. His themes come mostly from his observations of life in Peru. His greatest novel is Conversation in the Cathedral, *set in a 1950s military dictatorship. Another classic is* The War at the End of the World, *set in the middle of a rebellion in the backlands of Brazil. In 1990 Vargas Llosa was a candidate for president of Peru. He lost the election to Alberto Fujimori, and totally disillusioned, he left for Spain.*

(sahm-PONE-yahss), fashioned from sets of hollow reeds joined together in rows. Such music is often played at public festivals by folklore groups, some of international fame. Two contemporary Peruvian folklore groups that have become known outside of Peru are the Amaru and the Apu.

Modern Peruvians, though, are far more accustomed to other sounds. Of these sounds, *huaynos* (WHY-noess) (also known as waynos) are the most common and popular. The huayno is a kind of country music, Peruvian style, usually love songs set against a backdrop of the beauty of life in the countryside. The huayno is heard in much of coastal Peru, particularly at dances and festivals. In the small settlements and the towns of the Amazon region, the huayno and music of modern Western culture exist side by side.

Mestizos wearing colorful ponchos play Western instruments such as saxophones and clarinets at a festival in Cuzco.

PUERTO RICO

PUERTO RICO LIES IN THE GREATER ANTILLES ISLAND CHAIN, between Hispaniola and the Virgin Islands.

The island of Puerto Rico measures about 100 miles (160 kilometers) from east to west and just 35 miles (56 kilometers) from north to south. The territory also includes several smaller islands, including Vieques, Culebra, and Mona.

The center of the island is covered by a mountain range, the Cordillera Central, which rises to 4,389 feet (1,338 meters) above sea level at Cerro de Punta. Hillsides are blanketed by green rain forest. People primarily farm in the east, in the Turabo Valley, and on the plains that form a narrow strip around the coast. Some of the coastal land in the south is extremely dry. The northwest is made of limestone rock, which has been shaped and bored by water, forming small hills and sinkholes.

CLIMATE

Puerto Rico has a tropical climate, but is cooled by winds from the sea. Much of the coast and the higher mountain slopes remain cool, but some parts of the island can become very hot.

Average January temperature: *78°F (26°C)*

Average July temperature: *82°F (28°C)*

Average annual precipitation: *50 in (127 cm)*

Gateway to the Caribbean

The first Puerto Ricans were Native American peoples such as the Ciboney and the Igneri, who lived by gathering wild food in the forests and shellfish from the shore. About a thousand years ago the islands were settled by an Arawak-speaking people called the Taino (TIE-no). They called the island *Borinquen*, which in their language meant "land of the great lord." The Taino are usually described as a peaceful people who rarely engaged in violence unless provoked, as they were in the 1400s, when they came under attack from their more aggressive Carib (cah-REEB) neighbors. Like the Taino, Caribs had migrated to the Caribbean from South American rain forests.

In 1493 the Spanish, under Christopher Columbus, arrived on the island and declared that it was now ruled by Spain. Spanish settlers arrived in 1508, led by the adventurer Juan Ponce de León. The Taino were treated as slave labor for the island's gold mines. They rebelled, but most were killed or died of disease. A few survived and escaped to the central mountains or other islands.

The Spanish came under attack by the Caribs, and when the gold mines became depleted of their treasure, most Spanish settlers moved on to the mainland of Central and South America. Those who remained planted crops such as sugar and cotton or lived by smuggling. They imported slaves from western Africa, who

FACTS AND FIGURES

Official name: *Commonwealth of Puerto Rico*

Status: *Self-governing Commonwealth Territory of the United States of America*

Capital: *San Juan*

Major cities: *Bayamón, Carolina*

Area: *3,460 square miles (8,960 square kilometers)*

Population: *3,800,000*

Population density: *1,098 per square mile (424 per square kilometer)*

Peoples: *75 percent mixed (European-African-Native American) descent; 25 percent other, including Afro-Caribbean, European, and Chinese descent.*

Official languages: *English, Spanish*

Currency: *U.S. dollar*

National days: *Constitution Day (July 25); Grito de Lares (September 23)*

Country's name: *From the Spanish, meaning "rich port."*

The Taino of Borinquen

Who were the Taino? They were a highly developed and politically organized people who lived in farming villages, growing crops such as corn and cassava, from which they made bread. They ate turtles, shellfish, and iguana meat. The people grew cotton and used tobacco as a medicine and for spiritual ceremonies. Like the ancient peoples of Mexico and elsewhere throughout the Americas, they liked to play ball games. Playing courts have been discovered in the center of the island.

very soon outnumbered their masters. Spain showed little interest in the colony until the mid-eighteenth century when new settlers were brought in, new plantations were laid out, and new towns were built.

Despite these efforts to further build up the

Simple yet expressive, this fine carving of a bird shows off the artistic skills of the Taino people, who lived in Puerto Rico at the time of the Spanish invasion.

Timeline:	Igneri people join Ciboney people on island	Taino replace previous Native Americans	Christopher Columbus claims island for Spain	Spanish under Juan Ponce de León settle island	Slavery abolished
	ca. 200 B.C.E.	1000s C.E.	1493	1508	1873

The fortress of San Felipe del Morro in San Juan above the Atlantic breakers. Built between 1540 and 1783, it was last attacked in 1898 by the United States.

island colony, during the 1800s the whole of Spain's American empire began to break up. Spanish settlers living in the Americas wanted to rule themselves. Puerto Rico (poo-AIR-toe REE-koe) was no different, but Spain did its best to stifle all signs of protest.

Life on Puerto Rico was particularly harsh for the slaves, who lived under brutal laws based on race and did not receive their freedom until 1873. In 1897 Spain at last granted Puerto Rico a degree of self-rule. The island had barely tasted freedom, however, before the United States invaded as part of its campaign against Spain during the Spanish-American War. The United States defeated Spain, and in the following year Puerto Rico became a U.S. possession.

Under the United States the island was run even less democratically than it had been under the Spanish. Puerto Ricans were not made U.S. citizens until 1916 and were not allowed to choose their own governor until 1943. Throughout this time many Puerto Ricans demanded civil rights and democracy.

In 1952 Puerto Rico became a Commonwealth of the United States. Many Puerto Ricans still wanted full independence, but most were happy to reap the economic benefits of their link with the United States. More Puerto Ricans began settling on the U.S. mainland (see UNITED STATES OF AMERICA).

Many felt that the next step in the island's political development should be to become the fifty-first U.S. state. During the 1993 election, voters on the island rejected this option by a narrow margin. In March 1998 the go-ahead was given for another vote to take place on the status of the territory.

A Mixture of Peoples

Over the ages Puerto Rico has been a meeting place for many different peoples and cultures. While three-quarters of the population has mixed roots—mostly Taino, Spanish, and Afro-Caribbean—other peoples have also settled on the island over the years, including French, Irish, Scots, Cubans, South Americans, North Americans, Italians, and Chinese.

What remains of the Taino culture? Many Puerto Rican place-names, such as Mayagüez, date from the days before Columbus. Some of the Arawak words

Self-government for Puerto Ricans under Spanish governor	Treaty of Paris gives island to United States	Puerto Rico becomes Commonwealth Territory of the United States	Bid to make Puerto Rico the fifty-first U.S. state rejected	Vote on status of territory
1897	**1898**	**1952**	**1993**	**1998**

436

There is a strong Roman Catholic Church, which is supported by about 80 percent of all Puerto Ricans. Christmas, Easter, saints' days, and other Christian festivals play an important part in the island's life, just as they do in Spain. Another Spanish legacy is a love of horses and riding. Latin American music and dance are also strongly influenced by Spanish tradition.

African drumming and rhythms provide the beat in much of Puerto Rico's dance music. African words, such as *guneo* (gee-NAY-oh) (banana), also survive. Many of the masks and costumes worn at Christian festivals are similar to those worn at masquerades held by the Yoruba and Ibo peoples of southern Nigeria.

A baton twirler grins as she leads the festival parade in San Juan. Poise, passion, and style are all part of Puerto Rico's Spanish heritage.

used by the Taino, such as *tobacco* and *hurricane,* have passed into the English language we use today.

Of all the cultural flavors seasoning the Puerto Rican mix, probably the most evident are those that have survived the island's relationship with Spain. The chief survivor of Spanish rule is the language. Although English is also an official language, Spanish is more widely spoken. Puerto Ricans speak a dialect, or variety, of Spanish that is all their own.

Salsa and Bomba!

Salsa means "sauce"—but in Latin America the "sauce" referred to is hot, spicy dance music. Salsa is a mixture of traditional dance styles such as the mambo, rumba, and cha-cha. Its musical roots lie in Cuba, in a dance music called son *(SONE), which linked together Spanish and African styles. The term* salsa *was first used in its musical sense in Venezuela. The music is played with wind instruments, four-stringed guitars, and a wide variety of drums and percussion instruments. Salsa may be heard all over Latin America. Puerto Rican singers have their own distinctive style, heavily influenced by both Spanish traditions and the folk music of the countryside. Puerto Rican salsa has also been influenced by* bomba *(BOME-ba), a dance style with African rhythms that grew up around the towns of Loiza Aldea and Ponce.*

As citizens of the United States, Puerto Ricans are subject to U.S. military service and most federal laws. In Puerto Rico the traditional Latin American extended family, in which grandparents, aunts, uncles, and cousins all play a vital part, is becoming less common, as people begin to follow the North American pattern of smaller, more self-contained families.

In addition to baseball, which has become a national sport in Puerto Rico, American sports such as basketball and volleyball are very popular.

A police officer, dressed very much like a U.S. police officer, patrols the streets. Attire is not the only similarity; Puerto Rico and the United States have similar justice systems.

Ties with the Mainland

Since 1898 the United States has had a major influence on the Puerto Rican culture. U.S. goods are on sale in the shops, fast-food outlets serve up hamburgers and french fries, and many families have relatives living in the United States. English has become widely spoken. Many people slip from one language to the other without a second thought. Protestant religions have also gained followers, and today about 19 percent of all churchgoers in Puerto Rico attend Protestant churches.

The Cooking Pot

Traditional Puerto Rican food is still very popular. Traditional dishes are served in homes and by vendors at street stalls, or fondas *(FONE-thahss). Here is a sampling of traditional foods that have endured on the island:*

- *Asopao (ah-soe-PAH-oe) is a stew made with chicken or pork.*

- *Mofongo (moe-FONE-go) is a dish of plantain fried in batter.*

- *Frijoles (free-HOE-layss) (beans) are served in a hot, spicy sauce called sofrito (soe-FREE-toe).*

- *Surrilitos (soo-ree-LEE-toess) are cheese fritters made of cornmeal.*

- *Seafood fritters include* bacalao (bah-kah-LAH-oe), *a type of codfish, and* alcapurrias (ahl-kah-POO-ree-ahss), *which is crab.*

- *Lechón asado (lay-CHONE ah-SAH-thoe), a roast suckling pig, is served for Christmas dinner.*

- *Arroz con pollo (ah-ROESS cone POY-yo)—chicken and rice—is given a Puerto Rican flavor by adding coconut.*

The Caribbean Life

Puerto Rico's link with its powerful northern neighbor has made it one of the most developed islands in the Caribbean. U.S. aid and tax concessions have made San Juan a center of business and manufacturing, including chemicals and electronic goods. The island also produces textiles, garments, shoes, processed foods, and rum. Tourism has become big business in recent years, as Americans stream in from the mainland to enjoy the tropical climate and beautiful beaches.

By Caribbean standards, Puerto Rico is well-off, with decent education and health care systems and a prosperous middle class. By North American standards, however, Puerto Rico continues to face a great deal of poverty. Many people are unemployed, and people who have poured into the cities from rural areas in search of a better life find themselves living in shantytowns, in homemade shacks. In the countryside, farm laborers are often poorly paid.

Traditionally the Puerto Rican *jíbaro* (HEE-bah-roe), or peasant, lived in a thatched shack. Men wore straw hats called *pavas* (PAH-bahss) and walked barefoot to the fields. Women wore long skirts of colored cotton. Today the old way of life has largely disappeared, as villages have been modernized. Traditional crafts are still carried out on Puerto Rico, however, including woodcarving, leather tooling, and hammock making.

Crops grown on a large scale include sugar, tobacco, coffee, rice, and pineapples. Crops grown for eating locally include cassava (known in the Caribbean as *yucca*), corn, beans, bananas, and plantains (a large type of banana used in cooking). The bringing in of crops is celebrated with harvest festivals, or *crop-overs* as they are generally known in the Caribbean.

Despite its ties with the United States, Puerto Rico remains very much a part of the Caribbean. At no time is this more evident than in the Puerto Rican people's passion for carnival entertainment. Here saints' days such as the feast of St. John the Baptist (June 23) are celebrated with beach parties, dancing, and feasting. Traditionally, people ensure good luck by baptizing themselves— wading backwards into the sea.

Painted white faces and glittering costumes mark San Juan's own midsummer festival day. Every Puerto Rican town has its own special carnival, or fiesta.

SAINT KITTS-NEVIS

ALSO KNOWN AS SAINT CHRISTOPHER-NEVIS, these two Caribbean islands are part of the Leeward group in the Lesser Antilles chain.

Saint Kitts stretches about 23 miles (37 kilometers) from northwest to southeast. This island was formed by volcanic rocks that rise to 4,314 feet (1315 meters) above sea level at the northwest end and 3,792 feet (1156 meters) at Mount Misery. The forested slopes descend to coastal lowlands.

Two miles (three kilometers) to the south lies Nevis, a round island with lush vegetation, which rises to 3,232 feet (985 meters) at Nevis Peak.

The Twin Islands

"Fertile Isle" was the name given by the Caribs to green Saint Kitts. Nevis was named "Beautiful Waters" after its hot springs. The Caribs were a Native American people who were in possession of the islands when the fleet of Christopher Columbus passed by in 1493.

The islands had a fertile, volcanic soil but the only European settlers who dared risk attack by the Caribs were pirates. However, in 1623 Saint Kitts was settled by English colonists. The following year the French arrived and decided to settle Saint Kitts also. The English took Nevis in 1628. The French and English united to attack and kill off the Caribs but then began fighting each other. By 1713 the islands were British.

Sugarcane was planted and slave labor imported from western Africa. This cruel trade lasted until 1838. Other larger islands dominated the sugar market in the

CLIMATE

The two islands have a warm, tropical climate that features cooling winds from the sea. The driest months are from February to June.

Average January temperature: *77°F (25°C)*

Average July temperature: *80°F (27°C)*

Average annual precipitation: *55 in (140 cm)*

1800s, while the Kittitians and Nevisians lived in poverty. By the 1930s, few Europeans remained. Full independence was achieved in 1983 without the neighboring island of Anguilla, which decided it would rather be a British dependency than part of a federation with Saint Kitts and Nevis (see ANGUILLA).

440

In 1996 the premier of Nevis proposed secession from the federation with Saint Kitts, but the debate in the House of Assembly was boycotted by other political parties on Nevis. The Caribbean economic alliance, Caricom, proposed that a commission be set up to discuss the issue.

Today the great majority of Kittitians and Nevisians have Afro-Caribbean roots. The islands' British legacy lies in the old plantation architecture and forts and in a passion for the game of cricket.

Six out of ten people living on these islands are country dwellers. Sugarcane is still cultivated on Saint Kitts, while honey, vegetables, and cotton are produced on Nevis. Saint Kitts produces beer, clothing, and electrical goods, but the chief employer these days is the tourist industry. Visitors enjoy windsurfing and snorkeling in the coral reefs.

Tourism hasn't really changed the traditional Caribbean lifestyle on the islands. The lifestyle is easygoing and informal. Food includes seafood such as conch, shrimp, lobster, saltfish, and parrot fish, curried goat, *rotis* (ROE-teess), which

are pancakes with a curried potato and chicken filling, pumpkin soup, sweet potatoes, and green figs.

The festival highlight of the year is carnival. Held in Basseterre over Christmas and New Year, carnival includes costume parades, calypso music, and street dancing. A similar event, held on Nevis before the first Monday in August, is known as Culturama.

FACTS AND FIGURES

Official name: *Federation of Saint Christopher and Nevis*

Status: *Independent state*

Capital: *Basseterre*

Area: *118 square miles (306 square kilometers)*

Population: *42,000*

Population density: *355 per square mile (137 per square kilometer)*

Peoples: *94 percent Afro-Caribbean; 6 percent European or mixed descent*

Official language: *English*

Currency: *East Caribbean dollar*

National days: *Independence Day (September 19)*

Country's name: *Saint Christopher was named by Christopher Colombus after his own patron saint. Kitt is a common nickname for Christopher in English. Nevis was named Nieves (Spanish for "snow") by Columbus, after sighting the great white clouds hanging like snow over the central peaks.*

Young girls from Saint John's Primary School in Charlestown, a town on Nevis, jump rope on the playground during their morning break.

Timeline:	Caribs living on the islands they called Liamuiga and Oualie	English settlement of Saint Kitts by Sir Thomas Warner	Slavery abolished	Saint Kitts-Nevis becomes independent state	Nevis premier proposes secession
	1400s	1623	1838	1983	1996

SAINT LUCIA

SAINT LUCIA IS ONE OF THE MOST BEAUTIFUL ISLANDS IN THE CARIBBEAN.
It is part of the Windward group in the Lesser Antilles island chain.

Saint Lucia is about 27 miles (43 kilometers) from north to south and some 14 miles (23 kilometers) wide.

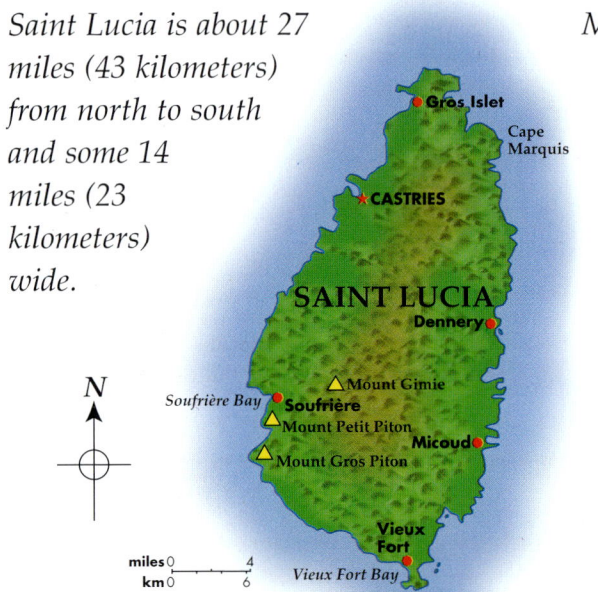

Mountains covered with forests on their upper slopes make up the center of the island, rising to 3,145 feet (959 meters) above sea level at Mount Gimie. Volcanic springs bubble and fume near the town of Soufrière. In the south of the island are two spectacular peaks, the Pitons.

CLIMATE

The climate is tropical and humid all year-round. The dry season lasts from January to April. The island frequently suffers from devastating storms and hurricanes in August and September.

Average January temperature: *74°F (23°C)*

Average July temperature: *79°F (26°C)*

Average annual precipitation: *60 in (150 cm)*

Carib, French, English, African

Between about twenty-five hundred and three thousand years ago, Saint Lucia (SAINT LOO-shee-ah) was settled by a Native American people from the mainland of South America. They were conquered about twelve hundred years ago by another Native people, the Caribs.

In the first half of the seventeenth century, the English tried to colonize the island. They were resisted by the Caribs, and most of them were either killed or driven away. In the second half of the same century, the French and English did settle the island, killing off the Carib population. The island changed hands no fewer than fourteen times. Finally, by 1814, it was the British who were left in control.

The colonists imported slaves from Africa to toil in the sugarcane plantations. They were liberated in 1834. In the same century, people from the East Indies (today's Indonesia and Malaysia) were also employed as laborers.

Saint Lucia achieved self-rule within the colonial system in 1967 and complete independence twelve years later.

French culture has lingered on the island. Today the island's Creole dialect, or patois, is still spoken by many people. It is based

FACTS AND FIGURES

Status: *Independent state*

Capital: *Castries*

Area: *238 square miles (616 square kilometers)*

Population: *143,000*

Population density: *600 per square mile (232 per square kilometer)*

Peoples: *85 percent Afro-Caribbean; 5 percent European descent and Southeast Asian descent; 10 percent mixed descent*

Official language: *English*

Currency: *East Caribbean dollar*

National days: *Independence Day (February 22); Saint Lucy's Day (December 13)*

Country's name: *Named in honor of Saint Lucy (Santa Lucia) by Spanish navigators, sometime before 1511.*

Today 85 percent of all Saint Lucians are Catholics. Three percent are Anglicans, and the remaining Christians are Pentecostalists, Baptists, Seventh-Day Adventists, Christian Scientists, and Methodists. Education is modeled after the British system.

The island's biggest industry is tourism, which has brought jobs, but often at the expense of the environment. The sugarcane industry came to an end in the 1960s in the face of competition from larger producers. Farmers today rely mainly on bananas, coconuts, and cocoa beans.

Over half of Saint Lucians are country dwellers. Food grown on smaller farms and in gardens is usually cooked with a French flair. Favorite dishes include callaloo soup (made from spinach), *soupe germou* (soop jer-MOO) (pumpkin soup flavored with garlic), and *pouile dudon* (PWAY dee-DOH) (chicken stew flavored with coconut and molasses).

Fruit and vegetables are sold at a Saturday morning market in Soufrière, a town of about nine thousand people beneath The Pitons, two conical mountains.

on French, with words borrowed from English and several African languages.

The Afro-Caribbean way of life is celebrated with food and dance at an October festival called *Jounen Kweyol* (joo-NEE KWAY-yahl). The island's biggest festival is carnival, which is held just before Lent. Carnival is celebrated with feasting, singing, and dancing. Saint Lucia's popular music includes calypso (in which singers make up satirical songs), reggae, and steel-band music, as well as music of the French Caribbean, such as *cadance* (cuh-DASS) and the techno-funk sounds of *zouk* (ZOOK) (from the Creole word for "party"). Carnival features costumed street parades and "jump-ups," in which dancers fall in behind trucks blaring out music.

Timeline:	Island settled by Native Americans	First peoples ousted by Caribs	English colonists from Saint Kitts arrive	Slavery abolished	Full independence
	ca. 1000 B.C.E.	ca. 800 C.E.	1638	1843	1979

SAINT-PIERRE AND MIQUELON

THESE TINY ISLANDS LYING OFF THE COAST OF CANADA are all that remain of France's once vast North American empire.

These islands lie 10 miles (16 kilometers) west of Newfoundland's Burin Peninsula. Miquelon is made up of two islands—Miquelon itself and the uninhabited island of Langlade—linked by a narrow stretch of sand.

The islands of Saint-Pierre and Miquelon have sandy shores, granite rocks, and cliffs. Inland, the damp climate has produced a terrain consisting of bogs, swamps, and bare hillocks. The soil is poor and supports little vegetation.

CLIMATE

Saint-Pierre and Miquelon have a cool, temperate, but wet climate, with sea fogs created by the meeting of warm and Arctic ocean currents. Their waters are ice-free all year round.

Average January temperature: *24°F (–4°C)*

Average July temperature: *58°F (14°C)*

Average annual precipitation: *55 in (140 cm)*

"As French as can be . . ."

That was how the French president Charles de Gaulle (1890–1970) described the tiny islands of Saint-Pierre (SAINT PEER) and Miquelon (MIK-uh-lohn).

Jacques Cartier, the French explorer, charted the uninhabited islands in 1536, and French fishers settled them during the 1600s. As Great Britain and France battled for control of Canada during the 1700s, the islands changed hands several times. It was 1814 before they finally became French.

The islands remained French-speaking communities that lived by fishing. During the 1920s Prohibition in the United States brought great changes to the islands. It

became illegal to manufacture or sell alcoholic beverages in the United States. Canada began to export vast amounts of hard liquor—quite legally—to Saint-Pierre and Miquelon. From there it was smuggled into the United States. When Prohibition came to an end in 1933, a huge source of income for the islands ran out.

The 1970s to the 1990s was a period marked by wrangling between Canada and France over fishing and oil rights in the North Atlantic. Because of overfishing, by

FACTS AND FIGURES

Official name: *Îles Saint-Pierre et Miquelon*

Status: *Part of France, but with a degree of autonomy*

Capital: *Saint-Pierre*

Area: *93 square miles (241 square kilometers)*

Population: *6,500*

Population density: *70 per square mile (27 per square kilometer)*

Peoples: *100 percent French citizens, mostly of Norman, Breton, and Basque descent*

Official language: *French*

Currency: *French franc*

National days: *Bastille Day (July 14)*

Country's name: *Saint-Pierre is named in honor of Saint Peter.*

Roman Catholic. Schools are run on the French educational system.

As in France, cooking is an important event. Traditional dishes—such as a tasty cod chowder called *tiaude* (tee-ODE)—are, not surprisingly, based on fish.

On August 4 the islanders commemorate the life of Jacques Cartier. August is also a time for remembering cultural roots with folk dance and music. A festival on Miquelon honors the Acadians, the French colonists driven out after the British conquest of Canada in the 1700s. Another festival on Saint-Pierre honors the Basques, the people whose European homeland is divided between France and Spain. Many Basque, Breton, and Norman fishers settled on Saint-Pierre. Ceremonies are also held traditionally to bless the fishing fleet. As in Brittany, model boats and holy statues are carried to the port through the streets.

the 1990s the fish stocks of the area were going into rapid decline. International fishing bans have been put into effect until stocks recover, leaving many families in Saint-Pierre without a livelihood.

Because the soil on the islands is poor and most foodstuffs and machines need to be imported, people in Saint-Pierre have never had as ready or obvious a source of income as fishing. The French government, which had to pay families compensation for their loss of income, is now trying to develop tourism, building a new airport and hoping that the lure of gambling casinos and duty-free goods will prove more attractive than the damp climate.

Most of the islanders live in the port of Saint-Pierre. The town has a large cathedral, and most of the population is

The port of Saint-Pierre (pictured) is reached by ferry from Fortune on Newfoundland's Burin Peninsula. Saint-Pierre is home to 90 percent of the islands' people.

Timeline:	Basque, Breton, Norman fishers settle	French settle and claim the islands	Islands finally confirmed as French	Islands become a Territorial Collectivity of France	Rapid decline in fish stocks is followed by international fishing bans
	1550s C.E.	1604	1814	1985	1980s–1990s

SAINT VINCENT AND THE GRENADINES

SAINT VINCENT IS A GREEN, VOLCANIC ISLAND IN THE WINDWARD ISLANDS, part of the Lesser Antilles.

Saint Vincent is about 18 miles by 11 miles (29 kilometers by 18 kilometers). To the south the territory also includes the Northern Grenadines, a string of small islands, cays, and coral reefs.

Saint Vincent is a fertile island whose forested hills rise steeply to a central mountain range called Morne Garu. The highest point is Soufrière, at 4,048 feet (1,234 meters). This is an active volcano, which last erupted in 1979.

CLIMATE

The climate is tropical, but it is cooled by the prevailing trade winds. Hurricanes may occur between June and November. The Grenadines are generally drier than Saint Vincent.

Average January temperature: *79°F (26°C)*

Average July temperature: *81°F (27°C)*

Average annual precipitation: *60 in (150 cm)*

Under the Volcano

When Christopher Columbus reached Saint Vincent in 1492, the islanders were Caribs, a Native American people who had seized the island from other Native people belonging to the Arawak culture.

In 1675 a Dutch slave ship was wrecked to the south, and its human cargo swam to freedom on Saint Vincent. Many of them married Native Caribs, forming a people who became known as Black Caribs, or Garifuna. As Britain warred with France through the 1700s, the islands changed hands between the two sides. The Europeans brought in slaves from western Africa to work on cotton and sugarcane plantations. The French encouraged the Black Caribs to rise up against the British,

but by 1797 the Black Caribs were defeated and over five thousand were deported to the island of Roatán, off the Honduras coast. Many of their descendants today live in Belize (see BELIZE).

Soufrière erupted in 1812, killing many of the remaining Native Caribs. The slaves were freed in 1834, and Portuguese and Asian laborers (from India and Southeast Asia) were brought in.

In 1979 Saint Vincent and the Grenadines became a fully independent nation.

Most of the people of Saint Vincent today are descended from the slaves. The European element includes British, Irish, French, and Portuguese. There are also descendants of the Asian laborers. The language of the islands is English, but a French dialect, or patois, can also still be heard. About three-quarters of the islanders are Protestant Christians, and about 10 percent are Roman Catholics.

Most islanders live off the fertile land, growing bananas, coconuts, spices, and cacao on big plantations. Saint Vincent is the world's largest producer of arrowroot, whose roots produce a starch used in making food and paper. Although tourism is a growing industry, about 20 percent of the workforce is unemployed.

FACTS AND FIGURES

Status: *Independent state*

Capital: *Kingstown*

Area: *150 square miles (389 square kilometers)*

Population: *113,000*

Population density: *753 per square mile (290 per square kilometer)*

Peoples: *66 percent Afro-Caribbean; 19 percent Afro-Caribbean-European descent; 2 percent African-Carib descent (Black Carib or Garifuna); 6 percent Asian descent; 4 percent European descent; 3 percent others*

Official language: *English*

Currency: *East Caribbean dollar*

National days: *Saint Vincent and Grenadines' Day (January 22); Independence Day (October 27)*

Country's name: *Saint Vincent was named by Christopher Columbus (the first known European to explore the island) on Saint Vincent's Day (January 22) in 1498. The Grenadines take their name from the island of Grenada (to the south), which was named after a town in Spain.*

Island residents share a passion for the game of cricket and a love of soccer. Vincy Mas' is Caribbean carnival time and is held in Kingstown each year in June and July. Reggae music booms out and steel drums give out fluid metal melodies as costumed crowds parade and dance. Singers compete in calypso, an off-the-cuff, amusing, and topical song style.

High school students pose for the camera at Barrouallie on Saint Vincent's Leeward Highway. Most islanders are Afro-Caribbeans.

Timeline:	Settled by Arawaks	Arawaks ousted by Caribs	African slaves land from Dutch shipwreck	Saint Vincent given to Britain by Treaty of Versailles	Slavery abolished	Full independence
	ca. 750 B.C.E.	ca. 800 C.E.	1675	1763	1834	1979

SURINAME

SURINAME, THE SMALLEST INDEPENDENT COUNTRY IN
SOUTH AMERICA, lies on the continent's north coast.

Suriname's north coast faces the Atlantic Ocean. To the south it is bordered by Brazil, to the east by French Guiana, and to the west by Guyana. Together Suriname, French Guiana, and Guyana used to be known as the Guianas.

Suriname has a narrow coastal plain, much of it swampy and crossed by sandy ridges. Behind the coastal plain are a hilly, forested region and savannahs. The remainder of the country is almost totally covered by tropical rain forest. This region includes the Wilhelmina central mountain range with the country's highest point, Juliana Top, at 4,035 feet (1,230 meters).

CLIMATE

Suriname is tropical and humid. The coastal region is influenced by the trade winds blowing from the Atlantic, so it is never uncomfortably hot. In the interior, temperatures vary according to the altitude. Rainfall is heavy most of the year; the main wet season extends from April to August.

Average January temperature: *70°F (21°C)*

Average July temperature: *90°F (32°C)*

Average annual precipitation: *72 in (183 cm)*

A street in Paramaribo, Suriname's capital city. Many buildings are made of wood and exhibit a traditional Dutch style.

448

In the Middle of the Guianas

The original inhabitants of Suriname (sue-ree-NAH-muh) were groups of nomadic hunters and gatherers of natural forest products. The earliest signs of people in the Guianas are mounds of shells left about six thousand years ago on the coast of Guyana. By the time the first Europeans arrived, these Native Americans, mainly Arawak- and Carib-speaking people, were settled tribes.

In 1499 Amerigo Vespucci, an Italian navigator who sailed for Spain, explored the Suriname coast. He found it covered with mangroves and swamps and peopled by Native Americans who resisted the European intruders. More than one hundred years passed before the first colonists arrived, a group of about sixty Englishmen, who planted tobacco.

The first serious attempt to colonize the country came in 1651 by the wealthy English landowner Lord Willoughby. The territory was known as Willoughbyland until a Dutch fleet seized control, and in 1667 a deal was struck giving Suriname to the Dutch and Nieuw Amsterdam (later New York) to the English.

Apart from two short periods when the land was again taken by the English, Suriname was a Dutch colony for over three hundred years. Its economy and government were administered from Amsterdam in the Netherlands. The Dutch needed labor for the large sugar plantations, and initially they turned to Africa and the already-established African communities in the West Indies for slaves.

FACTS AND FIGURES

Official name: *Republiek Suriname*

Status: *Independent state*

Capital: *Paramaribo*

Area: *63,251 square miles (163,820 square kilometers)*

Population: *440,000*

Population density: *7 per square mile (3 per square kilometer)*

Peoples: *33 percent East Indian descent; 33 percent Creoles; 15 percent Javanese descent; less than 10 percent African descent; 3 percent Native American; 6 percent Chinese, Lebanese, Jewish, Portuguese, and Dutch descent*

Official language: *Dutch*

Currency: *Suriname guilder*

National days: *Labor Day (May 1); National Unity Day (July 1); Independence Day (November 25)*

Country's name: *The Native Surinen people, who do not exist today, were the earliest-known inhabitants of the area that was given the name Surinam by European explorers. In 1978 the name was changed officially to Suriname.*

Some groups of Africans managed to escape from the plantations, fleeing deep into the rain forest to avoid recapture. They established a tribal way of life, and after signing peace treaties with the Dutch in the eighteenth century, these groups, known collectively as "Bush Negroes" (originally *bosnegers* in Dutch), were eventually granted their freedom.

Timeline:	First signs of inhabitants	Spanish reach coast	English settlers land and plant tobacco	Dutch establish trading post, now site of Paramaribo	English found first colony, Willoughbyland; African slaves imported
	ca. 4000 B.C.E.	1499 C.E.	1630	1633	1651

Deep in the interior rain forest of Suriname, some Bush Negroes build traditional palm-thatched houses using materials from the forest.

By the time slavery was abolished in 1863, Suriname was a flourishing colony, producing sugar, coffee, cacao, indigo, and wood. The colony needed more labor, and in 1853 the Dutch government brought Chinese and Madeiran (Portuguese) contract laborers to Suriname. By 1873 the Dutch government was also recruiting laborers from India, and by 1899 bringing in Javanese peasants from the Dutch East Indies (now Indonesia).

By the 1950s, the colony was actively seeking its independence from the Netherlands. The road to independence was given a push by the economic success of the bauxite industry (from which aluminum is produced). Mining started in 1916, and as the world demand for aluminum increased, so did the calls for

independence being issued by some of the political parties. In 1975 the country finally gained its long-sought independence but entered a period of instability. A military coup in 1980 threw out the elected government, and for ten years the country remained under a military dictatorship that was confronted by fierce opposition from guerrilla movements.

Elections took place in 1991, and a peace accord with the guerrillas came a year later. But the civil war had disrupted the economy. The people suffered and showed their discontent in street demonstrations. In 1996 further elections led to a coalition government, which continues to try to resolve the country's economic problems.

Who are the Surinamers?

For such a small country, Suriname has an impressive mix of peoples. The two largest groups in the population are the Creoles and the Hindustanis, each forming about one-third of the population. African slaves were first taken from their homelands between 1651 and 1667 to work on sugar plantations. The slaves soon greatly outnumbered the English, French, Dutch, and other European colonists, few of whom had brought families from Europe. Marriage between Africans and Europeans produced the mixed-race Creoles. On a lesser scale, Africans married with non-European immigrants as well.

England gives Willoughbyland to the Dutch in return for Nieuw Amsterdam (New York)	Slavery abolished	Suriname gains independence	Military coup	Guerrilla war begins	Elections held and democracy restored
1667	1863	1975	1980	1986	1991

Hindustani is the local name for the descendants of the contract Hindu and Muslim laborers brought from British India. Between 1873 and 1916 more than thirty-four thousand arrived. The Hindus and Muslims became independent farmers. Many educated their children in the Netherlands. Today Hindustanis have a prominent place in commerce and government.

Between 1899 and 1939 over thirty-two thousand Javanese entered the country, and Javanese descendants now form about 15 percent of the population. Most Javanese immigrants became small farmers, and today many are settled on the east bank of the Suriname River, around the village of Nieuw Amsterdam. Much of their vegetable produce is sold in the markets of Paramaribo. A few of the elderly women continue to wear traditional Javanese clothes. For the most part, however, their style of dress is Western.

Descendants of the escaped African slaves known as Bush Negroes number close to fifty thousand today. (Present-day Surinamers still use the term Bush Negroes.) This portion of the population consists of five groups: the Saramaccaner, Aukaners (or Djukas), Matuariërs, Paramaccaners, and Alukus (or Bonnis). Communities live in both the forested interior and near the coast. Many live close to rivers. Each tribal community is headed by a tribal, or paramount, chief, and a head captain. Bush Negroes are active politically, and they were at the core of the guerrilla movements that opposed Suriname's military dictatorship in the 1980s. A typical Bush Negro village has palm-thatched houses similar to those of local Native

Soccer is a favorite sport, and these boys are taking part in a competition near Paramaribo. Most of them are East Indian, with two or three of Javanese and Chinese descent.

Wood Carving: A Practical Art

Today's Bush Negroes are famed for their wood carving. The craftspeople produce wooden goods such as folding and reclining chairs. Each chair is made from a single solid piece of wood that is cut so it forms two interlocking and inseparable pieces. The two pieces can fold to form an X shape in which the owner sits. Many of the chairs and other items, such as plates, are carved with intricate designs drawn from the ancient spiritual world.

Bush Negroes produce fine woodcrafts. This folding chair began as a single slab of wood. It is carved all over with intricate designs.

American groups, and residents use slash-and-burn methods to clear the forest and grow crops. Most wear Western-style clothing.

Native Americans make up just 3 percent of Suriname's population. About 82 percent of all Native people are Carib or Arawak. (About fifty-four thousand are Carib and forty-nine thousand are Arawak.) Most of this population lives near the coast, in savanna regions, and on the fringes of more settled areas.

The remainder of Suriname's Native people live deep in the forest interior. They are the Waiyana (see discussion of the Wayana in FRENCH GUIANA), Trio, Wayarikule, Wama, and Akurio. Their homes are built of several straight poles standing upright and other poles sloped to form the shape of a roof. The roof itself is made of palm leaves interwoven and tied firmly with palm fibers. For the men, much

of daily life consists of hunting; for the women, it consists of planting cassava and collecting forest fruits. Some of the larger communities practice slash-and-burn agriculture and raise crops in gardens. By selling handicrafts, fish, and wood, they also have some contact with urban centers. A few communities also benefit from medical and educational services introduced by missionaries.

The remainder of Suriname's population is descended from a variety of other immigrant groups. Jews skilled in sugar production arrived in the 1660s. Today the Jewish community is quite strong and still maintains its religion and synagogues. Immigrants from China first arrived as contract laborers in the 1850s, and others have arrived since from Chinese

Native Americans in Suriname, such as this Palumeu woman, have been in contact with the outside world for a long time. Her fire, built in a traditional way, supports a modern bowl.

known as *Sranan tongo*, or *taki-taki*. Bush Negroes speak languages that are their own form of Sranan mixed with traces of English and Portuguese. Today Hindustanis speak a language known as Sarnami Hindi, which has its origins in Asia and is mixed with Sranan, Dutch, and English. The language of the Javanese, known as Suriname Javanese, is quite different from that of their homeland. Native languages are also spoken, although many younger Native people now speak Sranan as well. English is also becoming more common, especially in business.

communities around the world. Many Chinese immigrants became traders, and at one time the retail business of foodstuffs was entirely in their hands. Today many members of this closely knit community run restaurants.

Life in Suriname

The majority of people, about 80 percent, live and work near the coast. More than half live in the capital city of Paramaribo. The next largest town, Nieuw Nickerie, has a population of only eight thousand. The vast forested regions in the south are sparsely populated, with just a few settlers, scattered groups of Native Americans, and some Bush Negroes.

Suriname's official language is Dutch, and although this language is used in schools, it is not the most widely spoken. Most people communicate using Sranan (srrah-NAHN), a Creole English also

Food: A Gumbo of Possibilities

Few places in the world can equal the variety of food to be found in the city of Paramaribo. The staple for most of the cooking is rice, but many dishes include shrimp, cassava, sweet potatoes, plantains, and hot red peppers. Each of the ethnic groups has kept its own specialities, such as the Creole pinda soep *(PIHN-dah soop) (peanut soup with plantain dumplings) and the Javanese (Indonesian)* bami *(BAH-mee), which are fried noodles. One fast-food favorite is Hindustani* roti *(RROW-tee) (a wafer-thin unleavened bread) wrapped around curried potatoes, vegetables, and chicken. Hindustani snacks also include fried pastry* samosas *(sah-MOE-sahss) filled with spicy meat and vegetables and* phulawri *(pul-LAW-ree), or fried chickpea balls.*

Children at a school in Paramaribo receive a good basic education. Some will later go to local colleges. Most of these children are Creoles or of pure African descent.

Education is free and compulsory for children between six and sixteen. Some children continue in school until they are eighteen or nineteen and go on to the local university or to technical colleges. Younger people still tend to marry along strict ethnic lines, and although people from various groups meet on a friendly basis, the differences in the ways they live keep them fairly isolated from one another culturally. The Netherlands is the main point of contact with the world for Surinamers, and many have moved there.

Religious Life

Today in Suriname the principal religion is Christianity, followed by Hinduism and Islam. Most of the country observes the same Christian customs and holidays that people celebrate throughout the Americas. Hindu temples and schools are commonplace in Paramaribo, and mosques are seldom far away. The Hindustanis keep their own Asian festivals, with their main festival, Holi Phagwah, celebrated as a

An Islamic mosque dominates a street in Paramaribo. Few people wear the clothes of their original countries, but their religions are strongly maintained.

454

Hindu Weddings

Hindu weddings traditionally follow the Asian custom in which the bride and her future husband walk seven times around the room where they are to be married. They then sit on the floor of the house facing the bride's parents and a Hindu priest. After the ceremony, the guests dip their hands in rice and ginger and mark the wall of the home to wish the couple a happy future.

spring festival. Other festivals follow the Muslim (Islamic) lunar calendar. Islam is the religion of the Javanese community, and in the countryside Javanese Surinamers have built many small, green-painted mosques bearing the Islamic crescent.

Despite the efforts of missionaries to convert Bush Negroes to Christianity, their traditional beliefs remain strong. Many Bush Negro villages have both churches and a separate shrine dedicated to their own spirits. Many of the doors on their houses are painted with colorful designs related to African spirituality and beliefs.

The Musical Mix

In Suriname true Native American music is played on a variety of simple instruments, including gourd whistles or trumpets, bone or bamboo flutes, seed rattles, and reed panpipes. Over the years Bush Negroes and Europeans have introduced simple stringed instruments and drums. A large Bush Negro drum may be nearly 3 feet (one meter) deep and 20 inches (one-half meter) in diameter. The drums accompany dances and spiritual meetings, using a special "language" of their own to tell ancient myths. Javanese immigrants brought their distinctive gamelan (gah-meh-LAHN) music, thus contributing to the mix of musical styles in Suriname. Gamelan orchestras, consisting of drum, xylophone, metallophone, and several gongs, accompany songs, dances, and puppet plays.

Perhaps the best-known musical style coming out of Suriname is *kawina* (KAH-wee-nah), which features a solo singer and chorus accompanied by a band of drums of different sizes and the *cuatro* (KWAH-troe), a four-stringed guitar. In Paramaribo *kaseko* (kah-SICK-oh) bands—consisting of guitars, trumpets, clarinets, saxophones, trombones, piano, and double bass—accompany dances and entertain at celebrations.

Throughout Suriname, music is heavily influenced by the calypso and merengue styles of the Caribbean (see TRINIDAD AND TOBAGO and DOMINICAN REPUBLIC).

Bush Negroes still play some traditional instruments, such as this wooden board with strips, which vibrate when plucked.

TRINIDAD AND TOBAGO

TRINIDAD, THE MOST SOUTHERLY CARIBBEAN ISLAND, is the largest in the Lesser Antilles.

Trinidad lies just 7 miles (11 kilometers) off the coast of Venezuela, opposite the mouth of the Orinoco River. Tobago is a small island about 19 miles (31 kilometers) northeast of Trinidad.

Trinidad is about 50 miles (80 kilometers) long and 50 miles wide. The peak of Aripo in the north rises 3,085 feet (940 meters) above sea level. The center of the island is made up of fertile plains, and swamps lie along the coasts. Tobago is a little island of forests and tropical beaches.

CLIMATE

The climate is tropical and hot, with a dry season from January to June. The remaining months make up a wet season, but the islands generally escape the fury of hurricanes that pass to the north.

Average January temperature: *78°F (26°C)*

Average July temperature: *79°F (26°C)*

Average annual precipitation: *65 in (165 cm)*

A typical Tobago house. It is neatly painted and has a sheet-metal roof. Although fought over in the past, Tobago is a quiet place today.

Two Islands, Many Peoples

In 1498 a Spanish fleet commanded by the Italian explorer Christopher Columbus entered the southern Caribbean and spied two islands. The northern one, now called Tobago (tuh-BAY-goe), was occupied by Carib people, and Columbus did not land on the island. To the southwest was another island, which he named Trinidad (TRIHN-ih-dad). This island was so close to the South American mainland that it had been settled by a large number of Native groups. They called it Lere ("hummingbird island").

Most islanders were Arawak speakers. Although the Arawak people had been sufficently well organized four hundred years previously to fend off attacks by the Caribs, four groups of Caribs had by now gained control of the northern part of the island. Other indigenous peoples on the island included the Chaimas, Tamanaques, Salives, Chaguanes, and Quaquas. All these early Trinidadians lived in hut villages and hunted, fished, and farmed for food and tobacco.

The indigenous peoples fiercely resisted European attempts to settle the islands for many years, fighting off the Spanish in 1530. The Spanish returned, however, and under their rule the indigenous way of life gradually disappeared. Today only a few hundred Trinidadians are of Carib descent. Trinidad became a neglected outpost of Spain's empire, used as a base for exploring the mainland to the south. In 1783 the Spanish decided to clear and settle the island and encouraged immigration by

Roman Catholics. Many French settled on the island, and slaves of western African origin were used to plant sugarcane. These soon formed the majority of the population. Trinidad was captured by Great Britain in 1797.

In 1834 the slaves were freed and many set up homes, shops, and other small businesses. New settlers arrived from the United States and Europe. Plantation

FACTS AND FIGURES

Official name: Republic of Trinidad and Tobago

Status: Independent state

Capital: Port-of-Spain

Other towns: San Fernando, Arima

Area: 1,980 square miles (5,130 square kilometers)

Population: 1,262,000

Population density: 637 per square mile (246 per square kilometer)

Peoples: 41 percent Afro-Caribbean; 41 percent South Asian (Indian) descent; 16 percent mixed descent; 1 percent Chinese descent; 1 percent European, Syrian, Lebanese, and Carib descent

Official language: English

Currency: Trinidad and Tobago dollar

National days: Independence Day (August 31); Republic Day (September 24)

Country's name: The island of Trinidad was named La Isla de la Trinidad ("The Island of the Trinity") by Christopher Columbus, after he had seen three hilltops from out at sea. The name Tobago comes from the tobacco grown by the Carib people who originally lived there.

Timeline:	Arawak peoples arrive	Caribs attack Arawak peoples and settle northern Trinidad and Tobago	Christopher Columbus first encounters the islands	Spanish settle on Trinidad	Tobago ceded to Britain
	ca. 1000 B.C.E.	ca. 1000 C.E.	1498	1592	1763

workers were shipped in from India, Southeast Asia, and China. Most were on short-term contracts and soon returned home, but a large number did stay on and raise families. Their descendants today make up a large percentage of Trinidad's population.

In 1888 Trinidad was united with Tobago, to the northeast. In the previous two hundred years, this little island had changed hands many times, being settled or fought over by various Europeans from countries such as Latvia, the Netherlands, France, and Britain. Tobago was granted to Great Britain in 1763.

In the 1900s new settlers arrived, many from Syria and Lebanon. The worldwide economic depression of the 1930s led to unemployment and hardship on Trinidad, and the workforce organized strikes and protests against the colonial authorities. The same political radicalism spurred on the demand for civil rights and self-rule. Independence was finally achieved in 1962. In the 1960s many Afro-Caribbeans on Trinidad joined the Black Power movement, asserting their equality with the many other ethnic groups on the island. In 1976 Trinidad and Tobago broke their last links with the British crown, becoming a republic. In the 1980s Tobago achieved a degree of home rule within the republic.

Work and Society

The pattern of work on Trinidad has changed greatly since the days when most of the population labored on the plantations. Today, as in neighboring Venezuela, oil is king, providing about 70 percent of all export earnings. Oil and natural gas are produced mostly from offshore fields and provide work in production, refinery, petrochemical manufacture, and energy. Other resources on Trinidad include coal, iron ore, limestone, and a natural lake of black, sticky pitch at La Brea, which provides asphalt for road surfaces.

As the international price of oil has risen and fallen in recent years, the government has tried to vary the kind of industries based in Trinidad. Trinidad is now the home of clothing manufacturers and food and beverage processors. A tourism

A Tobago fisherman hauls in the nets. Fishing is important to the island's economy. The population of Trinidad's sister island is almost entirely Afro-Caribbean.

Britain captures Trinidad	Slavery abolished	Laborers imported from India, China, and Southeast Asia	Full independence	Trinidad and Tobago form a republic	Tobago has home rule within the republic
1797	1834	1844–1866	1962	1976	1987

Hot, Hot, Hot!

The street food of Trinidad is often hot and spicy and includes Asian, Caribbean, African, and European influences.

• **Shark and bake** is a sandwich of fried bread filled with firm, white shark meat.

• **Pow** (PAO) are small, white Chinese doughnuts, sweet or savory.

• **Rotis** (ROE-tee) is bread filled with any spicy curry or dhall (DOLL) (lentil) mixture.

• **Aripa** (ah-RAY-pah) is a patty or pie made of cornmeal dough and stuffed with meat.

• **Fish and chips** is the British classic fast food. The french fries (chips) are the same, but the fish is a tropical species, such as flying fish.

• **Phulori** (puh-LAOW-ree) are split peas, known to Indians as channa (CHAH-nah), fried in small balls of batter.

• **Fried plantain** is a Caribbean speciality. The plantain is a large cooking banana.

• **Curries** may include shrimp, pork, beef, chicken, goat, fish, and vegetables, and they may be served with hot, delicious chutneys and coconut rice.

industry is also being developed, especially on the quieter, more relaxed island of Tobago. In the last forty years many Trinidadians have sought work abroad, especially in Great Britain. Some of them send money back to their relatives at home.

Sugarcane is still a major crop and is processed to make the local rum. Rice, cocoa, coffee, coconut, and citrus fruit are also grown on a large scale. Fishing is important, especially on Tobago, with the local catch including shrimp, crab, flying fish, and shark.

Only one in ten Trinidadians now work the land, and 69 percent live in cities or towns. The capital, Port-of-Spain, is a busy, energetic city where picturesque Caribbean buildings with ornate, fretted woodwork mix with modern concrete offices and stores. Out in the country the green

Traders do business at Arima, a borough in northern Trinidad. Many of this town's inhabitants claim partial descent from Arawak and Carib communities.

"Playing Mas"

Almost every Caribbean town has its carnival, but Port-of-Spain has the best of them all. Trinidad's carnival is called Mas (short for masquerade). It dates back to the 1700s, when Roman Catholic settlers from Europe brought in the custom from their homelands. There, carnival was a chance to feast and make merry before the solemn Christian period of Lent, when eating meat and all revelry were forbidden. From the mid-1800s the festival in Trinidad was taken over by those of African descent, and it became livelier year by year. The wild celebrations became known as Bacchanal (from the Roman god of wine, Bacchus).

Today the carnival starts on the Friday before Lent and builds up over the Sunday and the Monday dawn procession. It culminates before midnight on Shrove Tuesday. Thousands of Trinidadians parade in the streets, dressed as devils and

angels in satin and sequins. There are stilt walkers and "jump-ups," at which people dance along behind trucks stacked high with loudspeakers. "Playing mas" (MAHS) means taking part in costume competitions and enjoying the music— calypso (satirical songs made up on the spot), loud soca (SOE-kah) (soul calypso, dance music swinging to a calypso beat) and steel-band music (played on "pans," which were originally adapted from oil drums). All of these musical forms were invented on Trinidad. So was the famous dance called the limbo, in which people bend over backward to fit beneath a pole that is gradually lowered during the dance.

The razzle and dazzle of Trinidadians erupt on the streets of Port-of-Spain during the annual carnival. Trinidad's carnival has been taking place for over two hundred years.

plantation fields are dotted with small villages, and white walls and red roofs rise from the water's edge around the coast. Tobago is much less developed and more peaceful.

Oil and gas have made only a few people wealthy, and many islanders remain poor. Although unemployment is high and is matched by a high crime rate, oil wealth has funded social welfare, and

there are good hospitals and schools. The islands have a high rate of literacy, and one of the campuses of the University of the West Indies is located on Trinidad.

The Melting Pot

The richness of Trinidadian life lies in the diversity of its cultures and peoples. English is spoken everywhere, but French dialect or Creole, Spanish, Hindi, and Chinese may also be heard in places. Traditionally, the Afro-Caribbean population has formed the majority of the working class, fishing, farming the land, and working in the oil industry. They have also worked in government and administration. The descendants of the Asian laborers who arrived in the 1800s started up shops and stores and soon formed a wealthier middle class. Cultural barriers are starting to break down, however, and the island has become a melting pot.

Calypso has its origins in French Trinidad of the late 1700s. Singers compete to put down their rivals with a well-placed insult, or *picong* (pee-KONG). Calypso has fused into new forms such as *soca* (soul calypso), *rapso* (RAP-soe) (calypso rap), and an Asian variant called *chutney* (CHUT-nee). *Parang* (pah-RAHNG) is an older music, dating back to the days of Spanish rule. It is heard before Christmas and consists of traditional Spanish carols backed by guitar, *cuatro* (CWAH-troe) (four-string guitar), maracas, bass, and fiddle.

The largest portion of the population is Roman Catholic Christian, followed by Hindu, Protestant Christian, and Muslim. The Christian festivals of Easter, Whitsun, Corpus Christi, and Christmas are all public holidays, and the Asian population has also introduced its religious festivals into public life. The major Hindu festival is Divali (dee-WAH-lee), a festival of light honoring the goddess Lakshmi. It is normally held in November, and families light candles and exchange presents and cards. The spring festival of Phagwa (PAH-gwah) (known elsewhere as Holi) is supported by Hindus and non-Hindus alike. Phagwa has a carnival atmosphere all its own as crowds of festivalgoers squirt colored dyes at one another.

Muslims of Asian descent who fast during the holy month of Ramadan mark the end of the month with the feast of Eid ul Fitr (eed ul FEE-tar). The Islamic New Year, a movable festival known as Hosay (hoe-ZAY), honors one of its ancient martyrs, named Hussein. Glittering models of the martyr's tomb are carried through the streets to the sound of drumming.

The legacy of British rule may be seen in the political and legal system, in the old colonial buildings of Port-of-Spain, and in the game of cricket. This bat-and-ball game is played wherever there is a level green space or even a beach or street.

The United States has exerted a considerable cultural influence on Trinidad. This influence is marked by a large number of U.S. programs on the television networks and the fact that many children from wealthier families study at U.S. universities.

A Muslim girl covers her head with a veil. Many Trinidadians are of Asian descent. About 6 percent of them are Muslim, and about 25 percent are Hindu.

461

TURKS AND CAICOS ISLANDS

THESE TWO SMALL ISLAND CHAINS EXTEND FROM THE SOUTHEAST OF THE BAHAMAS, in shallow blue-green waters.

The Turks and Caicos Islands are in two small groups. They number about forty and include low-lying islands, or cays, sandbanks, and coral reefs. The ocean seeps through limestone rocks to form salt ponds and marshes.

The only inhabited islands are Grand Caicos, Grand Turk, South Caicos, Middle Caicos, North Caicos, Providenciales, and Salt Cay. Grand Caicos is the largest, about 30 miles (48 kilometers) long by 2.5 miles (4 kilometers) wide. The capital, Cockburn Town, is on the island of Grand Turk.

Along the Cays

The Turks and Caicos Islands were settled a thousand years ago by the Taino, a people who belonged to the Arawak culture. They lived well by hunting, fishing, and planting crops such as corn, but their way of life was doomed as soon as Spanish soldiers set foot on Caribbean soil. The Taino were soon forced to work in the gold mines of Hispaniola (the island that now includes Haiti and the Dominican Republic), where they mostly perished.

CLIMATE

The Turks and Caicos Islands have a tropical climate that is kept moderate by fresh winds from the seas. Hurricanes sometimes sweep in over the islands in late summer or early autumn.

Average January temperature: 76°F (24° C)

Average July temperature: 83°F (28°C)

Average annual precipitation: 29 in (74 cm)

The islands were taken over by European pirates in the 1600s. From 1678 on, colonists of British descent arrived from Bermuda. They collected salt that had dried out from the ponds and marshes and sold it to British colonists along the North American coast. The Spanish took over the

FACTS AND FIGURES

Status: *British dependency*

Capital: *Cockburn Town*

Area: *166 square miles (430 square kilometers)*

Population: *14,000*

Population density: *84 per square mile (33 per square kilometer)*

Peoples: *100 percent Afro-Caribbean*

Official language: *English*

Currency: *U.S. dollar*

National days: *Emancipation Day (August 3)*

Country's name: *The Turks are named after the local Turk's Head cactus, which produces a red blossom shaped like the hat called a fez, formerly worn in Turkey. Caicos is from the Arawak caya hico, meaning "archipelago."*

The chief industry on the islands today is tourism. A growing number of visitors come to enjoy the beaches, seas, and coral reefs. Although farming is restricted by a lack of freshwater, many families have garden plots where they grow corn, sweet potatoes, and peas. People fish locally, catching snapper, lobster, and conch. Many islanders have left in search of work in the Bahamas or the United States

The islanders are mostly Christians, following Anglican, Baptist, Methodist, and Church of God forms of worship.

Afro-Caribbeans born on the islands are called "belongers." Other Afro-Caribbeans have come to the islands from Haiti and the neighboring Dominican Republic, and tourism and banking developments have brought in European and American visitors and workers. The islands share both British and Afro-Caribbean traditions. For example, the Queen's birthday is marked by parades, while August is the time for a Caribbean carnival on Grand Turk. Boat racing and fishing competitions are also popular.

islands after 1710 to protect their shipping from pirates. The French later invaded the islands, but in 1783 the British regained control. After the American Revolutionary War ended in 1783, some colonists who had supported Britain in the new United States settled on the Caicos Islands. There they planted cotton and sisal, a fibrous plant used to make rope and twine. Slaves of western African origin did the hard work. In the 1800s the salt industry and the plantations declined, and most of the plantation owners left. The slaves, freed in 1838, became the chief inhabitants of the Turks and Caicos. The Turks and Caicos finally gained home rule in 1976.

Front Street (bottom) in Cockburn Town, the islands' capital, on Grand Turk. A basket maker (top right) holds examples of her work, which she sells to tourists.

Timeline:	Islands home to an Arawak people called the Taino	Spanish enslave the Taino and ship them off to Hispaniola	Islands settled by salt producers from Bermuda	British gain control of the islands	Turks and Caicos gain home rule
	1000s c.e.	1500s	1678	1783	1976

Glossary

abolition: bringing a law or custom to an end; the abolishing of slavery.

adobe: sun-dried mud or clay.

agricultural reform: the redistribution of land to the poor.

black power movement: a radical movement demanding better conditions for black people. It emerged in the United States in the 1960s and had many supporters in the Caribbean.

cassock: a long gown, fastened up to the neck, worn mostly by priests or clerics.

cay: a small island or reef, usually formed by sand or coral. Also *key* and *cayo*.

cede: to grant or give up.

coalition: a temporary alliance between political parties or groups of people.

contract laborers: workers hired for an agreed period of time.

coup: a change of government brought about by force.

cricket: a bat and ball game played by two teams of eleven players each. It was first played in England and has spread from there to many parts of the world, including the Caribbean.

dialect: a nonstandard version of a language, as spoken in a particular region or by a particular group of people.

dictatorship: a form of government in which a ruler of a state has absolute authority.

exploit: to take advantage of something for selfish reasons.

fretwork: ornamental work in wood or metal, made up of interlacing or perforated designs.

guerrilla: a member of an irregular fighting force whose tactics include ambushes, surprise attacks, and sabotage rather than intense, close battles with the enemy.

indigenous: relating to a people who were born within a country or a region as opposed to being immigrants or settlers. Also *aboriginal* or *native*.

intact: untouched; left whole.

irrigation: watering of the land, often by using channels.

legacy: something handed down from one generation to another; an inheritance.

macabre: gruesome; often associated with death.

mestizo: a Spanish word for somebody of mixed descent, specifically a person of mixed European and American Indian descent.

mulatto: someone of mixed African and European descent.

nitrate: a chemical compound, sometimes occuring naturally, used in the making of fertilizer.

patois: a regional dialect, especially of the French language.

poncho: a garment made from a square or rectangular piece of cloth with a slit for the head.

premier: the head of a government, such as a prime minister or president.

radicalism: a belief in drastic or fundamental reform.

refugee: a person who flees to another country, usually for political or religious reasons.

savannah: a grassland dotted with trees.

stifle: to silence or suppress.

tax concessons: official agreements that allow someone to pay less taxes.

tubers: thickened, underground plant stems with buds from which other plants can develop.

viceroy: a person who governs a country or territory in the name of and with the authority of the supreme monarch or ruler.

viceroyalty: the office or term served by a viceroy.

Further Reading

Peru

Bickman, Connie. *Children of Peru.* Minneapolis, MN: Abdo & Daughters, 1994.

Deltenre, Chantal, and Martine Noblet. *Peru and the Andean Countries.* Hauppauge, NY: Barron, 1995.

Department of Geography Staff. *Peru in Pictures.* Minneapolis, MN: Lerner Group, 1992.

Falconer, Kieran. *Cultures of the World: Peru.* Tarrytown, NY: Marshall Cavendish, 1996.

Kalman, Bobbie, and Tammy Everts. *Land, People, and Cultures: Peru.* New York: Crabtree Publishing Company, 1994.

Lepthein, Emilie U. *Peru.* Danbury, CT: Childrens Press, 1992.

Puerto Rico

Abodaher, David J. *Puerto Rico: America's 51st State.* New York: Franklin Watts, Incorporated, 1993.

Aliotta, Jerome J. *Puerto Ricans.* New York: Chelsea House, 1995.

Fradin, Judith, and Dennis Fradin. *From Sea to Shining Sea: Puerto Rico.* Chicago: Childrens Press, 1995.

Hauptly, Denis. *Puerto Rico: An Unfinished Story.* New York: Simon and Schuster, 1991.

Johnston, Joyce. *Puerto Rico.* Minneapolis, MN: Lerner Group, 1994.

Johnston, Joyce. *Puerto Rico in Pictures.* Minneapolis, MN: Lerner Group, 1995.

Levy, Patricia. *Cultures of the World: Puerto Rico.* Tarrytown, NY: Marshall Cavendish, 1994.

Press, Petra. *Cultures of America: Puerto Ricans.* Tarrytown, NY: Marshall Cavendish/ Benchmark Books, 1996.

Saint Vincent and the Grenadines

Philpott, Don. *St. Vincent & Grenadines.* Lincolnwood, IL: Passport Books, 1996.

Suriname

Beatty, Noelle B. *Places and Peoples of the World: Suriname.* New York: Chelsea House, 1988.

Trinidad and Tobago

Bailey, Donna, and Ansel Wong. *Where We Live: Trinidad.* Austin, TX: Steck-Vaughn Library, 1990.

Urosevich, Patricia R. *Trinidad and Tobago.* Broomall, PA: Chelsea House, 1997.

Islands of the Caribbean

Mason, Antony. *The Caribbean.* Parsippany, NJ: Silver Burdett Press, 1988.

Mayer, T. W. *The Caribbean and Its People.* New York: Thomson Learning, 1995.

Springer, Eintou P. *The Caribbean.* Parsippany, NJ: Silver Burdett Press, 1987.

Walker, Cas. *The Caribbean.* North Pomfret, VT: Trafalgar Square Publishing, 1991.

Index

Page numbers in *italic* indicate illustrations.

Page numbers in *italic* indicate illustrations.

REFERENCE

PEOPLES
of the
AMERICAS

PEOPLES
of the
AMERICAS

Volume 7
Martinique–Paraguay

MARSHALL CAVENDISH
NEW YORK • LONDON • TORONTO • SYDNEY

Marshall Cavendish Corporation
99 White Plains Road
Tarrytown, New York 10591-9001

Consulting Editor: J. Patrick Gray, Professor of Anthropology, University of Wisconsin

Consultants: Jean-Marc Blais, Senior Interpretive Planner, Canadian Museum of Civilization, Hull, Quebec
        David Frye, Assistant Director, Department of Latin American and Caribbean Studies, University of Michigan

Spanish Consultant: Fran Kaplan

Contributing authors: D. L. Birchfield
                Marion Morrison
                Juliette Radcliffe Rogers
                Philip Steele
                Mary A. Stout

Discovery Books
    Managing Editor: Paul Humphrey
    Project Editor: Helen Dwyer
    Text Editor: Valerie J. Weber
    Design Concept: Ian Winton
    Designers: Barry Dwyer, Ian Winton, and Simon Borrough
    Cartographer: Stefan Chabluk

Marshall Cavendish
    Editorial Director: Paul Bernabeo
    Editor: Marian Armstrong
    Associate Editor: Debra M. Jacobs

The publishers would like to thank the following for their permission to reproduce photographs:
James Davis Travel Photography (frontispiece); Greg Evans International (351); Robert Harding Picture Library (Robert Cundy 373; G. A. Mather 403 top); Hutchison Library (J. G. Fuller 388; J. Henderson 379; Jeremy A. Horner 385); Panos Pictures (Gianni Muratore 360; Paul Smith 387); Edward Parker (359, 365, 374, 375); South American Pictures (Peter Dixon 390; Robert Francis 357, 370, 372, 383, 391, 393, 395, cover; Elin Hoyland 384; Tony Morrison 354, 355, 356, 358, 361, 362, 363, 364, 366, 367 top & bottom, 368, 376, 377, 386, 392, 394, 397, 398, 400, 401, 403 bottom; Chris Sharp 353, 371, 402); Tony Stone Images (Peter Poulides 381)

(frontispiece) Kuna girl on Panama's San Blas Islands.

Editor's note: Many systems of dating have been used by different cultures throughout history. *Peoples of the Americas* uses B.C.E. (Before Common Era) and C.E. (Common Era) instead of B.C. (Before Christ) and A.D. (Anno Domini, "In the Year of the Lord") out of respect for the diversity of the world's peoples.

Library of Congress Cataloging-in-Publication Data
Peoples of the Americas.
        p.   cm.
        Includes bibliographical references and index.
        Contents: v. 1. Anguilla–Belize — v. 2. Bermuda–Brazil — v. 3. Canada–Cayman Islands — v. 4. Chile–Costa Rica — v. 5. Cuba–French Guiana — v. 6. Greenland–Jamaica — v. 7. Martinique–Paraguay — v. 8. Peru–Turks and Caicos Islands — v. 9. United States of America — v. 10. United States of America–Virgin Islands
    ISBN 0-7614-7050-6 (set)
        1. Ethnology—America—Juvenile literature. 2. America—History—Juvenile literature. [1. Ethnology—America. 2. America—History.]
E29.A1P46   1999
970'.004—dc21   98-2801
                                                                                            CIP
                                                                                            AC

    ISBN 0-7614-7050-6 (set)
    ISBN 0-7614-7057-3 (vol. 7)

Printed and bound in Italy

Contents

MARTINIQUE

MARTINIQUE LIES AT THE CENTER OF THE GREAT ARC OF ISLANDS THAT MARKS THE EASTERN LIMITS OF THE CARIBBEAN SEA. It is one of the French Antilles.

The island of Martinique lies between Saint Lucia and Dominica, in the part of the Lesser Antilles known as the Windward Islands. It is about 19 miles (30 kilometers) from east to west and some 48 miles (75 kilometers) from north to south.

The north, with its lush rain forests, is dominated by Mount Pelée, a volcano that rises to 4,583 feet (1,397 meters) above sea level. The fertile plain of Lamentin lies in the center of the island, while the south has low hills known as mornes (MAWRN).

The Island of Flowers

Carib warriors inhabited the island when Europeans first reached the region around 1500. The Caribs had themselves seized the island from an Arawak people, who had settled there over a thousand years before.

The French were the first Europeans to settle the island in 1635. They fought the Caribs, cleared the land for sugarcane, and imported slaves from western Africa. Soon all the Caribs were killed or driven out. Martinique (mahr-tih-NEEK) prospered and became the chief French possession in the Caribbean.

After the French Revolution of 1789 the British occupied the island, but French rule was restored in 1814. Slavery was abolished in 1848. During the rest of the century, contract workers from southern India were brought in to work on the plantations.

In 1902 Mount Pelée erupted, killing more than thirty thousand people in what

---

CLIMATE

Martinique has a tropical, often humid climate. April is the driest month, and September is the wettest. The northern mountains are cooler and wetter than the central lowlands. Hurricanes are common in late summer and early autumn.

Average January temperature: *74°F (23°C)*

Average July temperature: *78°F (26°C)*

Average annual precipitation: *72 in (183 cm)*

FACTS AND FIGURES

Status: *Overseas department of the Republic of France*

Capital: *Fort-de-France*

Other towns: *Le Lamentin, Schoelcher, La Trinité*

Area: *425 square miles (1,102 square kilometers)*

Population: *394,000*

Population density: *945 per square mile (365 per square kilometer)*

Peoples: *90 percent Afro-Caribbean or mixed African-French descent; 10 percent Martinique French, expatriate French, and other*

Official language: *French*

Currency: *French franc*

National days: *Bastille Day (July 14); Schoelcher Day (July 21)*

Country's name: *Probably a corruption of the Carib Madinina ("island of flowers") or possibly from the Spanish name Martinica (after Saint Martin).*

cement plants. By far the fastest-growing industry is tourism.

About nine out of ten islanders are of African or mixed African-French descent. There is a small Asian population. The farmland and plantations are still largely owned by the descendants of the French settlers. Many people born in France have settled in Martinique to work in business, tourism, or government.

Most of the population speaks a Creole language based on French. The Roman Catholic faith is shared by more than 90 percent of the people. There are small Protestant, Hindu, and Jewish communities.

Religious festivals include All Saints, or *Toussaint* (TOO-seh), on November 1, marked by candlelit processions to the graves of loved ones. The chief festival of the year is carnival, leading up to Mardi Gras (Shrove Tuesday). African influence is shown in the masked costume parades and in the frantic drumming of a roots music known in Creole as *chouval bwa* (choo-VAHL bwah).

was then the island's chief town, Saint Pierre. In 1946 the island became a department of France, with its citizens having equal rights to French citizens. In 1974 Martinique was upgraded to an administrative region of France.

Sugarcane is still grown and is used to make rum, a leading export. Other crops include bananas, pineapples, eggplants, avocados, and limes. Many people work in small factories, food processing plants, oil refineries, and

A boat crosses the harbor at Le Vauclin, a fishing port on Martinique's coast. Today only about five percent of the island's workforce makes its living by fishing or farming.

Timeline:	Arawak peoples settle the island	Caribs drive out Arawaks	French colonize the island	Slavery abolished	Martinique becomes an overseas department of France	Martinique becomes an administrative region of France
	ca. 1 c.e.	1400s	1635	1848	1946	1974

MEXICO

MEXICO IS THE THIRD LARGEST COUNTRY IN LATIN AMERICA. It has the
largest Spanish-speaking population of any country in the world.

*Mexico shares a border with the United States
in the north and with Guatemala and Belize in
the southeast. It is bounded on the west and
south by the Pacific Ocean and on the east by
the Gulf of Mexico and the Caribbean Sea.*

*More than half of
Mexico is over 3,200
feet (915 meters) above
sea level. Two mountain
ranges, the Sierra Madre
Occidental and the Sierra Madre
Oriental, run north to south. A central
plateau lies between the two. The northern end
is dry and thinly populated. A range of
spectacular volcanoes crosses the southern end
of this plateau, most of which is over 8,000 feet
(2,438 meters) above sea level. Between the
volcanoes are valleys where Mexico City and
other large cities are located. To the south are
the lower ranges of the Sierra Madre del Sur
that line the southern Pacific coast. Low-lying
areas of Mexico include the deserts of the
northwest and Baja California, the coastal plain
along the Gulf of Mexico, and the flat, partly
forested Yucatán Peninsula.*

The Earliest Cultures

The earliest human artifacts found in
Mexico (MEK-sih-koe or MAY-hee-koe)
date from around 9000 B.C.E. The first
inhabitants of the area were hunters and
gatherers, but by about 2000 B.C.E. people
were cultivating crops, such as corn,
avocados, chili peppers, beans, and
squashes, and making pots.

FACTS AND FIGURES

Official name: *Estados Unidos Mexicanos*

Status: *Independent state*

Capital: *Mexico City*

Major Cities: *Guadalajara, Monterrey, Puebla, León, Ciudad Juárez, Tijuana*

Area: *756,066 square miles (1,958,201 square kilometers)*

Population: *95,700,000*

Population density: *127 per square mile (49 per square kilometer)*

Peoples: *60 percent mestizo; 30 percent Native American; 9 percent European descent; 1 percent other*

Official language: *Spanish*

Currency: *New Mexican peso*

National days: *Constitution Day (February 5); Birthday of Benito Juárez (March 21); Labor Day (May 1); Anniversary of the Battle of Puebla (May 5); Independence Day (September 16); Columbus Day (October 12); Anniversary of the Revolution (November 20)*

Country's name: *The early Aztec people were also known as the Mexicas; the country is named after them.*

Organized societies began to take shape about 1500 B.C.E. The first to emerge were the Olmecs (AWL-mekss) on the Gulf coast and in the eastern highlands. The Olmec culture was remarkable for the enormous stone carvings of heads and figures—many with a jaguar motif—which have survived to this day, and for the small figures and ornaments they made in jade. Olmec influence grew as the people traded and traveled the region in search of semiprecious stones. No one knows why, but their civilization came to an abrupt end about 400 B.C.E.

The Oaxaca valley was occupied from late Olmec times principally by Zapotecs (zah-puh-TEKS), whose main city was Monte Albán. There, giant stone tombs have revealed exquisite jewelry, fresco paintings with figures and ritual scenes, and some hieroglyphics. Monte Albán went into decline about 800 C.E., again for no obvious reason. After 1000 C.E. the Zapotecs were supplanted by the Mixtecs (mees-TEKS), who were fine wood-carvers

A gold pectoral, or breastplate, of the Mixtec culture found on the Monte Albán site. It was buried with an important chief in the fifteenth century C.E.

Timeline:	Earliest evidence of human settlement	Cultivation of crops	Olmec civilization on the Gulf coast and in the eastern highlands
	ca. 9000 B.C.E.	**ca. 2000 B.C.E.**	**ca. 1500–400 B.C.E.**

CLIMATE

The climate in Mexico is largely determined by altitude. There are three climate zones. The first, rising to just over 3,000 feet (915 meters), is hot and humid. The second, from that level to about 6,000 feet (1,829 meters), has a temperate climate but with sharp differences between day and night temperatures. The third zone, above 6,000 feet (1,829 meters), often has freezing temperatures and permanent snow. Mexico is generally a dry country, and only a few places in the south and along the Gulf coast get adequate rainfall year-round.

	Mexico City	La Paz, Baja California	Mérida, Yucatán
Average January temperature	55°F (13°C)	64°F (18°C)	72°F (22°C)
Average July temperature	61°F (16°C)	85°F (29°C)	83°F (28°C)
Average annual precipitation	30 in (76 cm)	6 in (15 cm)	38 in (97 cm)

and stonemasons. They made mosaics so intricately cut and pieced together that they did not need mortar.

From the sixth to the twelfth centuries, the Huastecs (WAH-steks) and Totonacs (toe-TOE-nahks) occupied the Gulf coast in the Veracruz region. The ruins of El Tajín, the Totonac capital, still stand and are best known for a pyramid that has 365 niches cut into its four sides.

Teotihuacán in the Valley of Mexico (the valley in which Mexico City stands today) was one of the most important cities in pre-Columbian America. Founded around 300 B.C.E., it flourished for about one thousand years before it too declined. At its peak Teotihuacán was a commercial, political, and religious center with a population of at least 100,000 people, who included skilled artists and builders. The area was covered with richly adorned temples and some of the largest pyramids ever built. The temples and pyramids were dedicated to various religious deities, including the sun god, the moon goddess, the rain god, and Quetzalcóatl, the feathered serpent.

One theory suggests that Teotihuacán fell to

The giant stone statues, known as the Atlantes, or Gigantes, of Tula, were built by the Toltecs sometime after 900 C.E.

Zapotec civilization in the Oaxaca valley	Teotihuacán civilization in the Valley of Mexico	Maya civilization begins
ca. 400 B.C.E.–800 C.E.	ca. 300 B.C.E.–700 C.E.	ca. 200 B.C.E.

the Toltecs (TOEL-tekss), whose cultural center was at Tula, also in the Valley of Mexico. They too were excellent craftspeople, responsible for the carvings of giant human figures still standing today. Tula lasted from about 850 C.E. to about 1200 C.E. Then, for reasons nobody today understands, their civilization collapsed, and the Toltecs were forced to disperse, some making their way to Maya lands in the Yucatán.

Surrounded by forest, the palace at the Mayan site of Palenque in the state of Chiapas has a maze of tunnels, galleries, patios, and a four-story tower.

The Maya: Architects and Mathematicians

The Maya (MY-uh) civilization dates from about 200 B.C.E. to the Spanish conquest, but was at its height between 300 and 900 C.E. The Maya homelands were the forests of Chiapas and the Yucatán, where they built pyramids of perfect proportions, finely decorated with stone carvings. They devised a form of writing using symbols, or hieroglyphs, to record their history and other important events. Many examples of hieroglyphic writing are found on the stone buildings. The Maya were also excellent mathematicians and astronomers, devising a 365-day calendar. A way of measuring time and the seasons was vital for the agricultural year, to indicate the right days for planting and harvesting. The Maya had many gods, including the gods of rain and of the earth. They would only decide when to plant and sow once they had consulted the gods and made sacrifices of animals, or perhaps children, to them.

The Maya lived in independent city-states, which were sometimes at war with each other. Theirs was a well-organized society, with rulers and nobles, highly skilled builders, engineers, and artisans. Populations were large; to feed so many people, farmers used slash-and-burn methods to clear patches of forest for growing food, and they built soil terraces in hilly areas for a variety of crops. They also devised irrigation techniques, which were essential in the Yucatán, where there is no surface water. The Maya had contact with other groups of people, mostly traveling by canoe on the rivers and along the sea coast. They traded textiles, pottery, crops, and salt and used cacao beans as money.

Huastec and Totonac civilizations in the Veracruz region	Toltec civilization at Tula in the Valley of Mexico	Aztec civilization
ca. 500–1200 C.E.	ca. 850–1200 C.E.	ca. 1200–1521 C.E.

The Ball Game of Ancient Mexico

A ball game was played throughout Mexico from the time of the Olmecs on. Many of the famous archaeological sites have ball courts. The largest court is at Chichén Iztá. El Tajín has twelve mounds known to be ball courts. Ball courts have been found all through South America, North America, and the Caribbean, all dating from before the Spanish came to these areas.

The Mexican game was played with a large, solid rubber ball that players could touch only with their bodies, not their hands. The goal was to get the ball through a relatively small stone circle placed high on one of the sloping stone sides of the court. Players wore protective knee and hip pads; gloves; wide, heavy belts of wood and leather; and sometimes helmets, since the weight and speed of the ball made the game very dangerous. The game was also full of religious symbolism: losing players were often offered to the gods as a sacrifice.

Although the sequence of events is not entirely clear, sometime after the fall of Tula in the mid-twelfth century, the Toltecs arrived in the northern Yucatán. Their architecture and objects can be seen in the great Maya-Toltec site at Chichén Iztá. They dominated the area for some two hundred years before being defeated by Maya people from another region.

Not much is known of the origins of the Tarascan (tuh-RASS-kuhn) people who inhabited Michoacán in western Mexico at about this time. From a history written by the Spaniards after the conquest, we know that their religion was based on volcanoes and their chief god represented the young sun. To honor him, the people lit fires on top of ceremonial centers. The Tarascans had their own language and were excellent potters and wood-carvers. They were strong enough to resist conquest twice by the most powerful people in the region, the Aztecs.

The Aztec Empire

The Aztecs (AZ-teks) probably originated in northern Mexico, making their way

The Sun Stone, or Aztec Calendar, sculpted in 1479. At the center is the Sun God. Around him hieroglyphs represent the days and months of the Aztec world.

Spaniards arrive	Spaniards take Tenochtitlán	Spaniards establish Mexico City	First call for independence from Spain
1519	1521	1527	1810

south to the Valley of Mexico sometime in the thirteenth century. According to legend, they saw an eagle with a serpent in its mouth perched on a cactus on an island in Lake Texcoco. Aztec priests had predicted that the people would see these signs; when they did, they were to settle in that place. So on this swampy island they founded their city, Tenochtitlán, which later became the site of Mexico City. At the heart of the city they built the great temple-pyramid of Huitzilopochtli. Within the lake they devised a system of irrigation and built *chinampas* (chee-NAHM-pahs), popularly known as floating gardens, where they grew a variety of crops. These crops, together with textiles, minerals, and other items, were traded in markets in Tenochtitlán and all around the empire.

In warfare the Aztecs were widely successful but very cruel. They imposed harsh taxes on their defeated enemies and were despised by them. By the end of the fifteenth century, the Aztecs had gained absolute power over an immense region, and their language, Nahuatl, was used in an area almost as large as present-day Mexico.

The Aztecs had created their empire with amazing speed, in something less than one hundred years, and the last few years were their greatest. Under Montezuma II, the ninth king (1502–1520), they built up a bureaucracy of political, military, and religious officials to govern the land. They produced codices, parchments of drawings and symbols, with details of how the empire was organized, as well as how each region was cultivated and taxed. The kingdom was arranged with political,

At the Festival of Our Lady of Guadalupe in Mexico City, people celebrate their heritage by dressing in Aztec-style outfits. This dancer has strings of rattles around her ankles.

military, and religious leaders, governors, and tax inspectors in such a way that everyone, from the slaves and serfs to the nobility, knew his or her place in society. Corruption was virtually unknown. Further progress, however, was disrupted by the arrival of five hundred Spaniards led by Hernán Cortés in 1519.

Mexico becomes independent	United States annexes Texas from Mexico	War between Mexico and the United States; Mexico loses half its land to the United States	Benito Juárez is president
1821	1845	1846–1848	1858–1864

Arrival of the Spaniards

Cortés and his men landed at Veracruz on the Gulf coast, marched into the interior without opposition, and reached Tenochtitlán. There Montezuma received them as guests, not realizing that the Spaniards' intention was to take the Aztec capital for themselves. After a lengthy campaign they succeeded in August 1521.

Mexico, or New Spain as it was then known, would become a Spanish colony for the next three hundred years. Within the first hundred years, the Spaniards subdued most of the Native Americans, helped in the north by Franciscan and Jesuit missionaries, whose purpose was to

The Conquest of Mexico is a mural by Diego Rivera in the Palace of Hernán Cortés in Cuernavaca. Here, a Spanish landowner oversees his slaves on a sugar plantation.

convert the people to Christianity. The Spaniards discovered valuable deposits of silver, founded many of today's important towns and cities, and introduced sugarcane and livestock.

The Native peoples suffered as slaves on the land and in the mines and as victims of European diseases such as smallpox and influenza. Those who could fled into remote areas. But within decades of the conquest, almost 90 percent of the Native population was wiped out. Some communities committed mass suicide rather than accept Spanish rule.

Archduke Maximilian of Austria is emperor of Mexico	Juárez is president for the second time	General Porfirio Díaz is president
1864–1867	**1867–1872**	**1876–1880**

New Spain was governed by a viceroy appointed by the Spanish crown, but power lay in the hands of an elite Spanish upper class. The population consisted of poor Spanish settlers; Spaniards born in Mexico (criollos); mestizos of mixed Mexican and Spanish parentage; black slaves brought from Africa to work the sugar plantations, farms, and mines; and the remaining Native Americans. By the eighteenth century, criollos and mestizos counted for about half the population.

In 1810, a move for independence from Spain began, led by the priest Miguel Hidalgo y Costilla. Until he was captured and executed, Hidalgo led rebels against the Spanish elite. He was followed by another priest, José María Morelos y Pavón, who in turn was imprisoned and shot in 1815. A general, Agustín de Iturbide, then joined the rebels and led them to victory in 1821.

Independent Mexico: An Uneasy Land

Soon after independence, conservatives and liberals in the country were at war with each other. The United States annexed the Republic of Texas from Mexico in 1845, then claimed more Mexican territory, including present day California, Arizona, and New Mexico. In 1846 the United States declared war on Mexico and a year later took Mexico City. In February 1848, with the Treaty of Guadalupe Hidalgo, the United States acquired all the land from Texas to California and from the Rio Grande to Oregon.

Benito Juárez came to power in 1858, promoting liberal ideas for education, freedom of speech, prohibition of slavery, separation of the state and the church, and a new constitution. Civil war continued, but Juárez won the day. The defeated conservative opposition then sought help from the French leader, Napoleon III, which led to the Archduke Maximilian of Austria becoming emperor of Mexico from 1864 to 1867.

Benito Juárez was a Zapotec Indian born in Oaxaca in 1806. He trained as a lawyer and was twice president of Mexico, from 1858 to 1864 and from 1867 to 1872.

General Porfirio Díaz ruled Mexico from 1876 to 1880 and from 1884 to 1911. He built up industries, organized the country's administration and finances, and built railroads and roads. However, the majority of Mexicans remained poor and oppressed. Díaz took away their land and gave it to a small, wealthy elite, who got richer by cultivating cash crops that they could

Díaz is president for the second time	Mexican Revolution	President Lázaro Cárdenas begins reforms
1884–1911	1910–1917	1934

export. Foreigners also owned vast tracts of land and had a huge stake in the country's industries.

Poverty, anger, resentment, frustration, and desperation among the mass of people eventually led to a peasant rebellion and Porfirio Díaz's downfall—and ultimately to the Mexican Revolution (1910–1917). Led by Emiliano Zapata and Francisco "Pancho" Villa, the revolutionaries' principal aim was to seize land from the rich and redistribute it to the poor. A new constitution (ratified in 1917) promised land, social, and educational reforms, but many were not implemented until the government of General Lázaro Cárdenas in 1934. World War II (1939–1945) was a turning point for Mexico, as the country could no longer rely on imports from Europe and the United States and had to develop more of its own industry.

Over the next decades people sporadically demonstrated against unemployment, high prices, and soaring inflation. In the 1970s it seemed relief was at hand when huge reserves of oil were discovered. This allowed the Mexican government to borrow heavily from international banks, thinking that it could repay the loans from money made from selling oil. But when the world price of oil fell in the early 1980s, Mexico could not pay its debts. The government imposed financial restrictions on its citizens and increased prices, which made life for ordinary Mexicans even more difficult. In 1994 the North American Free Trade Agreement (NAFTA) was ratified by the countries of Mexico, the United States, and

A member of the Zapatista National Liberation Army fighting in Chiapas. Many people have lost their lives in the struggle between the Zapatistas and the Mexican armed forces.

Canada to allow goods to be traded within the three countries free of tariffs.

Since 1994 the government has been faced with serious confrontation with Native American groups in Chiapas, who call themselves the Zapatista National Liberation Army. Chiapas is one of the poorest regions of Mexico, but the Native American fighters are representing poor Mexicans everywhere in their demands for employment, more schools, better health services, and a greater share of the land. They have proved they are willing to fight and die for their cause.

Large reserves of oil discovered	North American Free Trade Agreement (NAFTA) established between Mexico, the United States, and Canada; Indian groups in Chiapas confront the government
1970s	**1994**

Mexico's Booming Young Population

Since the end of World War II, Mexico's population has risen from 22 million to nearly 96 million. At least half the population is under twenty years old. The majority of Mexicans are mestizos of Spanish and Native American parentage. About 9 percent are descendants of Spanish or other European settlers. A tiny number of descendants of mixed African and Spanish or African and Native American marriages live around Veracruz and on the southern Pacific coast. They share much the same lifestyle as mestizos, as do the few Arabs and Chinese who have settled in Mexico. Ninety-five percent of the population speaks Spanish.

It is very difficult to calculate the number of Native Americans, since some Indians consider themselves mestizos.

What is more certain is that only about 7.6 million people speak one of the fifty Native languages as a first language. There are more than fifty groups of Native Americans, and about 95 percent of them are concentrated in just three areas of the country: the central plateau; the southern Pacific coast and the Oaxaca valley; and the Gulf coast and the Yucatán.

Mexico's three largest cities—Mexico City, Guadalajara, and Puebla—are all in the southern central plateau. The region covers just 14 percent of the country but contains more than half the population. Country people began drifting toward urban areas in the middle of the twentieth century, looking for a better way of life. Over two-thirds of Mexicans now live in cities and towns with populations over fifty

Guadalajara's central square is the Plaza of Liberation, with the cathedral on one side. People meet in the square to chat, play music, or to demonstrate.

thousand. Outside Mexico City, the fastest-growing cities are on the Mexican-United States border because there is more chance of getting employment in factories there. Hundreds of thousands of Mexicans have chanced entering the United States illegally.

Rapid population growth has tremendously strained Mexico's educational and health facilities. Central American refugees fleeing their own troubled countries, particularly in the 1980s, have added to the growing population problem in Mexico. Since the 1970s the Mexican government has worked to eliminate illiteracy and intends that all citizens should receive at least a primary education. Children ages six to fourteen are required to attend school, but nearly 15 percent do not. Most publicly funded schools are in rural areas, but the standard of teaching and equipment is low, and hardly a secondary school exists outside the towns. The best schools are privately funded, but few Mexicans can afford them.

The government also aims to provide health care for everyone, but facilities and standards vary greatly. While Mexico City and urban centers have the best hospitals and the most doctors and nurses, many rural areas have a medical clinic served only by a nurse. Certain rural areas, such as Chiapas, have a low standard of health care, and death rates are high.

There is no official religion in Mexico, and the government imposes strict regulations on churches. The number of priests that can be ordained is limited, and they are not allowed to vote, wear their robes in public, or make public political statements. People getting married must have a civil ceremony before a religious service. However, about 90 percent of the people consider themselves Roman Catholic, including many Native American peoples who still keep some of their traditional religious beliefs and practices. Other religions are allowed, and Protestant missionaries have been particularly successful in converting the urban poor.

In a high school in Mexico City, the teacher is giving a geography lesson. Subjects studied are much the same as those in the United States or Europe.

Traditional Food

The earliest peoples of Mexico found an abundance of useful wild plants that they gathered and then cultivated. Corn is perhaps the best known, but there are many others—the squashes of the gourd family, sweet potatoes, many chilies, beans, mushrooms, maguey cacti, prickly pear cacti, and countless herbs. Insects and their larvae were often used for food, and some still are. Lakeside people ate plenty of fish, lizards, frogs, and algae.

The natural pods from which chocolate is derived were thought to be of divine origin. Chocolate is still the basic ingredient in one of Mexico's most famous dishes, mole poblano *(MOE-lay poe-BLAH-no). Made into a rich sauce with different types of chilies, pumpkin seeds, peanuts, tomatillos (small, green fruits that are used in many dishes), and many herbs, it is served with turkey, chicken, or pork.*

Tortilla making is common throughout the country. Corn dough is first rolled into small balls and then patted by hand until it is very thin and flat. The circular tortilla is then cooked on a metal or clay griddle. It is then used for enchiladas, *rolled around a tasty filling; or as* chilaquiles *(CHEE-lah-kee-layss), pieces of dry tortilla added to a variety of dishes.*

Mexico City: A Sprawling Metropolis

Founded on a lake bed in a shallow depression between mountains, Mexico City is now home to 16 million people. By the year 2025 Mexico City is expected to be the world's largest city. The present population is mainly made up of mestizos and whites.

At this typically busy snack bar in Mexico City, the chefs are preparing thick tortillas served with cooked meats, chilies, and beans.

The city sprawls in every direction from its historic center, the main square called the Zocalo. Many buildings in streets around the Zocalo date from colonial times, and there are many churches. The cathedral is on one side of the square, and the National Palace is nearby.

For much of the day the central area is crowded with people looking for work. Each carries a small sign indicating his or her trade. Not far from the Zocalo, a wide tree-filled garden, the Alameda, provides a refuge where many poorer people stroll, sit, and make friends. At one time this was the

Virgin of Guadalupe

Every year on December 12, tens of thousands of Mexicans converge on a small suburb of Mexico City known as Villa de Guadalupe. For many it is simply a religious holiday, with families gathering to enjoy the company of friends over an open-air meal or snacks from sidewalk stalls. For others it is a deeply spiritual experience, and they walk slowly, some on their knees, along the road leading to Mexico's supreme religious center, the Basilica de Nuestra Señora de Guadalupe. More people visit this shrine than any other in the Christian world, except for the Vatican in Rome. For the Virgin of Guadalupe is not only revered as Mexico's principal religious symbol, she is also the country's patron saint.

The original basilica was built in 1533, but because of the massive growth of the population, a new basilica had to be constructed in 1976. Now as many as ten thousand people can crowd inside.

During the Festival of Our Lady of Guadalupe, a mass is held at the church, and many climb the small hill behind it to offer prayers and small gifts at a shrine. In the square outside the basilica, groups of musicians and Native Americans from all over the country parade and dance throughout the day.

great social center of the city where the rich and famous gathered. Times have changed, and parts of this area are often taken over by the homeless from around the city, protesting to the government about their plight.

Some people live in inadequate housing on the outskirts of the city. The poor construct makeshift dwellings of cardboard, grooved iron, and any other material they can find. Large families

The Festival of Our Lady of Guadalupe is celebrated in front of the new basilica. Thousands of people come to watch the dances and displays.

These brightly painted boats ferry people around the floating gardens, or chinampas, at Xochimilco in Mexico City. The Aztecs used these gardens for growing crops.

crowd into one- or two-roomed shacks with very little furniture. Few of these shacks have any running water, electricity, or sanitation services.

In contrast to the mass of the city's population, some extremely wealthy families live in fine houses with high walls and security guards. A typical middle-class family of a senior office worker will live in a modest suburb in a two-story house with perhaps four or five rooms. They will own a small car and a television.

Mexico City has a serious pollution problem. Exhaust emissions from traffic, pollution by industry, and millions of gas stoves have produced a greenish, choking pall that often completely obscures the sun.

Rural Life

Rural Mexico has many small, well-ordered towns. Often there is a church and a weekly market for local produce. The mestizos tend to be the traders and may speak both Spanish and the local Native American language.

The small towns offer many of the amusements that have made Mexico famous, and weekends are times for music and dancing, perhaps with some connection to a Native American or other

holiday. Skilled horsemen, known as *charros* (CHAH-roess), entertain crowds with their *jaripeos* (hah-ree-PAY-ohs), or competitions of roping and taming horses. The biggest events are held in Mexico City, but out in the country they are family affairs, drawing people from neighboring villages. Some small towns have bullrings that are well attended. At such times the little towns are crowded, and street vendors sell trinkets and snacks.

The Nahuas and Otomis of Central Mexico

The Nahuas (nah-WAHS) are Mexico's largest Native American group, with over a million people speaking the Nahuatl language, which has many regional dialects. They live in the Valley of Mexico

Charreadas, or rodeos, are held in rural areas throughout Mexico. In this village in the Western Sierra Madre, horsemen are preparing to demonstrate their expert skills.

and surrounding states, in the Eastern Sierra Madre, and on the Gulf coast around Veracruz. Often Nahuas are indistinguishable from rural mestizos, wearing the same clothes, living in similar homes, following the Catholic religion, cultivating crops such as corn and agave, and raising animals. Traditional dress of the men consists of coarse cotton pants tied at the waist and ankles, cotton shirts, sashes, and palm-leaf or straw hats. Women have long, straight skirts or full skirts gathered at the waist, blouses embroidered around the neck, embroidered white tunics called *huipiles* (wee-PEE-layss), and wool or cotton shawls called *rebozos* (ray-BOE-soess).

The Otomis (oh-TOE-meess) are also one of the largest ethnic groups, though only one-third the size of the Nahua group. They live mainly in the central highlands and have largely adopted a Western lifestyle. They are principally farmers but also make a living selling handicrafts. The Otomis have traditionally used the fibers of the agave plant to make cloth and baskets, but they also work with wool, clay, and leather. They weave carpets on vertical looms and paint bark paper with colorful abstract designs, flowers, and animals.

Like the Nahuas, the Otomis are Catholics but still cling to some of their Native beliefs. One of their most important festivals, shared with mestizos, honors the patron saints of their villages. The celebrations

(above) Mexico's Native peoples are skilled weavers. This Nahua woman is weaving on a back-strap loom, making colorful cloths and tapestries for sale to tourists.

include processions in which a statue of the patron saint is carried around the village, accompanied by music and dance. Sometimes the Otomis perform ritual dances in the church. Perhaps the most spectacular is the Dance of the Quetzal, with dancers wearing wheel-like headdresses interlaced with multicolored ribbons and tipped with feathers.

Small numbers of Otomi Indians in the highlands continue to live in traditional homes made from cactus and thatch. This Otomi woman is grinding corn between stones.

The Seris and Yaquis of Sonora

Sonora is in the northwestern corner of Mexico. Generally a dry region, irrigation has transformed parts of the state into a leading producer of cotton and wheat.

Other areas, including the Sonora desert, are arid and parched, empty landscapes of stony soil and weirdly shaped cacti.

The Seris (SEH-rrees) and Yaquis (YAH-kees) Indians live in Sonora. One of the Seris' traditional homes was on Mexico's largest island, Tiburón in the Gulf of California, but they were moved to the mainland in the 1960s. With only about seven hundred members, they are one of the smallest Native American groups in Mexico. They live by fishing, and catches

Native American Handicrafts

In the state of Michoacán, west of Mexico City, some 80,000 to 100,000 Tarascans, or Purépechas, live in the mountains and plains around Lake Pátzcuaro. They are skilled in making a wide variety of handicrafts, which include wood and beaten-copper articles; pottery and lacquered bowls; shawls and blankets of wool or cotton; leather goods; and items woven of palm-leaf or agave fiber.

The Zapotecs and Mixtecs of Oaxaca and the southern highlands also produce beautiful handicrafts. One Zapotec village, Yalalag, is renowned not only for the skirts worn by the women, which are dyed with natural colors, but also for crosses of hand-embossed silver. Traditionally, girls are given these crosses by their mothers when they marry. The Mixtecs are best known for their wooden animals, carved in all shapes and sizes and painted in brilliant colors, as well as for their finely woven colorful blankets, or serapes, which Mexicans carry over one shoulder, ready for use when the weather turns cold.

Traditional designs are painted on natural bark paper. They often depict country scenes, with birds, flowers, people, horses, and perhaps a church.

368

are large enough to sell the surplus in local markets or to traders who collect from them daily.

For centuries the Seris resisted Catholic teachings brought by the Spaniards and followed their own beliefs, in which the turtle and pelican, animals of their original homeland in the Gulf of California, were of supreme importance. They also worshiped the sun and moon. Today many have been converted to evangelical Protestantism. They have been persuaded to give up many of their old customs, including the women's ritual of decoratively painting their faces with vegetable dye.

The Seris make handicrafts, including shell necklaces, pottery, and ironwood carvings of animals. Ironwood is one of the hardest woods, rich in natural patterns in different shades of brown. The men carve designs based on animals they know well, particularly frogs, turtles, and fish. Women make baskets from a fiber called *torote* (toe-ROE-tay).

The Yaquis live on a reservation created for them in the 1930s, north of the Yaqui River. Their lands suffer from a lack of water, and they have no money for modern irrigation. In good years they grow a variety of crops, including corn, wheat, sorghum, cotton, fruit, and vegetables; at other times they hire themselves out as agricultural workers. They also fish and raise cattle.

The Yaquis have remained fiercely independent, with their own traditional authorities meeting weekly to sort out problems. They also have a master and a mistress of ritual, for although the Yaquis completely adopted the Catholic faith, they retained many of their festivals. One of the best known is the Stag Dance, which they perform during Holy Week. With the musical backing of harps, violins, drums, and a flute, two dancers representing coyotes (the spirit of evil) try to kill the stag (the spirit of good), who is represented by a third dancer wearing a dried stag's head. The stag is cornered by the coyotes, but he escapes, attacks, and kills one of them. The dead coyote comes back to life as a hunter who, with bow and arrow, kills both the other coyote and the deer, then falls dead again.

The Tarahumaras and Huichols of the Western Sierra Madre

The Tarahumara (tahr-uh-hoo-MAHR-uh) Native Americans, who number about 50,000, are in the northern part of the Western Sierra Madre and inhabit both cold, forested highlands and low, hot valleys. Today some Tarahumaras prefer to stay totally isolated, while others want schools, medical facilities, and better roads and communications. In their higher homelands they grow corn, squash,

Rarpipama: The Ball Race

The Tarahumaras have a reputation as great marathon runners, and their favorite entertainment is the ball race, or **rarpipama** *(rrahr-PEE-pah-mah). Two teams compete by running and kicking a ball in front of them. Their races are in laps, from 2 to 20 miles (3 to 32 kilometers) long, along narrow dirt tracks and through thick forests. They can run up to 100 miles (160 kilometers) nonstop and cover much greater distances than this over two or three days. The Tarahumaras also like to bet and will gamble a flock of sheep or goats on one of the teams.*

Tarahumara women weaving baskets on the railroad platform at El Divisadero in the Sierra Madre. They sell their baskets to the tourists who arrive by train.

houses made of wood, rocks, and adobe bricks built around a circular patio and surrounded by a low wall.

Although Huichol men increasingly favor Western-style shirts and pants, their dress is very colorful at fiesta time, with long white trousers and shirts elaborately embroidered in bright colors, one or more belts of brilliantly woven wool or cotton, and a decorated shawl or cape. They cover their hats with feathers and carry shoulder bags richly decorated with abstract patterns or stylized figures of animals.

potatoes, wheat, and barley; in the low valleys, beans, onions, and chilies are the main crops. All raise sheep and goats.

Tarahumara men sometimes work as farmhands, while the women make clay articles or baskets and weave shawls, blankets, and sashes on back-strap looms. Many men today wear Western clothing of manufactured shirts and pants, but traditional garments are a form of loincloth worn under a long shirt made of a rectangular length of cloth. Women wear square-shaped blouses with several full skirts, depending on how cold it is.

The Huichols (wee-CHOLES) also number about 50,000 and are even more isolated and independent than the Tarahumaras. They grow their own corn, beans, and squash, and they raise cows for milk to make cheese and sheep for their wool. But they also occasionally work on farms and sell their cattle and handicrafts to get money to buy other necessities. Related families generally live on *rancherias* (ran-chair-EE-ahs), groups of several

The Religious Ritual of Peyote

Peyote is a spineless cactus that grows in Central Mexico in a desert region northeast of where the Huichols live. The plant is central to their religious and social life, and every year they make a pilgrimage of over 600 miles (nearly 100 kilometers) to gather it. They regard the site in the state of San Luis Potosí as the birthplace of their gods.

A small dose of peyote—one to four buttons—staves off hunger and thirst. Larger doses produce hallucinations and are taken by Huichol shamans, or priests, to put themselves in touch with spirits who they believe help diagnose or cure illnesses. They also use peyote in ceremonies connected with the planting and harvesting of crops.

The Huastecs and Totonacs of the Eastern Sierra Madre

The Huastecs and Totonacs have much in common. They live in the Sierra Madre and on the Gulf coast, and both groups speak a form of Mayan. There are about 100,000 Huastecs and 150,000 Totonacs. Like most Native Americans, they are farmers, growing corn, beans, and chilies for their own use, as well as cash crops, such as coffee, cotton, tobacco, cacao, and sugarcane. Among younger men traditional rough cotton shirts and pants have largely given way to manufactured clothes. Women wear long skirts with white blouses and shawls lavishly embroidered in bright colors. In recent years the Totonacs have been threatened as the discovery of oil, combined with large-scale cattle ranching, has pushed them off the land.

The Voladores

The Totonacs are the Native Americans most closely associated with the Voladores (boe-lah-DOOR-ayss), or Flying Pole Dance. It is performed from a pole up to 100 feet (30 meters) high. Five men dressed in red pants, white shirts, and decorated hats climb to a platform at the top of the pole. While one plays music and dances, the other four secure ropes to their waists; on a given signal they drop together from the platform and swing into the air. As the ropes unwind, they glide around the pole thirteen times in widening circles. As they approach the ground, they perform a somersault and land on their feet. The total number of rotations, fifty-two, is a sacred number.

The Tzotzils and Tzeltals of the Chiapas Highlands

The Tzotzils (SOWT-tseelss), with possibly 200,000 people, and Tzeltals (sel-TAHLSS), with perhaps 50,000, are two large groups of Native Americans. The Tzotzils' home is high in the spectacular central highlands, while the Tzeltals live on the lower slopes. They are linguistically related, both speaking Mayan dialects, and have retained striking clothing. Scarlet and white are favorite colors, and embroidery and ribbons are widely used for decoration.

The five dancers taking part in the Voladores ritual begin their performance at the top of the one-hundred-foot pole. Today the dance is performed for tourists.

A Tzotzil girl from the Chiapas region. Her home is one of the poorest and most remote parts of Mexico, where Native Americans keep largely to their traditional ways.

In colonial times these peoples were treated very badly by the Spaniards, who seized their lands and forced them to work as slaves, exacted heavy taxes, and made them transport heavy bundles of produce over hundreds of miles from the mountains to the coast. The Spaniards were supported by the Catholic Church, whose teachings and orders the Indians have followed ever since, though they still respect their own gods and traditions.

The people rebelled, mainly demanding more land. Until the 1930s no Native American was allowed to walk on the sidewalks of the main town of San Cristóbal, and even today the Indians are still not accepted as equals by mestizos. Chiapas has remained one of the poorest areas of Mexico, and today Native Americans have taken up arms to fight for more land and a better deal for their families.

The Lacandones: People of the Chiapas Rain Forest

The traditional home of the two or three thousand Lacandones (lah-kahn-DOE-ness) is the dark, dense, and damp rain forest of Chiapas, close to the border with Guatemala. Their inaccessible villages deep within the forest enabled them to stay out of reach of the Spaniards and the missionaries, and for centuries they had little contact with other Mexicans. This started to change at the end of the nineteenth century, when lumbermen began searching for mahogany. Over the years access roads have been built, sawmills have appeared, and in their wake, hunters and colonists have arrived. In exchange for land or wood or by working for the lumbermen, some Lacandones have earned money, which they use for clothing, axes and machetes, alcohol, firearms, and even trucks.

The Lacandones' traditional way of life is to clear the forest, using slash-and-burn methods, and grow corn, cotton, yucca, and bananas for their own use and tobacco, which they sell. They hunt, fish, and raise chickens, turkeys, pigs, and bees. The forest provides them with medicinal plants and all the wood and thatch needed for building their homes.

The Lacandones live in small communities called *caribales* (kah-REE-bah-layss) and move on every four or five years to a different part of the forest. The head of each community is the oldest man. Clothing is a simple, full-length tunic of coarse cotton for men and a long skirt and blouse for women, who also wear necklaces made from beads and berries.

The Lacandones, unaffected by Catholic teachings, worship many gods of the natural world and gods related to their spiritual life. For example, they worship Hachakyum, who is the god of creation, and Nojoch Yum Chac, the Old Lord of Rain. The gods are represented by incense burners and clay figures and placed in the ceremonial hut of each caribal, where various ceremonies and rites are performed. Each year the incense burners are renewed, and offerings such as corn bread are made to the used burners.

Posadas and Piñatas

Christmas is celebrated in Mexico with posadas (poe-SAH-das) and piñatas. During a posada, candle-lit processions of people make their way along the street, knocking on doors until eventually at one door they are invited in and a party starts. This custom reflects the journey of Joseph and Mary searching for an inn. Piñatas are large clay pots covered in papier-mâché and shaped as an animal or fun figure. The pots are filled with candies and suspended from a rope. Blindfolded children try to hit the swinging pot with sticks; when they do, it crashes to the ground, and they scramble to get the candies.

This Lacandones man stands in front of a Mayan carving at Bonampak. Some Lacandones earn money by selling craft items to tourists at archaeological sites in the Chiapas region.

The Yucatecs of the Yucatán

The Yucatecs (YOO-kuh-teks), a Mayan people, live in the Yucatán peninsula, a largely flat land of rain forest, semiarid plains, and swampy areas close to the border with Guatemala and Belize. Today the Yucatecs live much like other Native Americans, as subsistence farmers and occasionally working on plantations. Recently the Yucatecs have been involved in tourism, which has been highly successful in Cancún and around the many Mayan archaeological sites left in Yucatán.

Traditional practices are still important to the Yucatecs. Every year they hold a ceremony to the rain gods, hoping to secure water for crops. When a Yucatec man marries, he must perform *muhul* (moo-HOOL) by taking gifts to his future wife. He must also agree with her parents on how long he will help on their land as part of his "bride service." This task is called *hancab* (hahn-KAHB), or "work of the groom." Once the agreement is made, the couple can marry.

Children are baptized in a ceremony called *hetzmek* (HETZ-mek), which means "astride" and refers to the first time a child is carried astride the hip of his or her godparents. At the ceremony the children are symbolically presented with tools of work, such as digging sticks or cooking bowls.

Music and Dance: A Mix of Styles

Mexican music is a combination of pre-Columbian and Spanish traditions, with additions from the Caribbean and other parts of Latin America and Anglo-American rock and pop. Instruments played at Native American fiestas include a small flute; the *chirimía* (chee-ree-MEE-ah), a horizontal wooden drum; the *teponaztle*

A Maya girl from the Yucatán sells homemade shell and bead necklaces to tourists. Tourism is a growing source of income for the region.

A group of mariachi players in Mexico City. Mariachi players regularly gather on weekends in city plazas, where they play tunes at the request of passers-by.

(tay-poe-NOTS-lay), a vertical drum; the *huehuetl* (way-WAY-tull), a giant conch shell; and rattles. The Spaniards introduced the violin, guitar, and harp. Mostly wind and brass instruments are played in Yucatán, while the marimba, which is like a xylophone with big wooden keys, is most popular in Chiapas and Oaxaca.

The music perhaps most associated with Mexico is mariachi. Mariachi groups wear cowboy costumes of large sombreros, tight-fitting black jackets, and pants decorated with silver. Often hired for weddings and parties, they play mostly romantic songs on stringed instruments and trumpets.

One of the best-known Native dances still performed in Mexico is the Dance of the Moors and Christians. Moors were the people from northern Africa who conquered Spain, and this dance celebrates their expulsion from Spain. Dancers are divided into two groups, each with a king or leader. They wear colorful capes or robes and tin-and-cloth crowns covered with mirrors and beads. Half-moons adorn the Moorish crowns, and a cross decorates the Christian crowns. Both groups of dancers usually wear masks decorated to look like Europeans with blond beards and blue eyes. A mock battle with wooden weapons takes place, with the Christians winning.

One of the oldest dances is the *Tarascan* (tah-rah-SKAHN), or Dance of the Old Men, which is dedicated to the Old God, or God of Fire. Old and young take part, wearing straw hats decorated with ribbons and masks depicting old men with wide, toothless grins. Mimicking old men, the dancers hobble out, using walking canes and appearing very tired. Then they suddenly jump and leap around.

Two men perform the Dance of the Moors and Christians. The Christian, with a sword, is on the left; the Moor, beating a drum, is on the right.

A Writer and a Poet

Carlos Fuentes is perhaps the best known of Mexico's writers. He has a strong international following, not least because of a book called *The Buried Mirror* and a lengthy television series based on it. His work portrayed the history of the conquest of Latin America and its effects on its people.

Mexican poet Octavio Paz, who died in 1998, was awarded the Nobel Prize for literature in 1990. His works reflect his own disillusion with the Mexican Revolution and with socialism in general. He has written much about the Mexican personality and how Mexico's many festivals are of great importance to the people, in some cases their only relaxation. To visitors, the festivals portray the richness of the country's national heritage.

Day of the Dead

Celebrating the Day of the Dead is particularly important to many Mexicans. They believe the spirits of their loved ones return on that day. Long before the event, people get busy baking breads and making candies in the shape of skulls or skeletons. Many Mexicans prepare small altars in their homes for their dead relatives or friends. The altars are decorated with masses of orange flowers and photos of the deceased. November 1 is dedicated to children who have died, and toys, cakes, candy, and honey are laid out on altars for their spirits. The next night, when adult souls are believed to visit, families take specially prepared dishes and gifts to cemeteries, which are lit by hundreds of candles as people spend an all-night vigil there.

Art on a Grand Scale: The Muralists

The most famous Mexican artists are the great muralists Diego Rivera (1886–1957), David Alfaro Siqueiros (1896–1974), and José Clemente Orozco (1883–1949). These men covered the walls of government buildings and many others with bold political art. One of Rivera's best-known works is in the National Palace and was painted between 1929 and 1935. The painting covers many separate walls. The central portion depicts the history of Mexico from the arrival of the Spaniards to the time of the Revolution.

Some of Siqueiros' best paintings are in the Palace of Belles Artes, and Orozco's finest, known as **Man of Fire**, with a huge flame surrounding figures representing earth, air, and water, is in Guadalajara, Mexico's second-largest city. Another muralist, Juan O'Gorman (1905–1982), covered the outside walls of the library of the National University of Mexico, Mexico City, with a mosaic of natural stones and colored glass. The mosaic, which covers almost 50,000 square feet (3,900 square meters), depicts the meeting of the cultures of Mexico and Europe.

A section of The History of Mexico, a huge mural by Diego Rivera in the National Palace in Mexico City. This portion depicts market day in the Aztec city of Tenochtitlán.

MONTSERRAT

MONTSERRAT IS THE SOUTHERNMOST OF THE LEEWARD ISLANDS, part of the Lesser Antilles chain in the eastern Caribbean Sea.

Montserrat is a small island, about 11 miles (18 kilometers) long and 7 miles (11 kilometers) wide. The interior is mountainous, rising to 3,000 feet (914 meters) above sea level at the island's highest point, Chances Peak, in the Soufrière hills.

This is a dangerously active volcano. The island is lush and fertile.

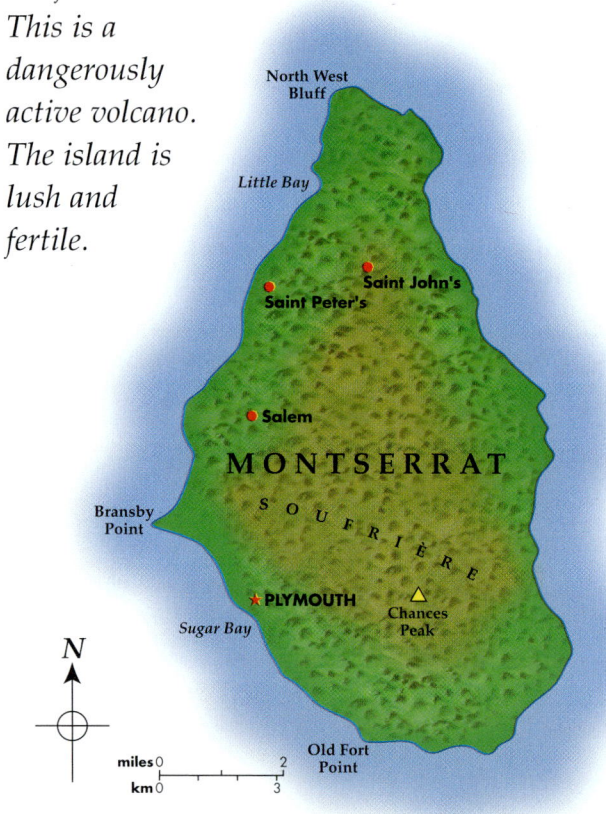

The Emerald Isle

When Christopher Columbus sailed toward the Caribbean Sea in 1493, the island was home to scattered Carib war bands. Today Montserrat (mahn-suh-RAT) is sometimes called "the emerald isle" because the island was settled by colonists from Ireland, which is also known by that name. The Irish arrived in 1632. The Caribs were killed or driven away, and African slaves were brought in to clear the land and plant sugarcane. Slavery was abolished in 1834, and the freed slaves worked their own small plots of land but remained desperately poor. The Irish intermarried or drifted away after the abolition of slavery, since the island's economy declined.

During the twentieth century many more Montserratians left the island in search of work on other Caribbean islands or in Great Britain. Recently their place has been taken by wealthy North Americans in search of a peaceful retirement and construction workers from elsewhere in the Caribbean. The latter were needed because in 1989 Hurricane Hugo damaged or destroyed most of the island's houses.

CLIMATE

Montserrat has a warm, tropical climate, at its coolest from December to February and its driest from February to May. Hurricanes and tropical storms frequently devastate the island in late summer and early autumn.

Average January temperature: *76°F (24°C)*

Average July temperature: *81°F (27°C)*

Average annual precipitation: *65 in (165 cm)*

FACTS AND FIGURES

Status: *British dependent territory*

Capital: *Plymouth*

Area: *40 square miles (104 square kilometers)*

Population: *4,000 since eruption of 1997 (12,000 pre-eruption)*

Population density: *100 per square mile (38 per square kilometer)*

Peoples: *100 percent Afro-Caribbean or mixed African-European descent*

Official language: *English*

Currency: *Eastern Caribbean dollar*

National days: *Saint Patrick's Day (March 17); Festival Day (December 31)*

Country's name: *Named by Christopher Columbus after the monastery of Santa Maria de Montserrate, near Barcelona, Spain.*

is English, often spoken with a strong Caribbean accent. The chief religion, surprisingly, is Protestantism rather than Roman Catholicism, the religion of the majority of Irish in Ireland.

The Irish influence does survive in the steps of some folk dances and in the instruments sometimes played, such as fifes. African influence, however, dominates most popular music. This includes calypso (Trinidad-style satirical songs) and soca (soul calypso). The aim of *jumbie* (JUM-bee) dances, in the African tradition, is to heal the ill. Favorite foods include goat water (a spicy goat stew flavored with rum), frog legs (served as "mountain chicken"), conch, and lobster.

Christmas is marked by processions and parades that build up to a carnival on New Year's Eve and New Year's Day. Saint Patrick's Day is celebrated partly as the national day of Ireland and partly as a commemoration of a slave uprising in 1768.

Eight years later a series of eruptions in the Soufrière hills killed nineteen people, destroyed Plymouth, and caused many people to flee the island. Scientists reported that further eruptions were possible, and the British government made plans to fully evacuate the island. Many Montserratians decided to stay, however.

The island normally produces all the fruit and vegetables it needs. These include potatoes, sweet potatoes, lettuce, tomatoes, and tropical fruits. One in ten workers are employed in small factories, producing electronic parts and leather goods.

The great majority of Montserratians today are of Afro-Caribbean descent; some are part-Irish. Irish surnames and place-names are common. The official language

A farmer and his wife take to the road near Saint John's, in the north of Montserrat. The island is one of the least developed in the Caribbean.

Timeline:	Island sparsely settled by Caribs	Christopher Columbus reaches the island	Catholic Irish settle on the island	Confirmed as British colony by Treaty of Paris	Abolition of slavery	Volcanic activity and eruptions prompt evacuation
	1400s C.E.	1493	1632	1763	1834	1995 and 1997

NETHERLANDS ANTILLES

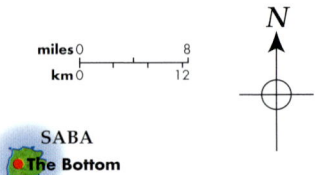

THIS FEDERATION OF CARIBBEAN ISLANDS IS MADE UP OF TWO WIDELY SEPARATED GROUPS. Sint Maarten, Saba, and Sint Eustatius lie in the Leeward Islands. Curaçao and Bonaire lie 500 miles (800 kilometers) to the south, near Venezuela.

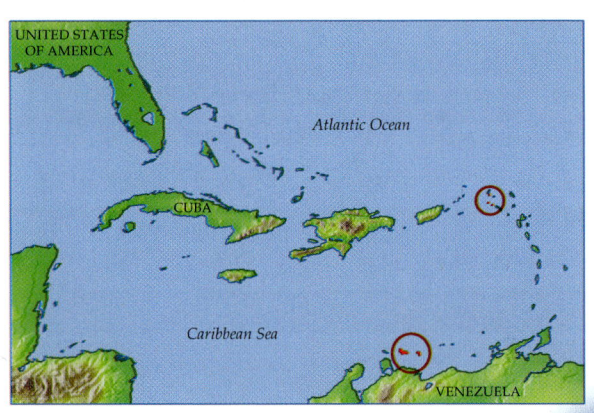

Sint Maarten covers 13 square miles (34 square kilometers) of a steep, forested island of which the northern half, Saint Martin, is part of French Guadeloupe. Saba, with an area of 5 square miles (13 square kilometers), and Sint Eustatius (commonly called Statia), with an area of 8 square miles (21 square kilometers), are both lush, volcanic islands.

The other two islands are larger, low-lying, and covered in cacti, stunted trees, and shrubs. Curaçao is 171 square miles (443 square kilometers) in area, and Bonaire is 111 square miles (288 square kilometers).

The Dutch Caribbean

The Netherlands Antilles have been united since 1845 and have had self-government since 1954. Aruba seceded from the federation in 1986 (see ARUBA).

The northern Leeward Islands of Saba, Sint Eustatius, and Sint Maarten were originally home to bands of Arawak-speaking Native Americans, but it was the

CLIMATE

The Netherlands Antilles have a tropical climate. While the Leewards in the north have considerable rainfall, the southerly islands are semiarid.

	Sint Eustatius	Curaçao
Average January temperature:	79°F (26°C)	79°F (26°C)
Average July temperature:	83°F (28°C)	82°F (28°C)
Average annual precipitation:	45 in (114 cm)	23 in (58 cm)

FACTS AND FIGURES

Official name: *De Nederlandse Antillen*

Status: *Autonomous region of the Netherlands*

Capital: *Willemstad (on Curaçao)*

Other towns: *Kralendijk (Bonaire), The Bottom (Saba), Oranjestad (Sint Eustatius), Philipsburg (Sint Maarten)*

Total area of islands: *308 square miles (792 square kilometers)*

Total population of islands: *208,000*

Overall population density: *676 per square mile (261 per square kilometer)*

Peoples: *No breakdown by race available.*

Official language: *Dutch*

Currency: *Netherlands Antilles guilder (florin)*

National day: *Queen's Day (April 30)*

Country's name: *Antillia was the name of a legendary island in the Atlantic that appeared on medieval maps. When Europeans found the Caribbean islands they used this name.*

seaport after slavery was abolished. Now it is a center for ship repairs and has factories producing textiles and beer. The name of the island is given to a famous liqueur, which is flavored with bitter oranges. Bonaire produces salt and textiles, and Sint Maarten is known for its rum distilleries.

The Netherlands Antilles are a cultural melting pot. The peoples there are descended from Afro-Caribbeans, South Americans, and Europeans of all descriptions.

The closeness of Venezuela has given the southern islands a South American feel. This is reflected in the popular music, which includes the Latin dance styles of merengue and salsa. The Dutch Leewards have more of an Afro-Caribbean feel, and the English language, brought in by settlers from the surrounding islands, predominates.

A ferry passes buildings that would not look out of place in Amsterdam. However, the water is much warmer! This is Curaçao, the largest island in the Netherlands Antilles.

warlike Caribs who controlled the region when these islands were settled by the Dutch in the 1600s. The colonists destroyed any Carib opposition, imported slaves from western Africa, planted crops, and exported salt. The Dutch abolished slavery in 1863.

An Arawak-speaking tribe called the Caiquetios were among several indigenous peoples who had settled the southern part of what became the Netherlands Antilles. The first Europeans to arrive were the Spanish in 1499. The Dutch took over Curaçao in 1634. Under their rule the island became a major depot for the slave trade. Curaçao remained an important

Timeline:	Arawak settlement on Lesser Antilles	Caribs seize Leeward Islands	Dutch settle Lesser Antilles	Federation of Netherlands Antilles formed	Abolition of slavery	Internal self-government throughout Netherlands Antilles
	ca. 700–1100 C.E.	1400s	1630s–1640s	1845	1863	1954

NICARAGUA

OF THE SEVEN SMALL COUNTRIES MAKING UP CENTRAL AMERICA, NICARAGUA IS THE LARGEST. It bridges the continent, with shores on both the Pacific Ocean and the Caribbean Sea.

Nicaragua is bordered on the north by Honduras and on the south by Costa Rica. In the north-central region, mountains rise to 6,898 feet (2,103 meters) above sea level at Pico Mogotón, near the northern border. From there many rivers descend eastward, flowing across a broad plain into the Caribbean Sea. This humid region of lagoons and estuaries is sometimes called the Mosquito Coast.

CLIMATE

Nicaragua has a tropical climate. The Pacific region is hot year-round, but temperatures are cooler in the north-central mountains. The Caribbean coast is the wettest region, with a heavy rainfall for much of the year.

Average January temperature: *79°F (26°C)*

Average July temperature: *86°F (30°C)*

Average annual precipitation: *45 in (114 cm)*

The most populated part of Nicaragua is the Pacific coast, a region of lowlands studded with volcanoes. It also has two very large lakes, Lake Nicaragua and Lake Managua.

Between Two Oceans

The Republic of Nicaragua (nih-kuh-RAH-gwah) is named after the Nicarao (neek-AR-oe), one of the many indigenous groups living in the region before the first Spanish arrived in 1522. They were farmers, growing corn and sweet potatoes. Like the Aztecs of ancient Mexico, the Nicarao were speakers of a Nahuatl language. Other Native peoples included the Chorotegas in the west and the ancestors of the Ramas and Sumos.

As the Spanish invaded the land, about two-thirds of the Native people were killed or died of diseases for which they had no resistance. The Spanish built splendid new cities named Granada and León; the latter had to be relocated after a severe earthquake in 1610. During the 1700s the two cities became increasingly bitter rivals. In 1821 Nicaragua broke away from Spanish rule, and after seventeen years as

FACTS AND FIGURES

Official name: *República de Nicaragua*

Status: *Independent state*

Capital: *Managua*

Major cities: *León, Granada, Masaya, Chinandega, Bluefields*

Area: *49,579 square miles (128,410 square kilometers)*

Population: *4,400,000*

Population density: *89 per square mile (34 per square kilometer)*

Peoples: *77 percent mestizo; 10 percent European (mostly Spanish) descent; 9 percent Afro-Caribbean; 4 percent Native American*

Official language: *Spanish*

Currency: *Cordoba*

National day: *Independence Day (September 15)*

Country's name: *Named by the Spanish after the indigenous Nicarao people*

Caribbean coast, which had been under British control for many years, was ceded to Nicaragua.

In 1893 a general named José Santos Zelaya seized power, but after a rebellion against him in 1909, the U.S. government forced him to quit. In 1912 the United States sent in twenty-five hundred marines, who remained in Nicaragua for most of the period up till 1936. The U.S. government used the soldiers to force through policies and personalities favorable to the United States. In 1926 a radical guerrilla movement led by Augusto Sandino attacked the marines, the beginning of a six-year guerilla war.

The U.S. Marines set up and trained a National Guard under the leadership of Anastasio Somoza García. In 1934 Somoza arranged the assassination of Sandino, and in 1936 overthrew President Juan Batista Sacasa. He received the backing of the

Ancient rock carvings of patterns, figures, and animals are found on islands in Lake Nicaragua. Nicaragua was inhabited for over five thousand years before the Spanish arrived.

part of Mexico and the ill-fated United Provinces of Central America, it became an independent nation in its own right. The quarrel between León and Granada erupted into a civil war, during which an American adventurer and soldier named William Walker intervened and ended up being elected president. Two disastrous years later, Walker was ousted. Managua was made the capital, and soon the

Timeline:	Earliest traces of human settlement	Spanish explorers reach Nicaragua	Independence from Spain	Civil war; city of Granada attacks and defeats city of León	U.S. Marines in Nicaragua to support government
	ca. 4000 B.C.E.	1522 C.E.	1821	1855	1912–1936

United States and remained in power, or acted as the power in the background, until his assassination in 1956.

This dictator was succeeded by his son Luis Somoza Debayle. In 1963 his brother Anastasio took over. The Somoza years were marked by corruption and violence. When Managua was laid waste by an earthquake in 1972, international aid was

Sandinistas gather for a rally. The revolutionary party, which came to power in Managua in 1979, has failed to be voted into power since the general election of 1990.

diverted to the ruling family. The Somozas continued to receive the support of the United States because they were against communism, an economic and political system the United States also strongly opposed.

In 1978 a leading critic of the Somozas, newspaper editor and opposition politician Pedro Joaquín Chamorro, was assassinated.

There followed a full-scale popular revolution, led by the socialist Sandinista National Liberation Front (FSLN), named in honor of Sandino. By 1979 Somoza had fled the country, and the rebels held power. The new Sandinista rulers set about rebuilding the shattered country and improving literacy and health care. However, centrist politicians such as Violeta Barrios de Chamorro, the widow of Pedro Joaquín Chamorro, soon distanced themselves from the left-wing FSLN. The United States was not prepared to condone a government that supported other guerrilla armies in the region. It funded right-wing rebels called Contras, whose ranks included many former supporters of Somoza. The Contras harassed the Sandinista government, staging guerilla attacks.

At the general election in 1990, Violeta Chamorro and her Unión Nacional Opositora (UNO) party won power. Although the Sandinistas' reforms were still popular, most Nicaraguans by now just wanted peace and an end to the civil war between the Sandinistas and the Contras. The Sandinistas split over future policy. They remain powerful today, despite having failed to win power once again at the 1996 general election.

Rebellion by anti-government guerrillas starts	Somoza dynasty heads Nicaragua	Foundation of FSLN, radical guerrilla group	Full-scale revolution erupts, Somoza flees, FSLN take Managua	FSLN wins election	UNO party wins election	Center-right Liberal Alliance party wins election
1926	1936	1961	1979	1984	1990	1996

Peoples, East and West

Only about 10 percent of Nicaraguans, or "Nicas," are directly descended from the Spanish who arrived in the country when it was still a colony. The great majority are mestizos, people of mixed Spanish and Native American descent. Those Nicarao and Chorotega people who survived the arrival of the Spanish soon became Christian and mixed in with them. In eastern and central Nicaragua their traditional way of life and customs disappeared. Many feared to retain their traditions, because Natives were treated little better than slaves. Today the Pacific coast, where most of the population lives, is mostly mestizo and 100 percent Spanish-speaking, with a pronounced local accent.

The Atlantic coast is very different. With poor overland communication through the mountains and the rain forest of the interior, it has remained isolated from Managua in the west, and its culture is influenced more by the Caribbean. There, only about half the people are Spanish-speaking mestizos, and English and indigenous languages may also be heard.

A large number of Miskito (miss-KEE-toe) Indians are scattered throughout the Atlantic region. This indigenous people has mixed with other peoples up and down the coast. Other Native American peoples include the Sumos, who number about eight thousand, and the Ramas, who number only about eight hundred. There are thirty thousand or more Afro-Caribbeans, some of mixed European descent known as Creoles.

Children displaced from their villages during the years of civil war make their home in a ruined building in Managua. Nicaragua faces severe economic and social problems.

There are also two thousand or so Garifuna (GAHR-rih-FOO-nah), also known as Black Caribs. These people descend from the indigenous Carib people and from Afro-Caribbeans. Their ancestors originally came from the Caribbean island of Saint Vincent (see SAINT VINCENT AND THE GRENADINES) but were expelled from there to Central America at the end of the eighteenth century, after a war with the British colonial authorities. Most Garifuna live to the north, in Belize (see BELIZE).

The Atlantic coast is the poorest region of a poor country. Contras attacked sites in the Atlantic region in the 1980s and kidnapped indigenous peoples living there, forcing them to join the Contras at their bases in Honduras. Successive governments in Managua have ignored the needs, languages, and traditions of those on the Atlantic coast, but recently local governments have gained some power from the national government.

How Nicaraguans Live, Work, and Play

Well over one-third of all Nicaraguans work as fishers or farmhands. Coffee and cotton are major exports, and important crops include bananas, sugarcane, rice, tobacco, corn, sorghum, and beans. About one-tenth of the workforce is employed in manufacturing, producing processed foods, garments, and chemicals. The largest number of workers are employed in the services sector.

Since the Sandinistas fell from power, services that were once provided by the government have been taken over by private businesses. Many jobs were lost in this transition. Vast numbers of people have no jobs or only minimal employment as street vendors. Many country people have moved into towns in a fruitless search for work.

The standard of living in Nicaragua is very low, and during the 1990s the new government cut down on the programs introduced by the Sandinistas, greatly reducing spending on education and literacy, health care, and public transportation. Cities are crowded; housing and public services are often very poor.

Ninety percent of Nicaraguans follow the Roman Catholic faith introduced by the Spanish, although many people on the Atlantic coast are Protestant. During the 1970s and 1980s the Roman Catholic Church was divided between priests who believed that the best way to

Shoppers check out a street stall in central Managua. Goods for sale include plantains, tomatoes, and mangos.

help the poor was to support the Sandinistas and those who opposed any kind of socialist politics. The traditional gods of the indigenous peoples are no longer worshiped, but some Christian festivals and processions include dances and music that date back to the days before the Spanish conquest.

Easter, Christmas, and saints' days are all celebrated with festivals. *Purísma* (poor-EEZ-mah), held on December 6 and 7, commemorates a miracle said to have taken place long ago when the Virgin Mary quieted an erupting volcano. In Masaya, carnival is celebrated with masks and disguises. On the Atlantic coast May Day is a festival marked by revelry and dances, some of which are said to have been introduced by English pirates in the 1600s.

Independence Day is a chance to set off fireworks and listen to military bands. More traditional folk music is played on instruments such as the marimba, which is a large xylophone, and the maracas, or gourd rattles. Reggae music is popular along the Caribbean coast.

The most popular sport is baseball, introduced to Nicaragua about sixty years ago by U.S. Marines. As in many other Latin American countries, soccer is another passion. Cockfighting, in which roosters fight to the death, is bet upon by gamblers, and there is also a local version of bullfighting, in which the bull must be ridden rodeo-style.

Nicaraguan cowboys show off their horsemanship in the ring at a rodeo. Cattle ranching and dairy farming are very important for the rural economy.

PANAMA

PANAMA IS IN CENTRAL AMERICA, part of the isthmus that joins North and South America. The 51-mile- (82-kilometer-) long Panama Canal crosses the narrowest point of the isthmus, linking the Pacific and Atlantic Oceans.

Panama has coastlines stretching 1,230 miles (1,980 kilometers) bordering the Caribbean Sea on the north and the Pacific Ocean on the south. To the west lies Costa Rica, and in the east lies Colombia in South America.

Panama has three mountain ranges. The country's highest peak is the inactive volcano Barú at 11,400 feet (3,475 meters) near the western border. Much of the land consists of small hills and lowland plains. The coasts have many bays, peninsulas, and white sandy beaches. Rain forests line the border with Costa Rica and in the east extend across the Darién region to the Colombia border. Panama has more than sixteen hundred islands: Off the Caribbean coast lies the San Blas Archipelago; off the Pacific coast, the Pearl Islands and Panama's largest island, Coiba.

A Link Between Oceans

The first humans in Panama (PAN-uh-mah) survived by hunting in the forest where deer, wild pigs, rodents, monkeys, and the tapir, were plentiful. They also fished and collected wild berries and nuts. Probably about two thousand years ago, people began cultivating corn, cassava, and a few other crops.

The main groups of Native Americans when the first Europeans arrived early in the sixteenth century were the Guaymí, the

Painted with red vegetable dye, a Chocó woman is dressed for a fiesta. A folded banana leaf is in her hair, and her necklaces are made from seeds and plastic beads.

388

FACTS AND FIGURES

Official name: *República de Panama*

Status: *Independent state*

Capital: *Panama City*

Major cities: *San Miguelito, Colón, David*

Area: *29,208 square miles (75,649 square kilometers)*

Population: *2,700,000*

Population Density: *92 per square mile (36 per square kilometer)*

Peoples: *70 percent mestizo; 14 percent Afro-Panamanians; 10 percent European or Asian descent; 6 percent Native American*

Official language: *Spanish*

Currency: *Balboa*

National days: *Labor Day (May 1); Discovery of America Day (October 12); Independence from Colombia Day (November 3); Flag Day (November 4); First Call of Independence Day (November 10); Independence from Spain Day (November 28)*

Country's name: *Panama means "an abundance of fish."*

las Casas, pleaded on behalf of the Indians to the Spanish crown; some new laws were introduced but with little effect. With the demise of the Native population, African slaves were imported to take their place.

Panama has always been geographically important because it could be used as a short route linking the Pacific and Atlantic Oceans. This route became known as the Royal Road because all the silver, gold, and other treasures of Spain's colonies were transferred along it by mule from the Pacific to the Atlantic coast for shipping to Europe. Pirates continuously attacked the route during the sixteenth and seventeenth centuries; they also besieged Panama City in 1671 before burning it down.

Spain had a monopoly on trade in the region that was resented by other European powers. Britain was allowed to sell slaves but, to undermine Spain's position, also began a contraband trade in many other goods. In 1731 the British stormed Portobelo, Panama's Caribbean port, and Panama's trading importance came to an end.

The people of Panama no longer wished to be ruled by Spain, but they had to wait until 1821 before they could break from it. Panama became part of Gran Colombia with Colombia, Ecuador, and Venezuela. When this federation broke up, Panama remained part of Colombia until 1903.

In 1845 Colombia granted the United States free access across the isthmus and permission to construct a railroad. The railroad took about five years to build and cost the lives of some six thousand workers. During the California gold rush

Kuna (or Cuna), and the Chocó, the same three groups that have survived to this day. The Native population at that time has been estimated at well over half a million.

Less than one hundred years later, all but a few had been wiped out. The man most responsible was Governor Pedro Arias Dávila, or Pedrarias the Cruel. He led the way in killing or enslaving thousands of Native Americans. Many also died from diseases caught from the Europeans. One man, Friar Bartolomé de

Timeline:	People cultivated corn in the area	Europeans cross the Panama isthmus	Independence from Spain
	ca. 1 C.E.	1513	1821

The Panama Canal is the shortest crossing between the Atlantic and Pacific Oceans. Ships of every kind, from oil tankers to cruise ships, pass through it every day.

thousands of prospectors traveled on this railroad, coming from the east coast of the United States by ship, crossing the isthmus, and picking up another ship that took them up the west coast to California.

It was only a matter of time before a canal would be built. The U.S. government decided to take up the project. The Panamanians went along with this, in return for U.S. support in gaining independence from Colombia. Panama became independent on November 3, 1903, and in a treaty signed a few days later, the United States gained the right to use, occupy, and control, in perpetuity, the land known as the Panama Canal Zone. Construction of the railroad and the canal brought immigrant workers to Panama,

mainly from Europe, the United States, and the Caribbean.

Control of the Panama Canal Zone has been a source of controversy between the United States and Panama since the first ship went through the canal in 1914. In the 1960s, anti-U.S. feelings erupted in riots and violent demonstrations. Eventually, in 1977, an agreement was reached by which Panama would take full control of the canal in 1999.

Politically, Panama has lived through turbulent times since World War II. The most popular leader was General Omar Torrijos Herrera. With much of his support from ordinary, rural Panamanians, he introduced agricultural and social reforms, made improvements in health and education, modernized the country's transportation network, and brought in foreign investment.

Panama railroad completed	Independence from Colombia; United States gains rights to Panama Canal Zone	Panama Canal completed	Omar Torrijos Herrera is head of government
1855	**1903**	**1914**	**1972–1978**

CLIMATE

Panama has consistently high temperatures, except in the highest mountains. Rainfall is heavy, with the Caribbean coast receiving more than the Pacific. The dry season lasts from January to April.

	Panama City	Colón
Average January temperature:	79°F (26°C)	80°F (27°C)
Average July temperature:	81°F (27°C)	80°F (27°C)
Average annual precipitation:	70 in (178 cm)	127 in (323 cm)

Panama's most notorious leader was General Manuel Noriega Moreno who in 1989 was removed to the United States to face drug trafficking charges. He was convicted in 1992 and imprisoned. In 1994 Ernesto Perez Balladares was elected president and introduced a program to address the problems of drug-related crime, unemployment, and poverty.

The People of Panama

By far the largest number of Panamanians are mestizos. However, because Panama stands at the crossroads between the Atlantic and Pacific Oceans and the two Americas, its population is extremely varied. There are some white Panamanians of old Spanish families or of North American families who arrived in the country to build the canal or to trade. These families tend to form the social elite and have wealth and political power, although education and modern business have opened the way for aspiring mestizos and newcomers to join the ranks of the elite. Other immigrants who arrived to help construct the canal included the Chinese. Today the Chinese are mainly traders or restaurateurs. There are also some Lebanese, Hindus, and Jews, who are involved in commerce and industry.

The first Panamanians of African origin were brought in as slaves, some of whom escaped and found refuge in the tropical rain forest. Small enclaves of their descendants have survived and today live in villages in the Darién region or on the Pearl Islands. Many other black people were drawn to Panama from the Caribbean islands at the time the railroad and the canal were built. Afro-Panamanians now live in many parts of the country but particularly in coastal areas.

Children from Bocas del Toro on Colón Island. In Bocas, English is spoken by many of the black population, whose ancestors came from other Caribbean islands.

General Manuel Noriega Moreno assumes power and becomes president	United States invades Panama; Noriega faces drug trafficking charges	Ernesto Perez Balladares elected president
1988	**1989**	**1994**

The arrival of the Spaniards in the sixteenth century pushed the Native Americans into remote parts of the country. To the east of the line now occupied by the canal, the tropical rain forest and swamps were the home of the Kuna (koo-NAH) and Chocó tribes. As contact with Europeans increased, the Kuna responded by seeking refuge in the San Blas Archipelago. Some Kuna still live along the Atlantic coast of Darién, but most are on the San Blas islands. The forested Chocó region in the south of Panama and across the border with neighboring Colombia is the home of the Wounaan (Waumeo or Noanama) and the Embera (see COLOMBIA). The north and west are inhabited by the Guaymí.

Panamanian Life

About half the population lives in cities, with Panama City and its suburb San Miguelito accounting for almost a million people. Most of the rural population inhabits the provinces on the Pacific side of

Many public buses in Panama City are brightly painted, sometimes with scenes of the countryside. The destination is painted in large letters on the windshield.

the country west of the canal. Spanish is the official language, but English is still spoken by some Afro-Panamanians on the Caribbean coast. Some Native Americans know only their own language.

Panamanian children are expected to attend school from the ages of seven to fifteen. After primary school, they have a choice of secondary schools, where they learn academic subjects, or vocational schools, which teach technical skills. A successful student can continue with higher education at a university.

Most Panamanians are Roman Catholics, but there are small groups of Protestants, Muslims, Hindus, and Baha'is. Most Native Americans have their own religious beliefs.

The people of the towns are mainly mestizos; they generally run businesses or work in shops and manufacturing industries. In Panama City, at the Pacific end of the canal, there is a wide range of jobs, many connected with the shipping trade. Bus drivers there have some of the most colorful vehicles in all of the Americas, painted with vibrant scenes and messages. Daily life and culture has been strongly influenced by North American fast food, music, television, and movies. Many people look forward to the weekends and longer national vacations to escape to the coast for swimming and sailing. Favorite places are Taboga Island off the coast near Panama City and the beaches along the coast in the west.

Colón, at the Atlantic end of the canal, is Panama's second-largest city, with a population of 140,000. Like Panama City, it is a busy center for the shipping trade and has a large area set aside as a duty-free zone. Thousands of people are employed in the business of importing, repackaging, and exporting a wide range of goods. The very poor in Colón live in high wooden tenements separated by narrow alleyways in one of the most overcrowded areas of any Latin American city.

The countryside produces bananas for export, and the coast is renowned for its shrimp. Both industries employ many people, from managers to those involved with transporting the goods.

Villagers prepare for an orange festival in the province of Chiriqui, piling oranges and other fruits on a stall in a local park. Chiriqui is an important agricultural area.

The Kuna of San Blas: An Independent People

The Kuna still live along the Atlantic coast of the Darién region, but most are on the San Blas islands. These places were at one time totally uninhabited and a haven for pirates. They still have little to offer except palms, coral reefs, white sandy beaches, and isolation.

Panamanian Dishes: From Seafood to Sancocho

With two very long coastlines it is not surprising that Panamanians choose to eat fish and other marine delicacies. Sea bass, or corvina *(kore-BEE-nah), is popular and can be prepared in many ways. Fish and shrimp are often prepared using fresh lime juice. The uncooked fish is left in the juice with sliced hot chilies and a touch of garlic until the flesh turns from translucent to white. Then it is ready to eat.*

Other foods include beef with potatoes, rice, peppers, and various spices. In country areas green bananas, or plantains, are often substituted for potatoes; for meat the people may catch iguanas or take turtle eggs from the beaches.

Sancocho (sahn-KOE-choe) is the traditional soup. It usually contains chicken, corn, yucca, plantains or potatoes, and spices, including coriander. Sometimes a raw egg is stirred in before serving.

In the early twentieth century, officials of the young Panamanian Republic tried to make the Kuna change their lifestyle. The women were forbidden to wear their traditional outfits, and images of their ancient spirits were destroyed.

By 1925, this oppression prompted the Kuna to rebellion. The government tried to intervene but failed, and in 1938 an autonomous Kuna region was established, known as the Comarca de Kuna Yala. It covers a strip of coastal land from the northeast of Panama City to the Colombian

A Kuna woman wears golden necklaces and a mola, *a cotton blouse decorated with layered designs. This traditional form of needlework is now sold worldwide.*

colored beads called *wini* (WEE-nee) around their arms and legs complete the women's outfits. Kuna men are less traditional; most wear cotton shirts with trousers or jeans.

The coast dwellers number about seven hundred in Panama, though up to another eight hundred live in neighboring Colombia. The Kuna of the islands number approximately fifty thousand, and a few Kuna live in Panama City.

Kuna Needlework

Kuna women have been making molas *(moe-LAHSS) for a long time. This blouse is made from several layers of colored cotton. The design, which may be an animal shape or perhaps a religious motif, is created by cutting narrow lines in each layer so the colors from below can be seen at the top. Once the pattern is formed, the layers are stitched together with great care. A good mola maker is considered a valuable wife, so the young women take enormous pride in fine needlework. Molas are offered to visitors on the islands, sold in Panama, and are now found in craft markets worldwide.*

border and encompasses more than 360 tiny islands. The Kuna make their own laws and also decide whom they will allow to visit their land. All fresh water and most fresh foods have to be transported from the mainland. The Kuna are excellent sailors and use large wooden canoes with a jib and small triangular sail.

Kuna houses are simple rectangular structures, built from split sugarcane and thatched with palm leaves. Kuna women's traditional dress is a long wraparound skirt and a very colorful cotton blouse, decorated with appliqué designs. Gold nose ornaments, silver rings on their fingers, colored head scarves, long necklaces of colored beads, and bands of

The Wounaan and Embera of the Chocó

Chocó (choe-KOE) is a forested region in the south of Panama and across the border in neighboring Colombia. It is also the general name given to the Native Americans who live there. They are divided into two main groups—the Wounaan (woe-NAIN), or Noanama, who live along the banks of rivers, and the Embera (em-BARE-ah), who live on higher land between the rivers (see COLOMBIA). In total they number about ten thousand, living in small groups of one or two families deep in the rain forests of one of the world's wettest places.

Although the Chocó way of life is changing, the traditional Chocó house is still built on piles of wood and is round without walls. The belief in ancient spirits remains strong, and the men carve small, wooden statues representing mythological figures. Clothing is simple, and women often wear wraparound skirts similar to the Kuna. They live by growing corn, yucca, and plantains and hunting birds, rodents, and larger mammals.

Native Americans in Northern and Western Panama

The traditional lands of the Guaymí (GWHY-mee) were the savannahs west of the line of the canal, toward the border with Costa Rica. Since the arrival of Europeans, the Guaymí have moved into higher land and the northern part of the country. About seventy thousand Guaymí live in small family communities. They grow crops such as corn by clearing the forest, and they supplement their diet by hunting or fishing. About twenty-five hundred Buglere (boog-LARE-ee) (or Bugle), also speaking a Guaymí language, live in the mountains in the west. A separate group, the Teribe (tare-EE-bay) (or Térrabas), numbering three thousand, live in the tropical forest of the northwestern area, near the Teribe River.

Music and Dance

Lively Panamanian music is played on a variety of instruments, including small five-stringed guitars, drums, and maracas, which are made from dried gourds filled with tiny stones. The national dance, the *tamborito* (tam-bore-EET-oh), uses African rhythms and is performed to the accompaniment of hand-clapping and beating drums. Another dance, the *cumbia* (KOOM-bee-ah), has roots in slave dances. Men and women form a circle, and the couples gyrate to rhythms from drums and maracas. The African element is also very strong in the festival of carnival, which spans four days at the beginning of Lent. The modern festival includes colorfully costumed street parades, dances, and many community parties.

Dancing at a fiesta, Panamanian children wear traditional outfits. The boy has a straw hat and white pleated cotton shirt, while the girl wears a full skirt and embroidered blouse.

PARAGUAY

PARAGUAY IS A LANDLOCKED COUNTRY IN THE MIDDLE OF SOUTH AMERICA.

Paraguay shares borders with Bolivia in the north, Brazil in the east, and Argentina in the south and west. The Pilcomayo, Paraguay, and Paraná Rivers run along much of the length of Paraguay's borders. Although Paraguay has no coastline, it does have access to the Atlantic Ocean through the Paraná River and the Río de la Plata (River Plate), which empties into the Atlantic near Buenos Aires in Argentina.

CLIMATE

Temperatures do not differ greatly throughout the year, though winter months from April to September are cooler and sometimes there is frost. Rainfall is heaviest in the north and east and sometimes results in the flooding of the main rivers. The Chaco region receives less rain and occasionally suffers from droughts. Some of the hottest temperatures in South America have been recorded in the northern Chaco.

Average January temperature: *81°F (27°C)*

Average July temperature: *64°F (18°C)*

Average annual precipitation: *53 in (135 cm)*

Land of the Guaraní

At the time of the Spanish conquest in the sixteenth century, the predominant and most widespread Native Americans in the region of Paraguay (PAR-uh-gwhy) were the Guaraní (gwahr-uh-NEE), whose ancestors practiced ritual cannibalism. Other peoples included the Aché in the east and several groups in the Chaco. Not a great deal is known of the original peoples,

The Paraguay River runs across the center of Paraguay, dividing it into two very different regions. West of the river is the Chaco, with low marshy plains near the river and thorny scrub elsewhere. It is part of the Gran Chaco, which extends into Argentina and Bolivia. Most of the people live east of the river on a fertile plain with wooded hills. There are hilly ranges in the northeast and southwest.

though undoubtedly they were hunters who survived on game, wild plants, and nuts from the forest and fish from the many rivers.

By the early sixteenth century when the Spaniards first appeared, the Guaraní were seminomadic. They cultivated corn, cassava, beans, and fruit in fields that they had cleared in the forest by slash-and-burn methods. After a few years, once the soil was exhausted, they moved on to another part of the forest.

The Guaraní built large rectangular houses of wood and thatch, where many families lived in separate quarters under the same roof. Four to eight houses made up a village, which, if necessary, was protected against potential enemies by a series of moats and a stockade. Inside their houses the families used cotton or palm-fiber hammocks, woven baskets, and a variety of pots and bowls. Large jars were kept for storing a mildly alcoholic drink made from corn, but they also served as funerary urns, vessels in which the dead were buried. Guaraní dress, when worn, was a loincloth or a simple cotton tunic. Some chiefs wore feather cloaks. Men wore

A Native American horseman from the central Chaco. Horses are the best form of transportation in this region where there are few roads and some land is seasonally flooded.

FACTS AND FIGURES

Official name: *República del Paraguay*

Status: *Independent state*

Capital: *Asunción*

Other cities: *Ciudad del Este, Encarnación, San Lorenzo, Concepción*

Area: *157,043 square miles (406,741 square kilometers)*

Population: *5,100,000*

Population density: *32 per square mile (13 per square kilometer)*

Peoples: *95 percent mestizo; 5 percent European, African, and Asian descent and Native American*

Official languages: *Spanish, Paraguayan Guaraní*

Currency: *Guaraní*

National days: *San Blás, Patron Saint of Paraguay (February 3); Heroes' Day (March 1); Labor Day (May 1); National Days (May 14–15); Peace of Chaco Day (June 12); Constitution Day (August 25); Columbus Day (October 12)*

Country's name: *The word Paraguay derives from the Guaraní language, but its meaning is unclear. It is thought to relate to water or a river, and one interpretation is "the place with the great river."*

huge necklaces made of shells, and the women hung shell pendants from their ears. They all decorated their faces and bodies with vegetable dyes from the forest.

Each community had a chief, but the most important person was the shaman, or priest, who was thought to have supernatural powers. Two of the most

Timeline:	Guaraní are widespread in Paraguay	Alejo García is the first European to travel through Paraguay	Asunción is founded	First Jesuit mission founded	Spanish expel Jesuits from Paraguay
	1400s	1525	1537	1609	1767

sacred Guaraní instruments were rattles used by the shamans and stamping tubes reserved for the women. These tubes were made from a section of bamboo, closed at one end, and decorated with feathers. The women pounded them against the ground to make a dull beat.

The Spaniards Invade, the Jesuits Follow

When the Spaniards first encountered the Guaraní, they were impressed by their gold and silver. However, they realized later that these treasures came from the Inca Empire in the Andes. The Guaraní had been invading edges of Inca territory for some time and were willing guides to the Spaniards in their search for riches. In 1525, Alejo García became the first European to cross Paraguay. Other Spanish expeditions followed, and in 1537 Asunción was founded as a base for operations. The explorers had little success, but Asunción remained the largest town in southern South America until 1580, when the Spaniards developed Buenos Aires.

After that the Paraguay region was virtually ignored by the Spanish authorities. Although the land was not rich in minerals, the eastern plain was good for farming. The Guaraní were made to work as slave laborers, and thousands died from smallpox, influenza, and others diseases brought by the Europeans. They were also hunted down by slave traders from Brazil.

The first Jesuit mission was established in 1609. The missions were the only place the Indians could turn to for help and protection. Naturally, they received Catholic religious instruction, but the Jesuits also taught them other things. Some Natives learned to read, write, and study academic subjects, while others learned to paint, draw, carve, and weave.

This fine carving of gold leaf is in a church in the town of Yaguarón. The Guaraní were taught to make these carvings by the Jesuits in the eighteenth century.

By the end of the sixteenth century, there were more than thirty missions housing about 100,000 Guaraní. The missions were self-sufficient and also produced crops and other items to sell. The Guaraní shared in the cultivation of cassava, corn, tobacco, cotton, sugarcane, and fruit; they also tended herds of cattle. The missions had plantations of maté, the tree that produces the leaves for a tealike drink that originated with the Guaraní but is now universally popular with Paraguayans.

Paraguay becomes independent	Dr. José Gaspar Rodríguez de Francia is head of government	Slavery abolished	Carlos Antonio López is first president	Francisco Solano López is president
1811	1814–1840	1842	1844–1862	1862–1870

The success of the missions caused great resentment among landowners, who conspired to get rid of the Jesuits, and in 1767 the Spanish Crown expelled them. It was a disastrous decision for the Guaraní, who had nowhere to go other than into slave labor or back into the forest.

Independence and Dictators

Paraguay became independent from Spain in 1811. Since then the country has been governed mostly by dictators and has been involved in two disastrous wars. The first president and dictator was Dr. José Gaspar Rodríguez de Francia, a highly educated but austere man who gave the country a period of peace by effectively sealing the borders so that no one could leave or enter. Slavery was abolished in 1842. Francia was followed by the López dictators, father and son. Carlos Antonio López tried to modernize the country by inviting foreign scientists, engineers, and medical experts to help build roads, railroads, schools, and hospitals. When he died in 1862, Paraguay seemed set for a bright future, but his son Francisco Solano López will be remembered as the man who led Paraguay into the War of the Triple Alliance (1865–1870), when Paraguay fought against its giant neighbors Brazil and Argentina and a reluctant Uruguay. It has been calculated that more than half the population of Paraguay died in that war.

In the 1930s Paraguay fought Bolivia in the Chaco War, from which it emerged victorious but at terrific cost to the economy and people. More dictators followed until General Alfredo Stroessner seized power in 1954. His regime was very repressive; opponents were silenced, tortured, exiled, or executed. There was no freedom of the press, and his secret service had spies in every quarter. He had many achievements, however, including turning Asunción into a modern capital, providing more schools and hospitals, improving the transportation system, and, with Brazil, building one of the world's largest hydroelectric dams at Itaipu on the Paraná River.

By the time Stroessner was deposed in 1989, Paraguay was deeply involved in contraband and drug trafficking. A few people were extremely wealthy, but the majority remained poor and with little hope. Democratic elections have taken place since, but the poor economic situation led to a general strike in 1994, the first in thirty-five years. The government of Juan Carlos Wasmosy, elected in 1993, also faced problems of corruption and widespread dissatisfaction in the army. In 1998 Paraguayans elected Raul Alberto Cubas Grau as president.

Paraguay Today

Most people are settled east of the Paraguay River, with about one-tenth of the total population in the capital, Asunción. Less than 5 percent of the population live in the Chaco, which covers nearly 61 percent of the country. About 95 percent of the people are mestizos of Spanish and Guaraní parentage. Most are bilingual and speak Spanish and Paraguayan Guaraní, which is

War of the Triple Alliance	Chaco War	General Alfredo Stroessner is president	Juan Carlos Wasmosy is president	Raul Alberto Cubas Grau elected president
1865–1870	1932–1935	1954–1989	1993–1998	1998

recognized officially as a second national language and taught in many schools. Outside Asunción most people speak Guaraní by choice.

The remaining 5 percent of the population are whites, Native Americans, a few blacks who live on the border with Brazil, and a small number of Asian immigrants. The whites include descendants of a few European immigrants who settled there at the beginning of the twentieth century, notably Germans, who have created their own farming colonies and continue to speak their native German. Some German refugee families arrived just before and after World War II. Other German speakers are members of Mennonite communities, a religious group. There are over fifty thousand Native Americans speaking five different languages, but the predominant language is pure Guaraní. This is distinct from Paraguayan Guaraní, which has been influenced by Spanish.

Most Paraguayan schools are run by the state or by the Catholic Church, though some are private. The best schools and colleges are in the cities. All children are supposed to start school at the age of seven and continue for at least six years. Often this does not happen, particularly in rural areas, sometimes because the school is too far from the family home or the children are needed to work on the farms. Despite these difficulties, the literacy rate is high at over 90 percent.

Daily Life in Town and Country

Life in Asunción and other cities like Ciudad del Este and Encarnación involves many of the routines of any Westernized

Old streetcars are still widely used in Asunción as public transportation. In springtime many streets in Asunción are lined with the colorful blossoms of jacaranda trees.

country. Government offices, banks, shops, and restaurants employ the largest number of urbanites. On the outskirts of towns stand small manufacturing industries.

In the capital, mansions of the wealthy contrast with the riverside shacks of poorer people, which are often flooded when the water rises. Other parts of the city still have an air of nineteenth-century grandeur left from times when Asunción was an important port for trade with the interior of South America. Flowering trees everywhere add a gentle, unhurried, tropical air.

The smaller towns and villages of the countryside are well kept and often colorful with flowers. Houses are built of wood, concrete, timber, or adobe bricks, many with Spanish-style red-tile roofs. In some parts horse-drawn carts are still used by farm and delivery people. Ox-drawn carts, once seen everywhere in many country areas, are being replaced by trucks and tractors.

For social functions at all levels of society, Paraguayans expect to be smartly dressed. Even if the event is informal, the men will have finely pressed shirts, some perhaps of the local hand-embroidered cotton known as *aho-poi* (ao-POI). Older people gather at restaurants and bars where there may be Paraguayan music; the younger ones find discos or their own social clubs.

About 45 percent of the population is involved in agriculture; crops include cotton, sugarcane, soybeans, corn, wheat, tobacco, and fruit. In some places forests are felled for timber and to expand the farmland. Men also find work on cattle ranches. At festival times people gather for a traditional beef barbecue with dancing, music, and informal bullfighting, the hallmarks of rural Paraguay.

A farmer and his son inspect their yerba maté trees, whose leaves are used to make maté. Many large orchards of yerba maté trees flourish in southern Paraguay.

The Mennonites of the Chaco

The Mennonite religious group dates from the sixteenth century and today has strong close-knit communities in many countries. In Paraguay the largest settlements are in the middle Chaco. The first group came to Paraguay from Canada and Russia in the 1920s, when they were offered land, tax incentives, and immigration advantages. The most recent settlement was founded in 1947 at Neuland, also in the Chaco.

Mennonite towns and colonies are noted for their organization. Long, straight roads bisect the landscape, and well-kept fields stretch to the horizon. Mennonites produce cereals and soybeans, and their many milk products are sold throughout the country. Outside the towns families have neat, often wooden homes at the edges of the fields. They visit the towns for religious meetings, education, and farm business.

Food and Drink

Most Paraguayans eat a lot of meat and fish. Fruit is plentiful although seasonal. Traditional dishes include sopa Paraguaya *(SOE-pah pahr-ah-GWHY-uh), which is a kind of dumpling made of ground corn and cheese, and* chipas *(CHEE-pahs), a corn bread flavored with lots of cheese and a small amount of anise, a licorice-flavored herb.*

Often when men gather to talk, they pass around a small gourd filled with Paraguayan tea, or maté, which is known as terere *(tare-air-AY) when cold water is used. It is sucked through a metal straw called a* bombilla *(bome-BEE-yah).*

Paraguay's Native Americans

Among Paraguay's fifty thousand Native Americans, the largest groups are the eighteen thousand Chulupí, also known as the Nivaclé, and the ten thousand Lengua in the Chaco, and the ten thousand Pai Tavytera and some seven thousand Mbya Guaraní, also known as Kadiweu, living in eastern Paraguay. About two-thirds of Native Americans live in the Chaco.

The way of life for the Native Americans of the Chaco has been changing since the seventeenth century, when Jesuit priests entered the area and began to draw the Native Americans into missions. The Native Americans today have lost the best of their past and gained the worst of modern life. Many now live in extreme poverty, their huts surrounded by trash they have gathered from nearby towns, while they either beg for food or work on farms for low wages or just for gifts.

The land of some groups, like the Chulupí (choo-loo-PEE) and Lengua, was given to the Mennonites. Until the 1940s the Native Americans made annual migrations to the sugarcane harvest in neighboring Argentina, but as the Mennonite farms grew, they went to those farms for work. Many are now settled around the Mennonite colonies, and besides working there, they grow subsistence crops on their own plots. Today many Chulupí settlements are poor and cluttered with the castoffs of their wealthier white neighbors. The Chulupí now have radio programs and education in Spanish and in their own language.

The three thousand or so Ayoreo (ah-joe-RAY-oe) people of the northern Chaco and Bolivian border are some of the Native Americans least affected by contact with the modern world, but even they exist in harsh conditions. Their homeland is very dry and among the hottest places in South America. They are constantly on the move in a maze

Most Native Americans are slowly adopting the ways of other Paraguayans. For the lucky ones like this Aché girl, there are schools in rural areas to teach basic subjects.

Maca women from the community near Asunción are often seen in the city with their specially made handicrafts, such as these decorated bows and headdresses, for tourists.

of dried-up watercourses and dry, cactus-studded forest. Priests in the region maintain the Ayoreo's contact with the missions, and in times of extreme drought the Ayoreo seek food at the missions or the small towns of the region. Traditionally, they live by gathering natural foods; they particularly like to eat land tortoises.

Outside the Chaco the worst-affected Native Americans have been the Aché (AH-chay); only about nine hundred survive. They are nomadic hunter-gatherers of the forests of eastern Paraguay. Much of their original territory has been taken for farming.

Native Americans along the Pilcomayo River are constantly threatened by ranching, new roads, and other incursions. One group, the Maca (mah-KAH), once occupied a large area immediately west of the Paraguay River, where eventually European settlement began to affect its land. In the 1930s the Maca were employed as trackers by an army general making a survey of the Chaco, and he won their friendship. In return he obtained for them a reserve of land not far from Asunción. The Maca soon adopted the poorest ways of

modern society. They gave up many of their customs, such as fiestas with corn beer, and turned to drinking pure cane alcohol. About one thousand Maca have survived in their reserve. They often travel to the capital, where they sell handicrafts and herbal remedies.

Wood Carving and Lace Making

Paraguayans produce fine handicrafts of carved bowls, plates, furniture, and other items. The woods of the dry Chaco are hard with a fine grain. Some are very dense, and some have subtle colors. One, the quebracho, meaning "ax breaker," is extremely hard.

Among the most popular handicrafts is the ñandutí (nyah-doo-TEE) lace made by the women of the town of Itauguá, not far from Asunción. The art was brought from Spain, but the designs are mostly Paraguayan. Almost all the women of Itauguá are employed making lace. Some work on small delicate goods such as mantillas, or women's head coverings, and others make colorful tablecloths and napkins.

Glossary

adobe: sun-dried mud or clay.

agave: a plant that produces fibers used for making ropes.

agricultural reform: the redistribution of land to the poor.

besiege: to surround with armed forces, cutting off communications and supplies.

cassava: a plant with fleshy tuber roots, used as a food.

commemoration: an act of remembrance, something by which to remember people.

communism a theory that suggests that all property belongs to the community and that work should be organized for the common good.

condone: to overlook or forgive an offense.

consecrate: to declare something sacred or holy.

contraband: goods that are sold or traded illegally.

dowry: money or something of value given by a bride's family to her new husband.

enclave: a small piece of territory surrounded by land belonging to others.

evangelical: refers to Protestant churches emphasizing personal salvation in their teachings.

expatriate: someone who lives in a country that is not his or her own.

fiesta: a Spanish word for a religious festival; a festivity or holiday.

fresco: a watercolor painting on fresh, moist plaster.

hieroglyphics: ancient form of writing using objects or figures to represent meanings and/or sounds.

incentive: something that gives a cause or motive that encourages a person to act.

isthmus: a narrow strip of land that connects two larger territories.

legume: any of a large family of plants and vegetables with seeds in pods, for example, beans and peas.

Lent: the forty days between Ash Wednesday and Easter in the Christian calendar.

monopoly: to be the only person or company allowed to trade in a particular product or with a particular country.

motif: a distinctive feature or pattern that is part of a design.

perpetuity: eternity; permanence.

restaurateur: a person who runs a restaurant.

scrubland: an area of land with low stunted trees and thickets.

services sector: that part of commerce or trade that makes money by providing services to the public (rather than by making or growing things). Examples of service industries are insurance, catering, and tourism.

slash-and-burn cultivation: the practice of felling trees and clearing the ground by burning, then using it for crops for a few years before moving on.

socialism: a political theory in which the community as a whole controls land, property, industry, and money, and organizes them for the good of all the people.

socialist: someone who believes in the theory of socialism.

social reform: to change and improve institutions, for example, education and health facilities, for the benefit of the people.

social welfare: services that aim to help people with problems such as poverty, unemployment, poor public health, and illiteracy.

sombrero: a broad-brimmed hat, usually made of felt or straw.

sovereign rights: the rights of a governor or ruler.

sporadically: from time to time.

tariffs: taxes usually imposed on imports and exports.

trade embargo: to prevent trading by not allowing goods to be carried in or out of a country.

viceroy: a person who governs a country or territory in the name of and with the authority of the supreme monarch or ruler.

Further Reading

Mexico

Alcraft, Rob, and Sean Sprague. *Mexico.* Crystal Lake, IL: Rigby Interactive Library, 1996.

Arnold, Helen. *Mexico.* Chatham, NJ: Raintree/Steck-Vaughn, 1995.

Dahl, Michael, S. *Mexico.* Mankato, MN: Bridgestone Books, 1997.

Dubois, Jill, and Eric Siow. *Cultures of the World: Mexico.* Tarrytown, NY: Marshall Cavendish, 1993.

Hopkinson, Amanda. *Mexico.* Chatham, NJ: Raintree/Steck-Vaughn, 1992.

Howard, John. *Mexico.* Morristown, NJ: Silver Burdett Press, 1992.

Irizarry, Carmen. *Passport to Mexico.* New York: Franklin Watts, 1994.

Kalman, Bobby. *Mexico—the People.* New York: Crabtree Publishing, 1993.

Parker, Edward A. *Mexico.* Chatham, NJ: Raintree/Steck-Vaughn, 1998.

Rummel, Jack. *Mexico.* Broomall, PA: Chelsea House, 1990.

Staub, Frank. *Children of the Sierra Madre.* Minneapolis, MN: Lerner Group, 1996.

Stein, R. Conrad. *Mexico—a Golden Past, A Hopeful Future.* Minneapolis, MN: Dillon Press, 1996.

Montserrat

Dyde, Brian. *Islands to the Windward: Five Gems of the Caribbean.* Edison, NJ: Hunter Publishing, 1990.

Nicaragua

Haverstock, Nathan A. *Nicaragua in Pictures.* Minneapolis, MN: Lerner Group, 1993.

Kott, Jennifer. *Cultures of the World: Nicaragua.* Tarrytown, NY: Marshall Cavendish, 1994.

Malone, Michael. *A Nicaraguan Family.* Minneapolis, MN: Lerner Group, 1998.

Panama

Hassig, Susan M. *Cultures of the World: Panama.* Tarrytown, NY: Marshall Cavendish, 1996.

Presilla, Maricel E. *Mola: Cuna Life, Stories, and Art.* New York: Henry Holt and Co., 1996.

Stewart, Gail B. *Panama.* New York: Crestwood House, 1990.

Vasquez, Ana M. *Panama.* Danbury, CT: Childrens Press, 1991.

Paraguay

Haverstock, Nathan A. *Paraguay in Pictures.* Minneapolis, MN: Lerner Group, 1987.

Morrison, Marion. *Paraguay.* Danbury, CT: Childrens Press, 1993.

Islands of the Caribbean

Mason, Antony. *The Caribbean.* Parsippany, NJ: Silver Burdett Press, 1988.

Mayer, T. W. *The Caribbean and Its People.* New York: Thomson Learning, 1995.

Ramdin, Ron. *West Indies.* Chatham, NJ: Raintree/Steck-Vaughn, 1991.

Springer, Eintou P. *The Caribbean.* Parsippany, NJ: Silver Burdett Press, 1987.

Walker, Cas. *The Caribbean.* North Pomfret, VT: Trafalgar Square Publishing, 1991.

Index

Page numbers in *italic* indicate illustrations.

Page numbers in *italic* indicate illustrations.

REFERENCE

PEOPLES
of the
AMERICAS

PEOPLES
of the
AMERICAS

Volume 6
Greenland–Jamaica

MARSHALL CAVENDISH
NEW YORK • LONDON • TORONTO • SYDNEY

Marshall Cavendish Corporation
99 White Plains Road
Tarrytown, New York 10591-9001

Consulting Editor: J. Patrick Gray, Professor of Anthropology, University of Wisconsin

Consultants: Jean-Marc Blais, Senior Interpretive Planner, Canadian Museum of Civilization, Hull, Quebec
David Frye, Assistant Director, Department of Latin American and Caribbean Studies, University of Michigan

Spanish Consultant: Fran Kaplan

Contributing authors: D. L. Birchfield
Marion Morrison
Juliette Radcliffe Rogers
Philip Steele
Mary A. Stout

Discovery Books
Managing Editor: Paul Humphrey
Project Editor: Helen Dwyer
Text Editor: Valerie J. Weber
Design Concept: Ian Winton
Designers: Barry Dwyer, Ian Winton, and Simon Borrough
Cartographer: Stefan Chabluk

Marshall Cavendish
Editorial Director: Paul Bernabeo
Editor: Marian Armstrong
Associate Editor: Debra M. Jacobs

The publishers would like to thank the following for their permission to reproduce photographs:
James Davis Travel Photography (290, 297, 299, 313, 339); Eye Ubiquitous (David Cumming 340, 341 top & bottom; L. Fordyce 308, cover); Getty Images (293, 324; Keystone 316; Ragnar Sigurdsson 295); Robert Harding Picture Library (Explorer 329 top; Adam Woolfitt 327); Hutchison Library (Sarah Errington 325, 328; J. G. Fuller 303); John Noble Wilderness Photography (291, 294); Panos Pictures (Neil Cooper 330, 334, 342, 343; Jean-Léo Dugast 323; Marc French 329 bottom, 337, 338; Duncan Simpson 317, 319, 321; Paul Smith 305, 307; Sean Sprague 326); South American Pictures (Jevan Berrange 315, 320; Robert Francis 301, 306, 312 bottom, 333; Tony Morrison 304, 310, 311, 312 top, 318, frontispiece; Chris Sharp 309, 331, 335)

(frontispiece) Maya mother and daughter at Chichicastenango market, Guatemala.

Editor's note: Many systems of dating have been used by different cultures throughout history. *Peoples of the Americas* uses B.C.E. (Before Common Era) and C.E. (Common Era) instead of B.C. (Before Christ) and A.D. (Anno Domini, "In the Year of the Lord") out of respect for the diversity of the world's peoples.

Library of Congress Cataloging-in-Publication Data
Peoples of the Americas.
        p.   cm.
        Includes bibliographical references and index.
        Contents: v. 1. Anguilla–Belize — v. 2. Bermuda–Brazil — v. 3. Canada–Cayman Islands — v. 4. Chile–Costa Rica — v. 5. Cuba–French Guiana — v. 6. Greenland–Jamaica — v. 7. Martinique–Paraguay — v. 8. Peru–Turks and Caicos Islands — v. 9. United States of America — v. 10. United States of America–Virgin Islands

    ISBN 0-7614-7050-6 (set)
        1. Ethnology—America—Juvenile literature. 2. America—History—Juvenile literature. [1. Ethnology—America. 2. America—History.]
E29.A1P46 1999
970'.004—dc21   98-2801
                                                                                                            CIP
                                                                                                            AC

    ISBN 0-7614-7050-6 (set)
    ISBN 0-7614-7056-5 (vol. 6)

Printed and bound in Italy

Contents

GREENLAND

GREENLAND IS ONE OF THE WORLD'S LARGEST ISLANDS. A remote region of the Arctic, it stretches far north of the Arctic Circle.

Greenland is separated from Canada by the Davis and Nares Straits and from Iceland by the Denmark Strait.

Although Greenland covers a vast area, 83 percent of its land surface is blanketed by the Arctic ice cap, which is 10,000 feet (over 3,000 meters) thick in places. The coastal regions form a bleak landscape of lakes, boulders, and tundra. A few stunted willows and birches grow on the inhospitable, cool grasslands. A ring of mountains around the coast rises to 12,139 feet (3,700 meters) at Gunnbjørn Fjeld. Massive glaciers edge their way coastward, breaking up into icebergs when they reach the sea. The coastline is rugged, with deep sea inlets called fjords.

Brightly painted houses look out on the icy waters of Greenland's west coast. This town is known to the Inuit as Ilulissat and to the Danish as Jakobshavn.

CLIMATE

Greenland has bitter winters and brief summers. It is mildest in the southwest, which is warmed by sea currents. Away from the coast, temperatures can plummet to −85°F (−65°C). Precipitation takes the form of snow or ice crystals.

	north	south
Average January temperature:	−9°F (−23°C)	5°F (−15°C)
Average July temperature:	41°F (5°C)	46°F (8°C)
Average annual precipitation:	2.6 in (6.6 cm)	46 in (117 cm)

FACTS AND FIGURES

Official names: *Kalaallit Nunaat/Grønland*

Status: *Self-governing Territory of Denmark*

Capital: *Nuuk/Godthåb*

Area: *840,000 square miles (2,175,600 square kilometers)*

Population: *57,000*

Population density: *0.07 per square mile (0.03 per square kilometer)*

Peoples: *83 percent Inuit and mixed Inuit-Danish descent; 17 percent Danish and Danish descent*

Official languages: *West Greenlandic (Kalaallisut) and Danish*

Currency: *Danish krone*

National day: *National Day (June 21)*

Country's name: *By naming the country something alluring, the Vikings who discovered this Arctic wilderness hoped to persuade their countrymen back in Denmark to settle there.*

Settling the Coast

The savage climate of central Greenland makes it extremely difficult for humans to survive there. Settlement has always been along the coast, where there is a strip of ice-free land.

Human beings first set foot in Greenland over four thousand years ago. Nomadic hunters of the musk ox, they had gradually moved through the Canadian Arctic from their Asian homeland. They were part of the successive migrations of Arctic peoples who became known as Eskimo or Inuit.

They were followed over the ages by new Inuit bands that crossed the Nares Strait into the district known as Qaanaaq (or Thule). Some moved on from there, down the eastern and western coasts. They lived by hunting caribou, seabirds, seals, walrus, and the whales that migrated to the melting ice cap each spring. Nothing went to waste in Inuit life. They lived off the meat and skins of their prey; hides were used to cover their canoes and make clothes. The Inuit house, or *illu* (IG-loo), was made of stones and turf, or wood where available. The Inuit also constructed a temporary hunting lodge called an *illuigaq* (ig-LOO-yee-gahk) from blocks of frozen snow.

The Arctic winter is long, dark, and very harsh. The small communities were not

A Greenlander breaks through sea ice to fish for halibut. Arctic waters are rich in plankton and attract a wide range of fish, including cod, Arctic trout, capelin, haddock, and pollack.

Timeline:	First ancestors of Inuit arrive in far north of Greenland from Canadian Arctic	A Viking called Gunnbjørn reaches Greenland by accident	Erik the Red founds settlements around Julianehåb	Norse (Norwegian) and Inuit trade goods
	ca. 2500 B.C.E.	920s C.E.	985	1200

united into anything like a state, and there were no rulers. The most important person in each community was the shaman, who contacted the spirit world to help heal sick individuals.

About 1,080 years ago a seafarer called Gunnbjørn was blown off course by an Atlantic storm and reached this great Arctic wilderness by accident. He was a Viking, or Norseman (Northman), one of the fearless European raiders and explorers from Scandinavia. Gunnbjørn's reported sighting was not forgotten. In 982 another Viking called Erik the Red followed the same course from Iceland and explored the coasts. He and his crew named the island Greenland, hoping to attract settlers to the new land. Their countrymen were persuaded, and three years later Erik led them to his not-so-green promised land.

In the following years Norse colonists founded settlements around Julianehåb Bay in the south and Godthåbfjord in the southwest. They were trading with remote Inuit settlements by 1200, living by sealing and raising sheep and Icelandic ponies on the bleak, coastal grasslands. However, the colonies failed. Why? There may have been skirmishes between the Norse and the Inuit—or at least competition for the same food supplies. The climate probably changed for the worse as well. By the 1350s the western settlements were abandoned, and the last boat to carry goods back to Europe sailed in 1410. By 1500 the eastern Norse settlements were also deserted.

English explorers sailed along the coasts of western Greenland in the 1570s and 1580s, making contact with the Inuit. In the following century they were followed by whaling fleets from Scotland, England, and the Netherlands, whose crews all traded with the Inuit settlements.

In 1721 the Danish king sent a Norwegian priest named Hans Egede to Greenland to see if there were still any Norse settlements. There were not, and Egede founded a Protestant mission and trading post near today's capital, Godthåb. Many Inuit became Lutheran Christians, and about 98 percent remain so today. The Danish government took over trade in 1726 and fifty years later founded the Royal Greenland Trading Company.

The Danish may have believed themselves to be superior to the Inuit, but

Stories in String

In the long, dark winter above the Arctic Circle, when lamps fueled by whale blubber flickered in the illu, the Inuit worked out a number of games to while away the time. One was rather like the cat's cradle games played in lands to the south. The player held out both hands as a frame to hold a length of string. He or she then looped the string in all sorts of patterns so that the string looked like a building, a face, a bird, or an Arctic fox. Some of the shapes could be made to "run," "fly," or "bite." An imaginative user could make up stories concerning the shapes, describing an old legend or a hunting expedition.

Norse settlements lose touch with Scandinavia	English explorers make contact with West Greenland Inuit	Scottish, English, and Dutch whaling fleets trade with Inuit	Danish government controls Greenland trade	Union between Norway and Denmark dissolved; Greenland becomes solely Danish colony
1410	1570s–1580s	1600s	1726	1814

Inside one of the wealthier Inuit homes in Greenland in 1877. The stove and lumber are Danish imports, but the people still wear the skins of the animals they have hunted.

they did treat them with a respect that was rare in this age of empires. They encouraged education and use of the Inuit language and tried to protect the traditional way of life, although the missionaries did their best to undermine the power of the shamans. People traditionally depended on hunting for their livelihood, but trade was now becoming more important. In the early twentieth century codfishing became a pillar of the Greenland economy.

As more and more Inuit received an education and traveled overseas, they began to demand to govern themselves. In 1953 Denmark made Greenland a part of Denmark instead of a colony, giving Inuit and Danes equal rights as citizens. Home

rule was granted in 1979, a Greenland national flag was designed, and a democratic parliament called the *Landsting* (LAHND-sting) was established with a wide range of powers.

Inuit and Danes

Greenland is the least populated land in the world except for Antarctica, with only one person per 15 square miles (39 square kilometers). An island three times the size of Texas, it has the population size of a small town.

Codfishing established	Greenland no longer a colony but an overseas territory of the Danish kingdom	Home rule for Greenland	Denmark transfers all political power to Greenland; now controls only Greenland's defense and foreign affairs
1911	**1953**	**1979**	**1993**

A young girl from Greenland's east coast cuddles a husky pup. Huskies are tough dogs with thick coats, bred for hauling sleds across the Arctic ice.

Inuktitut, but the remoteness of Inuit communities from each other has led to many regional variations and dialects. In Greenland the official version of the language, Kalaallisut, is a westcoast dialect, very different from the northern and eastern variants. The language was first written down in the 1800s, and since 1973 it has used a revised, more logical, system of spelling. It has adapted to the challenges of the modern world and is thriving as a medium for broadcasting and education.

Not all Greenlanders are Inuit. There is a sizable population of native-born Greenlanders of Danish descent. Although they speak Danish, they see themselves as distinct from the Danes born in Denmark, who now make up the majority of the Danish population in Greenland.

Living in the Arctic

The ancient Inuit way of life has, of course, changed greatly in the last two hundred

Eight out of ten Greenlanders are Inuit or people of mixed Danish-Inuit descent. The Inuit form three main groups. The largest group is the Kalaallit (kah-LAH-licht), or Egedesminde, who live on the west coast. *Kalaallit* is sometimes used as a general term for all indigenous Greenlanders. The Iit, or Angamagssalik, live on the east coast, while the Inughuit, sometimes referred to as the Polar Eskimos, live in the region of Qaanaaq. Their homeland is the most northerly one of all the Arctic peoples.

The language of the Inuit peoples of Canada and Greenland is known as

Making a Dome of Snow

The traditional overnight lodge of the Inuit hunter was cut from blocks of deep-frozen snow, each about 3 feet x 2 feet, and 6 inches thick (90 x 60 x 15 centimeters). These were laid out in a circle around an excavated area. The foundations were topped by a spiral of inward-leaning, angled blocks before being capped by a final block. A door was cut on the side sheltered from the wind. The dome took about three hours to build and provided a cozy shelter. Today many hunters use tents instead, but snow houses are still sometimes built and have proved to be much safer than tents in a severe blizzard.

years. Neat, modern houses, with timber imported from Scandinavia, have replaced the traditional village homes of stone and turf. Inuit hunters can keep out the wind and snow with modern waterproof clothing. They may buy supplies at stores, keep their money in the bank, go to church, travel on snowmobiles, watch television, and finish their education at the University of Greenland. The standard of living is high, with good social welfare programs, health care, and education.

However, the traditional Inuit way of life does survive in Greenland as well as anywhere. Many coastal communities still live by hunting, even though high-powered rifles have replaced many traditional weapons. Families may wear beautifully made leggings of hide and fur. They still know how to use a dog team to pull a sled or how to make a snow house. They also know how to wait for hours at a hole in the ice until a seal comes up for air. International bans on seal hunting do not cover the Greenland Inuit, to whom hunting is such an important part of everyday life and culture.

The Danish who work in Greenland may be employed as government officials, builders, bankers, or other office workers, or in the fishing industry. Sheep are still grazed on suitable land as they were in Viking times.

Denmark has been a member of the European Union (EU), an organization that works toward and oversees the economic and political integration of European states, since 1973. Greenland, however, pulled out

An Inuit from Kulusuk, in eastern Greenland, shows off a child's jacket made from sealskin. Traditionally, clothes were also made from the fur of the Arctic fox, hare, and polar bear.

in 1985. It has kept some economic ties with the EU, and Denmark is still its chief trading partner. Factories processing fish and other seafood are widespread and are still the major employer of Greenlanders. However, the decline of fishing stocks in the North Atlantic has affected the industry and led to a rise in unemployment.

In the 1990s Greenland's government decided to develop new industries. Mining and oil companies were given the go-ahead to prospect for mineral reserves, and tourism was boosted, as more and more people from North America and Europe sought adventurous holidays in remote locations. The fear is that these industries will damage the environment, as has already happened in other parts of the Arctic Circle.

GRENADA

GRENADA IS THE SOUTHERNMOST OF THE WINDWARD ISLANDS. It is in the Lesser Antilles chain of the eastern Caribbean.

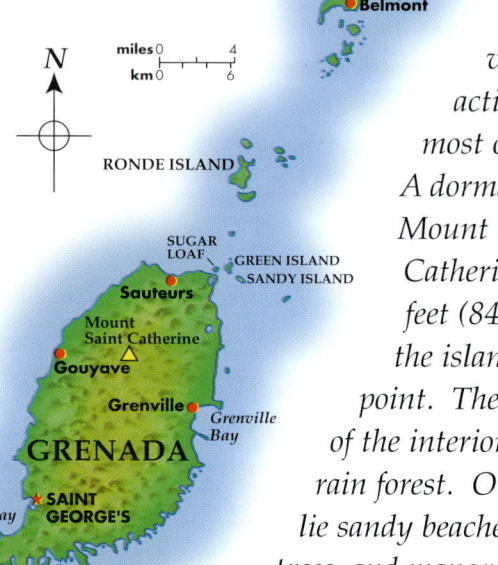

Ancient volcanic activity formed most of Grenada. A dormant volcano, Mount Saint Catherine, at 2,755 feet (840 meters), is the island's highest point. The mountains of the interior are clad in rain forest. On the coast lie sandy beaches, palm trees, and mangroves.

Grenada is 21 miles (34 kilometers) long and just 12 miles (19 kilometers) wide. Grenadan territory extends northward to include the most southerly of the Grenadines, a chain of tiny coral islands. These include uninhabited islands such as Sugar Loaf, Green Island, and Sandy Island, as well as two inhabited islands called Carriacou and Petite Martinique.

The Spice Island

About two thousand years ago Grenada (grihn-AY-dah) was the home of Native American peoples. About one thousand years ago, Arawak-speakers were ousted by more aggressive Caribs. The first Europeans to land were English colonists in 1609. They were repeatedly attacked by the Caribs. French settlers arrived in 1650, and soon they, too, were locked in a brutal war with Caribs. The French grew coffee, cacao, sugar, and tobacco, and imported African slaves to work on the plantations. The remaining Caribs were mostly absorbed into the population as a whole.

In 1783 the Treaty of Paris declared that Grenada was to be British. British authorities freed the slaves in 1833. Many former slaves became small farmers. Throughout the 1800s Grenada prospered exporting bananas, cacao, and spices.

CLIMATE

Grenada is warm and humid, with a rainy season that lasts from June to November. Over twice as much rain falls on the mountains as on Saint George's, the capital.

Average January temperature: *80°F (27°C)*

Average July temperature: *82°F (28°C)*

Average annual precipitation (coast):
60 in (152 cm)

Average annual precipitation (mountains):
160 in (406 cm)

FACTS AND FIGURES

Status: *Independent state*

Capital: *Saint George's*

Area: *133 square miles (345 square kilometers)*

Population: *110,000*

Population density: *827 per square mile (318 per square kilometer)*

Peoples: *82 percent Afro-Caribbean; 13 percent mixed descent; 5 percent European and Asian descent*

Official language: *English*

Currency: *East Caribbean dollar*

National day: *Independence Day (February 7)*

Country's name: *Grenada is named after the Spanish city of Granada. The spelling comes from the French, La Grenade.*

Grenada is a center of spice growing. The seeds of the nutmeg tree are processed into the spices called nutmeg and mace. Grenada also produces cinnamon, cloves, pimento, ginger, and vanilla. As well as being exported, the spices are widely used for flavoring local drinks and dishes.

Unstable prices on the international spice market have forced Grenadans to turn to tourism as a source of income. Despite this, there is very high unemployment.

Grenada holds its carnival in August, marked by parades and dancing to steel bands. Carriacou has its carnival in the period before Lent and a popular regatta each August. Carriacou is also known for its *parang* (pah-RAHNG) festival, a celebration of music and song in the weeks before Christmas. The cultural influence of Trinidad, to the south, is very strong and includes a love of calypso music.

Independence came in 1974. In 1979 the New Jewel Movement, led by Maurice Bishop, introduced a socialist program, building schools and improving health care. However, in 1983 some of Bishop's former supporters, who thought he was not doing enough, put him under house arrest and later shot him and many of his supporters. The United States, concerned about Cuban influence on Grenada, decided to invade, backed by their allies in the region. The conflict claimed 282 lives, and the troops stayed for two years.

The Grenadans are mostly Afro-Caribbeans. Others are of mixed Afro-Caribbean, British, French, or Carib descent. There are also some Grenadans of European and Asian descent, whose ancestors came to work on the spice plantations.

The Saturday market in Saint George's is one great splash of color—from the bright umbrellas to the vendors' clothes and the assortment of tropical vegetables, fruits, and spices.

Timeline:	Settlement by Arawak people	Invasion by Caribs	Island becomes British	Slavery is abolished	Independence from Great Britain
	ca. 1 C.E.	ca. 1000	1783	1833	1974

GUADELOUPE

GUADELOUPE LIES AT THE NORTHERN END OF THE WINDWARD ISLANDS, part of the long Caribbean chain known as the Lesser Antilles.

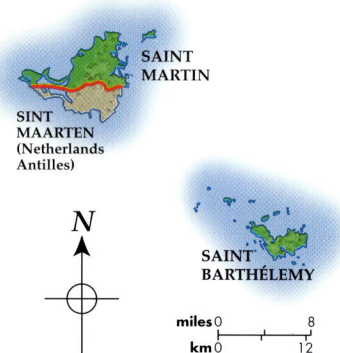

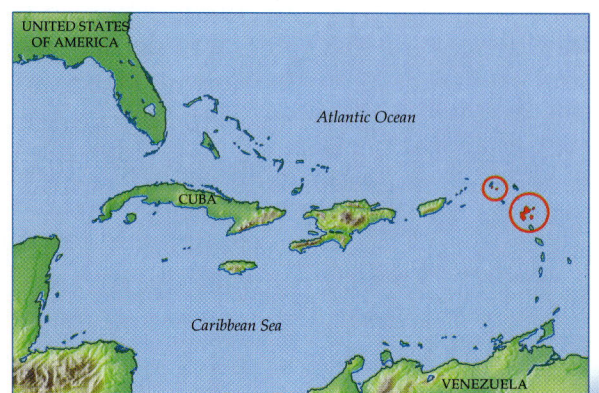

The highlands of Basse-Terre rise to 4,869 feet (1,484 meters) at the restless volcanic peak of Soufrière. To the east, Grande Terre is an island of coral reefs and sandy beaches.

Guadeloupe is made up of two parts, the islands of Basse-Terre and Grande Terre. They are joined together by a bridge over a narrow strait, the Rivière Salée. The territory also includes the islands of Saint Martin, Saint Barthélemy, Marie-Galante, Désirade, and Îles des Saintes.

CLIMATE

The climate is warm and humid but cooled by trade winds. L'hivernage (lee-vair-NAHJ), the rainy season, lasts from July to November. Guadeloupe suffered a severe hurricane during the 1989 rainy season.

Average January temperature: *74°F (23°C)*

Average July temperature: *80°F (27°C)*

Average annual precipitation (coast):
71 in (180 cm)

Average annual precipitation (mountains):
390 in (990 cm)

Tropical France

Guadeloupe (GWAHD-l-oop) was settled by Native American peoples about two thousand years ago. Arawak-speakers were displaced by the Caribs in the 1300s.

In 1635 heavily armed French settlers invaded the island and forced the Caribs to flee. The settlers then planted sugarcane and imported African slave labor.

It was not until 1848 that the slaves were freed. In the years that followed, many Asian workers were hired as laborers.

After World War II (1939–1945), Guadeloupe became an overseas department of France, which meant that it was governed in just the same way as any other part of France. This has given the island the

FACTS AND FIGURES

Status: *Overseas department of France*

Capital: *Basse-Terre*

Area: *683 square miles (1,770 square kilometers)*

Population: *427,000*

Population density: *625 per square mile (240 per square kilometer)*

Peoples: *80 percent mixed descent (African-European-Asian); 15 percent Afro-Caribbean; 5 percent French*

Official language: *French*

Currency: *French franc*

National day: *Bastille Day (July 14)*

Country's name: *Christopher Columbus named the island after a Spanish cult of the Virgin Mary—Santa Maria de Guadalupe de Extremadura. Guadalupe was spelled Guadeloupe by its French settlers.*

smaller islands include descendants of Breton fishermen. Most people speak a French-Caribbean dialect known as Creole. Most islanders are Roman Catholic, with a minority of Protestants and Hindus.

The island's architecture includes French colonial buildings and Hindu temples. French cuisine is served alongside Afro-Caribbean specialties—land crab, conch, snapper, and curried goat.

Carnival begins on January 6 and builds up until Lent. It is marked by street dancing, parades, and music. Many women wear traditional Creole costume, with shawls, scarves, blouses, and long skirts with petticoats for festivals.

African rhythms and vocal styles created the music called *gwo ka* (GWOE KAH) in Guadeloupe and in the 1980s contributed to a Caribbean techno sound called *zouk* (ZOOK).

Palms and verandas overlook a street market in Pointe-à-Pitre, a town of eighty thousand people. Here, you can buy cotton cloth, fresh fruit juice, pumpkins, and melons.

advantage of French and European Union aid and development. Nearly 90 percent of all export trade is still with France.

Most of the islanders work in farming, growing sugarcane, bananas, melons, and flowers for export as well as vegetables and fruit for the home market. Unemployment is quite high. Tourism is gradually providing more work for the islanders.

The capital is Basse-Terre, but Pointe-à-Pitre on Grande Terre is larger and busier. The population is largely of mixed descent. Africans, French, and Asians all intermarried over the years. About one in ten inhabitants are solely of African descent, and there are some French. The

Timeline:	Caribs invade, displacing Arawaks	French settlers drive off Caribs; African slaves imported	Guadeloupe becomes a French colony	Slaves freed; Asian labor brought in to work on plantations	Guadeloupe becomes an overseas department of France
	1300s C.E.	**1635**	**1674**	**1848**	**1946**

GUATEMALA

GUATEMALA IS THE THIRD LARGEST COUNTRY IN CENTRAL AMERICA after Nicaragua and Honduras.

Guatemala is bordered by Mexico on the north and west, Belize on the northeast, and Honduras and El Salvador on the southeast. It has a long Pacific coast on the southwest and a short Caribbean coast on the east.

Thirty-seven rivers run through Guatemala—the biggest being the Usumacinta—and mountains crisscross the country. Most of the over thirty volcanoes in Guatemala are still active, and some erupt often. Some of these volcanoes' cones hold beautiful lakes; the most famous is Lake Atitlán. The country also suffers from frequent and often disastrous earthquakes. Its forests and swamps are rich in plant and animal life.

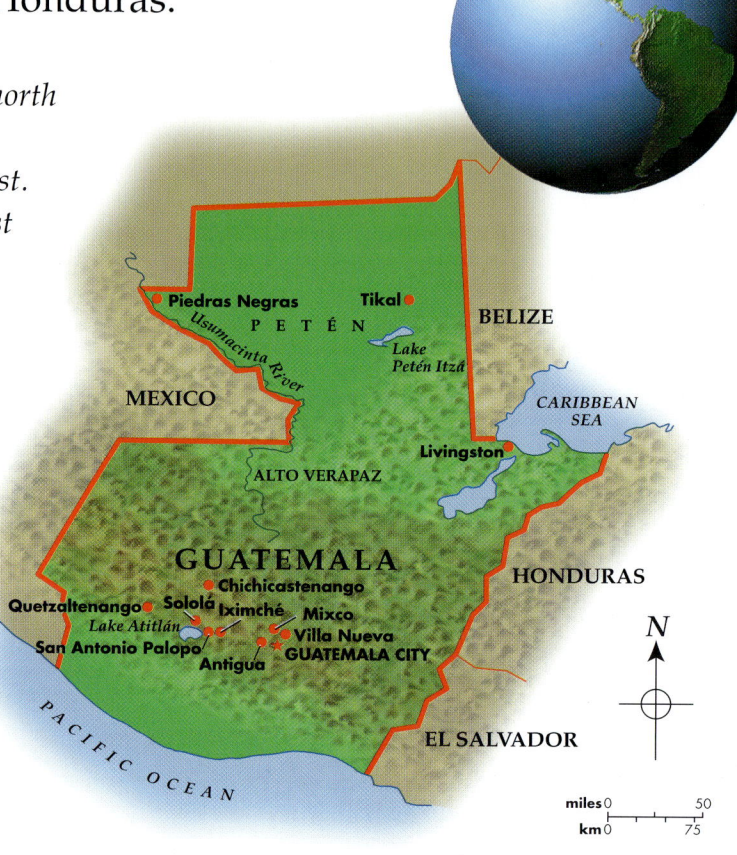

CLIMATE

There are two climate regions in Guatemala. The Pacific and Caribbean coastal lowlands have a tropical climate, where the temperature ranges from 77°F to 86°F (25°C to 30°C). Most of inland Guatemala is at a high altitude, with year-round cool weather. The average temperature for the highland regions is 68°F (20°C). Four mountain ranges cross Guatemala, and on the highest peaks the climate is generally cool to cold, averaging 59°F (15°C). Throughout Guatemala a rainy season lasts from May to October, and a dry season lasts from November to May.

Average January temperature: *62°F (17°C)*

Average June temperature: *68°F (20°C)*

Average annual precipitation: *60 in (152 cm)*

The First People and the Mayan Empire

The first people to come to Central America—and to live in the lands that are Guatemala (gwah-tuh-MAH-luh) today—are believed to have arrived around twelve thousand years ago. Depending on herds of wild animals and wild plants for food, people moved farther and farther through Central America. Very little is known of the life and culture before the rise of the great Mayan empire, except that people had begun to grow plants for food and fibers and to live in settlements by 2500 B.C.E. Archaeologists think most of the sites of these early peoples are under water

FACTS AND FIGURES

Official names: *República de Guatemala*

Status: *Independent state*

Capital: *Guatemala City*

Major cities: *Quetzaltenango, Mixco, Villa Nueva*

Area: *42,042 square miles (108,889 square kilometers)*

Population: *11,200,000*

Population density: *266 per square mile (103 per square kilometer)*

Peoples: *43 percent Native American; 57 percent ladino (Native American-European descent and Native Americans living a middle-class lifestyle)*

Official language: *Spanish*

Currency: *Quetzal*

National days: *Anniversary of the Victory of the 1871 Revolution (June 30); Independence Day (September 15); All Saints' Day (November 1)*

The country's name: *The root of the word Guatemala is unknown but of Native origin. It is not known which Native language it is in or what it means.*

From here developed the religion of the Maya, the focus of Mayan life. The Maya (MAH-yuh) believed that the wind, air, earth, sun, corn, and many other natural things had their own gods who controlled the natural world. They believed if the people flattered these gods, gave them gifts, and built great temples in their honor, the gods would favor them with good harvests and a safe world to live in.

In religious centers the Maya built temples shaped like tall, narrow pyramids topped with flat areas and buildings.

The Temple of the Great Jaguar and the Grand Plaza in the Mayan capital of Tikal have now been uncovered from the rain forest, which had completely hidden them for many years.

now because the oceans are higher than they were then.

Though they grew chili peppers for seasoning and gourds to make dishes, corn came to be the central crop. The success of a corn harvest was very important, determining whether people ate or starved. Farmers did their best, digging holes with pointed sticks and planting one corn kernel at a time.

Timeline:	First people move into the land that is now Guatemala	Development of agriculture	Rise of Mayan civilization
	ca. 10,000 B.C.E.	ca. 5000 B.C.E.	ca. 2500 B.C.E.–250 C.E.

Priests used these temples to make offerings and sacrifices to the gods of nature. The remains of these religious centers are still standing, some overgrown by the rain forest and others cleared by archaeologists. In Guatemala the most famous temples and ruins are at Tikal, Mixco, and Piedras Negras.

The religion grew more complex and began to use increasingly advanced mathematics, astronomy, calendars, and writing systems, which are the hallmark of Mayan learning. All these sciences were developed to help the Maya in their religion so that they could predict the actions of the gods and know how to please them the most.

Mayan Ritual Sacrifice

As the Mayan priests perceived it, the gods needed offerings of the blood of their worshipers and the lives of humans if they were going to give the Mayan worshipers the crops they asked for. Mayan people took prisoners of war from their raids on non-Mayan villages and sacrificed these people so they could prosper under the blessings of their gods. A series of murals found in a building archaeologists call Bonampak in Mexico, which means "Painted Walls" in Mayan, illustrates the story of a raid and the sacrifice of prisoners in great detail. Smaller offerings of beautiful and precious things and of incense such as copal were also made.

At its peak the Mayan civilization reached far north into Mexico's Yucatán Peninsula and included modern-day Belize and the northern rim of Honduras. However, it went into a decline by the year 900 C.E. The priests disappeared and building at the temple sites stopped. Archaeologists believe that the Maya population exploded and their agricultural techniques could not keep up with the demand for food. Other groups moved in on the edges of what had been Mayan territory, but Guatemala—the heart of Mayan civilization—stayed cut off from these groups until the Spaniards arrived in the sixteenth century. The people still lived the same way and practiced their old religion but without the organized religious and political system present at the height of Mayan civilization.

Spaniards Make Contact, Conquer, and Colonize

Spain sent many expeditions to the Americas looking for gold and wealth believed to be hidden in the new lands. They also wanted Catholic missionaries to convert the Native people from their old religion to the religion of Spain—Catholicism. Hernán Cortés sent Pedro de Alvarado from the Spanish base in Mexico to conquer Guatemala. Alvarado set up a Spanish city called Iximché in 1524 after a long fight with the Native people. The rain forests and swamps of Guatemala put up as much resistance to invasion as the people themselves. In 1527 it was clear that the Mayan warriors were still too strong for the

Building and use of Tikal	Decline of Mayan civilization	Spaniards arrive on Central American mainland
ca. 250–900 C.E.	ca. 900–1500	1502

The Tikal Museum displays some of the tools and works of art, such as these pottery vessels, that archaeologists have discovered as the temples and ruins have been uncovered.

Mexico, the Maya's territory north of Guatemala in present-day Mexico.

An area of dense forest populated by a few groups of Native peoples, the Petén was the last region left free of Spanish control. The biggest of these groups was the Itzá (eat-SAH), who were based on an island in Lake Petén Itzá in a settlement called Tayasal. Missionaries had tried to win converts there but were driven out or sacrificed to the Mayan gods. In 1697 the governor of Yucatán brought an enormous army to Lake Petén Itzá. He built a huge ship to carry the soldiers and attacked the island from the lake with continuous gunfire. The settlement was destroyed and its people were massacred within the day. The last stronghold of Mayan independence was crushed.

Life under Colonial Rule

Life under Spanish rule was a huge change for the Mayan people of Guatemala. The Spaniards sought to eliminate their traditional culture, especially their religion. Missionaries were so eager to convert them to Catholicism that they tortured the Maya until they gave up their old religion. Mayan land was divided among the Spanish colonists and officials, and the Native people had to farm their former lands for the Europeans. The Spanish colonists built huge farms and beautiful homes, all the work of Native people. They forced the Maya to build Spanish cities, a legacy of architecture that remains today in cities like Antigua and on plantations throughout the countryside.

few Spaniards to hold their ground at Iximché, so the Spaniards moved their center to Santiago de los Caballeros and established it as the first capital.

The Spaniards finally managed to conquer the Maya by turning them against each other. The Maya were a coalition of various tribes with a similar culture and religion but different political interests. When the Spaniards arrived, many of these Mayan groups were already at war with each other. As a result, the small Spanish army got invaluable help from local warriors who knew the land and the enemy. But as soon as the common enemy had been defeated, the Spanish turned on their Native allies and subjugated them as well. Most of Central America had fallen by 1546, when Francisco de Montejo conquered the Yucatán Peninsula of

Iximché, the first Spanish city in Guatemala, is established	Spanish conquer the last free Native peoples in Guatemala	Guatemala declares itself free of Spanish rule
1524	**1692**	**1821**

The Spanish conquerors forced the Maya to build and decorate Spanish towns and homes. This richly painted church is in the highland town of San Andres Xecul.

Independence and Beyond

In the early nineteenth century the Spanish throne was seized by the French, and Spain lost control of its overseas colonies. As a result, it was a relatively bloodless revolution that broke Guatemala and its Central American neighbors away from Spanish rule. By this time even the people of Spanish descent in Guatemala wanted independence. Their families had lived in Guatemala for generations, and Spain was a foreign country to them. They began to resent being ruled from Europe instead of being able to govern themselves. When Mexico declared independence in 1821, Guatemala was quick to follow.

At first Guatemala was part of a coalition of former colonies that tried to unite the countries of Central America so they could be stronger against outsiders like Spain and the United States. But many disagreements arose among politicians in Guatemala and neighboring countries, and soon all the former colonies became independent. Governments changed often, usually through revolutions and military coups, and there were many rulers throughout the nineteenth century. In 1839 Guatemala finally became an independent republic. Its leaders were usually dictators, some of whom did great things to improve life in their country, like building railroads and wiring for electricity. But they were usually better known for their cruel treatment, including torture, of people who disagreed with them.

In the late nineteenth century Justo Rufino Barrios seized power. In addition

The Maya died at a dramatic rate under Spanish rule; the biggest killer was probably disease, brought from Europe by the Spaniards. Diseases that were minor to a European were severe for people in the New World, who had no resistance to illnesses like smallpox and measles. Many others died trying to resist the Spanish or resisting conversion to Christianity. It is estimated that at least 75 percent of the Native people died as a result of contact with the Spaniards.

Guatemala becomes an independent republic	General Jorge Ubico elected president	President Jacobo Arbenz Guzmán is driven into exile by U.S. forces	A disastrous earthquake hits Guatemala, destroying thousands of homes
1839	**1931**	**1954**	**1976**

to improving schools and establishing strong banks, he promoted the growth of coffee to help the economy. As an owner of coffee plantations, he saw coffee as a commodity that could bring money into Guatemala. He forced all the Native people living in prime coffee-growing lands to move so that land could be used for coffee. These people were then forced to work on banana plantations.

In 1931 Guatemala elected a president, General Jorge Ubico, who also had strong ideas on how to improve the lives of his people. He tried to make labor laws and wages more fair for the common person. During his period in office, Ubico also stabilized Guatemala's economy. However, late in his administration he became more dictatorial and lost much support.

Jacobo Arbenz Guzmán, who was president from 1951 to 1954, tried to redistribute the plantations of the United Fruit Company, an American company, to the local people who had been farming it for slave wages. The Communist Party of Guatemala supported this idea and became involved in the takeover. Afraid that Guatemala would become a communist country under Guzmán, the United States sent in military forces to overthrow the president and replace him with a more conservative leader. The United States has supported noncommunist governments in Guatemala since then and uses Guatemala as a base for its political and military actions in countries neighboring Guatemala.

The Guatemalan government has been run by the military or by presidents working closely with the military since the 1950s. Since then, social protest has grown, protests that have been suppressed by military violence. Military coups have continued. Currently, military control is strongest in the countryside, where government forces make sure that the common people in the villages cannot plot revolution against the government. Political disagreements and unstable governments have sapped Guatemala's strength and slowed its growth right up to the present day. The military is still a dominant force in the people's daily life.

At demonstrations in Guatemala City, people carry pictures of loved ones who have "disappeared," demanding their release or an explanation of what became of them.

The army seizes control of the government	Guatemala elects its first civilian president in fifteen years	Rigoberta Menchu receives the Nobel Peace Prize for her work on human rights for all Guatemalans
1982	**1985**	**1992**

Preserving the Mayan Religion

Christian missionaries burned old Mayan religious books and, in the process, destroyed much of the history of the Mayan civilization. Oddly enough, one of the leading book-burning missionaries, Diego de Landa, also kept very careful records of what the life of the Mayan people was like and what they believed. Today his journal tells us most of what we know about the Maya when the Spanish came. Another source from the seventeenth century is the Popol Vuh *(POH-puhl VOO), a book written by a Maya who was educated by the Spanish. He described the myths of the old religion so they would not be forgotten.*

The People of Guatemala Today

Guatemalans descend primarily from the original Mayan peoples. Throughout their history the Maya have been divided into several groups. These groups are separated by their languages, which are really dialects of the same original language. Because the groups have lived in small groups of villages for centuries, the speech in each area has evolved differently. Today many people of different areas cannot understand each other. There are more than twenty dialects.

People identify themselves with their own group, not as Mayan. The largest of these are the Quiché (or K'iche), Cakchiquel (or Kaqchikel), and the Mam, most of whom live in the highlands, along with the Tzutuhil (or Tz'utujil), Chuh (or Chuj),

Lake Atitlán provides water for many villages that surround it. It is also the "laundry room," where women scrub their clothes and lay them out to dry in the sun.

Rigoberta Menchu: A Mayan Woman's Story

When she was twenty-three years old, Rigoberta Menchu told the story of her life and of the customs and sufferings of her people. Her book has helped the world understand the plight of the Native people of Guatemala. She decided to learn Spanish and become a leader for equal rights for her people after her mother, father, and twelve-year-old brother were murdered by the Guatemalan military. In 1992 she won the Nobel Peace Prize for her work.

When the Guatemalan army attacked villages where they suspected antigovernment activity, people hid in shelters they dug in the earth and covered with heavy logs or stones.

Aquatec (or Awakateko), Oxil, Uspantec, Kanjobal (or Q'uanjob'al), and others. The Kekchi (or Q'eqchi), Pikomchi, and a few others live in central Guatemala, most in the Alto Verapaz region. All these people have much the same customs, myths, and heritage. Their Native languages are still spoken in the villages, although most people also speak Spanish because it is taught in schools and necessary for official business. The Mayan peoples today have a strong cultural identity, which they keep alive in their clothing styles, language, and some religious practices. They are generally farmers, workers, and craftspeople.

A small minority of Guatemalans have ancestors who originally came from Spain and did not marry into the local communities. Called *criollos* (kree-OY-ohs), they are the elite of modern Guatemala and have the most powerful jobs in the government, military, and business. People who have both Spanish and Mayan ancestry are called *ladinos* (lah-DEE-nose). They make up the middle class of

shopkeepers, managers, politicians, and bureaucrats. Sometimes *ladino* is used to refer to people with some Spanish blood or even to people who are Native American who live a middle-class lifestyle. Together, these ladinos and criollos make up over half the population of Guatemala.

Fewer than two thousand Garifuna (gah-ree-FOO-nah), or Black Caribs, who are descendants of Carib Indians and African slaves, live on Guatemala's northern Caribbean coast. They are becoming fewer as they, like others, flee from the military violence in Guatemala across the nearby border into Belize (see BELIZE). The Garifuna are largely isolated from the lifestyle of ladinos. Although they are Catholics, they retain many Afro-Caribbean customs in their churches and in their music, which uses traditional African and Caribbean instruments.

In Livingston, on the eastern side of Guatemala, you may see blacks who are descendants of African slaves, along with the more common ladinos.

Life in Guatemala

Towns and cities have a higher percentage of ladinos and reveal more of their unique culture. The ladino way of life is based on

---

The Quetzal, Symbol of the Maya

The shy quetzal, a beautiful bright green bird with long, curving tail feathers, lives deep in the rain forest and is rarely seen. When taken into captivity, the quetzal usually dies. As more and more of its native forests are cut for farming and development, the quetzal's numbers decline, and the birds hide deeper and deeper in the forest. To the ancient Mayans, the quetzal was the symbol of life. Modern Mayan people see this threatened bird as a symbol of their own history, when their ancestors once disappeared into the dense forests to escape the Spanish and often died when captured.

---

old Spanish culture. For example, it is still possible to see young women promenading arm in arm with their friends in a circle around town squares while the young men look on, hoping to catch the eye of the girl they like. Even in the smallest of towns, boys are often eager to play an impromptu soccer game in the town square or in the street. A lot of social life, for all ages, takes place in the streets, from chatting with a friend on the doorstep to taking part in big church fiestas. During these church holidays people parade the statues of the saints through the streets amid celebration. The pavement is sometimes covered in designs made of brightly colored flower petals.

Despite some political instability, Guatemala has a small but steady export economy. Their largest export crops are coffee, bananas, spices, cotton, and sugar. They also export lumber, seafood, and

Before Easter, people in long robes carry religious statues through the streets of Antigua, which are carpeted with intricate designs of flower petals and colored sawdust.

Though the military presence in the countryside is not as violent or warlike as in some neighboring countries, it has gotten bad enough to force families who could afford it to emigrate to other, safer countries.

Work and Play in Guatemala City

About one-quarter of Guatemala's population lives in its capital, Guatemala City, the only industrial city in the country. The richest people, mostly the criollos, live in mansions with servants. Middle-class people live in smaller homes. The lower-class people, who are mostly poor workers of Mayan descent, live in very small, crowded apartments. In the last thirty years more and more people have moved to the city from their farms in the country, looking for work in the factories. The city has been overcrowded and polluted for decades and presents many problems that need to be solved to improve life there.

livestock. The government continues its efforts to gain ownership of large international businesses for Guatemalan people, not foreign people, so that the income can help Guatemala. Tourism gives Guatemala a large share of its income, too, and tourists' money often goes directly to the local people who need the income.

For all people, especially men, it is common to spend the night in a bar with friends whenever they have a little extra money and time. Bars are more than drinking places—they are the social centers of most neighborhoods for men and may have live music and dancing. Women are more likely to stay at home, weaving and

In Guatemala City, the country's capital and largest city, most people dress just like North Americans, as you can see from this group of students.

looking after children. They socialize more during the day, when their chores and errands bring them outside the home. Women sometimes work in groups while preparing food, doing the laundry, or other tasks, so they can talk while they work and help the time go by faster.

The Maya: Traditional Life in the Villages

Mayan families outside the cities often live in a thatched house called a *na* (NAH). The traditional houses in the colder highlands have no chimneys, and smoke from the cooking fire fills the house. Each family usually has a garden in which they grow some food for themselves. Some families may have farms on which they grow food for sale. Most of the farmwork is done by men, who work the very rocky earth by hand with hoes. Men often work on plantations and then go home in the evening to farm their own land to feed themselves and their families.

Grinding corn is considered women's work. Traditionally, corn is dried, broken off the ear, and put into storage. When it is time to cook, a woman takes a portion of this dried corn, pounds it to break it up, and then places handfuls on a flat, rough grinding stone called a *metate* (may-TAH-tay). She rubs the corn against the metate with a long stone bar until it is a fine flour. She uses this flour to make tortillas, tamales (steamed cornmeal dumplings filled with spiced meat or vegetables), and many other dishes.

The food of Guatemala also features a variety of peppers, both spicy and sweet,

Weaving and Textiles

Men and women may both make crafts to sell, bringing the family extra income. Most famous of all Guatemalan handicrafts is weaving, which is done by women. In many places people still spin the wool of their own sheep and dye it in bright colors with dyes made from plants and animals. They use the indigo plant for blue and the cochineal beetle for red dye. Now artificial dyes are also easily available, as are commercially spun and dyed yarns.

They weave the yarn into beautiful cloth on traditional looms called back-strap looms, which date back to before the Spanish came. Instead of having a solid wooden frame, as most looms have, the loom is kept tight and in place by tying it around the body of the weaver, who keeps pulling back on it to keep the loom's threads tight so the pattern is even.

The cloth woven on these looms is sewn into clothing, such as the woman's shirt called the **huipil** (hwee-PEEL). The huipil is a loose shirt that is usually covered in small, beautiful, colorful designs of animals, plants, people, and old traditional patterns, such as symbols of the old gods. Handwoven cloth is also used to make wraparound skirts for women, pants and shirts for men, and carrying cloths to wrap up bundles.

Each village in Guatemala has its own unique styles of weaving and designs its craftspeople use. You can tell which town a person is from by looking at his or her clothes. Over the last fifty years it has become less and less common to see Mayan people in traditional clothing, and men, especially, have started to wear ladino-style clothes instead. In the last few years, however, people have stopped being ashamed of their old-style clothing, and more Mayan people are beginning to wear their huipils and village clothing with pride.

Back-strap looms can be made from a few sticks and rolled up for carrying. To weave, women fasten one end to a tree limb and the other around their waist.

Village women often wear their traditional huipiles. People can tell from the colors and pattern of this woman's huipil that she is from San Antonio Palopo on Lake Atitlán.

dance. Mostly they wait until market day, when they can break their routine and go to town for more fun and excitement. Sunday is set aside by most people to go to church and is generally a more relaxed day.

The religion of the Maya today is particularly interesting. Though they were all converted to Catholicism by the Spanish, the Maya's religious practices are very different than the official church doctrine. Many old traditions are still practiced in Catholic churches by Guatemalan people, who burn old Mayan copal incense outside the church before entering and still decorate their clothing with images of the old gods. Many Mayan people will still go to a traditional healer, a

(below) Before Easter nearly every town has a procession. Here in Chichicastenango, Quiché Maya people carry a statue from the local church through the market.

many kinds of beans, rice, soft white cheese, and chicken or other small animals. A common meal is beans or shredded meat wrapped in a soft tortilla that has been cooked on a griddle. Children help their parents with their work, and young girls begin helping with cooking and sewing at an early age.

Life in the country can be very hard, and most days there is no time to relax. When people have free time from the farming, they work on something else. For fun, people may gather and drink, talk, and

On market days people from all over the highlands arrive by bus and on foot with huge bundles to set up stalls in Sololá, above Lake Atitlán.

shaman, when sick, in addition to or instead of a doctor. They want to be treated in the old way, invoking the old gods to cure sickness magically, as well as the new scientific way. Catholic missions in Guatemala today support the new kind of Catholicism practiced by the people and work with the people to improve their lives. They are anxious to make up for the wrongs done by the early Spanish missionaries.

The social position of the native Maya is improving at a snail's pace. Even though it is increasingly possible for them to attend school, get better jobs, and be active in the running of their country, it is by no means easy. For many, joining the military or moving to Guatemala City is the only way out of the hard life of a farmworker.

Market Day!

Markets are held once a week in many villages, and there are bigger festival markets at holiday times. Craftsmen and farmers alike bring their wares to markets to sell and trade.

Markets are noisy with people calling out their wares and bright with the variety of things for sale. Mounds of red peppers may be stacked beside a booth of painted carved masks, and a tamale vendor may stand beside a weaver's stall hung with a rainbow of sashes and huipils.

Women usually carry their smallest children tied to their backs with colorful cloths, and often small children are left to care for their younger siblings while the mother works or does the shopping.

GUYANA

GUYANA, ON THE NORTH COAST OF SOUTH AMERICA, was formerly a British colony known as British Guiana.

Guyana is bordered by Venezuela on the west, Brazil on the southwest and south, Suriname along the Courantyne River on the east, and the Atlantic Ocean on the north.

A narrow plain no more than 10 miles (16 kilometers) wide runs along Guyana's Atlantic coast. Most of it is below sea level, and it is crossed by four major rivers. A seawall keeps out the Atlantic Ocean, and a system of dikes and canals makes farming possible. Much of the center of the country is a hilly region of sand and clay covered in tropical rain forest. Along the western border with Venezuela and Brazil are steep, forested escarpments and spectacular waterfalls. The southwest is mostly open grassland, or savannah.

CLIMATE

Guyana has a typical tropical climate with high temperatures, heavy rainfall, and high humidity, though this is relieved by offshore winds. Temperatures change little throughout the year. On the coast a wet season extends from April to August, but seasonal drought can occur in July and August depending on the movements of the southeast trade winds.

Average January temperature: *79°F (26°C)*

Average July temperature: *81°F (27°C)*

Average annual precipitation: *87 in (221 cm)*

The Wild Coast

The first peoples in Guyana (GUY-ah-nah) were Arawak, Carib, and Warrau. By 1000 B.C.E. they were seminomadic, practicing agriculture but still hunting in the forests. When the Spaniards arrived early in the sixteenth century, they found Native Americans growing cassava, potatoes, beans, and peanuts, fishing with spears or hooks and lines, and using long dugout canoes.

The region was inhospitable; swamps close to the shore made access difficult, and

Rock carvings in the Rupununi Savannah. Ancient peoples fashioned these symbols, but precisely who, when, or why is not clear.

FACTS AND FIGURES

Official name: The Cooperative Republic of Guyana

Status: Independent state

Capital: Georgetown

Major towns: Linden, New Amsterdam

Area: 83,000 square miles (215,000 square kilometers)

Population: 800,000

Population density: 10 per square mile (4 per square kilometer)

Peoples: 49 percent East Indian descent; 36 percent African descent; 5 percent Native American; 1 percent Chinese and Portuguese descent; 9 percent mixed descent and other

Official language: English

Currency: Guyana dollar

National holidays: Republic Day and Mashramani Festival (February 23); Labor Day (May 1); Independence Day (May 26); Caricom Day (first Monday in July); Freedom Day (first Monday in August); United Nations Day (October 24)

The country's name: The word Guyana is derived from a Native American word meaning "land of waters."

the forests were dense. It became known as the "Wild Coast," and explorers avoided it for many years. Dutch and English colonists first attempted to settle the area early in the seventeenth century, and until 1796 the Dutch controlled most of the region. At first they built trading posts upriver, then they moved to the coast, where they introduced dikes and floodgates similar to those used in Holland to drain the land. They farmed tobacco, cotton, and coffee and, in the mid-seventeenth century, imported slaves from western Africa to work on coastal sugar plantations. In 1796 the British seized the territory, which was retaken by the Dutch in 1802 and then finally captured by the British in 1814. In 1831 the colony of British Guiana was formed.

When slavery was abolished in 1838, there were about 100,000 slaves, many of whom became small farmers. This left the large plantation owners without labor. By 1860 some 30,000 Portuguese from the Azores and Madeira Islands and about 14,000 Chinese had arrived in British Guiana. About 240,000 East Indians came as laborers between 1838 and 1917.

By the beginning of the twentieth century, many blacks, benefiting from the

Timeline:	Seminomadic Arawak, Carib, Warrau tribes are farming	First attempts to settle by Dutch and British colonists	British seize region from the Dutch, who recapture it in 1802	British retake territory
	1000 B.C.E.	1616 C.E.	1796	1814

compulsory education they received through the British 1876 Education Act, had become literate and numerate. This led to jobs in administration and other skilled professions. The East Indians shunned Guyana's school system because it was run by the Christian church. They developed rice farming, something they had done in India. Within a few years it became an important export. Politically, however, both groups had little say, and power remained largely in the hands of the few wealthy British landowners. Trade unions emerged to demand better working conditions and better pay. The British government made some political concessions, allowing a one-house legislature and giving more people the right to vote.

Forbes Burnham (in the front car) and Cheddi Jagan (in the second car) drive past cheering crowds of supporters in Georgetown in 1954.

Cheddi Jagan and Forbes Burnham

Cheddi Bharrat Jagan was one of eleven children of a Hindu sugar estate foreman. He was born in 1918, and when he died in 1997, his funeral procession drew the largest crowd ever seen in Georgetown. Jagan worked to pay for his education and made his way to Washington, D.C., and Chicago, where he studied dentistry. He returned to Guyana in 1943 with Janet, his American wife, daughter of a Jewish immigrant. He entered politics with a policy that aimed to reduce the gap between the rich and poor of his country.

Linden Sampson Forbes Burnham was born in 1923 in a village near Georgetown. His father was the headmaster at the local Methodist primary school, and as a young man, Forbes Burnham was encouraged to study. He won a scholarship that took him to Great Britain, where he became president of the West Indies Students' Union. He was a brilliant speaker, and that gift and his ideals led to politics. Initially a socialist, he soon disagreed with Jagan, whose policies he found too extreme.

Colony of British Guiana founded	Slavery abolished	Portuguese and Chinese immigrants arrive	240,000 East Indians settle	People's Progressive Party led by Cheddi Jagan gains power
1831	**1838**	**1830s–1850s**	**1838–1917**	**1953**

An important election was held in 1947, when an East Indian, Cheddi Jagan, was elected to the legislature for the first time. He founded the People's Progressive Party (PPP) with Forbes Burnham, an Afro-Guyanese lawyer. Together they won the 1953 election, and Jagan became president. But tension soon developed between the two, and Burnham founded the Afro-Guyanese People's National Congress Party (PNC). Between 1964 and 1992, the PNC regularly beat the PPP in elections, and Forbes Burnham was president until he died in office in 1985. The struggle between the two parties became increasingly bitter, with divisions along ethnic lines often erupting into violent street demonstrations.

British Guiana became the independent Cooperative Republic of Guyana in 1966 but remained a member of the British Commonwealth. It has moved between socialist and capitalist policies. In 1992 Jagan was voted back into office, but he died in 1997. Elections later that year resulted in victory for his wife, Janet Jagan.

Living and Working in Guyana

Ninety percent of Guyanese live in the habitable two-thirds of the narrow coastal plain. About one-quarter of the population live in Georgetown, the capital. The only other town of any size on the coast is New Amsterdam, where about twenty-five thousand people live. Outside the towns, most people work in farming, fishing, or herding dairy cattle. The main crops are sugar and rice. Coffee, cacao, cotton, fruit,

and vegetables are also grown. Rice farming is still largely a family affair, where the work is done by hand with water buffalo or oxen.

Guyana's second largest town is Linden, a bauxite-mining town inland on the Demerara River, with a population of about sixty thousand. For many years Guyana has been a leading producer of bauxite, used to make aluminum, but the main export and moneymaker today is gold. These minerals, together with valuable hardwood timber, are found in the central region of Guyana. Here, industrial development is leading to a gradual opening of the forest, with more prospectors and settlers moving in.

Education in Guyana is broadly based on the British system, but lack of funds since

Schoolchildren in blue-and-white sailor-style school uniforms wait in line to enter school. These pupils are at a high school for children between the ages of eleven and fifteen.

Afro-Guyanese People's National Congress Party led by Forbes Burnham gains power	British Guiana becomes the independent Cooperative Republic of Guyana	Cheddi Jagan elected president again	Cheddi Jagan dies and Janet Jagan elected president
1964	**1966**	**1992**	**1997**

Porknockers: Prospectors of Guyana

Porknockers is the name given to people who go into the forested interior and spend months or years searching for gold, diamonds, or other minerals. Men, and occasionally women, have been doing this for a long time. The name is believed to be derived from the custom in early days of stopping in town to pick up quantities of salt pork before setting off. Porknockers endure terrible conditions, working knee-deep in rivers and mud, risking disease and serious accidents, searching for the glimmer of a precious rock, in the hope that one day they will strike it rich. Some, although few, have become very wealthy.

Guyanese are Chinese and Portuguese. About 7 percent of the population descend from a variety of mixed marriages between blacks, East Indians, Europeans, and Native Americans.

The Indo-Guyanese came largely from hilly areas of southern India. They were given contracts for five years' work, housing, and rations. Some Indians returned to their homeland, but sufficient numbers stayed so that in time the East Indian population was established.

The Indo-Guyanese have retained some of their native culture, particularly their religion. The majority are Hindu, with minorities following the Islamic faith and some, Christianity. Hindu temples and Islamic mosques have been erected in East Indian areas.

An Indo-Guyanese girl from a village near Georgetown. She is descended from East Indian families who first arrived in Guyana at the beginning of this century.

the late 1960s has meant a decline in standards. There are too few teachers and not enough equipment; although all children are supposed to attend school from the ages of four to fifteen, many do not.

Rice and seafood are basic to the Guyanese diet, and tropical fruit and vegetables are varied and plentiful. One traditional favorite is pepper-pot, a spicy stew of meat cooked in bitter cassava juice with peppers and herbs. Dishes vary from English-style roast beef to Indian curries, Chinese sweet-and-sour meals, African dishes cooked in coconut milk, and, most recently, fast-food hamburgers.

A Mixture of Immigrants

Most people are Indo-Guyanese (of East Indian origin) or Afro-Guyanese (of African origin). There is a small number of Native Americans, and about one percent of the

Sunday worshipers leaving Bedford Methodist Church in Georgetown. Many Guyanese belong to Protestant and Evangelical churches.

The Indo-Guyanese are mostly coast dwellers, living in the country or town suburbs where they run profitable farms, shops, and food-trading businesses. Just over half the Guyanese East Indians speak Caribbean Hindi, a language with its roots in languages from India. Many speak English, but most talk in Creole English, the most widely spoken language in Guyana. This is a form of English that has absorbed African, Dutch, and other words.

The Afro-Guyanese work in every level of the Guyanese economy. After the abolition of slavery some of the slaves stayed on the plantations and joined together to buy them. Most Afro-Guyanese speak Creole English as a first language, although some speak English. Native African elements in their culture have long disappeared, and they are mostly Christians.

The Portuguese, whose forefathers arrived as laborers, came mostly from Madeira to work in the sugarcane fields. They soon found other jobs, and many opened small shops in the rural areas. Though some still have Portuguese names, very few speak Portuguese.

The Chinese came to work on the plantations. Those that stayed turned to other employment, and like the Portuguese, many became storekeepers. They are cautious businessmen and most have remained isolated as a community. Arthur Chung, the country's first president, was Chinese.

The Indigenous Peoples

Native Americans comprise about 5 percent of the present-day population and continue to use their own languages, mainly Arawak and Carib. Many live on enormous reservations set aside by the government. Although access to these areas is severely restricted, only the most remote tribes are isolated enough to have retained aspects of their original cultures. The work of missionaries sought to erase many of the customs of the indigenous peoples. Traditional languages are disappearing. Many Native Indians speak two languages, English learned in schools and their own native tongue, from which the name of the tribe is often drawn. Those living near settlements of miners, lumber workers, or farmers find work and earn money. A few find employment tapping trees for *balata* (bah-LAH-tah), a rubbery sap from the bullet wood tree.

The Lokono (loe-KOE-noe) are the largest Native American group, though

Kaieteur Falls

The Kaieteur Falls on the Potaro River in the Pakaraima Mountains are one of Guyana's main tourist attractions. Surrounded by unspoiled forest, the falls have a drop of 741 feet (226 meters), almost five times that of Niagara Falls.

According to legend, the falls are named after Kai, a chief of the Patamona tribe. Kai wanted to save his tribe from a rival Carib tribe and sacrificed his life to the Great Spirit, Makonaima, by going over the falls in a canoe.

other Guyanese country people, wearing similar clothes and working on small farms.

The Macushi (mah-KOOSH-ee), who live in the southwestern border area in the Rupununi Savannah and the foothills of the Pakaraima Mountains, number about seven thousand. Like their ancestors, they use slash-and-burn cultivation to clear land. They grow both sweet and bitter cassava.

About nine thousand Wapishana (wah-PEESH-eeah-nah) are scattered in villages in the southwest, south of the Kanuku Mountains. They speak both English and their own language. In many areas they have totally lost their original culture. Today there is a chance that they will find work in the eco-tourism industry, since they are receiving encouragement from conservation groups and tour operators.

One of the smallest groups of Native Americans, the Wai Wai (WHY why), live deep in the forests of the southwest near the headwaters of the Essequibo River. Some Wai Wai have retained much of the original life of forest people. They collect

fewer than fifteen hundred still speak their Arawak language. They live along part of the coast and the Courantyne River. They have had long contact with Europeans, and today they live in much the same way as

Two Wai Wai paddling their canoe on the Essequibo River. They are transporting goods wrapped in banana leaves and packed in homemade, woven baskets downriver to their village.

food from the forest and build their homes from natural materials. One symbol of ancient Wai Wai tradition is a large circular house in Georgetown known as Umana Yana. It was built in 1972 of traditional materials—bamboo, wood, vines, and palm leaves.

Other small groups include the Pemon, Patamona, and Warrau (see Warao in VENEZUELA). The Pemon, or Pemong, number about 475 and live in the north,

close to the Venezuelan border. About 4,700 Patamona live in thirteen villages in northern and northwestern Guyana. The same number of Warrau live in the northwest near the coast.

Sport in Guyana

The most popular sport in Guyana is cricket, a bat and ball game that was introduced into Guyana by British colonial settlers. Men and young boys use any spare patch of ground for a game. Cricketer Clive Lloyd is Guyana's most famous sportsman. A spectacular hitter and fielder, he represented his country on many occasions. He was also the most successful captain ever of the West Indies (the pan-Caribbean cricket team), which he led to thirty-six victories.

Another team game, rugby, was also introduced by the British. Other popular sports include volleyball, tennis, and boxing.

Holiday Time

Each ethnic group has its own religious holidays. Christmas and Easter are important occasions for the Christian community, and one feature of Easter time is the kite-flying competitions held in Georgetown. In January Muslims celebrate the birthday of their holy prophet Muhammad, and the Hindu festival of lights takes place in November. The Chinese celebrate the beginning of the lunar year toward the end of January by lighting firecrackers and performing a dragon dance.

One holiday that brings all groups together is Mashramani on the anniversary in February of the day Guyana became a republic. Celebrations start with the raising of the national flag. This is followed by parades, processions, and children's games, backed by steel bands and East Indian dancers wearing musical bells.

Revelers in Georgetown celebrate the Mashramani festival on February 23. This annual independence celebration is enjoyed by many of Guyana's different ethnic groups.

HAITI

HAITI TAKES UP ONE-THIRD OF THE ISLAND OF HISPANIOLA. It is east of the Jamaica Channel and the Windward Passage in the Greater Antilles chain of islands. The eastern part of the island is taken up by the Dominican Republic.

Haiti is dominated by high mountain ranges, including the Massif de la Hotte and the Massif de la Selle, which rises to 8,793 feet (2,680 meters) above sea level at Mount La Selle. On the map, two large peninsulas look as if they are the jaws of a beast poised to swallow a smaller island, the Île de la Gonâve.

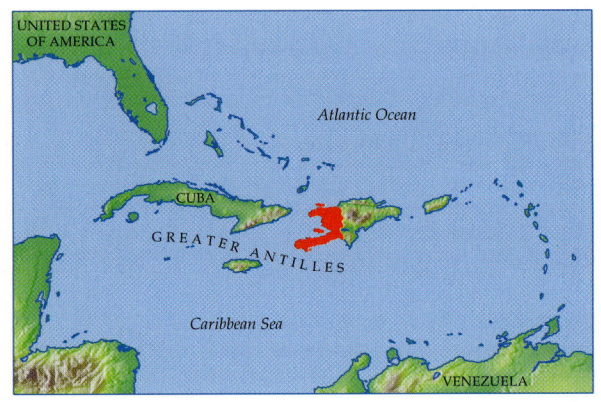

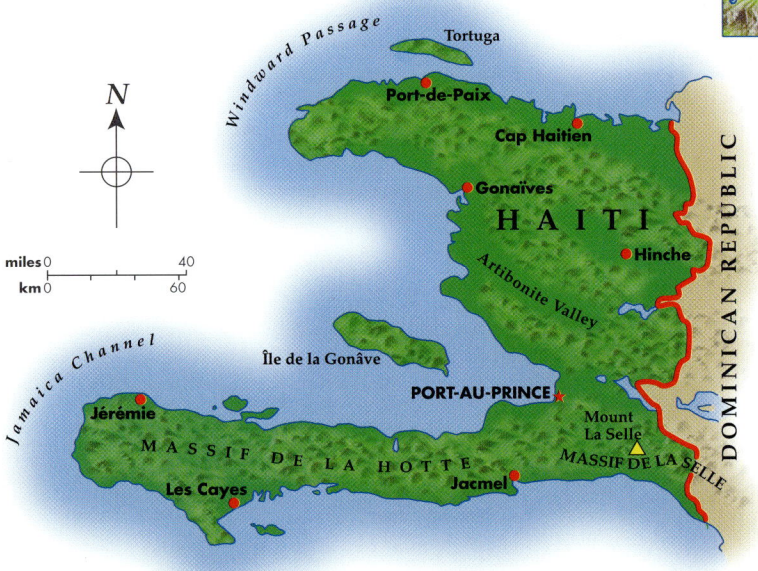

Haiti was once densely forested, but 95 percent of the cover has been stripped bare, mostly by farmers or by villagers burning wood into charcoal. The roots that once locked moisture into the soil are no longer there, and large areas of countryside are turning into dust. The problem is particularly acute in areas where mountains form a barrier to rains coming in off the ocean.

CLIMATE

The climate is warm and tropical, with two rainy seasons—the first from April to June and the second from August to November, when there is a high risk of tropical storms and hurricanes.

Average January temperature: *77°F (25°C)*

Average July temperature: *84°F (29°C)*

Average annual precipitation: *53 in (135 cm)*

A Troubled History

By about 7000 B.C.E. the Taino (TIE-no), a peaceful Native American people, were living on the island of Quisqueya ("big country" in the Arawak language). By all accounts these Arawak people were gentle and friendly. They lived in villages, farmed, and smoked tobacco.

In 1492 the Italian explorer Christopher Columbus claimed the land for Spain. He

FACTS AND FIGURES

Official name: *République d'Haïti*

Status: *Independent state*

Capital: *Port-au-Prince*

Other towns: *Jacmel, Les Cayes, Jérémie, Gonaïves, Port-de-Paix, Cap Haitien, Hinche*

Area: *10,710 square miles (27,739 square kilometers)*

Population: *6,732,000*

Population density: *629 per square mile (243 per square kilometer)*

Peoples: *95 percent Afro-Caribbean; 5 percent mixed French-African descent*

Official languages: *French, Creole*

Currency: *Gourde*

National days: *Independence Day (January 1); Heroes of Independence Day (January 2); Americas' Day (April 14); Labor Day (May 1); Flag Day (May 18); National Sovereignty Day (May 22); Dessalines Day (October 17); Toussaint-Louverture Day (November 1); Discovery Day (December 5)*

Country's name: *Haiti is the Arawak word for "highlands."*

gold mines and were soon broken by slavery and destroyed by diseases. The gold ran out, but the settlers planted sugarcane and imported new slaves from western Africa.

In the face of continuing Carib raids, many of the Spanish moved to the Central and South American mainland in search of new riches. They neglected the west of Hispaniola, and it was soon taken over by

named it Isla Española, or Hispaniola (meaning "Little Spain"). Leaving behind forty men, Columbus went back to Spain. Before he could return to Hispaniola, his colonists were all dead, as were many Arawak, probably killed in merciless attacks by the Carib people who were then swarming up through the Caribbean islands. However, more Spanish colonists lost no time building new settlements. The Taino were forced to work in Hispaniola's

Port-au-Prince's Catholic Cathedral is a legacy of Spanish colonists. Many Haitians practice both Catholicism and Voodoo, the African spirit religion.

Timeline:	Taino people from Central America settle	Christopher Columbus reaches the island and names it Hispaniola	Spanish enslave and murder the Taino and import slaves from Africa	French pirates settle western part of Hispaniola (Saint Domingue)
	7000 B.C.E.	**1492 C.E.**	**1500s**	**ca. 1664**

Toussaint-Louverture, A Haitian Hero

During the slave revolts of the 1790s, a black leader emerged who proved to be a brilliant soldier and a skillful politician. François-Dominique Toussaint, grandson of an African chief, was born on a slave plantation in Saint Domingue. His master taught him to read and write. On the battlefield he received the nickname Louverture, which means "opening" and probably refers to the gaps he made in enemy lines. His uprising caused the revolutionary government then in power in France to order the end of slavery on Haiti.

Toussaint was enrolled as a general in the French army and fought off invasions by England and Spain. Occupying eastern Hispaniola (Santo Domingo), Toussaint began to dream of independence. The French leader Napoleon Bonaparte began to worry that Toussaint was becoming too powerful. His troops captured Toussaint by treachery and ordered slavery to be reintroduced in Saint Domingue. Toussaint was spirited away to captivity in France, where he died of pneumonia in 1803. He is honored to this day as one of the first in the New World to champion African rights and liberty. In Haiti November 1 is dedicated to his memory.

François-Dominique Toussaint-Louverture wears the uniform of a French general. His faith in the motto of the French Revolution—"Liberty! Equality! Fraternity!"—proved ill-founded.

buccaneers from the pirate base on the offshore island of Tortuga. These were mostly French outlaws who raided Spanish shipping and lived by slaughtering wild cattle. Soon the remote west of the island was effectively French territory, and Spain ceded it to France in 1697. It was known as Saint Domingue.

The French colony prospered. Mulattos (people of mixed African-European

Saint Domingue ceded to France	Slaves revolt against French	Slavery abolished by French government	Toussaint-Louverture made commander in chief by the French	Slavery reintroduced. Slaves rise up and drive out French
1697	**1791**	**1793**	**1797**	**1802**

descent), known as *affranchis* (ah-FRAH-shee), or "freemen," became increasingly powerful on Saint Domingue and soon owned many of the sugar plantations. However, life for the 160,000 or so African slaves on the plantations was probably as brutal and cruel as anywhere in the New World. In 1791 they rose in revolt, inspired by the new ideals of liberty preached during the French Revolution. Violence erupted; mills were burned and owners slaughtered.

The revolutionary government in Paris freed the slaves, who fought off both British and Spanish invasions. However, when Napoleon Bonaparte rose to power in France, he promptly ordered freedom suppressed in Saint Domingue and a return to slavery. In 1804 a slave leader named Jacques Dessalines tore up the French flag and declared the first ever independent Afro-Caribbean republic, to be named Haiti (HAY-tee). Dessalines proved to be a tyrant and was assassinated in 1806.

Many years of civil war followed; fortresses built during this era still dominate the landscape. The French confirmed Haitian independence—for a costly fee—but the country saw a succession of corrupt and brutal rulers. Throughout the rest of the century, the former slaves led lives of grinding poverty, and there was racial violence, with whites and mulattos on one side and blacks on the other.

In 1915 the United States invaded Haiti after a period of extreme violence and instability threatened American business interests there. World War I, which began in Europe the previous year, was already becoming a worldwide conflict. The United States was not yet participating, but it still wished to secure its position in the Caribbean. The American invaders started to build up the country, but the racist attitudes held by many of them toward both blacks and mulattos were widely resented. Between 1918 and 1920 some two thousand Haitians died opposing the U.S. presence. The U.S. troops were withdrawn in 1934. Thousands of desperately poor

Life is tough for this young girl as she toils in the rice fields under a hot sun. Many Haitian children have to work instead of receiving a proper education.

Blacks declare independent republic of Haiti under Jacques Dessalines	United States invades Haiti	Two thousand Haitians die in uprising against United States	François "Papa Doc" Duvalier elected president	Duvalier's son, Jean-Claude ("Baby Doc"), takes power
1804	**1915**	**1918–1920**	**1957**	**1971**

A soldier from the Asian country of Bangladesh stands guard in Port-au-Prince, part of the United Nations peacekeeping force that arrived in 1995.

was ousted by Brigadier General Raoul Cédras the following year. Thousands of Haitians tried to escape the crushing poverty and political violence by sailing to the United States in leaking wooden boats. Many drowned and most were sent back on arrival. In 1994 the United States decided to intervene once again, and Aristide was returned to power, backed by U.S. troops. They were replaced by a United Nations force in 1995, and Aristide supporter René Préval was elected president.

Haitian emigrants sought work in the adjoining Dominican Republic, where they were treated appallingly. It is thought that ten thousand were murdered in 1937 alone.

In 1957 a Haitian doctor named François Duvalier (nicknamed "Papa Doc") was elected president. By 1964 he had become a dictator, unleashing a reign of terror and pouring public funds into his private purse. His secret police, the *tontons macoute* (TOEN-toen mah-KOOT), were everywhere. The name, from Haitian folktales, refers to a ghoulish kidnapper. In 1971 Duvalier died, and his nineteen-year-old son, Jean-Claude ("Baby Doc"), took power. He was overthrown in 1986.

With the election of 1990 it seemed that a new era would dawn, as a democratic Roman Catholic priest named Jean-Bertrand Aristide became president. However, he

Below the Poverty Line

Haiti is the poorest country in the Americas. One percent of the population controls 40 percent of the nation's wealth. Over half the labor force work on the land, many scratching a living from poor, overused soils. Most of the old plantations were divided into small farms in the 1800s. Today, peasants grow corn, millet, sorghum, plantains, yams, and beans and raise chickens and pigs. Gourds (calabashes) are grown, as they are in western Africa, to provide a fleshy vegetable as well as a useful container for carrying water. The Haitian currency, the *gourde* (GOORD), is named after them. Country cooking includes limes, coconuts, and spicy flavorings, and local dishes include tropical fruits, grilled goat, chicken, pork, seafood, rice, and beans.

Coffee, the chief export crop, is grown on Haiti's mountains. Along the Artibonite

Jean-Claude Duvalier flees Haiti amid rioting	Father Jean-Bertrand Aristide elected president	Aristide overthrown by coup	United States invades. Aristide is reinstated as democracy returns	U.S. troops replaced by United Nations force; René Préval elected president
1986	**1990**	**1991**	**1994**	**1995**

Valley rice is the main crop. Sugarcane is refined into sugar or turned into rum, but production has declined, as has the export of sisal, a coarse plant fiber used to make string and rope.

Haiti's factories are based primarily around Port-au-Prince, the capital. Industries include the manufacture of footwear and the processing of vegetable oils. While most Caribbean islands have developed profitable tourist industries in the 1980s and 1990s, Haiti's political violence has kept visitors away.

After Aristide was overthrown in 1991, the United States and other countries brought economic sanctions against Haiti to encourage political reforms. Democracy has returned, but the restoration of international aid and economic reforms has been much too slow, and investors have stayed away. In 1997 Haiti was admitted to the Caribbean Community and Common Market (Caricom).

Many unemployed Haitians live in unhealthy conditions in shantytowns around Port-au-Prince—districts of shacks

Makeshift shacks and muddy jetties line the waterfront near Cap-Haitien in the north of the island. Most Haitians live in very poor, often unhealthy, housing.

and cabins cobbled together from scraps and having no proper water or power supplies. In the countryside peasants live in simple, thatched cottages of timber and clay or in very basic shelters. Some rich Haitians live in old colonial houses, many of which have decorative woodwork and ironwork in the Caribbean style. Others live in modern houses and luxurious apartments.

The poor living conditions are reflected in a very low life-expectancy rate, with men on average living to only fifty-five years old and women to fifty-eight. Health care is poor, with most people relying on traditional medicines that vary from effective herbal remedies to worthless potions. Education, neglected because of generations of political violence, is minimal. Estimates of how many people can read and write vary greatly, but most people agree that the literacy rate is the poorest in the Americas.

People and Language

Haitians may have had little luck over the years, but they are a hospitable and eloquent people. The language of the middle and upper classes may be French, but the language of the nation as a whole is Creole, or *Kreyol* (KRAY-awl). Creole is French that has been heavily influenced by various languages from western Africa. First spoken by the plantation slaves, it was never written down until this century. Today it is recognized as a full language with its own grammar.

Ninety-five percent of the population is of Afro-

Voodoo

From the 1500s onward slaves were seized from the regions of Africa occupied today by Nigeria and Benin and transported to the plantations of the Caribbean. Uprooted and subjected to great cruelty and hardship, many Africans sought comfort in the spiritual beliefs and rituals of their homeland. In Haiti this worship mingled with elements of the Roman Catholic faith, such as a belief in guardian angels and saints, to form a type of worship known as Voodoo, or Vodun (VOO-doo) in Kreyol. Voodoo priests played an important part in inspiring the slave revolts of the 1790s and 1800s.

Voodoo remains at the center of Haitian life and is followed by many who attend Christian churches. It is based on a belief in spirits called loas (LWAH). Important loas include Papa Legba (who acts as a go-between for humans wishing to contact other loas), Erzulie (a kind of Voodoo Virgin Mary), Damballa (the bringer of rain), and Baron Samedi (lord of the graveyard). Animals such as roosters are sacrificed to the loas. Zombies are believed to be the living dead, people without souls.

Voodoo has its own priests and priestesses, and worship takes place in a building called an ounphor (OEN-fore) in Kreyol. Cornmeal is sprinkled into patterns on the floor, and drums are beaten. People dance until they go into a trance, faint, and speak in strange voices that are believed to come from loas.

Caribbean origin, and Haiti is probably the most African country outside Africa. The busy street markets are reminiscent of western Africa. People crowd onto *taptaps* (tap-TAPS), elaborately decorated minibuses and old trucks, painted with slogans and good-luck charms. These are common in many African countries too. There is a love of bright, bold colors on buildings and in dress. And there is Vodun, or Voodoo, the African spirit religion that exists alongside the Roman Catholic faith inherited from the days of French rule. Many people practice both religions. Protestant Episcopalian missionaries from the United States have been active in Haiti for over a hundred years, campaigning against Voodoo.

A Voodoo priest leads the dancing as a rara band takes to the streets. The weekends between carnival and Easter are filled with dancing and music making.

Sound and Color

As in other Caribbean countries, carnival is the chief festival of the year. It starts early in the year, on the Feast of Epiphany (Twelfth Night, January 6), building up to

Drums are at the heart of rara and of every Voodoo ceremony. They provide a direct link with the western African culture brought to Haiti by slaves in the 1600s.

Mardi Gras, the Tuesday before the start of Lent. It is marked by dancing in the packed streets of Port-au-Prince, behind trucks carrying stacks of loudspeakers pumping out music. In Jacmel revelers wear masks and costumes.

Costumed dancers are back on the streets before Easter, forming *rara* (RAH-rah) bands that demand money from passersby. Their music, heavily influenced by Voodoo, is played on drums and homemade trumpets of bamboo. Other major festivals celebrate the harvest and, on All Saints' Day (November 1), mourn the dead.

Music is the true expression of the spirit and has carried the long-suffering Haitians through ages of oppression. To the Voodoo worshipers, drumming is a sacred ritual with African roots. All kinds of other influences have come from France, Spain, and other Caribbean islands. Haiti competes with the Dominican

Republic in claiming to have invented the Latin dance craze called merengue and its close relative, *compas* (KOME-pah). In Haiti you can also dance to *cadance* (KAH-dahns) and *zouk* (ZOOK), pop music of the French Caribbean, and to Cuban salsa and Jamaican reggae. All over Haiti, people meet up for elaborate dance-and-drumming sessions known as *bamboches* (BAHM-boesh).

Haiti is home to many of the best artists and craftspeople in the Caribbean region. Paintings may include scenes of local life and bright and simple abstracts. Wood-carvers specialize in making beautiful drums.

Soccer is the most popular sport. A cruel traditional pastime is cockfighting, in which two birds attack each other in the ring. Haitians love to gamble and will place bets on cockfights, card games, and the national lottery.

Men encourage roosters to battle to death in the cockpit. Each cock tries to slash and wound the other bird with its sharp talons.

HONDURAS

HONDURAS IS THE SECOND LARGEST COUNTRY IN CENTRAL AMERICA.

Islas del Cisne

CARIBBEAN SEA

Roatán   Guanaja
Utila **ISLAS DE LA BAHÍA**

La Ceiba

San Pedro Sula
El Progreso

GUATEMALA

Copán

H O N D U R A S

NICARAGUA

★ **TEGUCIGALPA**

EL SALVADOR

miles 0   40
km 0   60

N

Honduras is bordered by Guatemala on the west, El Salvador on the southwest, and Nicaragua on the southeast. A long Caribbean coast stretches along the north. Its territory includes two groups of islands in the Caribbean. The larger group, 20 miles (32 kilometers) from the mainland, is called the Islas de la Bahía (Bay Islands) and includes three major islands—Utila, Roatán, and Guanaja.

The smaller group of islands, farther east about 60 miles (95 kilometers) from the mainland, is called the Islas del Cisne (the Islands of the Swan). Honduras has a short Pacific coastline on the south.

The lowlands bordering the Caribbean are low, fertile plains, where most of the country's crops are grown. The lowlands bordering the Pacific Ocean are also flat, and used by livestock ranchers. Mountain ranges are scattered over the country. At elevations above 7,000 feet (2,100 meters), the tropical rain forests grow.

CLIMATE

The weather in Honduras varies greatly from one region to another. In the lowlands the temperature is pretty constant at 79°F to 82°F (26°C to 28°C). The highlands average a chilly 58°F (14°C) year-round, with low humidity and cold nights, especially in December and January. On the coasts it rains year-round, as much as 70 to 110 inches (180 to 280 centimeters). The yearly total rainfall in the highlands is 60 to 80 inches (150 to 200 centimeters).

Average January temperature: *60°F (15°C)*

Average July temperature: *80°F (27°C)*

Average annual precipitation: *64 in (162 cm)*

Life on Honduras's Caribbean coast, with a warmer climate and plenty of fresh fish to eat, is much easier than in the interior mountains.

The Mayan Empire in Honduras

The first people to settle in Central America are believed to have arrived by 10,000 B.C.E. They lived by hunting and gathering food. As agriculture caught on and people began to form permanent settlements, variety began to develop in their cultures. Before the Spanish arrived, many groups of Native peoples lived in what is now

Honduras (hahn-DUHR-us). The peoples of the north and center had been part of the Mayan empire; there was a strong capital at Copán in what is now western Honduras, near the Guatemalan border.

In the ancient Mayan city of Copán, carved stelae commemorate Mayan rulers. Archaeologists can "read" some of them but cannot tell whom this one represents.

Timeline:	First people migrate into the land that is now Central America	Development of agriculture	Rise of the Mayan civilization	Peak of the Honduran Mayan site of Copán
	ca. 10,000 B.C.E.	ca. 5000 B.C.E.	ca. 2000 B.C.E.–250 C.E.	ca. 435–820 C.E.

The archaeological site of Copán remains one of the finest existing sites of the Mayan civilization. Copán was built after similar sites to the north (see GUATEMALA and MEXICO). Its growth and decline occurred between 435 and 820 C.E. Archaeologists have learned a lot about the history of Copán from reading the hieroglyphics that are carved on stones and buildings around the old city. Most information comes from tall stone pillars called stelae, made to commemorate a historical event. From them we know of the most powerful ruler of Copán, Smoke Imix, who ruled for sixty-seven years. Under Smoke Imix many battles were fought to win more land and more slaves for the ruling class of Copán. Archaeologists think that Copán may have been abandoned because there were too many people and not enough food for all of them.

The Spanish Colonial Era

Honduras was one of the first places on the Central American mainland to receive the Spaniards. After a decade of island hopping in the Caribbean, Christopher Columbus visited the Bay Islands, while his brother, Bartolomé, landed on the Caribbean coast and claimed it for Spain in 1502. The first decades of Spanish conquest saw as much fighting between groups of Spanish as it saw between the Spanish and the Native people defending their own land. Hernán Cortés tried to claim Honduras for Mexico, which he governed. He had to fight Panama's governor and one of his own soldiers to hold on to the territory. In 1570 Honduras was made part of the territory of Guatemala for the rest of the colonial era.

Life under the Spanish was very hard for the Native peoples. It is estimated that at least three out of four Native people died within the first century of colonialism. Native Americans were captured and forced to work in silver and gold mines or farm the colonial plantations. Those who refused were executed; those who did work under the Spanish died of disease and mistreatment. The greatest of Native leaders was Lempira, of the Lenca people, who led an army against the Spaniards and won. However, Lempira was killed by the

Piracy and the Riches of Honduras

Many mines produced silver and gold in Honduras. Ship after ship, filled with precious objects, headed for Spain to add to the wealth of the Spanish royal family. In the seventeenth and eighteenth centuries, whenever there were riches on a ship, pirates would soon follow. Ships left Honduras from the Caribbean coast and sailed through the Bay Islands on route to Europe. Several groups of pirates made their hideaways in the Bay Islands and preyed on these ships. Most famous of all the pirates was Henry Morgan, who hid on Roatán Island. In the eighteenth century British ships patrolled the coasts and ended all piracy.

Decline of Mayan civilization	Arrival of Spanish on Central American mainland	Honduras declares independence from Spain	Honduras becomes part of the United Provinces of Central America	Honduras declared an independent republic
ca. 900–1500	1502	1821	1823	1838

Large and beautiful churches, such as this church of the Virgin of Sorrows in Tegucigalpa, were built by Spanish colonists in the 1700s.

Spaniards, who broke the promises of a treaty they had made with him, and his people fell under Spanish rule.

The Era of Independence

Honduras claimed independence from Spain in 1821, and in 1823 it became part of the United Provinces of Central America. The United Provinces did not last very long, and Honduras became independent in 1838. Its history from then until the 1950s was a tug-of-war between the Conservative Party and the Liberal Party.

Conservatives favored political action by the Catholic Church, had strong ties to the military, and invested in the factories, plantations, ranches, and mines owned by the upper class. Liberals thought the common person should have political priority and were more active in breaking up the large plantations and factories and in giving poor people a chance to own their own farms and businesses.

In 1957 Honduras elected a Liberal leader who had more impact on his country than most leaders before or since. Ramón Villeda Morales made sure that roads were built and a welfare system was started to care for the poor and elderly. However, a military coup led by Colonel Osvaldo López Arellano overtook the government in 1963. He and the army became the law and the police.

Most of the governments in the twentieth century have been run by the military, and even when the military is not in power through its association with a president, it retreats to the countryside and harasses the government through guerrilla activities until it can regain power. The government and politics of Honduras have changed often and dramatically, so often that Honduran people know no one way of life.

A new president, Carlos Flores Facusse, was inaugurated in 1998. His Liberal Party has appealed to all Hondurans to join in overcoming poverty, improving education and health care, and improving the status of both women and workers. Facusse has reduced the power of the military and has begun to cut government spending.

Liberal president Villeda Morales makes many changes improving life for the poor	Military coup, led by Colonel López Arellano, brings down government	Honduras signs peace plan with Central American neighbors	Liberal Party wins election
1957–1963	**1963**	**1987**	**1998**

333

The People of Honduras Today

Most people in Honduras work in the mines or on farms. Exports to other countries vary, ranging from minerals to crops of bananas, coffee, and sugar. Shrimp from the Caribbean and a variety of wood from the forests are sold to other countries.

Most of the people are of mixed Spanish and Native ancestry. Along the Caribbean coast are the descendants of African and Carib slaves known as the Garifuna (gah-ree-FOO-nah), or Black Caribs (see BELIZE, GUATEMALA, and NICARAGUA). Their ancestors were expelled from Saint Vincent in the Caribbean by the British authorities and exiled to Roatán Island. These people speak their native Arawak, and they follow African and Caribbean customs, especially in their music and dancing, using traditional African-style drums. They are Catholics but combine this religion with practices

Many of the people on the Caribbean coast are Garifuna, the descendants of Carib Indians and Africans who were brought to the Caribbean as slaves.

from African religions. These include elements of ancestor and spirit worship.

Other groups that live separately are the Lenca, who migrated from South America in the eleventh century, and the Chorti, who descend from the Maya. The Lenca (LAIN-kah), who number about fifty thousand, live in farming villages in the west, and the smaller number of Chorti (CHORE-tee), along with the even smaller groups of Pipil (an Aztecan group) and Chorotega (see COSTA RICA), live mostly in the area around Copán. They have retained some of their Mayan customs and beliefs, and some dress traditionally; men wear simple shirts and loose pants; women wear long gathered or wraparound skirts and *huipiles,* shirts made of rectangles of fabric with a hole in the center for the head. All these people still farm in the old way, loosening the soil with hoes, by hand.

Small groups of Miskito (meess-KEE-toe) and Sumo (SOO-moe) Indians live in the forests of northeastern Honduras, in tiny remote villages. They hunt, fish, and plant root crops, much like their ancestors did. More Miskitos, refugees from neighboring Nicaragua, joined them in the 1980s.

Honduras also has some Arabic-speaking Christians from Lebanon and elsewhere in the Middle East, all of whom live in the cities. A small but financially important Jewish community is centered in San Pedro Sula.

Hard Lives in Honduras

Honduran people are some of the poorest in Central America. With high population growth, few jobs, and not enough houses, daily life is focused on meeting very basic needs like getting enough food, a place to live, and clothes to keep warm.

Many people have moved to the cities in hopes of finding work, which has created

A boy in a banana plantation removes white bags before the bananas are harvested. Bananas ripen more slowly and evenly when they are covered in bags.

crowded shantytowns that sprawl around the cities' edges. Life in these shantytowns is no better than it was in the villages, where people at least had a place to grow some food. Wealthier people enjoy all the benefits of city living, with shops, modern buildings, and a lively nightlife of bars, clubs, and restaurants, as well as theater and sporting events.

Most Hondurans, however, live in small villages in the country. Their simple, one-room homes are made of bamboo or sugarcane, often plastered with mud, with dirt floors. Food is cooked over a wood fire. Corn, beans, and rice are the main foods, with bananas and other fruits common but not always available to poor people. More prosperous families eat meat, vegetables, fruits, and fish. Even poorer people along the Caribbean coast eat fish, which they catch in the ocean and rivers.

The education system does not reach people who live deep in the mountains and forests, so many people cannot read or write. There are not enough doctors to look after the sick. As a result, the average life span is short, and many people, especially children, die of diseases like malaria and typhoid.

The biggest holidays for people to relax and have a good time are Catholic holidays and local saints' days. Each town has its own patron saint, whose day is a major festival. Religious festivals are often lively, with singing, dancing, eating, and drinking, and provide a good opportunity to see friends and family. In Native American villages these patron saint festivals are often replaced by traditional holidays that incorporate ancient beliefs.

Although Honduras is less known for its arts than neighboring Guatemala, there is a strong tradition of wood carving, basket making, and pottery. In many villages pots and dishes are still made by the old coiled technique, by laying long, snakelike strips of clay in a tight spiral, then building up the sides and smoothing the coils together before baking the piece to harden. The marimba, a large reed-and-gourd xylophone played by several people, is the national instrument—or was, until it was largely replaced by American-style instruments.

Soccer is the most popular sport, and it is common to see boys and young men playing a game in village squares or in the roads. Honduran people are very proud of their national soccer team. Most people cannot afford their own television sets, but many bars and restaurants have them, and people gather there to watch games with their neighbors. Men also gather in pool halls, which can be found in both cities and small towns.

JAMAICA

JAMAICA IS A MOUNTAINOUS ISLAND rising from the Caribbean Sea
about 90 miles (145 kilometers) south of Cuba.

*The island of Jamaica is part of the Greater
Antilles island chain. It is 146 miles (235
kilometers) from east to west and 51 miles
(82 kilometers) from north to south.*

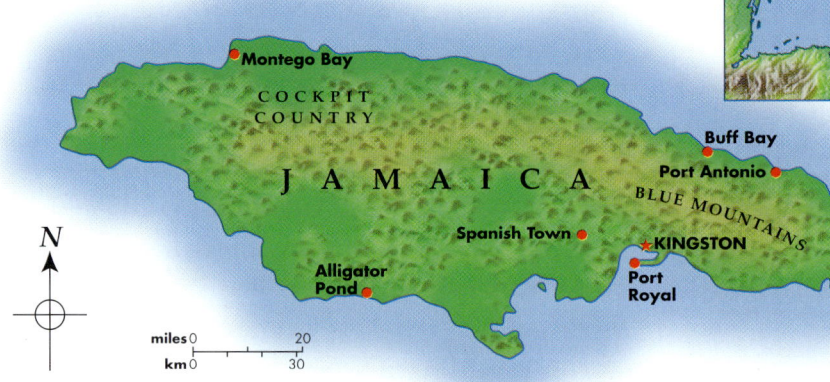

*Flat farmland makes
up the coastal strip.
The island has
sandy beaches
fringed by palms and
offshore coral reefs.*

*Green, forested mountain ranges
occupy the interior, climbing to 7,402 feet
(2,256 meters) above sea level in the Blue
Mountains. In the west, Cockpit Country is a
region of limestone eroded by rivers and rains.*

CLIMATE

*Jamaica has a warm, tropical climate, which is
coolest in the Eastern Highlands. The prevailing
trade winds are from the northeast. Rainfall is
heaviest on the windward side of Blue Mountain
Peak. Between June and November the island is
at risk from hurricanes, which sweep across this
part of the Caribbean.*

Average January temperature: *76°F (24°C)*

Average July temperature: *81°F (27°C)*

Average annual precipitation: *32 in (80 cm)*

Pirates, Planters, and Maroons

About a thousand years ago Arawak-
speaking farmers and hunters settled the
forested, mountainous island they called
Xamayca, the "land of wood and water."
The number of Arawak people on Xamayca
grew to about 100,000. But the Arawak
world was doomed on the day the
Europeans first arrived in the Caribbean.
The Italian explorer Christopher Columbus
landed on Xamayca, which he named
Santiago, in 1494. He thought it was one of
the most beautiful islands on earth.

The Spanish came to settle in 1509 and
built towns, the chief of which was
Santiago de la Vega (now Spanish Town).
They began to kill and enslave the
Arawaks and brought slaves from western

FACTS AND FIGURES

Status: *Independent state*

Capital: *Kingston*

Other towns: *Spanish Town, Montego Bay*

Area: *4,410 square miles (11,422 square kilometers)*

Population: *2,527,000*

Population density: *573 per square mile (221 per square kilometer)*

Peoples: *92 percent Afro-Caribbean or mixed African-European descent; 3 percent European descent; 3 percent Asian or mixed African-Asian descent; 1 percent Chinese or mixed African-Chinese descent; 1 percent other*

Official language: *English*

Currency: *Jamaican dollar*

National day: *Independence Day (August 1)*

Country's name: *Jamaica comes from the Arawak name for the island, Xamayca, meaning "land of wood and water."*

Africa to work for them. By the 1700s not one Arawak remained, though they left behind rock paintings that have survived to this day.

The island was never one of Spain's major colonies, and it was captured by an English task force in 1655. The English called it Jamaica (juh-MAY-kuh), from the Arawak word *Xamayca*.

The English faced some opposition from those Spanish who did not flee and also from African slaves, who had lost one set of masters and did not wish to exchange them for another. They were known as *cimmarón* (SIHM-mahr-rahn), meaning "wild," and

they were later called Maroons. These free Africans fought the authorities for much of the next 140 years.

The English built a fort and settlement at Port Royal, near modern Kingston. The port soon became a base for buccaneers and pirates. These were mostly French, Dutch, and English outlaws from the island of Tortuga (see HAITI). Many Maroons joined the buccaneers. The English were happy to let the buccaneers stay, as long as they attacked the Spanish ships transporting

Freshly netted fish are sold directly from the beach at Alligator Pond on Jamaica's south coast. Fishing provides many Jamaicans with an income.

Timeline:	Arawak peoples settle the island they call Xamayca	Christopher Columbus reaches the island and calls it Santiago; he claims it for Spain	Spanish begin to colonize Jamaica	Spanish kill off the Arawaks and import slaves from Africa
	ca. 1000 C.E.	1494	1509	1515

gold back to Europe. The buccaneers were contracted to form a large private army and attack Spain's mainland territories. One of their leaders, a Welsh rogue named Henry Morgan, was rewarded by being made lieutenant-governor of Jamaica.

In 1692 most of Port Royal was destroyed by a terrifying earthquake, which brought the buildings tumbling down into the sea. Two thousand died and two thousand more were killed by the diseases that then broke out in the devastated town. Many people claimed that Port Royal was being punished by God for its wickedness.

When the political usefulness of the pirates had expired, the English authorities turned against them. Many famous pirates were hanged in Jamaica well into the 1720s.

Women and children in Almond Town, Kingston. The capital's resources have been strained by the many country people who have come there in search of work.

Maroon uprisings and wars continued, but the sugar trade prospered and kept the plantation owners extremely wealthy. Slavery was finally abolished in 1833, but the Africans, who by now formed the majority of the population, were desperately poor. In 1865 they rose under the leadership of Paul Bogle, a preacher, and George William Gordon, a mulatto lawyer, but were crushed. Contracted laborers from China and southern Asia were brought to Jamaica in the nineteenth century.

During the twentieth century, Jamaicans were among the leaders in the Caribbean struggle for democracy. Following the tough years of international economic recession in the 1930s, Jamaicans formed trade unions and also political parties—the People's National Party (PNP) and the Jamaica Labour Party (JLP). As the Age of Empire drew to an end in the mid-twentieth century, Jamaicans received the vote, then home rule, and finally, in 1962, became the first islanders in the British Caribbean to gain full independence.

From the 1950s onward many Jamaicans left to seek work in Great Britain, where their descendants today form a large ethnic group that has made an important contribution to the culture of the capital city, London. Other Jamaicans ended up in the United States and Canada.

The 1960s and 1970s were marked by spectacular sporting

English invade Jamaica and build fort at Port Royal	Wars between English and Maroons	Earthquake destroys most of Port Royal	Maroons granted land	Maroons rebel against British rule	Abolition of slavery
1655	1655–1730s	1692	1739	1795	1807

success within the West Indian (Caribbean) cricket team and by the growing influence of its reggae music throughout the world. One of its leading exponents was singer, songwriter, and guitarist Bob Marley (1945–1981). He became a hero to young people all over the world, including many Africans, not only for his music but for speaking up for black rights.

The political scene was marked by shifts of power between the PNP and the JLP. Policy moved from sympathy for socialism

Bob Marley's house in Kingston is now a museum, with a statue of the late reggae star. This includes his guitar, a soccer ball, and a picture of Haile Selassie.

Marcus Garvey

During the 1800s and 1900s Jamaicans were struggling to improve not only the status of their own Afro-Caribbean population but that of black people everywhere. A leader in this campaign was Marcus Garvey, born in Jamaica in 1887 at the height of the colonial age. Garvey preached black self-respect and power and believed that the best way to achieve this was for Africans in the New World to return to Africa. He visited the United States in 1916 and received great support from African Americans. He went on to set up black-owned businesses in the United States, Africa, and Australia, but was accused of fraud in 1925. He died in London in 1940.

Garvey had a great influence on people of African descent and was an inspiration to later generations, being honored in the lyrics of many reggae songs.

and public ownership of industries to support for a capitalist free market. Elections were notoriously violent, and in 1980 five hundred people died in political mayhem. In 1995 a new political party was founded, the National Democratic Movement (NDM). It called for a new republican constitution, attempting to end the situation in which Jamaica's head of state is still the British sovereign. Thus far, the NDM has been unsuccessful at changing this situation.

Uprising against colonial authorities	Fall in world price of sugar	Full home rule	Jamaica becomes fully independent nation	Five hundred die during election riots	Severe hurricane damage
1865	1930s	1959	1962	1980	1988

Ras Tafari

Many Jamaicans follow the religious beliefs that have come to be known as Rastafarianism. The name comes from Ras Tafari, one of the royal titles of a former emperor of Ethiopia, Haile Selassie (1891–1975), who is still revered as a great spiritual leader.

The Rastafarian movement started in the slums of Kingston in the early 1930s. Rastafarians see themselves as one of the lost tribes of Israel, led into captivity in Babylon by the whites who enslaved them. The spirit of God, protector of the oppressed, is called Jah. The message of the Rastafarians is one of love and peace. Africa, and Ethiopia in particular, is believed to be the Promised Land. Because of this belief, Rastafarianism has been heavily influenced by the ideas of Marcus Garvey.

In the 1960s and 1970s Rastafarianism became closely associated with popular music and with radical politics. Many Rastafarians smoke the illegal drug marijuana, known in Jamaica as ganja *(gahn-JAH). Hair, which is never cut, is tangled into dreadlocks, as worn at times in the past by some of the peoples of eastern Africa.*

A Rastafarian family stands outside their home in Port Antonio. The man has dreadlocks, and the woman wears a long dress and head covering.

Jamaicans at Work

Jamaica's biggest moneymaker is bauxite, the ore that is processed to make aluminum. The island is the third biggest producer in the world. The industry is profitable, but it creates environmental hazards, such as acid dust. Developments in automation have led to a decline in employment; surface mining now employs less than one percent of the workforce. The island also has reserves of gypsum, used in making plaster of paris. Factories produce garments for export.

Tourism is now a major source of national income, with tourists arriving by plane or by luxury cruise liner. Wages in the tourist industry are low.

About 20 percent of the Jamaican population works the land. Sugarcane is

Young girls in neat dresses attend primary school. The Jamaican government provides free education for all children between the ages of six and fifteen.

chicken are served with rice. Jerked (barbecued) meats are sold from stalls. Food is often hot and spicy, with influences from Africa, China, and India.

While a few Jamaicans earn high wages and are wealthy, many others are very poor. Country people have headed into Kingston over the years, where many end up living in makeshift cabins in shantytowns, where there is a high rate of crime and little chance of getting work. This situation was vividly expressed to an international audience in a 1973 film called *The Harder They Come*, starring Jimmy Cliff. Today national unemployment stands at about 16 percent. Over half of Jamaicans are now city dwellers.

still the most important export crop, and the sugar industry is scheduled for expansion. One of its most famous by-products is Jamaican rum. Bananas, coffee, cacao, coconuts, and citrus fruits are also grown for commercial use.

Away from the big plantations, country dwellers produce food for their own families and for the local market. They grow yams, plantains (large bananas used for cooking), breadfruit, pigeon peas, and tropical fruits such as mangoes. They may also raise goats, pigs, and chickens. Traditional Jamaican foods include akee (a yellow fruit) and cod. Shrimp, crayfish, and snapper are popular, and meats such as curried goat or

Pineapples are among the fruits on display at the market in Port Antonio. This beautiful old town on the north coast is the center of Jamaica's export trade in bananas.

A woman goes into a state of trance, singing and dancing. She follows the kumina rituals of spirit worship that came to the Caribbean from Africa.

The education system is effective, and over 85 percent of the adult population is able to read and write. The reform of Jamaica's once generous welfare state has left hospitals short of funding in recent years. Life expectancy is seventy-one years for men and seventy-six for women.

Jamaica Talk

Most of the people of Jamaica are descended from the Maroons who escaped into the hills and from slaves brought into the Caribbean from western Africa by Spanish and English settlers. Over the years many mixed with the island's other peoples—the British or the various Asian peoples who arrived in the nineteenth century.

The language that survived this mixture is English mixed with African language structures and pronunciations. The island dialect is known as Jamaica Talk, or Creole. It varies a great deal. The Jamaica Talk of

the middle and upper classes is strongly influenced by the upper-class English pronunciation common in southern Great Britain today. The Jamaica Talk of villages and shantytowns, on the other hand, is very difficult for an outsider to understand. The Rastafarians too have introduced their own variant, a kind of "soul" language. Whatever the kind of Jamaica Talk, speakers share a love of words and wordplay, of humor and irony.

National Passions

The great majority of Jamaicans are Christians. They are keen churchgoers who wear their best clothes on Sunday. There are many different groups, from Seventh-Day Adventists to Church of God, from Anglican to Baptist. The small number of Jamaicans of Asian descent mostly follow the Roman Catholic, Muslim, or Hindu faiths.

African beliefs brought over by the slaves have also affected modern Jamaicans. There is a fairly widespread belief in spirits that can be summoned by drum music, and by magic and animal sacrifice. These rituals, known as *kumina* (koo-mih-NAH), are very similar to Haitian Voodoo (see HAITI). Traditional African and Christian beliefs merge in Pocomania, a form of worship that involves preaching, dancing, and speaking in "tongues," a form of religious ecstasy in which people speak in unknown languages.

Music not only plays an important part in Jamaican worship, it dominates everyday life. Loudspeakers are loud and pump out unique Jamaican sounds in many a city street. It all started with the work songs of the plantations in the 1800s. In the 1900s came a dance craze called *mento* (men-TOE), marked by humorous, outrageous lyrics. In the 1960s came the chirpy dance music of ska and bluebeat, which soon spread to Great Britain via Jamaican immigrants. The loud bass and drum line then developed the slow rhythms of rocksteady and dub, and from there to reggae, a somewhat faster music that became—and remains—popular all over the world. A reggae music festival called Sun Splash is held each year in Montego Bay. Rap and reggae have fused to form dancehall, which is dance music with indecent lyrics.

Another national passion is cricket, a bat and ball game introduced by the British. It is played all over the island wherever there is green space. This small island is also enjoying increasing international success with soccer.

Carnival only became a major event in Jamaica in recent years and is heavily influenced by the Trinidad celebrations. It is held around Easter. The word *festival* is used to describe the Independence Day holiday at the start of August, which is marked by parades and music. December is the time for a much older custom, dating back to the slaves who arrived from western Africa. John Canoe (originally from the African Jonkonnu) is a masquerade in which mummers dressed as animals or stock characters such as policemen, pregnant women, and Indians, dance through the street, demanding treats. The most important Christian festival of the year is Christmas Day, when many people attend church. Christmas food includes rich fruitcake and spiced wine.

Old-style mento music is re-created at Buff Bay. Mento, a type of folk music that reached its peak of popularity between 1900 and the 1940s, is a predecessor of reggae.

Glossary

bauxite: a mineral from which aluminum is made.

Breton: a person from Brittany, a part of western France that was once an independent country. The Bretons are descended primarily from Celts who fled from Britain during its invasion by Angles and Saxons during the sixth to ninth centuries.

buccaneer: an outlaw, usually European, who settled in the Caribbean from the 1630s onward.

cacao: a small, evergreen shrub, first grown in the American tropics. The seeds of the plant are used to make cocoa and chocolate.

capitalist policies: decisions based on an economic system in which land, factories, and other ways of producing goods are owned and controlled by individuals, not the government.

cassava: a plant with fleshy tuber roots, used as a food.

commodity: a product that can be traded or sold for a profit.

concession: a right that has been granted.

cooperative: a group of people working together to achieve the same thing. Craftspeople often form cooperatives to sell their work at a better price and to more people than they could on their own.

copal: an incense made from the dried sap of a tree, used by the Maya when they pray to their gods.

coup: a change of government brought about by force.

economic sanctions: measures taken to prevent or limit trade with a particular country. The aim is to force that country to change its political system or its policies.

eco-tourism: tourism that takes the environment, animals, and plants into account.

escarpment: the steep face or cliff of a mountain ridge or range of hills.

European Union: an alliance of European nations committed to economic union and closer political integration. It developed out of the European Economic Community (founded in 1957).

floodgate: A gate that can be opened or closed to allow water in or keep it out.

free market: an economy in which goods can be traded with minimal interference from the government.

guillotine: a wooden framework with a blade that drops, used to behead people.

home rule: self-government without full independence. For example, Greenland governs its own affairs (apart from foreign policy) but is still a dependency of Denmark.

house arrest: an official order banning someone from leaving their home.

impromptu: improvised, unplanned.

indigenous: relating to a people who were born within a country or a region as opposed to being immigrants or settlers. Also *aboriginal* or *native*.

Lent: the forty days between Ash Wednesday and Easter in the Christian calendar.

masquerade: a celebration at which people wear masks, disguises, or fancy outfits.

mayhem: violent rioting or fighting, causing injury or death.

mummer: a person wearing a festival costume, a mask, or a disguise. Mummers may perform plays or music in the street or call from house to house, demanding gifts.

plummet: to plunge or drop rapidly.

regatta: a boat race or series of boat races.

republic: a country in which power rests with the people and their elected representatives. A president usually heads a republic.

revolution: the overthrow of a government or political system; a complete change.

revolutionary: someone who supports or takes part in a revolution.

shaman: a Siberian word for priest, healer, or holy person. The word now refers to a religious healer or diviner in various cultures.

slash-and-burn agriculture: the practice of felling trees and clearing the ground by burning, then using it for crops for a few years before moving on.

socialism: a political theory in which the community as a whole controls land, property, industry, and money, and organizes them for the good of all the people.

socialist: someone who believes in the theory of socialism.

social welfare: services that aim to help people with problems such as poverty, unemployment, poor public health, and illiteracy.

sorghum: a grain crop commonly grown in hot countries.

speaking in tongues: calling out or making sounds during a religious trance.

trade union (or labor union): an organization of workers formed to benefit workers by trying to raise wages and improve working conditions.

tundra: a polar or mountaintop region where there are few, if any, trees. The climate is so cold that the soil remains frozen beneath the surface year-round.

Further Reading

Greenland
Alexander, Bryan, and Cherry Alexander. *The Eskimos.* New York: Crescent Books, 1997.
Buell, Janet. *Greenland Mummies.* New York: Twenty First Century Books, 1998.
Lepthien, Emilie U. *Greenland.* Danbury, CT: Childrens Press, 1989.
Levine, Charlotte. *Danish Dependencies.* Broomall, PA: Chelsea House, 1989.

Grenada
Eisenberg, Joyce. *Grenada.* Broomall, PA: Chelsea House, 1988.

Guatemala
Brill, Marlene Targ, and Harry R. Targ. *Guatemala.* Danbury, CT: Childrens Press, 1993.
Cummins, Ronnie, and Rose Welch. *Guatemala.* Milwaukee, WI: Gareth Stevens, 1990.
Hadden, Gerry, ed. *Teenage Refugees from Guatemala Speak Out.* New York: Rosen
      Publishing Group, 1997.
Nach, James. *Guatemala in Pictures.* Minneapolis, MN: Lerner Group, 1987.

Guyana
Brill, Marlene Targ. *Guyana.* Danbury, CT: Childrens Press, 1994.
Department of Geography Staff. *Guyana in Pictures.* Minneapolis, MN: Lerner Group, 1988.

Haiti
Anthony, Suzanne. *Haiti.* Broomall, PA: Chelsea House, 1989.
Goldish, Meish. *Crisis in Haiti.* Brookfield, CT: Millbrook Press, 1995.
Myers, Walter Dean. *Toussaint L'Ouverture: The Fight for Haiti's Freedom.* Old Tappan, NJ:
      Simon and Schuster, 1996.
Ngcheong-Lum, Roseline. *Cultures of the World: Haiti.* Tarrytown, NY: Marshall
      Cavendish, 1994.

Honduras
Targ, Harry R., and Marlene Targ Brill. *Honduras.* Danbury, CT: Childrens Press, 1995.
Weddle, Ken. *Honduras in Pictures.* Minneapolis, MN: Lerner Group, 1987.

Jamaica
Barraclough, John. *Jamaica.* Crystal Lake, IL: Rigby Interactive Library, 1996.
Capek, Michael. *Jamaica.* Minneapolis, MN: Carolrhoda Books, 1998.
Sheehan, Sean. *Cultures of the World: Jamaica.* Tarrytown, NY: Marshall Cavendish, 1996.

Islands of the Caribbean
Mason, Antony. *The Caribbean.* Parsippany, NJ: Silver Burdett Press, 1988.
Mayer, T. W. *The Caribbean and Its People.* New York: Thomson Learning, 1995.
Springer, Eintou P. *The Caribbean.* Parsippany, NJ: Silver Burdett Press, 1987.
Walker, Cas. *The Caribbean.* North Pomfret, VT: Trafalgar Square Publishing, 1991.

Index

Page numbers in *italic* indicate illustrations.

Page numbers in *italic* indicate illustrations.

REFERENCE

PEOPLES
of the
AMERICAS

PEOPLES

of the

AMERICAS

Volume 5
Cuba–French Guiana

MARSHALL CAVENDISH
NEW YORK • LONDON • TORONTO • SYDNEY

Marshall Cavendish Corporation
99 White Plains Road
Tarrytown, New York 10591-9001

Consulting Editor: J. Patrick Gray, Professor of Anthropology, University of Wisconsin

Consultants: Jean-Marc Blais, Senior Interpretive Planner, Canadian Museum of Civilization, Hull, Quebec
      David Frye, Assistant Director, Department of Latin American and Caribbean Studies, University of Michigan

Spanish Consultant: Fran Kaplan

Contributing authors: D. L. Birchfield
      Marion Morrison
      Juliette Radcliffe Rogers
      Philip Steele
      Mary A. Stout

Discovery Books
    Managing Editor: Paul Humphrey
    Project Editor: Helen Dwyer
    Text Editor: Valerie J. Weber
    Design Concept: Ian Winton
    Designers: Barry Dwyer, Ian Winton, and Simon Borrough
    Cartographer: Stefan Chabluk

Marshall Cavendish
    Editorial Director: Paul Bernabeo
    Editor: Marian Armstrong
    Associate Editor: Debra M. Jacobs

The publishers would like to thank the following for their permission to reproduce photographs:
James Davis Travel Photography (254, 257); Douglas Donne Bryant Stock Photography (John Mitchell 246; Suzanne Murphy-Larronde 245, 249); Eye Ubiquitous (Tim Page 241; Gavin Wickham 232); Hutchison Library (Eric Lawrie 255; N. Durrell McKenna 248; Nigel Sitwell 275; John Wright 265); Panos Pictures (Martin Adler 270; Trygve Bolstad 235; Jeremy Horner 247, 260; Philip Wolmuth 243 right); David Simson 243 left; South American Pictures (252; Robert Francis 271 top, 272; Edward Parker 266; Corinne Peignon 279 bottom; Rolando Pujol cover, 231, 233, 234, 236, 237, 239, 240; Tony Morrison frontispiece, 238, 251 top & bottom, 256, 258, 259, 261, 262, 263, 264, 267, 277, 279 top, 280 top & bottom, 281, 282, 283; Chris Sharp 269, 271 bottom, 273)

(frontispiece) Wayana boy in French Guiana using a cassava press.

Editor's note: Many systems of dating have been used by different cultures throughout history. *Peoples of the Americas* uses B.C.E. (Before Common Era) and C.E. (Common Era) instead of B.C. (Before Christ) and A.D. (Anno Domini, "In the Year of the Lord") out of respect for the diversity of the world's peoples.

Library of Congress Cataloging-in-Publication Data
Peoples of the Americas.
        p.   cm.
      Includes bibliographical references and index.
      Contents: v. 1. Anguilla–Belize — v. 2. Bermuda–Brazil — v. 3. Canada–Cayman Islands — v. 4. Chile–Costa Rica — v. 5. Cuba–French Guiana — v. 6. Greenland–Jamaica — v. 7. Martinique–Paraguay — v. 8. Peru–Turks and Caicos Islands — v. 9. United States of America — v. 10. United States of America–Virgin Islands

      ISBN 0-7614-7050-6 (set)
      1. Ethnology—America—Juvenile literature. 2. America—History—Juvenile literature. [1. Ethnology—America. 2. America—History.]
E29.A1P46 1999
970'.004—dc21
                                                         98-2801
                                                       CIP
                                                       AC

      ISBN 0-7614-7050-6 (set)
      ISBN 0-7614-7055-7 (vol. 5)

Printed and bound in Italy

Contents

CUBA

CUBA IS THE LARGEST ISLAND IN THE CARIBBEAN and lies 90 miles (145 kilometers) off the Florida coast.

Cuba lies at the western end of the Antilles chain of islands. Its nearest neighbor is Haiti, 48 miles (77 kilometers) to the east. Florida, in the United States, is 90 miles (145 kilometers) to the north.

Cuba boasts three mountain ranges. The island's highest peak, Pico Turquino at 6,476 feet (1,974 meters), towers in the Sierra Maestra range in the east. Swamps, marshes, and mangrove forests line the southern coast. Much of the northern coast is rocky. Cuba includes more than sixteen hundred islets and cays. Most people live along the coast and on fertile plains between the mountain ranges.

CLIMATE

The rainy season stretches from May to October and the dry season from November to April. Temperatures are higher in the rainy season than in the dry season. Between December and February cold fronts can arrive suddenly from the north; the sky remains overcast, it rains, and temperatures drop. Hurricanes have hit Cuba many times; Hurricane Flora killed four thousand people in 1963.

Average January temperature: *72°F (22°C)*

Average July temperature: *82°F (28°C)*

Average annual precipitation: *48 in (122 cm)*

Native Peoples Encounter the Spanish

The original inhabitants of Cuba (KYOO-buh) were the Ciboney, hunter-gatherers who probably migrated from South or Central America around 1000 B.C.E. Some anthropologists believe they date back to 3500 B.C.E. Traveling in canoes, the Ciboney gathered much of their food from the sea and lived in caves. Around 300 C.E. Taino people began to arrive in Cuba from the Orinoco River basin in Venezuela.

230

FACTS AND FIGURES

Official name: *República de Cuba*

Status: *Independent state*

Capital: *Havana*

Major cities: *Santiago de Cuba, Camagüey*

Area: *42,827 square miles (110,992 square kilometers)*

Population: *11,100,000*

Population density: *259 per square mile (100 per square kilometer)*

Peoples: *66 percent European descent; 21 percent mulatto; 12 percent African descent; 1 percent Asian descent and other*

Official language: *Spanish*

Currency: *Cuban peso, "convertible" peso (equal to one U.S. dollar), U.S. dollar*

National days: *Day of the Triumph of the Revolution (January 1); Day of the Workers/International Labor Day (May 1); Day of the Insurrection (July 26); Anniversary of the War of Independence in 1868 (October 10)*

Country's name: *Cuba was the name used by the indigenous people of the island.*

The explorer Christopher Columbus landed in Cuba in 1492, and the first Spanish invasion in 1511 met little resistance. The Spanish founded a settlement at Baracoa on the east coast in 1512. The Spaniards then marched west, massacring Native people along the way. By 1516 they had established seven garrison towns, including Santiago de Cuba, the capital until 1553.

The Spaniards divided the land among themselves and tried to enslave the remaining Native people. Within a few years of the Spaniards' settling in Cuba, the estimated 112,000 Native inhabitants had been reduced to 3,000. Whole villages committed mass suicide, and many Natives died through ill-treatment and diseases introduced from Europe.

Sugar grew well in Cuba, and during the sixteenth century the Spaniards brought black slaves from Africa to work the plantations. At the end of the eighteenth

Farmers and potters, these Arawak-speaking Indians lived in thatched huts in villages of up to two thousand people and had complex religious and burial customs. The Taino pushed the Ciboney into the far west of the island.

This nineteenth-century print of Havana shows the colonial fort and walls built by the Spanish. Some of the forts have survived to this day.

Timeline:	Ciboney settle in Cuba	Taino arrive from Venezuela	Christopher Columbus lands in Cuba	Spanish invade island
	ca. 1000 B.C.E.	ca. 300 C.E.	1492	1511

century, following a revolt in the French colony now called Haiti, some French settlers and slaves arrived in Cuba, settling mainly in the east.

The first half of the nineteenth century was a prosperous time for plantation owners. Cuba's sugar industry became the strongest in the Caribbean, and by 1860 Cuba was producing nearly one-third of the world's sugar. But plantation owners wanted to be free of trading restrictions imposed by Spain. The Spanish crushed the first Cuban rebellion (1868–1878); 250,000 Cubans died, and the sugar industry was virtually destroyed. U.S. landowners bought up Cuban sugar plantations at bargain prices.

The Spanish Leave, the Americans Arrive

A new uprising against Spain began in 1895. The United States wanted to extend its influence in the area, and in 1898 it intervened in the war on Cuba's side. This led to the Spanish-American War, which the United States won, establishing its influence over Cuba.

Cuba was declared a republic in 1902, and the American government left the island—but on the condition that Cuba give the United States the right to intervene in Cuban affairs. It was a false freedom for Cuba: U.S. businesses bought up land and plantations, and U.S. troops landed regularly to protect U.S. business interests.

Thousands of Spanish immigrants arrived, taking over trade and small businesses. U.S. companies dominated Cuba's big businesses, controlling the electricity, railroad, and telephone networks. At the bottom of the economic ladder, former slaves struggled to survive by working on the sugar plantations or farming their own meager plots. In 1912 they rebelled and approximately three thousand were killed.

Cuba became the playground of rich Americans, with new, modern hotels and casinos, many controlled by the Mafia. The decadent lifestyle was in sharp contrast to the poverty of most Cubans. In 1940 Fulgencio Batista y Zaldívar became president. Corrupt and cruel, he suppressed all opposition. In 1953 a group of revolutionaries led by Fidel Castro failed in an attempt to take the Moncada barracks in Santiago de Cuba. Castro was imprisoned and then exiled. He made his way back in 1956 with a small band of guerrillas and continued his attacks on the

Fidel Castro, who led the successful revolution in 1959 and has been the head of Cuba's government since then. Now in his seventies, he still enjoys popular support.

Black slaves imported from Africa	French and their slaves arrive from Haiti	Ten Years' War fails to make Cuba independent	Slavery abolished	Cuban War of Independence
1500s	**late 1700s**	**1868–1878**	**1886**	**1895**

government until, on New Year's Day, 1959, Batista was forced into exile.

Castro became prime minister and then president. One of his first actions was to nationalize, or take over, U.S. businesses, which immediately antagonized the U.S. government. At the same time, the Communist Soviet Union and eastern European governments offered Cuba help. In 1961 an invasion organized by the U.S. Central Intelligence Agency (CIA) to overthrow the Castro government was easily resisted. The next year the United States discovered that the Soviet Union was planning to use Cuba as a nuclear missile base. The United States threatened to

Che Guevara

Ernesto "Che" Guevara was born in Argentina in 1928. After graduating from medical school in 1953, he hitchhiked around South and Central America. In Mexico he met the exiled Fidel Castro and joined the guerrillas.

Guevara commanded units during the Cuban Revolution and, as a committed Marxist, later became an important member of the new government. He was affectionately known to everyone as Che, meaning "buddy" or "mate."

To the surprise of many people in 1965, Guevara gave up his posts in the Cuban government and set off for South America to ignite another revolution among poor peasants in the Andes. In 1967 he was captured by the Bolivian military and executed. He became a martyr and national hero; before school each morning Cuban children recite the slogan "Pioneers of communism, we shall be like Che."

Primary school children in the Plaza de la Revolución in Havana. Behind them is a metal sculpture of Ernesto "Che" Guevara, the revolutionary hero.

Cuba declared a republic	Fulgencio Batista y Zaldívar becomes president	Fidel Castro and his guerrillas unsuccessfully attack Moncada barracks	Castro and guerrillas return to Cuba	Batista flees into exile
1902	**1940**	**1953**	**1956**	**1959**

invade and to use nuclear weapons itself. The Soviets withdrew, but the U.S. government imposed a trade embargo to punish Cuba. As of 1998, American companies were still not allowed to trade with Cuba, and the U.S. government also passed a law forbidding U.S. trade with any other companies that themselves do business with the island.

Cuba became a Communist state in 1961 and, with the financial help of the Soviet Union, transformed its educational and health services. The 1970s were good years for Cubans, but by 1980 poor management of the economy created severe shortages, and many people wanted to leave. Cuba was also heavily criticized for its human rights abuses and its torture and execution of political prisoners.

The breakup of the Soviet Union in the early 1990s devastated Cuba, as financial aid and trading links were withdrawn. Since 1990, when Castro started rationing food, medicines, gasoline, and many other items under the Special Period in Peacetime decree, Cubans have undergone hard times. The program aimed to conserve energy—factories and offices were closed, public transportation became nearly impossible to find, and tractors gave way to horses and carts. Daily power shortages plague Cubans. Despite all their hardships, however, Cubans are among the warmest and most hospitable people in the Caribbean.

Life in Cuba

Cuba's population consists of whites, who are mainly descended from the Spanish, mulattos of mixed Spanish and black parentage, blacks, and Chinese. The revolutionary government has aimed for racial equality and has been largely successful in this, though there are still relatively few blacks in top jobs. Most blacks live in Havana and nearby Matanzas. For many years there was a Chinatown area in Havana, but this has almost disappeared, as the Chinese have died or intermarried.

The Cuban government's top priorities have been to improve Cubans' access to education and health care, which, before

Trinidad, founded in 1514, is one of the oldest cities in Cuba. Close to one of Cuba's main sugar-producing regions, it was a wealthy town in colonial days.

United States attempts to invade Cuba	USSR's missiles in Cuba provoke crisis with the United States	125,000 people leave Cuba for the United States	Special Period in Peacetime begins	30,000 people reach Florida in makeshift boats
1961	**1962**	**1980**	**1990**	**1994**

At the age of fifteen, Cuban girls celebrate their coming of age with a party, the Quinceañera, for family and friends. Their dresses are specially made for the occasion.

the revolution, were virtually nonexistent for poor people. In 1960 Castro vowed to eliminate illiteracy. He sent more than a quarter of a million teachers and schoolchildren into the countryside to teach peasants how to read and write. All Cuban children have free schooling and financial help with their school uniforms. Nurseries and kindergartens care for children from six months old to six years old so that their mothers can leave home to work. Most schools for younger children have a resident doctor or nurse and provide free meals. Today over forty universities provide college education.

Cuba also has an extensive health care system. Doctors and nurses work in every part of the island; every village has its own small medical clinic. Many serious diseases have been eliminated and others greatly reduced. Cubans can now expect to live to about seventy-five, a life expectancy similar to that in developed countries.

The Special Period has damaged this amazing turnaround in education and health services. Not enough equipment is available for either the schools or the hospitals, and standards are falling. Rationing food and other goods has also put a lot of pressure on family life, and the divorce rate is high.

The high divorce rate also reflects the newfound confidence of women, who now make up 40 percent of the workforce. But traditional family roles remain strong. In Cuba, as in many Hispanic cultures, the man is supposed to be the head of the family and the woman's role is as the mother and housekeeper. A girl's fifteenth birthday, announcing she is ready to consider marriage, is still celebrated.

The Spaniards brought Roman Catholicism to Cuba, and today about 41 percent of the population has been baptized. Since the revolution, religion has not been encouraged, although a visit by Fidel Castro to the Vatican and the pope's visit to Cuba in 1998 seem to herald change. People often go to church in time of trouble, and at the height of the Special Period (1993), church-going boomed, and many children attended Sunday school.

Habaneros: People of the Capital

Habaneros are the people of Havana, the capital, which today has a population of over two million. The city sprawls along the coast, divided from the sea by a four-mile- (seven-kilometer-) long road, the Malecón, where people fish, stroll, and meet to chat. The old colonial center, with

Celebrating the Day of the Kings, a fiesta in honor of the African gods, or orishas. Because of the Special Period, many of these fiestas are currently not taking place.

Santería: From Africa to Cuba

Many people in Cuba follow Santería (sahn-tay-REE-ah), an African-Cuban religion of the Yoruba people of Nigeria, the region from which most slaves came to Cuba. Central to Santería are orishas *(oe-REE-shahss), or gods, who rule people's lives and communicate with their followers on behalf of Orula, the supreme god. To keep their religion alive when their owners would have suppressed it, the slaves disguised their gods behind the names and images of Catholic saints. For example, Saint Lazarus is Babalú-Ayé; the Virgin of Charity, the patron saint of Cuba, is Ochún; and Saint Barbara is Changó, the god of fire, thunder, passion, and dance.*

Santería priests, who are all male, are called babalawos *(bah-bah-LAH-woess). They give advice and guidance. Among the various items used in their divination sessions is a chain with eight pieces of coconut shell. When swung, this can fall into over 250 different combinations, each of which has a meaning for the babalawo.*

forts, the cathedral, and the Plaza des Armas, stands near the harbor. Next to it is the suburb where fine mansions, hotels, and tree-lined streets were built during the first half of this century. Further along lie some once-affluent residential suburbs, and beyond these stand Soviet-style apartment complexes built after the revolution.

A housing shortage has become critical during the Special Period, with many families living in apartments in converted mansions that are now crumbling into ruins. Their kitchens have only the bare necessities, and water and electricity shortages occur frequently.

Transportation has also fallen victim to the Special Period. Havana has become a city of bicycles, vintage American cars, and

A group of cyclists wait for traffic to pass in Havana. Bicycles and buses are the most common means of transportation in Cuba today; private cars are rarely seen.

camellos (kah-MAY-yoess), enormously long vehicles shaped like camels. They run on regular routes, carry up to 250 passengers

Cubans in Exile

About a million Cubans are living in exile, mostly in Florida. Landowners and wealthy executives were the first to flee after the 1959 revolution. In 1980 public protests over the economic state of the country reached such a level that Castro allowed some 125,000 to leave in what became known as the Mariel boat lift.

A similar exodus occurred in 1994, when the effects of the Special Period were at their worst. Thirty thousand people fled in makeshift crafts and boats, mainly to

*Florida. They are known as **balseros** (bahl-SAY-roes), or rafters, since they risk their lives on flimsy rafts made from tires, barrels, and foam rubber, with bed sheets or sugar sacks as sails. The oldest known balsero was a ninety-one-year-old grandmother. Many did not make it.*

In 1994 the U.S. government changed its policy on fleeing Cubans; they are no longer granted automatic political asylum but have to join the line of other would-be legal immigrants into the United States.

who pay a twenty-cent fare, and are usually packed. Taxis cruise for those who can afford them, but very few people own private cars.

Economic Troubles Plague Cubans

Compared with Havana, other Cuban cities are small. Santiago de Cuba has a population of less than 400,000 people, and Camagüey, the third largest, has less than 300,000. All suffer the same difficulties as the Habaneros.

Finding enough to eat is most people's main priority. Since rationing began during the Special Period, families are restricted in what they can buy. All food, soap, matches, and even tobacco and rum, major products of the islands, are rationed. People line up for hours when they hear that bread or eggs might be coming into the government store. But if they have the money, everything, including imported goods, can be bought off the shelves of the black market or the "dollar stores."

The crisis has forced the government to make some changes to the currency. Now three types of currency circulate: the peso, the "convertible peso," and the dollar. One convertible peso equals one U.S. dollar. People are paid in all three currencies, but only dollars or convertible pesos can be used in the dollar stores.

Life for people earning just pesos is tough. The average income is equivalent to ten American dollars a month. Many must find other ways to make money—a second job, perhaps, or making and selling things in the market.

At the beginning of communism in Cuba, the government controlled all businesses. Now the government has made some private enterprises legal. People can apply for a license to be independent traders: hairdressers and barbers, knife sharpeners and shoe repairers, booksellers, and artists now work on Cuba's streets.

Campesinos: People of the Countryside

People living in rural areas are generally known as *campesinos* (kahm-pay-SEE-noess). Like the people of Havana and other towns, they have suffered during the Special Period, although many do have the advantage of a small plot of land where they can grow vegetables or keep a few chickens. The government allowed people who owned a piece of land before the revolution to keep it but nationalized the large estates.

Since the revolution, most villages have developed along roads or were built in specific places. Soviet-style apartment blocks of five or six stories, now rather run-down, form the core of some villages, with a store, a medical post, and a school, but no church.

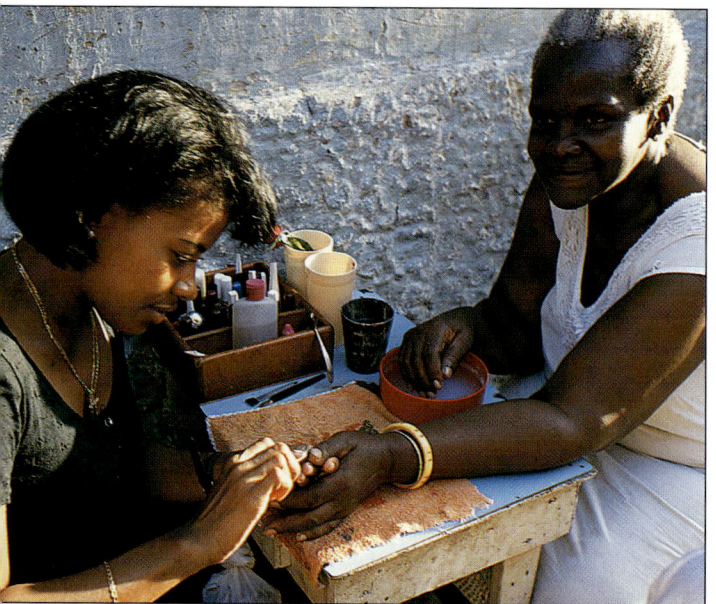

People in Cuba have recently been allowed to set up as independent traders, as long as they have a license. This manicurist works outside on a table on a Havana street.

Since the government introduced the Special Period in Cuba, it has been difficult for people to get enough food. In rural areas many people grow their own crops and raise animals.

West of Havana is the province of Pinar del Río, which provides the best tobacco in Cuba. Traditional peasant farmers, called *guajiros* (gwah-HEE-roess), live in *bohíos* (boe-EE-yoess), wooden houses with thatched roofs. Outside is a porch with a rocking chair or hammock. Farmers do most of their work by hand. There are few vehicles and little gas, so plows are drawn by oxen and seeds sown by hand. Crops include coffee, rice, a sweet potato called *boniato* (boe-NYAH-toe), bananas, citrus fruits, and the root vegetables *malanga* (mah-LAHN-gah) and yucca.

East of Havana, in the center of Cuba, lie large sugar plantations, fruit orchards, rice fields, and cattle ranches. The sugar plantations—and some cattle ranches—have housing for workers, a school, a church, and some even have a small hospital.

Ballet and Film

The two forms of art that have survived most successfully since the revolution are ballet and film. Alicia Alonso, affectionately known as the First Lady of Cuba, leads the Cuban National Ballet. Performing dances by Cuban choreographers, the ballet is widely acclaimed at home and abroad.

The film industry has grown since the revolution. Used at first for propaganda, some recent productions have been openly critical of aspects of the Cuban system and society. The film *Fresa y Chocolate (Strawberry and Chocolate)*, which deals with homosexuality, a subject not openly discussed in Cuba, won an award at the Berlin Festival in 1994. Since 1979 Cuba has hosted a Latin American film festival that attracts filmmakers from all over the world. It is important to the government that this continues, despite the hardships of the Special Period.

Music: From Son to Salsa

Cubans love music and dance, which are performed all over the island. There are many African-Cuban groups, like this one, who use mostly percussion instruments.

A rich musical tradition thrives in Cuba, much of it developed from the fusion of Spanish and African cultures. *Son* (SOEN) music is dance music with solo improvised singing and a repeated chorus. It came from the eastern provinces around Santiago de Cuba. Traditional son instruments include a double bass, bongos, maracas, a three-stringed guitar called a *tres* (TRAYSS), and sometimes trumpets.

From son music emerged the mambo, which became a popular dance music in North America in the 1950s, as did the Cuban-born cha-cha. Santiago de Cuba was also the birthplace of the conga, a popular street dance that dates back to Lenten carnivals of the seventeenth century. *Trova* (TROE-bah) is a form of ballad music sung in romantic Spanish style, from which *nueva trova* (noo-AY-bah TROE-bah), the first new musical movement since the revolution, has

developed. With its political overtones and experimental classical music, it took some time to catch on. During the 1970s the infinitely more popular salsa came to life, with a rhythm that derives from son and includes touches of the mambo, trova, cha-cha, jazz, soul, and rock.

Another famous dance music is the rumba, which originated in the late nineteenth century in black slave areas of Havana and Matanzas. Three drums of different sizes provide the rumba beat. Many African rhythms, including rumba, are associated with African-Cuban religions. *Batás* (bah-TAHSS), drums shaped like an hourglass, are sacred instruments used in Yoruba ritual music. Some of the best African-Cuban music used to be heard at the July Carnival held in Santiago de Cuba, but for the time being it has been canceled.

Sport: "The Right of the People"

After the revolution, sports were high on Castro's agenda. "Sport is the right of the people," he said. Sports were introduced at the earliest school level, and students with talent were filtered through to special coaching schools.

Cuba's successes in athletics have been outstanding. Heavyweight boxer Teófilo Stevenson became an Olympic gold medalist three times, and in 1976 Alberto Juantorena was the first athlete ever to win Olympic gold medals in both the 400- and 800-meter races.

In 1991 Cuba hosted the Pan-American Games, an amazing achievement given its poor political and economic situation, and won more gold medals than the United States. Cuba went on to dominate the 1993 Central America and Caribbean Games, winning seventy-five more gold medals than the combined total of the other thirty-one competing countries. At the 1996 Olympic Games in Atlanta, Cuba won seven gold medals, which in proportion to its size and population was an outstanding achievement.

Baseball

Introduced late in the nineteenth century by North Americans, baseball is Cuba's number one sport. As a young man, Fidel Castro was an accomplished athlete, and a professional American baseball team once offered him a contract. Cuba boasts some of the best players in the world, players who could earn a lot of money in the United States if they were allowed to enter the country. Some have gone to other countries to coach, but most remain in Cuba and take part in the National Series. The major teams are the Industriales (een-dooss-tree-AH-layss), meaning "the factory workers," from Havana; the Tabacaleros (tah-bah-kah-LAY-roess), meaning "the tobacco workers," from Pinar del Río; and the Azucareros (ah-soo-kah-RAY-roess), meaning "the sugar workers," from Villa Clara. Finals of the National Series bring the island to a standstill. People stop work to follow the games as they are broadcast live on television and radio.

A baseball game in progress at the stadium in Pinar del Río. Cuban players are some of the best in the world, and rivalry between the teams in their National Series is intense.

DOMINICA

DOMINICA IS A LUSH ISLAND in the Caribbean Sea, fringed by beaches of dark, volcanic sand. Part of the Lesser Antilles chain, it lies between Guadeloupe and Martinique.

Dominica is an island of towering mountains and high ridges. The misty slopes are clad in dense, green rain forest, with tumbling streams and waterfalls.

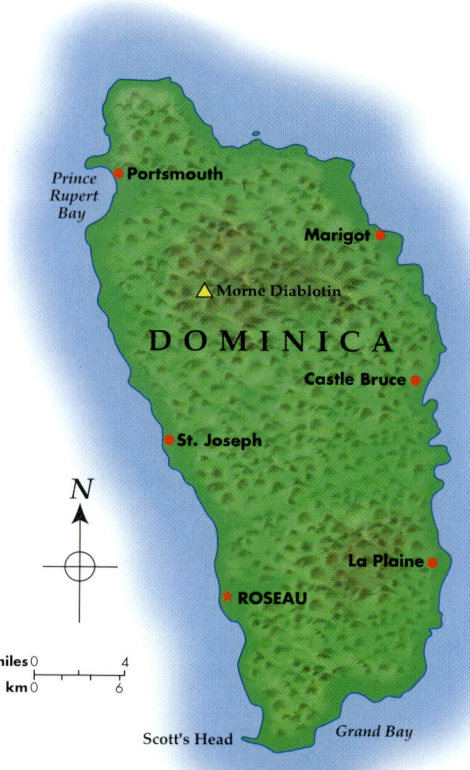

The Green Island

Carib-speaking Native Americans settled this mountainous island in the 1300s and called it Waitikibuli, meaning "tall is her body." The indigenous peoples fiercely and successfully resisted European settlers and invaders. The Spanish left the island alone, and in 1660 the French and English agreed to leave the island to the Caribs.

However, over the next century, the French settled and claimed parts of the island, leading a harsh war against the Caribs. The French planted coffee, and the port of Roseau became a market for slaves from western Africa, who worked the plantations. Some slaves, called Maroons, escaped to the hills, where they lived freely

CLIMATE

Dominica has a tropical, generally humid climate, with a high rainfall in August and a drier spell lasting from February to June. Hurricanes can cause severe damage.

Average January temperature: *76°F (24°C)*

Average July temperature: *81°F (27°C)*

Average annual precipitation: *78 in (198 cm)*

and raided plantations. Throughout the 1700s Dominica (dohm-uh-NEE-kuh) was caught up in the wars between Britain and France and changed hands several times. From 1805, the island remained under British rule, with its economy based on sugarcane and lime juice. When slaves were freed in 1834, many of them set up small farms in the desolate interior.

British rule ended in 1978. The early years of independence were marked by the

FACTS AND FIGURES

Official name: *Commonwealth of Dominica*

Status: *Independent state*

Capital: *Roseau*

Area: *290 square miles (751 square kilometers)*

Population: *90,000*

Population density: *310 per square mile (120 per square kilometer)*

Peoples: *98 percent Afro-Caribbean; 2 percent Carib (Native American)*

Official language: *English*

Currency: *East Caribbean dollar, French franc, British pound*

National day: *Independence Day (November 3)*

Country's name: *From the Spanish word for "Sunday," the day on which the island was sighted by Christopher Columbus.*

baskets and mats. They live in wooden houses built on stilts.

English is the official language, but the island's French background is reflected in the widely spoken Creole dialect.

Creole traditions are celebrated at an October festival called *Jounen Kweyol* (joo-NEE KWAY-yahl). Masquerade, or Carnival, is held before Lent with typical Caribbean music, dance, and costume. Popular sports include soccer and cricket.

Local cooking makes use of spices, tropical fruit, and coconut. The best-known dish is created from the legs of a giant frog, nicknamed "mountain chicken."

Over 40 percent of Dominicans live in towns such as Portsmouth and Roseau.

The islanders today mostly live by farming, growing coconuts, coffee, spices, limes, mangoes, guavas, and pineapples. Bananas have been the chief crop for many years, but prices have fallen greatly, as protected trading deals with Great Britain have ended.

election of the Caribbean's first woman prime minister, Eugenia Charles, in 1980.

This small island has a wealth of cultural influences. Most of the islanders are of Afro-Caribbean or mixed descent. About three thousand Caribs and people of Carib descent still live there, especially in the east, where they have their own special territory. They no longer speak a Carib language but still make dugout canoes and weave traditional

Two faces of Dominica—a Carib (above), whose ancestors were among the original peoples of the region, and (below) an Afro-Caribbean woman at the annual Masquerade.

Timeline:	Caribs settle Waitikibuli	Columbus lands on the island and names it Dominica	French settle and claim island	France cedes Dominica to Great Britain	Abolition of slavery	Independence from Great Britain
	1300s	1493	1720s	1763	1834	1978

DOMINICAN REPUBLIC

THE DOMINICAN REPUBLIC SHARES THE CARIBBEAN ISLAND OF HISPANIOLA WITH HAITI. After Cuba, it is the second largest country in the Caribbean region.

The Dominican Republic lies in the Greater Antilles island chain, bordered by the Atlantic Ocean on the north and the Caribbean Sea on the south. Puerto Rico lies to the east, across the Mona Passage.

Ranges of mountains run across the country, the largest of which is the Cordillera Central. Pico Duarte, which rises to 10,417 feet (3,175 meters), is the highest peak in the Caribbean. The highland forests have suffered in places from tree cutting. Valleys and plains are fertile and well watered, especially in the north and east, but the far southwest is extremely dry.

A Troubled History

The original inhabitants of the island, which was named Hispaniola or La Española ("Little Spain") by Christopher Columbus, were the Taino, a Native American people who spoke an Arawak language. The Taino led peaceful lives, catching fish, growing crops, and smoking tobacco. But the Spanish slaughtered or enslaved most of them in the early years of colonial rule. In the northeastern part of the island lived another Arawak-speaking group, the Ciguqyo, who were much more warlike than the Taino.

CLIMATE

The Dominican Republic has a hot, tropical climate, relieved by fresh winds. The rainy season lasts from May to November, with a high risk of hurricanes at that time.

Average January temperature: *75°F (24°C)*

Average July temperature: *81°F (27°C)*

Average annual precipitation: *56 in (142 cm)*

Columbus, an Italian explorer in the service of Spain, landed on the island on December 5, 1492. The following year the Spanish founded their first settlement in the Americas, in northern Hispaniola. The southern port of Santo Domingo, founded in 1496, was the base from which they conquered the Spanish Main, or the American mainland, during the 1500s. However, more and more Spanish adventurers moved on to seek their fortune on the mainland, and Santo Domingo became little more than a port visited by Spanish vessels shipping treasure back to Europe. Spain invested little in new settlements and forts, so French pirates managed to gain a foothold in the far northwest of Hispaniola. France and Spain soon had to fight for control of the west, and by 1697 Spain was forced to give up one-third of the island—the

The image of a lost people, this fine carving was made by the Taino, an Arawak-speaking people whose way of life was destroyed when the Spanish invaded Hispaniola.

FACTS AND FIGURES

Official name: *República Dominicana*

Status: *Independent state*

Capital: *Santo Domingo*

Major cities: *Santiago de los Caballeros, La Romana, San Pedro de Macorís*

Area: *18,700 square miles (48,400 square kilometers)*

Population: *8,200,000*

Population density: *439 per square mile (169 per square kilometer)*

Peoples: *70 percent Afro-Caribbean-European descent ; 15 percent European descent; 15 percent Afro-Caribbean descent*

Official language: *Spanish*

Currency: *Dominican Republic peso*

National days: *Independence Day (February 27); Restoration Day (August 16)*

Country's name: *From Santo Domingo, the capital and oldest European city in the Americas.*

colony of Saint Domingue, later known as Haiti—to France (see HAITI).

While the Dominicans raised cattle, their French neighbors planted sugarcane and prospered until 1793, when the slaves of Haiti rose in rebellion against the brutal plantation system, under their leader, Toussaint-Louverture. Spain at first supported the rebels but was rejected by them when slavery was abolished. By 1801 Toussaint controlled all of Hispaniola.

In 1809 Great Britain sided with Spain and recaptured Santo Domingo and the east. However, the Spanish of Santo

Timeline:	Taino arrive from Venezuela	Christopher Columbus lands on Hispaniola	Western Hispaniola lost to France	Dominicans declare independence	Haitian invasion
	ca. 300 C.E.	1492	1697	1821	1822

Domingo now wanted independence from the parent country and broke away, becoming the independent Dominican Republic (duh-MIHN-ih-kuhn rih-PUB-lick) in 1821. The following year the new country was invaded by the Haitians, who freed the slaves and held power until 1844, when the Dominican Republic was restored. Generals then ran the country, and one of them, Pedro Santana, returned the country to Spain in exchange for protection from Haiti. The Dominican Republic was finally restored in 1865.

In 1869, still unable to resist attacks and invasions by Haiti, the leaders of the Dominican Republic offered political control of the country to the United States but were turned down. However, the United States did control the troubled Dominican economy from 1905 until 1941. In 1916 U.S. Marines moved in, staying until 1924.

The year 1930 saw the start of a brutal dictatorship under Rafael Trujillo. It is believed that up to twenty thousand Haitians living in the border provinces of the Dominican Republic were massacred in 1937. Trujillo was assassinated in 1961, and four years later, following a period of great instability, the U.S. Marines were back in the country. In 1966 elections brought a corrupt

One legacy of Spanish rule is the Roman Catholic religion. Here, the faithful join a procession through the streets of Santo Domingo during Holy Week, just before Easter.

conservative, Joaquín Balaguer, to power, and he dominated Dominican politics, on and off, into the 1990s. The political system is still heavily influenced by the military and the powerful landowners. Leonel Fernández was elected president in 1996.

Land of Contrast

The Dominican Republic, like Cuba and Puerto Rico, is very much part of Latin America, with a strong Afro-Caribbean influence. The nation is Spanish-speaking, and 95 percent of the population worship as Roman Catholics. Christian festivals play an important part in Dominican life, with local fiestas marking saints' days.

Dominicans independent again	Spanish rule	Independence restored	United States controls Dominican economy	Brutal dictatorship of Rafael Trujillo	Leonel Fernández elected president
1844	1861	1865	1905–1941	1930–1961	1996

Dominicans celebrate the chief festival, Our Lady of Altagracia, across the nation on January 21. In country areas African spiritual beliefs such as voodoo have influenced a form of worship known as Santería, where worshipers go into trances and communicate with spirits (see CUBA).

Six out of ten Dominicans live in towns. The capital, Santo Domingo, was the first European settlement in the Americas and is dominated by a palace dating from 1510, the Alcázar de Colón, "the fortress of Columbus." Here, too, stands the first cathedral built in the Americas, Santa María la Menor, begun in 1523. Over the ages earthquakes and wars destroyed much of the old city. Now a large modern town with wealthy suburbs gives way to a fringe of shantytowns.

Plantains and Stews

The traditional dishes of the Dominican Republic use local vegetables and tropical fruits. Plantains (large bananas that are cooked) are served mashed, fried, or boiled with eggs, garlic, or spices. Tropical fruits include passion fruit, melon, mango, and guava.

Sancocho *(sahn-KOE-choe) is a stew made of goat meat or sometimes chicken, pigeon, pork, beef, or any available meat. Various vegetables such as potato and cassava—a starchy root crop known locally as yucca—flavor the stew. The dish is simmered long and slow in a pot. A cow's stomach, or tripe, forms the basis for* mondongo *(moen-DOEN-goe) stew.*

Many dishes use seafood, including shrimp, lobster, and clams. Seafood may also appear with chicken in a rice dish called locrio *(LOE-kree-oe).*

Life in the poorer districts of Santo Domingo can be a struggle, with the lack of adequate drainage, water, and power supplies affecting the health of many families.

Out in the countryside, fruit and sugarcane flourish on large plantations. But many people farm small plots, growing plantains (large bananas) and raising chickens. Villages consist of simple houses and wooden cabins, or *bohíos* (boe-HEE-oess). If they can spare the time, families sit out on their porches in the evening sunshine after working in the fields. Televisions receive broadcasts from Mexico and the United States as well as from local stations.

Although Dominicans have little leisure time, they all follow baseball. There are

The game of dominoes is very popular in bars, cafés, and homes in many parts of the Caribbean. This session is under way in the capital, Santo Domingo.

those who owned large plantations, but today the route to the top may include a career in banking or business. The Dominican upper classes shop in Florida, seek medical treatment in Cuba, and send their children to college in Spain. They make sure that they marry into other powerful, wealthy families. The middle

major stadiums in five cities. Boys practice hard, hoping one day to play professionally in the Caribbean, U.S., or Canadian leagues. Some of the best Dominican stars play in the United States for part of the year.

Many Dominicans live in great poverty. The peasants, or *campesinos*, include small landowners as well as a great number of migrant laborers. Health care is fairly basic, although life expectancy here is considerably higher than in neighboring Haiti, where years of corruption, poverty, malnutrition, and violence have destroyed health care facilities. About 15 percent of the population cannot read or write. Many country people come into the towns in search of work but rarely find it. The slums of Santo Domingo offer little comfort, with little access to water or electricity, no proper drainage, and too many people.

Just a few families are extremely wealthy. Traditional wealth used to lie with

The Merengue Beat

The Dominican Republic is a land of dance. Music is everywhere—on the streets, in bars, and on car radios. Merengue rules. This style of music started in the countryside. It was originally an acoustic sound, created by bands comprised of accordions, basses, saxophones, and tamboras *(tahm-BOE-rahss), drums with two ends. The lyrics often described the hardship of country life. Merengue then rolled into the towns and was copied by dance orchestras. After the 1960s a new style of merengue developed that grew into the modern sound, influenced by rock music and also by its Caribbean cousin salsa, the dance music. With its fast dance and vocal routines, merengue spread to New York City and around the world in the 1980s and 1990s.*

Merengue and salsa music may be heard at Carnival, celebrated each year in February and ending with Dominican Independence Day on February 27. This festival mixes African and European cultural influences; parades include dancers and people disguised in masks and fantastic costumes.

class is larger, making up about one-third of the population. Its members may work as businesspeople, shopkeepers, teachers, or administrators.

The Dominican Republic has a less troubled racial history than Haiti, but the fact remains that if you are extremely rich, you are probably white, while if you are a black Afro-Caribbean, you will probably find it hard to escape poverty in the countryside.

Working at Home and Abroad

The peoples of the Dominican Republic have had economic problems for most of their history. Like many of the world's poorer countries, the country is crippled by its need to repay international debts. It receives financial aid from the European Union (an alliance of European nations) and the United States, its chief trading partner.

The country has resources of nickel, and its gold mines lured the Spanish settlers to the island five hundred years ago. It also produces larimar (a form of turquoise unique to the Dominican Republic) and amber, a fossilized resin of transparent yellows and browns; both make beautiful jewelry. Tourists are increasingly important to the economy, attracted by the warm seas and beaches of fine sand fringed by palm trees.

The chief crop is sugarcane, which is turned into the thick, sweet syrup called molasses and used to make rum. Other export crops include cacao, coffee, and tobacco. Cattle and pigs are raised on a large scale.

One way out of the poverty trap is to flee the country. Many people travel in small boats to enter Puerto Rico illegally. Many Dominican exiles now live in the United States and send much-needed money back to their families at home.

Whether it is old-time routines or moving to the latest Latin merengue or salsa hits, the Dominicans' idea of enjoying life is to dance.

ECUADOR

ECUADOR IS THE MOST DENSELY POPULATED COUNTRY IN SOUTH AMERICA and lies on the earth's equator.

Ecuador lies on the northwest Pacific coast of South America, with Colombia to the north and east and Peru to the south and east. It also includes the Pacific Galápagos Islands, known locally as the Archipiélago de Colón.

The Andes cross the center of Ecuador from north to south. Snow-capped volcanoes dominate the ranges, including Cotopaxi, the world's highest active volcano.

In the mountain region, or sierra (see-EHR-uh), nestle valleys where people have lived and farmed for hundreds of years. Low hill ranges, valleys, marshlands, mangrove swamps, and sandy beaches cover the Pacific coast in western Ecuador. To the east is Ecuador's Amazon, called the Oriente or Selva, a land of rain forest and numerous tributaries of the Amazon River.

An Ancient Land

The first inhabitants of Ecuador (EHK-wuh-door) were hunters and gatherers. By about 3000 B.C.E., humans had begun cultivating crops in different parts of South America. Pottery and other objects have established the Valdivia culture on the Pacific coast of Ecuador as the oldest known in all of South America, dating back to at least 3500 B.C.E. The intriguing question is how it originated in a relatively isolated region. Evidence shows that the Valdivia people traded with the inhabitants of the Amazon and of present-day Mexico.

Coastal cultures flourished until the fifteenth century. The Tolita culture (600 B.C.E.–400 C.E.) produced exquisite gold work and sculptures, and the Manta culture (600–1500 C.E.) created gold and

FACTS AND FIGURES

Official name: *República del Ecuador*

Status: *Independent state*

Capital: *Quito*

Major cities: *Guayaquil, Cuenca, Ambato, Esmeraldas, Manta*

Area: *103,930 square miles (269,178 square kilometers)*

Population: *12,000,000*

Population density: *115 per square mile (45 per square kilometer)*

Peoples: *40 percent Native American; 40 percent mestizo; 20 percent European and African descent*

Official language: *Spanish*

Currency: *Sucre*

National days: *Patriotism and National Unity Day (February 27); Labor Day (May 1); Battle of Pinchincha Day (May 24); Bolívar's Day (July 24); Independence Day (August 10); Columbus Day (October 12)*

Country's name: Ecuador *is the Spanish name for the equator, which crosses the country just north of Quito, the capital.*

A gold mask of the Tolita culture of the Ecuadorian and Colombian Pacific coast. It probably represents a sun god and is about two thousand years old.

south, the Puruhás in the central region, and the Caras in the north. These tribes resisted the Incas for many years, and the Cañaris lost most of their male population in battle. Once Quito in the land of the Caras was taken, the Incas began to move groups of loyal Quechua peoples from Peru to settle in Ecuador, at the same time sending many Cañaris and Caras to other parts of their empire.

When Incan Emperor Huayna Capac died in around 1525, civil war broke out among his successors. In the middle of the fighting, a small group of Spanish soldiers arrived, led by Francisco Pizarro. The Spanish explorer

A ceramic statue made by the pre-Columbian Bahia culture of Ecuador's Pacific coast, portraying a mother with her baby in swaddling clothes.

silver objects, pots, and cotton textiles. Its people were also excellent seafarers; many archaeologists believe they, together with sailors from Peru, discovered the Galápagos Islands.

When the Incas from Peru invaded Ecuador in the fifteenth century, the indigenous groups they encountered in the sierra (mountain region) included the Cañaris in the

Timeline:	First peoples arrive	Valdivia culture established in Ecuador	Tolita culture thrives	Manta culture flourishes
	13,000–8,000 B.C.E.	3500–1500 B.C.E.	600 B.C.E.–400 C.E.	600–1500 C.E.

captured the emperor Atahualpa and later executed him. The Inca Empire fell, unable to resist the guns of the Spaniards, and Ecuador became a Spanish colony.

The Spanish divided the land in the sierra among themselves and forced the Indians to work on their farms and in workshops making textiles. The Spaniards also introduced horses, cattle, pigs, and wheat to the region. During the eighteenth century, black slaves were imported from Africa to work on cacao plantations on the coast. Many thousands of Native peoples died from diseases brought in by the Europeans, and thousands more escaped into remote parts of the highlands and into the Amazon forests.

Ecuador won its independence from Spain in 1822. For eight years it was part of Gran Colombia with Venezuela and Colombia, until in 1830 it broke off and became the Republic of Ecuador. The population included a small wealthy and powerful elite, but the majority of people were poor. The first president to address the country's social problems was Gabriel García Moreno, president from 1860 to 1875. Schools and hospitals were built, roads constructed, a railway linking the highlands and coast was started, and the economy improved.

With the successful production of cacao, sugar, rice, and, later, bananas, the coastal

The port of Guayaquil as it was in 1884. A few years later, fire destroyed many of the wooden buildings.

Inca conquest begins	Spaniards conquer the Incas	Black slaves imported to work on cacao plantations	Ecuador becomes independent	Ecuador part of federation of Gran Colombia
1471	1534	1700s	1822	1822–1830

CLIMATE

Ecuador's temperature is much the same all year-round. In the lowlands it is hot and humid, while in the main cities of the mountains the climate is generally warm and sunny. Higher in the mountains it is much colder. Rainfall varies from region to region. July and August are considered dry months in the mountains and on the Pacific coast. The Oriente has heavy rainfall for most of the year. From time to time a current of warm water collects offshore, creating El Niño, a weather phenomenon that can cause great storms.

	Quito	Guayaquil
Average January temperature	59°F (15°C)	79°F (26°C)
Average July temperature	58°F (14°C)	75°F (24°C)
Average annual precipitation	44 in (112 cm)	39 in (99 cm)

lowlands gained economic importance, causing a rivalry for power between the sierra and the coast that continues to this day. Early in the twentieth century, real power lay with the wealthy merchants and bankers of Guayaquil on the coast. In the 1920s a fall in exports, together with disease that devastated the cacao plantations, led to mass unemployment and huge unrest. Hundreds of people died in riots and massacres.

Late in the twentieth century, two events changed the face of Ecuador. In 1964 agricultural reform led to the breakup of the large estates owned by a few wealthy people. The land was distributed to farmers who now run large estates on a cooperative basis or have their own small farms. The other event was the discovery of oil in the 1970s, which led to an economic boom and increased prosperity for some people. In the 1980s the economy suffered from a drop in oil prices worldwide.

Today the gap between rich and poor is as wide as ever, while corruption is widespread. Charged with misuse of public funds, the vice president fled the country in 1995, and several ministers were impeached or had to resign. Perhaps in exasperation, the people voted Abdala Bucaram to power in 1996. A highly unconventional president, he was nicknamed el loco (el LOW-coe), meaning "the madman." Within a year he lost the confidence of the people. The military stepped in, and Fabián Alarcón was declared president.

From a Rural Society to an Urban One

Ecuador has the greatest population density of any country in South America. About 40 percent of the population is Native American, while another 40 percent is mestizo, descendants of mixed marriages between Spaniards and Native Americans.

Ecuador becomes a republic	Gabriel García Moreno is president	Agricultural reforms begin	Abdala Bucaram elected president	Military deposes Bucaram
1830	**1860–1875**	**1964**	**1996**	**1997**

Instead of *Indian* and *mestizo*, Ecuadorians prefer the terms *indígena* (een-DEE-hay-nah) and *blanco* (BLAHN-koe), which means white.

To be an indígena means to be of Indian descent, live in an Indian community, speak a Native language with or instead of Spanish, and, most important, wear a form of dress that identifies the person with a community. Indígenas describe themselves as coming from a specific community. They can become blancos by moving to the cities, speaking Spanish, and dressing in Western-style clothes.

The remaining 20 percent are whites; blacks; mulattos, people of mixed Spanish and black descent; and coastal *montuvios* (moan-TOO-bee-oess), who have white, Indian, and black parentage. Few immigrants have settled in Ecuador.

The population is fairly evenly spread between the highlands and the coastal lowlands. The Oriente, which covers more than one-third of the country, is home to only 5 percent of the population. Whites and mestizos live in both the highlands and the lowlands, but the majority of indígenas dwell in the highlands, with most of the blacks in the coastal lowlands.

Apart from Spanish, the most widely spoken language is the Quechua of many indígenas, the language imposed by the Incas. After the Spanish Conquest, missionaries also used it.

Until agricultural reform in the 1960s and the discovery of oil in the 1970s, Ecuador was a rural society. Agricultural reform left many peasants in the highlands without employment or land since there was not enough good land for everyone,

The Church and Monastery of San Francisco in Quito. Built in 1553, the church is said to be the first religious building constructed in South America by the Spaniards.

while the oil industry meant more jobs and better opportunities in the cities. Thousands of people moved from rural to urban areas and from the sierra to the coast. In less than twenty years a quarter of Ecuador's population moved from the countryside to the towns; today almost 60 percent of the people live in urban areas.

All Ecuadorian children between the ages of six and fourteen are supposed to attend school, which is free. But in practice many cannot. Those living in towns and cities have more schools, public transportation, and better educational resources. Their country cousins have a much harder time, since getting to school may mean long walks, lengthy horse rides, or hitchhiking. Another problem for poorer families in all areas is that children must work to help the family. Country children tend crops, look after cattle, or go to market, while in the cities many work on the streets, shining shoes, cleaning cars, or selling trinkets.

Medical facilities are much better in the cities and towns than in rural areas, but malnutrition and lack of good drinking water remain serious problems. Trucks must deliver drinking water to some parts of the country.

A Religious People

The Spanish imposed Roman Catholicism on the Native Ecuadorians, and attendance at mass and Catholic festivities have long been a part of daily family life. Godparents become intimate members of the extended family. A midmorning mass on a working day is typically celebrated by a cross section of the population, from grandmothers and grandchildren to businesspeople with briefcases and mobile phones. People drop into church from the street, light a candle, say a prayer, and go on their way again.

Evangelists like the Baptists and Seventh-Day Adventists have been hard at work in recent years, particularly among the poor, and with considerable success. Their small churches, made of wood or iron and surrounded by a few simple houses, even appear in remote parts of the country.

Ecuadorians celebrate religious festivals throughout the year. In some cases the Spaniards were able to make these coincide with pre-Columbian Native festivals associated with the

agricultural year. Corpus Christi is held at the time of the winter solstice in the third week of June, which the Incas celebrated with Inti Raimi, their Festival of the Sun. Most villages and towns also have their own saints' days. All are occasions for dancing, drinking, and eating, with colorful, noisy processions and parades.

Indígenas have accepted Catholicism but also have their own beliefs. Their spirits, gods, and shrines are part of the natural world around them. Mountain gods provide rain and make the land fertile, and indígenas make offerings to them. To have a good harvest or give thanks for one, they sprinkle drops of alcohol on the ground to please Pachamama, Mother Earth. Most communities have a shaman (a healer who acts as an intermediate between the spiritual and visible world), who helps with domestic or business problems and treats illnesses using native plants such as tobacco, and small animals such as guinea pigs and frogs.

On All Souls' Day people make special preparations to remember loved ones who have died. They take food and other gifts to the cemetery and spend many hours there.

Dishes of Ecuador

The wide variety of dishes in Ecuador reflect the different geographical areas of the country. Many people consider fanesca *(fah-NAYSS-kah), a soup eaten only at Easter, the most representative dish because it contains ingredients from so many regions. It includes fish, eggs, cheese, corn, onions, peanuts, rice, squash, beans, lentils, and peas, but no meat.*

A favorite dish along the Pacific coast is seviche, raw fish or seafood marinated in lemon or lime juice and served with onions and peppers. Rice and plantains (bananas), boiled or deep fried, are basic foods in the coastal region and the Oriente. In the Oriente are cassava and river fish, including enormous catfish and the fierce but delicious piranha.

Highland food is based on soups and stews. They range from thin, rather watery soups with a few chunks of potato, chicken, or meat, to barley and quinoa (the highland grain) soups, to locro *(LOW-croe), or* chupe *(CHOO-pay), which is a thick cream soup. Stews are made from corn, plantains, potatoes, cabbages, onions, and other vegetables. A hot sauce made from chili peppers, or* aji *(AH-hee), spices up many stews. At one time the* cuy *(KWEE), or guinea pig, provided the main source of meat in the Andes and was kept by* indígenas *in their homes, but today it is a delicacy.*

A trader prepares his booth with piles of specially made colored cookies in preparation for the annual fiesta to honor the patron saint of the small town of Montecristi.

Serranos: Living in the Mountains

Serranos (say-RAH-noess) are people who live in the Andean highlands. They include whites, mestizos, and indígenas who live in the cities and in the mountain valleys where they farm or trade in the small towns. Usually wealthy and of Spanish descent, whites form a small elite. Until the agricultural reforms they were the rich landowners, while indígenas were forced to work on the estates in return for a small plot of land to grow their own crops. Managers and clerks were generally mestizos, whose considerable authority over the indígenas was greatly resented.

A middle class emerged from the mass of mainly mestizo people who migrated to the towns in the 1960s and 1970s. Successful middle-class people are usually well educated and become executives, teachers, lawyers, or civil servants. They live in comfortable, spacious houses or apartments, drive cars or have chauffeurs, and employ at least one maid and probably a gardener.

Most Ecuadorians are far removed from this style of living and work at anything that will make them enough money to live. Less than half of Ecuador's workers have a full-time job. Traders selling almost anything from cooked food to watches pack city streets. Women lug huge pots of food from home to sell on the streets. Some women clean the homes of the wealthy or work in shops. Men find jobs driving buses, trucks, and taxis, or they work in construction, building houses and repairing roads.

The rush to the towns left the authorities unable to cope. There is a great shortage of housing and electricity, and garbage collection is a big problem. Huge garbage dumps line the roadsides near towns.

In the highland countryside wealthy landowners still own the best land at the bottom of the valleys, where it is flat. Small farmers, mainly indígenas, farm plots on the surrounding rocky, volcanic hillsides, where they also graze their few sheep or llamas. Unable to use tractors or motor vehicles on the steep slopes, farmers work with ox-drawn plows, wooden hoes, and digging sticks, and they sow their seeds by hand. Heavy rains constantly wash away the best topsoil, and few small farmers can afford chemicals or fertilizers.

Building homes is a communal task among indígenas, who have a strong belief

In the highlands, market day is a chance for people to socialize. Here, Otavaleño women bring pigs to the weekly animal market, where livestock and poultry are traded.

in community and family life. All families are expected to help in other communal tasks like repairing roads or digging irrigation ditches.

Today men dress much like their mestizo neighbors in Western-style pants and shirts. Women have kept their long, full skirts and embroidered blouses and shawls, with the colors differing from one village to the next. Communities are often distinguished from each other by the different styles of hats worn by their inhabitants.

Every week indígenas trek to their local market to trade their produce and animals. There they meet people from other communities to eat and drink with, share news, and discuss their problems.

A Black Community in the Andes

In the northern Andes, not far from the border with Colombia, is the hot, dry Chota valley, where sugar, bananas, and other tropical fruits grow. African slaves fled from plantations in Colombia and settled here, probably in the eighteenth century. Until recently their descendants lived in African-style homes of bamboo, mud, and thatch. It was the only black community in the sierra. Today adobe (mud brick) and brick houses have replaced the bamboo huts.

The people, too, are changing. Marriage with mestizos and indígenas is lightening their skin color. In a generation or two it is likely that most traces of their ancestry will

The volcano Cotacachi overlooks the daily market in the town of Cotacachi, where Otaveleños and blacks from the nearby Chota valley sell their fruit and vegetables.

have disappeared. Some older members still tell stories of their slave ancestors, and African music survives in the *bomba negra* (BOME-bah NAY-grah), a curious mix of Native highland music and African rhythms.

The Otavaleños

The most prosperous of all Ecuador's indígenas, the Otavaleños, live south of the Chota valley and less than 60 miles (100 kilometers) north of Quito in the Otavalo valley between the Cotacachi and Imbabura volcanoes. They claim to be descended from the Incas, but it is more likely their ancestors were the Caras, who lived in the valley before the Inca conquest.

Weaving has been key to the Otavaleños' success. Like other indígenas, most Otavaleños are rural people whose lives revolve around the land, and weaving has

Otavaleño Clothing

The distinctive woolen clothing of the Otavaleños is as close to Incan clothing as any seen in the Andes today. The men wear baggy, spotlessly clean, white pants that stop halfway down their shins, heavy white cotton shirts, and dark blue woolen ponchos. They have wide-brimmed felt hats and tie their shiny black hair in a long braid.

Women's dress includes two ankle-length skirts wrapped around the waist, with one over the other, fastened by a handwoven belt. They wear frilly white blouses embroidered across the front and around the sleeves, over which they drape a shawl either knotted in front or worn across the chest so that one arm is free. Strands of golden beads around the neck indicate the wealth of the family, and other jewelry includes beaded bracelets and earrings. Women wear their hair like the men but usually cover it with a scarf. Both men and women wear open-toed cotton sandals called alpargatas *(ahl-pahr-GAH-tahss).*

large-scale factories with electric looms that produce hundreds of ponchos a day. Besides ponchos, Otavaleños make tapestry wall hangings, embroidered blouses, dresses, gloves, socks, blankets, belts, shawls, scarves, capes, and bulky sweaters. They sell many of these to other Ecuadorians and to tourists at the local Sunday market. Otavaleños also travel abroad to sell their goods. Their export market to North America, Europe, and Japan makes millions of dollars every year.

Prosperity has brought a dramatic change in lifestyle for some Otavaleños, who now own restaurants, apartment buildings, and hotels, live in modern houses, and send their children overseas to be educated. Others, not quite so prosperous, have been able to buy land in the valley and acquire all sorts of consumer goods. They can also afford to give their children a good education. The Otavaleños' success has been achieved without their losing their indígena identity, clothing, or language. They have taken on, and been accepted by, the modern world on their own terms.

traditionally been scheduled around sowing, planting, and harvesting. Over three-quarters of the forty-five-thousand-strong community in the Otavalo valley are involved in some way, on a part- or full-time basis, in the textile business. A few Otavaleños have abandoned the land altogether and invested in

Otavaleños are renowned for their weaving skills. At their weekly market in Otavalo, mother and daughter are selling traditional woven wall and floor coverings.

The Salasacas

Another indígena group, the Salasacas, live near the city of Ambato. Most are still farmers, although their land is threatened by mestizo settlers. They, too, are well known for their weavings, mainly *tapices* (tah-PEE-sayss), strips of cloth that can be cut into wall hangings. The tapices repeat a particular design, often of a bird or animal in an angular shape, in different colors. The weavings form an important part of the Salasaca economy, and Salasacas sell them through a cooperative as well as in markets.

The Salasacas all wear distinctive black-and-white ponchos. The men sport white pants and the women long black skirts; both wear broad white hats with upturned brims. Their outfits are said to be worn to mourn the last Inca emperor.

The Cañaris and Saragureños

The Cañaris are an indígena community in the province of Cañar, between Ambato and the southern highland city of Cuenca. Armed with only slings, star-shaped stone clubs, and *chonta* (hard palm wood) spears,

Pase del Niño

Like many towns and villages in Ecuador, Saraguro celebrates the birth of Christ with the Pase del Niño *(PAH-say del NEEN-yoe). Each Saragueño community has its own statue of the Christ child, which inhabitants carry in a procession from the main church in Saraguro to the house of the statue's "godparents." Musicians with violins and drums lead the processions, and dancers dress as devils, bears, and fierce Native people whose job it is to guard the Christ child. Once in the home, the statue is placed on an altar decorated with flowers and vegetables. Everyone then takes part in a huge Christmas meal.*

they resisted the Incas for many years but were finally overcome. The Incas subsequently moved many of them to Peru.

Today most of the forty thousand remaining Cañaris farm, growing barley, agave, potatoes, or quinoa, a nutritious grain that grows only at high altitudes. Some also herd sheep and cattle. The mountain region in which they work, the *páramo* (PAH-rah-moe), has little vegetation, and the climate is constantly cold, wet, and misty. When they work, the Cañaris wear protective sheepskin covers over their pants.

The Cañaris make finely woven belts with motifs of native animals, Inca-style pots, and other designs. They wear *ikat* (EE-kaht) ponchos at fiestas. Ikat is a process in which

A Cañari man in his typical felt hat and poncho. The Cañaris live high in the southern highlands, and among their crops are agave plants, seen here alongside the path.

threads are tie-dyed before they are woven to form a design. Because it is so time consuming, the technique is gradually dying out.

The province of Loja, south of Cuenca, is the highest in Ecuador and the home of about twenty thousand Saragureños, another indígena group. They are independent farmers and cattle traders. With only poor pasture in their highland home, they regularly drive their cattle to the eastern lowlands to graze and fatten the herds before returning to sell the cattle in the highland markets.

Apart from their white felt hats, the Saragureños dress almost completely in black. Their outfits, like those of the Salasacas, are said to mourn the last Inca emperor. Men wear knee-length shorts and thick ponchos, and women dress in calf-length pleated skirts. Their shawls are held together with ornate silver pins called *tupus* (TOO-pooss). Fine tupus are often handed down from one generation to the next. The women also like to wear filigree earrings and beaded necklaces.

Costeños: People of the Coast and Lowlands

The coastal lowlands are crossed by many rivers that flow from the Andes into the Gulf of Guayaquil. These areas are prone to frequent floods. Known as *Costeños* (koess-TAYN-yoess), almost half the population lives in the coastal lowlands. Mestizos form the majority and live and work both in the towns and rural areas. Whites and the few descendants of Chinese and Lebanese immigrants dwell mainly in the cities and towns.

Some Chinese laborers who helped build the Quito-Guayaquil railway in the nineteenth century stayed in Ecuador, and early in the twentieth century Lebanese people arrived. Both have integrated with the local population. The Lebanese have become successful businesspeople and have entered politics. Many of the Chinese settled in Guayaquil and in the inland town of Quevedo, meaning "Chinatown," where the Chinese presence is most obvious in the advertisements and on the signs of shops and restaurants. The greatest concentration of coastal blacks and people of mixed black marriages is in the province of Esmeraldas in the north.

The fertile, green, warm, and wet lowlands of the coast are easier to live in than the tough, hostile environment of the highlands. The coastal region has been the hub of the country's economy for a long time, and Guayaquil is the country's main port and largest city. Yet political power rests with Quito, in the center of the country, which the Costeños resent.

Ecuador's large banana plantations are in the lowlands. After the bananas are picked, they are washed, dried, and packed in local factories, ready to be trucked to the Pacific coast ports.

Students in Guayaquil are taking part in a campaign to promote care of the environment. They are using brushes to demonstrate the need for cleanliness in the streets.

Large plantations of bananas and cacao, rice paddies, fruit orchards, sugarcane fields, and cattle ranches prosper inland on the fertile lowlands. Ecuador is the world's largest exporter of bananas. Farmers working their own small plots grow crops such as cassava, peanuts, bananas, plantains, coffee, cacao, and corn. They live in houses on stilts, with walls of flattened bamboo and roofs of thatch.

The Cayapas (ki-YAH-pahss), also known as the Chachi, are the only group of indígenas living near the coast. They have survived partly because their home is in a remote corner of the northwest. Between two and four thousand Cayapas live in small villages along the Cayapas River. Built on wooden stilts above the ground, their houses are constructed of bamboo with thatched roofs. Several families live in one house. The Cayapas clear areas in the forest where they grow cassava (manioc), cotton, vegetables, and fruit. They weave fine hammocks and baskets, which they sometimes sell in Esmeraldas, the nearest big town. The Cayapas are famous for their dugout canoes carved from strong hardwood trees, which they trade to anyone using the river and to mestizos and blacks living on the coast. At an early age children learn how to make and handle the canoes, an essential skill since the rivers are the only "highways" in this region.

The Cayapas have also survived because of their resistance to change. They have had contact with blacks and mestizos for many years and traded with them in a cash economy. But when they could have been involved in commercial rubber or banana production, they preferred to keep to their simple existence. Now they have less choice since their land is gradually being invaded by speculators and colonizers.

The original blacks were slaves from western Africa brought to work on the cacao, coffee, and banana plantations. Today the population includes mulattos and montuvios (people of white, Indian, and black descent), but the traditions of Africa have remained strong in spiritual beliefs and in music. Many follow the Macumba religion, which practices ancestor worship and rituals in which mediums call on spirits to cure illnesses or give guidance. During the rituals, dancers whirl to the beat of loud drums. *Esmeraldeños* (ayss-may-rahl-DAYN-yoess), as the people of the Esmeraldas coastal region are called, love the salsa music of the Caribbean. Their favorite instrument is the xylophone-like

Fishing is an important industry for towns and villages along the Pacific coast. Here on the beach at Manta, fishermen are selling their varied, early morning catch.

The Galápageños

The Galápagos Islands are best known today for their unique wildlife, which played an important role in the famous scientist Charles Darwin's book, On the Origin of Species. *Darwin visited the islands in 1832.*

From the time of their discovery in the sixteenth century, the Galápagos Islands have been used by European pirates, seal hunters, and whalers. The first permanent resident was an Irishman marooned on Floreana Island in 1807. In 1832 an Ecuadorian military officer tried to start a colony with a band of convicts and prisoners. He became known as the Dog King of Charles Island because he kept huge dogs to control the convicts.

In the 1930s colonists arrived from Norway and Germany. All but three of the Norwegians died when conditions turned out to be harsher than expected. The German settlers were an eccentric mix. They included a nudist doctor with steel teeth and a baroness who proclaimed herself Queen of Galápagos. A series of deaths and murders subsequently left only one woman and her children.

Today about eleven thousand people live on the islands. Most are from Ecuador, seeking a new life. They work for the tourist industry; catch sea bass, groupers, and lobsters; or farm in the highlands, where they breed cattle and grow coffee, bananas, avocados, sugar, and yucca.

marimba, often accompanied by a deep-pitched drum and a long conga drum.

Most people in the Esmeraldas region are involved in the fishing industry, working on shrimp and cargo boats or on shrimp farms. Others work on tobacco and cacao plantations and on cattle ranches along the coast.

The Colorados

Near Santo Domingo de los Colorados, an important market town in the western lowlands between Quito and the coast, live the Colorados (koe-low-RAH-thoess), or

Tsíchila (ZEE-chee-lah), as they call themselves. These indígenas, who number less than two thousand, live in villages that are now part of a reserve. Although they wear mainly Western-style clothes, on special occasions they smear their hair and paint their bodies with an extract from the achiote plant (*Bixa orellana*). They traditionally dress in one piece of cloth wrapped around them like a skirt. The cloth is dyed in horizontal black and white stripes for the men and in strikingly bright reds, blues, yellows, and greens for the women. All are naked from the waist up.

Peoples of the Amazon

The largest ethnic group in Ecuador's Amazon is the Quichua (KEE-chew-ah), with about sixty thousand people. It consists of smaller groups, such as the Quijos, Yumbos, and Canelos. The Shuar are one of the Jivaro groups and number about forty thousand. Other groups are very small. They include the Achuar, who, like the Shuar, extend into Peru; the Waorani, or Huaorani, who live on a protected reserve; and the Siona-Secoya and the Cofan, each with about six hundred members who live in the northern part of the Oriente.

Most of these people are now at least partially Westernized. In the past they worked on farms and cattle ranches, and today some find jobs in the oil industry. Some have learned to read, write, and speak Spanish. Homes are still traditional, made from split bamboo and palm thatch, and they are often built on stilts for protection from floods and animals.

Traditional dress is mainly worn for fiestas, special occasions, and showing

The Colorado Indians take their name from the tradition of coloring their hair and painting their bodies red. These customs are gradually dying out.

A Waorani Indian has painted her face red with the dye of the achiote plant. The seeds from which the dye comes are encased in the prickly plant she is holding.

wooden blowguns and poison-tipped darts. When oil was discovered in Waorani territory in the 1960s, missionaries were able to persuade many of them to move onto a reserve. Now most live a seminomadic life there, growing crops in temporary gardens or plots. After much effort, the Waorani have regained ownership of some of their former lands from the Ecuadorian government, which has, however, retained its right to develop any deposits of oil found there.

Most Native American communities in the Amazon rain forest live by farming crops, hunting animals, and gathering wild fruits, nuts, and honey from the forest. The Quichua, related to the Quechua-speaking people of the highlands, originally escaped into the Oriente when the Spanish invaded. Already farmers, they applied their skills in the forest, though with different crops, such

tourists. It includes knee-length cotton tunics, or *cushmas* (KOOSH-mahss), among the Siona-Secoya and Cofan, and a similar tunic draped over one shoulder and secured with a belt among the Shuar and Achuar. They also wear necklaces of many strands of beads, seeds, and animal and fish teeth.

The Waorani (wah-oe-RAH-nee) are the most nomadic of the forest groups. Until the mid-twentieth century, so little was known about them in the outside world that they were known only as *Aucas* (OW-kahss), the Quichua word for "savages." Naked, they roamed the forest, hunting monkeys, birds, and wild pigs with

Shamans

In Amazon cultures the most important person is the shaman. He or she has many powers; shamans treat the sick, make decisions in time of war, cast curses on people, and conduct the initiation ceremonies in which young men and women pass into adulthood. Shamans also preserve the history, myths, and legends of their people, passed down to them through the generations. Each shaman has a preferred piece of magic, perhaps stones or darts, and shamans in most Amazonian groups use ayahuasca (i-yah-WAHSS-kah), a hallucinogen taken from a forest plant. This induces visions that often feature jaguars, anacondas, and eagles, all important animals in the mythology of the indigenous people of the Amazon.

as cassava, yucca, and plantain. They rotate their use of plots, leaving one or two fallow after they have been used for several years. The Siona-Secoya and the Cofan practice slash-and-burn farming, making a clearing where they grow crops for a few years before they move on. The Shuar and Achuar use cassava, the main crop, as both a food and a drink.

The Amazon peoples make baskets and clay pots. Those made by the Shuar are particularly fine, intricately decorated with geometric designs. Perhaps the most beautiful are those made by the Canelos women, with designs depicting aspects of their life and mythology.

In the 1970s the discovery of oil in the Amazon devastated the Native people and their environment and added to the problems they already faced from colonists

and settlers arriving from the highlands and invading their land. Now they are fighting back, forming pressure groups, involving themselves in environmental issues, and publicizing their plight.

Ecuador's Music

Ecuador's oldest music comes from the highlands. The sounds of the Andean panpipes and flutes have drawn audiences worldwide. The small *rondador* (roen-thah-DOER), the Ecuadorian panpipe, is made from bamboo and is similar to the *zampoña* (sahm-PONE-yah) of Peru and Bolivia, which many Ecuadorians now also play. The bamboo *quena* (KAY-nah) is the main flute, but there is also the smaller *pingullu* (peen-GOO-yoo). Percussion instruments include large and small drums called *bombos* (BOME-boess), rattles made from gourds, maracas, and a variety of bells. The *charango* (chah-RAHN-goe), made from an armadillo shell, resembles a tiny guitar.

The Spanish introduced stringed instruments, including the guitar, violin, mandolin, and harp. A basic part of fiestas, brass bands provide music for parades. Many of the trumpets, trombones, and other instruments are old and battered, but they create amazingly loud background music. Ecuador's most extraordinary instrument must be the *coroneta* (koe-roe-NAY-tah), or *bocina* (boe-SEE-nah), made from as many as twenty cow horns bound together.

The main highland dance is the *sanjuanito* (sahn-wahn-EE-toe), while the most widespread dances, both of European origin, are the *pasillo* (pah-SEE-yoe) in waltz time and the *pasacalle* (pah-sah-CAH-yay), which is similar to the Spanish *pasodoble* (pah-sah-THOE-blay).

Cofan Indian women in Lago Agrio, an Amazon town in Ecuador's oil-producing lowlands. They are selling handicrafts made from the seeds of forest plants, shells, and feathers.

Panama Hats

Ecuador's most famous craft, for which it has long been denied recognition, is the Panama hat. Panama hats are made in Ecuador, not Panama. They got the name in the 1850s, when gold miners returning from Central America to New York mistakenly said their elegant straw hats came from Panama. They next came to the notice of the public when U.S. soldiers wore them at the end of the nineteenth century. Since then they have been very popular with film stars, kings, presidents, and fashion-conscious men worldwide.

The finest Panamas come from Montecristi near the coastal town of Manta. They are made from local **toquilla** *(toe-KEE-yah) straw, which has to be boiled and dried before it can be woven. Women and children do much of the weaving because small, nimble fingers are needed to handle the strands of straw, which are only fractions of an inch wide for the finest hats. A good Panama, or* **superfino** *(soo-pair-FEE-noe), takes three months to make and will cost $1,000 in Paris, London, or New York, yet the weavers receive only a tiny fraction of that sum. People have been making Panamas in Montecristi for 150 years, but many fear the end is in sight. The Panama hat is no longer as popular as it once was, and Costeños find they can make more money from farming and ranching.*

Today in Montecristi only a few small businesses continue making Panama hats, but a genuine Montecristi Panama still commands the highest prices on the international market.

Painting Ecuador's History

Several of Ecuador's leading painters, such as Eduardo Kingman and Camilio Egas, have indígena backgrounds and have used indígena subjects to portray suffering and oppression. Perhaps the best known and most controversial painter is Oswaldo Guayasamín. Many of his works portray social or political protest but often with rather ugly depictions of indígena people. Guayasamín's best-known mural is in the Congress building in Quito, where he depicts the course of Ecuador's history in twenty-three panels. Four of these, in black and white, are devoted to slavery and dictatorship. In one panel a skeleton wears a helmet bearing the letters CIA, meaning the U.S. Central Intelligence Agency. This caused a furious argument with the United States. The U.S. ambassador called for the letters to be painted out, and there was talk of cutting aid to Ecuador, but in the end the panel remained unchanged.

EL SALVADOR

EL SALVADOR IS THE SMALLEST AND MOST DENSELY POPULATED COUNTRY in Central America.

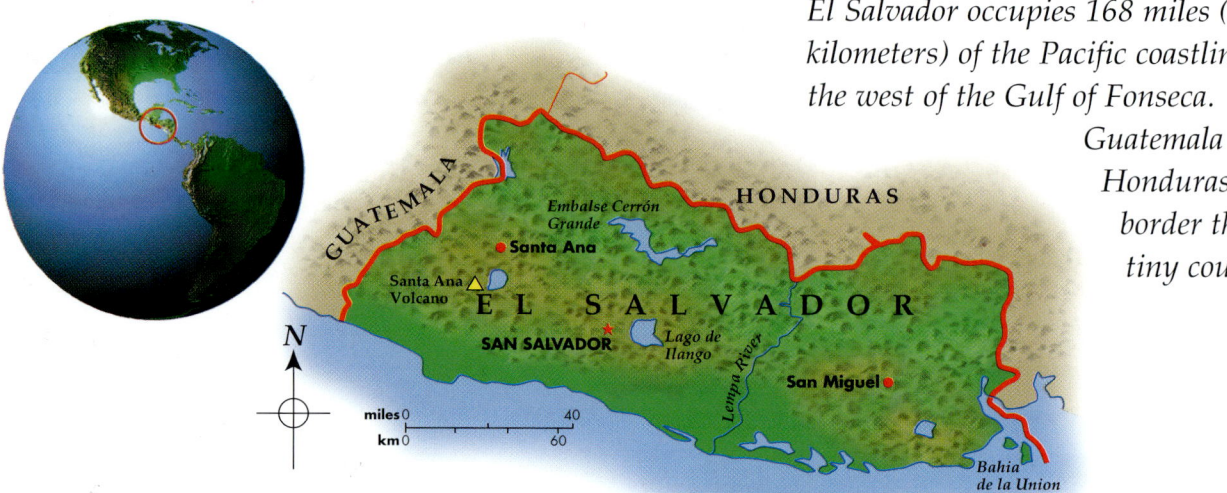

El Salvador occupies 168 miles (270 kilometers) of the Pacific coastline, to the west of the Gulf of Fonseca.

Guatemala and Honduras border the tiny country.

The Lempa, the longest river in Central America, meanders around El Salvador, and the country boasts several large lakes. Beyond a narrow coastal strip, fertile slopes and plateaus rise to volcanic mountains. The highest peak, at 7,825 feet (2,385 meters) above sea level, is Santa Ana Volcano. The country lies in a seismic danger zone, and in 1986 a devastating earthquake hit the capital, San Salvador. Over the ages it has suffered from other earthquakes, floods, and a volcanic eruption.

CLIMATE

The narrow coastal belt known as the tierra caliente *(tee-AY-rah kah-lee-AYN-tay), or "hot land," is typically tropical and humid. In the highlands and plateaus, conditions are cooler. The dry season lasts from November to April, although a light rain can fall. The wet season delivers a heavy rainfall along the coast.*

Average January temperature: *71°F (22°C)*

Average July temperature: *75°F (24°C)*

Average annual precipitation: *78 in (198 cm)*

From Cuscatlán to San Salvador

By 2000 B.C.E. the Native American peoples of Central America were sowing the seeds of great civilizations, and El Salvador (el SAHL-bah-door) was on the fringe of these remarkable cultures. A massive stone head found at Chalchuapa, in the west of the country, suggests that the Olmec culture, based around the Bay of Campeche in Mexico, had reached this area perhaps four thousand years ago. The Mayan culture, which started flourishing around twenty-three hundred years ago, was also based in the north, in Mexico's Yucatán peninsula. In El Salvador the Maya left behind stone ruins such as the impressive pyramids of Tazumal and San Andrés. The power of the Maya declined after 900 C.E.

At the time of conquest by the Europeans, eastern El Salvador was the home of Mayan groups known as the Lenca and Pokoman. The most powerful and numerous people were the Pipil, who

FACTS AND FIGURES

Official name: *República de El Salvador*

Status: *Independent state*

Capital: *San Salvador*

Major cities: *Santa Ana, San Miguel*

Area: *8,260 square miles (21,395 square kilometers)*

Population: *5,900,000*

Population density: *714 per square mile (276 per square kilometer)*

Peoples: *80 percent mestizo; 10 percent European descent; 10 percent Native American*

Official language: *Spanish*

Currency: *Colón*

National day: *Independence Day (September 15)*

Country's name: *El Salvador is Spanish for "The Savior" (Jesus Christ). The name is taken from the capital, San Salvador, which was named after the Christian festival of San Salvador del Mundo, meaning "Holy Savior of the World."*

then won a decisive battle against them. The land became part of Spain's Central American empire, governed by a viceroy (royal official) in Guatemala. A capital city, San Salvador, was founded in 1525 but was relocated several times.

In the 1800s, revolt against Spanish rule spread like wildfire through Central and South America. After uprisings in 1811 and 1814, Salvadorans finally joined their Central American neighbors in declaring independence in 1821. These colonies formed the United Provinces of Central America. In 1841, El Salvador broke away as an independent republic.

The region had few resources. Cacao was planted and its beans, used for making chocolate, were exported. From the 1860s on, coffee became the chief crop, bringing great wealth to the few landowners. Most people remained desperately poor.

In 1931 the coffee market collapsed, creating great hardship. The following year a revolution was put down with the

were related to two other great Mexican peoples, the Toltecs and the Aztecs. These peoples lived by hunting and growing corn, squash, and beans. They wove cloth and made baskets and pottery.

A Spanish conquistador, Pedro de Alvarado, invaded the region known as Cuscatlán, the "Land of Jewels," in 1524. At first he was defeated by the Pipil but

The step pyramids of San Andrés in western El Salvador were built by the ancient Maya. This site was discovered in 1977. Much of it is still to be excavated.

Timeline:	Native Americans settle in western El Salvador	Olmecs reach El Salvador	Start of classic Mayan civilization	Decline of Mayan civilization	Pedro de Alvarado defeats the Pipil and conquers region for Spain
	5000 B.C.E.	2000 B.C.E.	300 C.E.	900	1525

massacre of about thirty thousand rebels, many of them indigenous peoples. From 1944 until 1979 the army played a key role, controlling government policy. The 1980s saw increasing violence and turmoil as a civil war broke out between extreme right-wing governments, supported by the United States, and the Frente Martí Liberación Nacional (FMLN), left-wing guerrillas. Government-supported and U.S.-funded death squads murdered anyone they disliked, including liberal priests and the Roman Catholic Archbishop, Oscar Romero. It is believed the death squads killed over fifty thousand people. In retaliation, the FMLN blew up railroad tracks and destroyed plantations in order to weaken the national economy.

A Spoiled Paradise

El Salvador is one of the most polluted countries in the Americas. Waste poisons the waters of the Lempa and many other rivers; in a country where many people have no other water supply, this poses a serious hazard to health. The air pollution from traffic and factories in San Salvador also poses a danger. The loss of natural forest—only 5 percent of the land is still forested—has led to precious soil being washed away. The pressure on land is tremendous, since this tiny country could have a population of over seven million by the year 2010.

In 1992 the United Nations arranged a peace deal, and the rebels were recognized as a legitimate political party. They performed well in the 1997 elections to the National Assembly, winning as many seats as the right-wing ARENA party. Years of war have left the country war-weary, its infrastructure destroyed. Hundreds of thousands of Salvadorans left the country to escape the violence.

Hardship amid Beauty

El Salvador's indigenous peoples include the Pipil (the Panchimalco, Nahuizalco, and Izalco groups of the southwest, near the Guatemalan border) and the Lenca (whose

These two women guerrillas fought for the FMLN during El Salvador's tragic civil war in the 1980s. The long struggle ended in compromise and an uneasy peace.

Freedom from Spain	El Salvador is a member of the United Provinces of Central America	Army puts down revolution	Border war with Honduras	Civil war	Peace under UN agreement
1821	1823–1841	1932	1969	1980s	1991–1992

Local women wash their clothes in the open air in Laguna el Jocotál. This is in the east of the country, not far from El Salvador's third biggest city, San Miguel.

lands straddle the border with Honduras, in the northeast). Years of persecution, massacre, and civil war have virtually destroyed all Native traditions in El Salvador. Only a few Pipil still speak their Native Nahua language, which is related to the ancient language of the Aztecs. However, towns and geographical features, such as rivers and volcanoes, have kept their indigenous names. Only on Christian feast days does the traditional dress of Native Americans still appear. The everyday lives of Native Salvadorans are not so different from those of the mestizos (mixed-descent Salvadorans) who make up the vast majority of the population.

El Salvador is a land of extremes between rich and poor. About 20 percent of the people own 70 percent of the wealth. The rich own big coffee plantations and often have financial interests in the United States. The small middle class includes business managers, doctors, teachers, and store owners. About 70 percent of Salvadorans are poor. Health care and education resources are of a low standard because of a lack of funding and the destruction caused

by the civil war. Men can expect to live to sixty-four and women to sixty-nine. Nearly a quarter of all men—and even more women—cannot read or write.

Forty-four percent of Salvadorans live in cities such as Santa Ana in the west, San Miguel in the east, and San Salvador in the Valle de las Hamacas. San Salvador, the capital, is a bustling, modern city. Few old buildings survived the severe earthquakes that have shaken San Salvador over the years. Pick-up trucks, taxis, and minibuses jam the streets. Many city dwellers work for low wages in factories and stores. Country people come to the capital in search of work, but there are few profitable jobs. The poor must live in makeshift shacks, a world away from the homes of the wealthy, and earn a living by selling cigarettes or lottery tickets on the streets.

A farmhand, one of many people in El Salvador who depend on farming for their livelihood. About one-third of El Salvador is used for pasture and about one-third for crops.

Out in the country, people also lead a hard life. Villages are often of simple, thatched, single-story cabins called *chozas* (CHOE-sass). These may be built from whitewashed adobe (mud brick) or from wattle and daub (interwoven strips of wood coated with dried mud). There is little electricity, and power supplies are unreliable. The collection of firewood for cooking and heating only adds to the serious problem of deforestation, and water supplies are often of poor quality. Many people earn a living working on coffee plantations in season. Others grow just enough food to keep themselves fed or to sell at the market.

Corn has provided flour for cooking since the days of the Maya. As in neighboring countries, tortillas (flat cornmeal pancakes) are baked on a clay griddle and served with frijoles (beans, either boiled whole or mashed and refried). Another type of pancake, the *pupusa* (poo-POO-sah), is made of cornmeal or rice flour. It has various fillings, from cheese to beans, and makes a tasty snack served with pickles. Tropical fruits such as mangoes and bananas are plentiful and—naturally—so is good strong coffee.

The most popular sports in El Salvador are baseball, basketball, and soccer, which is the national passion. Riots at an international soccer match even sparked off a brief but bloody war with Honduras in 1969. The underlying reason for that conflict was the refugee problem between the two countries.

About 90 percent of all Salvadorans are Roman Catholic. The years of civil war divided the church, with some Catholics supporting the rebels and siding with the oppressed and poor and others supporting the wealthy and powerful. Indigenous traditions have influenced Catholic beliefs in places. Many people believe in evil

Catholics mark the Christian festival of Palm Sunday, which commemorates Christ's entry into Jerusalem. Some hold palm leaves as they join a procession through San Salvador.

cement, and pharmaceuticals. The country, once far too dependent on growing coffee, now also exports sugar, cotton, and textiles.

Poor peasants work on the coffee and sugar plantations, but small farmers also grow crops for local markets or their own use. These include corn, sorghum, tomatoes, cassava, bananas, and rice.

The long years under military control and the civil war wrecked the Salvadoran economy. About half of the labor force is unemployed. Many Salvadoran refugees remain abroad, especially in the United States, and send money back to El Salvador.

The berries picked by this coffee plantation worker contain seeds. These are the "beans" that make coffee. The economy of El Salvador depends on this crop.

spirits and witchcraft, or *brujería* (broo-hay-REE-ah). They often visit Indian *curanderos* (koo-rahn-DAY-roess), or herbal doctors, and take part in rituals in search of cures for illnesses. Protestant churches, including Evangelical and Baptist churches, have gained many converts since the 1980s.

Going to Work

El Salvador has very few resources, although the Lempa River is harnessed for hydroelectric power. Major industries include oil refining and manufacturing of garments, footwear, cardboard boxes,

A Country Named After a Festival

As in many lands where the Spanish have influenced the way of life, festivals play an important part in much of El Salvador. Every village and town has its own special fiesta in honor of its patron saint. The celebrations are Christian but influenced by indigenous traditions. Native American communities take this opportunity to wear customary outfits and perform traditional music and dances. A big festival on December 12 honors the Virgin of Guadalupe, whose banner symbolized the Central American struggle for independence in the 1800s.

The biggest festival of all is that of San Salvador del Mundo, held in the capital. In fact both the city and the country take their name from this festival, on the eve of which, in 1525, Pedro de Alvarado finally defeated the Pipil and won the country for Spain. The celebrations take place during the week before August 6 and are marked by processions and a big fair.

FALKLAND ISLANDS

THE FALKLAND ISLANDS ARE A BRITISH COLONY in the remote South Atlantic Ocean.

The Falkland Islands lie about 250 miles (400 kilometers) off the coast of Argentina and about 480 miles (770 kilometers) north of Cape Horn, the stormy tip of South America. They include about two hundred islands, scattered over a vast area of cold, gray ocean.

N

WEST FALKLAND

North Falkland Sound

Mount Adam

Mount Usborne

FALKLAND ISLANDS

Port Darwin

STANLEY

Mount Pleasant

Port Stephens

EAST FALKLAND

Falkland Sound

miles 0 — 20
km 0 — 30

East and West Falkland, divided by Falkland Sound, are each over 2,000 square miles (5,180 square kilometers) in area. The other islands are mostly small, uninhabited except by sheep. The coastline is rugged and rocky, with some sandy inlets, the haunt of penguins and seals.

CLIMATE

The cold Antarctic current flowing up from the southern oceans affects the climate of the Falkland Islands. The islands have a cool, temperate climate, driest in November. Violent gales can blow up from the southwest, especially during the southern spring.

Average January temperature: *49°F (9°C)*

Average July temperature: *35°F (2°C)*

Average annual precipitation: *27 in (69 cm)*

At the Bottom of the World

Indigenous peoples from Patagonia may have reached the Falkland Islands by canoe, but there is no evidence of settlement. The islands were uninhabited when they were sighted in 1592 by an English ship called *Desire*. In the following years the islands were claimed and occasionally settled by the French, the Spanish from Argentina, and the British. In 1833 the British expelled the Argentineans and declared the islands a British colony.

The islanders lived by sheep farming in the countryside. The port of Stanley, founded in 1844, served whalers and seal hunters as well as sailing vessels bound for the stormy waters of Cape Horn.

Argentina never gave up its claim to the islands, which it called Islas Malvinas. In 1982 it sent troops to invade the Falklands. British troops defeated the Argentineans in a short but tragic conflict that cost many lives.

Almost all of today's Falklanders are of English or Scottish descent. Over two-thirds are Falklands-born, while the rest have mostly come to settle and farm. Locally produced food is restricted to lamb, beef, fish, dairy products, and vegetables.

Boats and four-wheel-drive vehicles are essential for getting around, since most

FACTS AND FIGURES

Status: *United Kingdom Crown Colony*

Capital: *Stanley*

Area: *4,700 square miles (12,175 square kilometers)*

Population: *2,100*

Population density: *0.4 per square mile (0.2 per square kilometer)*

Peoples: *Of English and Scottish descent*

Official language: *English*

Currency: *Falkland pound (equal to one British pound)*

National day: *Falklands Day (August 14)*

Country's name: *Falkland is a Scottish place name, given to the Falkland Sound in 1690.*

fifteen are educated in Stanley, although there are small schools elsewhere and some traveling teachers. During February, when the weather is at its best, islanders gather for parties and traditional country sports, such as sheep dog trials.

The 1982 war ended the extreme isolation of the Falklands. British troops moved there and tourists came, eager to study the bird and animal life. New roads were constructed, and a new airport was built at Mount Pleasant on East Falkland. Money was put into education, communications, and health care.

The future of the islanders will depend on economics. Sheep breeding has always determined the way of life of the Falklanders, centered around shearing, peat cutting, and other tasks of the farming year. Since the 1980s the island government has also raised money by licensing fishing fleets, although this business has since suffered from competition with Argentina. The islanders may face great changes in the future if large reserves of offshore oil are exploited, as expected.

roads are little more than rough tracks over peat bog. The government runs a light aircraft service to carry medical supplies, mail, and equipment around the islands. Peat is widely burned as a fuel. Timber has to be imported (the islands are bare of trees), as do oil and the machinery needed for life on remote settlements.

Over half the population lives in Stanley, the capital, on East Falkland, a town with houses of stone, brick, and clapboard with roofs of tin. Dominated by Government House, the center of the British administration, and Christ Church Cathedral, Stanley is the center of the islands' broadcasting service. Most children between the ages of five and

Falkland Islanders pass by Saint Mary's Roman Catholic Church, which was built in Stanley in 1873. What will the future hold for this remote settlement in the South Atlantic?

Timeline:	French establish garrison at Port Louis	British found settlement at Port Egmont	Spanish take over Port Louis and Port Egmont	British expel Spanish; Falklands become a British colony	Argentina invades and is defeated by British troops
	1764	**1765**	**1767**	**1833**	**1982**

FRENCH GUIANA

FRENCH GUIANA LIES ON THE NORTHEAST COAST OF SOUTH AMERICA, facing the Atlantic Ocean.

French Guiana has three main land regions. The coastal strip contains swamps, palms, mangrove forests, and open grassland, or savannah. Behind the coast the land rises gradually to more savannahs that extend inland for about 50 miles (80 kilometers). Most people live on the coast and the savannahs. The rest of the country is covered with rain forest and is dissected by many rivers. The only significant mountain range, the Tumuc-Humac, runs along the southern border with Brazil.

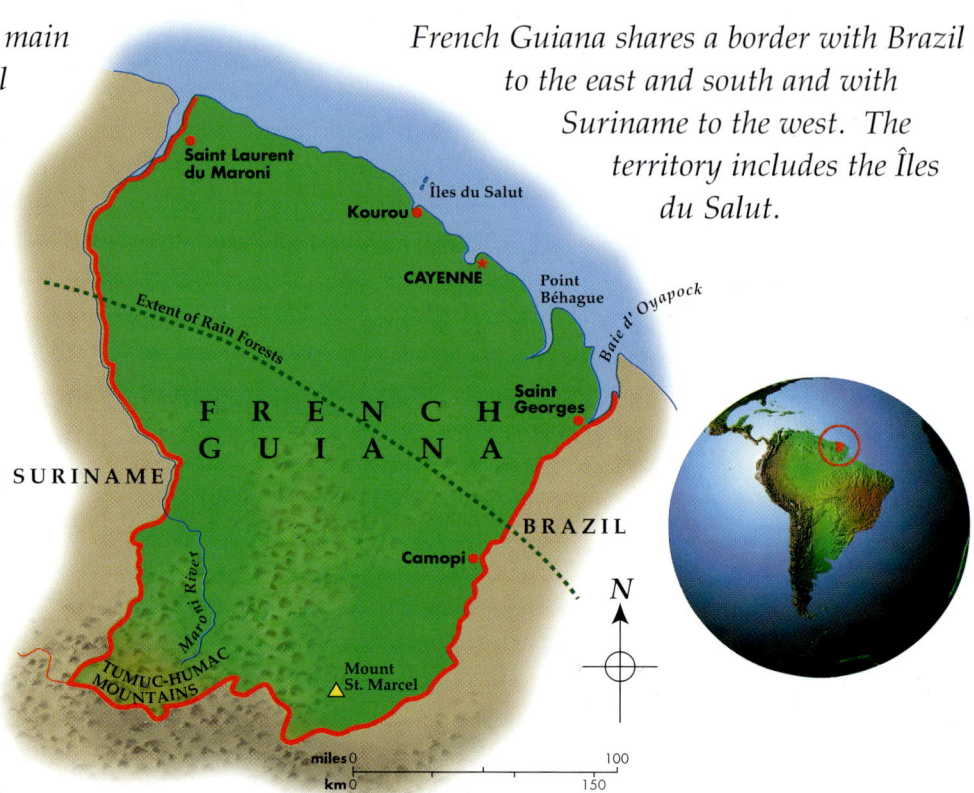

French Guiana shares a border with Brazil to the east and south and with Suriname to the west. The territory includes the Îles du Salut.

Settlers, Prisoners, and Refugees: A Hard Life for All

In 1500, when the first Europeans made landfall in the area covered by French Guiana (ghee-AH-nah) today, the land was inhabited by Arawak- and Carib-speaking forest Indians. These hunters and gatherers were descendants of the first Native Americans who came ten thousand to fifteen thousand years ago. During the seventeenth century, French, English, and Dutch settlers arrived. The French founded Cayenne, the present-day capital,

CLIMATE

French Guiana is hot and humid. The temperature varies little through the year, and it rains heavily most of the time, especially between December and July.

Average year-round temperature: *79°F (26°C)*

Average annual precipitation: *120 in (305 cm)*

in 1643 and eventually took control of the territory in 1676.

The first settlers traded in brazilwood for the red dye extracted from it; the dye became fashionable in Europe. Later colonists developed plantations of coffee, cacao, vanilla, cotton, and sugarcane. Late in the seventeenth century, black slaves

FACTS AND FIGURES

Official name: *Département de la Guyane Française*

Status: *Overseas department of the Republic of France*

Capital: *Cayenne*

Major cities: *Kourou, Saint Laurent du Maroni*

Area: *33,399 square miles (86,504 square kilometers)*

Population: *132,500*

Population density: *4 per square mile (1.5 per square kilometer)*

Peoples: *40 percent Creole (mixed African-European descent); 5 percent European descent; 4 percent Native American; 1 percent Maroon; 50 percent other, including Chinese, Indian, Lebanese, Haitian, and refugees from Laos and Suriname*

Official language: *French*

Currency: *French franc*

National days: *Labor Day (May 1); National Day (July 14); Armistice Day (November 11)*

Country's name: *The word Guiana is believed to come from a Native American word meaning "land of waters."*

authorities accepted the situation and declared them free.

The colonization of French Guiana progressed very little during the eighteenth century. The coastal region of swamps and mangroves was difficult to cross, and many would-be French settlers succumbed to local diseases. When slavery was abolished in 1848, there were twenty thousand slaves and a European population of twelve hundred. The former slaves left the plantations, and the planters tried unsuccessfully to attract labor from Asia. Only a few people from India and China came, and the economy went into decline.

Political prisoners had been sent to French Guiana since the French Revolution in 1789. In 1851, as a solution to the labor situation, the French emperor Napoleon III decided to send more—and dangerous

This illustration of people in Cayenne in the 1860s shows a mixed population. At that time there were a great many more descendants of African slaves than of European settlers.

were brought from Africa. Some escaped the harsh treatment and set up independent communities in the forest. They became known as *Marrons* (mah-RONS) (in English, Maroons), or "wild slaves." In time the

Timeline:	First Native Americans arrive	Dutch, British, and French occupy the area	French found Cayenne	Slavery abolished
	13,000–8,000 B.C.E.	1600s C.E.	1643	1848

Devil's Island

For almost 150 years the French government disposed of its enemies and criminals by sending them to French Guiana. Prisoners came by sea and were dispatched to different parts of the colony. All dreaded being sent to the Îles du Salut: Île Royale, Île Saint-Joseph, and Île du Diable (Devil's Island). Shark-ridden seas separated these islands; escape was virtually impossible. Dreadful conditions included underground cells where prisoners could be held in solitary confinement for months, sometimes years, on end.

Devil's Island had the worst reputation. Surrounded by strong currents, it covers just 35 acres (14 hectares). A wire carried food there from Île Royale. One convicted murderer, Henri Charrière, better known as Papillon, was there in the 1930s. He wrote a book describing his numerous attempts to escape and his eventual success on a makeshift raft.

criminals as well. France deported more than seventy thousand men between 1851 and 1939.

In 1946 French Guiana became an overseas department of France, with the same laws and administration as a department in France. In 1970 a pro-independence group emerged, and demonstrations arose against the French government, mainly about the poor state of the economy. In 1974 France granted French Guiana regional status and more aid. Little improved, however, and demonstrations and protests continue to the present day. More recent protests have often been against the thousands of refugees fleeing from a civil war in neighboring Suriname (see SURINAME).

The People Today: A Cultural Mix

Creoles make up the largest single ethnic group in French Guiana today. They are of mixed African and European parentage. Though French is their first language, they also speak a Creole dialect, a mixture of mainly French and African languages, with a few English and Portuguese words.

There are six surviving groups of Native Americans. The Galibi and the Arawak Indians on the coast have largely integrated into Creole society by marriage and dress, by speaking French or Creole, and by working for local farmers. However, the Palikur, another coastal group, prefer to remain in isolation, and though they, too, wear Western clothing, they show no desire to enter the mainstream economy. In the interior, contact with Europeans has devastated the Emerillon and most of the Oyampi Indians. Alcoholism and prostitution are big problems for these groups. One remote group of Oyampi still lives in a traditional way, growing crops, fishing, and hunting. The largest group in the interior is the Wayana. Although there are less than one

French Guiana becomes a penal colony	French Guiana becomes an overseas department of France	European Space Agency site and town of Kourou built	France grants French Guiana regional status
1851	**1946**	**1968**	**1974**

thousand of them remaining today, they still lead a traditional way of life and speak their own language. Other forest dwellers include several groups of Maroons, the descendants of African slaves who escaped and settled in the forest.

Immigrants in French Guiana come from around the world. Indians and Chinese were imported as workers in the nineteenth century. The Chinese now run restaurants and stores in the towns. Haitians have left their own desperately poor island in the

Carnival

Carnival in Cayenne starts in February and reaches a climax during the four days before Ash Wednesday. On Saturday disguised and masked women, known as Touloulous, ask men to dance with them in the streets. The men are not allowed to refuse. On Sunday are parades. On Monday people mock marriage as men dress as brides and women as grooms. On Tuesday, Vaval, the devil and soul of Carnival, appears, accompanied by dancers dressed in red costumes with horns and tails and carrying pitchforks. That night, a straw doll representing Vaval is burnt, and the following day, Ash Wednesday, everyone dresses in black and white to mourn him.

A Hmong mother and son. Two groups of Hmong, political refugees from Laos, have settled in two communities, one south of Cayenne, the other near Saint Laurent du Maroni.

Caribbean in search of better work in French Guiana. Brazilians come because they can get better paying jobs here than at home. Some Lebanese are involved in commerce and run textile and clothing companies.

In 1977 a group of five hundred Hmong from Laos were given French government aid and settled south of Cayenne. A second group arrived ten years later. The Hmong have become successful gardeners and sell much of the country's fruit and vegetables.

The most recent immigrants are refugees from Suriname, fleeing civil war in their own country. They have been housed in camps near Saint Laurent du Maroni, but

High school children outside their school in Saint Georges. Although many children are now attending school, the illiteracy rate is still high, at over 15 percent.

their presence—at one time ten thousand strong—has placed a great strain on the medical and educational facilities in French Guiana.

French Influence

The people of French Guiana are French citizens, and education is modeled on the French system, with compulsory, free schooling for children ages six to sixteen. Students usually go to college either in France or in Cayenne.

Most people are Roman Catholic, though many are joining evangelical churches such as the Assembly of God and Jehovah's Witnesses. Immigrant communities practice their own religions. Native Americans worship their own spirits and gods, related to the natural world around them.

Economically, French Guiana depends very heavily on aid from France, and the

French government is the largest employer. French Guiana grows a large variety of fruit and vegetables, and many kinds of fish flourish in its waters. Food is also flown in regularly from France, including cheeses, pâtés, and meat. Typical Creole food includes rice, beans, cassava flour, breadfruit, and various spices, including Cayenne pepper. In the towns are Chinese and other ethnic restaurants.

People of the Coast and the Savannahs

Although Cayenne, the capital, is mainly a Creole city, the French influence is everywhere. French-style *gendarmes* (ZHAN-dahrm), or police officers, direct French-made cars. People employed by the French government as civil servants, lawyers, teachers, and doctors receive the same pay and benefits as workers in

At the central market in Cayenne, there is a wide variety of fruit and vegetables for sale. This trader has locally grown lettuce, bananas, and ginger root.

Wayana Indians making a canoe. After scouring out wood from a tree trunk, they attach struts to secure the frame and dry out the wood to seal in the resins from the tree.

France. They have good homes and a high standard of living. They drive nice cars, buy imported French food, and some send their children to school in France. Others, such as traders and people running their own businesses, earn less money. Their homes are often old, wooden colonial buildings, and they buy their food in the local markets. About sixty thousand people live in Cayenne and about twenty thousand, mainly Creoles, in Saint Laurent du Maroni, a quiet colonial town on the Maroni River close to the border with Suriname.

In rural areas along the coast and on the savannahs, Creoles work as fishers and as farmers growing crops for their own use. A few are employed on plantations growing sugarcane or fruit.

People of the Forest Interior

The Wayana (why-YAH-nah) are the largest group in the forest interior. Their home is a protected area that visitors cannot enter without permission and a medical certificate. The authorities' attitude is one of protection alongside development. For example, in one Wayana school, children can watch television and videos powered by batteries charged from solar panels.

Yet much of Wayana life is still traditional. They clear land in the forest to grow cassava and other crops, and they hunt and catch fish. Wayana dress consists

A community of Maroons in the 1860s. Maroons were descendants of African slaves who escaped and were left to live in independent communities in the forest.

of a simple piece of cloth that covers the lower part of the body. They still make traditional handicrafts such as necklaces and bracelets of seeds and glass beads, cane baskets, bows and arrows, and pottery, all sold through a cooperative in Cayenne.

In every Wayana village stands a *tukusipan* (too-koo-SEE-pahn), a large, circular, communal hut made from dried palm leaves. There, the Wayana hold meetings and festivities. To the highest point on the inside of the roof, the Wayana attach a *maluana* (mah-loo-AH-nah), a circular piece of wood cut from the trunk of a *fromager* (froe-mah-JAY) tree. They paint the maluana in bright colors with geometrical designs and animals that have spiritual or mythological meaning.

The Wayana still hold one ceremony called the *marake* (mah-RAH-kay), or the "ant test," part of the ritual boys and girls undergo before they begin their adult life, around the age of eleven or twelve. A wicker frame full of stinging ants is applied to their bodies; to show strength, the children must remain silent.

French Guiana's forests are also home to groups of Maroons, whose slave ancestors escaped and settled in the forest. Some have come into French Guiana from Suriname. They live close to the Maroni River near the border with Suriname, where they live in houses made of wood and palm thatch, growing food and catching fish. Traditionally they paint their house doors in vivid colors and complex designs. They are experienced boatpeople, with a knowledge of the Maroni River's rapids and shallows that is unequaled. Sometimes they work as guides to prospectors or tourists. The Maroons speak their own language, Taki-Taki, a mixture of English, Dutch, and African words.

Les Métros: People of Space City

Kourou, on the coast to the west of Cayenne, is locally called the "white" city because of the large community of metropolitan French families, *les métros* (lay may-TROE), living there. These technicians, engineers, and administrators come on short-term contracts to work at the European Space Agency center, a rocket launch site. Kourou was built for them, with red brick housing and apartments of modern French design, landscaped lawns,

and wide avenues. There are upscale shopping centers and supermarkets, recreational and sports facilities, and a lake for boating. Between ten and twenty thousand people live there, much as they would in France. The European Space Agency provides work for local Creoles in spin-off jobs like construction and makes a substantial contribution to the economy.

The People at Play

In their free time some people head for the coast—to sail, fish, or go bird-watching in the swamps, which are rich in wildlife. Few people head for the beaches, as they are often muddy and the currents are strong. Thanks to the French influence, cycling is popular, and people take part in weekend road races. As elsewhere in Latin America, soccer is the most popular sport; even the Wayana boys and girls enjoy the game.

Cycling is one of the most popular sports in French Guiana. Races take place mainly on the paved roads along the coast. Here the riders are close to Cayenne.

Glossary

agricultural reform: the redistribution of land to the poor.

antagonize: to irritate, to go against someone or something.

black market: illegal trade, usually of goods that are otherwise difficult to get.

choreographer: a designer or arranger of dances, especially ballet.

clapboard: overlapping wood planking nailed on exterior walls of buildings to protect against the weather.

commerce: the buying and selling of goods; business.

Communist: a believer in communism, a theory that suggests that all property belongs to the community and that work should be organized for the common good.

compulsory: enforced, often by law.

cooperative: a group of people working together to achieve the same thing. Craftspeople often form cooperatives to sell their work at a better price and to more people than they could on their own.

Creole: an English word related to a French, Spanish, or Portuguese term meaning "native to the locality," but it has come to mean very different things at different times and places: (1) most generally, any Caribbean not born in Africa; (2) a Caribbean or Latin American who is descended from the original colonial settlers rather than later arrivals; (3) in the United States, a Louisiana citizen of French descent; (4) various patois, dialects, or accents of French or English as spoken in the Caribbean and the Americas. The Spanish equivalent is *Criollo*.

decadent: to be in a state of decline or decay; chacterized by self-indulgence.

department: a region within a country or state created for administrative purposes.

divination: the practice of foretelling future events by supernatural or magical means.

equator: the imaginary line that circles the earth midway between the North and South Poles.

fallow: a piece of land that is plowed but left without crops for a period of time.

filigree: delicate jewelry made from threads and beads, usually of gold or silver.

FMLN: the Frente Martí Liberación Nacional (FMLN) is a Salvadoran revolutionary movement. In 1979 the FMLN formed the largest group within an alliance of opposition groups. It fought a violent guerrilla campaign against the U.S.-backed Christian Democrat Party and the extreme right-wing ARENA party. It agreed to a cease-fire in 1992 and campaigned as a democratic political party.

garrison: a place where soldiers are housed.

godparents: people who, at the baptism of a child, agree to provide guidance and encourage spiritual growth and development.

guerrilla: a member of an irregular fighting force whose tactics include ambushes, surprise attacks, or sabotage rather than intense, close battles with the enemy.

hallucinogen: a substance taken that makes a person appear to see things that are not there.

illiteracy: the state of being unable to read or write.

impeach: to formally accuse a public official of misconduct. If the official is found guilty, he or she is removed from office.

indigenous: referring to a people who were born within a country or a region as opposed to being immigrants or settlers; also meaning "aboriginal" or "native."

left-wing: pursuing radical, progressive, or socialist politics.

Lenten: referring to the period of Lent, the forty days preceding Easter.

Mafia: a group of people opposed to the law who often resort to violent crimes; the original groups were from Sicily, Italy.

martyr: a person who suffers or dies for a cause he or she believes in.

massacre: a bloody, brutal killing of people or animals, often on a large scale.

mestizo: originally a Spanish word for someone of mixed descent, specifically a person of mixed European and American Indian descent.

motif: a distinctive feature or pattern as part of a design.

nationalize: to make something the property of the nation or state.

penal colony: a place where criminals are sent for punishment.

political asylum: refuge in another country because of one's political beliefs.

prime minister: the official head of government in many democratic parliamentary systems.

propaganda: ideas or information deliberately spread to influence the thoughts of others.

republic: a government in which power resides in a body of elected representatives.

revolutionary: a person who tries to overthrow a government or ruler by force.

right-wing: favoring conservative and antireformist politics.

seismic: of or relating to underground tremors and earthquakes.

shantytown: an area of makeshift housing, often illegally constructed by poor people on the edge of a town.

slash-and-burn cultivation: the practice of felling trees and clearing the ground by burning, then using it for crops for a few years before moving on.

solstice: one of two times in the year when the sun is farthest from the equator.

sorghum: a grain crop commonly grown in hot countries.

speculator: a person who takes risks investing in business or finance in hope of gaining.

trade embargo: to prevent trading by not allowing goods to be carried in or out of a country.

Further Reading

Cuba

Crouch, Clifford. *Cuba.* Broomall, PA: Chelsea House, 1991.

Cummins, Ronald. *Cuba.* Milwaukee, WI: Gareth Stevens, 1991.

Haverstock, Nathan. *Cuba in Pictures.* Minneapolis, MN: Lerner Group, 1993.

Morris, Emily. *Cuba.* Chatham, NJ: Raintree Steck-Vaughn, 1991.

Sheehan, Sean. *Cultures of the World: Cuba.* Tarrytown, NY: Marshall Cavendish, 1994.

Staelb, Frank. *Children of Cuba.* Minneapolis, MN: Lerner Group, 1996.

Stewart, Gail. *Cuba.* New York: Crestwood House, 1991.

Dominica

Staib, Frank J. *Children of Dominica.* Secaucus, NJ: Carol Publishing Group, 1998.

Dominican Republic

Foley, Erin. *Dominican Republic.* Tarrytown, NY: Marshall Cavendish, 1995.

Haverstock, Nathan. *Dominican Republic in Pictures.* Minneapolis, MN: Lerner Group, 1988.

Ecuador

Bickman, Connie. *Children of Ecuador.* Minneapolis, MN: Abdo and Daughters, 1996.

Foley, Erin. *Ecuador.* Tarrytown, NY: Marshall Cavendish, 1995.

Lepthein, Emilie U. *Ecuador.* Danbury, CT: Childrens Press, 1993.

Sly, Alexandra. *The Waorani: People of the Ecuadoran Rain Forest.* Morristown, NJ: Silver Burdett Press, 1993.

El Salvador

Bachelis, Faren M. *El Salvador.* Danbury, CT: Childrens Press, 1990.

Cheney, Glenn Alan. *El Salvador, Country in Crisis.* New York: Franklin Watts, 1990.

Cummins, Ronald. *El Salvador.* Milwaukee, WI: Gareth Stevens, 1990.

Foley, Erin. *El Salvador.* Tarrytown, NY: Marshall Cavendish, 1994.

Stewart, Gaul B. *El Salvador.* New York: Crestwood House, 1991.

Falkland Islands

Strange, Ian J. *The Falklands: South Atlantic Islands.* NY: Putnam Publishing Group Library, 1985.

French Guiana

Morrison, Marion. *French Guiana.* Danbury, CT: Childrens Press, 1995.

Islands of the Caribbean

Mason, Antony. *The Caribbean.* Parsippany, NJ: Silver Burdett Press, 1988

Mayer, T. W. *The Caribbean and Its People.* New York: Thomson Learning, 1995.

Springer, Eintou P. *The Caribbean.* Parsippany, NJ: Silver Burdett Press, 1987.

Walker, Cas. *The Caribbean.* North Pomfret, VT: Trafalgar Square Publishing, 1991.

Index

Page numbers in *italic* indicate illustrations.

Page numbers in *italic* indicate illustrations.

PEOPLES
of the
AMERICAS

PEOPLES
of the
AMERICAS

Volume 4
Chile–Costa Rica

MARSHALL CAVENDISH
NEW YORK • LONDON • TORONTO • SYDNEY

Marshall Cavendish Corporation
99 White Plains Road
Tarrytown, New York 10591-9001

Consulting Editor: J. Patrick Gray, Professor of Anthropology, University of Wisconsin

Consultants: Jean-Marc Blais, Senior Interpretive Planner, Canadian Museum of Civilization, Hull, Quebec
     David Frye, Assistant Director, Department of Latin American and Caribbean Studies, University of Michigan

Spanish Consultant: Fran Kaplan

Contributing authors: D. L. Birchfield
          Marion Morrison
          Juliette Radcliffe Rogers
          Philip Steele
          Mary A. Stout

Discovery Books
     Managing Editor: Paul Humphrey
     Project Editor: Helen Dwyer
     Text Editor: Valerie J. Weber
     Design Concept: Ian Winton
     Designers: Barry Dwyer, Ian Winton, and Simon Borrough
     Cartographer: Stefan Chabluk

Marshall Cavendish
     Editorial Director: Paul Bernabeo
     Editor: Marian Armstrong
     Associate Editor: Debra M. Jacobs

The publishers would like to thank the following for their permission to reproduce photographs:
Andes Press Agency (Carlos Reyes-Manzo 174, 187); Douglas Donne Bryant Stock Photography (Robert Fried 218, 221); Eye Ubiquitous (Omar Bechara Baruque 200, 208); Hutchison Library (Jeremy Horner 207, 213 bottom; Eric Lawrie 197, 205; Brian Moser 203, 211, 212; Titus Moser 206; Moser/Tayler 204, 209); Panos Pictures (Jeremy Horner 202); Edward Parker (176, 179, 181); South American Pictures (171, 184; Jevan Berrange 215, 216, 223; Grant Fleming cover, 194, 201; Peter Francis 178; Robert Francis frontispiece, 177, 182, 222; Bill Leimbach 185; Sue Mann 170, 173, 180, 183, 186; Rebecca Morrison 191; Tony Morrison 188, 190, 192, 193, 195, 196, 198, 199, 210, 213 top, 217, 219, 220)

(frontispiece) Young rider at a fiesta in Chile.

Editor's note: Many systems of dating have been used by different cultures throughout history. *Peoples of the Americas* uses B.C.E. (Before Common Era) and C.E. (Common Era) instead of B.C. (Before Christ) and A.D. (Anno Domini, "In the Year of the Lord") out of respect for the diversity of the world's peoples.

Library of Congress Cataloging-in-Publication Data
Peoples of the Americas.
          p.   cm.
          Includes bibliographical references and index.
          Contents: v. 1. Anguilla–Belize — v. 2. Bermuda–Brazil — v. 3. Canada–Cayman Islands — v. 4. Chile–Costa Rica — v. 5.
Cuba–French Guiana — v. 6. Greenland–Jamaica — v. 7. Martinique–Paraguay — v. 8. Peru–Turks and Caicos Islands — v. 9. United States of America — v. 10. United States of America–Virgin Islands

     ISBN 0-7614-7050-6 (set)
     1. Ethnology—America—Juvenile literature. 2. America—History—Juvenile literature. [1. Ethnology—America. 2. America—History.]
E29.A1P46 1999
970'.004—dc21

                                                                                                                98-2801
                                                                                                                CIP
                                                                                                                AC

     ISBN 0-7614-7050-6 (set)
     ISBN 0-7614-7054-9 (vol. 4)

Printed and bound in Italy

Contents

CHILE

A LONG, NARROW COUNTRY, Chile runs down
the west coast of southern South America.

*Chile is approximately 2,700 miles (4,345
kilometers) long and has an average width of a
little more than 100 miles (160 kilometers).
Peru and Bolivia border Chile on the north,
Argentina shares its long eastern border, and
the Pacific Ocean laps its western coast. Its
southern tip is barely 400 miles (644
kilometers) from the Antarctic. Chile has
many islands, including Easter Island, which
is 2,000 miles (3,200 kilometers) west of the
mainland in the Pacific Ocean.*

*Natural disasters are common in Chile. Over
two thousand volcanoes dot the landscape;
more than fifty are active. Many earthquakes
have shaken the land, and sometimes
tsunamis (tsoo-NAH-mees), huge sea waves
caused by earthquakes on the ocean floor,
devastate the coast.*

*The Andes run the length of
Chile's boundary with
Argentina and take up
between a third and a
half of the width of the
country. Between the
mountains and the sea
in the north lies
desert. Most of the
population live in the
fertile central part of
the country. Farther
south lies the lake
district, a land of
forests and lakes, while
the far south consists
of cold, windswept
plains, glaciers, and
deep fjords littered
with icebergs.*

A tourist ship approaching a glacier in the fjords of
southern Chile. Very few people live in this icy region,
which covers a third of the country.

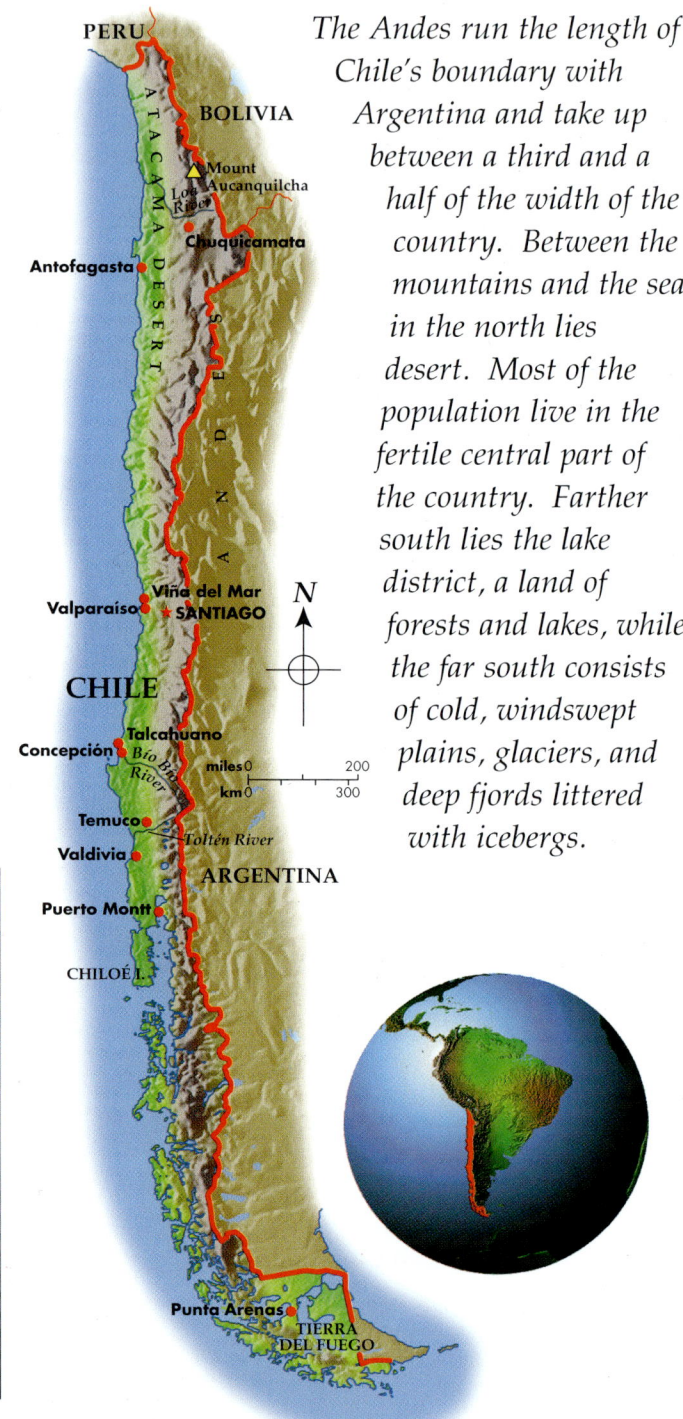

170

Native Tribes of the North and South

Native Americans settled in Chile (CHEE-lay) about ten thousand years ago. Tribes in northern Chile lived in the mountains, in the valley of the Loa River, and in other river valleys south of the desert. In the Andes were the Aymara (eye-MAH-rah) people, who also occupied parts of present-day Bolivia and Peru (see BOLIVIA and PERU). They lived by growing a few crops and herding llamas.

The main tribes in northern Chile were the Atacameño and the Diaguita, or Calchaquí (see ARGENTINA). They lived by fishing, hunting, herding llamas, and by cultivating corn, squash, cotton, and beans.

An early twentieth-century photo of an Araucanian Indian woman weaving. Her baby is strapped to a wooden, fur-lined frame, which the mother carries on her back.

These tribes lived in thatched-roof houses of adobe bricks or rough stones in small villages. They made and decorated pots, wove cloth and baskets, and used metal tools.

Araucanian-speaking peoples occupied the center of the country and the forests and lakes to the south. All these tribes fished and made a variety of watercraft from wood and reeds. They also lived in

Timeline:	First peoples arrive	Cultivation of crops begins	Incas invade
	ca. 8000 B.C.E.	ca. 1500 B.C.E.	ca. 1500 C.E.

CLIMATE

Chile endures great extremes of temperature and climate. The Atacama Desert in the north is one of the driest places on earth. Along Chile's coast, temperatures are moderated by the Peru Current, also known as the Humboldt Current, which carries cold water from the Antarctic. The central area is a temperate zone, with seasonal changes between summer and winter but no extremes of temperature. The south is very cold, wet, and windy.

	Santiago	Antofagasta	Punta Arenas
Average January temperature	67°F (19°C)	69°F (21°C)	50°F (10°C)
Average July temperature	46°F (8°C)	57°F (14°C)	36°F (2°C)
Average annual precipitation	15 in (38 cm)	0.5 in (1.3 cm)	17 in (43 cm)

thatched-roof houses with walls built of stone, wattle, mud, or wooden planks. Some, like the Picunches (pee-KOON-chase), cultivated crops. Clearings in the forests were home to the Mapuche (ma-POO-chay) and the Huilliche (wee-YEE-chay), who hunted and gathered nuts. The Pehuenche (pay-WAYN-chay) were a seminomadic hunting and gathering tribe who lived on the higher slopes and in the valleys of the Andes Mountains. Piñons, the nuts of the Araucanian pine, or monkey puzzle tree, formed the basis of their diet.

The far south of Chile was the cold realm of hunters—the Chono, Alacaluf, Haush, Yaghan, and Ona. The Ona (OE-nah) lived in present-day Tierra del Fuego, hunting animals and gathering seeds and berries. The other tribes lived on the islands and ate mostly shellfish, sea lions, and birds.

About forty years before the arrival of the Spaniards, the Incas (EEN-kahs) from Peru invaded Chile (see PERU). They soon overcame the northern tribes but failed to conquer the Mapuche. The Incas' hold over the region was still insecure when the first of the Spaniards arrived.

The Europeans Arrive

From 1536 on, Spanish explorers arrived in Chile looking for gold and silver; they founded Santiago in 1541. At this time an estimated 500,000 Native American peoples inhabited the region. The Mapuche resisted Spanish attacks, quickly learning to master horses and becoming effective guerrilla fighters. Throughout the colonial period they prevented the Spanish from taking any land south of the Bío Bío River, except the town of Valdivia and the island of Chiloé. But other Native peoples were forced to work as slaves on the land and in the copper mines. Many died from European diseases, from which they had no immunity. Marriage between the Spanish and Native peoples produced a mixed-race group called *mestizos*.

Portuguese explorer Ferdinand Magellan sights southern tip of Chile	Spanish explorer Diego de Almagro crosses northern Chile	Santiago founded	Mapuche Indians destroy all Spanish forts south of Bío Bío River
1520	1536–1537	1541	1598

During the eighteenth century some families from the Basque country on the border of Spain and France migrated to Chile. Mainly merchants and traders, they bought large tracts of land.

By the beginning of the nineteenth century, settlers were aware of independence movements in other American colonies. As the Spanish hold on its colonies weakened, the Chileans began to revolt. Argentina's revolutionary government sent an army over the Andes into Chile, defeating the Spanish in 1817 at the Battle of Chacabuco. A year later, after the Battle of Maipú, Chile became an independent country.

Relatively stable governments allowed for the growth of commerce and attracted British, Italian, French, and North American immigrants; all offered the new republic skills it lacked. They included accountants, bankers, miners, farmers, and engineers.

In 1879 Chile went to war with Bolivia and Peru (see BOLIVIA and PERU) over an area of the Atacama Desert rich in nitrates, minerals that are used as fertilizers. Chile won the War of the Pacific, gaining a large tract of land and enormous wealth. At the same time, Chilean troops at last subdued the Mapuche. The government then adopted a policy of persuading Germans, Swiss, and Belgians to colonize Chile's southern lake district. By the end of the century, these immigrants were playing an active role in businesses and government.

Other immigrants arrived at the turn of the twentieth century; a gold rush lured some twenty-five thousand Slav and Croatian miners to Tierra del Fuego. Some

Near Puerto Montt, in southern Chile, farming families still use ox-drawn wooden plows to turn the soil. In the river estuary in the background, fish farms have been established.

Basque families arrive	Spanish defeated at Battle of Chacabuco	Chile becomes independent	Immigrants from Europe and North America arrive	Chile fights in War of the Pacific against Bolivia and Peru
1700s	1817	1818	1800–1850s	1879–1883

British immigrants took up sheep farming and commerce in the same region, along with some Jews from eastern Europe, Christian Syrians, and Lebanese refugees.

Political Upheaval

The nitrate industry began to decline in the 1920s, mainly because new artificial fertilizers entered the market. This caused economic chaos in the region. The nitrate miners were ready for new, mainly socialist ideas about sharing political power, especially about decisions regarding producing and distributing goods. But the aristocracy who owned land clung to their power and wealth. Many left their land entirely, investing their money elsewhere, unconcerned about the needs of their tenant farmers.

It was not until 1964, under the leadership of President Eduardo Frei, that the first real efforts were made to tackle Chile's social problems. But, opposed by both the landowners and the army, he achieved much less than he had hoped. In 1970 Chile surprised the world by electing Marxist Salvador Allende as president. He nationalized industries and banks; that is, the government now owned and controlled these businesses. He also broke up large

During the military government of General Augusto Pinochet, many people "disappeared." In 1990 these protestors demanded to know what had happened to them.

Government troops subdue Mapuche Indians	Second wave of European immigrants arrive	Oil and gas discovered in far south	President Eduardo Frei attempts social reform
1881	**1883–1901**	**1945**	**1964–1970**

farming estates and gave the land to tenant farmers. In doing so, he made powerful enemies, not the least the U.S. government, which wanted payment for the

nationalization of U.S. copper mines in Chile. The United States stopped giving aid to the government and tried to ban its copper from world markets. The Allende government was doomed, and President Allende died under mysterious circumstances in September 1973. The military, led by General Augusto Pinochet, took over Chile's government.

Pinochet remained at the head of the most repressive government in Chile's history until 1989. Opponents were arrested, tortured, and exiled, and thousands just "disappeared." Political parties were banned, the constitution was suspended, and press and personal freedoms were curtailed. Pinochet eventually agreed that elections could take place, and in 1989 Chile came back under democratic rule. Elections in 1993 were won by Eduardo Frei, son of the earlier president. Many of the problems he faces are the same as those his father tried to solve.

Chile: Land of Mestizos and Europeans

Over 95 percent of Chileans are mestizo or of European descent; about 3 percent are Native American, mostly Mapuche. The remaining 2 percent include the Polynesian inhabitants of Easter Island. The majority of the population, about 77 percent, live in the central region, which covers less than a fifth of the country.

Spanish is spoken throughout Chile, though the Mapuche and some Aymara people living near the Bolivian border also

Victor Jara and the New Song Movement

The Chilean New Song Movement began in 1965, led by musician Violeta Parra and her daughters. Here was an outlet for folk music, using many of the traditional instruments of the Andes. The 1960s were a time of political and social change in Latin America; songs were full of protest and hope.

Victor Jara was a talented young theater director, actor, and musician. He came from a peasant background, and his songs reflected the poor, the hardworking, and the hungry. In 1969 Jara won the First Festival of Chilean New Song with "Prayer to a Worker." He helped form the group Quilapayún, which, together with the student group Inti Illimani, became known worldwide. Their music was used in Chile to educate people about electing Salvador Allende as president and, later, around the world to voice protest over the military coup of 1973 and at the regime that followed. But by that time Jara was dead. Along with thousands of students and professors, he was arrested, tortured, and killed when General Pinochet seized power.

Salvador Allende elected president	Military rule under General Augusto Pinochet	Democratic elections take place	Eduardo Frei (the son) elected president
1970	**1973–1989**	**1989**	**1993**

At a school near Temuco, Mapuche Indian boys are learning a traditional dance. The Mapuche value their cultural traditions, which are an important part of the school curriculum.

have their own languages (see BOLIVIA). The native language of the Polynesian people of Easter Island is Pascuense, and some immigrant groups, including the Germans, still speak among themselves in their native tongue.

Chile's upper and middle classes like to think of themselves as European and not mestizo. (The majority is mestizo.) Surnames are important to them because surnames link people not only to their ancestors but also indicate connections with other old families. This concern with social status means that people try to live in the right area, try to go to the right school, and try to appear in the newspapers' social pages. They are also interested in cultural activities, and it is not unusual for a politician to be a writer or for a doctor to be

an actor. At the other economic extreme are the five million or so poor Chileans, whose communities are rich in folklore and song, often reflecting the struggles and hardships they have survived.

Chile has a good educational system that provides free, compulsory schooling. In the far north and south, children may have to travel far to get to school. To help with this problem, the government provides some rural boarding schools where children live during the week and go home only on weekends.

Just under 90 percent of Chileans belong to the Catholic Church. About 10 percent are Protestant, mainly members of evangelical churches, where music and song play a large part in the services. There are also some Jews and Muslims. The Mapuche Indians have their own tribal religion. Chileans tend not to be strongly religious, but Catholicism can affect their lives in a number of ways. Many children go to Catholic schools, and the Church plays its part in helping the poor, working among the deprived in the slums and providing school lunches. At times the Church represents a solid force against unpopular governments, such as the Pinochet regime.

There are a number of religious holidays during the year. Some, like Christmas, are family occasions; others, like patron saints' days, are celebrated with pilgrimages, processions with decorated carriages and floats, elaborate costumes and masks, and music and dance.

Independence Day is celebrated throughout the country. Rodeos are in full swing, palm-roofed shelters are erected as temporary dance halls, bands play military music, and booths are stacked with food and *chicha* (CHEE-chah), fermented grape juice. Children, and very often their parents, are obsessed with flying kites.

With a coastline of over 2,500 miles (4,000 kilometers), it is not surprising that fish is the most widely eaten food in Chile. A huge variety ranges from conger eel to almost every kind of shellfish. Trout and salmon come from freshwater rivers in the south. Perhaps the most traditional dish, with Native American origins, is *porotos granados* (poe-ROE-toess grah-NAH-thoess), made of corn, squash, and beans, with onions and garlic. *Empanadas* (em-pah-NAH-thus), pastries filled with eggs, olives, cheese, seafood, or finely chopped meats, are another favorite, often eaten as

Priests and Bandits

At Easter time in central Chile, a festival called Domingo de Cuasimodo (doe-MEAN-goe day kwah-SEE-moe-doe) takes place. Its roots date back to the early nineteenth century, when priests and others were being robbed by bandits who still supported the Spanish crown. Huasos (WAH-soess), the Chilean cowboys, came to the rescue and, in their brightly colored ponchos and silver spurs, accompanied the priests, holding an image of Christ high and daring the thieves to attack. Today these events are celebrated with specially decorated carriages carrying priests, accompanied by horsemen in finest huaso dress and horses draped with beautiful capes like those worn by horses in medieval times.

At the head of the procession in the festival of Domingo de Cuasimodo, two riders represent the priests who were robbed by bandits in the early nineteenth century.

snacks. Equal to Chile's plentiful supply of fish is its abundance of fruit and vegetables, all grown in the central valley.

Miners of the Desert and the Mountains

In the north of the country, the Atacama Desert—dry, vast, and apparently empty—has been the main source of Chile's wealth for many years. At its heart sits Chuquicamata, the world's largest open-pit copper mine, which employs about eleven thousand miners. Because of their importance as a workforce, they can command good wages and benefits. Miners live on site and in the satellite town of Calama, and by Chilean standards they live well.

A Bolivian immigrant, accustomed to high altitudes in his own country, extracts sulfur from the world's highest mine, on Aucanquilcha Mountain.

A number of towns and ports sprouted along the coast to export minerals from the Atacama. Because the region is so devoid of natural building materials, supplies were brought in from elsewhere. Towns like Mejillones and Iquique are almost completely built from wood. Along the coast between the towns lie small villages where people make a living as fishers.

A very different mining operation takes place in the mountains that overlook the Atacama and form the border with Bolivia. Here is the world's highest mine, Aucanquilcha. Only people adapted to working at high altitudes can mine the sulfur, and the workforce includes many Aymara, some of whom cross the border from Bolivia (see BOLIVIA).

It is believed that there are about fifteen thousand Aymara in Chile. The majority live in small villages in the mountains, in houses made of adobe or stone. Their main occupation is herding llamas and alpacas, but they also grow a few crops, often using agricultural terraces that were built before the Incas. The animals feed on tough *ichu* (EE-chew) grass, which is also used as thatch. Bushes, resinous plants, and dried llama dung are used for fuel.

City Dwellers of the Central Valley

South of the Atacama, the central valley extends from about 50 miles (80 kilometers) north of Santiago to 300 miles (480 kilometers) south, close to the Bío Bío River. About 80 percent of Chileans live in cities, and of these some 40 percent live in Santiago, the capital, which has a population of over five million. More than half of the country's manufacturing industries are based there. The city's smog problem is now so serious that traffic is restricted, and newspapers print details

about the smog daily. People often wear masks when walking or bicycling.

Upper-class families in Santiago dwell in grand houses in the affluent suburbs, with large gardens, several cars, and a number of servants. The middle and lower classes live either in housing estates or apartment blocks. The poor are generally confined to shantytowns on the edge of Santiago, where a typical home, built of cardboard and grooved iron, has two rooms. Some homes have electricity, illegally tapped from overhead wires, but few have water. Many of the poor are migrants from the countryside who came hoping to improve their way of life.

There is a great contrast between the ways people earn a living. The elite upper class consists of a small group of people with a great deal of wealth and economic power. Middle-class men and women fill

This monument in Santiago's Plaza de Armas is dedicated to Chile's indigenous peoples. It was unveiled in 1992 on the five-hundredth anniversary of Columbus's arrival in America.

many professional and commercial positions or, like some of the working class, are employed in factories. People of the lowest class may get jobs as domestic servants or laborers, but many have to survive by selling trinkets, peanuts, or sweets; guarding or washing cars; cleaning shoes; or perhaps painting instant portraits. The Plaza de Armas, in the city's historic center, is always full of people with inventive ideas trying to make a living.

Chile's second largest urban concentration is in the cities of Valparaíso and, 5 miles (8 kilometers) to the north, Viña del Mar. Valparaíso is Chile's oldest city and its main port. Following the construction of a new congress building, it is now the home of Chile's Parliament.

179

Viña is a tourist center of steel, glass, and neon lights, full and bustling during the summer months from November to February, when most people are employed in businesses related to tourism.

Farmers and Winegrowers of the Central Valley

The central valley has the richest farmland in the country, and the climate is mild and virtually frost-free. The combination is ideal for growing fruit and almonds, which are replacing the older crops of wheat, grain, and animal fodder. Smaller farms make a profit by producing fruit for the out-of-season markets in the Northern Hemisphere. Over a million acres of pine tree plantations spread over the valley.

Old run-down farmhouses still dot the landscape, with faded colonial tile roofs, verandas, central courtyards, large kitchens, and stables. Animals still pull plows or carts laden with produce, but most farms use tractors and motorized vehicles.

Wine has been produced in the valley since the time of the first Spanish settlers. Today Chile is the largest exporter of wines in Latin America, with approximately half a million people employed in the industry.

The Rodeo: A Huaso and His Horse

In colonial times a rodeo in Chile was an opportunity for Spanish ranchers to display their skills with cattle. Today it is a contest of great skill where the Chilean huaso and his horse are stars. Two huasos work together to maneuver an animal to a particular place against the arena fence. To take part in the rodeo, a huaso has to be impeccably dressed in the traditional broad, flat-topped sombrero; a buttoned-up white shirt; a short striped poncho; brown pinstriped pants; fringed leather leggings; and heeled boots with spurs. After the rodeo everyone enjoys a hearty meal of meat and beans before the dancing begins. It is time for the cueca *(KWAY-kah), the Chilean national dance, led by the winning huaso and the rodeo queen. A form of courtship dance, it is performed with passionate stomping of feet and a graceful twirling of handkerchiefs.*

Two Chilean huasos at a local rodeo, dressed in traditional ponchos and sombreros. Rodeos take place throughout Chile, and are a chance for huasos to show off their riding skills.

The Native Americans

The Mapuche live south of the central valley, mainly in forest land around Temuco, between the Bío Bío and Toltén Rivers, but with a few communities farther south. Estimates of their numbers range between about 400,000 and 1,000,000. Fewer than 400 Pehuenche people have survived. They live close to the upper Bío Bío River. Their village is threatened by plans to create a hydroelectric dam on the river.

When, in 1881, the Mapuche lost their last fight against the army and government, most of their lands became state property, and they received little compensation. In the 1930s the Mapuche founded a movement to reclaim their lands and their culture. Old rites and traditions, such as *malones* (ma-LONE-ayss), which were meetings to listen to dreams and predict the future, and *machitunes* (mah-chee-TOO-nayss), collective prayers to the gods, were revived. The movement attracted support from some Chileans, and the Mapuche began to take part in political life, eventually electing representatives to the Chamber of Deputies (similar to the House of Representatives in the United States).

Some Mapuche have now left behind their old way of life and have headed for the towns. There, they are on the bottom rung of Chilean society, living in miserable slums, trying to find work. Others live in equally miserable conditions on reservations, where they grow wheat, potatoes, and other crops, and herd sheep, cattle, and horses. They add to their income by making finely crafted silver jewelry, pottery, and handwoven ponchos, sweaters, and other handicrafts for sale in the local town markets.

A traditional home, or *ruka* (ROO-kah), is circular and made completely of thatch. It

Today fewer than four hundred Pehuenche survive, the last to continue their traditional lifestyle. The monkey puzzle trees provide nuts, the Pehuenche's staple food.

usually houses a man, his wife, his parents, his children, and sometimes his brothers and sisters. Most Mapuche speak and understand Spanish but prefer their own language, Mapudungun. They believe in many gods; the most important is Ngenechen, the creator, who is all that is good. Wekufu brings death, disaster, floods, famine, disease, and all that is bad. Other gods represent the sun, the moon, the stars, the earth, the sea, and thunder. While the Mapuche have some male shamans, the majority of the shamans are women, known as *machis* (MAH-cheess); through the machis, the Mapuche seek to make contact with the gods.

A Touch of Europe: People of the Lake District

Chile's beautiful lake district runs south of Temuco and the Toltén River to the town of Puerto Montt and the fjords. Every year thousands of tourists visit this landscape of lakes, rivers, waterfalls, forests, and snowcapped volcanoes.

Country families grow potatoes and other crops, and there is plenty of pasture to raise livestock and dairy cattle. Small farms are sometimes cut off because the year-round rains make driving on the dirt roads very difficult. Slow and unreliable

Two students walk to Valdivia Technical University. Other universities include the University of Chile, with campuses in several towns, and a number of Catholic universities.

buses connect the rural areas to the towns; people often prefer to rely on their horses or ox-drawn carts.

It was in the lake district that many European immigrants chose to settle, perhaps because it reminded them of parts of their homelands. Three or four generations later, their descendants are Chilean in every way, except perhaps for some eastern European and German surnames and an older generation that may still speak its original language.

Some towns, like Valdivia, have obvious German influences in their architecture, cooking, and culture. Most Germans arrived here around the turn of the twentieth century. They included blacksmiths, locksmiths, tailors, carpenters, tanners, watchmakers, and brewers. Some became farmers, others turned their talents to commerce and industry, and by 1913 Valdivia was Chile's leading industrial center. The many different trees in the region were the basis of a highly successful timber and furniture trade.

Germans also settled around Puerto Montt, where, today, at festival time, men still play the accordion and dress in traditional German knee-length leather trousers, felt hats, and decorated socks and waistcoats.

People of Chiloé

The Chilotes (chee-LOE-tayss) are the people of Chiloé, an archipelago of islands close to Puerto Montt. Originally the islands were inhabited by the Mapuche and Chono. Then came a few Spanish and Jesuit priests. The people today are descendants of mixed marriages between the indigenous peoples and the Spanish settlers. Because they have had only limited contact with Chilean culture on the mainland, Chilotes have their own accent, similar to sixteenth-century Spanish but mixed with many indigenous words. They also have their own system of measurement, which uses an *almud* (ahl-MOOD), a wooden box of a fixed size.

Today Chilote men work as farmers and fishermen and in fish-processing factories, while the women weave blankets, ponchos, socks, and scarves, which they'll

Fishing boats and houses on the island of Chiloé. The wooden homes built on stilts are said to symbolize the people of Chiloé's close association with the earth and the ocean.

sell on the mainland. Many young people now look for work away from Chiloé, especially on sheep ranches in the south.

The Extinct Tribes of Tierra del Fuego

When the Portuguese explorer Ferdinand Magellan sailed around the southernmost parts of South America in 1520, Ona, Haush, Alacaluf, and Yaghan Indians inhabited the rocky shores and small islands. Spanish explorers did not get that far south, and few sailors were prepared to try their luck in the tempestuous storms of the region. For three hundred years these tribes continued to live in virtual isolation.

The Ona lived on land, hunting animals with bows and arrows and gathering berries and grass seeds. Tall in comparison to other tribes of the time, they wore cloaks made from guanaco skins.

The other tribes fished in the fjords. Their basic diet consisted of fish, shellfish, and seals, and was sometimes varied with

---

Twin Serpents: A Battle Between the Elements

Chilote beliefs are a fusion of Spanish and Native American ideas. In their legends are gods and goddesses, ghost ships, a lost city, mythical creatures, and wizards. One legend tells of a battle fought between twin serpents, Cai Cai and Tren Tren. The serpents may be interpreted as a volcanic eruption and a tsunami, both fairly frequent events in Chile.

Tren Tren, the friendly serpent, asleep in her mountain fortress, is unaware of the approach of her evil twin from the raging waters of the sea. Cai Cai is accompanied by her servants, the Pillanes, who cause thunder, lightning, and rain. Only a child's laughter wakes Tren Tren. As Cai Cai causes the water to rise higher and higher, Tren Tren pushes the roof of her cave ever closer to the sun, until eventually it is out of reach of the evil serpent, who falls with her servants into the abyss below.

A late nineteenth-century photo of the now extinct Ona Indians. They used the fur of guanaco and other animals to shield themselves from the cold of southern Chile.

birds, eggs, and the meat of stranded whales. The tribes had a variety of boats, some of bark, others of wooden planks. Their only domestic animals were dogs. They built huts of sticks and covered them with bark or skin. Clothing was made from bark and the skins of guanaco, seals, sea otters, and foxes. They made necklaces of shell and bone. Fire was important in their cold, windswept land, not only for heat but also to send smoke signals in times of danger. Using a stone and dried fungus, the Indians lit the fires and kept them going. The Yaghan (YAH-gahn) even had fires in their canoes.

The Yaghan often wore just cloaks made from fox or sea otter skins. The women were as tough as the men and swam and dove in the icy waters for shellfish. They lived in simple huts made of branches and roofed with turf and grass.

In the 1880s the first miners from eastern Europe arrived in Tierra del Fuego in search of gold. They were followed by people from Britain, Australia, and New Zealand, who set up large sheep ranches. For the Ona, traditionally accustomed to hunting guanaco on the open pampas, the sheep were an easy target. When their sheep were killed or stolen, ruthless

Darwin and the Yaghan

"I never saw such miserable creatures," wrote scientist Charles Darwin about the Yaghan peoples of Chile's far south. He was traveling onboard the HMS **Beagle**, a British survey ship, in 1828. Also on board were some Yaghans who had been taken two years earlier to Great Britain.

The intention had been to teach them the gospel and return them to their people to spread the message of Christianity. In Britain they were given rather silly names such as York Minister, Jemmy Button, and Fuegia Basket and were even presented to the king and queen. They surprised many people by quickly learning British culture. After they returned to their homeland, they once again adopted their original way of life.

No doubt Darwin would have been surprised to learn, as missionaries did fifty years later, that the Yaghan had a rich language with no less than thirty-two thousand words.

ranchers retaliated by killing the Indians. The tribes also had no immunity to the diseases brought in by the ranchers and miners. Today the Yaghan, Ona, and Haush have been wiped out, and the last surviving Alacaluf live in a remote fishing village.

Islanders in the Pacific Ocean

Chile owns the Juan Fernández Islands, about 400 miles (645 kilometers) west of its Pacific coast, and Easter Island, about 2,000 miles (3,200 kilometers) from its coast. In 1704 a Scottish sailor named Alexander Selkirk was marooned on the largest of the Juan Fernández Islands for four years and four months, surviving mainly on goats for food and clothing. His story came to the attention of Daniel Defoe, who based his famous novel *Robinson Crusoe* on Selkirk's adventures. The largest island in the archipelago is now named Robinson Crusoe Island, the next is Alexander Selkirk Island, and the smallest is Santa Clara. Over five hundred people of Chilean and European descent live on the main island in simple, wood-frame houses; many fish for lobster, which are sold on the mainland.

Easter Island is the world's most remote inhabited island. The original peoples were Polynesian, and today's population numbers about two thousand people of Polynesian descent and five hundred

Three Polynesian inhabitants of Easter Island, traditionally painted and dressed for a local festival. They are standing next to an ancient statue, or moai.

Chileans. The native islanders have retained some traditional Polynesian customs, as well as their language, Pascuense (pahss-KWEN-say), though they also speak Spanish. Their name for the island is Rapa Nui, and the only village is Hanga Roa. They enjoy traditional festivals, which they celebrate with music, singing, and special dances in which they wear grass skirts. For Tapati, a one-week festival at the end of January, everyone stops to celebrate. Most islanders are Catholics, though there are a few Mormons and Protestants. There is also a strong belief in native gods and spirits.

The islanders still depend on the mainland for services such as schooling and health, but an airstrip built in the 1960s transformed their lives. It opened the way for tourists, who now arrive daily to visit the most famous inhabitants of the islands, the six hundred or so huge, intricately carved stone statues, or *moai* (MOE-eye). Archaeologists are still debating when and why the Polynesian islanders built the statues and why they stopped doing so. Easter Islanders make a reasonable living by selling crafts and wood and stone carvings to the many tourists.

Poets and Protest Crafts

Poets have always been popular in Chile, and two very different Chilean poets have received the Nobel Prize for literature. Gabriela Mistral was a schoolteacher who wrote lyric poetry about lost love and everyday country people. A committed Communist, Pablo Neruda wrote about

Children dance the cueca as part of the celebrations in Santiago for Independence Day. The cueca is learned at an early age by all Chileans.

Courting with the Cueca

Chile's national dance is the cueca, a courtship dance where partners twirl and flick handkerchiefs to attract each other. Lively music, usually played on guitar or harp, accompanies the dancers, while spectators clap hands. Each region has its own version of the cueca. Sometimes it is performed by women in elegant costumes and men in huaso dress, but country people dance in simple outfits in their bare feet.

A Chilean arpillera—this one represents the dangers of AIDS—from an embroidery exhibition. Arpilleras are now made mainly for the tourist market.

scenes are equally popular. A good arpillera, completely covered in pictures and scenes, can take a year to make, and women in some communities are forming cooperatives to do the work, which sells well in tourist and other markets.

Chileans at Play

Skiing is very popular on the snow-covered slopes just an hour or two outside Santiago. The mountains also offer every opportunity for walking, hiking, riding, or mountain climbing. Two or three hours in the other direction are the beaches, used more for sunbathing than swimming, since the waters are cold. Hiking and backpacking are increasingly popular among young Chileans in the lake district.

Sports of every kind are played in Chile, but soccer is easily the most popular. Chile's national team has not reached the caliber of Argentina's, Brazil's, or some other South American teams, but its supporters are no less enthusiastic.

hunger, poverty, and the plight of factory workers. He died shortly before General Pinochet came to power, and his poems became a focus of hope for other artists throughout that repressive regime.

Handicrafts, such as pottery, baskets, carvings, and weavings, are on sale all over Chile, but there is one handicraft that stands out. An *arpillera* (ahr-pee-YAY-rah) is a plain piece of cloth onto which scraps of material are embroidered to create pictures and patterns. Arpilleras were first made by a group of women whose menfolk had been persecuted by the military regime. It was a way of earning some money but also of protesting against the government. The idea caught on, but now everyday

Competitive Kites

Kite flying is not just a pastime in Chile; to many people it is a national sport. Introduced in the eighteenth century by Catholic monks, it first became popular among the upper classes. Today everyone likes to fly kites, and the best time is from the beginning of spring in September until the cold weather arrives around June. Though many people do it for fun, there are teams that compete seriously. The object of one kind of competition is to break the strings of the opponent's kite while in flight. The strings are coated in glue and powder to make them very tough and difficult to break.

COLOMBIA

COLOMBIA IS THE FOURTH LARGEST COUNTRY IN SOUTH AMERICA and has the second largest population after Brazil.

Colombia is the only country in South America to have both a Caribbean and Pacific coast. On Colombia's northwestern border, Panama juts out between the Atlantic and Pacific Oceans. To the east, Colombia borders Venezuela and Brazil and to the south, Peru and Ecuador.

A varied landscape covers Colombia. In the west the Andes run from north to south. Among them loom many volcanoes. Between the mountains and the sea in the north are the Atlantic lowlands, crossed by the Magdalena River, and in the west, the Pacific lowlands, with swamps and forests. From the eastern foothills of the mountains, low-lying grasslands extend east for hundreds of miles. To the south of these are Colombia's Amazon rain forests.

Guajira Peninsula

Santa Marta
Barranquilla
SIERRA NEVADA DE SANTA MARTA
Cartagena

CARIBBEAN SEA

PANAMA

SIERRA DE PERIJA

Cauca River
Magdalena River

VENEZUELA

Cúcuta

PACIFIC OCEAN

ANTIOQUIA
Bucaramanga
Medellín
Quibdó
CALDAS
Manizales
Pereira
Zipaquirá
★ BOGOTÁ
Ibagué
Buenaventura
Cali
CAUCA
Silvia
Popayán
Pasto

L L A N O S

C O L O M B I A

N

miles 0 ——— 200
km 0 ——— 300

ECUADOR

BRAZIL

PERU

AMAZON RAIN FOREST

Leticia

Colombia is the world's second largest producer of coffee. Much of it is grown on small farms high in the mountains, where picking and sorting are done by hand.

Colombia's Native American History

When Spanish explorers first arrived in Colombia (koe-LOME-bee-ah) around 1500 C.E., an estimated 700,000 Native Americans inhabited the land. About one-third of these people were the Muisca, known also as the Chibcha, who lived around present-day Bogotá. Other groups included the Quimbaya of the Cauca River valley, the Tairona on the north coast and mountains, and the Sinú around the lower Magdalena River. The Panche and the Pijao had settled in the middle Magdalena River valley, and in the southern highlands lived the Pasto, Quillacinga, Páez, Popayanense, and Guambiano. They all lived in settled communities. Most of the tribes were organized into small chiefdoms, each with its own ruler and some with nobles and priests. They traded among themselves, with items such as gold being exchanged for salt.

Houses were mainly built with wood and thatch, and some of them were large communal or multifamily dwellings. Excavations in the 1970s revealed a large city of the Tairona culture, which showed that its engineers used stone for building houses, roads, irrigation canals, and bridges.

The majority of tribes grew crops, including corn, potatoes, and, in high areas, a grain called quinoa, together with many kinds of fruit. Their only domesticated animals were dogs and guinea pigs. To make the most of their hilly land, some tribes built terraces where different crops grew at different levels.

Most tribes made pottery, usually for household use, though some pots were beautifully painted for storing gold and other precious objects. They wove clothing from cotton or fashioned it from bark. The Muisca (moo-EESS-kah) wore two pieces of white cloth. The lower was wrapped around the waist. Men wore the upper piece knotted over the shoulder, while

FACTS AND FIGURES

Official name: *República de Colombia*

Status: *Independent republic*

Capital: *Bogotá*

Major cities: *Cali, Medellín, Barranquilla, Cartagena, Cúcuta, Pereira, Bucaramanga, Ibagué*

Area: *440,831 square miles (1,141,748 square kilometers)*

Population: *37,400,000*

Population density: *85 per square mile (33 per square kilometer)*

Peoples: *58 percent European-Native American descent; 20 percent European descent; 14 percent mulatto; 7 percent African and African-Native American descent; 1 percent Native American*

Official language: *Spanish*

Currency: *Colombian peso*

National days: *Labor Day (May 1); Independence Day (July 20); Battle of Boyacá (August 7); Columbus Day (October 12); Independence of Cartagena (November 11)*

Country's name: *Colombia is named after Christopher Columbus, the European explorer of the Americas.*

Timeline:	First peoples arrive	Incas conquer parts of Colombia	Spaniards reach Colombia	Cartagena founded
	ca. 10,000 B.C.E.	ca. 1450 C.E.	1500	1533

The early civilizations in Colombia crafted superb objects in gold, including this so-called Golden Man of Calima, made by craftspeople of the Quimbaya culture.

women fastened it at the front with a pin. They also wore ornamental jewelry in their noses and ears.

During the second half of the fifteenth century, some tribes in the southern highlands were conquered by the Incas, who created an empire that spread from southern Colombia to northern Chile (see BOLIVIA, CHILE, ECUADOR, and PERU).

The Spanish Arrive

The first Spanish settlement, Santa Marta on the Caribbean coast, was founded in 1525. The following year, the Spaniards traveled up the Magdalena River, subduing the Muisca people and founding the city of

The Legend of El Dorado

Soon after their arrival, the Spaniards heard of the legend of El Dorado, "the Golden Man." When a new Muisca ruler was about to take rule, he journeyed to Lake Guatavita to make offerings and sacrifices to the Muisca god. A raft of rushes was made, containing four lighted braziers to burn incense. The naked heir was then painted with sticky earth, covered with gold dust, and put on the raft along with heaps of gold and emeralds. Four of his chiefs went with him, also naked except for plumes, crowns, bracelets, and other golden jewelry.

As the raft left the shore, music began. Trumpets, flutes, and other instruments played, and people sang. The chiefs then threw their gold into the middle of the lake, and the heir dove into the water, washing off the gold dust. When he returned to the shore, he was recognized as lord and king. The Spaniards searched for El Dorado's gold throughout the sixteenth century but found little. Neither has anyone since.

Bogotá founded	First African slaves arrive	Viceroyalty of New Granada created	New Granada becomes independent	Gran Colombia collapses
1538	1564	1718	1819	1830

CLIMATE

The equator runs through Colombia's Amazon region. Low-lying parts of the country have a tropical climate, with high temperatures and no real seasons. Rainfall is generally heavy but differs greatly between the Chocó department of the Pacific coast, with a yearly average of nearly 400 inches (1,000 cm), and the Guajira peninsula in the north, with only 10 inches (25 cm). The most significant changes in temperature occur with altitude. The highest land is permanently covered with snow and ice.

	Bogotá	Barranquilla	Cali
Average January temperature	58°F (14°C)	80°F (27°C)	75°F (24°C)
Average July temperature	57°F (14°C)	82°F (28°C)	75°F (24°C)
Average annual precipitation	42 in (107 cm)	32 in (81 cm)	37 in (94 cm)

Santa Fé de Bogotá in 1538. In the south, following their conquest of the Inca Empire, the Spaniards entered Colombia from Ecuador. They subdued most of the tribes easily but met fierce resistance from the Pijao (pee-HOW) and the Páez (PIE-ayss). The Spaniards killed all the Pijao but never overcame the Páez, who were eventually left to retain their customs and traditions without interference.

The Spaniards forced many Native Americans to work in the gold and emerald mines; most Indians in the lowland interior escaped these hardships. Many Indians died of diseases introduced by the Spaniards. From the mid-sixteenth century onward, black slaves were imported from Africa as a labor force to replace the Native Americans.

In the seventeenth century a group of European Jewish refugees arrived, settling in the highlands of the Cordillera Central and later founding the city of Medellín. In 1718 the Spaniards

An eighteenth-century illustration of a street market in Barranquilla. Mulattos and blacks sell their wares, including wine and fruit, to well-to-do Spaniards and mestizos.

Country becomes known as Colombia	War of a Thousand Days (a civil war)	Panama becomes independent	La Violencia (a civil war)
1863	1899–1903	1903	1948–1962

created New Granada, an administrative region that included present-day Colombia, Venezuela, Panama, and Ecuador. From 1796 on, its people fought for independence from Spain, but this was not achieved until 1819, when Simon Bolívar and his army defeated the Spaniards in battle. New Granada became the short-lived Republic of Gran Colombia, of which Bogotá was the capital. This collapsed in 1830 when Venezuela and Ecuador separated from Colombia and Panama. Present-day Colombia only became known by that name in 1863, and Panama remained part of Colombia until it gained its independence in 1903.

The history of Colombia since its independence is one of frequent warfare between the Conservative and the Liberal parties. Two of the worst periods of civil war were the War of a Thousand Days, from 1899 to 1903, in which over 100,000 people died, and *La Violencia*, "the Violence," from 1948 to 1962, which left over 300,000 people dead. The two parties compromised in 1957, and coalition governments, each lasting four years, were governed by alternating Conservative and Liberal presidents.

Violence continued to erupt during the 1980s, and in 1990 two presidential candidates were assassinated. Colombia's principal problem in recent years has been the battle against the cocaine trade, which is controlled by cartels, or business groups, based mainly in the cities of Medellín and

Cali. Colombian governments, backed by the United States, have been unable to wipe out the trade, which has caused widespread violence, with countless bombs and assassinations.

In 1994 Ernesto Samper Pizano was elected president; his goal has been to tackle the drug trade and deal with political violence. His party has been accused of receiving funds from drug barons during the elections. Tension has developed between the United States and Colombia, since the United States believes the Colombian government is not doing enough to stop the drug trade.

Living in Colombia

Colombia's population is made up of people of European descent and mestizos, mulattos, zambos (SSAHM-boess), blacks, and Native Americans. Mestizos are descendants of marriages between the

Near the city of Popayán, a mulatto farmworker spreads sisal out on a line to dry. Sisal is used for making rope and comes from the agave plant, which grows in the highlands.

Popayán hit by an earthquake	Nevador Ruiz volcano erupts, destroying town of Armero	Two presidential candidates assassinated	President Ernesto Samper Pizano elected
1983	**1985**	**1990**	**1994**

For many country families, a horse and cart is their only form of transportation. The horse and cart are especially useful on steep dirt roads.

Spaniards and Native Americans and form the majority of the population. The people of European descent generally have a light skin color and can claim some association with the early Spanish families. Mulattos are descendants of marriages between the Spaniards and blacks. The children of Native American and African marriages are called zambos.

Colombia's rigid class structure makes it difficult for people to move from one level of society to another. At the top, although in a minority, are the whites, who hold many of the most important positions in government and business. Then come middle and working classes and, at the lowest level, the poor, who are usually illiterate.

About 70 percent of Colombians, mainly mestizos and whites, live in the highlands of the Andes. Settled by the Spaniards, this region was where the first farms and mines were developed. Blacks and mulattos have

mostly remained in the coastal lowlands and river valleys, where they were first brought to work on banana and sugar plantations.

Native American people now count for only about one percent of the population, but many indigenous tribes have survived. The most common language groups are Arawak, Chibchan, Carib, and Tupi-Guaraní. The greatest concentration of tribes is in the lowland forests of the Chocó in the west and the Amazon in the southeast. In the southern Andes, Native Americans have mostly integrated with other rural communities, but in the north, groups, like the Kogi in the mountains of the Sierra Nevada de Santa Marta and the Barí in the Sierra de Perijá, are more isolated. On Colombia's most northerly point is the Guajira Peninsula, where

Young schoolchildren with decorations they have made for Christmas. All Colombian children are supposed to attend school from age six to twelve.

support each other. Young married couples live with parents until they are ready to set up homes on their own. Children have godparents who are welcomed as part of the extended family.

Colombia has a long tradition of freedom of the press. Even so, several of today's leading newspapers clearly reflect the views of political parties, such as *El Tiempo* for the Liberals and *La República* for the Conservatives.

desolate salt flats are home to the Guajiro, the largest group of Native Americans in the country.

Spanish is the official language of Colombia. Most Native American groups understand Spanish, but many still use their own language. On San Andrés and Isla de Providencia, two Colombian islands in the Caribbean, some English is spoken, since most of the original inhabitants were of British descent.

Colombia is probably the most religious country in South America. Over 95 percent of Colombians are Roman Catholic. They regularly attend mass and observe religious holidays, especially Easter and Christmas. They also attach great importance to religious occasions such as baptism and confirmation. Even among the poorest families, money is found for a young girl's long white dress and veil for her first communion.

Family life is important to Colombians. Several generations often live together and

Traditionally, Colombia's economy has been based on agriculture, with coffee being the major crop. The number of people employed in farming has declined, however, as export earnings from oil and minerals have grown. Colombia has the largest coal reserves in South America and is the world's largest producer of high-grade emeralds.

A Salt Cathedral

One of the most unusual places of worship in Colombia is a cathedral built in a huge, rock-salt mine in Zipaquirá, a rich cattle-raising district not far from Bogotá. The cathedral was built by miners and dedicated to Señora del Rosario, the patron saint of miners. The main altar is an eighteen-ton (sixteen-metric ton) block of salt, and there is room in the main gallery for several thousand worshipers and visitors. The rock-salt mine is said to have enough salt to last the world for one hundred years.

The Bogotanos

Colombia's capital city stands on a flat plain in the eastern range of the Andes. Before European settlement began, it was the site of Bacatá, the center of the Muisca Indians' territory. Bacatá has been translated to mean "beyond the cultivated lands." Over the years the name became Bogotá. Today's population is mainly mestizo and white, and the people are known as *Bogotanos* (boe-goe-TAH-noess).

The heart of Bogotá lies in the old colonial center around Plaza Bolívar, where the cathedral and some old government buildings stand. Many of the houses are kept as they were in colonial days, with tiled roofs and ironwork balconies. The streets are narrow, cobbled, and lined with many colonial churches filled with magnificent gold and silver altars, fine paintings, and ornate carvings.

The commercial sector of Bogotá is always busy with well-dressed men and

Colombia's capital city, Bogotá, has a population of about seven million. It stands 8,695 feet (2,650 meters) above sea level and is surrounded by the plain, or Sabana de Bogotá.

Golden Treasures

Perhaps nothing demonstrates better the richness of Colombia's culture than the gold work of the early tribes. Bogotá's Gold Museum houses some thirty thousand gold objects made by the goldsmiths of the Quimbaya, Tolima, Sinú, Chibcha, and other cultures. An inner, sealed vault is filled from floor to ceiling with an amazing array of breastplates, jewelry, and hundreds of ornaments. They show that these ancient peoples knew almost all the techniques of creating gold objects known to goldsmiths today.

women making their way to work. Endless lines of cars fill the streets and modern high-rises of glass and steel are everywhere.

The older residential areas lie in the northern part of the city. Here, middle-class people live in large private houses on wide avenues. Newer areas of the city are

in the south and west, where workers are employed in manufacturing industries. Their homes are in new housing estates or apartment blocks, spacious enough for a family of three or four children and a housekeeper, if the family employs one.

On the outskirts of the city stand the slums of the poor. Families who arrive from the countryside, hoping to find something better in the city, live in run-down shacks with only the barest essentials for cooking and sleeping. They are often without lights or running water. Many of the new arrivals have few skills to offer. At best they can work in the streets, trading from stands or selling snacks.

The streets of Bogotá are home to many children whose families are too poor to keep them. Some are only eight or nine years old. They spend their days doing odd jobs like cleaning cars or shoes, or they beg. They find food where they can and at night sleep on the sidewalks, at times in freezing temperatures. Many turn to crime or become involved in the drug trade. The Catholic Church and other organizations try to help with food and shelter, but homelessness remains a huge problem.

Outside the city, a view across the plain reveals many large greenhouses where people work in the fresh-flower trade. Flowers, such as carnations and roses, are grown for the overseas market. The land and the temperate climate are ideal for this industry, and Colombia is now one of the world's largest exporters of flowers.

People of Antioquia and Caldas

Northwest of Bogotá, on the green slopes of the central range of the Andes, lie two of Colombia's main cities: Medellín and Manizales. Medellín is the capital of the department of Antioquia, and Manizales is the capital of the department of Caldas,

On a main street in downtown Medellín, traders sell all sorts of small items, including jewelry, watches, leather goods, hair clips, ties, and baskets.

which borders Antioquia in the south. This is the most dynamic and prosperous region of Colombia, where the people are known for their energy and enterprise.

In the seventeenth century, Jewish refugees arrived from Spain, looking for an isolated place to live. They chose the Aburrá River valley, and in 1616 they founded Medellín. Dividing the land into small farms, they grew corn, beans, sugarcane, and fruit. They usually married within their own community. Their farms prospered, and in 1848 they founded

Manizales. Some fifty years later, they found that the land was ideal for growing coffee.

The industry developed quickly, and soon Antioquia and Caldas were producing half of the country's crop. Much of the coffee from this region is grown by small farmers. Since it is not easy to use mechanized equipment on the mountain slopes, most farmers still work with traditional hoes and machetes. The entire family helps pick the ripened berries.

Today more than two million people live in Medellín. Many of the mestizo population work in the textile industry, which produces more than 80 percent of the country's textiles. There are also steel mills, chemical plants, and factories. Despite ever-increasing pollution, Medellín is known as the "City of Eternal Spring" because of its pleasant climate. Masses of orchids grow in the Botanical Gardens, and Medellín claims to be the world's center for orchids, which are exported daily to Europe and the United States. The Festival of Flowers is held every year in August, with floats, parades, and music. Dancers are weighted down with baskets of orchids, carnations, roses, and many other flowers.

Native Americans of the Southern Highlands

Two of the most important cities of the southern highlands, Popayán and Pasto, were founded in the 1530s. Popayán sits in a valley of palms and bamboos and is celebrated as one of the most beautiful cities in Colombia. The city was hit by an earthquake in 1983. Much of it has now been restored, but many of its churches were destroyed forever. Pasto is also in an

attractive setting. It overlooks green hills and is dominated by the Galeras Volcano, which has caused concern since it began to erupt in 1989.

Most people living in the region are farmers or cattle ranchers, and Pasto is a center for their agricultural businesses. People also earn a living making handicrafts, which include Panama hats and lacquer work.

There is a stronger Native American presence here than in other parts of highland Colombia. People often have slightly darker skin, a reminder of their Native ancestry.

Several thousand members of the Páez tribe occupy lands in Tierradentro, in the department of Cauca. There, on mountain slopes, they cultivate potatoes, beans, corn, fruits, vegetables, yucca, and cassava. Men and women work both on the family plot and communally on any large-scale project,

An elderly woman of the Páez people, who live in the southern highlands. Traditional clothing has mostly disappeared in favor of warm, knitted garments.

197

A young Guambiano Indian family. They live near the town of Silvia in the southern highlands, growing crops and keeping sheep on the hilly slopes.

such as coffee planting. Weaving is women's work; using wool and cotton, they make ponchos and other items, some of which sell in local markets. Páez Indians have a few domestic animals, including turkeys. The most common meal is *mute* (MOO-tay), a soup with boiled corn, cabbage, squash, and potatoes. It is often the first and only meal of the day until evening. Páez Indians chew coca leaves to sustain them during the day.

Another Muisca tribe, the Guambiano (gwahm-bee-AH-noe)—also known as Guambía or Coconuco—has survived, but in smaller numbers. About four thousand live close to the small town of Silvia. The Guambiano have lands on the steep hillsides above the Piendamo River, a tributary of the Cauca. Their tiny homes are made of mud and wooden poles. They grow onions, potatoes, corn, and wheat, which they sell in the market in Silvia.

The Statues of San Agustín

Near the headwaters of the Magdalena River is Colombia's most famous archaeological zone. San Agustín is a cluster of small sites, most of which feature stone statues. Some of the statues are life-size, some with big round eyes, others with slits. Several depict animals, such as eagles, serpents, and jaguars. Who made the statues? People have lived around these sites for at least twenty-five hundred years. The best guess is that the statues were made sometime between 50 and 600 C.E.

Around their plots the farmers leave a strip of open ground up to nine feet (almost three meters) wide where they keep their sheep.

Like the Páez Indians, the Guambiano have retained some of their Chibcha language and traditions. The women wear distinctive deep-blue skirts, the men either linen pants or a long kiltlike garment. Dome-shaped hats are made of tough felt. As a top layer, both men and women wear a heavy woolen poncho that is warm and waterproof.

The only remaining Inca group in Colombia is the Kamsa (also known as the Sibundoy), but their way of life is no longer that of the Native American. In most ways they live like rural mestizos, at the poor end of society, growing a few crops, wearing Western dress, and working in a cash economy.

In Cartagena, on the Caribbean coast, the patio of an old colonial building is filled with seamstresses and tailors, making, repairing, and pressing clothes.

Descendants of African Slaves: People of the Caribbean Coast

The first boatload of slaves from Africa arrived in Cartagena on the Caribbean coast in 1564. From that time on, Cartagena became the leading African slave market in the New World. The city prospered as huge fortunes were made selling the slaves to buyers from all over the continent. In Colombia the Africans were sent to work on sugar plantations in the Cauca and Magdalena River valleys and along the Caribbean coast. Others were dispatched to the Chocó region in the Pacific lowlands

to work in gold mines. Although some slaves escaped and set up enclaves called *palenques* (pah-LAYN-kayss) in the rain forest, most stayed in these areas, mixing to some extent with the white, mestizo, and Native American populations.

Along the Caribbean coast today, the majority of people are black or mulatto. Most are concentrated in Cartagena and Barranquilla, towns of very different character. Cartagena is a laid-back, tropical city with a happy atmosphere. Because of its well-preserved Spanish architecture, it is Colombia's leading tourist attraction, and most people are connected with the tourist industry or work on the docks. Even the unemployed can find odd jobs or set up stands selling snacks and trinkets to passersby.

Barranquilla is a modern industrial city with streets full of rattling, overcrowded buses that fill the air with smoke and pollution. Many unemployed people hang around on street corners, and poverty abounds in the shantytowns on the outskirts of the city. Yet the carnival in Barranquilla, just before Lent, is one of the best in the Americas. Preparations begin just after Christmas to perfect the ritual dances and make costumes, masks, and fancy outfits. The carnival lasts for four days, with parades, floats, and beauty contests; dancing and singing people fill the streets.

Music and dance are a vital part of life in the Caribbean lowlands. One of the best-known dances is the *cumbia* (KOOM-bee-ah), which is of African origin. It is performed by several couples, with men forming an outer circle and women an inner one. The men hold bottles of rum, the women bundles of candles. Instruments accompanying the cumbia include *gaitas* (GUY-tahss), flutes made from cactus and beeswax. Also very popular is the relatively recent *vallenato* (bye-NAH-toe) music. Played on the accordion, this music is backed by drums and *raspas* (RAHSS-pahss), instruments made from gourds.

The annual carnival in Barranquilla is one of the most popular in Colombia. These stilt walkers are typical of the performers to be seen in this four-day event.

200

Mulattos and Mestizos of the River Valleys

Two of Colombia's greatest rivers have their sources in the southern highlands: the Magdalena and its tributary, the Cauca. The Magdalena flows north between the central and eastern ranges for about 1,000 miles (1,600 kilometers) and empties into the Caribbean Sea near the port of Barranquilla. The Cauca, rising in the mountains close to Popayán, flows north between the central and western ranges and joins the lower Magdalena as it meanders across the swampy Caribbean lowlands to the coast.

These river valleys have some of Colombia's richest agricultural land, and today many of the mixed black and mestizo population work on the sugar plantations, in sugar-processing plants, and on cattle ranches. Others work on farms on the valley slopes, producing cotton, rice, tobacco, and coffee.

The bustling city of Cali is nestled in the Cauca valley. In the north are stylish hotels and expensive apartment blocks; in the south, commercial centers and poor housing. Cali's fine mansions and terrible slums reflect the huge gap between rich and poor. In the evenings life revolves around the street cafes and the salsa grills, where people meet to eat, drink, and chat.

Away from the cities people living along the banks of the rivers have homes built on stilts to protect them from floods and wild

A group of mestizo and mulatto children in their shantytown home on the outskirts of Cali. These children are from very poor families that have just arrived from rural areas.

animals. These dwellings are made of wood and sometimes corrugated iron. There is little furniture but always several hammocks, by far the best way to relax in the heat. Small towns provide meeting points for cattle markets or weekly fairs.

Peoples of the Pacific Lowlands

A group of children take part in the San Pacho Festival in Quibdó, the capital of the Chocó region. Most of the music and festivals of the region have African origins.

West of Cali and the Cauca valley are the Pacific lowlands, covered in swamps and forests. The population of the Pacific lowlands is predominantly black and mulatto, with scattered tribes of Native Americans, particularly in the northern Chocó region. Life for the blacks centers on Buenaventura, Colombia's main Pacific port, which handles 60 percent of the country's exports. Here, they work on the docks, toiling under the oppressive heat and daily rain. Outside the town, people make a living working in the timber trade, in gold mining, by fishing in the many rivers, or by growing their basic crops of yucca, plantains, and beans.

The black people of the Pacific lowlands have preserved the purest form of African music known in Colombia, possibly in all of South America. Typical instruments include the marimba; the *cununo macho* (koo-NOO-noe MAH-choe) and *cununo hembra* (koo-NOO-noe EM-brah), two single-headed drums; the *bombo* (BOME-boe) and *redoblante* (ray-doe-BLAHN-tay), double-headed drums; and the *guasá* (gwah-SSAH), a cylindrical rattle containing seeds. The energetic *currulao* (koo-roo-LAH-oe), the most common dance, plays an important part at fiestas.

Wakes, or ceremonies held after a person dies, are important in this region. Funeral rites last for nine days, while the mourners consume considerable amounts of alcohol and sing special songs of praise called *alabaos* (ah-lah-BAH-oess). During the fiesta of Saint Anthony in August, the statue of the saint is taken downriver, accompanied by a procession of canoes full of people singing an alabao in praise of the saint.

Tribes of the Chocó

The Chocó is the northernmost department of the Pacific coast. The capital, Quibdó, is one of the wettest towns in the world. Tribes of Native Americans, including the Cuna, Embera, Catio, and Noanama, live in the Chocó forests (see PANAMA). Today they are threatened by settlers and colonists invading the region, particularly those intent on destroying the forests, either for farming or the timber trade.

Many tribes, including the Noanama (noe-ah-NAH-mah), live close to the river and constantly move in their canoes between their villages and plantations. These tribes catch fish with nets, lines, and basket traps made of cane and lined with poisonous leaves to stun small fish. They use bows, blowguns, and arrows for hunting. For centuries some tribes have dipped their arrows in a poison taken from kokoá frogs.

Other work includes basket making, etching designs on gourds that are used as containers, carving figurines, and shaping new arrows. Men also make flutes and drums, which they like to play in the evenings and at festival time. Their religious traditions stem from a belief in the spirits of their ancestors. These spirits are

An Embera Indian of the Chocó fells an enormous tree with only an ax. Wood and thatch are needed to build homes and plants help cure sickness.

represented by figurines carved in wood, which the Noanama call *hai* (HI). When very small, children are each given their own hai to protect them throughout their lives. A *haibana* (hi-BAH-nah), or shaman, also helps protect them.

Although Native Americans have more and more contact with the ways of Western civilization, they still rely on the forest for palm thatch and other materials to build their homes, for wood to build their canoes, for animals and game to supplement their diet, and for plants to make dyes for decorating their bodies.

A Noanama Indian from the Chocó wears a headband and necklaces made of tiny glass beads. Beads of this kind were first given to the tribe centuries ago by early explorers.

English-Speaking People of the Pirate Islands

Colombia has two tiny islands: San Andrés and Isla de Providencia, some 300 miles (483 kilometers) north of the Caribbean coast. Late in the seventeenth century, English pirates arrived and used the islands as their base. For many years after they left, the islands were inhabited by only a handful of English settlers and blacks from other Caribbean islands. English is still spoken and many people are Protestant.

Recently tourism has transformed the islands and lured immigrants from the Colombian mainland, as well as some Chinese and Middle Eastern people. The islands are famous in Colombia for their music, which includes local forms of calypso, reggae, and church music.

The Kogi of the Sierra Nevada

Overlooking the Caribbean coast, in the northeast corner of Colombia, is an isolated range of mountains called the Sierra Nevada de Santa Marta. It is home to the Kogi (KOE-hee), or Cagabá, and the Arhuaco (ahr-WAH-koe) Indians, both descendants of the early Tairona (tie-ROE-nah) peoples. When the Spaniards invaded this part of the coast, the Tairona fought back stubbornly but finally had to concede defeat. A number escaped, fleeing deeper into the mountains' thick forests. For four hundred years these tribes have lived in their mountain home, isolated from the world. The Arhuaco are becoming absorbed into Colombian life, but the eleven thousand or so Kogi have deliberately remained remote. Visitors and intrusion into their way of life are not welcome.

At the center of a Kogi village stands the men's house, from which women and

A family of Arhuaco Indians in the Sierra Nevada de Santa Marta. Their traditional culture is changing as they have more contact with the Western way of life.

children are barred. It is surrounded by smaller huts, where the women and children live. The conical huts are made from thatch that reaches to the ground. These villages are used as meeting places or for ceremonies. Most of the time the Kogi men and women live in separate huts in their fields, some distance from the village. The fields are small family-owned plots, where they grow potatoes, cassava, corn, bananas, beans, and fruit. Virtually self-sufficient, the Kogi sometimes trade their domestic animals or sugar with neighboring peasants in exchange for salt or items such as cooking utensils and knives.

Tending to the fields is family work, but women harvest the crops. Men weave, make pots, and tend the agave plants, from which nets, bags, and ropes are made.

The Kogi Universe

The Kogi are a deeply religious people, and the mamas *(MAH-mahss), or priests, are the most powerful people of the tribe. Trained from a young age for the task, mamas become involved in every aspect of village and family life and preside over the nightlong meetings in the men's house. The Kogi believe in one supreme being, the goddess Nabulwe, the symbol of fertility, who peopled the world with her offspring. Their complex religious beliefs are related to the structure of the world, with the four main points—north, east, south and west—occupied by mythical ancestors of the Kogi.*

It is the mamas' principal task to keep order in the universe: to ensure that the sun rises and sets, that seasons come and go, that both the world and the people are fertile. To do this, they perform special ceremonies at remote temples and sites. There, Kogi gather to make offerings. Masked dancers, representing gods, ancestors, and spirits, are accompanied by songs and music played on flutes, seed rattles, and small drums. Kogi believe it is their responsibility to guard the world: they are the Elder Brothers, the rest of the world are the Younger Brothers.

A Kogi family travels to their remote highland home. Women have an inferior role in Kogi society. Here, the mother walks while the husband carries their child on horseback.

Kogi dress is very basic: coarse woven cloth is worn by men and women as knee-length tunics. Sometimes women wrap this around the body, leaving one shoulder uncovered. Men, especially, wear a variety of head coverings, including hand-braided sombreros, but only *mamas*, or priests, are allowed to wear pointed hats in the same conical shape as their houses. This shape is very important in Kogi religion.

The Guajiro of the Salt Deserts

At the extreme northern end of Colombia's Caribbean coast, on the border with Venezuela, the Guajira Peninsula juts out from the mainland. This vast, flat salt desert, dotted with cacti, is arid and hot for most of the year. Only between September and December, when the rains come, does the desert turn green. This inhospitable region is the home of the Guajiro (gwah-HEE-roe), also known as the Wayuu.

The Guajiro are the largest group of Native Americans in lowland South America, numbering perhaps eighty thousand in total in Colombia and Venezuela (see VENEZUELA). They owe their survival to their adaptability. Originally hunters and gatherers, they traded pearls with the Spanish in return for goats, cattle, sheep, pigs, donkeys, and chickens. The Guajiro became successful seminomadic herders, living on meat and milk. For many years they have also traded salt and gypsum, a mineral found in the desert, and at times they look for work over the border in Venezuela, in the nearby oil-producing area around Lake Maracaibo. For a long time, too, the border region has been the center of a thriving contraband business and, more recently, the drug trade. The Guajiro earn money by helping to move these goods across the desert.

However, cattle are still fundamental to the Guajiro way of life. Family groups, called *castas* (KAHSS-tahss), each have their own territory and animals. A casta is admired for the number of cattle it owns. If necessary, guns are used to protect the herds. Sick cattle are often treated by a shaman. Since families are often on the move, their homes are simple. While herding, the Guajiro protect themselves with a windbreak made from the branches of a cactus. Their more permanent traditional home is made from wattle and daub, with a roof of thatch and split cactus or of grooved iron. Newer houses are made of brick and cement. The Guajiro's greatest problem is the lack of water in the dry season. They have devised a system of wells, each about nine feet

The Guajiro Indian's home is the inhospitable salt desert of the Guajira Peninsula. Plants and trees, often larger than full-grown men, provide occasional shelter from the fierce sun.

Desert Dress

While Guajiro men wear mainly Western-style shirts and pants, women's dress is more traditional and adapted to the harsh conditions of the peninsula. They cover their bodies in long, flowing cotton robes called mantas *(MAHN-tahss) and tie bright cotton scarves over their heads to protect their faces from the hot sun and the sand that is whipped up by the wind. Also for protection, they paint their skin with a specially made mixture that contains goat fat and charcoal. A woman's most prized possession is a necklace made of gold beads and semiprecious stones, called a* tuma *(TOO-mah), which she inherits from her mother and passes on to her daughter. Both men and women protect their feet from the burning sand by wearing sandals with large colorful pom-poms.*

Guajiro Native American women blacken their faces with a mixture of fat and charcoal. The mixture protects their skin from the burning desert sun.

(almost three meters) deep and surrounded by cactus wood. However, the water seldom lasts from one rainy season to the next, and they now rely on government-built reservoirs.

While Guajiro men and boys wander over the peninsula, herding and watering the cattle, the women prepare meat, milk the cows, and make cheese. They also weave hammocks, belts, and bags from cotton and wool and make mats from a local reed.

The Barí of the Sierra de Perijá

South of the Guajira, lying along the border of Colombia and Venezuela, stand the Sierra de Perijá in the northernmost part of the Andes chain. This is the home of the Barí Indians, or Motilones, who were once widespread in both countries. Now just a few hundred Barí are left. Continuing their traditional way of life, they grow bananas and corn on the mountain slopes and hunt in the forests. Their homes are constructed of heavy thatch, designed to keep out the cold nighttime winds. Skillful hunters, the Barí use an array of different arrows to kill

This young Barí is playing a musical bow, using his mouth as a resonator. The Barí people also play bamboo panpipes and flutes made from human bones.

fish, birds, and mammals, and, occasionally, to shoot at their enemies. They use bird feathers to make arrows and colorful headgear, which is worn at the First Fruit and Corn Festivals. The festivals celebrate the fruit and corn harvests. Festivities include dancing and music played on panpipes.

The future of the Barí is uncertain. Their numbers were already severely reduced by disease when oil was found on their land in the 1920s; threats of violence from speculators forced them to retreat to the Perijá. The Colombian Barí live on a reserve and supposedly control their own land. But in reality they have struggled to survive in the face of the demands, sometimes violent, of oil men, plantation owners, and settlers. Hundreds have died defending their lands and rights. It seems unlikely that the Barí will survive much longer against such odds.

The Llaneros of the Plains

The land east of the Andes extending to the borders of Venezuela, Brazil, Peru, and Ecuador covers more than half the country, yet only 4 percent of the people live there. Much of it is *llanos* (YAH-noess), vast, open grassland plains crossed by countless rivers. For much of the year the llanos are impassable because of rains and swollen rivers, but during the dry season, from December to March, ranchers and farmers are busy transporting their meats and cereals to the highlands.

A llanero herds his cattle through the wooded edge of the grassland plains. In the rainy season llaneros drive the cattle to higher ground since lowland areas are flooded.

The cattlemen are the *llaneros* (yah-NAY-roess), a tough and resolute breed, able to defend themselves and survive the hardships of Colombia's backlands. They have their own music and dance. The *joropa* (hoe-ROE-pah) is the most popular dance of the region, and the harp is the main instrument, normally backed by the guitar, two smaller guitars called the *cuatro* (KWAH-troe) and the *tiple* (TEE-play), and maracas. Other dances are the *galerón* (gah-lay-ROEN), the *pasaje* (pah-SAH-hay), and the *corrido* (koe-REE-thoe). All are dances for couples. Some are slow and others are breathtakingly fast. Most involve a lot of heel tapping, reflecting their distant roots in Spanish flamenco dance.

The llaneros are mestizos with a strong pride in their Native American blood. The largest group of Indians in the llanos are the seminomadic Guahibo, whose homelands extend into Venezuela (see VENEZUELA). Their story is a good example of the difficulties facing tribes in the region. During this century wealthy landowners and ranchers have moved in and tried to persuade Native Americans to move away or to work on their farms. They erected fences around the land. The tribes resisted and began to defend their rights. Members, when provoked, became violent. The ranchers called in the national army on the grounds that it was a subversive Communist movement. The Guahibo fought back using guerrilla tactics but with only simple weapons of bows and arrows and a few revolvers and rifles captured from the enemy. The odds against them were too great. Most of the Guahibo abandoned their traditional life in the llanos and took refuge in the nearby forests.

Amazon Forest Tribes

Colombia's Amazon forests are even less accessible than the llanos grasslands. There are no roads, and the only means of getting around is by boat or plane. The main town is Leticia, a port on the Amazon River. Mestizos, who work as rubber tappers, fishers, or in the timber trade, are the main inhabitants of the forest, together with the surviving tribes, including the Tukano, the Huitoto, the Bara, and the Cofan.

The Tukano (too-KAH-noe) tribe, which extends into Brazil and is the largest group, includes a number of smaller tribes: the Desana, Cubeo, Tatuyo, Barasana, and Makuna to name a few. The individual groups live in communal thatched houses called *malocas* (mah-LOE-kahss). The malocas are spaced out along the river and are several hours from each other by canoe. This way the people feel they can make the most of the land around them and the natural food supply. They grow sweet potatoes, peanuts, plantains, and cassava. They hunt with traditional blowguns and arrows, but often use guns they have acquired from traders too. Before setting out to hunt, they seek permission to hunt and kill game from Wai masá, the Master of Animals. They believe that he will be angry if they fail to consult him or if they kill too many animals. In

this traditional way the tribes have kept a balance in the forest, ensuring they always have food.

The Tukano have shamans who use plants from the forest to induce hallucinations. While hallucinating, they communicate with their ancestors and spirits. Anthropologists believe that many of the designs these Indians use when

The Tukano are the largest Native American group in the Amazon lowlands of Colombia. This father and his son are members of the Barasana tribe.

A Barasana Indian paints a spirit guard on his hut. He is using a white river clay to outline the black charcoal figure and designs.

painting their bodies and decorating their pots and rock paintings relate to visions seen while taking these drugs.

The tribes have their own festivals, with traditional dances and costumes of colorful feathers and masks. Often made from bark cloth, the masks represent spirits, demons, animals, and plants. However, many of these traditions are disappearing as the tribes come into more contact with the outside world. During the Amazon rubber boom at the turn of the twentieth century, the forest peoples were forced to tap latex

and work in horrible conditions. Today they are threatened by destruction of their forest home.

Artists and Writers

Two of the leading artists in Colombia are Alejandro Obregón and Fernando Botero. Obregón is regarded by many as the father of modern painting in Colombia. Many of his images—animals, birds, plants—reflect the environment around him, and he is known for his semiabstract landscapes, inspired particularly by Colombia's Caribbean coast.

Fernando Botero's work is immediately recognizable by the roundness of the figures he paints; the people in his paintings are always "fat." Many of the scenes he depicts come from everyday contemporary life in Colombia and Latin America, at times including a wry look at military and political figures. Many of his sculptures can be seen in parks and squares in Europe and the United States.

Colombia's most famous writer is Gabriel García Márquez, who won the Nobel Prize for literature in 1982. His best-known and most loved work is *One Hundred Years of Solitude*, a novel about the extraordinary events that befall a peasant family over a period of one hundred years. Among his other well-known novels are *The Autumn of the Patriarch* and *Love in the Time of Cholera*.

Time to Relax

It is possible to enjoy virtually every kind of sport in Colombia, and the spectacular landscape makes climbing, walking, hiking, and skiing particularly attractive. Cycling is a favorite sport, although the terrain is very challenging for Colombia's many cyclists. The Caribbean coast is ideal for all

Bicycling competitions in Colombia are grueling, as courses range from the high altitude of the mountains to the tropical heat of the lowlands.

kinds of water sports, and the beaches are always crowded on public holidays.

Traditional recreational pursuits include bullfighting, introduced by the Spanish and still very popular. The origins of *tejo* (TAY-hoe) are even older. The game probably started among the Muisca people. It involves throwing a metal disk at a gunpowder detonator lodged in a metal ring. The person with the most disks within the ring, causing the most explosions, is the winner. Another similar game is *juego de la rana* (WAY-goe day lah RAH-nah), in which a small heavy ring is thrown from a considerable distance into a metal frog's mouth.

The number one sport in Colombia, as in almost all of Latin America, is soccer. Each city has its own team, and the national team frequently plays in the World Cup finals.

The national dance, the bambuco, and other traditional dances have complex movements. This folklore group is performing in the highland town of Nieva.

COSTA RICA

COSTA RICA IS THE THIRD SMALLEST COUNTRY IN CENTRAL AMERICA **after** El Salvador and Belize.

Costa Rica is bordered to the north by Nicaragua and to the south by Panama. Its eastern Caribbean coastline is 132 miles (212 kilometers) long. The Pacific coast, with many peninsulas and bays, is more than three times that length.

A mountain range runs from northwest to southeast, with valleys cutting through the range. Volcanoes, some of them active, are scattered throughout the highlands. Lowland plains in the north and east cover about one-fifth of the country, but much of the land is swampy. For most of the Pacific side of the mountains, only a narrow coastal region stands between the steep, forested mountains and the sea. Offshore lie a number of islands, of which Cocos Island is the largest.

Map labels: NICARAGUA; GUANACASTE MOUNTAINS; Lake Arenal; GUANACASTE; TILARÁN MOUNTAINS; Monteverde Biological Reserve; Puerto Limón; Alajuela; SAN JOSÉ; Desamparados; Cartago; Nicoya Peninsula; Puntarenas; COSTA RICA; TALAMANCA MOUNTAINS; PANAMA; N; miles 0 50; km 0 75

A Peaceful Land

By 1500 about twenty-seven thousand Native Americans inhabited the area now called Costa Rica (KOESS-tah REE-kah). Tribes included the Catapas, Votos, and Suerres in the north; the Térrabas, Guayamís, and Boruca on the southern Pacific coast; and the Bribri and Cabécar on the Caribbean coast and in the Talamanca mountains. In the northwest were the Chorotegas, who had contact with the Olmecs (see MEXICO) and the Maya (see GUATEMALA and MEXICO), two powerful civilizations to the north. The tribes were often at war with each other, though no single group became all-powerful.

CLIMATE

On the Caribbean coast it is hot and humid year-round, and it rains a great deal. The western coast is drier and cooler. In the highlands there is a temperate climate throughout the year. The wet season lasts from May to December and the dry season from December to April.

Average January temperature: *66°F (19°C)*

Average July temperature: *69°F (21°C)*

Average annual precipitation: *72 in (183 cm)*

A country home surrounded by mountain rain forest. The house has a veranda, and the roof is covered with tropical plants, which grow quickly in the hot, humid climate.

These Native Americans lived by hunting and gathering in the forests and by fishing. They cleared patches of forest and grew crops such as corn, tobacco, and cacao (from which chocolate is made). They used cacao as money in their markets, and they bartered with corn and cotton. Textiles were made of thread spun from cotton, agave, and palm fibers. One of their greatest skills was pottery making. Archaeologists have found pottery fragments that date back about one thousand years. Fine jade objects have also been found. Large, perfectly round stones, standing about six and a half feet (two meters) high, have also been discovered in the Diquís region in the southwest. No one is sure how or why they were made.

Christopher Columbus was on his fourth and last expedition to the Americas when a storm forced him to land on the Costa Rican coast in 1502. Spanish explorers first settled close to the shore, not venturing into the interior until the mid-sixteenth century. When the Spanish realized there were no worthwhile minerals, many went elsewhere in Central America. A few stayed, took up farming, and introduced cattle, horses, and pigs to the land.

Timeline:	First peoples arrive	Christopher Columbus lands in Costa Rica	Cartago founded	San José founded
	ca. 10,000 B.C.E.	1502 C.E.	1563	1738

The Spanish treated the Native peoples badly, and those who could escape fled into the forests and mountains. Others were used as slave labor on the farms, but the majority died from diseases brought from Europe.

Left to its own devices, the small colony barely progressed, and most families were very poor. The population remained small. The Spanish took wives from among the indigenous people, producing mestizos, who now form a large percentage of the population. The very lack of wealth and status within this colonial community left Costa Rica free of much of the greed and violence that affected so much of Central America, and it laid the foundation for the peaceful country it is today.

When other Central American countries gained independence from Spain early in the nineteenth century, Costa Rica followed. After independence the government encouraged people to grow coffee in the highlands. The climate proved ideal, and the crop was very successful.

Immigrants began to arrive soon after independence and continued to do so

Colorful Oxcarts

In the middle of the nineteenth century, Costa Ricans used oxcarts to transport coffee beans from the highlands to the Caribbean coast for export to Great Britain. Whole families made the journey, which took several days. On the trail, women and children were kept busy grinding corn for tortillas, cooking beans and plantains, and collecting water and forage for the animals. With the arrival of the railroad, the long trails of oxcarts disappeared.

However, they are still used in villages in the highlands and are an essential feature at fairs and festivals. The oxcarts have solid wheels and are painted with brightly colored, intricate designs. Originally the designs were of geometric patterns, but now they include flowers, leaves, and vegetables.

Cowboys and country folk gather to celebrate the Day of the Oxcarts in San Antonio de Escazu. Cart making is the country's most celebrated handicraft.

Independence from Spain	Chinese laborers arrive	Caribbean blacks begin to arrive	Jews arrive from eastern Europe	President Rafael Calderón Guardia introduces social welfare reforms
1823	1873	1874	1920	1940s

Revelers, some dressed as caricatures, are making fun of politicians. Others carry banners protesting their salaries in a Labor Day parade in San José.

throughout the nineteenth century. They came from North America and many parts of Europe and included engineers, doctors, veterinarians, miners, scientists, and entrepreneurs.

In 1871 construction of a railroad from the highlands to the Caribbean coast began. Chinese, Italian, and some East Indian laborers came to work on the project, but many died from yellow fever. Eventually blacks from the Caribbean islands, mainly from Jamaica and Barbados, completed the railroad. Banana plantations were established in the hot, tropical lowlands of the Caribbean coast, and again the black people of the

Caribbean islands were encouraged to come to Costa Rica to work on them.

By the turn of the twentieth century, Costa Rica was already a unique country in Central America. Where elsewhere there were wars, revolutions, and rebellions, Costa Rica was developing its trade and democratic traditions in a mostly peaceful way. This has continued throughout the present century, apart from a brief civil war in 1948 when the results of an election were disputed. In the following year a new constitution abolished the army. During the 1970s and 1980s the country became a refuge for people escaping war and upheaval in other Central American countries. In 1987 President Arias Sánchez was awarded the Nobel Peace Prize for his efforts to bring peace to the region.

Civil war erupts	New constitution abolishes the army	Costa Rica faces severe economic problems; much of Central America at war.	Earthquake hits Puerto Limón
1948	**1949**	**1970s–1980s**	**1991**

217

A Decent Standard of Living

About 98 percent of Costa Ricans are whites and mestizos. Whites are mainly descended from the immigrants who arrived during the nineteenth and twentieth centuries. Other whites include North Americans, many of whom have moved to Costa Rica for their retirement. Some of the mestizos are refugees from other Central American countries. The remaining 2 percent of the population is made up of blacks, some Asians, and a few thousand Native Americans.

Less than one percent of Costa Ricans are Native American. They include Bribri and Cabécar, who live in the Talamanca mountains, and the Boruca in the southwest. For the most part they live like the rest of the rural Costa Rican poor,

Many aspects of the traditional way of life of the Bribri Indians have disappeared, but here a boy is being taught basket weaving by an older man.

Festival of the Devils

The Festival of the Devils, which the Boruca still perform to celebrate the New Year, is essentially a replay of the Spanish Conquest—but with a very different outcome. A man dressed as a bull symbolizes the Spanish, and a number of "devils" wearing balsa wood masks represent the Native peoples. The story is played out over three days. The bull is taunted by the devils, while all move from house to house, enjoying the local corn drink, chicha *(CHEE-chah), and the village hospitality. Eventually, the bull, or Spaniard, is ritually killed, and the devils, or Native peoples, are victorious.*

speaking Spanish, wearing Western clothes, growing crops for their own use, and selling a few crafts to tourists. Very few of their Native traditions have survived, though some effort is being made to preserve the Bribri language. In 1976 the government established a reserve where the Bribri and Cabécar could live, but it did not allow them to own the land. As a result there is little to stop mining companies and others from exploiting the reserve.

Spanish is the official language of Costa Rica. English was the original language of the black laborers of the Caribbean coast and is still spoken by most of the older people there. They also use a form of pidgin English that combines Caribbean English with local Spanish words. Today few young people speak English because Spanish is the language taught and used in all schools. Costa Ricans refer to themselves by the nickname *ticos* (TEE-koess), which many people believe is a shortened form of *hermanticos* (air-mahn-TEE-koess), meaning "little brothers."

Mounted policemen ride through the streets of San José to keep law and order. They are easy to recognize in their brightly colored uniforms.

Although some Costa Ricans are still very poor, in general the country has one of the highest standards of living in Central America. The most obvious reason for this is that the economy has developed without the huge distractions of war and revolution experienced by other countries in the region. An advanced social welfare program ensures that people in need receive help from the state. In addition Costa Rica has a well-established educational system with free and compulsory schooling. Over 95 percent of the people are able to read and write.

Health is also a government priority. Life expectancy is high—seventy-six years for men and eighty years for women. There are clinics throughout the country, where visiting doctors and nurses can provide treatment and care. Even so, many

Chinese and Eastern Europeans

Descendants of immigrants from China and eastern Europe are most noticeable in Costa Rican commercial life. About six hundred Chinese arrived in 1873 to help build the railroad to the Caribbean coast. Today, descendants of those who survived run shops and restaurants, mostly in the smaller towns of the highlands. In the 1920s a group of Jews arrived from eastern Europe. Known in Costa Rica as polacos *(poe-LAH-koess), some of them became traveling salespeople, selling all sorts of household goods. They became regular visitors to towns and villages throughout the country and began a tradition that continues today.*

people still believe in traditional herbal medicines, and there is always a good supply in the markets.

Wealthy people in Costa Rica own spacious ranch-style or Spanish-style homes. In the cities row houses are popular, though there are also concrete and brick apartment buildings. Poorer people live in makeshift wooden homes or in crowded, run-down apartments. Homes in the countryside are usually built of adobe brick, painted white, with red tile roofs. Some homes are made of brightly painted wood.

Most Costa Ricans are Catholic, although they do not go to church regularly. Most households have some kind of religious ornament, maybe a figure of Christ or a poster on the wall or even a small, sacred shrine. A small number of Costa Ricans, particularly the black peoples of the Caribbean coast, belong to the Protestant church, and evangelical churches and missions are becoming increasingly popular.

People of the Highlands

Within the highlands is a large plain, the *meseta central* (may-SAY-tah sayn-TRAHL), also known as the central valley. The capital city, San José, is located here, overlooked by the impressive Poás and Irazú Volcanoes. Costa Rica's oldest city, Cartago, is located in another basin to the east.

Two-thirds of all Costa Ricans live in the central valley, with almost a million in San José and its outskirts. Many people are employed in the coffee industry. Some farmers have introduced new fruit crops and exotic garden and house plants, while others grow vegetables for the home market. Most of Costa Rica's manufacturing industry is also based on agricultural products. Around San José many factories produce processed foods and drink, textiles from locally grown cotton, and tobacco.

Beans and rice, with some meat and fish, are the bases of most family meals in the highlands. Local vegetables are often added. Sometimes known as the national dish, *gallo pinto* (GUY-yoe PEEN-toe), meaning "painted rooster," is a breakfast meal of red and white beans served with rice and sometimes scrambled eggs.

Many villages and towns in the highlands hold fairs and festivals. Some are to honor patron saints and include processions in which people carry images of saints through the streets. The most important saint's day honors Our Lady of the Angels, the patron saint of Costa Rica. A statue of her is kept in a basilica in Cartago, and every year pilgrims make their way there to honor her, walking on their knees down the aisle of the church.

Rides, booths with games, fireworks, and lotteries are all features of a good fair. There may also be soccer games between neighboring villages and horse-riding competitions.

In San José, Costa Rica's capital city, an entertainer performs on the street. A crowd gathers to watch his mime and the antics of his performing dog.

220

The Quakers of Monteverde

A quarter of Costa Rica is protected by national parks and wildlife reserves, which are visited by thousands of tourists each year.

One of the most successful, the Monteverde Biological Reserve, is run by Quakers from North America who settled in the mountains of Tilarán, northwest of San José, in 1951. At that time there was only an oxcart trail to San José, several days ride away. The Quakers worked extremely hard, clearing the forest and building houses, a school, and a meeting house. The climate and pasture proved to be good for cattle, and by 1954 the Quakers had built their first cheese factory. It was not long before their dairy products were in great demand in San José markets and sold throughout the country.

The Monteverde Biological Reserve, which was created in 1986, receives help from scientists all over the world. It contains a huge number of plants and animals, including the gorgeous quetzal, a spectacular Central American bird with magnificent blue and green plumage.

People of the Caribbean Coast

About one-third of the people of Limón Province on the Caribbean coast are descendants of the black laborers who arrived from the Caribbean to work on the railroad and the banana plantations. The banana plantations developed like small towns. The workers were provided with good housing, hospitals, and schools.

Although isolated from the highlands, this lifestyle suited the Caribbean peoples, who had their own culture. They were Protestant, not Catholic; liked their own kind of food; and enjoyed their own music and dance. Their language was English, the same as the American plantation owners, and many blacks themselves became managers. This was resented, however, by Spanish-speaking whites and mestizos from the highlands who, early in the twentieth century, moved to the Caribbean coast to find more profitable work.

Disaster struck in the 1920s and 1930s when disease destroyed most of the banana crop. Many of the plantations were moved to the Pacific coast. The government insisted that the work must first be given to

Most black Costa Ricans, like this man working in a restaurant, live in and around the town of Puerto Limón. This is one of the poorest areas in the country.

Caribbean Food

The Creole cooking of the Caribbean region has its origins in Africa. It uses coconut milk, yucca, plantains, and spices such as cumin, coriander, peppers, chilies, paprika, and cloves. Two favorite dishes are rundown *(RON-don), a vegetable and meat or fish stew mixed with plantains and breadfruit and cooked for many hours in coconut milk, and* pan bon *(PAHN BONE), a glazed sweet bread with cheese and fruit.*

native Costa Ricans, and, despite their protests, most of the black population were left behind on the Caribbean coast. They survived as best they could, clearing the forest, cultivating small patches of land, and fishing. The towns, schools, hospitals, and houses fell into ruin. It was only after 1949 that blacks were officially recognized as Costa Ricans.

Puerto Limón, the main town in the Caribbean lowlands, is crowded with slums, where drugs and crime are major problems. Together with cacao, bananas are still the main business of the region, though the plantations are always under threat from the major hazards of disease, occasional earthquakes, and hurricanes that can wipe out an entire harvest.

Perhaps the best known of Costa Rica's festivals is the carnival in Puerto Limón in October. Families spend many months preparing floats and brilliantly colored costumes. Work stops, and people from all over the country arrive to join in the party. The music is Afro-Caribbean, from reggae to calypso, and everyone loves to dance. Theater, bull-baiting (in which the bull is not harmed), and spectacular firework displays are common. Streets are lined

with booths selling every kind of food and drink. The climax of the festival is the *Grand Desfile*, or "big parade," which makes its way noisily through the streets, accompanied by the sound of tambourines and whistles.

The Sabaneros of Guanacaste

The province of Guanacaste originally belonged to Nicaragua and, in some aspects, remains different from the rest of the country. Many refugees, particularly from Nicaragua, have settled in this area. A high percentage of the people are mestizo, descended from the Spanish and the Chorotega Indians. In early colonial days Guanacaste was a region where cattle ranching was the most important activity. By tradition the *sabaneros* (sah-bah-NAY-roess), or cowboys, were seen as hardy, free-spirited horsemen, romantic figures sleeping under the stars and playing

Costa Rica has both Caribbean and Pacific coastlines, with waters rich in a variety of fish. Here, in the province of Guanacaste, fishermen bring their catch ashore.

Horseback riding is one of the most practical ways of getting around the countryside. Children learn to ride almost as soon as they can walk.

melancholy ballads on guitars and accordions. Some of this was true, but today they mostly work on their own small farms or on large ranches belonging to wealthy landowners.

The sabaneros display many of the traditional skills in rodeos at local fairs and fiestas. Against a background of bands with saxophones, clarinets, drums, and huge tubas, sabaneros demonstrate their amazing skills and tricks with horses, lassos, and cattle. During the intermission men and boys have wrestling matches, and after the rodeo everyone takes to the floor to dance.

Some traditions of the Chorotega people have been kept alive. One community makes and sells pottery styled on the black and red designs of the Chorotega. Corn, the mainstay of the Chorotega diet, is still the basic food of the region. It is used to make tortillas and *tamelas* (tah-MAY-lahss), or corn snacks, as well as the local alcoholic brew, *chicha*.

Relaxing in Costa Rica

When Costa Ricans want to take time off, they have a choice of almost any kind of sport or leisure pursuit. The simplest options are to head for the beach, which is never very far away, or into the mountains, to walk, climb, or ride. Costa Ricans learn to ride horses when they are young, and many are accomplished riders. Young people are enthusiastic about water sports, and the Pacific coast has excellent waves for surfing. Lake Arenal is known worldwide for windsurfing, and some rivers have fast-flowing water that is ideal for rafting and kayaking.

Traditional sports are still popular, and none more so than soccer, which draws large crowds. There are also facilities for golf, tennis, and many other sports.

Glossary

adobe: sun-dried mud or clay.

affluent: wealthy, well-off.

altitude: height above the ground or above sea level.

archipelago: a large group of islands.

barter: to exchange goods and/or services without the use of money.

basilica: an oblong-shaped religious building with a series of columns and a domed roof.

Basques: a European people whose homeland lies in southern France and northern Spain. The Basques have their own culture and a language that is related to no other language in Europe.

blowgun: a long tube, often made from palm wood, from which a dart is propelled by a sharp puff of breath.

brazier: a large, flat pan for holding burning charcoal, incense, etc.

caricature: a representation in which a person or object is shown in an exaggerated, uncomplimentary, or humorous way.

cash economy: economy based on earning and spending money instead of bartering.

cassava: a plant with fleshy tuber roots.

class (economic): level of society based on an individual's wealth and social status.

compulsory: enforced, often by law.

contraband: goods that are sold or traded illegally.

cooperative: a group of people working together to achieve the same thing. Craftspeople often form cooperatives to sell their work at a better price and to more people than they could on their own.

daub: plaster, mortar, or clay applied to wattle, or woven sticks or branches, to form a wall.

department: a region within a country or state created for administrative purposes.

detonator: a device that causes something else to explode.

devoid: to be without.

entrepreneur: someone who organizes, operates, and assumes the risks of a business to make money.

evangelical: refers to Protestant churches emphasizing personal salvation in their teachings.

First Holy Communion: the first time a person participates in the Christian Eucharist.

fjord: a long, narrow inlet of the sea between steep slopes or cliffs.

fodder: food for domestic animals.

forage: food for horses and cattle, especially dry food.

guanaco: a South American animal related to the camel.

kiosk: a light wooden building used for selling newspapers and small items like candy.

Marxist: a person who believes in the theories of German socialist Karl Marx. He proposed a theory of social change, based on struggles between economic classes, that incorporated socialism.

mestizo: someone of mixed Native American and European descent.

mulatto: someone of mixed African and European descent.

open-pit mine: an open hole in the earth from which minerals are extracted.

pampas: vast, flat grasslands.

pidgin: a simplified form of speech that is a mix of two or more languages. Pidgin languages are used for communication between groups that do not speak the same language.

plantain: a fruit similar to the banana. It is a staple food in many tropical countries.

regime: a form of government.

resinous: relating to resin, a substance found in most trees.

resolute: marked by determination.

row houses: similar houses built in a line and attached to each other.

semi-abstract: having subject matter that is partly based on real images.

shaman: a priest, healer, or holy person.

socialism: a political theory in which the community as a whole controls land, property, industry, and money, and organizes them for the good of all the people.

socialist: someone who believes in the theory of socialism.

speculator: someone who invests in business or finance with a risk of losing the money invested.

temperate climate: having a moderate temperature all year-round.

tenant farmer: a farmer who does not own the land on which he or she works.

veranda: a covered balcony, usually extending along the front of a building or a house.

waistcoast: a sleeveless garment, worn mostly by men under an open jacket.

wattle: sticks, twigs, or branches woven together to make fences, walls, and roofs.

Further Reading

Chile

Department of Geography Staff. *Chile in Pictures.* Minneapolis, MN: Lerner Group, 1988.

Dwyer, Chris. *Chile.* Broomhall, PA: Chelsea House, 1990.

Galvin, Irene. *Chile: Journey to Freedom.* Morristown, NJ: Silver Burdett Press, 1996.

Galvin, Irene. *Chile: Land of Poets and Patriots.* Morristown, NJ: Silver Burdett Press, 1990.

Hintz, Martin. *Chile.* Danbury, CT: Childrens Press, 1994.

Pickering, Marianne. *Chile: Where the Land Ends.* Tarrytown, NY: Marshall Cavendish, 1997

Winter, Jane Kohen. *Cultures of the World: Chile.* Tarrytown, NY: Marshall Cavendish, 1991.

Colombia

Department of Geography Staff. *Colombia in Pictures.* Minneapolis, MN: Lerner Group, 1987.

Dubois, Jill. *Cultures of the World: Colombia.* Tarrytown, NY: Marshall Cavendish, 1991.

Morrison, Marion. *Colombia.* Danbury, CT: Childrens Press, 1990.

Pearce, Jenny. *Colombia: The Drug Wars.* New York: Gloucester Press, 1990.

Stewart, Gail. *Colombia.* New York: Crestwood House, 1991.

Costa Rica

Cummins, Ronnie. *Costa Rica.* Milwaukee, WI: Gareth Stevens, 1990.

Department of Geography Staff. *Costa Rica in Pictures.* Minneapolis, MN: Lerner Group, 1987.

Foley, Erin. *Cultures of the World: Costa Rica.* Tarrytown, NY: Marshall Cavendish, 1997.

Forsyth, Adrian. *Journey Through a Tropical Jungle.* Old Tappan, NJ: Simon and Schuster, 1989.

Mallory, Kenneth. *Waterhole: Life in a Rescued Tropical Rain Forest.* New York: Franklin Watts, 1992.

Patent, Dorothy, and William Munoz. *Biodiversity.* Boston, MA: Clarion Books, 1996.

Peduzzi, Kelli. *Oscar Arias: Peacemaker and Leader Among Nations.* Milwaukee, WI: Gareth Stevens, 1991.

Index

Page numbers in *italic* indicate illustrations.

Page numbers in *italic* indicate illustrations.

REFERENCE

PEOPLES
of the
AMERICAS

PEOPLES

of the

AMERICAS

Volume 3
Canada–Cayman Islands

MARSHALL CAVENDISH
NEW YORK • LONDON • TORONTO • SYDNEY

Marshall Cavendish Corporation
99 White Plains Road
Tarrytown, New York 10591-9001

©1999 Marshall Cavendish Corporation

Consulting Editor: J. Patrick Gray, Professor of Anthropology, University of Wisconsin

Consultants: Jean-Marc Blais, Senior Interpretive Planner, Canadian Museum of Civilization, Hull, Quebec
David Frye, Assistant Director, Department of Latin American and Caribbean Studies, University of Michigan

Spanish Consultant: Fran Kaplan

Contributing authors: D. L. Birchfield
Marion Morrison
Juliette Radcliffe Rogers
Philip Steele
Mary A. Stout

Discovery Books
Managing Editor: Paul Humphrey
Project Editor: Helen Dwyer
Text Editor: Valerie J. Weber
Design Concept: Ian Winton
Designers: Barry Dwyer, Ian Winton, and Simon Borrough
Cartographer: Stefan Chabluk

Marshall Cavendish
Editorial Director: Paul Bernabeo
Editor: Marian Armstrong
Associate Editor: Debra M. Jacobs

The publishers would like to thank the following for their permission to reproduce photographs:
Bryan and Cherry Alexander (cover, 112, 113, 132, 137, 138, 147 top, 152, 153, 155, 156 top & bottom); Allsport (Glenn Cratty 159; David Leah 160); Bruce Coleman Collection (Gene Ahrens 136; Fred Bruemmer 120, 157; Harald Lange 119; Steffan Widstrand 154, 161); James Davis Travel Photography (148, 149); Greg Evans International (163); Mary Evans Picture Library (115, 116, 145, 151); Eye Ubiquitous (L. Fordyce 124 top & bottom, 127, 133; L. Johnstone 134); Getty Images (117, 126, 142; Wayne R. Bilenduke frontispiece); Robert Harding Picture Library (Robert Estall 130; Ken Gillham 140; Maurice Joseph 150; Norma Joseph 122; Ian Tomlinson 143); Hutchison Library (Robert Francis 129, 158; Michael MacIntyre 114, 147 bottom; Brian Moser 144; Trevor Page 146); Image Bank (André Gallant 139; Michael Melford 111); Rogers Associates (141); David Simson (118, 121, 123, 125, 128, 131, 135)

(frontispiece) Canadian Inuit girl holding a puppy.

Editor's note: Many systems of dating have been used by different cultures throughout history. *Peoples of the Americas* uses B.C.E. (Before Common Era) and C.E. (Common Era) instead of B.C. (Before Christ) and A.D. (Anno Domini, "In the Year of the Lord") out of respect for the diversity of the world's peoples.

Library of Congress Cataloging-in-Publication Data
Peoples of the Americas.
    p.   cm.
    Includes bibliographical references and index.
    Contents: v. 1. Anguilla–Belize — v. 2. Bermuda–Brazil — v. 3. Canada–Cayman Islands — v. 4. Chile–Costa Rica — v. 5. Cuba–French Guiana — v. 6. Greenland–Jamaica — v. 7. Martinique–Paraguay — v. 8. Peru–Turks and Caicos Islands — v. 9. United States of America — v. 10. United States of America–Virgin Islands

    ISBN 0-7614-7050-6 (set)
    1. Ethnology—America—Juvenile literature. 2. America—History—Juvenile literature. [1. Ethnology—America. 2. America—History.]
E29.A1P46 1999
970'.004—dc21
                                                                        98-2801
                                                                        CIP
                                                                        AC

    ISBN 0-7614-7050-6 (set)
    ISBN 0-7614-7053-0 (vol. 3)

Printed and bound in Italy

Contents

CANADA

CANADA IS THE SECOND LARGEST COUNTRY IN THE WORLD.
This huge area has a population of only thirty million,
about one-ninth that of the United States.

*Canada covers a vast area of North America,
stretching over five time zones. It extends
from the icy wastes of the Arctic to the
Great Lakes, from the shores of the
northern Pacific Ocean to the
northern Atlantic Ocean.
Canadian territory
borders the United
States on the west
and south.*

*Canada's northern shores are a maze of
ragged islands, large and small. On either side of
the vast inlet of Hudson Bay, bleak, treeless, deep-frozen
tundra stretches southward to lakes and forests. In the
far west of the country are the Rocky Mountains, which,
on their eastern side, descend to flat prairies. Farther east
still are the agricultural lowlands around the Great Lakes
and the Saint Lawrence River and Seaway. The
easternmost part of Canada has forested hills and a
rugged coastline exposed to the Atlantic Ocean.*

Mountain peaks rise from still, blue lakes in Waterton Lakes National Park in Alberta. This park is joined with Glacier National Park in Montana.

The First Canadians

During an ice age about thirty thousand years ago, the northern oceans were locked in ice, and the world's sea levels were very low. At this time it may have been possible to walk overland from Asia to North America, and many scientists believe that hunters from Siberia may have crossed into Alaska. Armed with tools and weapons of wood and stone, they gradually moved southward and eastward in search of bison and mammoth. Over many thousands of years their descendants spread throughout the Americas.

In the meantime new peoples were crossing into North America from Asia, walking over the ice or using boats. From about 3000 B.C.E. on, they traveled eastward through the Arctic. These were the

ancestors of the people whom the Ojibwe people later called *askimek* (AHS-kih-mek) and the Abenaki people called *eskimantis* (esk-i-MAN-tis). The Europeans were to name them *Esquimaux*, or Eskimos. They called themselves Inuvialuit (in-NOO-vee-

FACTS AND FIGURES

Status: *Independent monarchy*

Capital: *Ottawa*

Major cities: *Toronto, Montreal, Vancouver, Edmonton, Calgary, Winnipeg, Quebec, Hamilton, Halifax*

Area: *3,830,840 square miles (9,922,385 square kilometers)*

Population: *30,100,000*

Population density: *7.9 per square mile (3 per square kilometer)*

Peoples: *40 percent British descent; 27 percent French descent; 20 percent other European descent; 9 percent Asian and other descent; 4 percent Indian (First Nations People) and Inuit*

Official languages: *English, French*

Currency: *Canadian dollar*

National days: *Victoria Day (Monday before May 25); Canada Day (July 1); Labor Day (first Monday in September); Thanksgiving Day (second Monday of October); Remembrance Day (November 11)*

Country's name: *The term Canada was first used by French explorer Jacques Cartier to describe the region around the Saint Lawrence River. It is believed to have come from kanata (kuh-NAH-duh), a word used by the Huron and Iroquois peoples to mean "village" or "settlement."*

Timeline:	Possible date for hunters crossing from Asia into North America	First evidence of human settlement in Canada	First Inuit move into Canadian Arctic
	ca. 30,000 B.C.E.	ca. 13,000 B.C.E.	ca. 3000 B.C.E.

CLIMATE

In the far north, temperatures are below freezing for most of the year. The least extreme temperatures are on the west coast, where winters are mild but often cloudy and wet. Central Canada experiences cold winters and hot summers with little rainfall. The southern lowlands have snowy winters and hot, wet summers. Close to the Atlantic Ocean the weather is changeable, with snow in winter and fog for much of the year.

	Vancouver	Winnipeg	Toronto	Saint John's
Average January temperature	36°F (2°C)	–3°F (–19°C)	23°F (–5°C)	23°F (–5°C)
Average July temperature	64°F (18°C)	67°F (19°C)	69°F (21°C)	59°F (15°C)
Average annual precipitation	58 in (147 cm)	21 in (53 cm)	33 in (84 cm)	54 in (137 cm)

ah-loo-it), or simply Inuit (IN-yoo-it), meaning "the people."

Many different languages and ways of life developed among the first peoples in Canada. Before the arrival of Europeans there were probably about fifty main

An Inuit sits by his igloo. The Inuit word igdlu *means "house." However, Europeans used it to describe these overnight lodges built out of snow bricks by Inuit hunters.*

groups in Canada, each with its own way of life and language or dialect.

First, in the far north of the continent, were the Inuit peoples, who spoke Inuktitut. The Inuit formed small communities around the north coast. All the Inuit were experts at survival in the Arctic. They hunted seals, walrus, caribou, polar bears, seabirds, and whales. Dressed in warm skins and furs, they lived in family groups. Their homes included huts made of turf and stone, shelters of hide, and the temporary hunting lodges that we call igloos, made of blocks of frozen snow. The Canadian Inuit built sleds and the swift, hide-covered canoe they called the kayak, as well as a larger boat called the umiak.

Across the tundra regions and the great forests below the Arctic Circle, from the Yukon River to west of the Hudson Bay, the principal family of languages is called Na-Déné. Na-Déné includes mostly Athabascan languages. The Déné (deh-NAY) peoples include the Slavey, Beaver, Yellowknife, Dogrib, and Chipewyan tribes.

Second wave of Inuit settlement	Vikings sail from Greenland to Labrador and establish a colony called Vinland	John Cabot discovers Cape Breton Island; start of European fishing off Newfoundland
ca. 1000 B.C.E.	ca. 1000 C.E.	1497

These peoples traditionally lived by hunting caribou, moose, beaver, and hare and by trapping fish such as salmon. They lived in movable lodges made of poles. The tundra peoples covered the poles with hide, while the forest dwellers used bark and brushwood on their lodges. When European traders arrived, the Déné peoples, who were already experts at treating hides and pelts, supplied the fur trade with beaver, bear, fox, otter, and marten skins for hats and coats.

Another large language group is the Algonquian. The Algonquian languages were once spoken widely across North America. In Canada Algonquian languages could be heard in Labrador, Nova Scotia, and Newfoundland, around the shores of Lakes Huron and Superior, westward to the prairies, and northward into the Déné lands. Algonquian-speakers included the Algonquians, Cree, Ojibwe (also known as the Anishinabe and Chippewa), Naskapi

A Cree hunter paddles his canoe through the waterways of northern Quebec. Where possible, many of Canada's First Peoples still live by hunting, fishing, and trapping.

Months in the Cree Calendar

The living world of the Cree is reflected in their words for months and seasons. June is Sagipukawipizun, *the "month when leaves come out," while August is* Opunhopizon, *the "month when ducklings learn to fly." October is* Opinahamowipizun, *the "month when birds fly south," and November is* Kaskatinopizun, *the "month when rivers freeze."*

and Montagnais (together called the Innu), and Micmac. The Algonquian way of life varied from one region to another. Most were hunters and fishers, builders of fine birch-bark canoes.

The Ojibwe (o-JIB-way) were forest hunters, but some had learned how to cultivate corn from their neighbors in the Iroquois Confederacy to the east. On the wide open spaces of the northern prairies, Algonquian-speakers, such as the Blackfeet (BLACK-feet) and Plains Cree (CREE), hunted the buffalo.

Iroquois-speakers of the southeast lived in villages of wooden longhouses and grew

Jacques Cartier of France begins to explore Saint Lawrence River	Samuel de Champlain establishes French colony of Acadia	Henry Hudson reaches Hudson Bay
1534	**1604**	**1610**

corn, beans, squash, and tobacco. They formed three main groupings, or confederacies. There were the Neutrals, the Hurons, and a tribal alliance known as the Iroquois Confederacy (Mohawk, Seneca, Onondaga, Oneida, and Cayuga). The Confederacy was founded in 1570 by a Huron prophet called Deganawida. It expanded to six nations when the Tuscarora (tusk-uh-ROAR-uh) people joined the alliance in 1715.

However, from 1667 onward, many Mohawks (MO-hawks), and various other Iroquois peoples who had been converted to Christianity by French Jesuits, broke away from the Confederacy and settled around the Saint Lawrence River. Linguists link the eastern peoples, such as the Mohawk, with various prairie peoples, such as the Assiniboin and the Dakotas, or Sioux. Their languages are called Macro-Siouan.

The Indians of the Pacific Coast, such as the Tlingit, Salish, Kwakiutl, Nootka, and the Haida, belong to two small language groups called Salish and Wakashan. They survived by whaling, fishing for salmon, or hunting seals. These coastal peoples built villages of cedarwood houses that faced the sea and were skilled wood-carvers, basket makers, and weavers.

After Europeans arrived in Canada, the Native inhabitants were used as allies in the wars between the French and the British. Their ancient way of life was soon disrupted and eventually destroyed. Many died of diseases brought in by the Europeans, while others were poisoned by cheap alcohol sold by unscrupulous traders. Their lands were taken and many were forced onto reservations.

The Making of a Nation

The first Europeans to reach the shores of Canada were probably Vikings, about a thousand years ago. These Scandinavian seafarers had already raided and conquered large areas of Europe, including Iceland. They went on to settle Greenland (see

Kwakiutl peoples live on Vancouver Island and on the British Columbian mainland. Each clan has its own myths, which are acted out with drumming, singing, and masked dances.

New France becomes a royal colony of France	Founding of Hudson's Bay Company	British gain control of Newfoundland, Acadia, and shores of Hudson Bay	British defeat French at Quebec
1663	1670	1713	1759

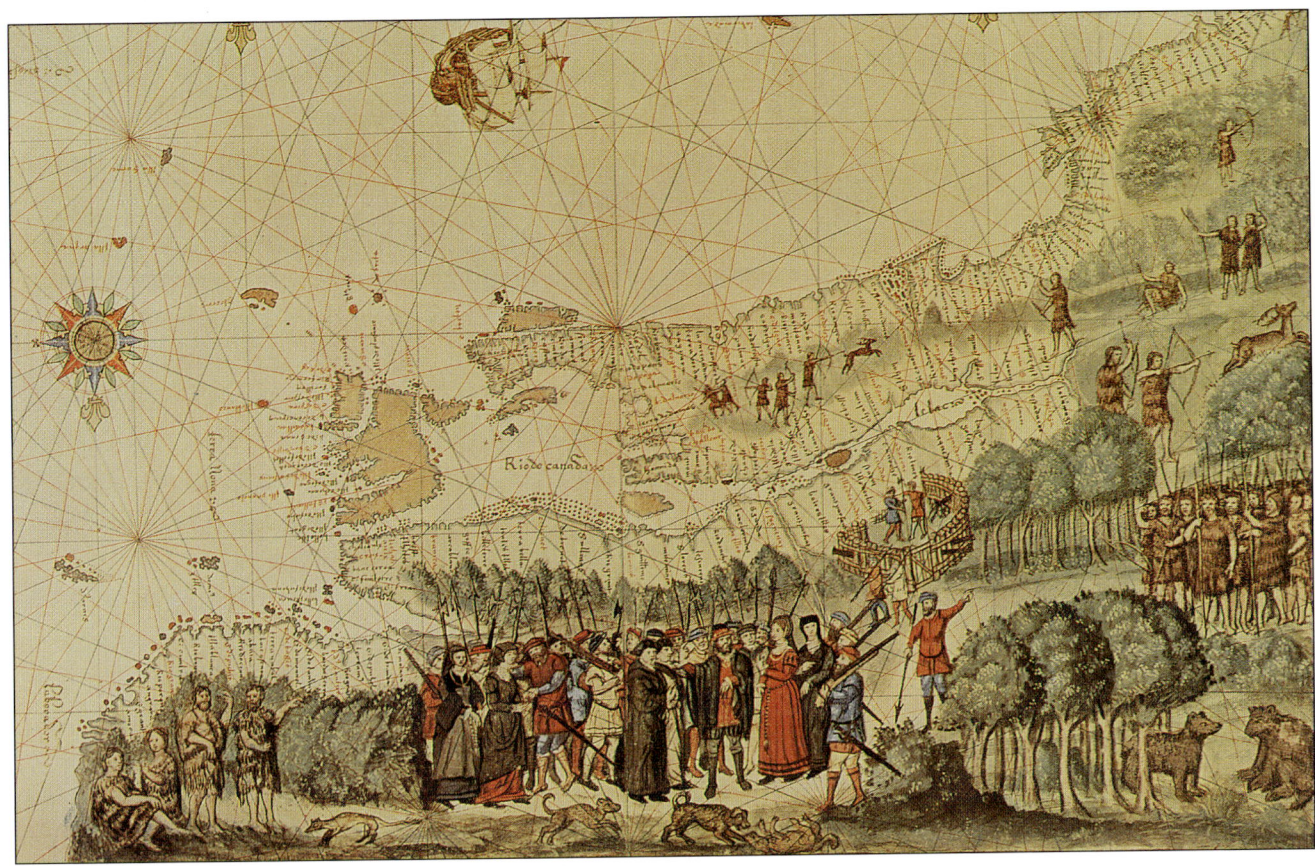

This map depicts Jacques Cartier and other French colonists arriving in Canada. Cartier made three voyages of exploration between 1534 and 1541.

GREENLAND) and sailed from there to Baffin Island, Labrador, and Newfoundland. They tried to establish a settlement they called Vinland; this was somewhere on the coast of Labrador or Newfoundland. Remains of Viking stone houses have been found in the far north of Newfoundland. These settlements were probably abandoned when attacked by local peoples, such as the Beothuk.

In 1497 John Cabot, an Italian-born explorer in the service of England, sailed to Cape Breton Island and Newfoundland. He was followed—or possibly even preceded—by the fishing fleets of western Europe. Waters around the Grand Banks, 75 miles (121 kilometers) south of

Newfoundland, were some of the world's richest fishing zones.

The first European fur traders in Canada were French fishermen. From 1534 onward they traveled from the coast up the Saint Lawrence River in search of good fishing zones. They bought furs such as beaver from the local peoples and shipped them back to Europe to be made into hats, the fashion rage of the time. The French king decided to develop this trade. In 1603 he ordered Samuel de Champlain, the navigator and explorer, to map out the river. The city of Quebec was settled in

Treaty of Paris: Canada made a British colony. New France becomes province of Quebec	U.S. War of Independence; British loyalists and people of African descent settle in Canada	Area of European settlement divided between Upper (English-speaking) and Lower (French-speaking) Canada
1763	**1775–1783**	**1791**

The Coming of the King-George-Men

"We see your ships, and hear things that make our hearts grow faint. They say that more King-George-men will soon be here, and will take our land, our firewood, our fishing-grounds; that we shall be placed on a little spot, and shall have to do everything according to the fancies of the King-George-men. . . . We do not want the white man. He steals what we have. We want to live as we are."

Conversation with a local chief as remembered by Gilbert Sproat, a British Columbian settler, 1800s

by the Native tribes living there. Trading posts were set up around the remote shores of Hudson Bay, where Native trappers would bring furs and skins to exchange for goods and supplies.

For over a hundred years the British and French struggled against each other for control of Canada and its fur trade. War followed war. Both powers allied themselves with local warriors, setting one indigenous tribe against another. In the meantime many French fur traders married Native women, and their descendants later became known as the *Métis* (MAY-tee), a French term meaning "of mixed descent."

1608 to handle the fur trade. The French allied themselves with tribes that supplied furs, stirring up hostility among many other tribes. Since furs were often paid for with weapons, including guns, the scene was set for tragedy.

The part of Canada west of the Saint Lawrence River became a French colony, the province of New France. However, the British claimed large areas of the continent to the south and also to the north, around Hudson Bay. Charles II, the British king, set up the Hudson's Bay Company in 1670 and gave it land and trading rights over a vast area of the Canadian sub-Arctic. However, this land was already occupied

In 1759 British troops defeated a French army at Quebec, and four years later Canada became a British colony. However, other British colonies to the south were soon in a state of rebellion. They broke away from British rule between 1775 and 1783 to form the independent United States of America. Thousands of Americans who were still loyal to Britain now moved north into Canada.

Frederic Remington's depiction of a French pioneer. Pioneers had to be tough, resourceful, and independent. They lived alongside and traded with Canada's First Peoples.

Act of Union joins Upper and Lower Canada	Oregon Treaty confirms U.S.-Canadian borders	Dominion of Canada founded (Ontario, Quebec, Nova Scotia, New Brunswick)	Britain recognizes Métis self-rule in former Hudson's Bay Company territories, but tensions break out into warfare
1840	1846	1867	1869

Many Europeans came to British Columbia in the nineteeth century, hoping to strike gold. This old-timer sits outside his cabin on the North Thompson River, in British Columbia.

During the nineteenth century, conflicts between French and British Canadians continued. Canada and the United States went to war and argued over the border during the War of 1812. Canada also experienced several uprisings by Native peoples and the Métis, whose lands were stolen by new European settlers. In 1867 Canada was given special self-governing status within the British Empire, becoming a dominion. Two years later it bought all the huge territories privately owned by the Hudson's Bay Company.

In 1885 Montreal was linked to the Pacific coast with a new railroad. The Canadian Pacific Railway united the country and boosted the economy. It brought immigrants to farm the prairies and transported the wheat they grew back east. These immigrants were mostly from eastern Europe—Ukrainians, Poles, Czechs,

Manitoba joins Canada	British Columbia becomes province	Prince Edward Island joins Canada	Indian Act severely limits rights of Canada's Native peoples	Uprising by the Cree Indians and Métis in Saskatchewan
1870	**1871**	**1873**	**1880**	**1885**

Slovaks, and Hungarians. They were seeking a new life, away from the grinding poverty and lack of political freedom in their homelands. Canada offered jobs in fishing, logging, mining, and the fur trade—and the country prospered.

In the 1890s gold was discovered in the far west. Fortune hunters from around the world risked their lives reaching the remote Klondike region. Many perished, but a few found gold. Some gambled away their new wealth in saloons. These were wild, colorful, and desperate times.

During the two World Wars (1914 to 1918 and 1939 to 1945), Canada fought as part of the Allies, along with Great Britain and the United States. As in many other countries, the years between the wars saw economic depression. Throughout the twentieth

The Mounties

The Northwest Mounted Police was formed in Ottawa in 1876. The force's original aim was to bring peace to the Canadian prairies, where lawless European settlers were robbing and killing settlers and Indians and selling whisky to the local Native peoples. Violence and the danger of war were widespread.

With their broad-brimmed hats and red jackets, the Mounties became one of the best-known police forces in the world. Hundreds of adventure stories and movies described their brave exploits and their legendary skill at tracking outlaws through snowy mountains and forests. "A Mountie," it was said, "always gets his man." The force was renamed the Royal Canadian Mounted Police (RCMP) in 1920. During the economic crises of the 1930s, the Mounties were used to break strikes in the cities. Today much of their work concerns the war on drugs and the prevention of smuggling.

A Mountie, wearing the traditional red jacket and broad-brimmed hat, parades in Ottawa. The Mountie is as much a symbol of Canada as the Houses of Parliament behind him.

Klondike gold rush; settlement in Northwest Territories	Alberta and Saskatchewan become provinces	Newfoundland joins Canada	Creation of Parti Québécois demanding a free Quebec	French declared official language of Quebec
1896–1898	**1905**	**1949**	**1968**	**1976**

The Alaska Highway runs from Dawson Creek, British Columbia, to Fairbanks, Alaska. This section passes through Kluane National Park in Yukon Territory, Canada.

century Canada steadily moved away from Great Britain politically and decided its own affairs. However, the growing self-confidence of Canada as a modern nation has been accompanied by growing demands for separation and self-government by French-speaking Quebec.

Canada Today: Meet the People

In remote areas of Canada, small towns and villages are linked by lonely roads and tracks that may be impassable in winter. Light aircraft or electronic communications may be the only link between small Arctic communities. Because of the harsh climate, it is hardly surprising that 77 percent of all Canadians live in towns and cities. They crowd into the big cities and suburbs of the south, linked by fast highways with the northern United States. Here, the winters are still cold and snowy, but the climate is generally milder and the summers are warm. Sixty-five percent of all Canadians live around the Great Lakes and the Saint

Quebec referendum: separatism rejected by 60 percent	Canada Act: removal of last British controls on Canadian law	Self-governing homeland for Inuit (Nunavut) approved for 1999	Quebec referendum: separatism rejected by only 51 percent
1980	**1982**	**1992**	**1995**

An Inuit statue stands outside Toronto's Lester Pearson International Airport. Stone figures like this were once used by Inuit hunters to frighten caribou into entrapment.

Lawrence River, a region that takes up only 5 percent of the country's land area.

Canada is divided into ten provinces and two territories. Because so few people live in the territories, they do not have the same degree of self-government as the provinces enjoy within Canada's federal system. In addition a new self-governing homeland for the Inuit people, Nunavut (previously part of Northwest Territories), came into being in 1999.

Canada has many place names derived from Native languages, such as Ottawa (named after the Algonquian-speaking Ottawa people) and Winnipeg (meaning "muddy water" in Cree). It also has Inuktitut names such as Inuvik, meaning "the place of man." Many other places, such as London, Windsor, Peterborough, and Hamilton, are named after towns in

Great Britain. Some names are French, such as Trois-Rivières, meaning "three rivers." Canada is a mixture of many different peoples and cultures. So who are today's Canadians?

About 40 percent of the population are descendants of people from Great Britain. Canadians of French origin make up about 27 percent of the population. Many other European peoples have also settled in Canada over the years, including Ukrainians, Hungarians, Poles, Russians, Finns, Germans, Dutch, Italians, Portuguese, Czechs, and Slovaks. Canada has a growing Asian population and is home to Japanese, Indians, Vietnamese, and Chinese.

Today about 625,000 indigenous, or Native, peoples live in Canada. Known as Native Americans in the United States, they are normally referred to as First Nations or First Peoples in Canada. In addition, there are about 29,500 Inuit and 64,500 Métis (of

French and First Peoples descent). Some indigenous peoples live in special areas called reserves set aside for them by the government. These reserves have their own laws and special treaties with the government. Other indigenous people live outside the reserves. While many of them work at the same kinds of jobs as other Canadians, a large number of them remain poor and lacking in opportunities. In the areas where it is still possible, they often live by fishing and hunting. However, they usually live in modern housing or cabins rather than traditional dwellings, and they wear traditional outfits only for special occasions and festivals.

But many Native peoples still speak their traditional languages and are interested in the cultures of their ancestors. The language of the Inuit, Inuktitut, is spoken

in the Arctic north. Many First Nations languages, such as Innu and Micmac, have also survived. However, both English and French are the official languages of the nation as a whole. The English accent spoken in Canada developed from the dialects of the early settlers—Scots, Irish, and English. It has also been strongly influenced by the accents of the United States, although Canadians still use more British spellings than American. The most widespread French dialect is very different from the French spoken in France today because of its strong regional accent and different expressions, some of which date back to the period of French settlement. The stronghold of the French language is the province of Quebec. Many European and Asian immigrants still speak their own languages.

Christianity is the most widely followed religion in Canada, with Roman Catholicism accounting for nearly half the

The oldest house in Kitchener, Ontario, belonged to German Mennonite Joseph Schneider. Today it is a museum in which people reenact everyday life in the 1850s.

Saint Jacobs, Ontario, is the site of a market that sells the produce of Mennonite farmers. Many of them reject modern technology and ride to the market by horse and buggy.

Christians. The remaining Christians include Anglicans, Baptists, Presbyterians, Lutherans, Eastern Orthodox Christians, and followers of the United Church of Canada. Small Protestant groups, such as Mennonites, originated in Europe and settled in Ontario and Manitoba in the 1800s. About 300,000 Canadians are Jewish, and there are small numbers of Muslims, Buddhists, and Sikhs.

Canadians Today: Questions of Identity

What does it mean to be a Canadian today? At one time it meant being a citizen of the British Empire. Ties to Great Britain were evident in Canada's laws and in the economy, as well as in the Canadian way of life. The British monarch remains the Canadian head of state today, and the soldiers changing the guard outside the Canadian Parliament look as if they have just marched off the streets of London. Many Canadians still keep in touch with relatives in the British Isles.

The United States, too, has always had a great influence on Canada. The two countries share a very similar history, geography, and way of life. The streets and shops of Toronto and Winnipeg are not so different from those of Chicago and Detroit. However, Canada is by no means a northern extension of the United States. Canadians have their own pace of life and their own view of the world. They pride themselves on having created a peaceful society that relies more on social welfare and less on individualism.

What does it mean to be a Canadian if you are French-speaking? Since the 1960s more and more Québécois (people of Quebec) have demanded complete independence from Canada. In a 1995 vote only 51 percent rejected a separate government for Quebec. The Québécois may one day be independent.

For the Inuit, becoming Canadian meant a change from the way of life that had helped them to survive in the Arctic for thousands of years. Self-sufficient bands of hunters were now governed from far away by people who did not understand their culture. Many suffered greatly from poverty, and suicide was common. However, the Inuit struggled and adapted to the new world while keeping up many of their traditions. For example, in 1981, a new television broadcasting company went on the air in the Inuktitut language.

Other First Nations people have also suffered as Canadians. Many still live in

In the last thirty years Canadian First Peoples have taken direct political action, organizing public protests to improve their land rights, living conditions, and civil rights.

poverty in poor housing on reservations. Their hunting grounds have been stripped by loggers, and their rivers have been polluted. In 1975 the Déné people issued a declaration: "We, the Déné of the Northwest Territories, insist on the right to be regarded by ourselves and the world as a nation. And while there are realities we are forced to submit to, such as the existence of a country called Canada, we insist on the right to self-determination." In 1989 Innu (IN-noo), First Peoples from Quebec and Labrador, protested against military jets conducting training runs over their homeland. A photograph at the time showed angry Innu women with a sign that read, "Get out of our land."

Today the unity of the nation is under great strain. The question of how Canadians see themselves and other Canadians is a very important one. It has been suggested that Canada should be seen as "a community of communities." Canada's mixture of peoples and cultures is one of its greatest riches, every bit as valuable as its wheat or its oil and gas.

Foods of Canada: Pancakes, Chowder, and Tourtière

The outdoor life in the Canadian countryside gives people a healthy appetite. The day might start with a breakfast of eggs, bacon, and hash browns, served with strong coffee or English-style breakfast teas. Pancakes and locally produced maple syrup are also popular.

A *Québécois fisherman guts cod at a pier on the Gaspé Peninsula. This is where the Saint Lawrence River reaches the open waters of the northern Atlantic Ocean.*

Canadian cities have much the same fast-food outlets, local diners, and ethnic restaurants as the United States, serving sandwiches and hamburgers, Italian pizzas, and Chinese, Japanese, Vietnamese, Greek, and Mexican meals.

Regional specialties are often based on locally caught fish and game and on farm produce such as cheeses and fresh apples, blueberries, or cherries. The east coast is famous for its seafood, especially clam chowder, lobster, herring, and other fish. In Quebec a thick pea soup and a pork pie

called *tourtière* (tour-tee-YAIR) are served. The lakes and rivers of Ontario and beyond provide freshwater fish, including walleye, trout, and whitefish. Ranches of the prairie provinces provide the cattle for barbecued beefsteaks. The west coast offers crab, oysters, and fresh fish, especially salmon.

Preserved and canned foods have changed the traditional healthy diet of the Arctic peoples, which included char and other fish, seal and whale meat, seabirds, and caribou. However, hunting and fishing

Sugar Shack Delight

Maple syrup, or sirop d'érable *(see-ROW dee ay-RAHBLE)—clear, golden in color, and sweet as sugar—is delicious with ice cream and essential with pancakes. It is produced on farms in Quebec, New Brunswick, and Ontario. The syrup is made from the sap of the sugar-maple tree. Buckets or tubes are attached to the trees to collect the sap as it oozes down the trunk. It is then poured into kettles or large pots in a* cabane à sucre *(kah-BAHN ah SOOK-ruh), or sugar shack, and boiled and boiled until it is thick and sticky and ready to eat.*

are still important to the Inuit and to indigenous peoples farther south. Native-American cooking may still include wild rice, venison (deer meat), fish, and even buffalo steaks.

Living in Canada: Social Issues

Canada is one of the world's wealthier nations. It has vast natural resources, including oil, gas, minerals, and timber. Its prairies are one of the world's great "breadbaskets," or grain-producing areas. This means that many Canadians enjoy a high standard of living and can afford a relaxed way of life.

Canada has a federal government, which means that the country is governed regionally as well as nationally. A national insurance plan funds most health care, although about a quarter of Canadians use private health care. The education system is set up regionally, allowing for variations in teaching policy, such as the mix of English and French language instruction. Most children go to free public schools, although there are some private schools too.

For most Canadians the social system works well. On average, women can expect to live to the age of eighty-one and men to seventy-four. Education is seen as very important and is well funded; 99 percent of all Canadians can read and write, and 75 percent of high school children go on to further education.

A kindergarten class from Ontario hangs on tight as they follow their teacher on a visit to Toronto City Hall. Education in Canada is organized by provincial governments.

Canada had economic problems in the 1990s, and the number of people without jobs climbed dramatically. The country has a system of social welfare to help look after the less privileged in society.

The environment is an important issue to many Canadians. This is the country where the international pressure group for the environment, Greenpeace, was founded. Greenpeace has opposed whaling and sealing, and its policies have been bitterly fought by many Canadian hunters and fur traders. Air pollution from traffic and factories to the south has resulted in acid rain and snow poisoning the rivers and lakes of the east.

People of Ontario: Life by the Lakes

The province of Ontario was given its name by the Iroquois peoples. It means "shining waters." In the north of the province are the shores of Hudson Bay. It is a lonely, flat part of the province, a wilderness of lakes, birch, and spruce. In the south of the province are four of the Great Lakes—Superior, Huron, Erie, and Ontario—and their cities, Thunder Bay, Sault Sainte Marie, and Toronto, linked to the open

Grey Owl: The First Environmentalist

During the 1930s the world was fascinated by the lectures and stories of a Canadian called Grey Owl. He had lived in the wilderness as a trapper, served as a forest ranger and national park warden, and worked to save the beaver from extinction. Many people assumed Grey Owl was from an indigenous tribe, but in fact he had been born in England as Archibald Belaney. A natural rebel, he had led a wild life and had been in trouble with the police. However, his love of the Ojibwe people and their way of life was genuine. He dressed like them and was as concerned as they were for the natural world in which they lived. He succeeded in waking people up to the importance of conservation and the environment— long before such issues were generally recognized.

Grey Owl arrived in Canada at the age of seventeen. His interest in the Ojibwe people began around the village of Temagami in northern Ontario. He died in 1938.

Two Ojibwe women meet up at a powwow. These festivals are held across North America and celebrate the outfits, music, and dance of the indigenous peoples.

Atlantic by the Saint Lawrence Seaway. This is a region of sprawling towns, suburbs, and highways.

People living in Ontario must learn to put up with harsh winters, but the summers are warm, and mild weather is common in the south. Living with snow and ice means keeping communications open, keeping pavements clear, keeping houses warm.

Ontario today has a population of over ten million. Many different peoples have settled here over the years. The Ojibwe people (also known as Anishinabe and Chippewa) lived around Lake Superior and the northern shores of Lake Huron, in the west and north of the province. Many

Ojibwes still live in reserves in southern Ontario. The lands to the west of Lake Ontario were the territory of the Ottawas and Petun, while the Hurons lived around the site of Toronto and the northern shores of Lake Ontario. The Nipissing people gave their name to the lake of the same name, while to their north and east were the Algonquians. Eastern Ontario bordered the lands of the Saint Lawrence Iroquois.

The province was rich in wildfowl, fish and game, berries, and wild rice. Birch trees provided bark for canoes, lodges, and woven mats. The Mohawk, members of the

Traditional German costume may still be worn at Kitchener, Ontario, where many of the people are descended from German immigrants.

Iroquois Confederacy, still live in Ontario, where they number about twelve thousand, as well as in neighboring Quebec.

After the American Revolution (1775 to 1783), Ontario was where many of the British loyalists settled, as well as Indians who had supported the British. It became English-speaking Upper Canada and attracted further settlement by Scots and English in the 1800s. English-speakers of British descent still form the majority of Ontario's population.

Many other ethnic groups have settled in Ontario over the years, and the festivals held there reflect this variety. There is the Grand River Powwow held by the Iroquois Confederacy at the Six Nations Indian Reserve near Brantford. In Kitchener, a city once called Berlin, six out of ten people are of German descent. During the annual

Oktoberfest, a beer festival, you might imagine you were in Germany.

Ontario is the wealthiest province and produces about half of Canada's exports. Ontario's farmers produce grain, vegetables, and fruit, including grapes for winemaking. They also raise beef cattle. Thousands work in the mines, which produce uranium, nickel, copper, gold, and zinc. The province's managed forests send hardwood and softwood trees to the sawmills. Factories produce paper, iron, steel, chemicals, and processed foods. Windsor is a center for the automobile industry, linked by tunnel and bridge with its U.S. counterpart, Detroit. Ontario's lakes and waterways provide the power to keep industry running and people employed.

Away from the industry of Ontario's cities, country villages are often very peaceful, perhaps a few houses and farms set alongside a rushing river, an old chapel, and a general store. The city dwellers of Ontario like to escape to their weekend lakefront homes in the countryside.

Ontario's Cities

Toronto is the largest city in Canada, with its population expected to reach five million by the year 2000. Today Toronto is the most important city of English-speaking Canada and the capital of Ontario Province. It is a center of publishing, media corporations, and finance and banking.

Spadina Avenue and Dundas Street West lie at the center of Toronto's Chinatown. Here, Chinese-Canadian women select live crabs for the cooking pot.

Toronto Chinese

Many Chinese Canadians are recent arrivals, successful businesspeople who moved to Vancouver from Hong Kong. Toronto, however, has an older Chinese community. Its Chinatown houses many families whose ancestors came from the paddy fields and villages of southern China earlier in the century in search of work. These Canadians retain a strong Chinese identity, speaking the Cantonese dialect of the Chinese language and following traditions such as the family festival of the Chinese New Year.

Toronto was originally a Huron word meaning "meeting place." It is a suitable name, for the city is chosen as a home by about half of all newcomers to Canada. The English and Scots who founded Toronto were conservative. But the 1960s saw an increase in the city's cultural diversity as immigrants from many parts of the world introduced different ways of life. Today you can explore Kensington Market and buy Jewish delicacies and Jamaica patties, pastries with hot, spicy fillings. On Gerrard Street East you are in Little India, and along Saint Clair Avenue West you are in Little Italy. In Greektown you can buy sticky Greek pastries such as *baklava*, and in Chinatown you can dine on Peking duck or the Cantonese snacks called *dim sum*. Many immigrant communities have their own languages and dialects, neighborhoods, restaurants, and festivals.

The British chose Ottawa as the national capital for Canada in 1857, when it was still a small logging town. Today Ottawa has a population of about 309,000. It's the home of the Supreme Court and other national institutions. The capital is bitterly cold during the long winter, but people make the most of the climate with skating, sledding competitions, and ice and snow sculpture. The people of Ottawa are mostly English-speakers, although most government workers need to speak both

In winter the frozen waters of the Rideau Canal provide 4 miles (7 kilometers) of skating for the people of Ottawa. The canal passes through the center of the city.

Blacks in Ontario

In the 1700s many people of African descent were brought to Canada as slaves by European settlers. During the 1800s many more fled from slavery in the United States to find freedom north of the border. Slavery was abolished in Great Britain and its colonies in 1833. From the 1820s onward, Windsor, Ontario, was the end of a network of escape routes for fugitive slaves. This network became known as the Underground Railroad. Many free African Americans also migrated northward in search of a better deal in life. By 1860 there were about fifty thousand African Canadians.

After the abolition of slavery in the United States, migration to Canada dropped. Many former slaves returned south. During the early 1900s migration to Canada was restricted based on race. Not until 1962 were new laws made that allowed large-scale migration from the Caribbean. Today, blacks make up about one percent of the Canadian population.

Some African Canadians have lived in Canada since the 1800s. Others have arrived more recently. This young woman is originally from Jamaica.

English and French. Ethnic groups who have made their homes in Canada's capital include Chinese, Italians, and Lebanese.

Just across the Ottawa River, in the province of Quebec, is the industrial town of Hull. Hull is mainly French-speaking. The Canadian Museum of Civilizations in Hull looks at all the different peoples who have made Canada what it is, from ancient times to the present day. Yearly festivals celebrate all the different regional cultures and communities. There is the First Peoples' Odawa Powwow in May, with drumming, singing, and dancing. June sees Italian and French festivals, and in the autumn are Japanese and Lebanese festivals. Each summer the Cultures Canada festival brings ethnic entertainers from all over the country.

Quebec: Peoples of French Canada

Kebec is an Algonquian word, meaning the "narrows" in a river. Canada's largest province takes up an area even larger than Alaska. The north of this vast wilderness is tundra country. Here, the soil stays frozen all year round. To the south lie great forests and countless lakes and, along the Saint Lawrence River, cities, farmland, and woods. The winter climate is severe, while the summers are warm.

The tundra and forest lands of the far north are the homeland of the Quebec Inuit. In the 1970s the Quebec Inuit clashed with the provincial government over the James Bay hydroelectric plan, which allowed large areas of their territory to flood. An agreement was eventually reached, but many Inuit were unhappy with it. Traditionally the Quebec Inuit lived by hunting, and the dam project forced them to adjust to a settled lifestyle, a difficult change for many. But the Quebec Inuit developed several successful enterprises, including a fishery and Air Inuit, an air service for the far north.

The East Cree people also live on the shores of James Bay, in small scattered villages. They, too, have had difficulty reaching an agreement with the government over the James Bay hydroelectric plan.

No More Dams

The first stage of the James Bay hydroelectric plan was finished in 1985. It flooded vast areas of land and drowned wildlife. It polluted the rivers and lakes of the region with mercury, which poisoned the fish and animals on which the Cree depended. It also brought outsiders into the region, and the outsiders had little understanding of the ancient Cree way of life.

The proposed second stage of the James Bay plan would have involved damming no fewer than eight rivers. Angered by the first plan, the Cree banded together to fight the power company in court. They took their campaigns across the border to the United States, where much of the electricity generated by the plan would be consumed, and made their objections known internationally. By 1994 the power company had abandoned the project.

A Cree woman chops logs into firewood in front of a traditional lodge. This snowy winter camp is near Lake Bourinot in Quebec.

To the north of the East Cree are the lands of the Montagnais (mon-tun-YAY), and to the east, the lands of the Naskapi (NAS-kuh-pee) stretch into Labrador. These two peoples call themselves the Innu and their remote homeland Nitassinan. They are closely related to the Attikamek (uh-TIK-uh-mehk) people, who also live in Quebec. The Montagnais were once nomadic caribou hunters, suppliers of furs to the French, and traditional enemies of the

Iroquois to the south. They suffered greatly from European contact, being forced to settle in villages. There are eleven Innu settlements within Quebec today and three Attikamek. While the Innu and Attikamek continue to fish and hunt, their Nitassinan habitat is under threat from logging and mining projects. Maliotenam, a Montagnais reserve east of Sept-Îles, hosts an annual celebration of traditional music, the Innu Nikamu festival.

Historically, the valley of the Saint Lawrence River was the home of the Saint Lawrence Iroquois tribes, including the Mohawk. Their territory bordered to the south of the Abenakis and Maliseet. The Mohawk settled near Montreal in the 1660s, when many were converted to Christianity by the French. Their numbers rapidly declined as wars and illness claimed many lives. Today they number about sixteen thousand in Quebec Province. In the last forty years much of their farmland and

fisheries have been taken over by environmental disruption and economic development around the Saint Lawrence Seaway. Rising poverty led to Mohawk demands for land rights and a revival of interest in the Mohawk language and religious traditions. In 1990 Mohawk people and security forces clashed violently in a dispute at Oka, a town near Montreal, when permission was given for a golf course to be built over a sacred burial ground.

The far east of Quebec, on the Gaspé Peninsula, falls within traditional Micmac territory. The dialect still spoken by the Micmac who still live here differs from that spoken by the much larger group of Micmac who live in Canada's Maritime Provinces.

The French-speaking Québécois have dominated the region since the 1500s.

The gentle farmland of the Île d'Orléans, an island in the Saint Lawrence River north of Quebec City, recalls the old country lifestyle of the Québécois.

French Quebec in an English-speaking Canada?

The problems between English-speaking and French-speaking Canadians go right back to the founding of Canada in the 1700s and 1800s. Although the French Canadians had their rights to language and religion guaranteed, many remained poor tenant farmers, or habitants *(ah-bee-TAHN), in a country where they had little political power. Real power remained with the landowners, or* seigneurs *(sayn-YEURS), and the priests. To the English-speaking rulers of Canada, French language and culture was a nuisance—to be ignored if possible.*

However, during the twentieth century the traditional Québécois way of life began to change. People left the country for the cities, and by the 1960s a new urban, educated middle class was politically active. At the same time the conservative Roman Catholic church began to lose its influence over French Canadians.

They came from a farming and Roman Catholic tradition. Many Québécois still work as farmers, growing corn, barley, buckwheat, oats, hay, and potatoes. Farmers also raise dairy cattle in the south. Coastal fisheries take catches of cod, herring, salmon, and lobster. Huge areas of forest are used for logging, and many people work in sawmills. Quebec produces one-fifth of all the world's wood pulp and paper. Others are miners, digging for copper, gold, and iron ore.

From the 1960s onward the Québécois demanded language rights and political reform. Some wanted increasing self-government within Canada; others wanted Quebec to become an independent country. Many of the political goals—short of independence—have now been achieved. French is now the official language of the province, used in business, education, and everyday life. The province is in reality largely bilingual. Quebec has a minority speaking English as their first language, mostly based around the Ontario and U.S. border.

Montreal and Quebec: Sprawling Cities of Quebec

Nearly half of all Québécois live in Montreal, Canada's second largest city and the largest French-speaking city outside France. It was developed by the French as Ville Marie, a center for fur trade, and during the 1800s it became the wealthiest town in Canada.

What's on the menu? People stroll past the terrace of a restaurant in Old Montreal. The people of Montreal are known for their love of good food.

The popular Montreal Jazz Festival is held each year in June and July. Both international stars and local bands perform around the city.

Culturally, Montreal is a meeting point between Europe and North America. Its old quarter, Vieux-Montreal, includes narrow streets and many historical buildings. Its strongly Roman Catholic background is seen in fine churches, while its role as a center of finance and commerce is seen in the modern office blocks, fashionable stores, and street markets. It has long been the liveliest city in Canada. People chat at street cafés, eat well at restaurants, and visit theaters and art galleries. They enjoy the first-rate sports stadium built for the 1976 Olympic Games, and weekends may be spent skiing in the Laurentian Mountains north of the city.

The population of Montreal today numbers about three million; the greatest number of its people are of French descent.

The French character of the city keeps a high profile, seen on street signs, stores, and advertisements. The province still has a large number of English-speakers, although many left when French became the official language of Quebec Province. Other small communities include Jews, Italians, Greeks, Chinese, Afro-Caribbeans, and people from central and eastern Europe. Most of the immigrant communities are English-speaking.

About 140 miles eastward of Montreal, down the Saint Lawrence, is Quebec City, capital of the province. The people of Quebec City today live in one of the most historic cities in North America, a World Heritage Site recognized by the United Nations. City landmarks include a number of impressive churches and chapels. The people of Quebec are strongly Roman Catholic, and the city has always been a center of Catholicism in Canada.

Carnival, Quebec Style

As in many Roman Catholic lands, the Québécois celebrate the period before the Christian fast of Lent with a festive carnival. Despite the bitter cold of a Quebec winter, parades take to the streets, presided over by the Bonhomme (bun-HUM), a jolly snowman in a red hat. For eleven days music, dancing, ice sculpture, sledding, and drinking abound.

Quebec City has a population of over 500,000 people, nearly all of French descent. Quebec has less of the international bustle of Montreal. It is very much the provincial capital, proud of its history. In July the city hosts a summer festival of the arts, with music and dance.

Peoples of Newfoundland and Labrador

Newfoundland and Labrador make up a single Canadian province, but the two are very distinct regions. Newfoundland is an island in the Gulf of Saint Lawrence; its eastern shore is open to the gray, stormy North Atlantic. The foggy coastline is ragged, with deep sea inlets, offshore islands, and high cliffs.

We know that the Vikings were in Newfoundland, at L'Anse aux Meadows, nearly five hundred years before Columbus landed in the Americas. After John Cabot's discovery of Newfoundland in 1497, the local fishing grounds brought untold wealth back to Europe. Newfoundland

Trinity, with its white picket fences and narrow streets, lies on Newfoundland's rugged east coast. It is one of the oldest towns in the province, dating back to at least 1580.

Heavy rain drenches fishermen as they haul in cod on Saint Mary's Bay on the south coast of Newfoundland. In the past fish always provided the island with its food and its livelihood.

itself became settled by English and Irish fishermen. The European settlers fought among themselves and, at the same time, completely destroyed the Native people of the island, the Algonquian-speaking Beothuk (BAY-uh-thuck). Not one of them survived into modern times. The Europeans called them "Redskins," or *"Peaux-rouges"* (poe ROUJ), because they painted their faces with red patterns. At one time this misleading term came to be used by Europeans for all Natives.

The age-old way of life in Newfoundland revolved around the sea, fishing in small boats and hunting the harp seal. Later came the trawlers and then the huge factory ships of modern times. The seemingly endless supply of fish went into sharp decline during the 1980s. By the early 1990s, fishing and sealing were placed under strict legal limits.

Unemployment is very high and many young islanders have left the island in search of work. An economic hope for the future lies in the growing oil industry, which is already bringing many changes to the island.

Most Newfoundlanders ("Newfies" to other Canadians) are of Irish or English descent, and these roots are revealed in

Songs Across the Sea

Newfoundland has a strong tradition of dance and folk music, often played on fiddle and accordion. Many of the tunes were brought across the Atlantic by the old-timers from Ireland and England. Traditional songs may be sung without accompaniment and often tell tales of seafarers, fishing, and shipwrecks. Other musical styles have been added over the years and can be heard at folk festivals.

their strong regional accent. A small number of Micmac live at Conne River. The only large town is Saint John's, with a population of 102,000. Around the coast are small towns and remote fishing villages of painted timber and board houses.

Labrador is a great triangle of the Canadian sub-Arctic, just 11 miles (18 kilometers) from Newfoundland. It is a remote, harsh wilderness of lakes, bogs, and forests, bitterly cold in winter.

Its Native peoples include the Labrador coast Inuit. These hunters and fishers occupied the southernmost of all Inuit settlements and were the first to meet European settlers. From the eighteenth century onward they were converted to Christianity by Moravian missionaries and traders, who brought literacy and education and encouraged the Inuktitut language. The missionaries were soon outnumbered by other European settlers, mostly fishermen. In 1978 the Labrador

Inuit, like other Canadian Inuit communities, presented claims to the provincial government for land rights and control of the environment and local government. Negotiations continued into the 1990s.

The Innu (Montagnais-Naskapi) today number about twelve thousand in Labrador; they are represented by a tribal government, the Innu Nation. They occupy a wide area of Labrador around the remote locations of Goose Bay (*Sheshatshiu* in the Innu language) and Davis Inlet (*Utshimassit*), their territories extending into northern Quebec. Traditionally, Naskapi, dressed in caribou skins, hunted across the remote sub-Arctic, wearing snowshoes or paddling their canoes along the swift rivers that are today harnessed for hydroelectric power. Since the 1950s their way of life has

Fog rolls in from the North Atlantic as the lighthouse keeper raises the Canadian national flag on the island of Baccalieu, east of Newfoundland, where the climate is cool and moist.

been threatened by logging and mining, which destroy the habitat of the game they have traditionally hunted. New mineral discoveries at Voysey's Bay may bring further changes to the region.

Today the majority of Labrador's inhabitants are of European descent. Some of the population are descended from the fishermen who came to settle the coast in the 1800s. Descendants of these old-timers are known as "liveyers" (LIV-yuhrs). More recent arrivals include Canadian workers from the big cities who come here to mine for iron ore, copper, and gold.

Peoples of the Maritimes

The three southernmost of Canada's Atlantic provinces—Nova Scotia, New Brunswick, and Prince Edward Island—are often called the Maritimes because they jut out into the ocean. Fishing and lumberjacking are the traditional occupations of the region, along with farming and mining.

Nova Scotia is a long, windswept peninsula extending into the Atlantic from New Brunswick. Birch, maple, and conifers fill its woods, while fishing villages of timber houses cling to the coastline. The provincial capital is Halifax.

The province of New Brunswick is low lying, rising toward the northern Appalachian ranges. The province is officially bilingual, using both French and English. This is a quiet, peaceful part of Canada that depends on its farms, forests, and mines for a living.

Prince Edward Island is Canada's smallest province. Originally, it was linked to the mainland only by ferry or plane. Prince Edward Island is now joined to New Brunswick by the Northumberland Strait Bridge, one of the longest in the world. Many Canadians come here on holidays to

A lumber truck loads up in the snowy forests of New Brunswick. Thousands of people in this province are employed in forestry, sawmills, and paper mills.

enjoy the quiet farmland, fresh sea air, sandy shores, and ocean drives.

The original peoples of the Maritimes were Algonquian-speakers, the Maliseet (MAL-uh-seet) and the Micmac. These were hunters and gatherers who lived off salmon, shellfish, wildfowl, and seals. They built the conical shelter covered with birch bark that the Algonquian peoples called the wigwam. Their clothes were beautifully decorated with beads and quills. When the French arrived in greater numbers in the seventeenth century, the Micmacs became trappers, and in the eighteenth century they turned to catching porpoises and trading in their oil. The Micmacs were converted to the Roman Catholic faith and later turned to farming. Many intermarried with Europeans.

In the 1600s both France and Great Britain claimed territory here. The British called the colony Nova Scotia ("New Scotland" in the Latin language). The French settlers called it Acadia. In the 1700s Britain gained political control of the region. Any Acadian French who would not pledge loyalty to the British were expelled from the country. Many went south to Louisiana, where their descendants are still known as Cajuns (from *Acadians*).

In the 1700s colonists who had been loyal to Britain in the American Revolution came to both Nova Scotia and New Brunswick. The loyalists brought with them African-American slaves. In the 1800s over fifty thousand Scots who had been evicted from their homes in the Scottish Highlands settled in Nova Scotia, while Germans arrived in Lunenburg, which was once a busy shipbuilding center. The people of the Maritimes today are descended from all these roots.

The Gaelic language of Scotland may still be heard in Nova Scotia, and Scottish Highland dancing and costume may be seen at festivals such as the Gaelic *Mód* (MAWD). This week-long festival,

The port of Lunenburg, in Nova Scotia, was founded in 1753 by German immigrants. Today its waterfront is more likely to be busy with tourists than with shipbuilders or fishermen.

The sound of bagpipes and drums is often heard in New Glasgow, a town in Nova Scotia. Immigrants from Scotland played an important part in shaping modern Canada.

featuring bagpipe music, folk dances, crafts, and sporting contests, is held at Saint Ann's on Cape Breton Island, where a Gaelic College of Arts and Culture is located.

The Prairie Provinces: Farming the Grasslands

Completely straight lines on the map mark out the borders of Canada's three prairie provinces—Manitoba, Saskatchewan, and Alberta—indicating that they were drawn up according to the political needs of the nineteenth and early twentieth centuries rather than by following more natural frontiers. The easternmost of the three provinces is Manitoba, whose name may come from the Algonquian *Manito Waba*, meaning "Strait of the Great Spirit." The Manitoba landscape includes a maze of rivers and lakes, the largest of which is Lake Winnipeg. The central prairie province is Saskatchewan. *Kis-is-ska-tche-wan* means "swift-flowing" in the Cree language. In the west, where the prairies meet the Rocky Mountains, is Alberta, named after a

daughter of Queen Victoria, the former ruler of both Great Britain and Canada.

Prairie is the word used across North America for a large area of natural grassland. Prairies take up the southern part of all three provinces and extend southward over the border into the United States. Today the grasslands are largely used for cattle ranching, grain production, and the cultivation of sunflowers, cattle fodder, flax, canola, and potatoes. Saskatchewan includes some of the largest fields of wheat in the world. These fields provide about two-thirds of Canada's wheat, and they feed people as far away as Russia. During the harvest huge combines swarm over the prairies in teams. The grain is stored for rail transport in high towers called silos or elevators, typical landmarks of the prairies.

The way of life in Canada's prairie provinces has changed a great deal over the years. The farmers have always led hard lives, toiling with the cattle roundup or the harvest. In the past they were often political radicals, campaigning for a fair deal for farmworkers. Modern farming methods may have made working on the prairies much easier, but the new methods have also greatly reduced the number of people working on the land. Today, changes in the price of grain on the world market are a main cause of anxiety.

The central belt of the provinces is taken up by hills and mixed woodlands called parkland. North of this is the great belt of northern coniferous forest that eventually meets the tundra. The northern regions of the provinces provide timber, freshwater fish, and minerals—nickel, zinc, and copper.

In the southwest, in Alberta, the peaks of the Canadian Rockies soar into the skies between Banff and Jasper. The Rockies act as a barrier to rains sweeping in from the west, creating a fringe of dry, rocky

Big blue skies, white clouds, and wide open spaces—all are characteristic of the Saskatchewan prairie. Cattle graze on the grasslands, and the province produces vast amounts of wheat.

badlands. Unlike the prairies, these are useless for farming. People living in the southern parts of Alberta welcome a famous winter wind called the Chinook. It blows up from the southwest and its warmth melts the snows.

The cities of these three provinces are mostly in the southern strip. They are modern, prosperous cities that are growing rapidly. About half of all the people in Manitoba live in Winnipeg, the capital of the province. Many work there in factories, processing food, flour, hides, and furs or manufacturing machinery and textiles. Saskatchewan's chief towns are Saskatoon and Regina, the capital.

The greatest number of Albertans live and work in Calgary and Edmonton, cities where wealth is based on oil. With its stockyards and surrounding farmland, Calgary still keeps up some of the traditions of its famous rodeo, but these

days its citizens are more likely to work in communications, electronics, and banking than in ranching. The city of Edmonton lies on the Saskatchewan River. It is farther north than Calgary and experiences harsh winters. It is a big retail center for the surrounding region, and a stopping point for visitors on their way to national parks and wilderness areas.

Before the arrival of the Europeans, the provinces of Manitoba, Saskatchewan, and Alberta were home to various indigenous peoples. The lands between Lake Winnipeg and Lake Athabasca were home to the Western Woods Cree; their lands were bordered on the east by the West Main Cree and on the north by the Chipewyan (chip-uh-WHY-un) and the Northern Ojibwe. To the southwest of Lake Winnipeg was a branch of the Saulteaux (SOE-toe) people. The northern tribes of the woodlands were nomadic hunters of deer and moose, and they fished on the lakes, later earning a living by trading furs with the Europeans. They lived in conical-shaped wigwams or domed shelters.

The southern lands and prairies were home to the Plains group of Indians, whose lands stretched southward into what is now the United States. Peoples of the Plains included the Plains Cree; the Assiniboin (uh-SIN-uh-boin); the Atsina (at-SEE-nuh), or Gros Ventre (grow VAHN-truh); and the Blackfeet, or Siksika (SITS-ih-kah), a group of peoples who included Piegan (pee-GAN) and Blood as well as the Siksika themselves. They lived in tepees, following the great herds of buffalo (North American bison) that once thundered across the prairies in their millions. The Blackfeet used to drive herds of buffalo over cliffs, and one of these sites, known as

Estipah-Siki-Kini-Kots, or Head-Smashed-In, may still be visited near Fort Macleod. From the eighteenth century onward, the Plains peoples hunted on horseback,

The Calgary Stampede

Hang on for your life! Bucking broncos, bulls, and buffalo are the highlights of the Calgary Stampede, Canada's big summer rodeo. The show includes competitions and displays of cowboy skills, such as lassoing and branding, wrestling steers, and racing chuck wagons. Locals and tourists, duded up in cowboy hats and cowboy boots, gather for ten days of parades, music and dancing, fireworks, and barbecues. The Stampede, Alberta's most famous festival, was first held in 1912.

Cowboys need skill, strength, and stamina, all of which are displayed at the annual Calgary Stampede, one of the most famous rodeos in North America.

Blackfeet and other Plains peoples gather at Edmonton, Alberta, for a powwow. These First Peoples of the northern Plains are related to the Cree peoples to the east.

Buffalo Country

The North American bison provided the peoples of the Plains with a great range of useful items. The hide was used for making tepee covers and clothing. The horns and bones were carved into spoons and tools. The tendons were used as tough thread for sewing. The meat was eaten fresh or mixed with animal fat and berries and dried in the sun. The strips of dried meat, called pemmican (from the Cree word pimikan, *meaning "grease"), were easily carried on hunting trips. Nothing was wasted.*

trading or capturing the wild horses that had begun to spread across the Americas since the arrival of the Spanish, far to the south.

The coming of the European hunters with modern firearms was a disaster for buffalo, which were brought to the edge of extinction, and also for the nations of the Plains. In the 1870s bitter wars were fought between the Plains nations of the south and the United States cavalry. After the cavalry was defeated at Little Bighorn in 1876, the great chief of the Dakotas (Sioux), Sitting Bull, led his people into Canada and remained there in exile for four years. The

First Nations of the Plains suffered greatly from European contact: they were herded onto reserves, dying from disease, starvation, and alcoholism.

Today, Indians make up about 5 percent of the region's population. The Ojibwe and Cree live on reserves in Saskatchewan. Blackfeet live on three Alberta reserves, their lands stretching south into the United States. Indigenous peoples have used their reserve lands to start up successful businesses. Although many still suffer from poverty, the indigenous peoples have revived a pride in their history and a concern for their treaty rights, backed by the Assembly of First Nations (AFN). The AFN is a forum where the chiefs of all the First Nations communities meet to devise common strategies on issues that concern all their peoples. The traditional dances, arts, and crafts of the region's First Peoples may be seen each year at numerous local powwows and at Calgary's Native Arts Festival, held each August.

The first Europeans to enter the region that became the provinces of Manitoba, Saskatchewan, and Alberta were *voyageurs* (voy-ah-JURZ)— French explorers, trappers, and traders—who reached the west of the region during the 1600s. Many

Litkhansahba (Black Bird) was the son of a Sioux chief. He was one of many First Peoples who joined forces with the Métis during their rebellion against the Canadian government.

adopted the Native-American way of life and intermarried with the indigenous peoples. They were the ancestors of today's Métis. Each February the city of Winnipeg recalls those pioneering days with the *Festival du Voyageur* (fest-ee-VAHL due voy-ah-JUR).

In 1670 the British granted the vast area of Canada to the west of Hudson Bay, then known as Rupert's Land, to the Hudson's Bay Company. This included most of the region that later became the three prairie provinces. In the northern part of the region, around the shores of Hudson Bay, the company traded in beaver and other furs supplied by the local peoples. In 1812 a new farming colony was founded on the Red River by Scottish, English, and Irish settlers. There were soon clashes with the Métis over land rights, and these broke into open rebellion in the 1870s and 1880s, when the Canadian government bought all of the Hudson's Bay Company territory. The prairie regions joined the Dominion of Canada and later became full provinces.

The Canadian government advertised in European newspapers that there was

145

Doukhobors and Hutterites

The New World attracted many different religious groups who fled persecution in Europe. They came to create utopias—communities where they could put their ideals into practice without interference from governments or churches. Some succeeded and some failed. Most were absorbed into mainstream Canadian or American society.

The Doukhobors (DUKE-uh-boors), meaning "spirit fighters," were an idealistic group from Russia, who arrived in Saskatchewan one hundred years ago. Their leader was a man named Peter Veregin, and they were supported by the great Russian writer Leo Tolstoy. The Doukhobors were anarchists and vegetarians. They believed in sharing property. They refused to fight as soldiers, to marry, and to accept the authority of the state. They soon clashed with the government of their new homeland. Some decided to stay in Saskatchewan; others moved to British Columbia.

The Hutterites (HUT-uh-rites) were another idealistic group who came to North America from Europe in 1874. They were originally from Slovakia and Moravia and took their name from an early leader of the group named Jacob Hutter. They still farm the prairies of Saskatchewan. Their Protestant faith has led them to a communal life and the rejection of all modern luxuries.

"free land" to be had in the Canadian prairies. A flood of newcomers poured west during the 1880s, including Scandinavians, Icelanders, Germans, Dutch, Austrians, Poles, Ukrainians, and Russians. Life was very tough for the newcomers. Freezing in winter and sweating in summer, they worked on the prairie. The Native peoples of the Plains lost their lands as quickly as the buffalo they hunted.

In the 1930s long periods of drought, combined with poor land management, led to large areas of North America turning to dust. The farmers of the Canadian prairies suffered alongside their southern neighbors in the United States.

The descendants of nineteenth-century immigrants make up the bulk of the population in the prairie provinces today. Many have kept an interest in the traditions

It is harvest time near Lethbridge, a large town serving the farming communities of southern Alberta. Here, the barley crop is being unloaded into storage.

The Church of the Immaculate Conception near Winnipeg is built in Eastern European style. It serves the Ukrainian community, many of whom are Eastern Orthodox Christians.

Columbia share the continental climate of central Canada. As the ground rises to the Rockies, the high altitude lowers the temperature, and winter snowfalls are heavy. Down near the coast the climate is very different. Thanks to the sea, the winters here are cool but not bitterly cold, and rainfall is high. This type of climate has created temperate rain forests in the far west, a land of green ferns and mosses.

The Natives of the inland regions included the Lillooet, Shuswap, Thompson, Carrier, Kutenai, Okanangan, and Interior

of their original homelands; the needlework of the Ukrainians and their beautiful Easter eggs, decorated in intricate patterns, may be seen in homes and museums. Customs have remained, but the languages and old way of life have changed. The Ukrainians, like their neighbors, have been Canadians for over a hundred years, and they are as likely to work in business or in the oil industry as in farming.

British Columbia: The Thunderbird Coast

Canada's westernmost province lies across the snowy ridges of the Rocky Mountains. South from the Alaskan border, Canada meets the Pacific Ocean in a ragged maze of coastal islands and inlets. The largest of these is Vancouver Island.

With harsh winters and warm, dry summers, the east and north of British

Elders of the Kwakiutl people in British Columbia gather together at a potlatch ceremony. Traditionally, older people were respected as leaders.

Salish tribes. They lived by gathering berries, by hunting moose and migrating herds of caribou, and by trapping salmon on their runs upstream. Housing included sunken shelters dug out of the ground, roofed with poles and turf, as well as conical lodges made of wooden poles covered with mats.

Along the coast, the First Peoples were the Tlingit, Haida, Nishga, Gitskan, Tsimshian, Bella Bella, and Bella Coola in the north and the Kwakiutl, Coastal Salish, and Nootka in the south. Their villages were of large cedarwood houses facing out to sea. They hunted fish, especially salmon, and they made baskets, cloth from bark and dog hair, and wooden masks for their dances and ceremonies. A chief would hold a special feast called a potlatch (from the Chinook word meaning "to give"), in which he gave away gifts and food to the accompaniment of songs and dancing. A chief would give as much food and property as he could. The more the chief gave away, the more he was respected. In fact, sometimes potlatches were competitive. His guests were obligated to repay the debt and add a little extra in the next feast. This went on until one chief could not repay the debt and lost the competition.

Totem Poles

The peoples of the Northwest culture were brilliant wood-carvers. Their chiefs liked to show off their personal wealth and prestige by having beautifully carved roof beams and gables. Over a hundred years ago it became fashionable for them to place separate tall poles made of cedarwood outside their houses. These totem poles were carved with mythical creatures, such as the thunderbird, and with people, birds, and animals. They represented the badges and history of the chief's family or tribe. Some old totem poles have survived to this day, and new ones are still being carved along the coast of British Columbia. The word totem *comes from the Algonquian word* ototeman, *meaning "brother-sister," that is, "relations" or "clan."*

Many Indians still live in British Columbia today, proud of their ancient traditions, skills, and crafts. Many live by fishing, providing services to backpackers and tourists, or selling craft items. Some are well-known artists. Some reserves run their own industries and businesses. However, many indigenous people are unemployed, and their ancestral lands and rivers are often threatened by logging and other industries that deplete their land of fish and wildlife. Many groups within British Columbia

Totem poles were traditionally carved by the Tlingit, Haida, Tsimshian, and Kwakiutl peoples. A feast was held to mark their completion.

are now standing up for their rights. For example, Haida bands joined with each other in 1980 to set up the Council of the Haida Nation.

The European part of British Columbia's population of about 3.3 million is mostly made up of English, Scots, and Irish. Many of these are descended from seafarers or from the prospectors who rushed to the Fraser River in 1859 hoping to discover a fortune in gold nuggets. British Columbia, like its neighboring provinces, is also home to Germans, Dutch, Scandinavians, and Ukrainians. Asians are numerous in British Columbia and include Japanese; Indians, including a very large Sikh community; Indonesians; Vietnamese; and Chinese, many of them from Hong Kong.

The port of Vancouver is the busiest in the North American Pacific. It has a population of over 1.6 million. The Cantonese language of southern China may be heard in the restaurants, offices, and stores of Vancouver's busy Chinatown district, and the city is a great place to celebrate festivals such as the Chinese New Year and the June Dragon Boat Race.

Modern high-rise offices and hotels rise from the yacht harbor in Vancouver, British Columbia. Canada's third biggest city has close trading links to the West Coast of the United States.

An art student of Asian descent sketches in a Vancouver park. Vancouver is home to many immigrants from the other side of the Pacific Ocean.

Vancouver is also a center for theater, the arts, and all types of modern music.

British Columbia has strong links with parts of the United States, such as Washington, Oregon, and California, which lie to the south. Increasingly its business people look for trading links with other places in the Pacific region—Japan, China, Australia, New Zealand, and the nations of Southeast Asia.

Only 3 percent of British Columbia is good for farming. Its mountains and wilderness produce timber, copper, coal, oil, and natural gas; these bring great wealth to the province. The environmental impact of these activities is closely monitored, and there have been clashes over the cutting down of ancient forests.

Yukon Territory: Gold Rush Country

Yukon Territory is a remote land, with bleak, treeless tundra, high mountain passes, and snowy forests. Roads are few and far between and are not the best places to run out of fuel. They are mostly lonely stretches of gravel traveled by mining trucks. Most people live in the south, around the city of Whitehorse.

Before Europeans arrived, the inhabitants of Yukon Territory were the Inuit and the Athabascan-speakers of the Déné culture, such as the Kutchin (kuch-IN), who fished in the rivers and hunted on the tundra and in the forests. Indigenous peoples still live in the Yukon today, and many still live by hunting and fishing.

In the 1800s Europeans entered the territory in search of wealth from furs and minerals. They struck gold near the

Rhymes of a Rolling Stone

Robert Service was born in England in 1874. He went to Canada and traveled around the country, working as a reporter and a bank official. He was sent to Dawson City in 1908, where he soaked up stories of the old days on the Klondike and described the larger-than-life characters of the gold rush in rhyming ballads. Robert Service's heroes and villains had colorful names like Dangerous Dan McGrew. They fought and brawled and died in the freezing wilderness. Robert Service's poems are funny, sentimental, and melodramatic. His love of the raw beauty of the Yukon lasted until his death in France in 1958.

Klondike River in 1896. From all over the world people poured into this remote region, crossing high mountain passes with mule trains. Some were old hands at prospecting, but many were inexperienced pioneers, coming directly from the cities of Europe. Many perished in avalanches and rockfalls. A few made their fortunes, but they were rarely the prospectors. They were the businesspeople who sold the shovels and tents to the newcomers or who

The main street of Dawson City in 1899. Hundreds of fortune seekers died in the ice and snow, trying to reach this remote outpost on the Yukon River.

opened saloons in Dawson City, the hard-drinking frontier boomtown.

The old days have passed, but this remains a land for pioneers. Gold is still mined in the Yukon, as are lead, zinc, and silver. The mining industry attracts temporary workers from the south, but few stay long. Other industries do provide a living for the more permanent population, and the most important of these is tourism. Canadians and Americans make the journey north to Dawson City to get a feel of the old gold rush days and to see the landscape of the north.

Northwest Territories: On Top of the World

The Northwest Territories take up an area larger than the whole of India. However, while India has a population of nearly 900,000,000, this Arctic wilderness is home to about 56,000 people. This is one of the most isolated places in the world.

The northern part of the region is made up of tundra, a region of mosses and lichens, of bogs and lakes. It freezes solid during the long winter, and it is a breeding ground for insects in the summer. Few trees can survive on the tundra, but to the south are the great forests of northern Canada, the haunt of the owl and the timber wolf. The border between the two zones is called a tree line. The Arctic section of the Northwest Territories is home to the Inuit people. However, in 1999 this region

Young men of the Slavey tribe, part of the Déné group of peoples, chant and drum in the time-honored tradition at Trout Lake, in the southern Northwest Territories.

The Northwest Passage

It's the meanest, toughest sea voyage in the world. For hundreds of years Arctic explorers tried to sail ships around the north of the continent to seek out a "northwest passage" from Baffin Island to the Beaufort Sea. The ocean is locked solid with pack ice for nine months each year. The climate is bitterly cold, the winter is dark and menacing, and the summer melt releases huge icebergs into Baffin Bay and the sounds that lead off it. John Cabot and Henry Hudson failed; Sir John Franklin and all his crew perished in the attempt in 1845—some of their bodies were preserved where they were buried, in the Arctic's permanently frozen soil. It was Norwegian explorer Roald Amundsen who first broke through, sailing the passage in a boat called Gjöa *from 1903 to 1906. Five years later he became the first human to reach the South Pole, at the other end of the earth.*

became a separate territory named Nunavut (NOON-ah-vuht), the name traditionally given to the ancestral home of the Inuit of the central and eastern Arctic.

The remaining part of the Northwest Territories will probably be renamed. This area comprises the forested sub-Arctic region, traditionally home to First Peoples of the Déné culture, who today number about ten thousand. This region

also includes about forty-five thousand Métis and some twenty-five thousand people of European descent, including both French- and English-speakers.

Once hunting, fishing, and trapping were the only means of survival in the Northwest Territories. Then came the whalers, the loggers, and the miners. Oil was discovered in the 1920s, and today zinc, gold, silver, and lead mining are the most important northern industries. Many of the workers are temporary visitors to the far north. Indigenous peoples still live by fishing, hunting, and trapping, but Native arts and crafts and tourism have offered new opportunities for work. Festivals in the small towns of the Northwest Territories may include dogsled races, competitions in igloo-building and

Déné girls of the Slavey group flex their muscles during a log-sawing contest in the Northwest Territories. Such competitions are popular in most parts of rural Canada.

skinning animals, and the song and dance of the Inuit and First Peoples.

The Arctic is a fragile environment and is easily disrupted by industry. The changes of the last fifty years have created environmental challenges and have raised disputes over land rights with Native peoples, such as the Déné.

Nunavut: A Future for the Inuit

The scattered communities of Inuit have had a long struggle to gain recognition. In 1962 it was suggested that the western part of the Northwest Territories split away from the eastern part and become a

An Inuit hunter from the Pond Inlet area of Baffin Island takes aim with his rifle. In the past, hunting was necessary for the Inuit to survive.

province. This never came about, but the idea was followed by growing demands from the Inuit of the eastern region for their own system of self-government. They suggested that the Northwest Territories be divided along the tree line, the point where the Arctic tundra, the Inuit homeland, gives way to the northern forests of the Déné peoples.

The Inuit and the Canadian government negotiated for many years. However, some Inuit mistrusted the whole idea because it meant that land claims in other parts of the Northwest Territories would have to be forfeited. Even so, the people of the Northwest Territories voted for separation, and in 1982 the government announced that separation would take place. However, it took until 1992 to sort out all kinds of claims for land and mineral rights.

Nunavut means "our land" in the Inuktitut language of the Inuit. In 1999 this new territory became a reality, the first in which indigenous North Americans have gained self-rule. Parts of the land are completely owned by the Inuit, while other parts are jointly owned with the Canadian government. About 136,500 square miles (350,000 square kilometers) of Arctic wilderness are separated from the Northwest Territories and governed as a separate region, with the small town of Iqaluit as its capital. Nunavut includes

Baffin Island, Ellesmere Island, part of Victoria Island, and the mainland from Coppermine River to Hudson Bay—an area making up about 20 percent of Canada as a whole. About 80 percent of the population of Nunavut are Inuit, and they have the right to hunt and control mining throughout the territory. Any other Canadian citizens may also belong to the new territory as long as they are

Inuit schoolchildren listen to their teacher on Southampton Island. The chart on the wall behind them shows the shapes called syllabics, which make up the Inuit alphabet.

Darkness and Light

In the lands of the Arctic, winters are long, and darkness fills the winter days. The summer is brief, but its days are long and light. This tale, told by the Canadian Inuit, explains how light first broke into the world.

"Long ago, at the beginning of time, gloom covered the land. There was no day, no night. High in the icy mountains there lived a chief. Children who visited his hut saw two balls hanging from the ceiling. The children wanted the balls for their games, but they always seemed to be carefully guarded.

"They waited and waited until the chief went out hunting. The guards soon fell asleep. Quick as a flash, the children ran in and stole the balls. Laughing and shouting, they bounced the balls all the way down the mountainside. Suddenly, the balls broke open. Out of one jumped the spirit of Light, dazzling the world. Out of the other jumped the spirit of Darkness. The two spirits battled and argued, but in the end they agreed to take turns to rule the world. . . ."

permanent residents. Nunavut does not contain all of Canada's Inuit, for many of them still live outside its boundaries in other territories and provinces.

The Inuit's traditional way of life has changed forever. Today they live in modern houses, shop at stores, and drive snowmobiles, small motor vehicles with skis. Inuit communities are linked with each other and with the lands to the south by satellite television, radio, and the Internet. Their clothes are as likely to be made of the latest waterproof fibers as of traditional sealskin and fur. However, many Inuit have kept up their cultural traditions and their hunting and survival skills.

During the twentieth century the Inuit have suffered from unemployment, and this has led to personal breakdowns, alcoholism, and health problems.

An Inuit woman from Igloolik teaches a teenage girl how to make clothing in the traditional way from sealskin and caribou hide. Such clothes are warm and waterproof.

However, hunting and fishing still provide a means of living, and many Inuit are employed by the government in administrative jobs.

Since the 1960s Inuit art and craft items have been greatly valued and exported around the world. Sealskin products have been affected by antisealing campaigns around the world, but small animal statues carved in a soft mineral called soapstone are especially popular. During the long winter nights of northern Canada, statues like these were passed around from hand to hand for feeling, as well as looking.

Music and the Arts

Canada today is a country where people have a taste for public art, music, and theater. Artists and writers are taken

Churchgoers prepare to go home after a Sunday morning service in Igloolik. Before Christian missionaries reached the Arctic, the Inuit believed solely in a world of nature spirits.

seriously and widely supported and enjoyed. The larger cities have excellent art galleries, drama festivals, and concert halls.

The story of Canadian music begins with the First Peoples and Inuit, whose dances may still be seen at powwows and other festivals, accompanied by chanting and drumming. Their music is similar to that of the peoples of Siberia, the region of Asia from which their ancestors probably came. The Métis and French fur trappers who traveled westward over remote rivers and lakes sang canoeing songs to help with the rhythm of paddling. The Bretons, French, English, Irish, and Scots brought country dances and fiddle music, jigs and reels. Dances from the regions of old Europe spread like wildfire across Canada with the pioneers. Some traditional folk music has been rediscovered by new generations of Canadians, while others have turned to modern folk, country, rock, or jazz.

The opening up of the wilderness inspired many Canadian painters in the 1700s and 1800s. In the 1900s the Canadian art world was dominated by artist Tom Thomson and his followers, who after Thomson's death became known as the Group of Seven. Rather than paint European landscapes, they preferred to paint Canada's lakes and pines. Montreal was the center of a very different school of art in the 1940s and 1950s, inspired by abstract shapes and geometry.

At this time the National Film Board of Canada was breaking new ground in cinema with some first-rate documentary films and some original animation directed by Norman McLaren. In recent years Canada has also produced some successful commercial films, such as *Jesus of Montreal*.

Indian and Inuit art may be seen in many of today's galleries, with fine carvings in wood, soapstone, and bone. Prints and paintings, inspired by traditional subject matter, now explore new mediums and forms of expression.

The writers who came to Canada in the 1800s and early 1900s wrote romantic tales of the great outdoors, of the wildlife, and of the Klondike gold miners. The Canadian landscape

This fine piece of soapstone was carved by Inuit artist Abraham Etungat. A human figure and Arctic wildlife form a pyramid shape.

The Call of the Wild

Jack London was an American writer who was born in San Francisco in 1876. He was a sailor, a wanderer, and a gold digger. In 1897 he was working in Whitehorse, Yukon Territory, and decided to head north to the Klondike River. He was inspired by the northern wilderness and its wildlife and went on to write the novels Call of the Wild *(1903) and* White Fang *(1906), which became popular around the world. Jack London died in 1916.*

remains an inspiration for many writers. It is often portrayed in literature, for example, the novels of E. Annie Proulx and the short stories of Alice Munro.

The Land and Its People

Canada's national and provincial parks provide some protection for its wildlife and forests. There are thirty-seven national parks; they include vast areas of the Rocky Mountains, lakeside birch woods, and sandy dunes. There are dense forests of spruce, lodgepole pine, and fir. Coastal parks on the foggy Pacific Ocean have ferns and red cedars, while in the east the Cape Breton Highlands National Park looks out over the rolling waves of the Atlantic.

Canada's national parks and reserves offer a chance for the Canadians of the southern cities and farmland to experience the wilderness, to walk through ancient forests, to get away from the crowds and

Southern Canada has many places where city dwellers can escape in their free time. These people are preparing for a boat trip on Big Hawk Lake in central Ontario.

the noise. In a way, the national parks are an aid to human survival just as much as they are a haven for animals and plants.

Canada is a vast, rugged country, the land of the Rockies and the great forests. The need to survive under such harsh conditions has shaped the characters of Canada's First Peoples, of its French and Scottish pioneers, and of the farmers from central and eastern Europe who built their farms on the prairie.

At the same time Canada is surprisingly fragile. Industrial developments can cause the permafrost of the tundra to melt. Fish stocks can run out, as in Newfoundland, and salmon runs can be blocked by dams and hydroelectric schemes. All such developments affect the everyday livelihood and quality of life of Canadians.

Sports: On Ice and Turf

Canadians love sports, and if they're not playing them, they're watching them. The most popular game of all is ice hockey. It was invented in Canada, and the first rules

The Maple Leafs bring glory to their home town of Toronto. Canadians love ice hockey; there are seven Canadian teams in the North American National Hockey League (NHL).

The Great Gretzky

If ice hockey is Canada's game of games, then Wayne Gretzky has helped to make it so. He is one of the greatest players of all time. Gretzky was born on January 26, 1961 in Brantford, Ontario, and was already skating at the age of three on the frozen river by his grandparents' farm. Gretzky began his career in the National Hockey League in 1979. In 1981–1982, playing for the Edmonton Oilers, he scored the highest number of goals in a season, ninety-two. In the same season, including Stanley Cup and World Championship games, he scored an incredible 238 points (103 goals and 135 assists). He achieved seven assists in a single game on at least three occasions; playing for Edmonton against Washington (1980), against Chicago (1985), and Quebec (1986). In his eleventh season (by then playing in the United States for the Los Angeles Kings), Gretzky overtook the previous NHL points record of 1,850, held by his childhood hero, Gordie Howe. "It's a true honor to have my record broken by a man like Wayne Gretzky," said Howe. Going on to play for the St. Louis Blues and the New York Rangers, Gretzky has played 1,335 games, scoring a total of 2,705 points (862 goals; 1,843 assists). He holds the records for the most goals, most assists, most points, most games scoring three or more goals, most consecutive 40-or-more-goal seasons, and most 100-or-more-point seasons. Gretzky has become a household name throughout North America.

Canada meets Sweden in the women's curling championships at the 1988 Olympic Games in Calgary. Canada's teams are regular winners of the world curling championships.

War games

To many Native American peoples in history, from Mexico to the shores of the Saint Lawrence River, ball games were sacred to the gods. One game they played, called lacrosse *(lah-CROSS) by the French, was not only holy, it was useful training for war. The game, in which a ball was hurled from a thonged scoop at the end of a stick, went on for days on end and could involve hundreds of people. This is the game on which modern lacrosse is based, only today it is played on a field between two teams of ten people. Enthusiastically fought, it is regarded as the national game in most parts of Canada.*

for the game were drawn up in Montreal in 1879. The game, in which a puck is hit across an ice rink with hockey sticks, is one of the world's fastest. There are two teams, each with five skaters and one goalkeeper, but substitutes can be called in to replace a player at any time. It is a tough game of body checks and collisions. The game of ice hockey spread from Canada to the United States and Russia, and today it has a growing following around the world.

Curling is another team game on ice, though less strenuous. It was brought over to Canada by settlers from Scotland and is still very popular. A curling competition is called a bonspiel (BAHN-speel). There are two teams of four players. A curling stone—a heavy disk with a handle—is slid across the ice toward a target circle. The closer you get to the circle, the more points you score. The ice is swept smooth with brooms so that the stone slides faster.

Canadian football is very much like American football, except that it has teams of twelve and a larger field. The Canadian Football League (CFL) is divided into two leagues, the Western and Eastern Conferences, and the season lasts through the fall. Most rising stars in the CFL are lured away by the big money offered by the American game, south of the border.

In Canada, as in the United States, soccer is less popular than elsewhere in the Americas. Rugby, a team game played with an oval ball, is mostly played in British Columbia, and Canadian rugby teams are beginning to get noticed internationally. Baseball, which is played by American rules, is very popular during the summer.

Skating is a popular pastime for all, either on rinks or on rivers and lakes during the winter. Canada, with its wide open spaces, is the ideal country for windsurfing, hang gliding, swimming, white-water rafting, and hiking.

A kayak heads up the Firth River in Yukon Territory, Canada. The kayak, an Inuit invention originally made from sealskin, is now used by sports canoeists all over the world.

CAYMAN ISLANDS

THE CAYMAN ISLANDS LIE IN THE HEART OF THE CARIBBEAN.
They form the largest remaining British
colony in the West Indies.

*The Cayman Islands lie about 150
miles (240 kilometers) northwest of
Jamaica. Grand Cayman is the
largest of the three islands, with an
area of 76 square miles (197 square
kilometers). Little Cayman and Cayman
Brac lie about 70 miles (110 kilometers) to
the northeast and together make up a total of
only 24 square miles (62 square kilometers).*

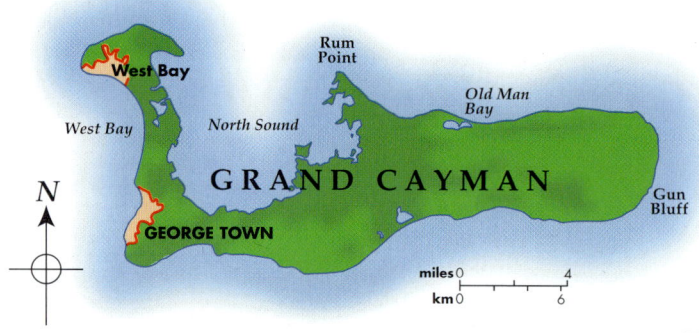

*Large areas of coast are fringed by
mangrove swamps. The coasts are rocky
and surrounded by coral reefs. The
beaches are beautiful stretches of sand,
backed by coconut palms.*

Turtles and Ships

For thousands of years the only population
of the Cayman (KAY-man) Islands was
turtles, who laid their eggs in the islands'
sandy beaches. The islands may have been
discovered by Native American peoples,
but none seems to have settled here
permanently.

The islands were deserted when
Christopher Columbus first reached them
in 1503. As English and French voyagers
followed the Spanish into the Caribbean,
the islands became a place where ships
stopped for repairs or to load supplies.

CLIMATE

*The climate in the Caymans is tropical, warm for
most of the year, with a rainy season from May
to November, when hurricanes are common.*

Average January temperature: *78°F (26°C)*

Average July temperature: *85°F (29°C)*

Average annual precipitation: *56 in (142 cm)*

The islands were claimed by the British
in 1670. The first permanent settlers,
Europeans accompanied by African slaves,
arrived on Grand Cayman from Jamaica in
1734. Little Cayman and Cayman Brac
were not settled until 1833. Slaves were
given their freedom by the British in 1838.

FACTS AND FIGURES

Status: *British dependent territory*

Capital: *George Town*

Area: *100 square miles (259 square kilometers)*

Population: *32,000*

Population density: *320 per square mile (124 per square kilometer)*

Peoples: *50 percent Afro-Caribbean-European descent; 25 percent Afro-Caribbean; 25 percent European descent*

Official language: *English*

Currency: *Cayman Island dollar*

National days: *Discovery Day (mid-May); Constitution Day (July 6)*

Country's name: *Cayman comes from caimán, the Spanish word for "alligator."*

Because the Caymans were not ideal for farming, the plantation system common in the rest of the Caribbean, with a wealthy landowning white elite, did not develop here, and the gap between rich and poor was not as great as on other islands.

Life on this remote outpost was quiet. During World War II, from 1939 to 1945, the islands were open to air traffic, and the development of the islands began. The colony was assigned an administrator, a position that became a full colonial governor in 1972. The islands became a center of finance and banking.

About one-quarter of all Caymanians are Afro-Caribbean, and one-quarter are from

Chatting outside the store in the evening sun, on Grand Cayman. Not all the islanders have benefited from the wealth brought into the islands by the international bankers.

British or other European backgrounds. About one-half of the islanders are of mixed descent. They speak English with various accents; some also speak Spanish.

Religion plays an important part in the life of the community. Most Caymanians are Protestant. The islands have a good record of health care and education, and there is no shortage of work. Most people live in George Town, which is linked by air and sea with the other islands. Roads link the main towns and villages on the islands.

The soil of the Caymans is not ideal for farming. Farms do produce tropical fruit, such as coconuts, and yams, but a large amount of food has to be imported. Fuel is also imported. Many islanders work in office or government jobs. Some work as fishers and shrimpers. Tourism accounts for 70 percent of the islands' income.

Craft items made on the islands include tortoiseshell (turtle) souvenirs. Some turtles are raised for this purpose.

Timeline:	Christopher Columbus reaches the islands	Settlers arrive on Grand Cayman	Settlers arrive on Little Cayman and Cayman Brac	Slavery abolished	Cayman Islands have their own colonial governor
	1503 C.E.	1734	1833	1838	1972

Glossary

abolition: bringing a law or custom to an end.

anarchist: an individual who calls for getting rid of governments in favor of informal agreements between free individuals.

boomtown: a city enjoying population growth and economic success.

Breton: a person from Brittany, a part of western France that was once an independent country. The Bretons are descended primarily from Celts who fled from Britain during its invasion by Angles and Saxons during the sixth to ninth centuries.

bronco: a pony or mustang that has not been broken in or trained yet. The term comes from a Spanish word meaning "rough" or "rude."

combine: a harvesting machine that reaps (cuts), threshes (beats), and cleans grain. The first horse-drawn combines were invented in the United States in 1836.

conifer: a tree or shrub that produces bare seeds, usually in cones. Most conifers are evergreens, such as pines and firs.

dialect: a nonstandard version of a language, as spoken in a particular region or by a particular group of people.

dominion: an area of rule. The term was once used to describe self-governing countries within the British Empire, such as Canada or New Zealand.

dude up: in U.S. slang, to dress up in fancy clothes; often used to describe how a city person dresses as a cowboy.

economic depression: a period of decline in business and trade, marked by debt, bankruptcy, and unemployment.

First Nations people: descendants of some of the first inhabitants of Canada who entered the region many thousands of years ago. They are also referred to as Indians or Native Americans.

free market: an economy where goods can be traded with minimal interference from the government.

gable: the triangular end of a roof.

hydroelectric: of or related to production of electricity from waterpower. The force of a waterfall or dammed river may be used to produce electricity in a power station.

independent: not ruled by another country.

Iroquois Confederacy: an alliance of five Native American nations of the northeast—the Cayuga, Mohawk, Oneida, Onondaga, and Seneca. It was founded in 1570; later the Tuscarora Nation joined the Confederacy.

linguist: someone who studies languages.

loyalist: someone who remains loyal to a cause. When the American Revolution broke out in 1775, many colonists remained loyal to the British government and fought against the rebels.

maritime: relating to the sea. Canada's eastern coast provinces—Nova Scotia, New Brunswick, and Prince Edward Island—are known as the Maritimes.

pack ice: in polar regions, the slabs of ice that are driven together by wind and ocean currents.

paddy: wet land in which rice is grown.

powwow: from the Algonquian word *po-wah*, meaning a conference, meeting, ceremony, or feast. Today's powwows are festivals in which Native Americans or First Nations people celebrate their traditions, such as dancing and drumming.

province: a district or division of a country.

Québécois: the French word for someone from Quebec Province.

radical: someone who tackles the cause of a problem; someone who favors drastic political action.

skipper: the captain of a yacht or small ship.

social welfare: services that aim to help people with problems such as poverty, unemployment, poor public health, and illiteracy.

trawler: a boat or small ship that fishes with a net. Trawlers drag nets along the seabed.

tundra: a polar or mountaintop region where there are few, if any, trees. The climate is so cold that the soil remains frozen beneath the surface year-round.

turf: a cut section of matted grass and soil.

United Nations: an alliance, founded in 1945, that today includes most of the countries in the world. Its aim is to encourage international cooperation and peace.

unscrupulous: lacking in principles; having no concern for others.

utopia: an ideal society. The word was first used as the title of a book by Sir Thomas More in 1516. It was taken from the ancient Greek word for "nowhere."

World Heritage Site: a place that is listed by the United Nations as being of great historical interest, scientific importance, or natural beauty.

Further Reading

Canada

Ayer, Elizabeth. *Canada.* Vero Beach, FL: Rourke Publishing Group, 1990.

Bakken, Edna. *Alberta.* Danbury, CT: Childrens Press, 1992.

Barnes, Michael. *Ontario.* Minneapolis, MN: Lerner Group, 1995.

Bender, Lionel. *Canada.* Parsippany, NJ: Silver Burdett Press, 1987.

Campbell, Kumari. *New Brunswick.* Minneapolis, MN: Lerner Group, 1996.

Department of Geography Staff. *Canada in Pictures.* Minneapolis, MN: Lerner Group, 1989.

Emmond, Kenneth. *Manitoba.* Danbury, CT: Childrens Press, 1992.

Gann, Marjorie. *New Brunswick.* Danbury, CT: Childrens Press, 1994.

Hancock, Lyn. *Northwest Territories.* Danbury, CT: Childrens Press, 1993.

Kalman, Bobbie. *Canada Celebrates Multiculturalism.* New York: Crabtree Publishing, 1993.

Kessler, Deirdre. *Prince Edward Island.* Danbury, CT: Childrens Press, 1992.

Law, Kevin. *Canada.* Broomhall, PA: Chelsea House, 1991.

Lotz, Jim. *Nova Scotia.* Danbury, CT: Childrens Press, 1992.

MacKay, Kathryn. *Ontario.* Danbury, CT: Childrens Press, 1992.

Malcolm, Andrew H. *The Land and People of Canada.* New York: HarperCollins Children's Books, 1991.

Margoshes, David. *Saskatchewan.* Danbury, CT: Childrens Press, 1992.

Pang, Guek-Cheng. *Cultures of the World: Canada.* Tarrytown, NY: Marshall Cavendish, 1994.

Richardson, Gillian. *Saskatchewan.* Minneapolis, MN: Lerner Group, 1995.

Sateren, Shelley Swanson. *Exploring Cultures of the World: Canada.* Tarrytown, NY: Marshall Cavendish, 1996.

Shepherd, J. *Canada.* Danbury, CT: Childrens Press, 1992.

Sunday, Jane. *Canada.* Chatham, NJ: Raintree Steck-Vaughn, 1992.

Templeman-Kluit, Anne. *Yukon.* Danbury, CT: Childrens Press, 1994.

Thompson, Alex. *Nova Scotia.* Minneapolis, MN: Lerner Group, 1995.

White, Marian. *Newfoundland—Labrador.* Danbury, CT: Childrens Press, 1993.

Cayman Islands

Smith, Hunter. *Cayman Islands—The Beach and Beyond.* Edison, NJ: Hunter Publishing, Inc., 1995.

Islands of the Caribbean

Mason, Antony. *The Caribbean.* Parsippany, NJ: Silver Burdett Press, 1988.

Mayer, T. W. *The Caribbean and Its People.* New York: Thomson Learning, 1995.

Springer, Eintou P. *The Caribbean.* Parsippany, NJ: Silver Burdett Press, 1987.

Walker, Cas. *The Caribbean.* North Pomfret, VT: Trafalgar Square Publishing, 1991.

Index

Page numbers in *italic* indicate illustrations.

Page numbers in *italic* indicate illustrations.

REFERENCE

PEOPLES
of the
AMERICAS

PEOPLES
of the
AMERICAS

Volume 2
Bermuda–Brazil

MARSHALL CAVENDISH
NEW YORK • LONDON • TORONTO • SYDNEY

Marshall Cavendish Corporation
99 White Plains Road
Tarrytown, New York 10591-9001

Consulting Editor: J. Patrick Gray, Professor of Anthropology, University of Wisconsin

Consultants: Jean-Marc Blais, Senior Interpretive Planner, Canadian Museum of Civilization, Hull, Quebec
        David Frye, Assistant Director, Department of Latin American and Caribbean Studies, University of Michigan

Spanish Consultant: Fran Kaplan

Contributing authors: D. L. Birchfield
                Marion Morrison
                Juliette Radcliffe Rogers
                Philip Steele
                Mary A. Stout

Discovery Books
    Managing Editor: Paul Humphrey
    Project Editor: Helen Dwyer
    Text Editor: Valerie J. Weber
    Design Concept: Ian Winton
    Designers: Barry Dwyer, Ian Winton, and Simon Borrough
    Cartographer: Stefan Chabluk

Marshall Cavendish
    Editorial Director: Paul Bernabeo
    Editor: Marian Armstrong
    Associate Editor: Debra M. Jacobs

The publishers would like to thank the following for their permission to reproduce photographs:
Allsport (Shaun Botterill 103); Bruce Coleman Collection (Luiz Claudio Marigo 60, 72 bottom); James Davis Travel Photography (50, 81, 86); Eye Ubiquitous (Bruce Adams 52, 53; John Miles 77); Edward Parker (cover, 79, 80, 82, 93, 98, 99, 100); South American Pictures (Bill Leimbach 88, 95, 96; Kimball Morrison 57, 68; Tony Morrison frontispiece, 54, 56, 58, 59, 61, 62, 63, 64, 65, 66, 67 top & bottom, 69, 70, 71, 72 top, 73, 74, 75, 78, 83, 84, 85, 87, 89, 90, 91, 92, 94, 97, 101); Tony Stone Images (Ary Diesendruck 102)

(frontispiece) Aymara mother and baby in Bolivia.

Editor's note: Many systems of dating have been used by different cultures throughout history. *Peoples of the Americas* uses B.C.E. (Before Common Era) and C.E. (Common Era) instead of B.C. (Before Christ) and A.D. (Anno Domini, "In the Year of the Lord") out of respect for the diversity of the world's peoples.

Library of Congress Cataloging-in-Publication Data
Peoples of the Americas.
        p.   cm.
    Includes bibliographical references and index.
    Contents: v. 1. Anguilla–Belize — v. 2. Bermuda–Brazil — v. 3. Canada–Cayman Islands — v. 4. Chile–Costa Rica — v. 5. Cuba–French Guiana — v. 6. Greenland–Jamaica — v. 7. Martinique–Paraguay — v. 8. Peru–Turks and Caicos Islands — v. 9. United States of America — v. 10. United States of America–Virgin Islands

    ISBN 0-7614-7050-6 (set)
    1. Ethnology—America—Juvenile literature. 2. America—History—Juvenile literature. [1. Ethnology—America. 2. America—History.]
E29.A1P46 1999
970'.004—dc21   98-2801
                                                                            CIP
                                                                            AC

    ISBN 0-7614-7050-6 (set)
    ISBN 0-7614-7052-2 (vol. 2)

Printed and bound in Italy

Contents

BERMUDA

BERMUDA IS A GROUP OF CORAL ISLANDS IN THE NORTHWEST ATLANTIC. They are 656 miles (1,056 kilometers) due east of the nearest land, which is Cape Hatteras, North Carolina.

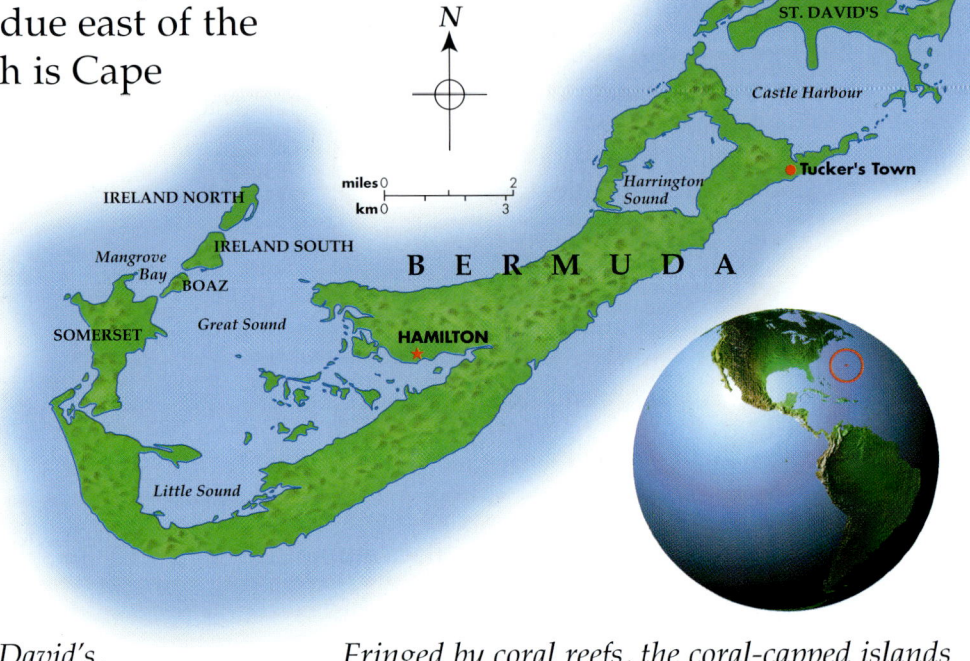

Bermuda has a total of 178 islands and islets. The largest and main island is Bermuda, which is 14 miles (23 kilometers) long. The capital, Hamilton, is in the center of this island. The next six largest islands are Saint David's, Saint George's, Somerset, Ireland North, Ireland South, and Boaz. These seven islands are connected by bridges and a causeway.

Fringed by coral reefs, the coral-capped islands are made of a 200-feet-thick limestone base. The land averages 262 feet (80 meters) above sea level and in one place reaches 344 feet (105 meters). Lush, green, fertile valleys lie between the low, rolling hills. Bermuda's soil is so porous that almost all drinking water must be collected from rainfall and stored.

CLIMATE

Rainfall is spread fairly evenly throughout the year; September and October are the wettest months. July and August are the warmest months, but the sea helps keep the temperatures tolerable.

Average January temperature: *63°F (17°C)*

Average July temperature: *79°F (26°C)*

Average annual precipitation: *57 in (145 cm)*

A police officer in British uniform directs the traffic in Hamilton, the capital of Bermuda. The islands remain British, although many Bermudians would like their independence.

FACTS AND FIGURES

Status: *British dependent territory*

Capital: *Hamilton*

Area: *21 square miles (54 square kilometers)*

Population: *61,000*

Population density: *2,905 per square mile (1,130 per square kilometer)*

Peoples: *58 percent African descent; 41 percent European descent; 1 percent Asian descent*

Official language: *English*

Currency: *Bermuda dollar (U.S. dollar also used)*

National days: *Bermuda Day (May 26); Cup Match Day (July 31); Somers Day (August 1); Labor Day (September 1)*

Country's name: *Bermuda is named after the Spanish navigator Juan de Bermudez, who was shipwrecked on the reefs around 1503. The name Somers Island is also used for official state matters. This name commemorates British admiral Sir George Somers, who landed there in 1609.*

A Voyager's Sailing Hub

Until the arrival of Europeans, Bermuda (bur-MYOO-duh) was uninhabited. The Spanish knew of its existence in the sixteenth century but made no attempts to colonize the islands. In 1609 Admiral Somers was on his way to the colony of Virginia in North America with 150 British settlers when they were swept ashore onto a Bermudian reef during a storm. They stayed ten months, surviving partly on pigs left behind by various European sailors who had been shipwrecked there. When the admiral and his passengers arrived safely in Virginia, they sent back reports to the British Virginia Company that Bermuda was a good place to settle.

Two years later, the company sent sixty settlers to colonize the islands. They soon brought in African slaves to work the land. In 1620 Bermuda became self-governing, and in 1684, it became a British colony.

The early settlers found that farming was not successful on the thin, porous soil, so they turned their skills to shipbuilding and constructed fast-sailing ships of Bermudian cedar wood. These vessels could outsail French and Spanish privateers, pirate vessels that preyed on merchant ships. With these ships, the Bermudians sailed on trading voyages between Britain and British colonies in North America and the Caribbean. They collected salt from Caribbean islands and took it to eastern Canada. This salt was traded for salted fish that, in turn, was exchanged for sugar and rum in the West Indies. These goods were traded in the American colonies for salted meat, which was then bartered in England for other goods, such as clothing.

Bermuda has a long history of illegal trade with its larger neighbor to the west, the American colonies. During the American Revolution, Great Britain stopped this trade with America. However, firearms and ammunition were smuggled secretly from Bermuda to the American rebels. During the American Civil War from 1861 to 1865, Bermuda was again a center for blockade runners, ships making the hazardous dash to ports in the southern

Timeline:	Islands first sighted by Europeans	Admiral Somers and 150 English passengers marooned for ten months	Group of British settlers arrive to colonize the islands	Beginning of self-government for the islands
	1503 C.E.	1609	1612	1620

The British governor of Bermuda attends a reception in ceremonial dress, which includes a hat of plumed feathers. The male guests wear typical British top hats.

states. During Prohibition from 1920 through 1933, when alcohol was banned in the United States, fast boats smuggled rum from Bermuda.

Bermuda's position in the Atlantic makes it important strategically. In 1941 land was leased to the United States for an air base. American military personnel remained on Bermuda until 1995, when the United States decided that there was no longer a Soviet military threat.

A new constitution was created in 1968 stating that a governor appointed by the British monarch has responsibility for external affairs and national security. There is also a two-chamber government. Bermudians elect the lower-house members.

Race relations in Bermuda are a source of discontent to the black population. The white population controls both the economy and government, and blacks are very dependent on the white elite for jobs and housing. During the 1970s tensions increased, racial riots took place, and in 1973 the governor, Sir Richard Sharples, was assassinated. In 1977 the government tried to end racial discrimination. Many blacks would like independence from Great Britain, but despite many discussions, the majority of the people prefer to remain part of Great Britain.

Land of Immigrants

Today the majority of Bermudians are of African descent. Some of these are descendants of slaves from other islands in the Caribbean, and most of today's Bermudians are descended from these islanders. Other black Bermudians arrived voluntarily in the twentieth century.

When slavery was abolished in the 1830s, Portuguese laborers were brought in from the Azores and Madeira, Portuguese islands off the northern coast of western Africa. Today there are roughly two thousand residents of Portuguese descent.

Other residents include British, Americans, and Canadians. The Canadians are the most numerous group of guest workers and have many jobs in the Bermudian government, educational system, and finance and tourism industries. Links with Canada have been strong since the 1780s, when Canada became a main supply source for Bermuda's food and timber. A small number of Asians live in Bermuda, working primarily in domestic service or the hotel industry.

Islands become British colony	United States granted ninety-nine-year lease on an air base	New constitution created with provision for a governor appointed by British monarch	Governor Sharples assassinated	U.S. lease on air base terminated
1684	1941	1968	1973	1995

Bermuda Shorts: A Fashion Necessity

Created in London at the turn of the twentieth century by the British Army, Bermuda shorts were designed so that soldiers and sailors would be lightly dressed for tropical climates. In those days, the British Empire stretched around the globe. The official tropical uniform became khaki shorts, knee-length socks, and highly polished shoes. When British regiments were stationed in the islands in the 1920s, the Bermudians adopted their dress. Today, worn with knee-length socks, Bermuda shorts are as well made as a good pair of pants and are the preferred dress of business people on the islands.

Many Bermudians are involved in the tourist industry, which attracts over 400,000 visitors each year, mostly from North America. The other major industry is finance. Because Bermuda has no income tax, thousands of international companies are registered there, although less than one in twenty of them have offices and staff.

About 4 percent of the land is used for farming, including onions, potatoes, and green vegetables. A wide variety of subtropical fruits are grown in Bermuda. However, the land cannot produce enough food for the population, and large quantities of food have to be imported.

Bermuda has many places of worship. About a third of the population belongs to the Anglican Church. Others are Roman Catholics, African Methodist Episcopalians,

Methodists, or belong to evangelical groups such as the Seventh-Day Adventists.

Most Bermudians celebrate religious holidays such as Easter and Christmas. When the weather is dry on Good Friday, the children fly kites made of tissue paper. It is thought that this custom originally had religious significance, representing Jesus Christ's ascension to heaven. Good Friday is also a day for eating codfish cakes, perhaps as a substitute for meat, which in the Christian tradition is not eaten on Fridays during Lent.

On Bermuda Day the main event is a parade. Dancers and the island's pipe and drum band join the parade as it moves through the city of Hamilton. Restaurants are open, and stands serve buffets of food.

Bermuda has some specialty foods made from local ingredients with names that reflect Caribbean, British, and American influences. Hoppin' John and Paw Paw Montespan is a savory dish of black-eyed peas with ground beef, cooked with tomatoes, rice, and pawpaws, fruit from the papaya tree. Bermuda onions, which are grown locally, are famous and appear in casseroles, biscuits, bread, soups, pies, and souffles.

Fishermen in Mangrove Bay sort their catch. Local fish provide the basis for dishes such as shark fritters, baked red snapper, and wahoo (mackerel) steaks.

BOLIVIA

BOLIVIA IS A LARGE, LANDLOCKED COUNTRY in South America, surrounded by five other republics.

The Andes Mountains divide into two ranges in Bolivia. Between them is a high, cold, treeless plain called the altiplano (ahl-tee-PLAH-no). To the east, the mountains drop through dense forests and fertile valleys. From the northern foothills, Amazon rain forests extend for hundreds of miles. To the south of the forests are extensive plains that flood annually. Farther south are the dry grasslands known as the Chaco.

Early Native Civilizations

People first reached South America between ten thousand and fifteen thousand years ago. They survived by hunting, fishing, and gathering nuts and fruit from the forests. Cultivating crops and domesticating animals came much later, probably about two thousand to three thousand years ago.

On the altiplano, Aymara women in traditional skirts, one with the traditional bowler hat, walk to La Paz. They and their mule are carrying produce to sell in the markets there.

FACTS AND FIGURES

Official name: *República de Bolivia*

Status: *Independent state*

Capital: *Sucre (officially); La Paz (seat of government)*

Major cities: *Santa Cruz, El Alto, Cochabamba, Oruro, Potosí, Tarija*

Area: *424,165 square miles (1,098,587 square kilometers)*

Population: *7,800,000*

Population density: *18 per square mile (7 per square kilometer)*

Peoples: *50 percent Native American; 25 percent mestizo; 20 percent European descent; 5 percent other*

Official languages: *Spanish, Aymara, Quechua*

Currency: *Peso Boliviano*

National days: *Labor Day (May 1); La Paz Municipal Holiday (July 16); Independence Day (August 6); Columbus Day (October 12)*

Country's name: *Bolivia was named after Simon Bolivar, the soldier who freed much of South America from Spanish rule in the early nineteenth century.*

Remains of an early civilization called Tiwanaku exist in Bolivia (bo-LEEV-ee-ah) near Lake Titicaca on the western border. From 500 to 1000 C.E., this site was the center of an empire including half of Bolivia, southern Peru, northern Chile, and northwestern Argentina. It was a ceremonial and trading center with pyramids, temples, and palaces. It is now thought that perhaps twenty thousand people lived there, supported by a farming system that produced all the crops they needed. No one is sure why the Tiwanaku empire declined around 1000 C.E.

Before Europeans arrived, many other peoples lived in what is now Bolivia. Chicka and Lipez people lived in the region of present-day Potosí in the south. The Yampara and Cochapampa inhabited valleys near Sucre, today's capital, also in the south. In the eastern lowlands lived many tribes speaking Tupi-Guaraní and Arawakan languages. The northern highlands were inhabited by Aymara-speaking tribes, who fought among themselves, and by Uru and Chipaya peoples, who spoke Puquina.

In the fifteenth century, the Aymara, Uru, and Chipaya were conquered by the Incas, a powerful Quechua-speaking people from Peru (see PERU). They tried, unsuccessfully, to impose the Quechua language throughout the area.

The Incas' victory was short-lived, as the Spanish conquistador, Francisco Pizarro, defeated them with a small band of men in the 1530s; the Spaniards had the advantage of horses and weapons unknown to the Incas. Peru and Bolivia, like much of South America, became Spanish colonies. In 1559 Sucre became the center of a Spanish territory called Upper Peru.

The Spaniards Dig In

The Spaniards settled and developed the colonies for two reasons: they wanted to get rich and convert the local people to Christianity. The first was quickly

Timeline:	First peoples arrive	Greatest years of Tiwanaku culture	Incas invade the highlands	Pizarro conquers the Incas
	13,000–8,000 B.C.E.	500–1000 C.E.	1438–1493	1533

accomplished. They soon found great wealth in the Cerro Rico, or "Rich Hill," of Potosí. During the sixteenth and seventeenth centuries, more silver was taken from Potosí than had ever been seen before. Native Americans were forced to work under dreadful conditions in the mines; thousands died. They were also forced to work the land for the Spaniards. But European diseases killed many more people than these hardships did. Lowland Native peoples fared better because they were out of the reach of Spanish authorities. They were also helped by missionaries who set up schools and workshops.

Since few Spanish settlers brought families with them, marriage with Native Americans gradually produced a people of

These Aymara men are taking part in the Dance of the Conquest at a fiesta in La Paz. Their masks represent the white faces of the Spanish conquerors.

mixed origins known as mestizos. Also, slaves were imported from Africa during the 1500s to work in the Potosí mines.

Settlers and their descendants in the Spanish colonies in South America resented the control Spain had, especially in matters of trade and taxes. Eventually, after many years of rebellion and unrest, Bolivia won its independence when General Antonio José de Sucre defeated the Spaniards at the Battle of Tumula in 1825.

For the next 125 years, a succession of generals and dictators, many of them corrupt and ruthless, ruled Bolivia. In the War of the Pacific (1879–1884), Bolivia lost its only port on the Pacific coast to Chile. During an Amazon rubber boom at the turn of the twentieth century, Bolivia sold its northern territory of Acre to Brazil in exchange for navigation rights on Brazilian rivers. The discovery of tin at the turn of

Spanish settlement begins	Silver discovered in Potosí	Independence from Spain won	War with Chile over ownership of land on Pacific coast leads to loss of Bolivia's only port	Bolivia gives up Acre territory to Brazil
1538	**1545**	**1825**	**1879–1884**	**1903**

CLIMATE

Throughout most of Bolivia a dry season usually extends from June to August, and a rainy season lasts from December to January. However, in parts of the lowlands, it rains all year-round. Climate varies according to altitude. In the highlands, there is a great contrast between day and night temperatures. On the altiplano, the average daytime temperature is much lower than in the lowlands. Cold winds from Argentina, the surazos (soo-RAH-sos), often cause severe drops in the altiplano's temperature.

	La Paz	Santa Cruz	Sucre
Average January temperature	53°F (12°C)	90°F (32°C)	55°F (13°C)
Average July temperature	47°F (8°C)	70°F (21°C)	49°F (9°C)
Average annual precipitation	23 in (58 cm)	54 in (137 cm)	27 in (69 cm)

the twentieth century brought some prosperity and formed the basis of Bolivia's economy for many years. A devastating war with Paraguay in the 1930s led to the loss of a vast area of the Chaco.

Political parties that emerged at the beginning of the century resulted in the victory in 1952 of the Movimiento Nacionalista Revolucionario (MNR) and a government that, for the first time, tried to improve conditions for the masses. In 1964 the MNR was deposed by a military government, but democratic elections have been held every four years since 1982. In all these elections, no candidate has received an overall majority, and Congress has chosen the president. In June 1997 General Hugo Banzer Suarez became president, a remarkable feat for a man who headed the military government from 1971 to 1978.

On Independence Day in La Paz, the national flag and portraits of the generals who ended Spanish rule in South America hang from the presidential palace.

War with Paraguay leads to loss of vast area of the Chaco	Movimiento Nacionalista Revolucionario (MNR) wins election	Military coup deposes MNR	Return to democratic elections	General Hugo Banzer Suarez elected president
1932–1935	**1952**	**1964**	**1982**	**1997**

Land of Native Americans

About one half of Bolivia's population is Native American, the highest percentage of Indians in any country in South America. The two largest groups are the Aymara (EYE-mah-rah), who live mainly in the north of the country, and the Quechua (KEH-choo-ah), most of whom have settled in valleys in the southeast. In the highlands are also a few surviving members of the ancient Chipaya tribe, and in the forests and plains of the lowlands dwell perhaps 50,000 to 150,000 members of several forest tribes and the Chiriguano of the Gran Chaco.

The remaining population is made up of mestizos, a very small number of descendants of the seventeenth-century African slaves, and small groups of immigrants. These include Europeans and Japanese, the majority of whom have arrived during this century. In 1954 about four hundred people arrived from Okinawa, Japan; their settlement near Santa Cruz is now a thriving community. In all, about ten thousand Japanese have settled in Bolivia. Mennonite farmers, members of a fundamentalist Protestant sect founded in the 1500s, also arrived in the second half of the twentieth century, mostly from the United States and Canada.

The principal language is Spanish, especially in the towns. But Aymara and Quechua are also widely spoken, and there are many villages and communities where these are still the only languages. A tiny number of Native Americans on the altiplano still use the ancient language of Puquina, while many of the lowland tribes speak their native Guaraní.

Since 1952 many schools have been built in rural areas. Nevertheless, these Quechua and mestizo children in southern Bolivia still walk many miles to school.

Traditionally, most Bolivians worked on the land or in the tin mines. But in the last thirty years, many thousands have made their way to La Paz and other towns, looking for a better way of life. There, they live in makeshift houses, often in very poor conditions, without electricity or running water, and make a living as best they can. Usually this means menial jobs or setting up as tradespeople in the streets. For the educated, there are good professional jobs, such as doctors, lawyers, or teachers.

Miners have always had a special place in Bolivian society, since tin has been the mainstay of the economy for most of the twentieth century. Miners have worked under tough conditions, often many miles underground and without adequate equipment. Many suffer from chest illnesses, and most have a short working life. But in the 1980s the world tin market collapsed, and many of the mines closed. The majority of miners are now out of work.

Bolivia has considerable mineral wealth, but it is still a poor country. A major economic problem is its geography. While most people live in the highlands, only very few inhabit the eastern lowlands, which have rich oil, gas, iron, gold, and timber reserves and are suitable for agriculture. Travel between the two is difficult because heavy rains often wash away roads on the steep slopes of the Andes Mountains.

Bolivia has few hospitals and medical clinics and not enough schools. On average, men can expect to live about sixty-one years, women about sixty-five. (By contrast, in the United States men can expect to live to seventy-two years old and women to seventy-nine.)

Many Bolivians suffer from malnutrition because they cannot afford to buy sufficient food. Those in the countryside depend on what they can grow.

A Quechua woman from Cochabamba sells her vegetables, including beans, onions, tomatoes, and chilies, on the roadside. The traditional hat she is wearing is now going out of fashion.

The basic foods are potatoes, quinoa (a cereal rich in protein), rice, and bread; little meat is eaten, though pork, chicken, or mutton (the meat of a mature sheep) are added to several dishes. Meals vary from region to region. In the highlands, soups and stews are popular and can include all kinds of vegetables and chunks of chicken, pork, or occasionally beef. They are very spicy, since strong *aji* (ah-HEE) peppers are often cooked with the dish or added as a sauce. On the table there is always a small dish of *locoto* (lo-KO-to), another very strong pepper, which can be green, yellow, or red. In the lowlands yucca (a tuber which takes the place of a potato), rice, bananas, and other fruits are the most common foods, mainly because they are locally grown. Because of the heat, which would spoil fresh meat without refrigeration, beef is often cut into thin slices and dried in the sun. It is fried and served with onions, tomatoes, or green-pepper sauce. Bananas, often the first meal of the day, are also fried.

Religion: Part of Family Life

Family life is important in Bolivia, with several generations often living in one house. Friends also become part of the extended family by being godparents to the children. Most Bolivians are Catholic, and families celebrate religious occasions such as First Holy Communion and marriage. They also enjoy festivals that mark the end of harvest or honor a local saint.

The religion of the Aymara people is a mixture of pre-Columbian traditions and Christian beliefs. Pachamama, or "Mother Earth," is as much revered as the Virgin

Inside a silver mine in Potosí, a boy miner chews coca leaves as he makes an offering to a god. For many Bolivians religion is a mixture of Native American and Christian beliefs.

Native American Gods Surround the Land

The Aymara and Quechua believe that gods and spirits exist in the world around them. Mountains, animals, and plants are a source of endless myths and legends. Many Aymara and Quechua celebrate the sun, Inti, who gives light and life; the moon, Pajsi, who sets the time for sowing and the harvest; and the stars, Warawara, who light the way for travelers at night.

A popular Aymara god is Ekeko, the god of good fortune and plenty, who is celebrated every year at the Alacitas fair in La Paz. The tiny god is represented by a small squat figure covered with all sorts of things, from pots and pans to sweets and foods. Everything sold at the fair is miniature, and you hope that you will get whatever you buy in abundance during the year.

Mary (mother of Jesus Christ) and Catholic saints. The blessing of Pachamama is always sought at important times, such as the beginning of harvest or the building of a new home. Offerings of coca leaves and liquor are sprinkled on the ground.

Bolivians from all areas gather to celebrate the fiesta of Copacabana, a small village on the shore of Lake Titicaca. On Good Friday thousands of people climb the Hill of Calvary above the village. Another celebration observed by people all over the country is *Todos los Santos* (To-dos los SAHN-tos), All Saints' and All Souls' Day. Families visit cemeteries to pay their respects to dead relatives, taking food, including specially baked candied bread, beer, and liquor, to place on the graves. It is a festive occasion, with people chatting, laughing, and occasionally dancing and making music.

Life on the Altiplano

The Andes Mountains run the length of South America and are at their widest in Bolivia. Here, the mountains divide into two ranges, or *cordilleras* (kor-deel-YEH-rahs). Between the two cordilleras is the high, cold, treeless plain called the altiplano. Most of this plain lies over 13,000 feet (4,000 meters) above sea level. About 70 percent of the population live on the altiplano, though it represents only about 10 percent of the land.

Lake Titicaca is the world's highest navigable lake. It lies at the northern end of the altiplano and is 12,500 feet (3,800 meters) above sea level. It lies on the border between Peru and Bolivia, with about half the lake in each country.

In the north, the altiplano is crossed by the Desaguadero River, which drains from the southwest corner of Lake Titicaca and meanders south to the dried-out Lake

In the village of Achacachi on the altiplano, Aymara women dance all day long at the Fiesta of the Indian. Behind them the men are dressed in carnival costumes.

The Creation of the World

Lake Titicaca is central to the creation myth of the Aymara people. They believe that in the beginning, the god Viracocha rose out of the lake and created a dark world without the sun, light, or warmth. Into this world he brought a race of giants, but they angered him and he destroyed them in a great flood. Then Viracocha reappeared from the lake to create a new world with a sun, moon, and stars and a new race of ordinary men.

Poopó. West and south of Lake Poopó, the altiplano continues with a series of salty lakes and brilliant white salt pans. Local traders use llamas and trucks to carry crude blocks of salt to small, often remote, villages. The salt is refined for sale throughout Bolivia. South of the salt pans, the land begins to rise gently again to a barren desert rimmed by volcanoes, some still active.

The Aymara who live on the altiplano have a hard, simple way of life. The climate is usually hot during the day but well below freezing at night. To combat the cold, the Aymara build homes of adobe brick (mud that is dried in brick form in the sun) and thatch. Often the only opening is a door. Inside are usually one or two rooms where the family eats and sleeps. Cooking is often done outside the hut in a dome-shaped, mud-brick oven.

Without irrigation, it is difficult to grow crops on the barren, dry soil, and few families can afford to buy fertilizers to enrich the soil. Most still use oxen and wooden plows. The Aymara grow potatoes, beans, and some cereal grains. Their working day begins at sunrise, and everyone is back home before sunset. Young sons and daughters often spend the day looking after sheep and llamas. The women of the family prepare food and may help with the farming, but one of their main tasks is weaving cloth, which they do during the day on a wooden loom outside their home.

In a village called Chipaya (chee-PAH-yah), at the edge of one of the salty lakes of the altiplano, a thousand or so people live

A Chipaya woman weaves on a horizontal loom with a bone tool. Chipaya clothing is of natural colors, made from the wool of sheep and llamas.

How to Dry a Potato

More than two hundred varieties of potatoes originated in the Andes, and the Andean peoples have developed a unique way to preserve them long after harvest has finished. The potatoes are spread on the ground, and women step on them to press out water. The potatoes are then left to dry in the hot sun and freezing night air until they become small and hard. In this state they are known as chuño *(CHOON-yo), or* tunta *(TOON-tah); they only need to be soaked in water and boiled in order to be used like fresh potato.*

in isolation. The Chipaya speak Puquina. They took refuge from the Incas and the Spaniards in the wilderness. Their houses are round and made of mud, with domed roofs cut from a tough grass. Doors are made from dried cactus wood. The Chipaya survive by tending llamas and sheep. The llamas provide wool, from which the Chipaya weave their clothes and shawls in natural colors of brown, beige, and black. Chipaya women spend many hours braiding each other's hair into many tiny braids in traditional style.

The Chipaya hunt wild birds living in marshes and small streams. To catch the birds, they use a bolas, a Y-shaped cord with weighted ends. When thrown skillfully so that the Y spins in the air, the weighted ends wrap around the bird.

Today some Aymara have homes on islands in the lake, but most live in villages along the shore. Around the neat one- and two-story houses, they grow a variety of crops and vegetables on the well-watered land. Lying close to the shore are beds of *totora* (toh-TOH-rah) reed that the Aymara

Gateway to the Sun

The Tiwanaku culture flourished from 500 to 1000 C.E. Today, Tiwanaku is an archaeological site not far from Lake Titicaca. The fine palaces, temples, and pyramids are in ruins, and only a few huge carvings of stone, godlike figures stand. Still standing, too, is the impressive Gateway to the Sun. Across the top of the gateway are finely made carvings of winged figures and a central figure, often referred to as Viracocha, the creator god. At one time thin sheets of beaten gold covered this arch and some other buildings.

The people who lived at Tiwanaku were probably ancestors of the Aymara. They wore rings, bracelets, armbands, and necklaces of copper, bronze, silver, and gold, fashioned by the city's many skilled craftspeople. For decoration, men of high rank wore earplugs of turquoise, seashell, wood, and gold. The emperor was revered as a god. No one is sure why Tiwanaku declined, but a massive earthquake or a prolonged drought may have devastated the area.

use as thatch for roofs, for mats and baskets, and for the reed boats, or *balsas* (BAHL-sahs), that traditionally have been used on the lake. When the reed is fully grown, it is cut and dried on the edge of the lake. Bundles of the reed are then tied together to form the body of the boat, which is shaped so that both ends rise out of the water. Nets cast from these boats catch fish for the local Aymara families.

An Aymara boatman on Lake Titicaca, wearing a traditional poncho and knitted hat. His boat is made from reeds that grow around the edge of the lake.

Paceños of La Paz

La Paz, Bolivia's largest city, lies at nearly 12,000 feet (3,650 meters) in a sheltered, deep valley of the altiplano at the foot of Mount Illimani.

At the heart of the city stands the commercial center, with modern high-rise buildings made of glass and concrete straddling the main avenue. From here, a road descends through the river valley to affluent residential suburbs. Above the main avenue and stretching up the side of the La Paz canyon are poorer houses, those of brick more sturdy than those of mud, grooved iron, and wood. Heavy rains often wash away fragile homes built near the rim of the valley.

Over the last twenty years thousands of people have migrated from the altiplano and made their way to La Paz. Today some villages on the altiplano are virtually uninhabited. Many of these people now live in El Alto. El Alto is a city above a city, situated on the altiplano over 1,300 feet (400 meters) above La Paz.

The people of La Paz are known as *Paceños* (pah-SEHN-yos). Most are mestizo descendants of Spaniards and Aymara. The men are often referred to as *cholos* (CHO-los), and the women as *cholas* (CHO-las). They are accomplished traders and a vital part of every Bolivian market. A typical chola is just as comfortable selling sophisticated electronic equipment as she is making clothes. And although town life is very important to them, many cholos still choose to keep their houses on the altiplano, staying close to their roots in Aymara communities.

On the Day of the Dead in November, chola women visit the graves of friends and relatives in a cemetery above La Paz, bringing food and gifts.

Aymara Dress

The traditional dress of cholas and Aymara women consists of several layers of brightly colored skirts called polleras (poy-YEH-rahs), which are gathered at the waist and very full. They are worn with simple cotton blouses, sweaters, or cardigans, and an aguayo (ah-GWHY-o), or striped shawl, which holds a baby or some produce on the woman's back. The most easily recognizable part of their dress is the bowler hat, thought to have been copied from similar hats worn by British railway workmen who arrived in Bolivia early in the twentieth century. A style of hat worn by Aymara men, a chullo (CHOOL-yo), is also distinctive. It is a brightly patterned knit hat shaped to cover the ears. In town many men prefer felt hats with conventional pants and jackets. A long, natural-colored poncho is essential for the cold nights.

An Aymara couple are married in their finest clothes. The bride wears many layers of skirts and a blue shawl. In front of her is the groom, while the bridesmaid walks behind.

The People of the Yungas

From the snowy heights east of Lake Titicaca, the east-facing slopes of the Andes drop through a wilderness of deep canyons and narrow valleys to Amazonian lowlands over 16,400 feet (5,000 meters) below. These slopes are known as the Yungas. Much of the Yungas is wreathed in clouds from the warm, moist air of the Amazon system rising to meet the chill of the mountains. Until the Spanish Conquest, the slopes were an impenetrable barrier between the peoples of the Amazon and the Andes.

Trade in forest goods, such as feathers and medicinal plants, was established long ago, but the Yungas were never heavily exploited until the Spaniards arrived. The main crop for the Native Americans was coca; its leaves produce the drug cocaine today. Yungas farmers still produce coca, though its use is strictly controlled.

To Bolivia's Native Americans, coca is considered a sacred plant. They chew the mildly narcotic leaves to stave off cold and hunger and use specially selected leaves for magic and divination.

The Kallawaya (kahl-yah-WAY-yah), or Qolawayu, are a small group of Aymara who live in an isolated valley above the Yungas. Their name is derived from *qola* (KO-la), an Aymara word meaning "medicine," and over the centuries they have learned the curative secrets of a host of valuable plants. Their knowledge has been handed down through families for generations. The Kallawaya have created a secret language, *Machaj-Juvai,* to use when healing, so that outsiders never learn their secrets. The men travel widely, carrying pouches crammed with herbal cures. Among the many plants from the humid forest, they collect the *quina*, containing quinine used for easing malaria symptoms. The Kallawaya speak Spanish and the Native American languages of the region, including Puquina.

The arrival of the Spaniards led to some valleys being opened for farming. Later,

when roads were built, the small settlements swelled with people from different regions of the country. The majority of the villages are populated and organized by cholos and cholas who have left the altiplano or La Paz to try their business skills in "pioneer country."

Apart from the population of cholos and cholas of the Yungas, inhabitants include the occasional settler, missionary, and miner from Europe or the United States.

There are few communities of black Bolivians. They are descended from the African slaves who were imported to work in the silver mines of Potosí. The Africans did not acclimatize to the high altitude and were taken to the lower, warmer Yungas,

Bolivian roads from the highlands to the rain forest are usually unpaved and descend steeply. Trucks are often the only form of transportation available for people.

Kallawaya medicine men travel around the country, treating the sick with their special knowledge of the plants of the Andes and the forests.

where they were employed on the sugar and coca estates.

About seventeen thousand black Bolivians live in the country's lowlands; most are in the Yungas, where their communities are quite distinct. They even had their own king until the last died in the 1950s. Today they are farmers, growing coffee, citrus fruits, and bananas. The men use the now-traditional shirt and trousers of the cholo, while the women often wear the bowler hat and pollera of the chola. The folklore of the black Bolivians is famous throughout the country. *Saya* (SAH-yah), a music that combines African drumming and chanting, has crept into many Bolivian festivals, where masks with black faces are worn to symbolize the slaves.

The Quechua of the Spanish Heartland

About 80 miles (130 kilometers) south of La Paz, the descent to the eastern lowlands is far more gradual than the slope to the Yungas. The landscape is dominated by some long, well-irrigated valleys set

The Virgin of Guadalupe

Before leaving Spain for the Americas, many adventurers visited a shrine in the small town of Guadalupe. There they prayed to an image of the Virgin Mary (mother of Jesus Christ) for a safe journey and success. The name of the town and the Virgin were carried to many places in the Spanish colonies, including Sucre in Bolivia. Today pilgrims from all over the country and many parts of the world visit the Virgin of Guadalupe in Sucre Cathedral. Over the years they have left so many small gifts that the total value of the shrine is priceless. The image of the Virgin is adorned with emeralds and gold, an estimated twenty-nine thousand pearls, and about twenty-one thousand diamonds. The local people, who after almost five hundred years of Spanish influence are of largely mixed origin, revere the Virgin as a part of their new religion as well as a figure that symbolizes their ancient love of the Earth Mother.

between mountain ranges. Native Americans settled this territory more than five thousand years ago and developed their own cultures. By the late fifteenth century, the Incas had arrived, taking over their land and insisting that their language, Quechua, should be used. The Incas transferred many Quechua-speaking people to the valleys   sometimes entire village populations from their own heartland in Peru (see PERU). Today, there are more Quechua people here than in any other part of Bolivia.

When the Spaniards arrived, the Quechua occupied three large valleys and the surrounding countryside. In these valleys, towns were founded that are now cities of considerable importance. One of them, Sucre, is the original capital. The people of the area today are a mixture of the Quechua, cholos and cholas, mestizos, and descendants of the Spanish settlers.

Clothing worn by the Quechua, either in a natural color or dyed, is usually handwoven from llama or sheep wool. At one time natural dyes were used, and some of these colors have survived. Today's colors are mostly artificial. Each area and community uses distinctive patterns in its weavings. The dress of the Quechua, most of whom live in isolated valleys, is especially distinctive, with many Spanish elements. Men from Tarabuco, not far from Sucre, wear a close-fitting helmetlike hat made from goatskin, similar to those worn by the Spanish conquerors, while women wear a boat-shaped hat covered with sequins.

Men from the province of Chayanta have strong helmets of cow skin that they use as protection during ritual battles, or *tinkus* (TEEN-koos).

The Macha (MAH-chah) is a Quechua group that lives in valleys 74 miles (120 kilometers) north of Sucre. Most Macha families have small farms in a valley, where they grow barley and corn. They also hold ancient rights to land higher on the mountainside, where they can grow potatoes. Far below, in the warmest parts of the valley, they can find work on other farms, some growing citrus fruits and sugar. Each year the Macha make a trek; using their llamas, they trade all their crops up and down the valley. Some even trek as far as the salt lakes on the altiplano, where they trade their crops for salt.

Quechua men from Tarabuco have very distinctive clothes. Their leather helmets resemble those worn by the Spanish conquerors.

This old house in the Quechua Macha village of Ocurilucho has a fine grass-thatched roof. The Bolivian national flag is painted on its wall.

Peoples of the Oriente

The Oriente, or literally the "eastern region," covers three-fifths of Bolivia, but only about 15 percent of the people live there. It extends from the foothills of the Andes for hundreds of miles to Bolivia's borders with Brazil and Paraguay. In the north of the Oriente are great Amazon rain forests, while the central area includes savannahs and the plains of Moxos. To the south are the dry grasslands and forest known as the Gran Chaco. The greater part of the Oriente is drained by rivers connecting to the Amazon River system.

Before the arrival of the Spaniards, this land was isolated from the Andean world of the mountain people. The tribes of the Oriente hunted wild animals and collected plants, both of which were in abundance. Some tribes settled in one place and grew staple crops such as corn or cassava, a tuber from which a flour is made. These lowland Native Americans were of the same basic language groups, including Arawak and Tupi-Guaraní, as many of the original forest people of Amazonia.

Some groups, like the Moxos, Sirionó, Chimané, and Chiquitano, have survived, living simply in palm-thatch houses with gardens where they grow crops. They still retain some of their traditional customs. At fiesta time, modern dress is put aside, and

69

Colonists from the highlands begin a new life in an area of cleared forest in the lowlands near Santa Cruz. Outside their palm-thatched home, women prepare food and wash dishes.

Moxos dancers wear feathered headdresses, white cloaks, and colored capes.

Although in the past most Native Americans of the Amazon Oriente went unclothed, some, like the Yuracaré (yoo-rah-kah-REH), wore simple clothing of native cotton, or bark cloth, made from a layer just under the bark of certain trees. They used designs cut on wood to stamp patterns on their skin and on bark cloth. Today, less than one hundred Yuracaré remain. They live in the lowland forest of the Chaparé River to the east of Cochabamba and have become almost totally westernized.

In a region that has been invaded by colonists and investors, the greatest problem for these peoples is defending their right to own land. Vast tracts of the tropical forest have been cleared for cultivating crops, cattle ranching, and searching for minerals, depriving the Native Americans of their home.

The Jesuit Missions

Jesuit priests of the Catholic Church followed the Spanish explorers to the Andes and established missions along the way. A typical mission consisted of a church, workshops, and living quarters for the Native Americans.

The Jesuits taught Native people the basic ideas of Christianity and employed them to make goods or grow crops that the Jesuits sold in Buenos Aires, in Argentina, or traded in Europe. Eventually the Jesuits became so rich and powerful that the Spanish monarch expelled them from South America.

Relics of some of the missions remain, especially in the southern part of the Bolivian lowlands, in Paraguay, and in Argentina. Some old mission towns and churches, such as those near Concepción in Bolivia, have been carefully restored.

Spanish settlement of these lowland areas was modest, but even so there was sufficient intermarriage with the Native Americans to produce a mestizo group of people. The mestizos worked mainly as laborers on ranches or moved to towns like Trinidad, the largest in the northern Oriente. Lowland mestizos together with Native Americans are known locally as *cambas* (KAHM-bahs), a name dating from early Spanish times. Cambas retain little of their Native American heritage apart from a few words used with everyday Spanish, such as *yuca*, the name of a sweet cassava root.

A cowboy from the lowlands. His work includes herding cattle on the open plains, branding on the ranch, and driving the cattle to market.

People of Santa Cruz

The largest city in the Oriente and Bolivia's second largest city is Santa Cruz. The spectacular growth of Santa Cruz from a population of 25,000 in 1950 to over 600,000 today has been due to a 1950s government policy to exploit the agricultural potential of the land. People from the altiplano and highland towns were offered incentives to colonize the area. The highlanders who arrived and settled are known as *collas* (KOL-yahs), to distinguish them from their camba neighbors. At first they did not adjust easily to the low altitude, and many suffered from tropical diseases. But over the years they have acclimatized and are now an integral part of lowland life.

As well as Bolivian settlers, the government attracted foreign immigrants, including groups of Okinawans from Japan and some members of a Mennonite religious sect, mainly from the United States and Canada. These peoples farm near Santa Cruz. The Japanese were given land cleared of rain forest and provided with tractors and other farm equipment. Today they are successful farmers, producing rice, soybeans, wheat, sugarcane, and dairy products. Older people tend to stay in their own communities and practice the Shinto religion that they have known from birth. Followers of Shinto worship *kami*, the basic forces, or spirits, of nature, such as mountains, rivers, and trees. Creativity, growth, disease, and healing are determined by these forces. Younger Japanese people have adopted a Bolivian way of life and are usually Roman Catholics.

The Mennonites mostly speak their original German dialect. Their farms are models of efficiency with a simple home and barn. Their traditional clothes—blue dungarees and straw hats for men, floral

A group of Mennonites in Santa Cruz. Members of this religious community are easily recognized by their clothing: floral dresses for the women, dungarees for the men.

dresses and straw hats for women—can be seen on the streets of Santa Cruz.

Oil and gas were discovered under the dry scrub forest of the Oriente between Santa Cruz and Tarija. The principal oil refinery is at Camiri, and a network of pipelines carries the product around Bolivia. Another oil field close to Santa Cruz produces gas, which is now Bolivia's most important source of income.

Native Americans of the Gran Chaco

In the extreme southern corner of the Oriente lies a region of Bolivia that is distinct from the rest of the country. A dusty, scrub-forested plain noted for the country's highest temperatures, it is part of the Gran Chaco, a huge lowland plain that

extends into Argentina and Paraguay.

The Chiriguano (chee-ree-GWAH-no) living here are a mixed group. A Guaraní-speaking tribe of the Gran Chaco migrated into Bolivia during the sixteenth and seventeenth centuries, looking for "a land without evil" promised to them by their leaders. A fierce group, they subjugated other tribes on the way and fought tenaciously against the Spaniards when they arrived; they were never fully defeated by the Europeans. They intermarried with the peaceful Chane group and became the Chiriguano. Today, few Chiriguano traditions remain, and the Chiriguano have blended with other peoples in this rural corner of southeastern Bolivia. They work as cowboys, ranching

A Guaraní Indian fixes the thatch roof of his sun-dried, mud-brick home. He is from the village of Kwarirenda in the Gran Chaco.

and making leather goods. They have retained some of their language and still prepare much of their food from corn.

At the Oruro Carnival the devil dancers wear colorful and elaborate costumes. The masks are made of plaster of Paris, with painted lightbulbs for the eyes.

The Music and Dances of Bolivia

In recent years the music of the Andes has become familiar to worldwide audiences through recordings and live performances of a number of Bolivian and Peruvian music groups. The instruments they play are part of the Native American tradition of the Andean highlands, where the music is still as strong and popular as ever. These instruments include the *zampona* (sahm-POHN-ya), a panpipe made from reed, and three flutes called *quena* (KEH-nah), *pinkullo* (peen-KOOL-yo), and *tarka* (TAHR-kah).

Carnival in Oruro

Of the many fiestas in Bolivia, the most colorful and popular is Carnival in the mining town of Oruro. It features the diablada (dee-ah-BLAH-dah), or "devils' dance," performed in honor of the Virgin of the Socavón, the patroness of miners. In the pageant, Lucifer and his devils are dressed in magnificent costumes and grotesque masks with protruding eyes and horns intertwined with serpents. Lucifer's woman and her companions wear bright red masks, wigs, and dresses, while bears and condors, which are huge Andean vultures, are made of feathers and fur.

Once only miners took part in Carnival, but today hundreds of dancers arrive from all over Bolivia to portray early tribes, the Incas, the blacks, the Kallawaya, the llama herders, and the many different peoples of the highlands and lowlands. Some of the most spectacular costumes, decorated with glass beads and feathers, are worn by morenada (mo-reh-NAH-dah) dancers, who represent black slaves and wealthy slave owners. Brass bands accompany each group of dancers. The procession makes its way through the streets for many hours until it reaches the shrine of the Virgin, where a mass is held in her honor.

73

At a fiesta on the altiplano, a group of Aymara men are playing large flutes. These are carved from wood, unlike panpipes, which are made from local reeds.

More exotic instruments are the *pututu* (poo-TOO-too), a bull's horn with a low, deep, trumpetlike sound, and the *charango* (chah-RAHN-go), which resembles a small guitar and is made from the shell of the armadillo. Indigenous music almost always includes drums; there are also tambourines and occasionally the *ch'ullu ch'ullu* (ch-OOL-yoo ch-OOL-yoo), shells or goat bones tied to each other. While Spanish influence is heard in the sound of the guitars, violins, and accordions, it is the haunting lilt of the panpipes that is most associated with the Native Americans.

Bolivia has many traditional dances with themes from Native American folklore. These dances often relate to the Spaniards' conquest of the area. A prime example is the *huayño* (WHINE-yoh), a Native American dance in origin that was made more sophisticated during Spanish colonial times. Another popular dance, the *cueca* (KWE-kah), is more directly descended from Spanish tradition, though Spanish castanets have been replaced by handkerchiefs held gracefully in the hands of both partners.

Some regions have distinctive music and dance. In Tarija the influence is Spanish. The special dance is the *chapaqueada* (chah-pah-KEH-ah-dah), and the instruments include the *caña* (KAHN-yah), a very long bamboo flute with a horn at the end; the *erke* (AIR-keh), a wind instrument similar to the pututu; the *caja* (KAH-hah), a type of drum; and the *chapaco* (chah-PAH-koe), a three-stringed violin.

Weaving: Part of Andean Life

Weaving is one of the finest expressions of art in Bolivia. Native American families weave their own cloth, a tradition that dates back to pre-Columbian times. All

74

members of the family get involved, using simple looms and spindles that can be worked while walking around. Many of the designs and patterns have particular significance to the family, their community, or the gods. But change is taking place. Where once natural dyes from forest plants were used, now there are synthetic colors; modern machine-made fabric, cheap and easy to buy, is replacing the handwoven textiles. The art of extremely fine weaving is now confined to just a few areas.

The best weavings are from near Calcha in southern Potosí, where ponchos are particularly fine. Dark maroon to wine colors are for daily use, black for mourning, and bright stripes for fiestas.

Some of the most beautiful Quechua weavings are from Potolo and Candelaria, two villages near Sucre. Potolo weavings depict birds like the Andean condor, and those from Candelaria are decorated with designs of tiny horses. Among the Aymara communities, some of the most beautifully woven and dyed textiles come from Sicasica and are made from alpaca wool. The usual background colors are brown or purple, sometimes black or pink. Within the weaving are bands with elaborate designs of many stripes and bird motifs.

Good weavings are prized by the communities. Traditionally they were given to the Inca emperor, and today they decorate statues of the village patron saint. Young women who make fine cloth are sought after as brides, as their skills are highly valued.

Highland peoples in Bolivia traditionally wove shawls and ponchos for their own use. Today they sell weavings, alpaca wool sweaters, and machine-made clothes to tourists.

BRAZIL

BRAZIL IS THE LARGEST NATION IN SOUTH AMERICA. It is the fifth largest country in the world and has the world's sixth largest population.

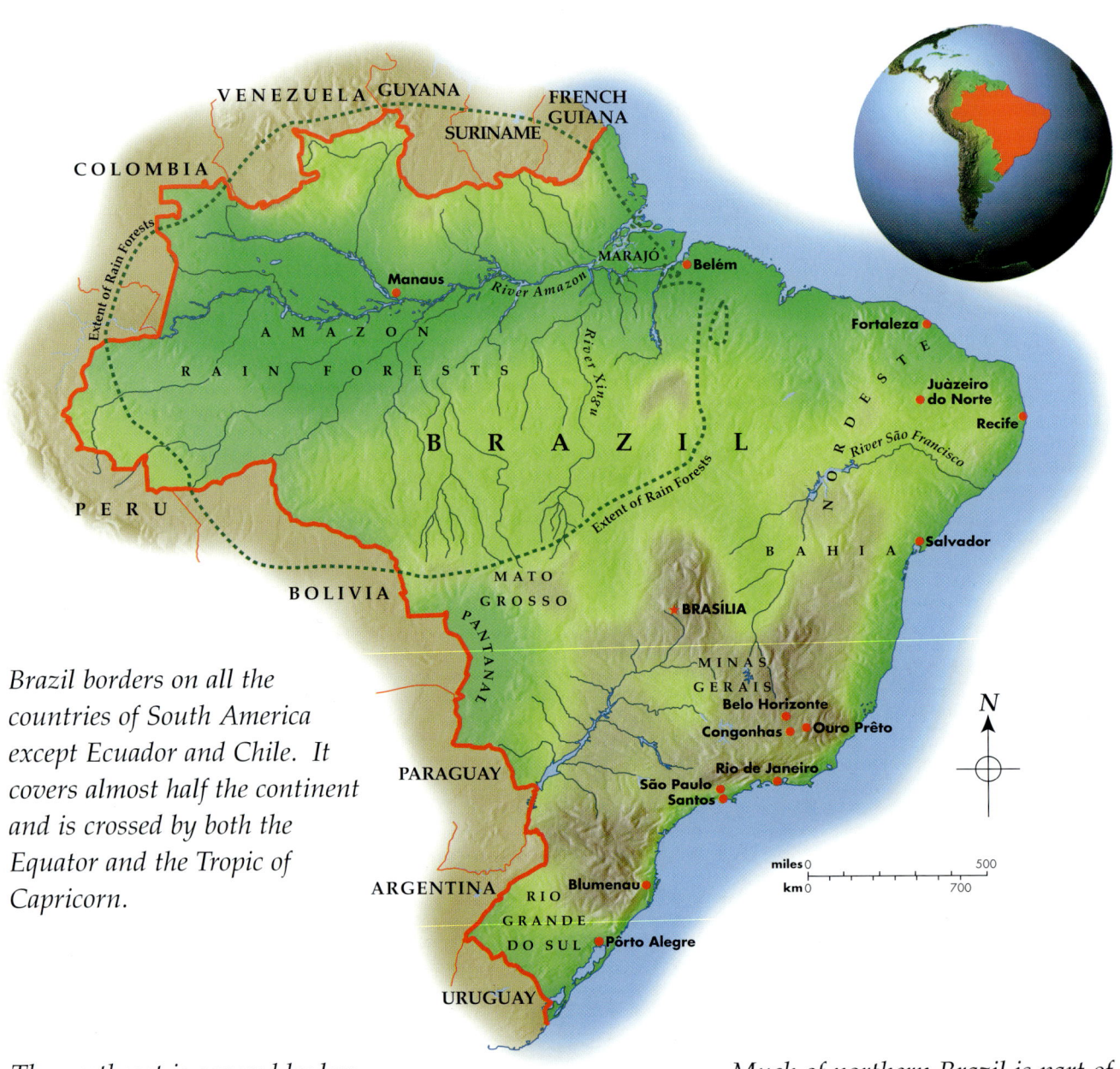

Brazil borders on all the countries of South America except Ecuador and Chile. It covers almost half the continent and is crossed by both the Equator and the Tropic of Capricorn.

The northeast is covered by low, thorny forest. A high plain of dry grasslands and scattered forests extends across the center, while the south is a region of rich, cultivated land.

Much of northern Brazil is part of the Amazon River basin, covered not only by the world's greatest rain forest but also with swampy mangroves, open savannahs, tropical forests, and flood plains.

FACTS AND FIGURES

Official name: *República Federativa do Brasil*

Status: *Independent state*

Capital: *Brasília*

Major cities: *São Paulo, Rio de Janeiro, Belo Horizonte, Salvador, Pôrto Alegre, Recife, Belém, Manaus*

Area: *3,285,630 square miles (8,511,996 square kilometers)*

Population: *160,300,000*

Population density: *49 per square mile (19 per square kilometer)*

Peoples: *53 percent European descent; 34 percent mestizo and mulatto; 11 percent African descent; 2 percent Native American and Asian descent*

Official language: *Portuguese*

Currency: *Real*

National days: *Tiradentes Day (April 21); Labor Day (May 1); Independence Day (September 7); Our Lady of Aparecida (October 12); Proclamation of the Republic (November 15)*

Country's name: *Brazil was named after the brasil, a tropical redwood exported by the first Portuguese settlers.*

Native Americans Encounter the Portuguese

When Europeans first came to the area in 1500, it was inhabited by between two and five million Native Americans. These were descendants of peoples who had arrived in South America between ten thousand and fifteen thousand years ago. The Native peoples were divided into four main language groups. Speakers of Gê and Tupi-Guaraní occupied much of the south and east of Brazil (bruh-ZIL), while the vast Amazon forests were occupied by Carib- and Arawak-speakers. Few of these peoples lived in settled communities, instead surviving by gathering nuts and fruits in the forests, by hunting, and by fishing. As they moved around, they grew cassava and sweet potatoes on patches of ground cleared by burning.

The Portuguese admiral Pedro Alvarez Cabral was the first European to land in Brazil, and Portugal claimed the land. The Portuguese found an abundant hardwood tree from which a red dye could be extracted. The Native peoples called it *brasil* (brah-ZEE-il), and it became the basis of a thriving trade with Europe, where the dye was highly valued.

Young Arara boys from the Xingu Indigenous Park play bamboo flutes. Body painting, using dyes made from plants, is traditional among the peoples of the Amazon rain forest.

Timeline:	First peoples arrive	Portuguese admiral Pedro Alvarez Cabral lands in Brazil	First building on site of Rio de Janeiro erected	Portuguese divide Brazil into fifteen *captaincies*, or regions
	13,000–8,000 B.C.E.	1500 C.E.	1503	1533

CLIMATE

The northeast suffers long periods of drought; the country's hottest temperatures have been recorded here. The central region is tropically hot and wet, though it is cooler in high-altitude areas. The south has a varied climate and often has snow and frost in midwinter and high temperatures in summer. The rainy season in the south is from December to March. The area of the greatest rainfall is in the Amazon basin, where it is hot and humid year-round.

	Manaus	Rio de Janeiro	Brasília	Pôrto Alegre
Average January temperature	79°F (26°C)	83°F (28°C)	72°F (22°C)	75°F (24°C)
Average July temperature	81°F (27°C)	67°F (19°C)	68°F (20°C)	62°F (17°C)
Average annual precipitation	87 in (221 cm)	67 in (170 cm)	63 in (160 cm)	67 in (170 cm)

Settlers arrived from Portugal during the sixteenth century, soon creating successful sugar plantations in the northeast and capturing Native Americans to use as slaves. Many tribes resisted and were virtually wiped out. When thousands died from ill-treatment and European diseases, the settlers imported black African slaves to do the work.

The Portuguese also settled on the coast in the south in the mid-sixteenth century and began exploring the interior of the country to capture more Native Americans as slaves. During the 1600s tough men called *bandeirantes* (buhn-deh-RUHN-tes) opened up trails into the center of Brazil, searching for gold and diamonds. When gold was found in Minas Gerais, many more Portuguese followed to make their fortune. The south now became economically more important than the north, and Rio de Janeiro became the country's capital in 1763. The Portuguese king saw this economic success as a chance to impose heavy taxes and duties, which were greatly resented by the colonists. Calls for independence grew.

Salvador was built by Portuguese settlers and was the first capital of Brazil. Some fine old colonial buildings remain today.

Salvador de Bahia becomes first capital	French seize harbor of Rio de Janeiro but are later forced to surrender by the Portuguese	City of Rio de Janeiro founded	Colony divided into two, north and south, with capitals in Salvador and Rio de Janeiro	Dutch occupy part of northeast coast
1549	**1555**	**1567**	**1572**	**1624–1654**

This woman in Bahia is a descendant of the African slaves who were brought to work in this area. Up to four million slaves came to Brazil between the 1630s and the 1880s.

In 1807 the Portuguese prince regent, exiled from Portugal as a result of Napoleon's invasion, introduced favorable reforms to the colonists and modernized Brazil. The following ruler, his son Dom Pedro, continued to stand up for the colonists' rights. Brazil became independent in 1822, led by Dom Pedro, who was proclaimed emperor.

Dom Pedro I was succeeded by his son, Dom Pedro II, who ruled Brazil wisely for almost fifty years. He developed trade, built the first railroad, encouraged education for all, and invited immigrants from Europe to settle in Brazil. He wanted to abolish slavery but met fierce opposition from wealthy landowners. When slavery was finally abolished in 1888, many rich planters were ruined, and they conspired for the emperor's downfall. They were successful; the following year Dom Pedro II was overthrown, and Brazil became a republic.

With the onset of independence, a trickle of immigrants began to settle in Brazil. The majority, over four million, arrived between 1887 and 1934. These included Italians, Germans, Spaniards, Japanese, people from central and eastern Europe, some Syrians and Lebanese, and people from other parts of Latin America.

Attempts to Modernize

Around the turn of the twentieth century, the worldwide demand for rubber from the Amazon forests created immense wealth for a few people and some towns along the river. But it further devastated the Native American peoples in the region, who worked like slaves collecting the latex sap.

Gold found in Minas Gerais	Jesuits expelled from country	Rio de Janeiro becomes capital	Brazil declares independence with Dom Pedro I as emperor	War with Argentina leads to loss of area now known as Uruguay
1695	1759	1763	1822	1825–1828

The Amazon rubber boom began toward the end of the nineteenth century and collapsed around 1912. Some rubber tappers still collect latex from wild rubber trees.

Nor was much being done for the general mass of the Brazilian population, who had to wait until the 1930s before President Getúlio Vargas, known as "The Father of the Poor," began to improve basic social and educational conditions. The military deposed him in 1945 when he threatened to become a dictator.

Juscelino Kubitschek, elected president in 1956, was responsible for building the new capital, Brasília, in the interior of the country. He was also determined to modernize the country. Within five years

huge dams were built, highways were constructed to improve the transportation system, and the iron, steel, petroleum, and coal industries were expanded. However, by the end of his term, the country was running out of funds.

In 1964 the military seized power. They borrowed huge sums of money from international banks to spend on projects designed to make Brazil an industrial nation, leaving the country with enormous debts. Later governments tried to reduce these debts by opening up the Amazon for cultivation and cattle ranching and encouraging settlers to move there. But the large-scale destruction of the forests led to

Slavery abolished	Dom Pedro II is deposed, and Brazil becomes a republic	Getúlio Vargas becomes president	Juscelino Kubitschek becomes president	Brasília inaugurated as new capital
1888	**1889**	**1930**	**1956**	**1960**

the loss of numbers of plant and animal species and to forest tribes dying out. Many countries condemned Brazil's actions. In 1992 countries from all around the world took part in an Earth Summit in Rio de Janeiro to discuss and promote environmental issues and development. Brazil recognized its special responsibility for its rain forests and has since taken steps to reduce forest destruction. However, in 1997, Amazon landowners continued to set fires on huge tracts of rain forest land, trying to clear it for agriculture and cattle grazing.

When a civilian government was returned to office in 1985, Brazil had built up enormous debts. Fernando Henrique Cardoso was elected president in 1994. His main goals were to restore the economy and bring about social reform. Brazil has vast mineral resources with great economic

potential, but it also has one of the largest populations in the world and many still live in considerable poverty.

A Multicultural Society

Just over half of Brazil's population is white and is descended from European immigrants. About a third of the people are of mixed race. They include mestizos of European and Native American parentage and mulattos of European and African marriages. The remainder are blacks, immigrants from Asia, and the surviving 300,000 Native Americans. The majority of blacks and mulattos live along

These young men are playing volleyball on Ipanema Beach in Rio de Janeiro. Other beach facilities include soccer fields and parallel bars for fitness enthusiasts.

Beach Life

Some magnificent beaches cover Brazil's 4,569-mile (7,353-kilometer) coastline. A few remain empty, just miles and miles of beautiful white sand beaches backed by coconut palms. But on a good day in Rio de Janeiro, Copacabana Beach is packed with people. Some just relax in the sun, while others work out energetically, playing soccer, volleyball, and various ball games. They arrive at dawn and leave at dusk—a scene repeated near towns all along the coast.

Xingu Indigenous Park, a reserve for Native peoples near Xingu River, created	Military seizes power	Democratic government restored	Earth Summit in Rio de Janeiro	Fernando Henrique Cardoso becomes president
1961	1964	1985	1992	1994

Slum districts, or favelas, *surround most of Brazil's large cities. Here, in a slum in Bauru in the state of São Paulo, women wash clothes at the only public faucet.*

Paulo and the south, these languages include Japanese, Arabic, and several European languages, including German, Italian, and Polish.

The distribution of Brazil's population is uneven; 75 percent of all Brazilians live in cities and towns, most of them on or near the coast. Recently, great numbers of people have moved from rural areas to towns and cities, searching for employment and better health and education facilities. Many end up living in squalid conditions in slums, or *favelas* (fuh-VEL-uhs). The problem is made worse by an increase in the population. This has resulted in an acute housing shortage, causing many more people to live in slum conditions.

Outside the towns, homes are generally built with materials that are available locally. In the south wood is widely used, and in the northeast mud-brick houses with tiled roofs are typical. In the Amazon forests the Native Americans live in wood and palm-thatch homes. These are often built on stilts for protection against flooding along riverbanks.

About a quarter of all Brazilian workers are employed in some kind of agriculture, from wine production and coffee growing to collecting nuts and palm oils. Industry also accounts for about a quarter of workers. Many Brazilians are employed in factories, producing everything from canned orange juice to cars. However, the majority of workers are involved in service industries, such as banks, or in the government or army.

A wide gap has grown between the wealthy and poor in Brazil. Many of the latter survive in rural areas by growing

the coast, while most of the German, Italian, and central and eastern European immigrants are settled in Brazil's three most southern states.

The indigenous peoples are divided into about two hundred groups, speaking some 170 languages. Most live in the Amazon region and the Mato Grosso in south-central Brazil. Some groups are seminomadic and live in forests, growing some crops, hunting, fishing, and gathering nuts. Other groups live in parks and reserves that the government has set aside for them since the 1960s to protect them from settlers and developers. Unfortunately, large-scale development in Amazonia threatens these reserves, and Native Americans must often protest in an attempt to keep their lands.

Portuguese is the official language of Brazil, but such a diversity of peoples means that many other languages are also spoken. Some Native Americans speak only their own languages, although an increasing number speak Portuguese. Among themselves, immigrant groups often talk in their native languages. In São

crops to feed their families and raising a few animals. In towns poor people may trade on the street or take low-paying jobs. Family life is very important, but often poor families are very large. Some children in the cities leave home to work and live on the streets. Because of the poverty, there is a great deal of crime and theft.

Brazil has a large number of national and provincial newspapers and extensive television coverage. The biggest TV station can boast the largest TV audience in the world, and even the most remote parts of the country receive programs. The most popular programs are *novelas* (noh-VEL-as), or romantic soaps, of which there are two or three every evening. People also enjoy films imported from the United States.

All Souls' Day, or the Day of the Dead, is celebrated in most parts of Latin America. In a cemetery in Juàzeiro do Norte in northeastern Brazil, people light small fires beside the graves.

Catholicism and Candomblé

Roman Catholicism has been Brazil's main religion since the Portuguese settled. Many Brazilians celebrate saints' days and important dates in the Christian calendar and walk many miles on pilgrimages. They look to their faith for miraculous cures for illness and other problems, and churches and shrines are adorned with offerings, thank-you cards, and trinkets. Catholicism is being challenged by evangelical churches, which are claiming many new converts, particularly in São Paulo.

Perhaps a fifth of Brazilians belong to African spiritual religions. These developed from the religions and gods brought by slaves from Africa and are mixed with Native American as well as Christian ideas. The main religions are *Candomblé* (kuh-dome-BLEH), which is centered in Bahia

In Brazil's arid Northeast it is difficult to grow many crops, so many men work as cowboys, or vaqueiros. They spend long hours in the hot, dry scrubland, looking after cattle.

and most reflects its western African roots, and *Macumba* (muh-COOM-buh), a more recent development centered in Rio de Janeiro, which brings together beliefs from western and southern Africa with European spiritualism.

Nordeste: Land of Drought and Poverty

Nine states make up the region known to Brazilians as the *Nordeste* (nor-DES-tay), meaning "Northeast." The most southerly is Bahia; the northernmost is Maranhão. Low, thorny forest covers the interior, called the *sertão* (sehr-TAO). This region suffers from long periods of drought.

Before the development of road and air routes, the Northeast was isolated from the rest of Brazil. The simplest connection was

---

Padre Cícero

For millions of people in the Nordeste, one man stands out as a spiritual leader.

Padre (Father) Cícero from Fortaleza settled on a small farm in a well-irrigated valley in Juàzeiro do Norte. During the great drought of 1877 to 1879, he organized local people to dig wells and plant crops to feed the thousands who flocked to the farm. The refugees believed he had been sent to them by God, and he became known as a miracle worker throughout the region. Later he organized a rebellion against the authorities and defended Juàzeiro do Norte against government forces. Padre Cícero died in 1934, but his name is still revered. Every year millions of pilgrims visit his shrine in Juàzeiro do Norte.

by sea, or alternatively, by paddle steamer along the São Francisco River, which flows north to south through much of the region.

The present population of the Northeast is small and varied. Living along part of the coast are descendants of black African slaves. Elsewhere there are mestizos from mixed Portuguese and Native American marriages. Descendants of the seventeenth-century Dutch, who occupied land near Fortaleza, still live in the Northeast. A few groups of Native Americans have survived in reserves; the most numerous are the Pankararu and the Fuini tribes, each with about three thousand members.

When drought occurs in the Northeast, crops fail and people have to move. Sometimes entire villages are abandoned by inhabitants looking for work and food. Thousands of cattle die in the thorny scrub, and the leather-clad *vaqueiros* (vah-KAY-rose), or cowboys, move on. The poverty caused by these extreme conditions has

tested many governments, and the region has been the scene of many rebellions.

Along the coast of the Northeast, fishermen use a sailing raft they call a *jangada* (juhn-GAH-duh). The men themselves are called *jangadeiros* (juhn-gah-DAY-rose). The rafts are modeled from a design used by Native Americans when the Portuguese first arrived. The original jangadas were log rafts; the sail is a recent addition. Now the construction is changing as jangadeiros increasingly replace wooden logs with plastic tubes. Many raft owners use advertising on their sails to help pay for their materials. The jangadeiros work long hours and sometimes spend days at sea in primitive conditions. Fishing is not very profitable; although it provides meals for the jangadeiros' families, they are poor by comparison to many Brazilians.

The traditional fishing boats of the Northeast of Brazil are called jangadas. *It takes many helpers and a lot of effort to pull a jangada with a full sail out of the water.*

Women of Bahia in traditional white dresses take part in a ceremony to honor Yemanjá, the goddess of the sea. African spiritual beliefs came to Brazil with African slaves.

The Blacks of Bahia

The state of Bahia is approximately 930 miles (1,500 kilometers) north of Rio de Janeiro. In the sixteenth century Portuguese settlers established sugarcane plantations there, and from 1630 on, Africans were brought as slaves to work on the plantations. By the time slavery was abolished in the 1880s, between three and four million Africans had been brought to Brazil.

Although the slaves came from many parts of Africa with different languages and customs, they worked together for freedom. Many revolts and rebellions arose, and groups of runaway slaves, called *quilombos* (kee-LUM-bose), set up "free" territories to which other slaves could escape. The slave trade has left a strong black presence along the coastal lands of not only Bahia, but as far as Rio de Janeiro in the south and Maranhão in the north.

Salvador is the capital of Bahia and Brazil's fourth largest city. Because there is so much evidence of African culture and way of life, it has been called "Africa in Exile." Food sold on Salvador's streets is similar to that from western Africa, music is dominated by African rhythms, and an Afro-Brazilian religion called Candomblé is practiced in over one thousand temples throughout the city.

Candomblé originated in the northeast of Brazil among the Yoruba peoples brought as slaves from the Guinea coast of Africa. Forbidden to practice their own religion, the Yoruba solved the problem by associating their gods, the *orixas* (oh-ree-SHAS), with Christianity. So the chief god of the Yoruba religion, Olurun, was identified with God the Father, while Oxalá, the most important of the gods, through whom Olurun communicated with humankind, was represented as Jesus Christ. Yemanjá, mother of the orixas, was seen as the Virgin Mary, while Ogun, the god of war, was identified with Saint George.

Followers of the Afro-Brazilian religions believe that mediums act as contacts with spirits in another world. Encouraged by chanting, singing, and the thunderous pounding of *atabaques* (uh-tah-BAH-kes), or tall drums, the congregation persuades a spirit to enter the body of a medium, who enters a trance and adopts the character of the spirit. Followers can then consult the spirit and seek solutions to their problems.

For the black Brazilian, everyday dress is simply a T-shirt and pants for men, a

Coconut and Shrimp

Typical food of coastal Bahia has its origins in Africa. Women of Bahia, or baianas *(buh-ee-YAHN-us), cook with oil from the* dendé *(den-DAY) palm, coconut milk, coconut, and sugarcane syrup, as well as cashew nuts, corn, and cassava flour. Many of the dishes prepared by the baianas have religious connections as well as being a meal. Certain dishes are made for individual ancient gods and are left as gifts for them at their shrines on a feast day.* Caruru *(kuh-ru-RU), which is made with dried shrimp, peanuts, and ginger, is offered to Xangô, the god of thunder.* Acarajé *(uh-cur-ruh-JAY), containing garlic, dried shrimp, and dendé oil, is sold by street vendors in Salvador and given as an offering to Iansa, goddess of the tempest.*

A woman sells snacks on the roadside in Salvador. The African-style food includes acarajé in the foreground and shrimp, meat, and corn in the bowls.

Yemanjá, Goddess of the Sea

Every New Year's Eve hundreds of followers of the Afro-Brazilian religions flock to Copacabana Beach to celebrate the Festival of Yemanjá, goddess of the sea. As the sun sets, women and men dressed in pale clothes, the women with full-skirted dresses, gather around bonfires and sand altars lit with many candles to sing and dance to the beat of drums. The climax comes at midnight when they rush to the water's edge to throw gifts of flowers, mirrors, combs, and jewelry into the sea in honor of the goddess, hoping that she will bless them with a good year to come. If the gifts are returned to the water's edge, the people know they have been rejected, but if the gifts float out to sea, all will be well.

simple dress or blouse and skirt for women. On certain occasions, baianas, the women of Bahia, wear a voluminous white dress and white head scarf. This impeccably clean clothing is traditionally used by the women who wash the steps of Bomfim Church in Salvador and by those who take part in other religious ceremonies. This type of dress is featured in Carnival, where the processions are headed by women dancers.

The Cariocas of Rio de Janeiro

Along the coast south of Bahia lies the city of Rio de Janeiro. Its setting, between high, eroded rocks surrounding Guanabara Bay, is a natural wonder. The urban growth along the coast since the 1950s has been spectacular, and now the suburbs extend 25 miles (40 kilometers) to the south. Rio's

Followers of the Macumba religion in Rio de Janeiro enter the sea to offer gifts to Yemanjá. Afro-Brazilian religions are becoming popular among a wide range of Brazilians.

Children take part in Rio's Carnival. Most samba schools have a children's section. These children are dressed in jaguar costumes that reflect an Amazon theme.

port is one of the world's biggest, handling exports and cruise ships that bring tourists from around the world.

Rio has many poor areas, including some of simple housing on the surrounding hillsides. Other poorer suburbs have grown on the routes leading into the city.

The people of Rio are called *Cariocas* (kah-ree-OH-kus). Carioca is the name of a river that flows through part of the city. The population is approximately 11 percent black African. Many more people are mestizos and mulattos of mixed marriages. Religion, though nominally Catholic, has African elements, especially in parts of the city where there are concentrations of black Brazilians.

Cariocas are known for their sense of fun and humor and their passion for soccer, and Rio itself is famed worldwide for its

spectacular Carnival procession held in February or March each year. The main parade involves thousands of dancers and an audience of almost 200,000 in the Carnival stadium, or *Passarela do Samba* (puh-suh-RELL-uh doe SUM-bah). People of all backgrounds, from television stars to children from the slums, take part and, for an hour or two, leave their daily cares behind. To create the spectacle, thousands of people work for a year making colorful floats and costumes. The parade is not simply a spectacle but is also a competition between the various samba schools, or clubs, from different parts of the city. Samba is a dance of African origins. It has a syncopated rhythm and is accompanied by drums.

Rio boasts the world's largest soccer stadium, the Maracanã, which holds 170,000 spectators. The Maracanã draws out the special enthusiasm and good-natured humor of the Brazilian crowd. Throughout the match, spectators wave huge banners in the national colors and chant samba rhythms.

The Miners of Minas Gerais

Brazil's third largest city, Belo Horizonte, or "Beautiful Horizon," is 267 miles (430 kilometers) inland and to the north of Rio de Janeiro. It is one of the fastest growing cities in Brazil and has a population of over 2.5 million. The people of Belo Horizonte work in manufacturing industries, in steelworks, and in the automobile industry.

Belo Horizonte is the capital of Minas Gerais State, whose people are known as the *mineiros,* meaning "miners." The name *mineiro* comes from the past, when this region of the country was a rugged land noted for its mineral wealth. As minerals were discovered, mines and towns were established. The Native Americans living there were either killed or forced to move.

One of the most famous towns is Ouro Prêto, a town of cobblestone streets set on a steep hillside. With its wealth of seventeenth-century churches and other buildings, Ouro Prêto has been declared a site important to Brazil's national heritage.

The prosperity of Minas Gerais today lies in its agriculture, animal farming, mining, and steel production industries. The state produces over half of the country's iron ore. Outside the main towns, people work on coffee plantations and large cattle ranches. Minas Gerais and the neighboring states of Rio de Janeiro,

Antônio Francisco Lisboa

Antônio Francisco Lisboa (1738?–1814) is considered one of Brazil's most famous artists. He was the son of a Portuguese architect and a black African slave. Born deformed, he became known as O Aleijadinho, *meaning "the little cripple." Although disabled, he carved some of Brazil's finest sculptures on his side and on his back. He worked ceaselessly until the end of his life, at which point he was blind and worked with tools strapped to his wrists. He designed, built, and decorated Bom Jesus de Matozinhos, a sanctuary in the old mining town of Congonhas, and the Church of São Francisco in Ouro Prêto. His sculptures still abound in Ouro Prêto, a town his father helped build.*

This statue of Isaiah by O Aleijadinho is one of a set of twelve prophets he carved. They stand on a wall surrounding a church in the colonial town of Congonhas.

São Paulo, and Espiríto Santo make up the richest part of Brazil, producing roughly 70 percent of the nation's wealth.

The Paulistas

With over eleven million inhabitants, São Paulo is Brazil's largest city. It is also the capital of São Paulo State, which is noted for its rich agriculture and industry. The city is built at an altitude of about 2,624 feet (800 meters) at the edge of a steep slope that overlooks the Atlantic. At the beginning of the nineteenth century, immigrants began to arrive from Europe, Lebanon, and Syria. In the years between 1887 and 1898, over half a million Italians emigrated to São Paulo State.

The rapid growth of the city began in the 1950s. By the 1960s, the population was over three million, and the city was the fastest growing in South America.

The *paulistas* (pow-LIS-tas), as the people of the state are known, seem quite different from their neighbors. Their commercial drive is recognized throughout the country. A typical paulista may work at several jobs and attend evening classes as well. On a normal working day, São Paulo is like any large city in North America, with crowds of shoppers and dark-suited executives filling the streets. Traffic is dense, and pollution is a very real problem.

Much of the nineteenth-century prosperity of São Paulo and nearby land was based on coffee production. For many years Brazil was known as a "coffee economy," and millions of sacks of dried beans were exported through the port of Santos, 43 miles (69 kilometers) from São Paulo. Santos is now the country's largest port. The coffee plantations are vast, and many people are still involved in the production process. Others work on farms that produce oranges, rice, cotton, and

The countryside in central and southern Brazil resembles that in parts of Europe. Many European immigrants settled here and became farmers and cattle ranchers.

The Japanese of São Paulo

Early in the twentieth century, immigrants arrived from Japan. Many came from rural regions and settled in the country areas around São Paulo. São Paulo State is dotted with Japanese farms, and many Japanese industries and banks are based in its capital. Later, more Japanese settlers inhabited other parts of Brazil, especially the state of Para, close to the Amazon, where they grow jute and pepper.

Liberdade, the Japanese area of São Paulo, is close to the original center of the city and is filled with Japanese restaurants, shops, and services. The Japanese language is visible in local newspapers and on all the shop signs. Liberdade is the largest Japanese community outside of Japan.

The heart of Liberdade, São Paulo's Japanese district, is always busy with shoppers and office workers. Japanese newspapers are sold here, and restaurants serve Japanese food.

soybeans. Cowboys work long hours on large cattle ranches.

The Immigrant South

The states of Rio Grande do Sul, Santa Catarina, and Paraná make up the southernmost part of Brazil and are the most European. Immigration began in the eighteenth century with the arrival of people from the Azores, Portuguese islands in the Atlantic. They settled around Pôrto Alegre on the coast. Later, immigrants came from Germany, Italy, and the Slavic countries. Many settled in the south in the last century. Some cities, such as Blumenau in Santa Catarina, look a lot like towns in southern Germany.

These southern states attracted immigrants because much of the land resembled parts of Europe, and the climate is varied, unlike the rest of tropical Brazil. In the south snow and frost are not uncommon in midwinter, while rainfall and temperatures can be high in the summer.

Most of the settlers became farmers. The Germans worked small farms and concentrated on rye, corn, and pigs. Other settlers developed large estates and took on tenant workers to grow rice. The Italians came with a knowledge of the wine industry; today, about three-quarters of all Brazilian wine comes from the state of Rio Grande do Sul.

Much of the southern part of Rio Grande do Sul is flat, open grassland, or pampas, extending to Brazil's borders with Uruguay and Argentina. More than thirteen million cattle graze these grasslands, and the people of Rio Grande do Sul call themselves *gaúchos* (gah-OO-shose), a South American word for cowhands or cattle herders used largely in neighboring Argentina (see ARGENTINA).

The cowhands have a special place in Brazilian folklore. The original gaúcho was usually a mestizo of Portuguese and Native American descent accustomed to the wild pampas. Cattle roamed free over huge areas, and the gaúchos' work consisted of herding, branding, and watching over the cattle. They led a seminomadic life,

feeding off the land and sleeping outdoors or in rural homesteads. They wore, and some still do, *bombachas* (bohm-BAH-shahs), or baggy pants; flat, wide-brimmed black hats; and ponchos. Even today, a gaúcho is never without his *mate* (MAH-tay), a form of herbal tea, which he traditionally sips through a silver tube from a gourd or a glass.

A few thousand Native Americans live in the southern states. Gradually they are being drawn into Brazilian society and Western ways. Members of the Kaingang tribes arrived from the Mato Grosso region in the 1920s and now number about seven thousand in all three states. The Xokléng, a Kaingang group of about seven hundred, have kept their own language. Recently, they have joined evangelical churches.

A businessman in Caxias do Sul in southern Brazil passes a mural that depicts a religious procession honoring a patron saint.

Brasília: Vision and Impact

A vast, high plain extends across central Brazil. Brazilians call this the *planalto* (pluhn-OWL-tow), or upland. It is covered largely by *campos cerrado* (KUHM-poos say-HAH-doe), a local name for dry grasslands with scattered, stunted trees.

The interior of Brazil was an empty place as recently as the 1950s, with towns connected only by poor, simple roads. One man, Juscelino Kubitschek, had the vision to change the face of Brazil. When he

The interior of Brasília's Metropolitan Cathedral, designed by Oscar Niemeyer, is shaped like a crown of thorns. The aluminum angels were sculpted by Alfredo Scesciatte.

became president in 1956, Kubitschek proposed moving the country ahead "fifty years in five." His vision included a new capital in the empty interior, a hub of roads, air services, and government. The site for this capital, Brasília, was put in the center of the highlands in Goiás State, halfway between the Atlantic and Brazil's western border.

Brasília has brought a new energy to the area and so have connections with Amazonia to the north. Roads now cross the region, linking many places that were once isolated. Huge farms yield a variety of agricultural produce, from corn to soybeans. The ranches of the region have many millions of cattle, and mines yield a variety of useful minerals. The one-time backwoodsy country has become part of a thriving national economy.

Change Brings Problems for Native Inhabitants

The changes of the past fifty years have placed enormous pressure on Native Americans. The Xingu Indigenous Park was created in 1961 to protect the Native Americans from interference from settlers and developers. A flat region in the north of Mato Grosso at the southern edge of the Amazon forests, it is crossed by the Xingu River and its tributaries. The forests are rich in wildlife, and the rivers teem with fish.

About twenty-seven hundred people from fifteen tribes live in the park today. The most numerous are the Kayabi (kie-yah-BEE), with about eight hundred people. They came originally from other rivers to the west, escaping from rubber collectors in the 1950s and 1960s. Another tribe living inside the forest are the Suyá (soo-YAH), with about 140 people dwelling in seven houses. They maintain a semitraditional way of life, growing crops of cassava from which they make cassava bread, or *beijo* (BAY-zhoe), and sweet potatoes.

Conflict still exists between the tribes and settlers who try to take their land. The Kayapo, who have always lived in the Xingu, have worked hard to publicize their problem internationally, even traveling to the United States and Europe. Within Brazil in 1989, they protested against the construction of dams that would threaten their territory in the Amazon. They succeeded in getting most of these projects postponed or cancelled.

Elsewhere in the central states, some tribes survive but in greatly reduced numbers. The Nambiquara live in the western Mato Grosso, where they have settled near an Indian post established to look after their affairs. Traditionally, they

Kayapo men of the Xingu region perform a ritual dance after killing a jaguar, a large, spotted forest cat. Its skin hangs to the right of this picture.

lived like nomads, looking for wild fruits and small animals. Diseases caught from contact with settlers reduced the population from an estimated twenty thousand in the early twentieth century to seven hundred today. The Karaja (kuh-rah-JAH), numbering about twelve hundred, live along rivers in the north of Mato Grosso and Goiás. They keep canoes hollowed from logs for fishing.

The Xavante (shah-VAHN-tay), estimated at about six thousand, is the most numerous tribal group in eastern Mato Grosso. Today they are settled farmers and live on the open grasslands. Most dress like Brazilians, in shorts and T-shirts. Some of their folklore, especially music, has survived. Another large group, the Guaraní, lives in southern Mato Grosso. Their language, Tupi-Guaraní, is of one of the most common of the ancient language groups in South America. Most of the Guaraní now live a

Roani, chief of the Kayapo, has painted his face with red dye. His headdress is made from reed and bird feathers. The custom of enlarging the lower lip is now dying out.

The Pantanal is a vast area of seasonally swampy land in the west of Mato Grosso and Mato Grosso do Sul. Much of the area is used for ranching, but part has been set aside as a national park. The Pantanal swamps have long been a wilderness, but the land around the swamps has attracted settlers. They arrived first in the 1930s, when the government promoted a "march to the West" program to open up the region. Then, in the 1950s, colonies were established near the rivers leading north to the Amazon.

Colonel Rondon

Cândido Mariano da Silva Rondon was of almost pure Native American ancestry. Brought up on a cattle station near Cuiabá, the capital of Mato Grosso, he spent more than twenty-four years exploring the highlands of the planalto. He organized the laying of 3,100 miles (5,000 kilometers) of telegraph wire to connect isolated outposts of the interior.

He also saw the plight of the Native Americans firsthand and determined to fight for their rights. In 1910 he helped establish the Indian Protection Service. Its aim was to give Native Americans their own land until they could be assimilated into Brazilian society. Not knowing how he would be received, Rondon put himself in considerable danger making friendly contact with Native Americans. His slogan was "Die if necessary, but do not kill." In recognition of his work, the state of Rondônia was named after him.

settled life around special government-run stations, but at one time they had large villages of up to sixty families.

Beyond Goiás to the Mato Grossos

West of Brasília and Goiás are the states of Mato Grosso and Mato Grosso do Sul. Portuguese interest here began in the sixteenth century with the search for gold, but for three hundred years much of the country remained a wilderness occupied only by hardy ranchers and numerous groups of Native Americans.

People of the Amazon River

When the Portuguese arrived in 1500, contact was made with forest tribes, but the first real exploration of the Amazon occurred during the nineteenth century. Toward the end of that century, the Amazon experienced an amazing economic boom. The reason for the boom was rubber. Latex for waterproofing clothes and making tires was in great demand. The boom lasted less than fifty years, but it transformed life on the Amazon. The forests were scoured for rubber trees and men able to tap them. Mestizos and immigrants from the Northeast became laborers, while Native Americans and black Africans were treated as slaves. By the end of the boom in 1912, the Native population of Amazonia was severely reduced. Many

Shoppers wander around the Ver-o-peso fish, fruit, and vegetable market in Belém, a busy port at the mouth of the Amazon River.

survivors retreated to the forest depths to avoid diseases and ill-treatment.

The rubber boom made immense fortunes for a few rubber barons and brought great wealth to the cities of the Amazon. In Belém, the port on the Amazon mouth, and Manaus, 990 miles (1,600 kilometers) upstream, huge mansions and fine public monuments appeared, electricity and telephones were installed, and luxuries of all kinds were imported from Europe and the United States. When the rubber boom collapsed, so did the cities, and many people went bankrupt.

In the 1960s Manaus had a population of 150,000, but it has grown to 1.25 million and has become the most important city in the region as a result of a government plan in the 1970s to open up Amazonia. Part of its newfound prosperity is derived from a duty-free zone, where many goods, especially electronic items, are manufactured for export. Modern,

air-conditioned factories provide employment for thousands of people.

The people of Manaus and other Amazon cities are mainly mestizos, some from families of Europeans, Lebanese, and Syrians who set up businesses during the rubber era. Other Amazon dwellers are *caboclos* (kuh-BOE-kloos), descended from marriages of forest tribes with Portuguese and other settlers. They gather nuts, tap rubber, or make their living as fishers.

Some of the most striking early remains of the original peoples have been discovered on the huge island of Marajó at the mouth of the Amazon. The land is flat and almost at sea level. The first people of Marajó lived above the water by building earth mounds. On one site, archaeologists found that the people had large circular

Caboclos are people of mixed descent who have lived and worked in the Amazon rain forest for several generations. A typical caboclo house appears in the background.

houses and made pottery. These remains date from about 1000 B.C.E., when it is believed that the people were growing sweet potatoes and cassava. No Native Americans have survived on Marajó Island, and the population today is largely mestizo. Cattle are kept in places where there is open grassland, and many people use horses for transportation. Water buffalo, introduced from Asia, are used for their milk and for pulling carts.

Riches of the Amazon Forest

As the world enters the twenty-first century, the Amazon forests are still home to small numbers of Native Americans. The size of the wilderness is so immense that a few groups of these people have never had lasting contact with the civilization outside and are known only from traces they leave in the forest or from the occasional unexpected meeting.

All the surviving forest people have one common bond—generations of experience surviving in an environment that most outsiders consider hostile. The forest is their home and provides everything they need. The full list of forest products covers such items as food from both animals and plants, medicines, dyes, glues, ceremonial dress, bags, baskets, bows, arrows, poisons, fish hooks and lines, housing materials, and more. The few remaining Native Americans are totally self-reliant in their environment. Theirs is a unique partnership in which they live in harmony with the ecosystem.

Typical Native American communities have large communal houses in which each family slings its hammocks. They clear patches of ground near the houses by slashing

A caboclo boy practices fishing with a harpoon. Local people also use spears and nets. More than two thousand species of fish breed in the flooded Amazon forests.

and burning the trees. Here they grow cassava, the staple diet of most tribes. Cassava is a poisonous tuber, but it can be made edible by soaking it in water, grating it, and squeezing it through a tube woven from palm or vine. It is then used to make cassava bread. Other crops include corn and yams.

Most of the food comes from the forest, where the people collect plants, fruit, nuts, honey, and spices. Fish is an important part of their diet, and the forest tribes catch them by spearing, netting, trapping, or using poisoned blowguns. The men hunt forest animals of all sizes, while the women tend the crops. Cooking is usually done over hot embers, traditionally in turtle or armadillo shells.

Most members are equal within the tribes. The only person with a specialized role is the shaman, who acts as a healer and makes contact with spirit gods, often by using hallucinatory drugs.

The single largest group of Native Americans today are the nine thousand Yanomami (ee-on-oh-MA-mee), who cling to their traditional way of life in the distant northern forests along Brazil's border with

Food from the Forest

One of the lessons that the Yanomami can teach the outside world is that the rain forest holds many riches. Trees produce useful resins and other materials, and a number of plants may have medicinal properties that are just being explored by scientists. The fish in the rivers can be harvested, but the Yanomami are closely dependent on fruits from the trees for food. A study of the potential cash return from two and a half acres (one hectare) of rain forest showed that the plot could make over six thousand dollars a year if its products were carefully harvested, six times better than the once-only profit gained from felling trees for timber.

The staple food in the Amazon forests is cassava. It is peeled, grated, and squeezed into a woven tube to get rid of its poisons. Then it can be baked to produce cassava bread.

some aluminum pots. In most ways they live like other Native Americans, by hunting, fishing, and growing crops.

In 1988 nineteen small patches of land were set aside by the government as Indian land, but this was far short of the original area used by the tribe. Other zones were set aside for mining by the *garimpeiros* (gah-reem-PAY-rose), mestizo gold seekers. The scheme to separate the two has not worked, and the garimpeiros have time and time again intruded on Yanomami territory, either killing the people or unwittingly introducing diseases. The Yanomami are under increasing threat; one study predicts that the tribe will not survive long into the twenty-first century.

In 1966 the Brazilian government decreed that a large part of Amazonia should receive special funds, tax incentives, and planning coordination to bring it fully under the country's economy. The plan

Venezuela (see VENEZUELA). Several Yanomami families, perhaps as many as a hundred people, live within a large circular shelter, or *yano* (ee-ON-oh), which is made of poles and palm thatch. Each family has space beneath the roof where they hang hammocks, build a fire, and keep their personal possessions.

At one time the Yanomami made all their goods from forest materials, but today, through a network of contacts, they obtain some goods from the world beyond the forest. They have matches, knives, machetes—the all-purpose, steel cutting blades used by most forest people—and

Tribal Art

Tribal people use dyes from plants of the forest to paint their bodies. Red comes from annatto and blue black from genipa. Body painting is an enjoyable communal activity, especially at festival time, and designs include spirals, spots, and lines. Many decorations are added as part of festival dress, such as feathers, seed necklaces, and pieces of animal bones or shells, which they put through their noses. The festivals celebrate many things, including the moon, birth and death, the spirits of the natural world, and the supernatural. There is dancing and music, played on panpipes and flutes made of bamboo, gourds with seeds that sound like maracas, and rattles and drums made of animal skin.

was called Operation Amazonia. Roads were the key to opening up enormous tracts of wilderness. In 1970 work on the TransAmazonica Highway began in earnest. Laborers were flown to selected points in the forest, where, armed with chain saws and machetes, they began to clear the route. Dozens of construction camps sprung up. These were followed by villages, then towns, farms, and all the trappings of modern civilization.

In 1960 the estimated total population of Amazonia was no more than 3.5 million. Today, after thirty years of Operation Amazonia, the total exceeds 20 million, with people drawn from all over Brazil. The Amazonian caboclos who knew the forest from childhood are being replaced by a generation of settlers, construction workers, farm hands, and garimpeiros. Many of the small towns, and even villages, are connected to the outside world by telephone, television, and the Internet. Bars, restaurants, all-night discos, and small supermarkets have appeared in many places. The changes in the forest have been so great that the surviving Native American inhabitants are threatened with extinction.

The Beat of Brazil

With its many regional variations and its enormous wealth of different people, Brazil has a rich cultural life. For most people, its music is the samba. Samba was originally a rural dance based on African circle dances and accompanied by singing. It was introduced to Hollywood and the rest of the world by the movie and club star Carmen Miranda. Samba is at the heart of Brazil's Carnival, when samba schools dance to *batucada* (buh-too-CAH-duh), or percussion groups, whose main instruments are tambourines, drums, and bells.

Most radio stations transmit Brazilian popular music. Many of the performers are from Bahia and the Northeast. Some, like Milton Nascimento, were protest singers during the time of the military government. Later from the same region came the "Tropicalismo" of Gilberto Gil, Caetano Veloso, and Gal Costa. The most recent development of popular music has been the *música sertaneja*, or "backlands music." It is the Brazilian equivalent of country music and accounts for 40 percent of all recordings sold in Brazil.

At carnival time in Olinda in northeastern Brazil, jazz musicians join the revelers. African rhythms and traditions strongly influence music and carnival processions in this region.

Brazilian popular music is different than the sounds of the original cultures. Native Americans have ceremonies at which they play on simple instruments, such as drums hollowed from a section of tree trunk, long flutes of hollow bamboo, and rattles of nutshells.

In Bahia music and festivals of African origin abound, and a dance called the *capoeira* (kup-oh-AY-rah) is performed to the sounds of the *berimbau* (beh-ring-BOW). This curious sounding instrument is a bow with a single string to which a hollow gourd is attached at one end to act as a resonator.

Young men in Bahia perform the capoeira, a dance of African origin. Two musicians are playing the berimbau, a stringed instrument shaped like a bow and hit with a stick.

Brazilian Art and Literature

Some Brazilians have become famous worldwide for their inspiring work. The architect Oscar Niemeyer is especially well recognized for his designs in Brasília, such as the National Congress, the Planalto Palace, the Supreme Court, and the Metropolitan Cathedral. Roberto Burle Marx (1909–1994), known internationally for his garden designs, was born in São Paulo to a Brazilian mother and German father. He used plants and sweeping patterns very effectively in some of his most famous works. Among them was the pavement and mosaic along Copacabana Beach in Rio de Janeiro. Cándido Portinari (1903–1962), is Brazil's best-known twentieth-century artist. From the 1920s until the end of World War II, Portinari produced murals and canvases depicting social themes. His work can be seen in the United States in the United Nations General Assembly Building in New York City and in the U.S. Library of Congress in Washington, D.C.

Brazil's best-known international writer is Jorge Amado, who was born in Bahia in 1912. His novels have been translated into many languages and used as themes for films. Amado's earlier works concentrated on poor but good people of the lower classes and evil men of power. His later stories, such as *Gabriela: Clove and Cinnamon* and *Dona Flor and Her Two Husbands*, are more sophisticated and humorous. These portray the society of the distant provincial capital where he grew up.

Brazilians at Play

Brazilians excel at many sports but are phenomenally successful at soccer, a passion in Brazil. There are more than twenty thousand teams in the country, with matches played regularly in every village, town, and city. From an early age, children knock a ball around in the street or on a bare patch of land. Becoming a

Pelé

Pelé's real name is Edson Arantes do Nascimento, and he was born on October 23, 1940. He first played soccer for Brazil in 1957 when he was sixteen, and he represented his country in four World Cup Tournaments: in Sweden in 1958, in Chile in 1962, in England in 1966, and in Mexico in 1970. He scored twelve goals in fourteen World Cup matches. Pelé is the only person to have won three World Cups as a player, and his lifetime goal average is just less than one goal for each of the 1,363 professional games he played. After leaving Brazilian soccer, he played for three years with the New York Cosmos. He is regarded by many as the greatest soccer player ever. Once in Nigeria, opposing sides in the Biafra Civil War agreed to stop fighting for forty-eight hours so they could watch him play.

Many people believe that the team that won the 1970 World Cup in Mexico was the greatest soccer team of all time.

Apart from their love of soccer, Brazilians enjoy every sort of sport. Volleyball is now the country's second favorite sport, and beach volleyball has a good following. Brazil has also been successful in Grand Prix racing, producing some of the world's finest drivers, including three world champions. Brazilians are great fitness fanatics. Many use the beaches for exercises, where parallel bars are conveniently in place, and for jogging. Not surprisingly, perhaps, with so much coastline, water sports are also very popular, with conditions that are ideal for windsurfing and sailing.

There are excellent facilities for sports such as golf, bowling, and tennis, but many people cannot afford the club fees. In the main cities, horseracing stadiums attract many spectators on the weekends.

Brazil's soccer teams reflect the ethnic diversity within the country. Soccer is the country's most popular sport, and the national team is the most successful in the world.

professional soccer player is a dream most children have, a guaranteed way of leaving poverty behind.

Many Brazilians follow national and international matches with great excitement. A World Cup match brings the nation to a standstill, and, if Brazil wins, everyone turns out into the streets for a rowdy but good-humored celebration. There is much flag-waving, and car horns blast throughout the night. Brazilian teams have given the people good cause for celebration; Brazil is the only nation to have won the World Cup four times.

Glossary

acclimatize: to adjust to a new or unusual climate.

alpaca: an animal of the Andean highlands, related to the llama and reared for its wool.

Amazonia: the area in Brazil and in adjoining countries (Bolivia, Colombia, Ecuador, French Guiana, Guyana, Peru, Suriname, and Venezuela) that contains the Amazon River or its tributaries.

blockade-runner: a ship or person that attempts to enter a port that is shut off to keep people and supplies from leaving or entering.

cassava: a plant with fleshy tuber roots, used as a food.

castanet: instrument made from hard wood or ivory shells that produces a rattling sound.

causeway: a raised mound of earth forming a highway across low or flooded ground.

colony: (1) a territory that is governed by another country; (2) an overseas settlement by people of another country.

colonial: relating to a colony.

colonialism: a policy of governing other countries as colonies.

colonist: somebody who lives in a colony.

communal: of or relating to a community.

conquistador: originally a Spanish word meaning "conqueror." It usually refers to the Spaniards who conquered Central and South America in the sixteenth century.

criollo: a person born in Latin America of Spanish parents.

divination: the foretelling of future events by magical or supernatural means.

dungarees: overalls made from a coarse, tough cloth.

duty-free zone: a place where goods can be bought without paying taxes on them.

godparent: a person who, at the baptism of a child, promises to provide guidance and encourage spiritual growth and development.

hallucinatory: giving the effect of seeing something that does not exist.

incentive: something that gives a cause or motive that encourages a person to act.

indigenous: relating to a people who were born within a country or a region as opposed to being immigrants or settlers. Also *aboriginal* or *native.*

integral: to be essential for completeness.

jute: a plant whose fiber is used to make a coarse material used for sacks, cords, and rope.

latex: a milky liquid found in plants; some trees produce latex from which rubber is made.

Lent: the forty days between Ash Wednesday and Easter in the Christian calendar.

Lucifer: another name for Satan or the Devil.

mestizo: someone of mixed Native American and European descent.

mulatto: someone of mixed African and European descent.

panpipe: a musical instrument made of reed, cane, or bamboo tubes of different lengths.

patroness: a woman who uses her influence, power, or money to support others.

poncho: a garment made from a square or rectangular piece of cloth with a slit for the head.

pre-Columbian: a term used to describe the time before Christopher Columbus arrived in the Americas.

province: a region or division of a country, similar to a state in the United States.

republic: a country in which power rests with the people and their elected representatives. A president usually heads a republic.

resonator: an appliance for increasing sound.

savannah: a grassland dotted with trees.

shaman: a priest, healer, or holy person.

tax incentives: the lowering or cancellation of taxes to encourage people to manufacture goods or provide services.

tenaciously: to adhere or hold on to in a determined or persevering way.

trilby: a soft, felt hat usually worn by men.

voluminous: of great volume; massive; bulky; large.

Westernized: accustomed to Western or modern American or European lifestyles, values, and customs.

Further Reading

Bermuda
Raine, David F. *Islands of Bermuda.* Boston: Houghton Mifflin, 1990

Bolivia
Blair, David Nelson. *The Land and People of Bolivia.* New York: Lippincott, 1990.
Department of Geography Staff. *Bolivia in Pictures.* Minneapolis, MN: Lerner Group, 1987.
Ikuhara, Yoshiyuki. *Children of the World: Bolivia.* Milwaukee, WI: Gareth Stevens, 1988.
Morrison, Marion. *Bolivia.* Danbury, CT: Childrens Press, 1988.
Pateman, Robert. *Cultures of the World: Bolivia.* Tarrytown, NY: Marshall Cavendish, 1995.
St. John, Jetty. *A Family in Bolivia.* Minneapolis, MN: Lerner Group, 1986.
Schimmel, Karen. *Bolivia.* Broomall, PA: Chelsea House, 1991.

Brazil
Ashford, Moyra. *Brazil.* Chatham, NJ: Raintree Steck-Vaughn Publications, 1991
Bender, Evelyn. *Brazil.* Broomall, PA: Chelsea House, 1990.
Carpenter, Mark. *Brazil: An Awakening Giant.* Parsippany, NJ: Silver Burdett Press, 1988.
Dawson, Zoe. *Brazil.* Chatham, NJ: Raintree Steck-Vaughn Publications, 1995.
Galvin, Irene. *Brazil: Many Voices, Many Faces.* Tarrytown, NY: Marshall Cavendish, 1996.
Galvin, Irene Flum. *Exploring Cultures of the World: Brazil.* Tarrytown, NY: Marshall Cavendish, 1996.
Haverstock, Nathan. *Brazil in Pictures.* Minneapolis, MN: Lerner Group, 1987.
Lewington, Anna. *Antonio's Rain Forest.* Minneapolis, MN: CarolRhoda Books, 1993.
Marshall, David. *Brazil.* Cary, IL: Rigby Interactive Library, 1996.
Reynolds, Jim. *Amazon Basin: Vanishing Cultures.* San Diego, CA: Harcourt Brace and Company, 1993.
Richard, Christopher. *Cultures of the World: Brazil.* Tarrytown, NY: Marshall Cavendish, 1991.
Schwartz, David M. *Yanomami: People of the Amazon.* New York: Lothrop, Lee and Shepard Books, 1995.
Waterlow, Julia. *The Amazon.* Chatham, NJ: Raintree Steck-Vaughn Publications, 1994.

Index

Page numbers in *italic* indicate illustrations.

Page numbers in *italic* indicate illustrations.